I
ENCYCLOPEDIA OF
WORLD

SPORT

From Ancient Times to the Present

I
ENCYCLOPEDIA OF
WORLD

SPORT

From Ancient Times to the Present

David Levinson and Karen Christensen, Editors

ABC-CLIO

Santa Barbara, California
Denver, Colorado
Oxford, England

Berkshire Reference Works Project Staff

Writers
Bonnie Dyer-Bennet
John Townes
Alan Trevithick

Technical Support
Qiang Li

Editorial Assistants
Bonnie Dyer-Bennet
Patricia Welsh

Library of Congress Cataloging-in-Publication Data

Encyclopedia of world sport : from ancient times to the present /
       David Levinson and Karen Christenson, editors.
            p.   cm.
         Includes bibliographical references (p.   ) and index.
         1. Sports—Encyclopedias. I. Levinson, David, 1947–   .
       II. Christensen, Karen.
       GV567.E56   1996
       796'.03—DC21   96-45437

ISBN 0-87436-819-7

02 01 00 99 98 97 96 95   10 9 8 7 6 5 4 3 2 1

ABC-CLIO, Inc.
130 Cremona Drive, P.O. Box 1911
Santa Barbara, California 93116-1911

This book is printed on acid-free paper ⊚.
Manufactured in the United States of America

Andrea Abbas
Keele University, Keele, UK

Harvey Abrams
State College, Pennsylvania

E. John B. Allen
*Plymouth State College, Plymouth,
New Hampshire*

Gary Anderson
International Shooting Union

G. Whitney Azoy
*Lawrenceville School, Lawrenceville,
New Jersey*

William J. Baker
University of Maine, Orono, Maine

John Bale
Keele University, Keele, UK

Ralph B. Ballou, Jr.
*Middle Tennessee State University,
Murfreesboro, Tennessee*

Robert Knight Barney
*Centre for Olympic Studies, University of
Western Ontario, Canada*

Dawn Bean
United States Synchronized Swimming

A. Gilbert Belles
*Western Illinois University,
Macomb, Illinois*

Kendall Blanchard
*University of Tennessee,
Martin, Tennessee*

Tim Boggan
USA Table Tennis

Anne Bolin
Elon College, Elon, North Carolina

Gherardo Bonini
*European Community Historical Archives,
Florence, Italy*

Douglas Booth
*University of Otago,
Dunedin, New Zealand*

Linda A. Bowlby
World Sidesaddle Federation

Maynard Brichford
University Archives, Urbana, Illinois

Anthony Bush
Waltham Cross, UK

Michael B. Camillo
*World Pulling International,
Worthington, Ohio*

Kevin Carr
*Amherst College,
Amherst, Massachusetts*

Richard Cashman
*University of New South Wales,
Kensington, Australia*

Joan M. Chandler
University of Texas, Dallas

Timothy J. L. Chandler
Kent State University, Kent, Ohio

Jeffery A. Charlston
*George Washington University,
Washington, D.C.*

Karen Christensen
Great Barrington, Massachusetts

Garry Chick
*University of Illinois,
Urbana-Champaign, Illinois*

Annie Clement
*Cleveland State University,
Cleveland, Ohio*

Tony Collins
*Sheffield Hallam University,
Sheffield, UK*

Mary Conti
American Horse Shows Association

Pamela Cooper
Allentown, Pennsylvania

Frank Cosentino
York University, Toronto, Canada

Sally Crawford
*National Louis University/
Full Circle Fitness*

Scott A. G. M. Crawford
*Eastern Illinois University,
Charleston, Illinois*

Simon J. Crawford
Illinois Wesleyan University

Michael Cronin
*Sheffield Hallam University,
Sheffield, UK*

Lewis C. Cuyler
*Berkshire Sculling Association,
Pittsfield, Massachusetts*

Michael G. Davis
*Truman State University,
Kirksville, Missouri*

Wolfgang Decker
*Deutsche Sporthochschule Köln,
Cologne, Germany*

Lisa Delpy
*George Washington University,
Washington, D.C.*

Michael A. DeMarco
Journal of Asian Martial Arts

Richard Dingman
International Jugglers Association

Jon Griffin Donlon
Baton Rouge, Louisiana

Contributors

Peter Donnelly
McMaster University,
Hamilton, Ontario, Canada

Andrew Doyle
Auburn University
at Montgomery, Alabama

Margaret Carlisle Duncan
University of Wisconsin,
Milwaukee, Wisconsin

Eric Dunning
Centre for Research into Sport and
Society, University of Leicester, UK

Tom Dunning
University of Tasmania, Launceston,
Tasmania, Australia

Brooke Dyer-Bennet
Monterey, Massachusetts

Bonnie Dyer-Bennet
Berkshire Reference Works (staff)

Mark Dyreson
Weber State University, Ogden, Utah

Henning Eichberg
Gerlev Idrætschøjskole,
Slagelse, Denmark

Raymond Farrell
British Association for Sport & Law,
Manchester Metropolitan University, UK

Albert J. Figone
Humboldt State University,
Humboldt, California

Dennis J. Foster
Masters of Foxhounds Association
of America

Joel S. Franks
San Jose State University,
San Jose, California

Richard Friary
Skate Sailing Association

Marco Galdi
ANSA News Agency, Rome, Italy

David W. Galenson
University of Chicago,
Chicago, Illinois

Heiner Gillmeister
University of Bonn, Bonn, Germany

Matti Goksøyr
Norges Idrettshøgskole,
Oslo, Norway

Allen Guttmann
Amherst College,
Amherst, Massachusetts

Astrid Hagenguth
New York, New York

Steve Hick
Falls Church, Virginia

Hajime Hirai
Shiga University, Shiga, Japan

Richard Holt
De Montfort University, UK, and
Katholieke Universiteit, Leuven, Belgium

Ronald L. Holt
Weber State University, Ogden, Utah

Peter A. Horton
School of Physical Education,
Singapore

Maxwell Howell
University of Queensland,
Indooroopilly, Australia

Reet Howell (deceased)
Queensland University of Technology,
Australia

Joan Hult
University of Maryland,
College Park, Maryland

Duncan Humphreys
University of Otago,
Dunedin, New Zealand

Steven J. Jackson
University of Otago,
Dunedin, New Zealand

Wesley V. Jamison
University of Arkansas,
Fayetteville, Arkansas

Ian F. Jobling
University of Queensland,
Brisbane, Australia

Don Johnson
East Tennessee State University,
Johnson City, Tennessee

Gary Kemp
University of Waikato,
Hamilton, New Zealand

Jane Kidd
British Equestrian Centre,
Kenilworth, Warwickshire, UK

Donald G. Kyle
University of Texas, Arlington

Horacio A. Laffaye
Yale University School of Medicine,
New Haven, Connecticut

Mary Lou LeCompte
University of Texas, Austin, Texas

Michael Letters
University of Queensland,
Brisbane, Australia

David Levinson
Human Relations Area Files,
New Haven, Connecticut

Katherine Lincoln
Bernardsville, New Jersey

Sigmund Loland
Norges Idrettshøgskole,
Oslo, Norway

John Lowerson
University of Sussex,
Brighton, Sussex, UK

John W. Loy
University of Otago,
Dunedin, New Zealand

Stu Luce
National Air Racing Group

Contributors

Ruth P. Ludwig
Balloon Federation of America

John McClelland
University of Toronto,
Ontario, Canada

C. D. (Kit) McConnell
Auckland, New Zealand

R. C. McConnell
Massey University (Albany),
Auckland, New Zealand

Richard V. McGehee
Southeastern Louisiana University,
Hammond, Louisiana

Heather McMorrow
United States Luge Association

Michael McNamee
Cheltenham and Gloucester College of
Higher Education, UK

Teresa Baksh McNeil
Cuyamaca College,
El Cajon, California

Anita H. Magafas
Western Illinois University,
Macomb, Illinois

Maurice Mars
University of Natal Medical School,
Kwa Zulu Natal, South Africa

Tony Mason
University of Warwick, Coventry, UK

Walter Miller
Monument, Colorado

Andrew W. Miracle
Texas Christian University,
Fort Worth, Texas

Timothy Mitchell
Texas A & M University,
College Station, Texas

Linda Mojer
American Amateur Racquetball
Association

William J. Morgan
University of Tennessee,
Knoxville, Tennessee

Morris Mott
Brandon University,
Manitoba, Canada

Susan Nattrass
Bedford, Nova Scotia, Canada

John Nauright
University of Queensland,
Brisbane, Australia

Dennis Pagen
United States Hang Gliding
Association

Victoria Paraschak
University of Windsor,
Ontario, Canada

Roberta J. Park
University of California, Berkeley

A. R. Parr
Broad Haven, Pembrokeshire, Wales

Katharine A. Pawelko
Western Illinois University,
Macomb, Illinois

Benny Josef Peiser
Liverpool John Moores University,
Liverpool, UK

Gertrud Pfister
Institut für Sportwissenschaft,
Berlin, Germany

Richard Pillsbury
Georgia State University,
Atlanta, Georgia

Philip A. Pines
Trotting Horse Museum,
Goshen, New York

Bill Plummer
American Softball Association

Michael Poliakoff
Pennsylvania Department of Education,
Harrisburg, Pennsylvania

S. W. Pope
Journal of Sport History

Rudi Prusok
American Single Shot Rifle
Association

Rivka Rabinowitz
Pierre Gildesgame Maccabi Sports
Museum, Ramat Gan, Israel

Benjamin G. Rader
University of Nebraska,
Lincoln, Nebraska

Gerald Redmond
University of Alberta,
Edmonton, Canada

Shirley H. M. Reekie
San Jose State University,
San Jose, California

Roland Renson
Katholieke Universiteit,
Leuven, Belgium

Mary E. Ridgway
University of Texas, Arlington, Texas

James Riordan
University of Surrey,
Guildford, Surrey, UK

Joachim K. Rühl
Deutsche Sporthochschule Köln,
Cologne, Germany

Allan J. Ryan
American College of Sports Medicine

Yasuhiro Sakaue
Fukushima University,
Fukushimashi, Japan

Thomas F. Scanlon
University of California,
Riverside, California

Andy Seeley
US Amateur Confederation
of Roller Skating

Roland Seiler
Sport Science Institute,
Magglingen, Switzerland

Contributors

K. G. Sheard
Centre for Research into Sport and Society, University of Leicester, UK

Ron Shepherd
East Melbourne, Victoria, Australia

Stan Shipley
University of London, UK

Fumiaki Shishida
Waseda University, Tokorozawa, Japan

Martti Silvennoinen
University of Jyväskylä, Jyväskylä, Finland

Ronald A. Smith
Pennsylvania State University, University Park, Pennsylvania

Chet Snouffer
U.S. Boomerang Association

Kathleen M. Spence
U.S. Badminton Association

B. James Starr
Howard University, Washington, D.C.

Sharon Kay Stoll
University of Idaho, Moscow, Idaho

Nancy L. Struna
University of Maryland, College Park, Maryland

Kim Taylor
University of Guelph, Ontario, Canada

David Terry
Ruislip, Middlesex, UK

George Theriault
New London, New Hampshire

Jeffrey R. Tishman
Associated Press Archives

John Townes
Berkshire Reference Works (staff)

Alan Trevithick
Berkshire Reference Works (staff)

Horst Ueberhorst
Wachtberg-Niederbachern, Germany

Wray Vamplew
De Montfort International Centre for Sports History and Culture, Leicester, UK

Robin S. Vealey
Miami University, Oxford, Ohio

Mark V. Wiley
Charles E. Tuttle Publishing Company, Tokyo, Japan

Ian D. W. Wright
Squash Rackets Association, UK

Daniel G. Yoder
Western Illinois University, Macomb, Illinois

Darlene Young
Western Illinois University, Macomb, Illinois

Philip B. Zarilli
University of Wisconsin, Madison, Wisconsin

Frank Zarnowski
Mount St. Mary's College, Emmitsburg, Maryland

Dean A. Zoerink
Western Illinois University, Macomb, Illinois

CONTENTS

List of Entries, xiii
Preface, xvii
Acknowledgments, xxi

ENCYCLOPEDIA OF
WORLD SPORT
From Ancient Times to the Present

VOLUME I

**Acrobatics to
Gymnastics**

VOLUME II

**Handball to
Rugby Union**

VOLUME III

**Sailboarding to
Yachting**

Bibliography, 1207
Illustration Credits, 1255
The Contributors, 1259
Index, 1265

Acrobatics
Aerobics
African Games
Aggression
Aikido
Air Racing
Animal Baiting
Animal Rights
Anthropology
Archery
Arm Wrestling
Armed Forces Games
Art
Asian Games
Associations
Badminton
Ballooning
Bandy
Barrel Jumping
Baseball, Finnish
Baseball, Japanese
Baseball, Latin American
Baseball, North American
Basketball
Biathlon
Billiards
Bobsledding

Bodybuilding
Boomerang Throwing
Bowls and Bowling
Boxing
Bullfighting
Buzkashi
Camogie
Canoeing and Kayaking
Carriage Driving
Chariot Racing
Coaches and Coaching
Cockfighting
Commercialization
Commonwealth Games
Conditioning
Coursing
Cricket
Croquet
Cross-Country Running
Cudgeling
Curling
Cycling
Darts
Definitions
Diffusion
Disabled Sports
Diving

Drag Racing
Drugs and Drug Testing
Duathlon
Environment
Ethics
Ethnicity
Exercise
Extreme Sports
Falconry
Fencing
Fishing, Freshwater
Fishing, Saltwater
Flying Disc
Footbag
Football, American
Football, Australian
Football, Canadian
Football, Gaelic
Formula 1 Auto Racing
Foxhunting
Gambling
Gay Games
Geography
Golf
Gymnastics

LIST OF ENTRIES

VOLUME II

Handball, Court
Handball, Team
Hang Gliding
Highland Games
History
Hockey, Field
Hockey, Ice
Horse Racing, Harness
    (Trotting)
Horse Racing, Steeplechase
Horse Racing, Thoroughbred
Horseback Riding, Dressage
Horseback Riding,
    Endurance
Horseback Riding, Eventing
Horseback Riding,
    Gymkhana
Horseback Riding, Hunters
    and Jumpers
Horseback Riding,
    Sidesaddle
Horseback Riding, Vaulting
Horseback Riding, Western
Horseshoes
Hunting
Hurling
Iaido
Ice Boating
Indy Auto Racing
Intercollegiate Athletics
Jai Alai
Jousting
Judo
Juggling

Jujutsu
Karate
Karting
Kendo
Kite Flying
Korfball
Lacrosse
Law
Leadership
Leisure
Literature
Luge
Maccabiah Games
Management and Marketing
Marathon and Distance
    Running
Martial Arts
Martial Arts, Philippines
Martial Arts, South Asia
Masculinity
Media
Medicine
Mesoamerican Ballgame
Modernization
Motocross
Motor Boating
Motorcycle Racing
Mountain Climbing
Movies
Mythology
Native American Sporting
    Competitions
Netball
Olympic Games, Ancient

Olympic Games, Modern
Orienteering
Paddleball
Pan American Games
Parachuting
Patriotism
Pedestrianism
Pelota
Pentathlon, Ancient
Pentathlon, Modern
Philosophy
Physical Education
Pigeon Racing
Politics
Polo
Polo, Bicycle
Polo, Water
Powerlifting
Psychology
Race Walking
Racquetball
Rafting
Religion
Ritual
Rock Climbing
Rodeo
Rounders
Rowing
Rugby Fives
Rugby League
Rugby Union

Sailboarding
Sailing
Sailing, Ice Skate
Sailing, Icewing and Roller
    Skate
Sailing, Parawing
Sand Yachting
Senior Games
Shinty
Shooting, Clay Target
Shooting, Pistol
Shooting, Rifle
Shooting, Single-Shot
Shuffleboard
Skateboarding
Skating, Figure
Skating, Ice Speed
Skating, In-line
Skating, Roller
Ski Jumping
Skiing, Alpine
Skiing, Freestyle
Skiing, Nordic
Skiing, Water
Sled Dog Racing
Snowboarding
Snowshoe Racing
Soaring
Soccer

Sociology
Softball
Spectators
Speedball
Squash Rackets
Stickball
Stock Car Racing
Sumo
Surfing
Swimming, Distance
Swimming, Speed
Swimming, Synchronized
Tae Kwon Do
Tai Chi
Takraw
Technology
Tennis
Tennis, Paddle
Tennis, Platform
Tennis, Real
Tennis, Table
Tobogganing
Track and Field, Decathlon
Track and Field, Jumps and
    Throws
Track and Field, Running
    and Hurdling
Traditional Sports, Africa
Traditional Sports, Asia

Traditional Sports, Europe
Traditional Sports, North
    and South America
Traditional Sports, Oceania
Trampolining
Trapball
Triathlon
Truck and Tractor Pulling
Truck Racing
Tug of War
Turnen
Umpires and Umpiring
Values
Vintage Auto Racing
Violence
Volkssport
Volleyball
War Games
Weightlifting
Women's Sports, Europe
Women's Sports, North
    America
Worker Sport
Wrestling, Freestyle
Wrestling, Greco-Roman
Wushu
Yachting

We watched the 1996 Olympic Games in Atlanta as this project was being completed. These Centennial Games told us much about the nature of sport and sports in the contemporary world. *Sport is global.* Athletes from 197 nations competed. People around the world consider sport an important form of individual, group, and national achievement and, in some cases, of human expression, innovation, and creativity. *Women's involvement in sport continues to expand.* The number of female competitors approached that of male competitors, and women's softball, soccer, gymnastics, and swimming were among the most popular events. *Victory in sport increasingly depends on technological innovation.* Training requires sophisticated facilities and equipment, scoring in many sports relies on electronic timers rather than the human senses, and uniforms and equipment are precision-manufactured at high cost. *Sports are spreading,* especially from the developed to the less developed world. Athletes from 57 nations won medals and African athletes won twice as many medals in 1996 as they did at the 1992 Barcelona Olympics. *Sports are big business.* Many competitors are paid or supported by their governments, many have agents, victory in high profile sports yields lucrative endorsement contracts, and corporations—as well as host cities for major sporting events—use sports to promote themselves and their products and services. *Sports are more varied and more specialized.* Some 271 sports, including many variants of single sports, were contested at the 1996 Centennial Olympics, by contrast with the 42 events contested at the first modern Olympics in 1896 and the single sport—the *stadion,* a sprint of about 200 meters—contested at the first Olympics in ancient Greece.

The *Encyclopedia of World Sport* covers these and other trends in sport and sports today. In addition, this three-volume work includes information never before assembled about the history and evolution of sport as a societal institution and about the history and evolution of individual sports—Olympic and otherwise—from ancient times to 1996.

What Is Sport?

It is important that we clarify what we mean by "sport" and "sports." By "sport" we mean sport as a societal and cultural institution that is composed of a complex mix of individuals, activities, events, and material objects, as well as beliefs and values associated with the practice of sports. By "sports" we mean all the different types of sport. We have defined sports very broadly in putting together this encyclopedia, and we have also included an entry on scholarly definitions of sports, as they are distinguished from games and other leisure activities. Our goal has been to bring sports, as practiced throughout the world, together in an accessible and comprehensive reference work.

In choosing topics to cover, we first included activities characterized by the following definition: (1) rules of play that allow a winner to be determined; (2) a primary goal being victory; (3) competition between two or more individuals or teams; and (4) victory determined by the relative physical ability of the competitors, although strategy and chance may also play a role. We have tried to cover all activities—both sports currently contested and many sports now obsolete—that fit this definition.

We also included several categories of activity generally treated as sports although they do not fit this definition. First, we have included coverage of sports in which the outcome is determined mainly by the physical ability of animals that are trained or controlled by humans. These sports include equestrian sports, covered in 12 separate entries, as well as bull fighting, cock fighting, dog racing, pigeon racing, animal baiting, and chariot racing. Second, we cover competitive activities that rely on mechanical technology and nonhuman energy: auto racing in several forms, as well as speed boat racing, air racing, and other sports.

While some experts do not consider these activities to be sports because of their reliance on nonhuman energy and the absence of direct human competition, we have chosen to be inclusive. There is little doubt that the competitors, their sponsors, and spectators consider them to be sports, and all depend on human skill, knowledge, and physical ability.

Even so, this list of sports represents a Western and male view of physical challenge. While the major global sports continue to be competitive team sports like soccer and basketball, we have also chosen to include substantial coverage of traditional sports, including Native American games, of the martial arts, and of emerging female perspectives.

The *Encyclopedia* has broad coverage of martial arts, both in a general entry and in ten specific sports entries. While martial arts increasingly tend, especially in the West, toward competitive practices that are similar to those of major Western sports, the traditional practice of martial sports emphasizes competition only in conjunction with the goals of fair play and self-mastery. By self-mastery the martial arts participant means self-control and personal development in terms of philosophical, moral, or spiritual goals. This comprehensive approach to sports practice is a significant global influence.

Another significant influence is the involvement of women at all levels of sport. Women's increasing participation in major sports and the different emphases they place on teamwork, cooperation, and physical activity challenge the dominant model of Western sport. Many women also treat as sports a wider variety of activities—for example, dance, one of the few ways women in many societies could be physically expressive and active, and noncompetitive outdoor and adventure activities. We have included entries on the development of women's sports in North America and Europe and given attention to women's participation in sport in many entries.

Coverage

With sports so broadly defined, we cover nearly 300 sports in this work, and also include refer-

ences to hundreds of other related activities and games. Many sports and variants of a single sport—such as football— are covered in separate articles, while some sports that are closely related—such as the many types of bowling—are covered in a single long entry. The criteria we used in deciding whether to consolidate coverage of similar sports were the amount of information available, the relative similarity of the varieties of the sport, and the variation in the societal contexts in which the sports are contested.

The increasing interest in preservation of local traditions and local culture is also an important aspect of world sport. Many contributors have discussed traditional sports that were precursors of modern sports in their coverage of the history of a given sport. We have also included general articles on the traditional sports of all regions of the world as well as extensive coverage of modern sports important in Asia, Oceania, Africa, and the Americas and coverage of these regions within major entries such as "Soccer."

Many sports are contested at various levels. Baseball in the United States, for example, is contested in informal pick-up games, in organized leagues for children and teenagers, in organized community leagues, in high school and college leagues, in the minor professional leagues at three levels, in the Olympics, and in the major professional leagues. This situation is much the same for many other major sports around the world. In a work of this size, it is impossible to cover each sport at all levels of competition. We have tended, therefore, to concentrate on each sport at its highest level of competition, either at the professional level or, for amateur sports, at the international level. Thus, the four articles on baseball (North American, Japanese, Latin American, and Finnish) stress professional baseball in these four regional contexts. Baseball as it is played at the collegiate level and in communities across America in American Legion, Babe Ruth, and Little Leagues is not covered in detail. While we would have liked to cover many sports at the community or recreational level, we found that there is very little literature—journalistic, academic, or participant—to draw on. Because a majority of people involved in sports around the world are not professional players, we need to learn much more about recreational sports in order to understand the role of sports in human culture.

The idea of community, a related and important aspect of sport and society, has not been covered in a separate entry for the same reason. While scholarly study has often focused on the negative effects of professionalized sports on local communities, sports are a vital way in which people have, throughout history, preserved a sense of community—or *communitas*—and community theorists have begun to revitalize the notion of sports as a character building activity and an essential aspect of strengthening communities. While there have been criticisms of the competitive aspects of sport in educational circles (in Britain, for example, only noncompetitive games are played in some schools), young people in many nations spend much time training for and competing in sports, and the role of sports in promoting good relations between individuals, communities, ethnic groups, and nations deserves further study.

Sport and Society

While it is obvious that sport is a societal institution, what is less clear is the exact nature of the relationship between sport and society. Experts suggest that sport and society might be related in three different ways. First, the way sports are organized and played may be a reflection of other institutions in a particular society. In this sense, the composition of an American football team is a reflection of the management structure of American corporations, with a single leader, the quarterback (CEO), finesse players called running backs and receivers (corporate division heads), offense (marketing), and defense (legal department). Second, sport may be a symbolic expression of the core values of the culture, such as achievement, individuality, teamwork, and winning. As a symbolic expression that takes place in public, sport plays the important role of communicating core values to all members of society and is especially important as a way for adults to communicate values to children.

These first two interpretations suggest that sport is basically a conservative activity that reinforces or reflects the existing social order. The third interpretation takes the opposite view and conceptualizes sport as an agent of social change. Title IX, for example, the U.S. law that opened college sports to women, also encouraged greater participation by women in other aspects of society. Similarly, the success of African athletes at the 1996 Olympics calls attention to African potential in other areas of human endeavor.

Sport as a societal institution is covered from four perspectives in the articles that follow. This coverage is the single most important feature of the *Encyclopedia of World Sport*. The four perspectives are (1) sport in society, (2) the culture of sport, (3) sporting competitions, and (4) the scholarly study of sport. Sport in society refers to societal institutions that influence sport, as well as the influence sport has on society. Some fifteen different articles cover the sport-society relationship. These range from commercialization to gambling and sports law to the mass media. By the culture of sport we mean aspects of the sport experience, other than the competition itself, that influence outcomes. These topics range from umpiring to drug use and spectators to technology. The globalization of sport is reflected in the spread and growth of international sporting competitions, some fifteen of which are covered here, including the ancient and modern Olympics, regional games, and games for special groups such as the Senior Games and Gay Games.

Scholarly Study of Sport

Finally, because this work is based to a significant degree on information produced by scholarly research and writing, we have included articles on the major scholarly disciplines in which there is an interest in sport. These articles provide important background information for many of the entries in the encyclopedia by setting forth the interests, paradigms, and methods used in the study of sport. Although the study of sport has been a widely accepted activity in academia for only ten to fifteen years, sports scholars have nonetheless made major contributions to our understanding of sport in human societies.

The primary disciplines active in the study of sport are psychology, history, sociology, anthropology, geography, and history. Psychologists inform us about the psychodynamics of competition and the group dynamics of sport elements such as teamwork and spectatorship. Historians produce major sport and sports histories and provide us with much detailed information about specific events and people in sports from ancient times to today. Sociologists provide us with a number of frameworks for interpreting the complex relationship between sports and society. Anthropologists provide a growing body of information about sports in cultures around the world and allow us to compare sport across cultures. Geographers inform us about the relationship between sport and the environment and about the spread of sports across time and place. Finally, classical scholars tell us about sport in the ancient world and its relationship to sport today.

Globalization

One of the major developments in sport since World War II and especially in the last two decades is the globalization of sport and sports. There has been a wholescale spread of various sports from nation to nation, a broader and deeper interest in sport in general across nations, a greater linkage between sports, politics, and the economy, and a diffusion of athletic success across nations. With the spread of certain sports around the world, sports have become a global language, a way in which people of diverse backgrounds and different cultures and languages come together. While there is no doubt that Americanization is having a dramatic effect on the practice of sport around the world, just as the British Empire in the last century carried British team sports to all corners of the globe, sports from other parts of the world—many of the martial arts, for example, and takraw, an important footbag sport from southeast Asia—are also becoming global.

We have made a determined effort to make the encyclopedia reflect the global nature of modern sport and sports. Our editorial advisers and authors represent sixteen different nations. Attention is given to cross-national variation in sports, by covering both sports that are played in many nations and sports whose appeal is limited to a specific region, nation, or even group within a nation. In addition, cross-national variations in the same sport are given considerable attention. Finally, a number of articles such as those on international sports competitions and diffusion focus explicitly on the global nature of sport.

We have by design placed less emphasis on sporting facts—events, winners, scores, averages, records, biographies, and accounts of performances. This type of information is available in great detail in numerous books, magazines, sports newspapers, almanacs, and materials compiled by sports associations. Providing it here would have detracted from the coverage we have given to the history of sports, the culture of sports, sports in society, and the global nature of sport. This does not mean we have ignored sport statistics and individual athletes; many articles (particularly those on lesser-known sports) do provide information on world records, and many articles cover athletes and other individuals who have played a pivotal role in the development of a sport. We give less attention to detailed rules of specific sports because this information is also readily available elsewhere and rapidly goes out of date (rules in many sports change, to greater or lesser degree, every year). We have, however, included overviews of the basic rules of all sports, diagrams of playing surfaces, descriptions of how each sport is played, and many photographs showing actual competitions.

This is the first time a work of such global scope has been compiled, and there are undoubtedly omissions we will want to rectify in future editions. Readers should feel free to send corrections and suggestions to the editors care of the publishers.

David Levinson & Karen Christensen,
October 1996
Great Barrington, Massachusetts

T he idea for the *Encyclopedia of World Sport* came from our publisher, ABC-CLIO, who asked us to develop the project. We recruited an editorial advisory board of scholars specializing in the study of sport to help us refine our list of entries and find contributors. These scholars represented different disciplines—anthropology, geography, history, literature, physical education, and sociology—and different parts of the world. Their contribution was invaluable: they helped to shape the work, recommended contributors, wrote some entries themselves, and reviewed portions of the final text. Richard Holt and Allen Guttmann were especially helpful and encouraging in early stages; their broad view of sports and culture helped to clarify the unique perspective of this encyclopedia. Alyce Cheska, now retired but a pioneer in the field, encouraged us, and advisory board members Garry Chick, John Loy, Donald Kyle, and Roberta Park made major contributions to the final work. The editorial board and the contributors they helped us to recruit are leading figures in the scholarly sports community, most of them experts on the topics they write about in these volumes.

The global nature of the encyclopedia can be seen not only in its contents but in its 150 contributors, who come from Australia, Belgium, Britain (England and Wales), Canada, Denmark, Finland, Germany, Israel, Italy, Japan, New Zealand, Norway, Singapore, Switzerland, and South Africa, as well as the United States. We have aimed for consistency between articles but also to maintain the range of authors' voices and approaches, rather than imposing uniformity on what is meant to be truly global. This cooperative global endeavor is exemplified in the process of locating an author for the entry on polo: a British contributor suggested an Italian colleague then based in Norway, who responded by e-mail, suggesting an Argentinean surgeon and polo player working at a Connecticut hospital only 150 miles from our base office.

Sports participants and nonacademic writers sometimes feel that scholars focus on the negative aspects of modern sports—injuries or drug use, for example—instead of on character building, fair play, and the joy of competition. But most of our scholarly editors and contributors are sports enthusiasts, practitioners as well as spectators. One contributor is an Olympic gold medalist, others are coaches at college or community level, and many help to run clubs and local sports organizations. We also recruited writers from national and international sports organizations, and, finally, had some entries written by staff writers.

Many contributors also helped us to recruit other authors, especially for the less well-known sports, and sometimes took on extra topics out of interest in the project. William Baker wrote the entry on sport and religion and was then persuaded to contribute two further entries; he tells us that scholars of sport tend to be evangelists for the cause. In working on encyclopedia projects we have found that the subject of a work determines the process of compiling it. Where political scientists would posture and negotiate, scholars of sport agree on rules, look for the goal, recruit the best teammates, and race to the finish line. They have our thanks for prompt and careful work and for their wonderful team spirit.

Developing an encyclopedia is a cooperative effort and we have been helped by several people whose names do not appear in the work itself. Phillips Stevens, for example, an anthropologist at SUNY/Buffalo, helped us locate contributors for the articles on traditional sports. Other scholars around the world kindly answered questions by e-mail and offered suggestions and specific information. To all these people we offer our

Acknowledgments

thanks, and a work we hope will define the field, provide a standard body of information, and encourage further study of world sport.

We also thank the editorial and production team at ABC-CLIO for the weeks and months they have spent bringing this mammoth project to completion: Richard Bass, Amy Catala, Amanda de la Garza, Barb Dinneen, Carol Estes, Todd Hallman, Jennifer Job, Liz Kincaid, Susan McRory, Jeff Serena, Kristi Ward, and Martha Whitt.

Acrobatics

Acrobatics, the practice of performing physically unusual feats with one's body (sometimes with apparatus), has a long recorded history and many noted practitioners. Acrobatic stunts have, however, always seemed morally as well as physically dangerous. Defying death was for a mortal an appropriately symbolic part of ancient funeral ceremony, but doing so for reasons of pure spectacle is an act of hubris. Acrobatics has thus traditionally been both applauded and derided. It has hovered on the fringes of dance and the theater, provided an aesthetic alternative to sport, and, masquerading as physical culture, insinuated itself into preventative medicine. Complete respectability has, however, always eluded acrobatics, possibly because, cut off from its symbolic origins, it was, unlike the pursuits to which it tried to attach itself, devoid of meaning. Perhaps for that reason, the practitioners of acrobatics have almost always been outsiders—or portrayed themselves as such—to Western European culture.

Origins

Acrobatics is principally the art of jumping, tumbling, and balancing; it often involves the use of apparatus such as poles, one-wheel cycles, and flying trapezes. By strict definition, however, an acrobat is simply one who "walks [Greek *bateo*] on the extremity [Greek *akra*]," which is usually taken to mean on tiptoe, but which might also denote walking on one's hands (ancient Greek statuettes depict acrobats doing just that). But whether on toes or hands, an acrobat is one who walks in a manner that is unnatural and inherently unbalanced. As such, acrobatics was part of the ritualistic act of dancing (ballerinas are still required to perform *en pointe*, i.e., on the very tips of their toes). Subsequently, the term "acrobat" came to designate a gymnast who walked on ropes or otherwise performed while hanging from them. This adaptation of the term may have come from the balletic gait required of rope dancers.

In any case, it was only in the limited sense of rope-walking that "acrobatics" entered the modern languages. The subsequent popularity of the word and its eventual extension to the range of physical activities listed above seems owing largely to advances in the techniques and technology of rope gymnastics. The invention of the flying trapeze (1859) and the exploits of Blondin and Farini, who in 1859 and 1860 walked on tight-ropes across the Niagara gorge, took acrobatics literally to new heights. The development of the great traveling circuses and the rise of the music-hall gave acrobatics both a venue and a respectability it had not previously enjoyed.

In addition to walking or dancing in a state of disequilibrium, often on a surface ill-suited to any form of locomotion, the other fundamental act of acrobatics is the somersault. From its simplest form—frontwards, with head and hands touching the ground—it developed many complex and increasingly difficult variants.

It was only in the later Middle Ages that the basic range of acrobatic feats was enlarged. Changes in the technology of warfare meant that cavalrymen had to acquire the skills of rapid dismounting and remounting, and horse-vaulting was born. By the late sixteenth century, it had become an exercise independent of any real military goals, and it thereby enlarged the panoply of acrobatic feats, as did the invention of the bicycle in the late nineteenth century. Acrobatics has always been ready to turn technology to its own ends and to turn purposeful activities into spectacle.

Significance

The successful performance of acrobatic feats requires considerable physical exertion, the painstaking acquisition of unusual athletic skills, and a high degree of muscular and psychological control. Acrobatic training is at variance, however, with training for most sports, whose goals are not the execution of gestures that are both preternatural and graceful—an acrobatic feat that is not graceful is unthinkable—but the performance of natural gestures, whether gracefully or not, in a way that supersedes all previous and simultaneous performances of those gestures. Acrobats are less motivated by the creed of faster, higher, stronger and by the quest for records than by the goal of performing more inventively than others. Since the ultimate purpose of the acquisition of acrobatic skills is not to compete but to acquire skills that are even more spectacular, acrobatics remains outside the realm of sport. The basic criteria by which we appreciate acrobatics—control, gracefulness, innovation—are not susceptible to objective measurement. Acrobatics cannot be competitive in the conventional sense and hence remains largely spectacular. Yet there are Olympic sports that are judged more on aesthetic than on quantified bases: gymnastics and figure-skating, to name but two.

Though acrobatics has not been integrated into the schema of culturally sanctioned pursuits, it has nonetheless contributed to them. The degree of grace and control required of acrobats—as specifically opposed to the skills of the competitive athlete—was an essential part of the physical culture advocated by Plato as the necessary counterpart to education in the intellectual disciplines. Domination of the body was a means to domination of the more violent impulses to which the personality might give vent. The physician Claudius Galen (130–200 C.E.) believed that exercises based on these principles possessed hygienic, prophylactic, and even therapeutic worth (Galen actually prescribed walking on tiptoe). In the Renaissance the revival of Platonic philosophy and Galenic medicine in Europe renewed an interest in the physiological benefits of strenuous gymnastics.

The link between acrobatics and dance appears to have been dissolved by the latter's increasing categorization into a set of regulated steps and positions that could be taught in dancing schools. Acrobats and dancers performed on the same stage, and some of the former rivaled the latter in celebrity, but acrobatics and dance were clearly distinct specialties and only dance remained part of high culture. This may be because acrobatics "is an art, not of the body as corporeal realization of a human person, but of the body as an innervated system of weights and levers" (Sparshott 1988). Acrobatics was also part of the *commedia dell'arte*, the traditional Italian theater that required actors to perform stunts we think of as more appropriate to the circus. But by the end of the seventeenth century the *commedia dell'arte* had been largely relegated to the fairground. The history of acrobatics is the history of its constant marginalization—but also of its constant presence—in Western civilization.

The ambiguous status of acrobatics may derive

Students from the western state of Maharashtra, India, form a human pyramid in New Delhi in preparation for a cultural pageant to be held on the country's Republic Day.

from its forgotten symbolism. Whether walking a tight-rope or performing a somersault, the acrobat is exposing himself to serious injury and is thus defying death. By making the feat more complicated, he is multiplying this defiance. For that reason, from the early Egyptians to the European Middle Ages, acrobatic feats (particularly somersaults) were an integral, if unofficial, element of funeral rites. The acrobat who survives the danger to which he has willfully exposed himself embodies our belief that immortality is possible, and he signifies our wish to be divine. By both their root meanings and later extensions, terms like "acrobatics, "funambulist," and "mountebank" denote postures, gestures, and means of locomotion that challenge the limits imposed by both the anatomical configuration of

The Training of a Young Acrobat, 1599

One of the most significant practitioners of acrobatics was Arcangelo Tuccaro (ca. 1535–ca. 1610). Originally employed by the Austrian emperor Maximilian II, he entered French royal service in 1570, with the title *saltarin du roi* (the king's acrobat). In 1599 he published in French the first and most complete account of his profession (*Trois Dialogues de sauter et voltiger en l'air*). Tuccaro's purpose was to achieve for acrobats the status enjoyed by other artists, and to that end he invokes at length ancient and contemporary authorities on the military and medical value of gymnastic exercises.

The most important part of the book, however, lies in the lengthy, copiously illustrated second section, in which Tuccaro prescribes the training of a young acrobat. He outlines some preliminary exercises, then proceeds through a series of 54 somersaults arranged from the simplest, a front-flip, to the most difficult, an elaborate feat involving apparatus. Each of the somersaults is carefully analyzed and described in terms of precise geometry and a surprisingly sophisticated biomechanics. The accompanying woodcuts (88 in all, some with geometrical schemata) demonstrate the successive configurations of the body from initial to final posture.

Tuccaro is wise enough to know that the most spectacular feat is not necessarily the hardest to perform. Hence his greatest crowd-pleaser—a somersault through 10 hoops (no other acrobat used more than 8)—comes in the middle, because although it is the most ostentatious, it is not the most difficult. Perhaps the most significant contribution of the book lies in Tuccaro's insistence that any acrobatic feat must first be abstractly conceived in the mind as a set of independent movements of the head, limbs, and torso. These movements must be imagined as constructed into an interlocking whole composed of a carefully timed sequence of acts. Only then can the stunt be successfully performed. The *a priori* imaging of the acrobatic feat is the means to controlling not only the movements of the body, but also—and Tuccaro is explicit about this—those of the emotions. By conceiving of himself merely as a mechanism executing a maneuver whose evolution is determined by mathematical necessity, the acrobat eliminates fear and hence failure.

Together with the work of Hieronymus Mercurialis (*Artis gymnasticae*, Venice, 1569; frequently reprinted), Tuccaro's book had a decisive influence on Giustiniano Borassatti (fl. mid-eighteenth century), whose *Il Ginnasta in Pratica, ed in Teoria* appeared in 1753; and on Johann Friedrich Guts Muths (1759–1839), who published in 1793 a *Gymnastik für Jugend*. These books influenced in their turn the development of physical education and physical culture throughout the nineteenth century and well into the twentieth. In some places, Tuccaro remained a manual for teaching acrobatics until World War II.

—John McClelland

our bodies and the decorum that is the mark of the civilized adult.

Any defiance of our physical limitations involves the risk of injury or death. But at the same time, defiance of decorum is a subconscious reminder of our animal nature. In an acrobatic feat humanity is seen to triumph over death, but the reversion to nonhuman gestures that is thereby entailed signifies that this aspiration to immortality is pure hubris, undoubtedly of evil or even diabolical inspiration. Ritual displays of acrobatics thus provoked disturbing and conflicting emotions that were undoubtedly cathartic and certainly not unwelcomed by the spectators. The acrobat was a kind of social pariah, blamed for performing what the public wanted excitedly to watch (for the Greeks acrobatic stunts were *thaumata*, acts that partook of the marvelous).

Because the vicarious thrill of seeing someone gratuitously risk his life might be enjoyed for its own sake, acrobatic feats were performed independently of the ceremonial occasions for which they had been devised and for purely spectacular and monetary purposes. The consequent debasing of gestures that had been highly symbolic compounded the unease that acrobatics occasioned in the best of circumstances. Deprived of its semantic content, acrobatics appeared to be a purposeless activity, the risking of life and limb for no discernible higher reason. In a Western world increasingly obsessed with rationalizing all human pursuits, acrobatics became necessarily subversive.

In early modern times acrobatics had been the prerogative of the Italians, who tended to valorize acrobatics by a combination of agility and equilibrium—the display of mind over matter. Later it came to be an Eastern European specialty that was characterized by exhibitions of great strength. The appearance in the West of the Peking (Beijing) Circus in the 1970s profoundly altered Western perceptions of acrobatics, since the Chinese stress less the notion of strength and more that of lightness. Chinese acrobats even go so far as to introduce humor into their acts, a fact that suggests that acrobatics has become so institutionalized in Asiatic culture that there is nothing to fear.

Finally, the Cirque du Soleil (founded in the 1980s) added a new notion to acrobatics, that of a narrative based on elements drawn from the *commedia dell'arte*. The Cirque's shows are not simply a string of acts consecutive to each other according to principles of sheer spectacle. Each act is actually part of a story; hence the flow is mimetic in addition to being rhetorical and aesthetic. The acrobatic spectacle involves the working out of human problems and relations as well as the successive amplification of the emotional thrill caused by witnessing the marvelous and the death-defying.

—John McClelland

Bibliography: Borassatti, Giustiniano. (1753) *Il ginnasta in pratica, ed in teorica.* Venice: Gio Battista Rossi.

Bouissac, Paul. (1973) *La mesure des gestes.* The Hague: Mouton.

Burgess, Hovey. (1976) *Circus Techniques: Juggling, Equilibristics.* New York: Drama Book Specialists.

Christout, Marie-Francoise. (1965) *Le merveilleux et le theatre du silence en France à partir du XVIIe siècle.* The Hague: Mouton.

Deonna, W. (1953) *Le symbolisme de l'acrobatie antique.* Brussels: Berchem.

Duchartre, Pierre-Louis. (1929) *The Italian Comedy.* Trans. by R. T. Weaver. London: Harrap.

Guts Muths, J. Chr. (1793) *Gymnastik für jugend.* (1804) 2d ed. (much modified). Schnepfenthal.

Lambranzi, Gregorio. (1716) *Neue und curieuse theatralische tanz-schule.* Nuremberg: Wolrab English translation by D. de Moroda. Brooklyn: Dance Horizons, 1966.

Mercurialis, Hieronymus. (1569) *Artis gymnasticae libri sex.* Venice: Giunti.

Sparshott, Francis. (1988) *Off the Ground. First Steps to a Philosophical Consideration of the Dance.* Princeton, NJ: Princeton University Press.

Strehly, Georges. (1892) *L'acrobatie et les acrobates, texte et dessins.* Paris: Delagrave.

Toole-Scott, R. (1960) *Circus and Allied Arts, a World Bibliography.* Vol. II. Derby: Harpur and Sons, 19–24.

Ulmann, Jacques. (1965) *De la gymnastique aux sports modernes.* Paris: Presses Universitaires de France. (1977) 3d ed. Paris: Vrin.

Aerobics

The term "aerobic" means "with oxygen," or "living and working with oxygen." Aerobics is a system of exercises designed to promote the supply and use of oxygen in the body. Some of these exercises include biking, running, dancing, rowing, skating, and walking. Aerobic exercise increases cardiorespiratory fitness, which is the heart's ability to pump blood and deliver oxygen throughout the body. Some benefits of cardiorespiratory fitness are increased endurance and energy, weight control, decreased blood pressure, decreased heart disease, decreased cholesterol, and an increased ability to manage stress.

Development

The word "aerobics" is relatively new in the context of sport and exercise. In 1968, Dr. Kenneth Cooper, a U.S. Air Force physician published a book entitled *Aerobics*, which came from Cooper's research on coronary artery disease. At their peak in the 1960s, cardiovascular diseases accounted for 55 percent of all U.S deaths annually. Cooper developed his aerobics exercise program in the spirit of preventive medicine. He felt that the contributions of aerobic types of exercise to cardiovascular health and fitness were significant. Cooper felt if people controlled their weight, lowered their blood pressure and cholesterol, and ate a proper diet they could lower the incidence of cardiovascular disease. One intent of aerobics was to develop a prescription for exercise, a specific program to follow. The book identified the quantity, kind, and frequency of desirable exercise. Cooper continued to spread his message with follow-up books, *The New Aerobics* (1970), *Aerobics for Women* (1972), and *The Aerobics Way* (1977). These books have been translated into German, Portuguese, Spanish, Swedish, Japanese, Hebrew, Russian, and Dutch. Cooper traveled all over the world lecturing and explaining his beliefs and methods. Cooper believed that "aerobics, exercise, and preventive medicine have no language, ethnic, or cultural barriers" (1977). In May 1968, the Congress of International Military Sports adopted Cooper's aerobics program for the coun-

Celebrities such as Jane Fonda (center) produced their own aerobics programs, including commercial videotapes. Such promotions helped to popularize the activity during the fitness craze of the 1970s and 1980s as a way of improving cardiovascular fitness.

tries of Sweden, Austria, Finland, Korea, and Brazil as well as the United States. From the military influences, the aerobics program spread to civilian populations. In Brazil, runners ask "Have you done your Cooper today?" when they want to know if you've done your running or jogging.

In 1968, about the same time Kenneth Cooper was promoting his aerobics program, Judy Sheppard Missett was beginning an aerobic exercise program called "Jazzercise," a highly choreographed set of exercises set to music. This type of exercise incorporated muscle group work with new dance trends. In 1969, Jackie Sorenson started "Aerobic Dance," which was also a choreographed set of dance patterns set to music with the goal of increased cardiovascular fitness. By the early 1970s, aerobics, aerobic dance, and dance exercise were used interchangeably to describe the combination of exercise and dance movements set to music. Most participants in the early aerobic dance classes were women.

By the late 1970s and early 1980s, in order to attract more men, the name "aerobic dancing" was simply shortened to "aerobics." Coeducational classes were now offered and the aerobics boom followed. Aerobics classes were offered in a variety of settings—churches, community centers, schools, and of course health clubs. Jane Fonda and Richard Simmons contributed to the tremendous growth of aerobics and the boom spread all over the world. U.S. instructors began to travel to other countries to train new instructors. In the United States in 1978 there were an estimated 6 million participants, in 1982, 19 million participants, and in 1987, 22 million participants. Forty-five percent of the aerobics participants were women aged 30–50, and this was their sole form of exercise. Another 45 percent of the participants added aerobics to their menu of sport and recreational activities. Ten percent of the participants were instructors. Aerobics quickly evolved from its early choreographed dance format to a varied and diverse form of dance, sport, and exercise movements set to music. Today more than 25 million people participate in the aerobic fitness industry. Virtually every community offers some sort of aerobic exercise class. Aerobics has even expanded into the home, as one can find aerobic dance leaders on television at just about any hour of the day or rent or buy aerobics videos from a variety of sources.

Many of the early aerobics classes were what is called "high impact," that is, both feet may be off the floor at any given time. High impact was characterized by running or jogging in place, jumping jacks, and small jumps or hops. This was an exciting beginning to aerobics; however, this style created a tremendous amount of stress on the joints, and many of the participants developed impact-related injuries. So, "low impact" aerobics was developed in response to the increase in injuries. Low impact means that one foot is on the floor at all times; the routines are characterized by marching in place and traveling from one side of the room to the other. Variable impact aerobics came next, which is a combination of high and low impact moves. This combined the intensity of high impact with the safety of low impact. From the creativity of aerobic instructors and the industry in general have come many new and varied types of aerobic classes. These include water aerobics, sculpting, strength, abdominal, sports conditioning, and circuit or interval classes. Step aerobics, which was developed by Gin Miller while she was recovering from a knee injury, is a trend that took the aerobics industry by storm. This extremely popular style involves stepping up and down from a platform 15 to 30 centimeters (6 to 12 inches) high while performing different step combinations.

Aerobics is extremely beneficial for developing overall physical fitness. Aerobic dance can improve a participant's flexibility, strength, cardiovascular fitness, and body composition, or percentage of body fat. The rhythmic movements performed to music also help to develop balance and coordination. The popularity of aerobics is also attributable to the social support and reinforcement inherent to a group exercise situation.

To ensure safe and effective aerobic exercise programs, training and educational organizations emerged to help guide this fast-growing industry. In the United States, the International Dance Exercise Association (IDEA) and the Aerobic and Fitness Association of America (AFAA) developed into two of the largest in the world, helping to promote aerobics in virtually every country. In 1990 IDEA had over 23,000 instructor members in over 70 countries. These organizations helped to develop some fundamental components of the aerobic exercise class. A well-designed aerobic dance class consists of five segments: the warm-up or prestretch (10 minutes), the aerobic segment (20–45 minutes), cool down (5–10 minutes), strength work (10–20 minutes), and the final stretch (5–10 minutes).

Competition

A natural progression of aerobic exercise classes has been the addition of competitive aerobics. The National Aerobic Championship (NAC) was created in 1983 by the founders of the sport, Karen and Howard Schwartz. It was the first national competition for aerobics presented in the United States. Today, its format and rules have become the international standard for aerobic competition around the world. In 1989, the International Competitive Aerobics Federation (ICAF), which became the governing body of the sport, was founded by Howard Schwartz. The growth of this new sport has been impressive. The first World Aerobic Championship was held in 1990, with 16 countries represented, and it was televised in 30 countries. Thirty five countries were represented in 1994. The World Aerobic Championships were broadcast to 175 countries in 1995.

Championship aerobics has been called the "toughest two minutes in sports." It is a rigorous display of both compulsory and freestyle moves choreographed into a two-minute routine set to music. The performance showcases incredible amounts of strength, flexibility, and endurance as well as creativity and dance. The competitors follow specific rules and regulations and are judged by an international panel of judges. There are 8 categories of competition: Novice Men's Individual, Novice Women's Individual, Masters Division *M* (over 35) men's individual, Masters Division *M* women's individual, Advanced Men's Individual, Advanced Women's Individual, Advanced Mixed Pair (male/female combination), and Advanced Teams (of three; any gender combination). In 1996, the governing bodies of the sport were developing new guidelines for competitive aerobics.

—Sally Crawford

Bibliography: Bishop, J. G. (1992) *Fitness through Aerobic Dance*. Scottsdale, AZ: Gorsuch Scarisbrick Publishing.

Casten, C., and P. Jordan. (1990) *Aerobics Today*. St. Paul, MN: West Publishing.

Cooper, Kenneth. (1968) *Aerobics*. New York: M. Evans and Co.

———. (1970) *The New Aerobics*. New York: M. Evans and Co.

———. (1972) *Aerobics for Women*. New York: M. Evans and Co.

———. (1977) *The Aerobics Way*. New York: M. Evans and Co.

Francis, Lorna. (1993) *Aerobic Dance for Health and Fitness*. Madison, WI: Brown and Benchmark.

Mazzeo, K. S., and L. M. Mangili. (1993) *Fitness through Aerobics and Step Training*. Englewood, CO: Morton Publishing.

Thomas, D. Q., and N. E. Rippe. (1992) *Is Your Aerobics Class Killing You?* Chicago: Chicago Review Press.

African Games

With a population of 820 million people, Africa is the second-most-populous continent after Asia. In the 1960s, the economic, educational, and linguistic problems inherited from colonial regimes and the contrasting cultural and political traditions present throughout Africa posed major problems for the newly independent African nations. In 1965, the Organization for African Unity (OAU) sponsored the first African Games. With shaky financial resources in a period of wrangling for power within the OAU, sports organizations found a common cause in the political struggle against South African apartheid. They benefited from the timely recognition by, and financial support from, the International Olympic Committee (IOC). In the April 1987 issue of *Olympic Review,* Banzouzi Malonga noted that the "national treasuries cannot sustain the organization of large-scale games" and called for a formula to save the regional games and "avoid the image of the Continental Games which have been held only three times in 22 years. By 1995, determined African leadership with IOC support had held six African Games. Though political and economic problems persisted, South Africa was now a participant and the games had provided a test case for the Olympic ideal of athletic competition as a means of securing peaceful international understanding while increasing cultural and national identity.

Origins

In the twentieth century, improved communications and transportation systems broadened the viewpoints of national and local sportsmen and sportswomen and made regional or continental games possible. Books, motion pictures, and television featuring international competitions reached worldwide markets. The renewal of the Olympic Games in 1896 awakened the sporting world to the possibilities of international athletic competitions. The early Olympics were confined to a collection of track and field, shooting, and swimming events. They were also dominated by the western and northern European nations and the United States, which had been populated by immigrants from western and northern Europe. Despite the European orientation of the IOC, its ideological commitment to open competition gradually extended its influence to other continents. With strong economic and political ties to European nations, South Africa and Egypt were the first African nations to obtain IOC membership. In 1908 and 1912, South Africans won four gold medals. In 1912, an Egyptian entered the fencing competition, and two Egyptian athletes won gold medals at the 1928 Olympics.

Colonial politics, language differences, the lack of communications systems, and economic difficulties delayed the organization of African games. At the close of his Olympic career in 1923, Baron Pierre de Coubertin (1863–1937), the founder of the modern games, sought to involve the IOC in the development of African sports. Unsuccessful attempts were made to hold All-Africa games in Algiers in 1925 and Alexandria in 1929. The economic crises of the 1930s and World War II delayed international competitions. While few Africans participated on national teams, Olympic successes brought international attention. In 1928, a Moroccan won the marathon while competing for France. From George Poage's two bronze medals in 1904 to Jesse Owens's four gold medals in 1936, Americans of African descent were successful in track events.

After World War II, the termination of colonial rule led to the creation of 32 new nations, 17 in 1960 alone. Many of the new national governments included a culture, youth, and sports ministry. In 1957 and 1959, Egypt won the first and second All-African soccer (association football) championships at Khartoum and Cairo. In 1959, French-speaking athletes competed in games at Bangui, in what is now the Central African Republic. In the independence year of 1960, East and West African games were held. In the same year, former French colonies held the Games of Friendship in Tananarive (now the capital, Antananarivo), Madagascar. In 1961, athletes from France and 22 African countries participated in the second games at Abidjan, Côte d'Ivoire. The third Games of Friendship were held on 11–23 April 1963, in Dakar, Senegal. French athletes joined those from 19 francophone and 5 anglophone countries in competing in track and field, boxing, soccer (association football), cycling, swimming, basketball, volleyball, handball, and judo. Women competed in track and field and basketball. The walls established by colonial powers were crumbling. Athletes from Mediterranean Africa, such as Egypt, Tunisia, Algeria, and Morocco, participated in the Mediterranean Games and athletes in anglophone Africa took part in the Commonwealth Games. In the 1960s, police and army units provided training opportunities for athletes, and foreign coaches provided instruction in techniques. By 1968, 45 African countries were involved in international sports. Table tennis was played in 21 countries, soccer (association football) in 12, track and field and boxing in 11, swimming in 9, and basketball and tennis in 8. The nations most active in Olympic sporting events were Egypt, Tunisia, Morocco, Ethiopia, Ghana, Sudan, Kenya, and Uganda.

The appearance of African victors in the Olympic Games coincided with the political emergence of new African nations. Ethiopia's Abebe Bikila won the marathon in 1960 and 1964 and his compatriot Mamo Wolde won in 1968. In 1980, Ethiopia's Miruts Yifter won the 5,000-meter (5,468-yard) and 10,000-meter (10,936-yard) runs. From 1968 to 1996, Kenya's runners won 11 gold medals in the 1,500-meter (1,640-yard) to 10,000-meter Olympic events. Moroccans won three gold medals and a Tunisian won one. In the 1996 women's events, Ethiopia's Fatum

A poster for the second African Games, first organized in the heady days of the independence period of the 1960s.

Roba won the marathon and silver and bronze medals were won by athletes from a variety of African nations.

In December 1966, 32 nations in the three-year-old OAU formed the Supreme Council for Sports in Africa. Composed of sports ministers, national sports committee heads, National Olympic Committee presidents, IOC members, and sports federation presidents, the Supreme Council's general purpose was to coordinate and promote sports, but the "primary motivating force in its formation" was "an attack on South Africa's apartheid sport." Under Secretary General Jean-Claude Ganga's astute management, the Supreme Council played the leading role in staging the African Games and opposing South African participation in international sports. Its policy of racial apartheid led to South Africa's

African Games

Reasons for Success

In 1990, Matthias O. Ukah, a professor in the Department of Physical Education, College of Education, Katsina Ala, Benue State, Nigeria, listed seven major sociocultural factors in the African Games:

Pan-African nationalism
The Supreme Council for Sports in Africa
The "sport for all" concept
The high public esteem enjoyed by African athletes
The International Olympic Committee
Foreign influences, particularly from the United States
Traditional sports and dances.

He concluded that the aim of African sport was "to foster African unity, peace, and brotherhood."

—Maynard Brichford

disbarment from the 1964 and 1968 Olympics and expulsion from the Olympic movement in 1970.

Development

On 18 July 1965, Congolese President Alphonse Massamba-Débat opened the first African Games at Brazzaville. More than 1,000 individuals from 30 nations competed in track and field, swimming, basketball (male and female), soccer (association football), handball, volleyball, boxing, cycling, judo, and tennis. Soccer was the most popular sport and attracted the largest crowds. The FIFA (soccer federation) reporter noted an evident rivalry between former French and British colonies and instances of pushing, holding, and striking, but commended the management of the games and the progress they represented. IOC President Avery Brundage spoke and approved the OAU's aid to the games, provided no "political pressure" was exercised.

On 7 January 1973, Nigerian head of state Yakubu Gowon opened the second African Games in Lagos. Delegations from 41 countries participated in the ceremonial march before 50,000 spectators. The crowd listened to the anthem for the games, which included refrains about "games and culture," "united in brotherhood," and "reflect the

common good." Originally scheduled for Bamako, Mali, a coup had forced the postponement of the games from October 1969 to January 1973. The Lagos newspaper headlined its report of the host Nigerian team's first gold medal in the table tennis competition. Both the 1973 and 1978 games benefited from the oil revenues of the host countries.

On 13 July 1978, the third African Games opened with nearly 3,000 athletes from 45 nations assembled before 70,000 spectators in the sports stadium in Algiers. The host committee had mobilized 9,000 people for service on commissions for protocol; beautification; housing, transportation, and food services; equipment and material; sports organization; medical services; press and information; and cultural activities. More than 300 journalists covered the games, and Algerian television provided the first live broadcasts and distributed three-hour summaries to 40 countries. The Algerian team of 265 athletes dominated the contests. Henry Rono of Kenya won gold medals in the 10,000 meters and the 3,000 meter steeplechase. The report to the IOC commended the games for "transcending the current political divisions."

The fourth African Games were held in Nairobi, Kenya on 7–12 August 1987. Approximately 4,000 competitors from 38 nations participated. After nine years during which the games had been postponed twice, the tenacity of the Supreme Council for Sports in Africa and the Organizing Committee helped stage the Nairobi games. Funds from the People's Republic of China provided facilities. Budgeted as an $18 million event, entry fees, IOC support, and income from broadcasting rights produced only $4 million. Part of the shortfall was made up by sponsorships proposed by a U.S. fund-raising firm and a national lottery organized by the Kenyan government's sports ministry.

Egyptian President Hosni Mubarak opened the fifth African Games in Cairo on 20 September 1991. Forty-two nations participated in 16 sports. Meeting before the games, the General Assembly of African National Olympic Committees admitted South Africa and Namibia to membership. The IOC provided substantial financial support through participation subsidies, technical assistance, and a grant. It reported that "the situation is a lot better" than in previous games. The Egyptian government invested $120 million in facilities and staged opening and closing pageants featuring

Egyptian history. Qualifying rounds were held in each of the Supreme Council for Sports in Africa's development zones. Egypt, Nigeria, and Kenya dominated the games, and newcomer Namibia won several medals.

The sixth African Games were held in Harare, Zimbabwe on 13–23 September 1995. A cash crisis caused by drought, World Bank restrictions, and a lack of sponsors limited participation and hampered the preparation of venues. A South African team participated for the first time. Despite poor attendance, the officials overcame organization problems, and athletes and spectators celebrated with "gay abandon."

—Maynard Brichford

Bibliography: Allison, Lincoln, ed. (1986) *The Politics of Sport.* Manchester: Manchester University Press.

Baker, William F., and James A. Mangan. (1987) *Sport in Africa.* New York: Africana Publishing Company.

Avery Brundage Collection. Box 196, University of Illinois Archives.

Lapchick, Richard E. (1975) *The Politics of Race and International Sport, The Case of South Africa.* Westport, CT: Greenwood Press.

Olympic Review. (September 1977; August–September 1978; April–June 1987; October 1987; September–November 1991; August–September 1995).

Ukah, Matthias O. (1990) "Socio-cultural Forces in Growth of All African Games." *Journal of the International Council for Health, Physical Education and Recreation* 26, 2: 16–20.

Wagner, Eric A., ed. (1989) *Sport in Asia and Africa.* New York: Greenwood Press.

Aggression

What level of aggression is acceptable in sport, what promotes it, and what can be done about it? Some theorists have viewed sport as a cathartic outlet for individuals' aggressive tendencies, holding that aggression is an internal drive. Others have viewed aggression as socially learned and thus potentially elevated by sport participation. Although it is often assumed that sport reflects the culture of which it is a part, it seems that some sports are more likely than others to promote aggressive behavior.

Recent research has also explored the relationship between sport and warfare and between sport and violence against women. Other investigators have examined the role of media in sport violence and the causes of fan violence. The prevailing conclusion from these studies is that violence is part of a more general cultural pattern wherein aggressive behavior, which may be acceptable or even endorsed in the controlled environment of sport, spills over into other areas of life where it is less acceptable (Loy and Chick 1993; Baron, Straus, and Jaffee 1988).

Defining and Measuring Aggression

As applied to sport, aggression is an ambiguous concept, having both positive and negative connotations. For example, public approval is typically given to assertive actions by individuals attempting to achieve appropriate goals using acceptable tactics; but public disapproval is expressed when individuals' excessively assertive actions willfully cause harm to others. However, as Russell (1993) observes, in a sport context, ambiguity can be mitigated by adopting aggressive rule violations as a standard and thus leaving judgments of excessive and illegal aggression to experts (e.g., officials, umpires, and referees).

Following an early distinction made by Buss (1961), sport psychologists distinguish between *hostile* and *instrumental* aggression. The primary purpose of hostile aggression is to inflict physical or psychological injury on another, whereas the main aim of instrumental aggression is to attain an approved goal, such as winning a game. These two forms of aggression can generally be distinguished clearly in most sport situations but, in the case of extreme contact sports such as boxing and ice hockey, it is not always possible to determine the reasons for athletes' aggressive actions. Moreover, recent research suggests that ambiguity in the understanding and use of aggression may be a factor that leads instrumental aggression in sport to spill over into hostile aggression outside of sport, for example, male athletes involved in sexual assault against women.

Aggression in sport typically is measured through questionnaires or interviews. For example, moods may be assessed through an adjective checklist or by querying a subject's evaluation or retaliatory reactions to various scenarios pre-

Do aggressive sports promote aggression or merely reflect patterns in society? Certainly contact sports such as rugby produce higher levels of aggression—in both players and spectators—than do noncontact sports.

sented in written descriptions, photographs, or films. Aggression may also be measured behaviorally by evaluating the assessment of penalties (e.g., Lefebvre and Passer 1974; Vokey and Russell 1992). Aggression has been studied from the perspective of morality by investigating the egocentricity of athletes and their willingness to violate rules in an effort to win (Bredemeier, Shields, and Smith 1986). Longitudinal studies that follow the same individuals over a significant period of time, noting changes in aggression for those who play sports, as well as for those who do not play sports, is the ideal way to address this issue. Such studies, however, have been rare.

Theorizing Aggression

In the first half of the twentieth century, many psychologists assumed that participation in sports might serve as a cathartic outlet for individuals' aggressive tendencies. Such assumptions generally were grounded in the view that aggression is an internal drive based on frustration and/or instinct. However, more recent research has consistently indicated that participation in sports is likely to increase an individual's aggression, supporting the notion that aggression is, at least to some degree, socially learned (Bandura 1973). Leonard Berkowitz (1969) combined elements of frustration-aggression theory and social learning theory, pointing out that frustration often leads to arousal and anger. In turn, arousal and anger may lead to aggression in particular contexts when the presence of socially learned cues indicates that aggression is appropriate.

Other theorists (e.g., Elias 1986) have argued that sport historically has developed as a constraint on aggression, or at least as a means to channel aggression into culturally acceptable forms. It also has been argued that sports do not necessarily increase aggression, but that sports reflect and enhance the dominant values and attitudes of the culture of which they are a part. For example, if competitiveness is defined as aggression, then the "killer instinct" is highly valued. There are, however, societies in which cooperation, which links the organization of social relationships and responsibilities of the individual to the group, is more highly valued than competitiveness (Allison 1980). In such societies aggression in sports is likely to be negatively sanctioned.

Some theorists (especially Bredemeier, Shields, and Smith 1986) have suggested that sport creates a separate moral sphere, distinct from the real world, and one in which the goal of winning negates the stated norms and rules of the game. Others have applied the notion of positive deviance to explain athletes' use of inappropriate aggression. Positive deviance is a form of overconformity to the perceived goals and norms of sport. Display of machismo, playing with pain, or intentionally injuring an opponent may be "grounded in athletes' uncritical acceptance of and commitment to what they have been told by important people in their lives ever since they began participating in competitive programs; in a real sense, it is the result of being too committed to the goals and norms of sport" (Hughes and Coakley 1991, 311). Where winning is valued above all else, athletes may use aggression to show their total commitment to sport or, more particularly, to winning in sport.

> In the case of athletes in highly visible sports, this process of developing fraternity, superiority, and disdain for outsiders might also lead some of them to naively assume they are somehow beyond the law, and the people outside the athletic fraternity do not deserve their respect. This could lead to serious cases of negative deviance including, for example, assault, sexual assault, and rape (including gang rape), the destruction of property, reckless driving, and alcohol abuse (Hughes and Coakley 1991, 314).

Contexts for Aggression
Aggression and the Individual
Although individuals who participate in sports seem to exhibit higher levels of aggression than

those who do not, it cannot be assumed that sport participation leads to elevated levels of aggression. It is equally possible that sports simply attract individuals who are innately more aggressive than nonathletes. This possibility underscores the theoretical issue of selection versus change or the relative influence of innate personality versus socialization through sport. In order to examine this important issue, it is necessary to measure individuals' levels of aggression before they begin to play sports and then to determine whether there is an increase in aggression that occurs over the time that they are playing sports.

Some sports are more likely to be associated with violence and inappropriate aggression than others. Under conditions of provocation, for example, participants in contact sports reveal much higher levels of aggression than participants in noncontact sports (Rees, Howell, and Miracle 1990). Other research has shown that aggression may be an effective strategy when applied early in a contest, or it may be employed as a reaction to failure (e.g., Widmeyer and Birch 1984). Even contact sports, however, do not have to promote unacceptable aggression and violence. It has been shown that a variety of contextual factors affect aggression levels in sports. For example, the presence of officials in organized sports increases the number of fouls since the athletes assume it is the referees' job to control inappropriate aggression (Rees and Miracle 1984).

Studies of martial arts also have demonstrated that sport participation does not necessarily promote aggression. In one experiment (Trulson 1986) a group of 13- to 17-year-old males classified as delinquent were divided into three groups matched on aggression and personality adjustment. One group received traditional training in Tae Kwon Do. During this training, the philosophical component of Tae Kwon Do, which includes maintaining a sense of responsibility, emphasizing respect for others, and building confidence and self-esteem, was stressed. Physical skills and meditation also were included. The second group practiced a modern form of Tae Kwon Do in which only the fighting and self-defense components were taught. The third group received no martial arts training but played basketball and football instead. After six months, the youths in group one showed lower levels of aggression, those in group two showed higher levels of aggression, and those in group three showed no change.

Aggression and the Group

Roberts, Arth, and Bush (1959) argued that games are models of culturally relevant activities and that events that provide the greatest opportunity to practice and to learn about salient cultural activities are also those most likely to be found in association with the activities they model. In technologically simple societies, games and sports provide relatively unambiguous models of other activities. American football, for example, with its "men in the trenches" (offensive and defensive linemen), "field generals" (quarterbacks), efforts by teams to move the ball into "enemy territory" and, ultimately, scoring by "invading" the opponent's end zone, is an unmistakable model of warfare. Baseball, on the other hand, is a much less straightforward example of any single culturally relevant activity, although running, clubbing, and missile throwing were all important activities in human evolutionary history.

Other theorists (e.g., Loy and Chick 1993) have found evidence for a cultural pattern model for sport and aggression and suggest that differences in aggressive behavior are primarily learned. Cross-cultural studies (Sipes 1973; Chick, Loy, and Miracle 1995) have shown, for example, that there is a positive association between the existence of combative sports and the prevalence of warfare in particular cultures. It seems that societies long ago devised sports in order to prepare young men for the inevitability of war. As noted previously, contact sports are effective in increasing aggression while channeling it into acceptable forms until it is necessary to redirect it to warfare.

Although aggression is appropriate, even essential for success in war, what happens to individuals with heightened levels of aggression during periods of peace or when there is no active war in which to channel their aggression? Recently, this question has most often been asked with regard to violence toward women. Several studies indicate that athletes are disproportionately represented among perpetrators of rape and other forms of violent physical abuse of women (Loy 1992; Loy and Chick 1993; Benedict, Crosset, and McDonald 1994). It has also been suggested that sports contribute to male hegemony by linking maleness with positively sanctioned aggression while belittling women and their activities (Bryson 1987; Messner and Sabo 1994). These issues are controversial, however. Some researchers believe that athletes are unfairly stereotyped due to their visibility and the fact that they are typically held to higher standards than others.

Aggression and Fan Violence

Violence by sport spectators or fans has become an issue of considerable concern in the second half of the twentieth century. Soccer (association football) hooliganism in Great Britain has received much attention (e.g., Pearton 1986), as have the eruptions of violence between European soccer fans. Soccer is even held responsible for the initiation of war between Honduras and Nicaragua in 1969.

One study (Phillips 1983) found a significant effect of sport aggression as presented through the mass media. Immediately after heavyweight championship prizefights from 1973 through 1978, homicides in the United States increased by more than 12 percent, with the greatest increase coming after heavily publicized fights. These findings persisted even after controlling for extraneous variables, suggesting that prizefights stimulate fatal, aggressive behavior in some Americans.

What is it about sports that excites spectators to violent aggression? Various possibilities have been suggested. For example, it has been hypothesized that such aggression is the direct result of: simply observing athletes' aggression (Arms, Russell, and Sandilands 1979); or of fans' desire to create and maintain a positive social identity (Wann 1993); or that spectator violence is largely ritualistic (Marsh 1982).

Drugs, especially alcohol, appear to be another element that is common to spectator aggression. During the 1995 U.S. National Football League season, a national audience was treated to a game-long spectacle of fans throwing snowballs and ice at players, coaches, and officials on the field, as well as at each other, during a game between the New York Giants and the San Diego Chargers. Alcoholic beverages were subsequently banned from Giants Stadium for the next home game to be played there, although it involved the New York Jets rather than the Giants. Drugs have also been implicated in aggressiveness by players. In particular, steroids, which are usually taken surreptitiously by athletes to promote muscular development, appear to heighten aggressiveness.

Aggression, Sport, and Mass Media

Instant replays, a result of advances in broadcast technology, have brought to the surface an interesting but chilling phenomenon in modern sport spectatorship. Scoring plays or other exciting or exceptional plays are commonly replayed. But, in addition, plays that involve exceptional aggressiveness, such as a "good hit" or a particularly devastating down-field block in American football, a hard-body check in ice hockey, or a powerful pick in basketball, are also commonly replayed even when they have little apparent effect on the outcome of the game or the particular play. Aggressive acts that lead to actual violence, in terms of fights among players, are frequently replayed or rebroadcast on sports shows. Spectators appear to enjoy exhibitions of aggression and even violence, while players in many sports believe that aggressive play is instrumental in winning (DeNeui and Sachau 1996). Aggressive play is often seen as evidence of trying hard to win and, thus, is as meritorious for the vanquished as it is for the victors.

Summary

Learning how and when to use violent forms of aggressive behavior may begin early in the sport socialization process. Young athletes observe the behavior of role models and learn from interactions with coaches, parents, and others (McPherson, Curtis, and Loy 1989). When such learning takes place early in life, it seems reasonable that it might have long-lasting consequences for individuals and for society.

Can there be sport without increased aggression? Social scientists can only analyze real behavior. Thus the studies of sport-related aggression are grounded in the reality of typical sports activities as they have been observed in societies around the world. However, there have been numerous suggestions in the extant literature that sport could be reformed so that it would not necessarily lead to increases in aggression. This idealized version of sport would require some changes in the way that sport is currently experienced by many players and spectators, though not by all. The suggestion that sport could be enjoyed without the promotion of inappropriate aggression is

supported by the fact that various cultural and contextual factors are known to contribute to increased levels of aggression in sports.

—Andrew W. Miracle, Garry Chick, and John W. Loy

See also Violence.

Bibliography: Allison, Maria T. (1980) "Competition and Cooperation: A Sociocultural Perspective." *International Review of Sport Sociology* 15: 93–104.

Arms, Robert L., Gordon W. Russell, and Mark L. Sandilands. (1979) "Effects on the Hostility of Spectators of Viewing Aggressive Sports." *Social Psychology Quarterly* 42: 275–279.

Bandura, Albert (1973) *Aggression: A Social Learning Analysis.* Englewood Cliffs, NJ: Prentice-Hall.

Baron, L., M. A. Straus, and D. Jaffee. (1988) "Legitimate Violence, Violent Attitudes, and Rape: A Test of the Cultural Spillover Theory." In *Human Sexual Aggression: Current Perspectives*, edited by R. A. Prentsky and V. L. Quinsey. New York: New York Academy of Sciences, 79–110.

Benedict, Jeffrey, Todd Crosset, and Mark A. McDonald. (1994) "Student-Athletes Reported for Sexual Assault: A Survey of Campus Police Departments and Judicial Affairs." Paper presented at the Conference of the North American Society for the Sociology of Sport, Savannah, GA.

Berkowitz, Leonard. (1969) *Roots of Aggression.* New York: Atherton Press.

Bredemeier, Brenda Jo, David L. Shields, and Michael D. Smith. (1986) "Athletic Aggression: An Issue of Contextual Morality." *Sociology of Sport Journal* 3, 1: 15–28.

Bryson, Lois. (1987) "Sport and the Maintenance of Masculine Hegemony." *Women's Studies International Forum* 10: 349–360.

Buss, A. H. (1961) *The Psychology of Aggression.* New York: Wiley.

Chick, Garry, John W. Loy, and Andrew W. Miracle. (1995) "Sport, War and Rape." Paper presented at the annual meeting of the American Anthropological Association, Washington, DC.

DeNeui, D. L., and D. Sachau. (1996) "Spectator Enjoyment of Aggression in Intercollegiate Hockey Games." *Journal of Sport & Social Issues* 20: 69–77.

Elias, Norbert. (1986) "An Essay on Sport and Violence." In *Sport and Leisure in the Civilizing Process*, edited by Norbert Elias and Eric Dunning. Oxford: Basil Blackwell, 150–174.

Hughes, Robert, and Jay J. Coakley. (1991) "Positive Deviance among Athletes: The Implications of Overconformity to the Sport Ethic." *Sociology of Sport Journal* 8: 307–325.

Lefebvre, L. M., and M. W. Passer. (1974) "The Effects of Game Location and Importance on Aggression in Team Sport." *International Journal of Sport Psychology* 5: 102–110.

Loy, J. W. (1992) "The Dark Side of Agon: Men in Tribal Groups and the Phenomenon of Gang Rape." Presidential Address, Annual Meeting of the North American Society for the Sociology of Sport, Toledo, OH, November.

Loy, John W., and Garry Chick. (1993) "A Cross-Cultural Test of the Cultural Spillover Theory of Rape." Paper presented at the annual meeting of the Society for Cross-Cultural Research, Washington, DC.

Marsh, Peter. (1982) "Social Order on the British Soccer Terraces." *International Social Science Journal* 34: 247–256.

McPherson, Barry D., James E. Curtis, and John W. Loy. (1989) *The Social Significance of Sport.* Champaign, IL: Human Kinetics.

Messner, Michael A., and Donald F. Sabo. (1994) *Sex, Violence and Power in Sports: Rethinking Masculinity.* Freedom, CA: Crossing Press.

Pearton, Robert. (1986) "Violence in Sport and the Special Case of Soccer Hooliganism in the United Kingdom." In *Sport and Social Theory*, edited by C. Roger Rees and Andrew W. Miracle. Champaign, IL: Human Kinetics, 67–83.

Phillips, David P. (1983) "The Impact of Mass Media Violence on U.S. Homicides." *American Sociological Review* 48: 560–568.

Rees, C. Roger, and Andrew W. Miracle. (1984) "Conflict Resolution in Games and Sports." *International Review of Sport Sociology* 19: 145–156.

Rees, C. Roger, Frank M. Howell, and Andrew W. Miracle. (1990) "Do High School Sports Build Character? A Quasi-Experiment on a National Sample." *Social Science Journal* 27: 303–315.

Roberts, John M., Malcolm J. Arth, and Robert R. Bush. (1959) "Games in Culture." *American Anthropologist* 59: 497–504.

Russell, G. W. (1993) *The Social Psychology of Sport.* New York: Springer-Verlag.

Sipes, Richard G. (1973) "War, Sports and Aggression: An Empirical Test of Two Rival Theories." *American Anthropologist* 75: 64–86.

Trulson, Michael E. (1986) "Martial Arts Training: A Novel 'Cure' for Juvenile Delinquency." *Human Relations* 39: 1131–1140.

Vokey, John R., and Gordon W. Russell. (1992) "On Penalties in Sport as Measures of Aggression." *Social Behavior and Personality* 20: 219–225.

Wann, Daniel L. (1993) "Aggression among Highly Identified Spectators as a Function of Their Need To Maintain Positive Social Identity." *Journal of Sport and Social Issues* 17: 134–143.

Widmeyer, W. Neil, and Jack S. Birch. (1984) "Aggression in Professional Ice Hockey: A Strategy for Success or a Reaction to Failure?" *Journal of Psychology* 117: 77–84.

Aikido

Aikido is a Japanese martial art that includes techniques for bare-handed wrestling, using weapons, and dealing with the armed enemy. It was promoted throughout Japan by Morihei Ueshiba (1883–1969). Aikido is known for its joint-twisting and pinning techniques (*kansetsu-waza*) and its thrusting and stunning blows (*atemi-waza*). The advanced student is a master of techniques to break the opponent's balance or ward off a thrust or grasp. Aikido techniques have the power to kill or injure, but fundamentally their purpose is to seize and control the opponent. All of the principles of swordsmanship (eye contact, proper distance, timing, and cutting methods) are incorporated into aikido movements. The methods of training and spiritual teachings vary from school to school.

Ueshiba learned several different kinds of martial arts during his lifetime, but the major techniques of aikido were derived from the Daito-ryu Jujutsu style, which he learned from Sokaku Takeda (1860–1943) in Shirataki, Hokkaido between 1915 and 1919. Takeda stood only about four feet, nine inches (1.45 meters) tall, but he had an extremely strong personality and was an outstandingly gifted jujutsu practitioner. Ueshiba developed his own techniques and named the resulting style "aikido," since he believed his methods were different from his teacher's both philosophically and technically. He also needed different nomenclature for his martial art to be economically independent from Takeda.

In 1919, Ueshiba moved to Ayabe, Kyoto and started to train as a live-in disciple of Onisaburo Deguchi (1871–1948), a master of a new Shinto-ism school called Omoto-kyo. There, Ueshiba taught Daito-ryu Jujutsu and engaged in religious services. From that point, Deguchi's Omoto-kyo doctrines became Ueshiba's personal spiritual basis.

In 1922, Takeda visited Ueshiba in Ayabe and coached him further in martial arts during his six-month visit. Upon leaving Ayabe, he granted Ueshiba credentials as an acting instructor of Daito-ryu Aiki Jujutsu. Takeda then changed the official name of his school from Daito-ryu Jujutsu to Daito-ryu Aiki Jujutsu, and Ueshiba followed suit, teaching his martial arts under this new name until about 1935.

At that time, the popularity of Omoto-kyo was spreading across the country, and some high-ranking Japanese naval officers who went to the school in Ayabe also came to have an interest in Ueshiba's martial arts, which were still being taught on the sacred grounds of Omoto-kyo in

Ayabe. Some of the officers passed on information about Ueshiba's school to Isamu Takeshita (1869–1949), a retired admiral in Tokyo, the capital. In 1925, Takeshita saw a demonstration of Ueshiba's Daito-ryu Aiki Jujutsu techniques for the first time and was so impressed that he took up the practice and continued it for the rest of his life. With Takeshita's tremendous support and Deguchi's approval, Ueshiba left Ayabe and moved to Tokyo.

In the capital, Takeshita introduced Ueshiba to influential people in military, financial, and political circles, as well as people connected to the imperial household, even organizing a society to support his martial arts teacher. This enabled Ueshiba to become entirely independent from Takeda and Daito-ryu Aiki Jujutsu. During this process, in 1928, Ueshiba changed the name of his martial arts school to Aioi-ryu Aiki Bujutsu. He again renamed his school Aiki-Budo or Ko-Budo, and finally settled with aikido in 1942. Aikido became an official term when it was approved at a conference of the Dai-Nippon Butoku-Kai, the association of all martial arts in Japan.

Like Takeda, Ueshiba had a strong personality and excellent technique and his genius received full attention following Takeda's death after World War II. He and his gifted disciples are responsible for the current position of aikido as a popular Japanese martial art.

Aiki and Daito-ryu Aiki Jujutsu

Aiki, the core concept of aikido, can be traced back to martial arts literature of the Edo era. According to *Toka Mondo* (Candlelight Discussion), written by the master of Kito-ryu Jujutsu in 1764, aiki means that two fighters come to a standstill in a martial arts bout when they have focused their attention on each other's breathing. Many other authors in the 1800s gave similar definitions. However, the volume entitled *Budo-hiketsu Aiki no Jutsu* (Secret Keys to Martial Arts Techniques) published in 1892 gave a new definition of the term. It says that aiki is the ultimate goal in the study of martial arts and may be accomplished by "taking a step ahead of the enemy." According to the volume, the prerequisites for such a preemptive move are to read the enemy's mind and use a battle cry. Unfortunately, no details on specific exercises have been recorded.

One of the less aggressive martial arts, aikido emphasizes internal harmony as opposed to competition.

It is no longer possible to reconstruct the precise definition of aiki in the Daito-ryu school of jujutsu. This is primarily because Takeda closely guarded his technical secrets, as earlier martial arts practitioners had done, and chose not to transcribe his teachings in written form. However, Nenokichi Sagawa, one of Takeda's closest followers, was mentioned sporadically in Takeda's 1913 notebook, "Exercise aiki." This suggests that Daito-ryu Jujutsu practitioners had used the term aiki and practiced techniques developed through this concept even before they changed the name of their school to Daito-ryu Aiki Jujutsu. Nevertheless, Takeda's failure to leave a clear-cut definition of aiki led to ambiguity in Ueshiba's interpretation, although Takeda still appointed Ueshiba to the important post of acting instructor. Later, as Ueshiba's school grew, his disciples and followers added some new meanings to aiki to compensate for the ambiguity. Since the term is composed of a combination of two Chinese characters—ai (unification) and ki (spirit or mind)—they decided that aikido is a way to become one with the universe or harmonize with the movement and rhythm of nature.

Ueshiba was only one of many Daito-ryu Jujutsu instructors who graduated from Takeda's school. There are many outstanding practitioners who trained with him and later organized their own schools under the name Daito-ryu Aiki Ju-jutsu. Taiso Horikawa and his son Kodo Horikawa (1894–1980) are prime examples. Kodo organized Kodo-kai in 1950. Another school called Roppo-kai is a splinter group of Kodo-kai. Takuma Hisa (1895–1979) was the only person to whom Takeda granted menkyo kaiden (the high-est-level teaching credentials) in Daito-ryu Aiki Jujutsu. This loyal student initiated Daito-ryu Aiki Jujutsu Takuma-kai in 1975. Toshimi Mat-suda (1895-?) was another talented student of Takeda. Ryuho Okuyama, one of Matsuda's stu-dents, later established Hakko-ryu. Yukiyoshi Sagawa (1902–), another highly credited practi-tioner, is now teaching his martial arts techniques to followers under the name Daito-ryu Aiki Bu-jutsu. Tokimune Takeda (1916–1993), one of Sokaku Takeda's sons, had started teaching Daito-ryu Aiki Budo in a combined form of Daito-ryu Aiki Jujutsu and Ono-ha Itto-ryu Kenjutsu (swordsmanship). However, after his death, the organization was split into several minor schools.

Popularization

Aiki-kai

Aiki-kai, the association founded by Morihei Ueshiba, has been promoted all over the world since World War II, and is said to have the great-est number of followers compared with other schools of aikido. This is due to the ceaseless ef-forts of Ueshiba's son, Kisshomaru (1921–), and those of Kisshomaru's full-time disciples. Kisshomaru inherited his father's foundation and ran it on the assumption that Morihei Ueshiba had come late in life to advocate a spiritual nobil-ity in aikido that he believed would enable man to become one with the universe and, in contrast to what he had pursued before the war, had con-demned meaningless competition. Kisshomaru has gone a step further to claim that there should not be any kind of competition in aikido—a stance in sharp contrast with judo and kendo (swordsmanship) promoters who have tried to develop their martial arts as systematic athletic events. The younger Ueshiba has demanded that his students practice aikido only for self-disci-pline and to seek the truth. This pacifist policy has come to be widely accepted, but some of Morihei Ueshiba's most distinguished disciples have disagreed with Kisshomaru and left his

school to establish their own. Some of these are mentioned below.

JAA (Japan Aikido Association)

Kenji Tomiki (1900–1979) founded the JAA in 1974. Tomiki, who joined Morihei Ueshiba in 1926, in 1940 became the first person to receive the eighth dan degree, the highest-level teaching credentials, from the master. Afterward, Tomiki became a professor of physical education and cre-ated a randori (training match) system of aikido. However, his new proposal caused a sharp con-flict of opinions on what aikido should be.

Yoshin-kan

Gozo Shioda (1915–1994), who had trained at Kobu-kan (an old name for Ueshiba's school) since 1932, founded his own school in Tokyo with the backup of business concerns. He developed a new practice system with an emphasis on mas-tery of basic techniques and a stratagem for street combat. He also made a great contribution to the promotion of aikido after World War II.

Ki no Kenkyu-kai (Ki Society)

Koichi Tohei (1920–) joined Kobu-kan in 1940 and later became chief instructor in Aiki-kai. Consequently, he was once seriously considered to be Morihei Ueshiba's successor. But when he was offered the position at Ueshiba's death, he declined and gave it up to Kisshomaru Ueshiba. Later, however, Tohei and Kisshomaru disagreed on instruction methods and began to struggle for leadership. Tohei founded the Ki Society and left Aiki Kai in 1974. He describes aikido as a way to assimilate man into the "Ki" of the universe.

Yosei-kan

Minoru Mochizuki (1907–) started training with Morihei Ueshiba in 1930 on the recommendation of Jigoro Kano (founder of Kodo-kan Judo). He studied aikido as a live-in disciple of Ueshiba. Then he built Yosei-kan in Shizuoka, where he developed a unique system for all-around mar-tial arts training with integrated judo and karate techniques.

Other Aikido Schools

Noriaki Inoue (1902–1994), Morihei Ueshiba's nephew, initiated the foundation of Shinei-Taido.

He and Ueshiba were both followers of Omoto-kyo, but after a 1935 police crackdown on the practice they disagreed on how to cope with religious oppression. So, he left Ueshiba and opened a new school of aikido. Kanshu Sunadomari (1923–) founded Mansei-kan in Kumamoto. He published several books on aikido spirit and breathing power. Minoru Hirai (1903–), who became general manager of Kobu-kan at Ueshiba's request in 1942 and continued to support Ueshiba until after World War II, opened Korindo. Kenji Shimizu (1940–), a live-in disciple of Ueshiba in the latter's twilight years, established Tendo-ryu. Technically speaking, the existence of many excellent aikido instructors with varying characteristics and backgrounds has made present-day aikido much more colorful than ever before. But, unfortunately, there is virtually no communication between the different schools.

Aikido as an Athletic Event

It is worthwhile to consider why judo and kendo have established completely unified associations, while aikido, like its forerunner, Daito-ryu Jujutsu, has been divided into many small groups. Judo and kendo federations have been able to maintain solid bonds because they have both developed a "training match" system so that all practitioners, regardless of their styles and schools, can meet and compete with each other based on the same rules. By participating in the same tournaments, they are able to measure their improvement objectively. Different kendo schools have come to organize a joint committee and hold unified tournaments while preserving their individual characteristics. They do this by teaching original techniques to their followers by means of kata (a practice of basic forms in martial arts). Nationwide—and sometimes worldwide—tournaments have brought different groups into contact. As far as judo is concerned, everyone has learned the same Kodo-kan judo, in which they practice randori and kata simultaneously. This uniformity has produced virtually no factional divergence.

On the other hand, Ueshiba, since the time of Daito-ryu Jujutsu, always encouraged his students to devote themselves to solitary, repetitive kata practice. The implication is that the absence of an objective method to measure students'

skills and strength has resulted in the phenomenal growth of different styles and schools, each of which has different philosophies and training methods. They do not try to understand each other's spiritual principles, causing miscommunication and mistrust among members of different organizations. It is ironic that aikido, which was originally meant to be a "martial arts of harmony and unification," is currently suffering this chaotic division.

As one solution to this problem, Kenji Tomiki incorporated randori practice into aikido in 1960. He advocated an integrated training process using kata and randori, claiming that aikido should be reformed as a competitive athletic event like modern judo and kendo. Tomiki proposed a system for randori aikido modeled on judo and kendo, two martial arts that were being taught in regular physical-education classes in Japanese schools. He argued that it was the only way to promote aikido. He came up with his idea when he was studying the history of kendo. In most kendo schools, kata practice had been the only way to teach or learn kendo techniques until about 1750. Then some instructors developed a training-match system with a bamboo stick and protective gear, which gained popularity with time and finally constituted the bulk of kendo training. However, although Tomiki's proposal made good sense to teachers of other martial arts, Ueshiba and his followers rejected it. Therefore, he established the Japan Aikido Association as an entity separate from Aiki-kai.

Aikido in Other Countries

The increasing popularity of aikido is attributable to Aiki-kai and other aikido schools' activities outside Japan. Stanley Pranin, editor of the internationally circulated aikido magazine *Aiki Journal*, reported that as of 1993 aikido had the greatest numbers of followers in France, the United States, Japan, Germany, and England, in that order. Minoru Mochizuki was the first person to teach aikido in France. He coached French people in martial arts from 1951 to 1953. Then Tadashi Abe and Nobuyoshi Tamura of Aiki-kai followed in his footsteps. The promotion of aikido in France was carried out in affiliation with the French Judo Federation, making it easier for French aikido instructors to receive governmental subsidies and to rent fully equipped gymnasiums at minimal cost. Consequently, tuition is reasonable, which has also helped to draw followers. Some of the students have chosen to be professional aikido instructors, and aikido schools have sprung up everywhere. According to the membership lists of two major aikido associations in France (Pranin, 1993), there are more than 2,500 schools in that country.

Aikido was first introduced to the United States by Kenji Tomiki in 1952 when he traveled through 15 states with a team of judo instructors. In the same year, Koichi Tohei taught aikido in Hawaii for the first time. They were regarded as two of the best instructors in Aiki-kai at the time. Tohei, in particular, laid the groundwork for the further promotion of aikido in the United States by making return visits to Hawaii. Yoshimitsu Yamada and other younger instructors contributed to the rapid popularization of aikido in North America in the late 1960s. In 1993, Pranin estimated the number of U.S. aikido schools at anywhere between 1,200 and 1,500. The same year, there were 1,300 to 1,600 aikido schools in Japan, but the number of students enrolled at each school is generally smaller, making Japan come in third after France and the United States in world rankings.

Aiki-kai established the International Aikido Federation in 1976 with affiliated clubs and schools located in 29 countries. Then, Yoshin-kan founded the International Yoshin-kan Aikido Federation in 1990. In 1993, the JAA initiated the Tomiki Aikido International Network (TAIN) represented in nine countries. The TAIN has held an international aikido competition every two years since 1989. Other aikido schools have also been engaged in active promotions of their own and have been steadily expanding their territories. But in terms of membership and political influence, Aiki-kai is currently the greatest aikido organization in the world.

The most obvious reasons for Aiki-kai's progressive popularity seems to be its instructors' unsparing efforts and enthusiasm. From the very beginning, no instructors were able to make a living by teaching aikido. They all had to find outside jobs to support themselves, so most of the young wrestlers who demonstrated excellence while they were students decided to stop training and look for regular jobs when they graduated.

However, there were still many people in Aiki-kai who were so dedicated that they chose to travel around the world as volunteer instructors. On the other hand, Kisshomaru Ueshiba, burning with ambition to expand his organization, kept founding new aikido clubs at Japanese universities and businesses. With their ceaseless efforts, Kisshomaru and the pioneers who taught aikido abroad have come to establish their positions as administrators and instructors of the world's largest aikido organization.

Outlook

One of the features of aikido that has drawn many followers is its unique practice system. The training is made up mainly of kata practice, which is well-suited for the elderly or female trainees who learn aikido for physical fitness or self-defense. Also, people in Western countries have come to accept this type of aikido as a way of Zen meditation or as a way to gain insight into the mysticism and philosophies of the East. Such interest of a cultural nature has helped make aikido even more popular.

However, today's aikido associations are faced with two major problems. One concerns diversification. Traditionally, the Japanese people are inclined to favor a school of great prestige and authority. But recently, even the Japanese are beginning to make their judgments based on cultural relativism—a philosophy centered on accepting different values shared by people in other parts of the world. And there is a new trend among young people to join an aikido school operated by a truly gifted teacher with a likable personality instead of choosing a large and traditionally credited school. In the long run, such a trend may present a challenge to the gigantic aikido organizations that have always enjoyed such authority.

The second problem concerns some aikido schools' rigid policy of prohibiting competition. Now that students in general are beginning to show an interest in competitive aikido, it will be increasingly difficult for the traditional schools to justify this policy. It is true that competitive aikido has a "negative" side in that contestants have a tendency to place priority on winning. But it also offers the trainees a wonderful opportunity to develop unflinching courage, a tense and serious attitude, and practical skills for self-defense. Games and tournaments are an excellent form of socialization. Not only do competing wrestlers sometimes form friendships among themselves, they also learn to demonstrate courtesy and manners toward their opponents. Despite these benefits, the traditional ban on aikido competition presents a large obstacle to the process of making aikido an Olympic event. However, an increasing number of groups like TAIN are hard at work to organize international tournaments.

—Fumiaki Shishida

Bibliography: Pranin, Stanley (1991) *The Aiki News Encyclopedia of Aikido*. Tokyo: Aiki News.
———. (1992) *Takeda Sokaku and Daito-ryu Aiki Jujutsu*. Tokyo: Aiki News.
———. (1993) *Aikido Masters: Prewar Students of Morihei Ueshiba*. Tokyo: Aiki News.
Shioda, Gozo. (1985) *Aikido Jinsei* [My Aikido Life]. Tokyo: Takeuchi-shoten-shinsha.
Shishida, Fumiaki. (1992) "Martial Arts Diary by Admiral Isamu Takeshita and Morihei Ueshiba in about 1926" (in Japanese with English abstract). *Research Journal of Budo* 25, 2: 1–12.
Shishida, Fumiaki, and Tetsuro Nariyama. (1985) *Aikido Kyoshitsu* [Aikido Class]. Tokyo: Taishukan.
Sunadomari, Kanemoto. (1969) *Aikido Kaiso Ueshiba Morihei* [A Biography of Morihei Ueshiba: The Founder of Aikido]. Tokyo: Kodansha.
Tomiki, Kenji. (1991) *Budo-ron* [Budo Theory]. Tokyo: Taishukan.
Ueshiba, Kisshomaru. (1977) *Aikido Kaiso Ueshiba Morihei Den* [A Biography of Morihei Ueshiba: The Founder of Aikido]. Tokyo: Kodansha.
———. (1981) *Aikido no Kokoro* [The Spirit of Aikido]. Tokyo: Kodansha.
Westbrook, Adele, and Oscar Ratti. (1979) *Aikido and the Dynamic Sphere*. Rutland, VT, and Tokyo: Charles E. Tuttle.

Air Racing

Origins and Development

Orville and Wilbur Wright's 12-second flight over a cold, windy North Carolina beach on 17 December 1903 gave birth to the air age. The incredible growth of this new era is apparent with the staging of the first air races less than six years later.

James Gordon Bennett, publisher of the *New York Herald,* was then living in self-imposed exile in Paris, the result of some flamboyant behavior not found acceptable by New York society. He was easily persuaded to offer a cash prize and a trophy for "the best speed record by an airplane over a closed course" at an air meet to be held annually. The first such prize would be awarded at the International Air Meet scheduled for Rheims, France, on 22 to 29 August 1909. There were daily contests for speed, altitude, and time and distance. Twenty-eight pilots and thirty-eight airplanes entered this historic event. The altitude contest was won by Hubert Letham of France, who climbed to the amazing altitude of 153 meters (503 feet). The time and distance prize of $10,000 went to Henry Farman, the son of a British correspondent stationed in France, who stayed aloft for just under 3 hours, 5 minutes, and flew 180 kilometers (112 miles).

The main event, the Bennett Cup, was held on 28 August, the next-to-last day of the meet. The weather was clear, sunny, and still for the final five contestants: three Frenchmen, one Englishman, and one American. Each flew separately for two laps over a 3.8-kilometer (6.21-mile) course. Glenn Curtiss, the American, went up first, flying a pusher biplane with a 50 horsepower water-cooled V-8 engine of his own design. He posted an average speed of 76.62 kilometers per hour (kph) (47.65 miles per hour [mph]), besting the second-place Frenchman, Louis Bleriot, by six seconds! Curtiss, the American "dark horse," won the beautiful silver cup, a representation of the Wright Flyer above a winged figure, and a $5,000 prize in the world's first closed-course air race.

Curtiss also participated in the first air meet held in the United States. From 10 to 20 January 1910, the West Coast watched airplanes vying for prizes in speed contests, altitude tries, and cross-country distance awards. Curtiss was the winner in the speed races but Louis Paulhan of France won the $10,000 award for the cross-country race, making him the overall money winner. In October 1910 the Bennett Cup race was held at Belmont Park, Long Island. Curtiss attempted to build a monoplane in which to compete, but he was unable to finish on time, and the first Bennett Cup race held in the United States was won by the English pilot, Grahame-White. A total of six Bennett Cup races were held, with the United

States winning twice, England once, and, in 1920, France winning the trophy for the third time and taking permanent possession.

To stimulate interest in designing and developing seaplanes, Jacques Schneider, an affluent French aviation enthusiast, offered a trophy for an annual race of aircraft capable of taking off and landing in open water. The first of the Schneider Cup races took place 6 April 1913, as part of a water meet held at Monaco. One American, Charles Weymann, and three Frenchmen qualified for the 28-lap, 280-kilometer (174-mile) race. A Deperdussin monoplane flown by Maurice Prevost of France won, flying at an average speed of 73.7 kph (45.8 mph) (adjusted downward from 110.7 kph [68.8 mph] after the judges sent him back around a marker they judged he had missed). The Schneider Cup series continued in 1914, then was suspended during World War I, resuming in 1920. England dominated the Schneider series, winning five of the eleven competitions and taking permanent possession of the trophy by winning three consecutive races in 1927, 1929, and 1931. Italy won three races, the United States two, and France one. By 1931 the winning speed had increased to 547 kph (340 mph).

After World War I there were hundreds of ex-military pilots and several thousand military surplus aircraft (including an estimated 6,000 Curtiss Jennys) in the United States. Many of these pilots turned to "barnstorming" to make a very marginal living until, in 1926, the U.S. Congress passed the Air Commerce Act. Under the administration of the Aeronautics Branch of the Department of Commerce, air traffic would be regulated, pilots and mechanics licensed, and aircraft registered and certified. That, coupled with the strict regulations written into the Civil Aeronautics Act of 1938, effectively brought to an end aviation's barnstorming period.

Some of the air shows featuring the barnstorming acts also included one or more speed competitions. In 1920 a trophy to promote higher speeds was offered by Ralph Pulitzer, publisher of the *New York World* and the *St. Louis Post Dispatch.*

The United States Army and Navy were intensely interested in developing faster, more powerful aircraft. With this in mind, funds were allocated to improve performance of planes they entered in the Pulitzer race. The first of this series was held 27 November 1920, starting at Mitchel Field, Long Island. The air over the 29-mile (46.7-kilometer) triangular closed course was crowded with the 37 entrants who took off individually and were timed separately as they flew the four-lap course. Twenty-five aircraft finished, with Captain C. C. Moseley, U.S. Army Air Service, winning in a specially built Verville-Packard plane using a 638-horsepower engine turning an average speed of 248.6 kph (154.5 mph). When the series was discontinued after the 1925 race, the winning speed had increased by almost 100 mph.

Air racing grew in popularity with the inception of the National Air Race series, organized under the sanction of the National Aeronautics Administration, which were first held in September 1926 at Model Farms Field, Philadelphia. Nineteen race events were scheduled for the week-long air meet plus numerous air show acts. Airplanes competed in various classes: Curtiss Jennys, Curtiss P-1 Hawks, observation planes, and greatly modified civilian planes such as the Waco, Ford, Travel-Aire and others. The feature race was the Kansas City Rotary Club Trophy held on Saturday, 11 September, for Army, Navy, and Marine Corps pilots. The trophy was awarded to Lieutenant George Cuddihy, Navy, flying a Boeing FB-3 fighter, who established a new world's speed record for this class at 290.4 kph (180.5 mph).

Military expenditures for development of racing aircraft soon dried up and for the next thirteen years the National Air Races would feature civilian designed and tested aircraft such as the Laird Solution, Seversky SEVs, Gee-Bees, Weddell-Williams, Howard's "Mr. Mulligan," and Wittman's "Bonzo," to name just a few. Between 1927 and 1939 eight of the National Air Races were held in Cleveland, three in Los Angeles, one in Spokane, and one in Chicago. The series is well remembered for two trophies awarded during the meet: the Thompson and the Bendix.

The Thompson Trophy events held between 1930 and 1939 were closed course speed races featuring unlimited aircraft (no restrictions on horsepower or airframe modifications). Pilots whose names are recognized today flew in the Thompson races: Charles "Speed" Holman, James Doolittle, James Wedell, and Roscoe Turner, who kept the trophy after winning three consecutive times. When the series resumed after World War II some of the pilots who had flown

Air Racing

Air races have been held almost as long as airplanes have been in existence. This photograph shows pilot Henri Farman winning the Grand Prix d'Aviation "Deutsch-Archdeacon" in January 1908.

the races before the war were back to try again.

The Bendix Transcontinental Speed Classic was inaugurated in 1931. Pilots were timed against the clock in the first dash from Los Angeles to Cleveland. Jimmy Doolittle won the 1931 race in a Laird Super-Solution with an average speed of 375 kph (223 mph). Winners in the following years were James Haizlip, Roscoe Turner, Douglas Davis, Ben Howard, Louise Thaden, Jacqueline Cochran, and two-time winner Frank Fuller, Jr.

There were other races held in the 1920s and 1930s—cross-country, across oceans and continents, and events at state and county fairs. The climax for air race fans was the National Air Races.

The National Air Races resumed in Cleveland from 30 August to 2 September 1946. Bendix offered two cross-country trophies: one for piston engines and one for jet aircraft. Paul Mantz, in a P-51, won the piston engine division flying from Van Nuys, California, to Cleveland in 4 hours, 42 minutes at an average speed of 700.7 kph (435.5 mph). The jet trophy went to Colonel Leon Gray, U.S. Army, flying the same route in an P-80A Shooting Star in 4 hours, 8 minutes, at an average speed of 796.1 kph (494.8) mph. There were also

two Thompson trophies. The piston engine division was won by Alvin "Tex" Johnston in a P-39 Bell Aircobra at an average speed of 601.6 kph (373.9 mph). The jet division race, the world's first closed course jet race, was won by Major Gus Lundquist, flying another P-80 Shooting Star, at an average speed of 830.1 kph (515.9 mph). The four-day event also featured a women's race and several consolation races for the slower ex-wartime planes.

World War II fighter and jet planes continued to dominate the National Air Races until 1949 when a P-51 flown during the Thompson race lost control and crashed into a home near the airport killing the pilot, a woman in the house, and her 13-month-old baby. The public outcry that followed concerning civilian safety during air races has haunted air race promoters ever since.

A group of pilot/designers who felt the warbirds were too expensive and wanted a more competitive class began designing small race planes. They convinced the Goodyear Tire and Rubber Company to put up prize money, and at the 1947 National Air Races they made their first appearance. Weighing about 227 kilograms (500 pounds) and with 80-horsepower engines, these tiny planes could fly a smaller radius course bringing them closer to the stands where the spectators could see them. The winning plane, "Buster," was a Steve Wittman design flown by Bill Brennand at 266.8 kph (165.8 mph). This new class of racer, eventually called the Formula I, kept air racing alive in the years after the end of the big National Air Races. The list of cities and towns where the Formula I's raced stretches from East to West and from North to South. The pilot/designers such as Steve Wittman or Art Chester are legends.

Bill Stead, a Nevada rancher/businessman, promoted the first Reno National Championship Air Race in a nine-day September event at Sky Ranch airport near Reno in 1964. There were air show acts, balloon racing, aerobatics and the U.S.A.F. Thunderbirds to keep the crowd entertained. Three classes of airplanes raced: Formula I's, Sport Biplanes, and the vintage World War II aircraft now designated "Unlimiteds." Robert Porter won the Formula I race at 311.2 kph (193.4 mph) flying a Miller "Little Gem." Clyde Parson won the Sport Biplane class at 232.5 kph (144.5 mph) in a Knight Twister. The cross-country Unlimited race, from St. Petersburg, Florida to Reno, was won by Wayne Adams in a P-51D flying 7 hours, 4 minutes, at an average speed of 512.9 kph (318.8 mph). The Unlimited closed course race, 10 laps over an 13.2-kilometer (8.2-mile) course, saw Mira Slovak the points winner in Bill Stead's F8F Bearcat, although Bob Love crossed the finish line first in a P-51D. The points system of scoring was later abandoned as confusing for the fans.

In 1995 the Reno National Championship Air Race celebrated their 32st consecutive event, making this the longest running series in air racing. The present format has qualifying of pilots and aircraft from Monday through Wednesday, with the races and air show held Friday through Sunday. The AT-6 class was added in 1969. Military precision teams, aerobatic flyers, and sky divers perform to the delight of the fans. Some astonishing records have been made at Reno: Ray Cote, in "Shoestring," winning the Formula I class eight straight years (1968–1975), plus an additional win in 1981; Darryl Greenamyer winning the Unlimited division six times in his F8F Bearcat, "Conquest I," and once in the RB-51 "Red Baron." Prior to the 1984 races the top winning speed in each class was: Unlimited—Mac

McClain in a P-51D, at 696.7 kph (433.0 mph) in 1980; IF-1—John Parker at 400.7 kph (249.1 mph) in 1980; AT-6—John Mosby at 358.6 kph (222.8 mph) in 1981; Sport Biplane—Don Fairbanks at 277.9 kph (172.7 mph) in 1982; Racing Biplane—Pat Hines at 336.9 kph (209.4 mph) in 1982.

Air races have been and continue to be held at locations all around the United States. Most of these events have featured one or two racing classes, usually limited by the size of the field or the prize money available. In the mid-1970s several exciting four-class races were held at Mojave, California. Lacking adequate financial backing, this series was discontinued after the 1978 season.

Since 1970 there has been considerable interest in the Formula I class in Europe, with annual races in both France and England under the direction of the International Formula I Air Race Association. As long as there are at least two airplanes still flying, there will be an air race somewhere.

The Four Classes of Air Racing
Unlimited

Unlimited air racing aircraft are the fastest racing machines in regular competition in the world. Their roots stem directly from the Thompson Trophy of the post-war era, which were ex-military fighter aircraft. After 1949, Unlimited air racing almost totally disappeared from the scene, but it was revived with the advent of the Reno National Championship Air Races in 1964 and has grown steadily in popularity since. The aircraft themselves may still be ex-World War II fighter aircraft, but there the kinship ends since most of the machines in this class have been highly modified and achieve performance far beyond that of stock military fighters.

Average winning speeds in unlimited competition are well in excess of 650 kph (400 mph), and a pilot in competition in this class cannot really expect to be competitive unless his mount is capable of those speeds. The current record in the class for average race speed is now in the neighborhood of 775 kph (480 mph), and there are several aircraft in the class that are capable of matching or beating that record.

The Unlimited class of air racing is the least restrictive of all the classes, with only two major restrictions. One is that the aircraft must be propeller driven and the other is that it must have a piston-type engine. Extensive modifications may be made to engines and to airframes, and most Unlimited aircraft of today have clipped wings, modified fuselages, cut-down canopies, and highly exotic racing engines as well as hundreds of other smaller refinements that are engineered into these racers for just one purpose: speed!

Unlimited Aircraft race on a closed-pylon course and use an "air start," with the aircraft in formation extending back from the pace aircraft.

T-6

T-6 air racing is extremely close and exciting for the simple reason that these aircraft are raced in basically a stock configuration. This "round-engined" plane, one of the world's leading training aircraft, has been around for many years and is a familiar sight to almost anyone in aviation. In the summer of 1968 it also became a racer.

The North American AT-6 made its initial appearance just prior to World War II and was used during the war as a military training aircraft by virtually every Allied Air Force in the world. The Air Force called it the AT-6. The Navy called it the SNJ. The Canadians, who also built this aircraft under franchise, and the British called it the Harvard. Nevertheless, it was the same airplane and it saw military service throughout the world well into the 1950s.

To make the new T-6 class competitive, it was decided to race them in a stock configuration. Stock means that the parts, engine configuration, etc., must have been standard on some type of T-6/SNJ/Harvard aircraft as assembled by North American or Canadian manufacturers. No engine or airframe modifications are permitted. However, it is permissible to remove lights, beacons, antennas, and rear seats for racing as well as factory installed roll bars, steps on the fuselage, and other extraneous equipment. Waxing, taping, and a certain amount of filling, particularly in the wing leading edge are also permitted, but the engine blower is limited to a 10:1 ratio for competition.

A T-6 in its normal military configuration was normally considered to be a 290 kph (180 mph) aircraft and these speeds were typical in the early years of the class. Since then, however, racing speeds for T-6s have climbed and now, if an aircraft is not at least in the 320 kph (200 mph) category, it is not competitive.

Formula I

International Formula I racing aircraft first raced at the 1947 Cleveland National Air Races. The whole idea in creating this class of racing was to provide aircraft that could be designed and built for a relatively low cost, would be safe to fly, and would provide close competition. The Formula I's met and continue to meet all of these standards and then some. Originally sponsored by the Goodyear Company, these airplanes were referred to as the Goodyear Midget Racers back in the 1940s, and, later, as the 190 Cubic Inch Racers. In the 1960s a rule change permitted engines of 200 cubic inches; at the same time, the class name was changed to International Formula I.

Normally built and often designed by those who race them, a Formula I aircraft is usually constructed of steel tube and fabric with wood wings. A Formula I normally has a wingspan and fuselage length between 4.6 and 6.7 meters (15 and 22 feet) and has an empty weight of 227 to 363 kilograms (500 to 800 pounds). All of these aircraft are designed and built to rules and specifications set up by International Formula I, and all are powered by four-cylinder, 200 cubic inch engines that deliver 100 horsepower.

Many of these aircraft are of original design and many are versions of popular types such as the Cassutt Racer, Shoestring Racer, and Owl Racer. The builder may incorporate some of his own ideas and originality into an established type. or he may design and build an aircraft from the ground up that is entirely his own design.

The Class Specifications and Rules for International Formula I Air Racing have been approved for International Competition by the Fédération Aéronautique Internationale in Paris.

Biplanes

For some time, there had been many single-place sport and aerobatic biplanes flying and Bill Stead, the organizer of the Reno Races, felt that these aircraft would make a good racing class. Consequently, he gathered a group of these aircraft together for that first Reno race in 1964, and, thus, the sport biplane class was born.

The early participants in the class and many that still compete today were primarily plans-built machines such as Pitts Specials, Stardusters, Mong Sports, EAA Biplanes, Smith Miniplanes and Knight Twisters. As in the Formula I class, the majority of these aircraft were raced by the men who built them. Construction materials and methods are also much the same as those used in the Formula I class: steel tube frames with fabric covered fuselages and wood wings. The average sport biplane is 4.6 to 5.2 meters (15 to 17 feet) long, has a wing span of 5.2 to 5.8 meters (17 to 19 feet), and weighs between 270 and 360 kilograms (600 and 800 pounds). By class rules, they are most normally powered by a Lycoming 0-290 engine of 125 horsepower and are restricted to an engine that displaces no more than 290 cubic inches. These engines are 4-cycle, direct-drive, and must not be supercharged. The wings must have at least 7 square meters (75 square feet) of area, not including that area displaced by the fuselage itself, and the smaller of the two wings must be 30 percent of the total wing area. Propellers must be of fixed-pitch for competition, and the landing gear must be fixed and nonretractable. The sport biplane aircraft also race on a 4.8-kilometer (3-mile) course and use a "race horse start" as do the Formula I's.

—Stu Luce

Alpine Skiing

See Skiing, Alpine

Animal Baiting

Animal baiting is a form of animal fighting in which men undertake the harassment, torment, or provocation of one animal by another for the purposes of entertainment, which usually includes wagering. The oldest type of animal fighting is cockfighting, which is at least 2,500 years old. For the past several centuries, men have set dogs on other animals such as bulls, bears, badgers, and rats. This practice has been labeled

animal baiting and has become what the term means historically.

Since the late eighteenth century, middle-class moralists have condemned this sport as being an undesirable public recreation of the poor. The vast majority of participants in this sport are men. The defenders of this sport have emphasized its value in producing a desirable masculinity based on the values of courage and bravery. Recently many scholars have studied animal fighting as a symbolic activity that can tell us a great deal about the societies in which it is held.

Origins

Animal baiting is a form of animal fighting. The oldest recorded type of animal fighting is cockfighting. This sport dates back over 2,500 years. Cockfighting occurs in most places in the world, being absent only as an indigenous sport in a few areas such as sub-Saharan Africa and Northwestern Europe.

Other types of animal fighting have existed in a variety of societies. Aside from cockfighting, dog fighting is perhaps the most widespread in both the past and the present. The type of fighting animal used, in many cases, has been regional, e.g., elephant fighting in India. There are also exotic, local fights, such as tarantula fights in South Africa and fish fights in China.

There have also been matches between different animals such as between boars and tigers in India and between bulls and bears in Spain. There have been fights between human beings and animals, the most famous being the Spanish bullfight.

Practice

Animal baiting is a form of the ancient practice of animal fighting. The best documented occurrences of this sport are from Great Britain during the seventeenth century, when it became an important public recreation. By the late eighteenth century, middle-class reformers attacked it. This eventually led to its illegality in the mid-nineteenth century. In the twentieth century, it became a rare, clandestine sport rather than a popular, public sport. The principal animals used in the sport were bulls, bears, badgers, and rats.

Bull baiting, the most popular type of animal baiting, was an event held on special occasions,

Animal Baiting

Controversy has raged since the eighteenth century over the morality of animal baiting, which occurs in many cultures. In this show fight in Chanpir village in India a dog attacks a Himalayan black bear to rescue another dog from the bear.

often at fairs, wakes, and even at elections. Many butchers considered meat from a baited bull superior to that from an animal that was merely slaughtered. In bull baiting, men attached the bull to a strong stake and unleashed dogs on it. The dogs seized the bull about the head. The one who retained its hold the longest won a prize for his master. Frequently the bulls tossed the dogs high into the air. Owners attempted to catch them before they fell to the ground and were injured.

Bear baiting was similar. The venue was a room or indoor pit in contrast to bull baiting, which always occurred in the open, usually a publican's yard, an open field, or a marketplace. Men tethered the bear to a wall with strong collar and chain. One man further controlled the bear with a rope that was fastened to the collar. This allowed the man to help a dog that the bear had grabbed and "hugged" with a sharp pull of the rope that would bring the bear to its knees, causing it to release the dog. A well-trained dog could

grab the bear by the nose or lower jaw and pull its head between its legs, causing a complete somersault which left the bear helpless at the end of a chain.

Bull running was a variant activity. It was usually held on a holiday. It began with the baiting of the bulls, usually with liquid irritants or a red effigy. This was followed by a free-for-all through the streets of the town. It was similar to contemporary bull running in France and Spain, the most famous being at Pamplona.

Badger baiting was another form of the sport. Again the animal was tied to a stake and a dog was loosed on it, worrying it while the badger fought back with its jaws and claws. A variation of this sport was badger drawing, in which a badger was placed in a box. The dog's master held the dog by the scruff of its neck and by the tail, letting the dog into the box and then drawing it out by the tail. The dog was supposed to have hold of the badger and draw it entirely out of the box.

Terrier versus Opossum

An Account of a Well Matched Fight between a young Terrier Bitch, Belonging to Mr. Ferguson, and an Opossum, Brought from New South Wales by Mr. Jenkins.

News has been received from London, of this extraordinary match, which excited exceeding interest amongst the sporting fraternity in the *Old Dart.*

Local boys need no introduction to the fighting attributed of the Vulpine Opossum, our *bushy-tail*, whose remarkably strong claws have left many a mark on incautious Europeans, both man and dog.

Mr. Ferguson's young terrier bitch was about sixteen months old, liver and white, weight about 25½ lbs. Mr. Jenkin's opossum from New South Wales was supposed to be about three years old and weighed 27 lbs.

The bitch and opossum fought on the 6th January, 1829, and the day being very rough, the fight was obliged to take place in a barn instead of Hempton Green, Norfolk, as had been contemplated, to the vexation of numbers, who could not get admission at any price; so much stir did the affair make in the neighborhood.

A great deal of betting took place previous to the match, at guineas to pounds, Possey the favourite. Some of our Norfolk knowing and learned country swells, who were acquainted with the *nature of the beast*, (after seeing the excellent trim he was got into by his trainer *Jemmy Neal*) even went as high as three to two, and it was said that even two to one was offered on the New South Wales favourite.

ROUND 1ST. Possey looked very fit, shook his bushy tail, and darted at the bitch as quick as lightening, caught her by the shoulder, and tore a piece out of it; he then drew back, made another spring at the fore leg, but missed it. Meantime, the bitch was not idle—she made several attempts at a hold, but the gentleman's furry coat deceived the poor bitch, who brought away a mouthful of his outer garment every time she sprung at him; at length, she caught him *where the Irishmen put their lundy*, and punished him severely, while he returned by making use of his claws, with which he scratched dreadfully. At length he got away, and was taken to his house; and after two minutes rest, began

ROUND 2ND. Both darted at one another, their heads met, and both were knocked over. Returning, Possey seized the bitch by the throat, and almost knocked all the wind out of the bitch (four to one on Possey freely offered—no takers). The bitch fought shy till she got a little wind, then made for him, seized his *proboscis*, and pulled him about in good style, in spite of his claws which made dreadful havoc with the bitch; Possey got away and was taken to his house. This lasted nine minutes and a half.

ROUND 3RD. The bitch made first play, and began by taking Mr. Possey by the nose, where she held him, and pulled him about for two minutes and a half he keeping his claws in exercise all the while when she lost her hold, and sprang at his neck (which in the previous round she had cleared of the fur) which she lacerated in a shocking manner, when he got away and was led to his house. Possey became rather weak from the loss of blood, but was restored by something being applied to his nostrils.

ROUND 4TH, AND LAST. The bitch again made for the foreigner's neck, where she left the marks of her toothy work; she then seized him by the shoulder, got an excellent hold, and for the first time Possey uttered a dismal yell, and, on getting away, made for his house, from whence he could no more be brought to the scratch. The bitch was consequently declared the winner.

The fight lasted thirty-seven minutes.

—Pierce Egan, *Book of Sports.* 1832. Reprinted in Ingleton 1952, 119.

Wagering was based on how many times the dog could successfully draw the badger from the box.

A third variation of this form of the sport was a fight between a badger and a dog. Badgers bit very hard and were difficult opponents. It was usually a safe bet that a dog could not kill a badger within an hour. (See sidebar for a newspaper account of such a fight.)

Rat baiting or rat killing was another form of animal baiting. Men placed dogs, usually terriers, in a small, wire-enclosed pit with a large number of rats. The dogs killed the rats by shaking them before the rats could bite. Each dog's handler had a small cane to assist the dog. The handler picked up the dog and placed the dog directly on a rat.

At this moment the timekeeper started his watch. When the dog had the last rat in his mouth, the timekeeper stopped the watch. The dog that killed the most rats in the shortest time won. Experts considered five seconds a rat good work. A rare variation of this form of the sport was a competition among men and dogs involving who could kill the most rats, men using their teeth to tear off the head of the rat.

A final entertainment of this type was throwing rocks at cocks, which was often held on Shrove Tuesday. It was the precursor to side-show amusements. This was a privately financed event rather a community one. A promoter charged twopence for three throws. The customer attempted to knock the bird down long enough to reach it and grab it before it regained its feet. If successful, he kept the prize.

These sports had gender, class, and racial components. Attacks and defenses of these sports involved these issues. Opposition to these sports began in the late eighteenth century, culminating in the introduction of the Bull-Baiting Bill of 1800 in the British Parliament. Reformers achieved further success in 1835 with the passage of the Act Against Cruelty of Animals. The middle class led the movement against these popular sports. Characteristically in 1801, Joseph Strutt claimed that bear baiting "is not encouraged by persons of rank and opulence in the present day; and when practiced, which rarely happens, it is attended only by the lowest and most despicable parts of the people, which plainly indicates a general refinement of manners and prevalency of humanity among the moderns."

Rational and radical individuals, who opposed the indifference to suffering and pain of a prehumanitarian age, and conservative moralists, who valued social control and feared these sports because they attracted large crowds in a revolutionary age, led the attack. Many moralists wanted to substitute Sunday Schools as orderly, structured, and useful alternatives to the time-wasting and unproductive Sabbath pastimes of the poor. One nineteenth-century Sunday school described its students as "semi-barbarous youths who previous to attending the schools spent Sabbath days in wrestling, fighting, bull-baiting, cock-fighting and football playing." There was a class bias to these attacks, as these individuals denounced the popular recreations of the poor, but not the blood sports of gentlemen, such as fox hunting, shooting, and fishing.

Many males advocated animal-fighting sports. Their arguments were race- and gender-based, emphasizing the values of bravery, valor, and courage of the English "race." The defenders endowed the dogs that participated in the various baitings with these values, which the Anglo-Saxon youth of Great Britain needed to defend Empire.

Beginning with Clifford Geertz's seminal 1972 essay, "Deep Play: Notes on a Balinese Cockfight," scholars have used cockfights as a means to analyze the social meaning of the event, the values of participants, and the structure of the

host society. Similar work can be done with the gender, racial, and class aspects of animal baiting

—Tom Dunning

Bibliography: Dundes, Alan. (1994) *The Cockfight: A Casebook.* Madison: University of Wisconsin Press.

Fitz-Barnard, L. (1983 reprint) *Fighting Sports.* Surrey, UK: Saiga Publications.

Ingleton, Geoffrey Chapman, ed. (1952) *True Patriots All or News from Early Australia as in a Collection of Broadsides.* Sydney: Angus and Robertson.

Malcolmson, Robert W. (1973) *Popular Recreations in English Society, 1700–1850.* Cambridge: Cambridge University Press.

Walvin, James. (1978) *Leisure and Society, 1830–1950.* London: Longman.

Animal Rights

During the late twentieth century, many tacitly accepted relationships between humans and the environment have come under scrutiny. One need only look as far as the local newspaper or sporting goods show to find evidence of tension between communities that extract natural resources and those that attempt to preserve them. From concerns about logging to protests over endangered species, environmental concerns permeate modern society. Nowhere do these concerns appear more contentious than in the realm of human/nonhuman animal relationships. Whether at a greyhound track or pigeon shoot, on a deer hunt or at a horse show, there is evidence of an emerging mass movement that questions the morality of sportsmen who interact with animals.

Indeed, the animal rights movement attempts to protect animals from human exploitation. The movement is an intellectual and cultural phenomenon that has landed on modern Western culture's front porch. Like a newborn child abandoned on the doorstep, its seemingly sudden, unanticipated appearance and loud cries have left casual observers startled and perplexed, wondering, "Where did it come from?" "Why is it here?" "To whom does it belong?" and "What can we do now?" It did not spring full blown from the brow of contemporary philosophers and intellectuals. Rather, the movement has a historical precedent, and like its predecessor, the contemporary animal rights movement represents a profound reaction to societal change. Unlike its predecessor, however, contemporary animal rights advocates carry the symbolic cause of animals out of the laboratory, beyond the barnyard gate, and into the realm of sport.

The animal rights movement is marked by utilitarianism and moral rights philosophy, is located within the middle class, and is currently notable for the diversity of its criticism. The underlying causes for the movement's emergence and rapid growth include a unique convergence of four factors: rapid urbanization, scientific evidence linking animals and people, changes in the anthropomorphic images of animals, and the ascendancy of egalitarianism as a universal political value. The animal rights movement poses many questions regarding relationships between animals and people. Indeed, animal rights activists ask, "If science tells us that we are related to other animals and they are very similar to us, and if my experience tells me that animals are similar to us, than why shouldn't we extend protection to animals?" This question has already had a profound impact on sports involving animals and the answer will continue to affect sports enthusiasts and animal rights activists alike far into the future.

Origins

Historians and social scientists trace the origin of the contemporary animal rights movement to the nineteenth-century antivivisection movement. The movement arose out of profound social reactions to increasing technological change and was concerned with the symbolic position of animals as liaisons between recently urbanized people and nature. Originally a Puritan reaction to both the Industrial Revolution and Victorian materialism, the antivivisection movement responded to perceptions of the increasing human exploitation of, and intrusion into, the natural world. Social scientists have discovered that, during periods of intense technological change and social displacement, there has often been receptivity to criticism of forces in society that appear responsible for

change. Hence, whether in the realm of agriculture or industry, technology came to be identified as the culprit. When placed in this context, the antivivisection movements of the nineteenth and twentieth centuries as well as the current animal rights movement reflect widespread and deeply felt anxiety regarding social change.

The Victorian antivivisection movement used sensationalized publicity along with popularized exposes of animal mistreatment and apocalyptic literature to mobilize public sentiment against animal experimentation, animal baiting, and the use of animals in sport. The movement depended heavily on aristocratic noblesse oblige as a reservoir of support, and played heavily upon public sensibilities concerning morality and brutality. The antivivisectionists opposed the relativistic ideology of science, which to the Victorian was symbolic of the irreversible pollution and corruption of existing social order. Indeed, the relativistic ideology of science, with its technological Frankensteins, seemed responsible for the disintegration of society.

The Victorian movement had little impact upon the use of animals. Eventually the movement disintegrated; however, the symbolic reaction against the utilization of animals did not disappear all together. The movement's radical agenda for the transformation of society eventually dissolved into the social milieu, leaving the reformist animal welfare movement as its legacy. The antivivisectionists, although extreme in their abolitionist zeal, had sensitized society to the plight of animals. Less committed, and indeed less radical, people were motivated in part by antivivisectionist publicity to join animal welfare groups. Such groups, which sought reform of societal attitudes toward animals, perpetuated the cause.

Through the turn of the century animal welfare groups carried the torch, seeking to abate animal suffering, and antivivisection sentiments reemerged briefly in the 1950s in the form of a social reaction to various scientific phenomena. Nonetheless, animal welfare groups continued to predominate. Beginning in the 1960s, the cause of animal protection was transformed from reformist calls for animal protection into the radical calls for societal redemption.

Whereas the nineteenth-century movement focused upon the experimental dissection of living animals and the mistreatment of companion animals, the contemporary animal rights movement has evolved to question virtually all forms of animal utilization and control. Like its Victorian predecessor, the animal rights movement has used publicity, exposes, and apocalyptic literature to frame the issues surrounding the status of animals in moralistic terms. However, unlike its progenitor, the radical animal rights movement extends rights-based claims for moral consideration and legal protection to animals.

Philosophies

The movement's claim to moral equivalency between human and nonhuman animals originates in two opposing philosophical schools: Utilitarianism and Moral Rights. First, the utilitarian argument posits that ethical decisions are dependent on their utility, stating that ethical decisions should maximize pleasure while minimizing pain. It cites the utilitarian creed, "The greatest good, for the greatest number, for the longest time," as its justification. Animal liberationists argue that since animals and people both feel pain and pleasure, that the utilitarian creed should be expanded to include nonhuman animals. In other words, they argue that the interests of nonhuman animals should be equivalent to those of humans in determining ethical decisions. Extending the evaluation of utility outward from humans to nonhumans can be traced to a school of utilitarian Oxford philosophers originating in the 1960s and 1970s. Finding its most popularized expression in Peter Singer's *Animal Liberation* (1975), the utilitarian justifications for moral consideration of animals are considered seminal to the movement's current growth.

Whereas utilitarian justifications rely on the utility of moral extensionism, the rights argument emphasizes similarities in the physiology, and therefore the inherent value, between higher mammals. Rights-based philosophers consider utilitarian moral considerations of nonhuman animals to be flawed in two aspects. First, utilitarianism is based on the assumption that types of pains and pleasures are qualitatively different, and, second, utilitarianism allows the exploitation of nonhuman animals if it is deemed necessary for the greater good. In response to utilitarianism's situational protection of animals,

The animal rights movement seeks to protect animals from human exploitation of all kinds, including in such sports as hunting, fishing, bullfighting, and polo.

Tom Regan, an animal rights philosopher and university professor, advocates a rights-based approach. He believes that rights are dichotomous and absolute, thus extending protection under all circumstances. He argues that since nonhuman animals have consciousness, expectations, and desires, they likewise have personal autonomy. He stated that "unless or until we are shown that there are better reasons for denying that these animals have beliefs and desires, we are rationally entitled to believe that they do." He attempts to protect their expectations and desires by granting personal autonomy through the extension of moral claims. Differentiating between moral and legal rights, he states that legal rights are provided to enfranchised citizens and consist of valid claims that have correlative duties. In his extension of moral rights to nonhuman animals, however, Regan argues that social justice calls for the respectful treatment of all beings who have inherent value.

The Animal Rights Movement

Each of the schools of thought has produced potent political and social critics of animal exploitation. The animal rights movement consists of various organizations, which can be subdivided into roughly three categories. According to James Jasper and Dorothy Nelkin in their book *The Animal Rights Crusade* (1992), these groups are the Welfarists, the Pragmatists, and the Fundamentalists. Welfarists believe that animals are objects of compassion, deserving protection, and that there are some boundaries between species. Their goals include avoiding animal cruelty, limiting animal populations, and adopting animals. Welfarist strategies include reformist legislation and humane education, funding of animal shelters and animal birth control programs, and cooperation with existing agencies. The Pragmatists believe that animals deserve moral and legal consideration, with a balance between human and nonhuman interests, and that there is some hierarchy of animals. Their explicit goals include the elimination of all unnecessary suffering by reducing and replacing existing uses of animals, and their strategy includes protests and debates, with pragmatic cooperation, negotiation, and acceptance of short-term compromises. The Fundamentalists argue that animals have absolute moral and legal rights to personal autonomy and self-determination, with equal rights across species, especially among higher vertebrates. They seek total and immediate abolition of all animal exploitation and use moralistic rhetoric and public condemnation in conjunction with civil disobedience and direct actions to protest the use of animals.

Each of these groups is composed of dedicated activists who believe firmly in the morality of their cause. Yet who are the activists? While the animal rights movement is not monolithic, its activists tend to fit a uniform demographic profile. Social science data indicate that activists tend to be highly educated, middle-aged, middle-class Caucasian females from urban areas with the inclination and the political will to effect change. Although most animal protection activists are portrayed as ignorant, socially marginal individuals who are overly emotional about animals, what emerges from the data is a composite of a movement that is broad-based and politically sophisticated, and of activists who are neither ignorant nor marginal. Indeed, animal rights activists are motivated by moralistic concerns rather than scientific, economic, or leisure-use justifications for animal exploitation.

Hence, in the 1960s the philosophical groundwork had been laid for a radical reinterpretation of the way people treated animals. Whereas people had traditionally viewed animals as objects to be used, albeit within some form of highly personal, existential moral constraint, the animal rights movement argued that animals had personal autonomy and moral agencies and therefore should be protected from human exploitation through the provision of rights. Likewise, data indicate that the movement draws its activists from within the middle class, that these activists are far from ignorant and uninformed, and that its message is finding increasing resonance with the greater public.

There are a few reasons for broader animal rights awareness. First, the rapid urbanization of American culture since 1920 has facilitated a sentimental longing to return to an idealized rural life with its proximate relationships to nature and animals. Second, since the 1970s, researchers who have studied primates and marine mammals have concluded that these animals have cognitive ability, complex social groups, and even forms of language. These conclusions, in turn, have further accentuated human empathy with animals. Third, evolutionary theory has indicated that humans and animals are biologically related, and indeed that people are directly descended from other animals; in effect, scientists have argued that animals are much more similar to humans than previously thought and that people are biologically related to their fellow animals. These findings tantalized an urban population whose experience with animals came as highly anthropomorphized versions of themselves. Hence, the philosophical justifications of Singer and Regan for the moral consideration of animals were not widely rejected among the lay public. If indeed animals can think and feel and are intelligent, if indeed they are physically similar to people, if indeed they are evolutionary brothers and sisters of humans, and if indeed animals act almost "human," then why should they not be treated as the moral equivalent of people?

With these factors established within the public psyche, calls for moral and legal protection for animals were a given. In other words, animal rights philosophers and activists argue that the ethical distinction between animals and people has been dissolved by science and changing attitudes about animals; therefore, animals deserve rights. They believe that the exclusion of nonhuman animals from egalitarian protections based upon species constitutes 'speciesism,' a form of arbitrary discrimination no less repugnant than racism and sexism.

What has been the effect of this reinterpretation? In the case of the animal rights movement, activists are reacting to social unease. Confronting this unease, they seek a return to a simpler, less confusing and complex time and to a bygone era where people live in closer harmony with nature. Thus, animals assume highly symbolic roles as representations of an idealized natural world; they manifest iconographic status as bucolic exemplars of the purity and innocence of the prescientific, preindustrial world. In effect, the animal rights movement attempts to protect its symbols of uncorrupted nature (animals) from desecration, and its mechanism has been through collective action. Once egalitarianism is uncoupled from the traditional boundaries of universal human suffrage by evidence of evolutionary linkages between humans and nonhumans, the extension of rights to animals is not only logical but inevitable. And once egalitarian protections in the form of rights are extended outward to domesticated animals, their extension inexorably includes wild animals as well. Thus, whether it comes as critiques of animal-based biomedical or cosmetic research, feral and exotic animal control, the use of animals for sport or leisure, or the industrialized agricultural production of animals, animal rights philosophy extends egalitarianism to all animals in all contexts.

Implications of the Movement

What are the implications for sports that involve riding, chasing, hunting, or just simply enjoying animals? The animal rights movement does not claim that animals have the right to vote; however, it does claim that animals have the right to life,

liberty, and the pursuit of their own happiness. As philosopher Bernard Rollin states, "A deer has a right to its 'deerness,' a wolf to its 'wolfness,' and a pig to its 'pigness,'" independent of human-caused pain and suffering. The implications of this philosophy for sports cannot be overstated. Indeed, the impact of the animal rights movement upon sport is ubiquitous in nature and global in geography.

In England, blood sports such as foxhunting have come under attack by the Hunt Saboteurs, an animal rights group whose protests and confrontational disruptions of fox hunts have been highly publicized. The Saboteurs, who believe that foxes have a right to their "foxness," oppose hunters who exploit the animals for mere pleasure. In response, some hunts now chase human marathon runners rather than foxes, ending when the hounds catch the runners, and a good time is had by all. In continental Europe, the movement is found in all sporting contexts. In Spain, animal rights activists protest bullfighting, albeit unsuccessfully. In Germany, catch-and-release fishermen have been attacked by animal rights activists, and the promenades of Vienna find activists accosting the Viennese for wearing fur. In Australia, the animal rights movement opposes kangaroo hunts, while in Africa animal rights groups protest big game trophy safaris and claim to have been responsible for the shift toward noninjurious "photo-safaris." In the Arctic, animal rights groups protest subsistence trapping as well as trophy hunting, and they have significantly impacted both the fur industry and sportsmen. In the United States, rodeos have been forced to justify their existence in the face of animal rights publicity. They have been picketed, and they now include contingency plans for disruptions caused by animal rights activists in their overall event planning. From greyhound racing to pig wrestling, from pigeon shoots to rattlesnake roundups, animal rights activists have periodically appeared at events to protest and disrupt, thus gaining publicity for their cause. Whether it be deer hunting to control overpopulation or provide pleasure, whether it be falconry or competitive sheep herding, animal rights activists believe that the animals involved have the right to be left alone, regardless of human justifications. Activists use a variety of methods, from protest and disruption to lawsuits intended to

Animal Rights and Billfishing

Animal rights activists believe that the ethical boundaries separating people from animals should be dissolved, thus mandating animals' moral consideration, and that these animals deserve inalienable rights that protect them from human exploitation. This philosophy has moved beyond the laboratory, barnyard, forest, and zoo to encompass oceans and streams. Activists argue that wild animals and fish deserve moral consideration and rights, so should wild animals and fish just as much as domesticated animals. Having extended equality outward from humans to animals, they ask, "If animals have inalienable rights, how can hunters and fishermen justify killing them?"

A case in point involves the tag-and-release program adopted by the Billfish Foundation in response to diminished fish numbers and the negative public perception of trophy fishing. Supporters contend that this program allows the thrills associated with the sport without damaging existing fish populations, all the while providing scientific research intended to perpetuate the species. In this program, sport anglers cooperate with researchers who tag the billfish, then release them to collect data.

Animal rights activists contend that billfishing is cruel and unacceptable. The tag-and-release program fails to account for the rights of the individual fish. Activists also assert that tag-and-release fails as a conservation tool because the struggle involved in landing some big game fish results in death or exhaustion to the fish; big-game fishing is the cause of, not the solution to, diminished game fish numbers. They likewise insist that very little "science" has actually emerged from the program. But more important, animal rights activists criticize the morality of subjecting fishes to repeated pain and exhaustion, hooking them, playing them, damaging them to the point of death, then releasing them, all for the pleasure of humans. The activists scoff at the idea of killing animals to save them. They ask, "How can people justify killing, torture, and maiming, all in the name of pleasure?"

Indeed, they attack all forms of fishing as repugnant. Nonetheless, they argue that subjecting an innocent animal to repeated torture through catch-and-release is worse than killing the animal outright. Hence they oppose the Billfish Foundation, and all such organizations, who in their ethical calculus fail to account for the rights of the fish they catch.

—Wesley V. Jamison

the very presence of the activists indicates that the movement is growing, and the dismissals of the movement's impending demise have been greatly exaggerated.

Perhaps the most striking example of the potential success of the animal rights movement came in California in 1990. California voters passed an initiative on the state ballot that banned mountain lion hunting despite the opposition of hunting, gun, and agricultural groups. This is significant to sportsmen for a variety of reasons. First, the California Department of Fish and Game (CDF&G) had conducted scientific studies that projected that mountain lions were sufficiently numerous to allow a lotteried hunt. Although the lion had been both hunted and protected numerous times in state history, biologists for the CDF&G believed that the cats were multiplying and that a hunt was justified as a management tool. Animal rights activists, on the other hand, disputed the scientific justification, arguing instead that hunting the lions was morally wrong and evil. Second, the animal rights groups who passed the initiative contained a significant minority who wanted to ban hunting outright. The leadership of the animal rights groups agreed that an outright ban on hunting was premature and would have failed. Instead they identified a strategy of legislation, which had a high likelihood of passing, banning the hunting of individual, charismatic megafauna. Third, the animal rights groups formed a coalition with environmentalists to redirect $900 million over 30 years from within other segments of the California budget toward habitat acquisition. This accomplishment is significant because the animal rights coalition redirected money away from the CDF&G and other hunter-friendly agencies as punishment for opposing them.

In California, animal rights activists were able to completely ban one facet of sports (hunting) that they found to be offensive. They were likewise able to convince the electorate that the cats needed protection. And they were able to punish state agencies that opposed them. Furthermore, a California ballot initiative to rescind the original legislation protecting the cats, and thus effectively subject them to renewed hunting, was resoundingly defeated in the spring of 1996. Most important, activists intend to extrapolate the success in California to other areas of sports. As a result,

block the event, to impose their philosophy. It is often argued that animal rights activists, although highly visible at sporting events, have had little success in ending them. Nonetheless, other states such as Oregon and Colorado have passed bans on specific types of hunting as well as hunting of certain species. In the fall of 1996, Massachusetts voters will decide whether or not to significantly regulate trapping. Hence, the lesson learned from the California initiative, regardless of whether or not it is ever repealed, is that the animal rights movement can effect its philosophy over the objections of sportsmen. Whether it comes as protests, event disruptions, lawsuits, legislation, or even violence, animal rights activist interventions should be anticipated in sports that involve relationships between people and animals.

What are the implications of animals rights for people who interact with animals in general? The contemporary U.S. animal rights movement has attempted to realize nothing less than the radical extension of egalitarianism. Animal rights are a peculiar hybrid of liberal egalitarian ideals with a reaction to modernity. Having framed animal use issues in moral terms, having usurped the nomenclature of rights in the cause of animal protection, the animal rights movement has left its opponents unprepared to contest its philosophical underpinnings. Sporting enthusiasts are generally unprepared to discuss political theory, and their tacit reliance upon utilitarian justifications for animal uses are increasingly remote from the concerns of the culture within which they must exist.

Animal rights attack all delineations between human and nonhuman animals as arbitrary, and in their place posits new arbitrary distinctions based upon sentience, species, or inherent value. How will hunters interact in a world devoid of hunting? How will sportsmen find solace in a world where their interactions with animals are strictly delimited to the recognition of those animals' right to be left alone? Animal rights pose just such a dilemma.

—Wesley V. Jamison

Bibliography: Dizard, Jan. (1994) *Going Wild: Hunting, Animal Rights, and the Contested Meaning of Nature.* Amherst: University of Massachusetts Press.

French, Richard. (1975) *Antivivisection and Medical Science in Victorian England.* Princeton, NJ: Princeton University Press.

Herzog, Harold. (1993) "'The Movement Is My Life': The Psychology of Animal Rights Activism." *Journal of Social Issues* 49: 103–119.

Jamison, Wesley, and William Lunch. (1992) "Rights of Animals, Perceptions of Science, and Political Activism: Profile of American Animal Rights Activists." *Science, Technology & Human Values* 17, 4: 438–458.

Jasper, James, and Dorothy Nelkin. (1992) *The Animal Rights Crusade: The Growth of a Moral Protest.* New York: Free Press.

Nash, Roderick. (1989) *The Rights of Nature: A History of Environmental Ethics.* Madison: University of Wisconsin Press.

Regan, Tom. (1985) *The Case for Animal Rights.* Berkeley: University of California Press.

Singer, Peter. (1975) *Animal Liberation: A New Ethics for Our Treatment of Animals.* New York: Avon Books.

Sperling, Susan. (1988) *Animal Liberators: Research and Morality.* Berkeley: University of California Press.

Anthropology

The anthropology of sport is an approach to the study of sport in which sport is treated as a distinct component of culture and analyzed from a cross-cultural or comparative perspective. Particular attention is paid to the description and interpretation of sport as it occurs in small-scale, traditional, or tribal societies. The anthropology of sport is also a technique by which the researcher or observer uses sport behavior as a perspective on a particular culture. In other words, sport in any given cultural setting is viewed as a reflection of general cultural values and as a window on that culture.

The major objectives of the anthropology of sport include the definition and description of sport from a cross-cultural perspective; study of sport in preliterate, tribal, non-Western, or third world countries; analysis of the role of sport in culture change; study of sport in prehistory; analysis of the language and symbols of sport; and the application of insights gained from the anthropological study of sport to improve sport and leisure programs, especially those that serve a multicultural clientele.

Even though by implication the anthropology of sport is an academic pursuit engaged in by persons calling themselves anthropologists, it is more an approach or perspective than a separate subdiscipline. Thus, members of various academic disciplines—including psychology, history, kinesiology, linguistics, journalism, sociology, and political science, as well as anthropology—contribute to the anthropology of sport by their involvement in its cross-cultural study.

Origins

The anthropology of sport has its roots in the work of early anthropologists who took an interest in the sports and games of non-Western, preliterate, and tribal peoples. For example, Sir Edward Burnett Tylor (1832–1917), sometimes referred to as the "father of anthropology," wrote an article in 1879 called "The History of the Games." In this article, he described a number of simple and natural sports (e.g., tossing a ball and wrestling) and argued that these had been invented independently in many different geographical settings. However, other more complicated games, like the parent game of modern football and soccer, he viewed as not so easily invented and as evidence of prehistoric diffusion and contact among the major cultural centers of the world.

Perhaps the most important figure in the history of anthropology's interest in sport and games was Stewart Culin (1859–1929). Culin was a businessperson who early in his career developed an interest in archaeology and eventually became a museum curator. In this capacity, he was particularly fascinated by the games of non-Western, tribal, and preliterate people. Spending most of his career as curator of ethnology at the Brooklyn Museum, he collected thousands of sport and game artifacts from around the world and amassed volumes of information about those artifacts. As a result of these efforts he published several major books on games, perhaps his most important being *Games of the North American Indians* (1907).

During the first half of the twentieth century there were other occasional articles and books written about sport and games by anthropologists. For example, Alexander Lesser's *The Pawnee Ghost Dance Hand Game: A Study of Cultural Change* (1933) is a classic monograph on change. It illustrates how in some cases ritual activities such as the ghost dance may have evolved from sport and games.

Anthropology of Sport Today

The most important impetus to the recent emergence of a distinct anthropology of sport subdiscipline came from anthropologist Clifford Geertz. One of the foremost thinkers and theoreticians in twentieth-century anthropology, Geertz published an article in 1972 entitled "Deep Play: Notes on the Balinese Cockfight." This article, a brilliant analysis of the illegal cockfighting he witnessed in Bali in the late 1960s, illustrates clearly the depth, complexity, and broad meaning of sport in human society. For many in anthropology as well as those in other disciplines, this article soon became a message about the potential of sport as a tool for understanding and interpreting culture. The importance of this article and its impact are illustrated in a collection of articles published in a special edition of the journal *Play and Culture* in 1992. This collection of invited articles is dedicated to the analysis of Geertz's "Deep Play," which is notable for the many times it has been reprinted, referred to, or quoted by other scholars. The authors of the articles are generally in agreement that the Geertz piece has provided for the anthropological study of sport and play an important academic legitimacy (Duncan 1992).

During the 1970s and 1980s, several interdisciplinary and international groups emerged as scholars everywhere began to pay more attention to the cross-cultural study of sport. One of the most important developments occurred in 1974. That year, thanks to the efforts of pioneers among those who studied sport from an anthropological perspective (e.g., Alyce Cheska, Edward Norbeck, Michael Salter, and Allan Tindall), a group of scholars came together in London, Ontario, to form The Association for the Anthropological Study of Play (TAASP). This organization, composed of historians, kinesiologists, sociologists, psychologists, ethnomusicologists, primatologists, archaeologists, and anthropologists, has over the past two decades hosted meetings, maintained a newsletter, and published journal and special collections of articles. Recently, the organization changed its name to The Association for the Study of Play, but many of its members continue to focus on the anthropological study of sport.

Other interdisciplinary groups have taken an interest in the cross-cultural study of sport. The

Anthropology

North American Society for Sport History (NASSH) and the North American Society for the Sociology of Sport (NASSS), for example, have many members who study sport from a cross-cultural perspective and make regular contributions to the understanding of sport in non-Western, tribal, or third-world settings. Also, organizations devoted to the study and preservation of traditional, ethnic, or folk sport have sprung up in Europe and Japan. These organizations involve the efforts of many scholars, including anthropologists, who are devoted to collecting information about little- or lesser-known sport activities that occur in the out-of-the-way places and rural areas of the world.

Regardless of one's particular academic training or background, the person engaging in the anthropological analysis of sport is guided by the following major theoretical concerns:

1. Understanding sport as an institution, as an element of culture, and as a complement to other aspects of culture. To watch an American football game without being struck by the very American cultural qualities with which the game is embellished is to miss a major point.
2. A critical perspective on sport and its role in human society and culture. Those who study sport from an anthropology perspective must be sensitive to the potential problems and excesses within the institution and be prepared to address these critically.
3. The importance of play and playfulness in sport. Play is vital to individual health as well as to group dynamics and adaptation. For this reason, anthropologists who study sport are serious about play.
4. The evolution and history of sport. Many questions about the origin, development, and details of early sport (e.g., the rubber ball game of the prehistoric Maya) remain unanswered.
5. The relationship between sport and general culture change and the role of sport in affecting that change. Sport is both a product of culture change and a factor underlying that change. It can be a mechanism for the maintenance of culture (e.g., learning the game of baseball as a child in the United States). It can also be a novelty that provokes culture change (e.g., the introduction of American baseball into Japanese society). And, from another angle, sport can simply be a perspective by which the anthropologist monitors, measures, and analyzes the general change and evolution of culture in a particular society or group of societies.
6. Making practical application of the theoretical insights provided by the anthropology of sport. In many ways, the anthropology of sport is a form of applied anthropology. Many of the world's social problems are reflected in its sport institutions. These same institutions provide unique opportunities for addressing and solving these problems. The anthropology of sport is particularly sensitive to issues of violence, international relations, gender equity, athletics and education, race and ethnic relations, sport language and the media, class conflict, and aging.
7. The importance of understanding and appreciating the sport of other cultures. Basic to a mutual respect among peoples is a recognition by all parties of the legitimacy and importance of sport and leisure activities other than one's own.

—Kendall Blanchard

Bibliography: Azoy, G. Whitney. (1982) *Buzkashi: Game and Power in Afghanistan*. Philadelphia: University of Pennsylvania Press.

Baker, William J., and James A. Mangan, eds. (1987) *Sport in Africa: Essays in Social History*. New York: Africana Publishing.

Blanchard, Kendall. (1981) *The Mississippi Choctaws at Play: The Serious Side of Leisure*. Urbana: University of Illinois Press.

———. (1995) *The Anthropology of Sport: An Introduction*. 2d ed. Westport, CT: Greenwood Press.

Blanchard, Kendall, and Alyce Cheska. (1985) *The Anthropology of Sport: An Introduction*. South Hadley, MA: Bergin and Garvey.

Culin, Stewart. (1907) *Games of the North American Indians*. Twenty-fourth Annual Report of the Bureau of American Ethnology. Washington, DC: Government Printing Office.

Duncan, Margret C., ed. (1992) *Play and Culture* 5.

Geertz, Clifford. (1972) "Deep Play: Notes on the Balinese Cockfight." In *The Interpretation of Cultures*, edited by Clifford Geertz. New York: Basic Books, 412–453.

Guttmann, Allen. (1978) *From Ritual to Record: The Evolution of Modern Sport*. New York: Columbia University Press.

———. (1994) *Games and Empires: Modern Sports and Cultural Imperialism*. New York: Columbia University Press.

Harris, Janet C., and Roberta J. Park, eds. (1983) *Play, Games and Sports in Cultural Contexts*. Champaign, IL: Human Kinetics.

James, C. L. R. (1983 [1963]) *Beyond a Boundary*. New York: Pantheon.

Klein, Allan M. (1991) *Sugarball: The American Game, The Dominican Dream*. New Haven, CT: Yale University Press.

Lesser, Alexander. (1933) *The Pawnee Ghost Dance Hand Game: A Study of Cultural Change*. Columbia University Contributions to Anthropology 16. New York: Columbia University Press.

Lewis, J. Lowell. (1992) *Ring of Liberation: A Deceptive Discourse in Brazilian Capoeria*. Chicago: University of Chicago Press.

MacAloon, John J. (1981) *This Great Symbol*. Chicago: University of Chicago Press.

Miracle, Andrew W., and C. Roger Rees. (1994) *Lessons of the Locker Room: The Myth of School Sports*. Amherst: NY: Prometheus Books.

Oxendine, Joseph B. (1988) *American Indian Sports Heritage*. Champaign, IL: Human Kinetics.

Poliakoff, Michael (1987) *Combat Sports in the Ancient World: Competition, Violence, and Culture*. New Haven, CT: Yale University Press.

Sansone, David. (1988) *Greek Athletics and the Genesis of Sport*. Berkeley: University of California Press.

Tylor, Edward B. (1879) "The History of Games." *Fortnightly Review, London*, 25, n.s. (1 January–1 June): 735–747. Also in *The Study of Games*, edited by Elliot Avedon and Brian Sutton-Smith. (1971) New York: John Wiley.

Vennum, Thomas, Jr. (1994) *American Indian Lacrosse: Little Brother of War*. Washington, DC: Smithsonian Institution.

Archery

Sport historians from the materialist (Marxist) tradition such as Eichel (1953) claimed that all sports originated in the production process and that *Homo ludens* (the playful human) was thus preceded by *Homo faber* (the tool-making human). One of these tools, which had a revolutionary impact on our culture, was the bow and arrow. Bows and arrows appear as hunting equipment in prehistoric cave paintings in Spain and France, and stone arrowheads have been found in a wide number of excavations as archaeological evidence of the first human hunters. Moreover, the evidence of archery can be found in almost every part of the world. Hence it can be assumed that it did not spread from one particular cultural site, but that it originated independently in various areas. Bows and arrows were also used as lethal weapons in warfare. The training of these military skills led to interindividual or team competitions, which can be considered as prototypes of organized sport.

An opposing interpretation of the origin of sports is the so called cultic historical school, which locates the origin of all sports in cultic rituals (see, for example, Diem 1971, 3). Archery was often linked with magic and full of symbolism, as shown in examples cited by James Frazer in his *Golden Bough* (1890). Among the ancient Hittites, for instance, it was part of a magic rite to cure impotence or homosexuality. A treatise dedicated to this subject tells how the patient dressed in a black cloak and how chants were intoned by a priest. The subject then had to undress and walk through a sacred gateway, carrying a spindle, symbolizing womanhood, in his hand. Once passed through the gateway, he replaced the spindle by a war-bow, the symbol of manhood. A magical formula then confirmed that he was cured and that all female elements had been expunged (Brasch 1972, 8).

From a historical and anthropological perspective it is often difficult to differentiate where, when, and how archery was practised "for its own sake." The links with hunting, warfare, and cultic rituals are never far away, but they have throughout history often been invoked as a rationalization for practicing shooting for pleasure. Although archery as a sport is a contest between archers and not a matter of subsistence (hunting for survival) or military intent, it is virtually impossible to sketch a history of archery without mentioning these technological and strategic aspects.

Archery in the Ancient World

When Tutankhamen's tomb was discovered in Egypt in 1922 by Howard Carter (1873–1939), it revealed, among other artifacts for hunting, bows, arrows, quivers, arm guards, and a bow case belonging to the king's hunting chariot. The bows were of three kinds: composite, made of wood, horn, linen, and bark; self-bows of single stave; and bows of two staves. The bows ranged from 69 to 124 centimeters (27 to 49 inches) in length and one 36-centimeter (14-inch) self-bow was probably used by the king during his childhood. Carter also found 278 arrows in the king's tomb, ranging from 25 to 91 centimeters (10 to 36 inches) in length and one 15-centimeter (6-inch) arrow, probably for the king when a child. Pictures show that the king's hunting with bow and arrow took place not only from a sitting or standing position, but also from a moving chariot, in which he stands with the reins tied to his waist while shooting with his free arms. The king of course displayed these hunting skills not out of economic necessity, but for pure enjoyment. These royal hunting scenes were, moreover, symbolic representations of the king's military preparedness and his physical fitness (Habashi 1976).

The pharaohs also demonstrated their marksmanship before an admiring public. A granite relief from Karnak shows Amenophis II shooting at a target from a moving chariot. The inscription reads: "His Majesty performed these feats before the eyes of the whole land." A text found at Luxor stated that the pharaoh not only challenged his soldiers to a shooting match, but offered prizes for the victors. A stele from Giza recalls the outstanding sporting achievements of Amenophis II, aiming at four targets of Asian copper, thick as a man's palm, that had been set up for him at distances of twenty ells (an ell was originally the length of an arm and thus the perfect length for an arrow shaft):

Then His Majesty appeared on his war chariot like Mont in all his might. He bent his bow and seized four arrows at once. Then he started up his chariot and shot at all four targets, like Mont in all his glory. His arrow sped through one target and hit the next post; he let fly his arrow at the copper target so that it came out again and fell to the ground—a deed no one else had ever performed and of which no one had ever heard.

Sport Egyptologist Wolfgang Decker has argued though that these surprising shooting records should be interpreted rather as mythological statements than as actual facts," they reflect the dogma of the kingdom under the new rule, that is, improvement over previously attained performances" (Decker 1990).

The motif of the king hunting with bow and arrow in a two-wheeled chariot is also frequently found in Ancient Mesopotamia, where King Asshurnasirpal was depicted in ninth- and seventh-century B.C.E. reliefs, performing his hunting skills before a crowd of spectators (Olivova 1984).

Archery contests are described in Homer's epic poems, the *Iliad* and the *Odyssey*. A series of sporting contests were organized in honor of the Greek hero Patroclus, who had been killed by Hector during the siege of Troy. As part of these funeral games, Achilles had a ship's mast set up in the sandy soil, with a pigeon tied to it by one leg, for the archery contest. The two entrants drew lots from a metal helmet and Teucrus won first shot. His arrow hit the ribbon and the pigeon flew off. The second archer, Meriones, snatched the bow from Teucrus and aimed at the bird as it circled in the clouds. His arrow struck the bird in the chest, went right through its body, and came down to bury its tip in the ground at the archer's feet. So Meriones victoriously carried away ten double axes, while Teucrus was given ten ordinary ones. This scene from the *Iliad* is an early predecessor of popinjay shooting, which even appeared on the program of the modern Olympic Games in 1900 and 1920.

Another story from Homer's *Odyssey* tells about the archery skills of the wandering hero. When Odysseus returned home after 20 years' absence, he found his wife Penelope besieged by a hundred suitors, eating and drinking at his expense. Odysseus' bow had lain idle for twenty years. Penelope had declared that she would choose for her husband the man able to string it and shoot an arrow at a target through the eyes of 12 axe-heads set up in a row, just as her husband used to do. One by one, the suitors tried the feat, but could not even string the bow. Then the bow was handed to Odysseus, disguised as a beggar. Without effort he strung the great bow and shot an arrow through the tops of all the axes to the target. Then he revealed himself, took aim at his wife's suitors, and struck them down one by one.

The training of Roman soldiers included archery, but they excelled more in handling the sword. Until the fifth century C.E. Roman legionaries shot their bows by drawing the string to the chest, instead of the longer draw to the face, which gives the arrow far more accuracy. However, faithful to their slogan "Castris uti, non palaestra" (barracks are important, not the sports field), historical evidence is lacking on archery for pleasure during the Roman period. Ironically, Saint Sebastian was martyred by being pierced with arrows because of his Christian faith around C.E. 300, he was a Roman officer of the Imperial Guard. He became the patron saint of many medieval archery guilds.

Archery from a Worldwide Perspective

Archery seems to have been among the first sports for which records were set. A Turkish inscription from the thirteenth century praises Sultan Mahmud Khan for a shot of 1,215 arrow lengths. A seventeenth-century miniature also portrays archers on Istanbul's Place of Arrows, where shots of astounding length were recorded (Guttmann 1978). Saracen, Arab, and Turkish archery have been thoroughly documented in the standard works of Latham and Paterson (1970), Faris and Elmer (1945), and Klopsteg (1934 and 1947).

Just as Attila and his Huns had terrorized the eastern borders of Europe with his horsemen-archers in the fifth century, Genghis Khan rode westward with his Mongolian cavalry in the thirteenth century. The Mongols used powerful composite bows, and their archery tradition survives in present-day Mongolia, where champion archers receive high social prestige. The so-called Mongolian draw or thumb lock for drawing the bowstring refers to this cultural heritage. This technique consists of drawing the bowstring with the thumb of the shaft hand rather than the fingers.

Kyudo, the traditional Japanese art of archery, is a branch of Zen Buddhism, in which the bow and arrow are used as a means to achieve a spiritual goal via physical and mental discipline. The famous samurai warriors were not only expert swordsmen but also skillful archers. They practised shooting from a galloping horse, which is still known today as *yabusame*. Shooting on foot with the seven-foot laminated bamboo bow (*yumi*), in which the thumb lock is used, has been amply described in the works of Herrigel (1948 and 1953), Acker (1965), and Sollier and Györbiro (1969). A gallery in one of the ancient religious temples in Kyoto served as a shooting range in the so-called Oyakazu contest, which took place between 1606 and 1842 and consisted of shooting a maximum number of arrows in a period of 24 hours through an aperture of 4.5 meters (14 feet,

9 inches) without touching the walls of the gallery. Interest in this contest dropped off drastically after 1686, when an archer scored 8,132 successes with 13,053 arrows, because it seemed virtually impossible to break this record (Guttmann 1978, 53–54).

In Africa archery is still used for hunting among isolated groups such as the Khoikhoi in the Kalahari and Pygmy in the rainforests of Central Africa, who employ rather small bows and poisoned arrowheads. Archery contests for non-utilitarian purposes have not been recorded, except for children's play activities.

North American Indians have always been associated with the bow and arrow. Bow types and arrow forms varied widely among the different tribes. The Inuits of North Alaska moved archery indoors in winter and used miniature bows and arrows for shooting at small wooden bird targets hung from the roof of the communal center. After horses were introduced by the Spanish conquistadors in the sixteenth century, the Indian archers quickly adapted themselves to shooting from horseback. Artist George Catlin (1796–1872), who visited the Plains Indians in the mid-nineteenth century, painted a vivid scene of shooting for distance. Contests are listed, such as shooting for accuracy at an arrow standing upright in the ground; arrows arranged upright in a ring; an arrow locked in a tree; a suspended woven grass bundle or a roll of green cornhusks (Culin 1907). Archers attempted to have their first arrow in flight for as long as possible because the winner was the one who could shoot the most arrows in the air before his first one hit the ground.

Archery is also widespread in South America. Shooting contests are usually organized as contests of dexterity in which the archers aim at a stationary or a mobile target (such as a ball, a doll, or fruits). Shooting for the longest distance is also common, especially in the southern areas. A thrilling variant (for instance, among the Yanomamö of the Brazil-Venezuela border) consists of shooting blunt arrows at opponents who try to parry their blows.

The British Legacy

The traditional English longbow occupies a special position in archery's evolution. The secret of the longbow lay in the natural properties of yew (*Taxus baccata*), which was cut in such a way that a layer of sapwood was left along the flattened back of the bow. The heartwood of yew withstands compression, while the sapwood is elastic; both return to their original straightness after the bow is loosed. This combination had already been applied in prehistoric times, as shown by Neolithic bows discovered in a peat bog in Somerset, England. The Saxons used bows for hunting purposes only, not for warfare, as they considered only man-to-man combat with handheld weapons appropriate. This would change, however, after the Norman invasion of England in 1066, in which William the Conqueror used massed archery.

A more proficient longbow, most probably developed by the Welsh, would make England a first-class military power. Folktales celebrated the lore of bow and arrow and featured such legendary bowmen as Robin Hood.

Of special importance for the spread of the English longbow was the victory in 1346 at Crécy, where the English archers completely routed the Genoese crossbowmen of the French army. The terrible showers of arrows cruelly wounded the horses of the onrushing French knights, who were unseated. Edward III's victorious army, which had been largely outnumbered by the enemy, consisted of some 13,000 men, half of whom were archers. Even more notable was the English victory in the battle of Agincourt in 1415, in which Henry V faced a French army five times as large as his 5,000 archers and 900 men-at-arms. Here, again, the victory was won by the "rare English bowmen." The yeoman archer became feared and respected and was therefore imitated on the continent, where the swift longbow was adopted side by side with the much more precise but slow-to-load crossbow.

The first law concerning archery was passed in the twelfth century; it absolved an archer from charges of murder or manslaughter if he accidentally killed a man while practising. From the thirteenth to the sixteenth century all servants, laborers, yeomen, and other menfolk were enjoined to have their own bows and to practise at the butts on Sundays and holy days. Target archery thus gradually lost its exclusive military character and also became a social pastime.

During the reign of Henry VIII (1491–1547) several acts were promulgated to encourage

Archery's origins lie deep in human history as a means of hunting and a tool of war. Today it is practiced as a pacific but competitive sport.

archery. One ordered all physically fit men under the age of 60, except for clergymen and judges, to practice shooting the longbow. During the famous Field of the Cloth of Gold tournament in 1520, Henry VIII demonstrated his skill with the bow at the particular request of his great rival, Francis I (1494–1547) of France. He also established and gave privileges to the Guild or Fraternity of St. George, a very exclusive and elite corps whose concern was "the science and feate of shootinge" with longbow, crossbow, and handgun.

Militarily speaking, however, firearms made the bow obsolete. Despite all the official encouragement and the publication of a specialised treatise on archery, called *Toxophilus, the Schole of Shootinge* in 1545, the bow's decline had begun. The author, Roger Ascham (1515–1568), an archer himself, made a plea for the retention of archery, which in itself is a sign of its decline: "So shotinge is an exercyse of healthe, a pastyme of honest pleasure, and suche one also that stoppeth or auoydeth all noysome games gathered and increased by ill rull . . ." (Schröter 1983, 51).

Continental Archery

Many Frankish knights had bravely joined the First Crusade (1096–1099) not only out of religious zeal but also for the sake of adventure. During these expeditions to the Holy Land, they became acquainted with a new weapon, the crossbow, a bow made by fastening a bow at right angles to a stock or tiller. This instrument proved to be so deadly that it was forbidden to Christians by the second Lateran Council of 1139—another antiwar decree that has never been observed!

By the end of the thirteenth century special elite troops had been set up within the urban militias; these were the guilds of the crossbow-men. The oldest records refer to the Saint George guilds of crossbow-men from the County of Flanders and the Duchy of Brabant such as those of Saint Omer, Ypres, Bruges, Ghent, Brussels, and Louvain, all of which were established around 1300. In the Battle of the Golden Spurs of 1302, the Flemish town militias killed 6,000 of the fine flower of French chivalry, who had zealously stormed into battle as if to the joust. During the battle, a French sally had been beaten off from Courtrai Castle by a company of crossbow-men from Ypres.

Stimulated by the dexterity and skill of the English longbow-men and their successes against the French in 1346 and 1415, several Saint Sebastian guilds of handbow-men arose on the continent. These guilds obtained their charters and received privileges during the fourteenth century. In the course of the fifteenth century the military role of the crossbow and longbow guilds was seriously affected by the invention of firearms. Moreover, as a result of their revolts against centralised authority, many of the precious privileges of the proud cities were severely pruned and their city walls and arms destroyed. The main pursuit of the archery guilds tended more and more toward the function of representing the prestige and status of the leading citizens.

They were never surpassed in the organisation of huge shooting festivities and banquets with plenty of food and heavy drinking. Although the archery guilds thus lost the character of training schools for military pursuits, they maintained their traditional social status position and political power.

In contrast to England and France, no legislative regulations were needed to promote archery in Flanders, in the Netherlands, and in the Rhineland. On the contrary, the rulers had serious problems in dealing with the numerous claims from villages, all asking to obtain proper guild status for their archers. Peasants shot at the butts (mounds of earth or stacked turves against which a shooting mark, or target, was placed) or at the popinjay (a wooden bird, set on a high mast as a target for archers to knock down). Their cheerful sixteenth-century world has been masterly painted by Pieter Brueghel (1525–1569).

Popinjay shooting has survived and still is a popular sporting activity in the Northern (Flemish) part of France, in Belgium (mostly in Flanders but also in Wallonia) and in the Catholic southern provinces of the Netherlands. This can most probably be attributed to the fact that these regions were much less affected by the drastic cultural changes of the Reformation or by the social changes of early industrialisation.

A few cities in Italy still keep their medieval crossbow tradition alive. During the magnificent yearly Palio della Balestra in Gubbio or San Marino, two rival societies of crossbow-men compete each other in full medieval attire, accompanied by their flag wavers and drum corps.

Numerous *Schützen* (rifle clubs) societies in Austria, Germany, and Switzerland found their origins in archery guilds. They have retained a martial character throughout the years, bringing together marksmen equipped with sophisticated firearms in local rifle associations.

Revival of Archery as a Sport

The Toxophilite Society of London, which was formed in 1781 for the practice of archery as a sport, set off the great revival of archery at the end of the eighteenth century and influenced most of the later societies. At that time the form of the game varied from one society to another, but rules for scoring, the number of arrows to be shot, and the distances for shooting would slowly evolve in an attempt to standardize the sport of competitive archery. Thomas Waring, who had inspired Sir Ashton Lever to create the Toxophilites, played a primary role in this process. Archery, which until then had been linked with the lower classes, was now rapidly adopted by the wealthy "leisure class." Archery tournaments took place in the grounds of fine country houses and drew large crowds of spectators. The Royal British Bowmen was the first society to admit ladies as shooting members in 1787. The archery field thus became an arena of fashion, coquetry, and elegance. *The Sporting Magazine* of November 1792 expressed the wish to "see the time when it can be said 'it is a reproach to be unskilful with the bow.'" In the same year *General Orders* were drawn up for a meeting on Blackheath, which reflect the national organization and growing bureaucratization of archery tournaments. The Prince Regent's patronage of archery also contributed to its successful revival, which extended to Scotland. When King George IV finally visited Scotland in 1822, the Royal Company of Archers, founded in 1676 in Edinburgh, was given the honor of acting as Royal Bodyguard everywhere in Scotland. Two members of this elite society fought a duel with bows and arrows in 1791. Although they shot three arrows at each other "at point blank," nobody was hurt.

In England, the first Grand National Meeting was held at York in 1844. It was agreed to shoot a "York Round," which consisted of shooting 72 arrows at 100 yards (91 meters), 48 at 80 yards (73 meters), and 24 at 60 yards (55 meters). The championship of Great Britain is still based on these rules, decided upon by the Archers of the United Kingdom, assembled in 1844 on the Knavesmire racecourse near York. The circles on the targets were scored as followed: gold, 9; red, 7; blue, 5; black, 3; and white, 1. Women competed for the first time in the second Grand National Archery Meeting of 1845, although some had already been members of various societies previously. These meetings were still restricted for the Victorian upper classes, and the best newspapers reported the sport in their society columns. Queen Victoria herself, before her accession to the throne, had not only been a patron of the Queen's Royal St. Leonard's Archers, but she had actively shot with them.

A Royal Archer

During the period of the Commonwealth, Oliver Cromwell's iron fist reigned over England and King Charles II had to seek refuge on the Continent. From 1651 to 1656 he first stayed in France and later in Germany. In 1656 Charles moved his residence to Bruges in Flanders.

Generally speaking his sojourn in Bruges was marked by its peacefulness. There was something in Charles' character through which he soon won all the hearts . . . not only those of lovesick ladies. The rough Irishman Lord Taaffe, once declared of him: "May I never drink wine, if I had not rather live in six sous a day with him than have all the pleasures of the world without him." But of course, where Charles came, pleasures and amusements were never far away.

From the very year of their arrival, Charles and his brother Henry, Duke of Gloucester, were registered as members of the old Saint George Crossbow Guild of Bruges. Later Charles also became an active member of the Saint Sebastian (archery) guild and the Saint Barbara (culverin) guild. Here follows the English translation of the original report, laid down in the Saint George Guild Book:

Charles II, King of Great Britain, enforced to leave his throne because of riots, has established his residence within the walls of Bruges.

On the 11th June 1656, the Gild has been shooting the bird of honour in the presence of His Majesty and His Highness the Duke of Gloucester, his brother, with many other noblemen both from England and from this Country, as well as the members of the illustrious Guild.

The King shot as first and he hit the popinjay; his brother continued shooting until the popinjay was finally shot down by mister Pieter Pruyssenaere, wine merchant, residing in the Old Castle . . .

Only two weeks after their entrance in the Saint George Crossbow Guild the Stuarts were already present at the shooting grounds of another guild: the Saint Sebastian Archers. Honouring the English longbow traditions, the king and his brother made archery their favorite sport and daily they were seen practising in the gild's lanes. As the king and his brother were not familiar with Flemish long-distance shooting, the Saint Sebastian Archers even arranged for two special butts at shorter distance to meet this problem.

—Roland Renson, "Play in Exile"

The English archery tradition spread to the United States, where the first archery club was founded in 1828 on the banks of the Schuylkill River, under the name the United Bowmen of Philadelphia. It was a semisecret society whose members adopted cryptic names. They ordered a complete set of archery tackle from Thomas Waring junior in London, which they then copied.

In the United States, the Civil War (1861–1865) was partly responsible for the renewed interest in archery. After the war, men who had been soldiers in the Confederate army were no longer permitted to use firearms. Two war veterans, the brothers William (1846–1918) and Maurice (1844–1901) Thompson spent the period from 1866 to 1868 in the wilderness of Georgia's swamps and Florida's Everglades, living for the most part on the game they killed with bow and arrow. Maurice Thompson's book *The Witchery of Archery*, published in 1878, captured their love of the sport. The book was widely read and interest in archery spread throughout the country. American archery tackle had rapidly improved and was now at least of equal quality to the English. The National Archery Association was founded and held its first Championship Meeting in Chicago in 1879. Will Thompson won, and he repeated this victory in the following five tournaments. Archery declined, however, almost as rapidly as it had expanded. Americans sought their thrills in rival fashionable outdoor games such as tennis, rowing, baseball, and golf.

Archery was also exported to the British colonies. In Australia, for instance, it was one of the rare socially acceptable competitive sports for women, and together with tennis was organized in mixed clubs.

Archery's Precarious Olympic History

Originally archery was included in the Olympics only at the request of the national archery association of the host country. International rules did not exist; the rules of the host country were used. Archery made its first appearance during the 1900 Games held in Paris. Strictly speaking, these Games were national and international championships, both for professionals and amateurs, and they were accredited Olympic status only afterward. Archery consisted of horizontal target shooting (*tir au berceau*) both with the crossbow and with the handbow and vertical popinjay shooting (*tir à la perche*) with the handbow. The crossbow contests were held at 35, 28, and 20 meters (38, 31, and 22 yards). The horizontal handbow contests, at 50 and 33 meters (55 and 36 yards), had two different events: shooting at the large target (*au cordon doré*) and the small target (*au chapelet*). Popinjay shooting at a tall 28-meter (31-yard) mast was practised *à la herse* and *à la pyramide*. All prizes were shared among French and Belgian entrants, among whom Hubert Van Innis from Belgium excelled with two gold medals in the 33-meter target events and one silver medal in the 50-meter target *au cordon doré*.

Archery reappeared during the 1904 Olympic Games, at which rain turned the tournament grounds into a sticky, muddy mess. Women participated for the first time in Olympic archery. All competitors, male and female, were Americans. The men shot the Double York Round (100, 80, and 60 yards [55, 46, and 37 meters]) and the Double American Round both individually (60, 50, and 40 yards) and in teams (60 yards). The famous American archery pioneer William Thompson won two bronze individual medals and one gold as a team member of the winning Potomac Archers from Washington, D.C. Among the women, Mrs. M. C. Howell won three gold medals: in the Double National Round (60 and 50 yards), in the Double Columbia Round individually (50, 40, and 30 [27 meters] yards) and in teams (60, 48 [44 meters], and 50 yards) as member of the Cincinnati Archery Club. During the so-called Anthropological Days, American archers competed against a number of "savages" from different parts of the globe. Where the white Americans put practically all their arrows at the 4 foot square target board at 40 yards, the "savages" hardly hit the target at all. This carnivalistic event with racist undertones upset Pierre de Coubertin, who had not been present and who called it a vulgar experiment not to be repeated.

For the 1908 Olympic Games, held in London, the Grand National Archery Society and the Royal Toxophilite Society joined efforts to organize three days' shooting in the newly built stadium at Shepherd's Bush. Clear concise rules of competition were drawn up, including a zealous regard for courtesy; for instance, one rule stated: "Gentlemen will not be allowed to smoke at the ladies' targets." The competing teams consisted of 25 women and 15 men from Britain, 11 men from France, and a lone male competitor from the United States. British archers won gold and silver in the York Round, but Henry B. Richardson, the U.S. champion, won the bronze medal. The only female competitors were British. French bowmen won all prizes in the Continental Style (50 meters).

The next Olympic appearance of archery occurred in 1920 in Antwerp, Belgium. Archery was Belgium's national sport par excellence, but it was rather idiosyncratic. Hence the Royal Toxophilite Society of England decided not to enter, as the rules restricted archery to popinjay shooting and to target shooting at "uncommon" distances. Only archers from Belgium, France, and the Netherlands showed up, and there were no women's events. Popinjay shooting was practised at a 31-meter (34-yard) mast both in teams (six archers plus two reserves) and individually. Belgian archers collected practically all the gold medals. After already having won three Olympic medals in Paris 20 years before, Hubert Van Innis of Belgium collected three more gold and two more silver medals, making him the absolute archery "olympionike" ("Olympic champion" in Greek) in history. Archery then disappeared from the Olympics for more than half a century, probably because of the lack of an international guiding body. In 1931 the Fédération Internationale de Tir à l'Arc (FITA) was founded at Lwow, Poland, with representatives from Belgium, France, Poland, and Sweden. This started a new era in international archery. FITA rules and regulations were internationally adopted. The United Kingdom joined one year later. Under the leadership of Oscar Kessels from Belgium (1957–1961) and of Mrs. Inger K. Frith of Great Britain (1962–1977), archery was voted back into the Olympic Games at the meeting in Mexico City in 1968.

FITA rules were recognized throughout the world and by 1972, archery was adopted again at the Munich Games. In the single FITA round, competitors shoot six sets of six arrows from distances of 90, 70, 50, and 30 meters (98, 77, 55, and 33 yards). Women's rounds have distances of 70, 60, 50, and 30 meters (77, 66, 55, and 33 yards). In Olympic competitions a double round is shot, which comprises 72 arrows at the same distances.

During the 1972 Olympics, two young Americans, 18-year-old John Williams and Wilber

Doreen, won the gold in the men's double FITA and the women's double respectively. Both established new Olympic and world records.

The 1976 Olympics in Montreal brought together men and women archers from 25 countries. At the boycotted Games of 1980 in Moscow and 1984 in Los Angeles, archery was represented but without particular splendor. In the 1988 Seoul Games, the South Koreans dominated the team and the 25 women's competitions, and South Korean women dominated the individual and team competitions at the 1992 Barcelona Games as well as the 1996 Games in Atlanta.

Some Variations on the Archery Theme

Archery lends itself to a variety of organized forms. Shooting from a wheelchair, for example, has become a standard sport among many paraplegic persons. It was introduced in 1948 by Frank L. Bilson (1902–1980) at Stoke Mandeville in England.

An alternative to formal target archery is field shooting, based on conditions as they might be encountered in hunting. Strangely enough, this more "natural" type of archery has also become standardized and is practiced either as the Field Round or as the Hunters Round. In both forms 56 arrows are shot from 14 different shooting positions, but in the first one at specified ranges and in the second at unknown ranges.

Flight shooting, or shooting for maximum distance, is a reminder of the technique developed by the Turks, once an honored pastime of the sultans. It has modern adepts both in the United States and in Great Britain. Distances of over 1,100 meters (1,200 yards) have been recorded.

In clout shooting arrows have to be shot with a high trajectory to fall into a target zone, marked by circles on the ground. It is still practiced by a few traditionalist societies in England and Scotland.

International crossbow shooting is regulated by the Union Internationale de Tir à l'Arbalète (UIA), which was founded in 1956 and has its seat in Switzerland, the land of the legendary Wilhelm Tell. The first Crossbow World Championship took place in 1979 after 11 European championships had been previously held. Several variants exist both in terms of traditional crossbow types (for instance, the bullet crossbow, still practiced in Belgium) as in terms of the targets (for instance, popinjay shooting with the crossbow).

Popinjay shooting is not only practiced at a tall mast, from which feathered "birds" have to be shot down, but is also horizontally in lanes, especially in Belgium, where this is a most popular form of archery.

—Roland Renson

Bibliography: Acker, William R. B. (1965) *Japanese Archery*. Rutland, VT: Tuttle.

Brasch, R. (1972) *How Did Sports Begin?* London: Longman.

Burke, Edmund Holley. (1957) *The History of Archery*. New York: William Morrow.

Culin, Stewart. (1907) *Games of the North American Indians*. Washington: U.S. Government Printing Office.

Decker, Wolfgang. (1990) "The Record of the Ritual: the Athletic Records of Ancient Egypt." In *Ritual and Record*, edited by John Marshall Carter and Arnd Krüger. New York: Greenwood Press, pp. 21–30.

Diem, Carl. (1971) *Weltgeschichte des Sports: Vol. 1*. Stuttgart: Cotta.

Dubay, Pierre. (1978) *Arc et Arbalète*. Paris: Albin Michel.

Eichel, Wolfgang. (1953) "Die Entwicklung der Körperübungen in der Urgemeinschaft." *Theorie und Praxis der Körperkultur* 2: 14–33.

Faris, Nabih Amin, and R. P. Elmer. (1945) *Arab Archery*. Princeton, NJ: Princeton University Press.

Frazer, James George. (1890) *The Golden Bough: A Study of Magic and Religion*. London: Macmillan.

Guttmann, Allen. (1978) *From Ritual to Record*. New York: Columbia University Press.

Habashi, Zaki. (1976) "King Tutankhamun, Sportsman in Antiquity." In *The History, the Evolution and Diffusion of Sports and Games in Different Cultures*, edited by Roland Renson, Pierre Paul De Nayer, and Michael Ostyn. Brussels: BLOSO, pp. 71–83.

Heath, Ernest Gerald. (1973) *A History of Target Archery*. Newton Abbot, UK: David & Charles.

Herrigel, Eugen. (1948) *Zen in der Kunst des Bogenschiessens*. Konstanz: Weller. (English translation by R. F. C. Hull [1953]. *Zen in the Art of Archery*. New York: Pantheon.)

Klopsteg, Paul E. (1934) *Turkish Archery and the Composite Bow*. Evanston, IL: Author (second edition in 1947).

Lake, Fred, and Hal Wright. (1974) *A Bibliography of Archery*. Manchester, UK: Manchester Museum.

Latham, J. D., and W. F. Paterson. (1970) *Saracen Archery*. London: Holland Press.

Michaelis, Hans-Thorald. (1985) *Schützengilden*. Munich: Keyser.

Loades, Mike. (1995) *Archery: Its History and Forms*. Knebworth, UK: Running Wolf Productions (video).

Olivova, Vera. (1984) *Sports and Games in the Ancient World*. New York: St. Martin's Press.

Paterson, W. F. (1984) *Encyclopaedia of Archery*. New York: St. Martin's Press.

Payne-Gallwey, Ralph. (1903) *The Cross-bow*. London: Longman.

Renson, Roland. (1976) "The Flemish Archery Gilds: From Defense Mechanisms to Sports Institutions." In *The History, the Evolution and Diffusion of Sports and Games in Different Cultures*, edited by P. P. De Nayer, M. Ostyn, and R. Renson. Brussels: BLOSO, pp. 135–159.

———. (1977) "Play in Exile: The Continental Pastimes of King Charles II (1630–1685)." In *HISPA VIth International Congress*. Dartford: Dartford College of Education, 508–522.

Schröter, Harald. (1983) *Roger Ascham, Toxophilus: The Schole of Shootinge. London 1545*. St. Augustin: Richarz.

Sollier, A., and Zsolt Gyobiro. (1969) *Japanese Archery: Zen Is Action*. New York: Walker/Weatherhill.

Stamp, Don. (1971) *The Challenge of Archery*. London: Adam & Charles Black.

Stein, Henri. (1925) *Archers d'autrefois; archers d'aujourd'hui*. Paris: Longuet.

Van Mele, Veerle, and Roland Renson. (1992) *Traditional Games in South America*. Schorndorf: Hofmann.

Weiler, Ingomar. (1981) *Der Sport bei den Völkern der alten Welt*. Darmstadt: Wissenschaftliche Buchgesellschaft.

Arm Wrestling

Arm wrestling is a contest of strength and willpower between two people. The contestants sit or stand facing each other across a table or other flat surface. Each places one elbow on the table, holding his or her arm upright at a V-shaped angle, and grips the opponent's hand with knuckles facing out. When the match begins, each person presses in an arc toward the table, attempting to force the opponent's forearm, wrist, and hand onto the surface beneath. The arm wrestler who succeeds is the victor.

Wrist wrestling is a specific form of arm wrestling. Although the terms are occasionally used interchangeably, wrist wrestling refers to a particular technique in which the opponents grip each other's unused arm across the table. In contrast, arm wrestlers grip a peg or other object with the free hand or keep it loose. Today, wrist wrestling is less common.

Arm wrestling has long been a popular, informal activity. However, since the 1960s it has also become an international organized sport with many tournaments and dedicated participants and fans. It is popular in many regions of North

Two sailors, one Russian, the other Ukrainian, arm wrestle at the Black Sea port of Sevastopol in 1992. At the time their respective nations were battling for control of the former Soviet Union's Black Sea fleet, giving an added edge to the seemingly friendly competition.

America. In India, where it is called punjah, it is among the most popular of sports, and national championships there attract thousands of spectators. Arm wrestling has also become increasingly recognized in Russia and other states of the former Soviet Union, and in Brazil, England, and other nations.

Origins

Arm wrestling is a variation of the basic sport of wrestling, in which contestants try to pin their opponents' shoulders to the ground. Wrestling has been present virtually throughout human history. Many cultures developed specific forms of wrestling, including versions for individual parts of the body. Although there is no extensive documentation of arm wrestling in early history, it is generally believed that people in ancient societies engaged in it as one of these specialized

forms of wrestling. The arm wrestling common today is usually traced to the indigenous people of North America, where it was adopted by later settlers. One traditional name for the sport, Indian wrestling, refers to these origins.

In addition to spontaneous individual matches, arm-wrestling tournaments have long been conducted at fairs, taverns, and other social settings. Organized arm wrestling gained momentum in the 1960s with a movement to coordinate and publicize it as a serious competitive sport. This modern arm-wrestling movement was originally most active in California, Connecticut, Virginia, and Pennsylvania. It subsequently spread to other regions of North America and other nations.

The 1987 movie *Over the Top*, which starred Sylvester Stallone as a competitive arm wrestler, gave the sport wider publicity, although some enthusiasts believe the film reinforces unwanted stereotypes. In 1988, organized arm wrestling gained major corporate backing when Heublein, a liquor company, began to sponsor a large annual circuit of tournaments called the Yukon Jack World Arm-Wrestling Championships.

Development

Contemporary arm wrestling reflects its varied history. Some aspects of the sport are very colorful, and emphasize belligerence and machismo. In other respects, arm wrestling is a serious athletic activity that focuses on technique and discipline.

Because it is straightforward and easy to set up a basic match, arm wrestling has traditionally been an informal, spontaneous sport. Young boys often arm wrestle each other to test their strength. Arm wrestling has also traditionally been associated with bars, work sites, and other situations in which physical strength is considered an important attribute.

People usually engage in arm wrestling on a friendly basis, but matches have also been held for more serious purposes. Arm wrestling has been used to settle disputes physically, express animosity, or compare strength without engaging in actual combat. Like most other sports, arm wrestling has also been a basis for gambling, with two wrestlers betting each other on a match or spectators placing wagers on the outcome. Traveling arm wrestlers have earned an income by challenging people to matches for money.

In the mid-1990s, an estimated 100,000 men and women competed seriously in organized arm wrestling. The sport has produced many top athletes well known among its followers, including David Patten, Cleve Dean, John Brezek, Moe Baker, and Dot Jones, among others. Individual arm wrestlers have very diverse personalities and wrestling styles. Some contestants are flamboyant, with extravagant tattoos and costumes. They have outrageous nicknames and growl, pound the table, or engage in other antics before a match. This reflects a sense of showmanship, but is also intended to intimidate opponents. Other arm wrestlers have more subdued personalities and approach the sport with quiet discipline and concentration.

The major goals of many contemporary proponents of arm wrestling are to change the sport's rough-and-tumble image and increase appreciation of it as a serious athletic competition. In the 1980s and 1990s, enthusiasts also initiated a drive to have arm wrestling included in the Olympics eventually.

The sport's largest sanctioning body is the nonprofit World Armsport Federation (WAF), based in Scranton, Pennsylvania. The WAF coordinates regional and national affiliated organizations in over 50 countries, including the American Arm-Wrestling Association (AAA) in the United States. Affiliates of WAF hold local and national competitions, with the winners representing their countries at an annual world championship. The Yukon Jack tournaments are a separate, corporate-sponsored, WAF-sanctioned series of events for prize money, with remaining proceeds donated to charity. Smaller independent arm-wrestling associations also sponsor tournaments. Some private entrepreneurs organize tournaments as profitable business ventures.

While the number of organized tournaments with cash prizes has increased since the 1980s, arm wrestling remains primarily an amateur sport, and most arm wrestlers pursue it as an avocation while holding other jobs. Many tournaments do not have cash prizes, and even for the top wrestlers prize money usually only covers travel costs and other expenses.

Practice

In arm wrestling, a match is called a pull. When it begins, each contestant presses his or her arm and hand in a downward arc toward the table. In right-hand matches, they press in a counterclockwise direction and in left-hand matches in a clockwise arc. Each opponent presses in the same direction, but because they are facing each other their arms and hands strain in opposite directions. A match ends in a pin, when one opponent forces and keeps the other's forearm, wrist, and hand down. Matches are not timed, so their length depends on the time it takes for a pin to occur. Often a pull may last less than a minute, although they can also be several minutes long. Flashing is a term used to describe a contest in which one opponent pins the other especially quickly.

Arm wrestlers use specific strategies in the way they hold themselves and use their muscles and energy during the match. In wrist wrestling, the physical position of contestants tends to focus on the overall use of the upper body. In standard arm wrestling, contestants have more mobility, and they emphasize techniques that use their shoulders, arms, and hands. Basic movements include the shoulder-roll, in which the wrestler exerts pressure from the shoulder and triceps; the hook and drag, which emphasizes the use of wrist and triceps to press the opponent's arm down; and the top roll, which focuses on bending the opponent's wrist. There are many variations of these movements.

While arm wrestlers are often large and obviously muscular, many successful competitors are small and wiry or of average size. Although strong, well-developed upper arms and shoulders give a wrestler an obvious advantage, well-developed tendons and ligaments in the forearm and hand are particularly important. In addition to physical strength, psychological attributes and technical strategies are vital to an arm wrestler's success. A contestant must have the willpower to maintain determination and sometimes endure intense physical pain during the strenuous match. They develop techniques to focus their mental energy and to gain a psychological advantage over their opponents.

Organized, sanctioned events have specific rules and guidelines governing how a match is conducted and judged. These rules prohibit movements or physical positions that give a contestant an unfair advantage or that might harm the opponent. The matches are refereed, and various illegal movements, such as letting go of the peg or removing one foot from the floor, result in a foul. The specific rules may vary somewhat among different sponsors, although many are consistent throughout the sport. In tournaments, for example, contestants are often required to keep their shoulders squared and to grip each other's hands at the thumb with the first knuckle visible. Tournaments are generally organized by weight classes and gender so the contestants will be well matched physically. Typical basic weight classes include divisions for less than 75 kilograms (165 pounds), between 75 and 90 kilograms (166 and 198 pounds), and over 90 kilograms (199 pounds). Official matches often take place on special tables equipped with elbow pads, a pinning mat, and gripping pegs.

—John Townes

Bibliography: Berkow, Ira. (1995) "Wrist Wars on the Waterfront." *New York Times* (26 August).
   Jordan, Pat. (1987) "In Florida: 'Lock Up!' And the Pulse Pounds." *Time* (2 November).
   Junod, Tom. (1993) "Arms and the Man." *Sports Illustrated* (14 June).

Armed Forces Games

Sports probably originated as games designed to teach human beings hunting and warfare skills. Throughout history and across cultures, members of armies have practiced various sports to hone their warrior skills or break the monotony of camp life. The industrial revolutions of the eighteenth, nineteenth, and twentieth centuries transformed war. In order to wage modern warfare, societies needed new and complex forms of social organization animated by the skills necessary for corporate endeavors. The new realities of warfare led to the institutionalization of sports in modern armed forces. By the mid-nineteenth century most military leaders in industrializing nation-states thought modern soldiers needed athletic competitions to practice their military craftsmanship, to teach the essentials of "teamwork" necessary for modern warfare, and to inculcate nationalism. In the emerging nation of Germany and in Scandinavia mass gymnastics (the Turnen movement) served as both a military drill and a platform for romantic nationalism. In Great Britain and its empire, in the United States, and eventually in France, modernized Anglo-American games such as track and field athletics, boxing and wrestling, various forms of football, and baseball became staple practices of modern armies and navies.

Origins

Modern armies began to sponsor sporting competitions during the Industrial Revolution. In the midst of one of the first "modern" wars in world history, the U.S. Civil War (1861–1865), troops played sports to divert their attentions from combat. In both the Union and Confederate armies soldiers played cricket, baseball, soccer (association football), and quoits. They also wrestled, boxed, ran foot races, swam, hunted, and fished.

Baseball enjoyed a particular popularity in Union army camps in which New Englanders introduced the regional game to Westerners and Southerners. Some Confederate prisoners of war even learned the "New York game" in Union prison camps. Promoters of baseball insisted that it prepared men for the rigors of modern battle. The baseball competitions in Civil War camps sparked a rapid spread of the game throughout American culture. By the end of the nineteenth century baseball had become the U.S. "national pastime," symbolizing the triumph of the nation-state over regional and other loyalties.

Development

In the United States following the Civil War, sports retained an important connection with the military. National Guard units helped to spread modern sports throughout the United States, and armories served as centers of the new sporting life. In the active services, sports had become a central feature of military life. A baseball craze swept the U.S. Navy during the 1890s. By the end of that decade every ship in the North Atlantic Squadron had a baseball team. In 1897 the cruiser U.S.S. *Detroit* won the title "Champions of Uncle Sam's Navy" by besting all Atlantic fleet rivals. In 1900 the battleship U.S.S. *Iowa*'s team beat the cruiser U.S.S. *Philadelphia*'s team for the championship of the Pacific Coast Squadron. Armed forces teams also competed in boxing, fencing, football, track and field, rowing, and other sports. In 1897 the armed services created a Military Athletic League.

Other industrialized nations also employed sporting competitions to inspire martial nationalism in their armed forces. The major imperial powers of the late nineteenth century—Great Britain, France, and Germany—used sports to train their armies and navies. Japanese sailors learned baseball from U.S. naval crews. The colonial powers, including the United States, also used sports in efforts to impose Western styles of civilization on the peoples of Asia, Africa, and the Pacific.

Advocates of modernization in the military promoted sport as a device for building morale and training the martial spirit. Legions of military and political officials who encouraged

In a kick-off event for National Fitness Month, two U.S. Navy tug-of-war teams from the aircraft carrier George Washington *compete while the carrier was in port Jebel Ali, United Arab Emirates, in May 1996.*

industrial nations to build new modern armies and navies insisted that athletic games and sports were crucial components in programs of military preparedness.

The outbreak of World War I entrenched sporting competitions in the military practices of the major powers. During the war, the United States armed forces fully incorporated sports into training regimens. Millions of servicemen played sports in programs designed to prepare them for combat. The military employed sports to dissuade soldiers from engaging in more dissolute activities and to train combat teams for the rigors of trench warfare. The U.S. armed forces organized regimental and divisional competitions in a variety of sports. The man whose name had become synonymous with the growth of modern college football, Yale's Walter Camp (1859–1925), served during the war as the general commissioner of athletics for the U.S. Navy. The U.S. Army worked with closely with the Young Men's Christian Association (YMCA) to organize army athletic activities.

The armed forces athletic competitions during World War I wove sports even more firmly into the fabric of American life. Indeed, in the wake of the war, the United States attempted to re-create through sport some semblance of a community of nations by reinvigorating the tottering Olympic movement with an armed forces competition. The United States thought that an athletic festival could help to resuscitate war-ravaged Western civilization. The Inter-Allied Games of 1919 sprang from the athletic genius of Elwood S. Brown, a leader of the YMCA movement and the director of athletics for the American Expeditionary Force (AEF). In order to hold the Inter-Allied Games, or "Military Olympics," the AEF constructed a stadium in Paris and named it after their commander, General John J. "Black Jack" Pershing (1860–1948). Before the actual games, Brown organized some mass athletic competitions and the AEF championships. Gene Tunney (1897–1978), the "fighting marine" who in the 1920s would win the world heavyweight boxing championship, won a boxing title in the AEF championships.

Brown modeled the Inter-Allied Games on the Olympic Games. According to the official U.S. report, the Inter-Allied Games of 1919 were motivated by the American love of fair play, a belief that athletics had helped to win the war, and a desire to maintain the comradeship built by shared experiences on battlefields. In the summer of 1919 nearly 1,500 athletes from Australia, Belgium, Brazil, Canada, China, Cuba, Czechoslovakia, France, Great Britain, Greece, Guatemala, Haiti, Italy, Japan, Liberia, Montenegro, Nicaragua, New Zealand, Panama, Poland, Portugal, Romania, Serbia, South Africa, and the United States gathered in Paris to compete. No athletes from the defeated Central Powers—Germany, Austria-Hungary, and the Ottoman Empire—were invited to participate.

Allied athletes contested in baseball, basketball, American football, soccer, and rugby, golf, boxing, track and field athletics, rifle and pistol shooting, swimming, fencing, equestrian events, cross-country racing, Greco-Roman wrestling, tennis, a sailing regatta, tug-of-war battles, and a "hand-grenade throw" contest. U.S. athletes, according to the American press, dominated the competitions, winning 12 first and 7 second places on the 24-event schedule.

The Inter-Allied Games prepared the ground for a revival of the Olympic cycle that had been interrupted by war, canceling the scheduled 1916 contest in Berlin, and paved the way for the celebration of the seventh modern Olympic Games at Antwerp, Belgium, in 1920. The success of the Inter-Allied Games kindled a resurgence of the modern Olympic movement in the wake of the European disasters spawned by the "Great War." The "Military Olympics" was also a unique event that was never repeated by the Allied armies.

In the years since, national armed forces competitions have continued to be an important institution in many countries. In the United States the military service academies compete in a variety of intercollegiate sports, and the Army-Navy football game has historically occupied an important place in the national fascination with college football. Well-organized sports programs play a prominent role in the U.S. military. Many other nations also use sports as training devices and morale builders for armed services.

Sports with important warfare components, such as shooting contests, the modern pentathlon, and the biathlon have remained a part of the Olympic program and been dominated by military competitors. Since World War II armed services in many nations have adopted sporting competitions and served as training grounds for world-class athletes. The Soviet Union's Red Army Hockey Club became the best team in the world from the 1960s through the 1980s. Olympic champions from Europe, Asia, Africa, Latin America, and North America, such as 1960 and 1964 marathon victor Abebe Bikila (1932–1973), who served in the Ethiopian Imperial Bodyguard, were members of their nation's armed forces, which encouraged and subsidized their athletic accomplishments. Various forms of armed forces competitions continue to play important roles in the global development of sport.

—Mark Dyreson

Bibliography: Baker, William. (1982) *Sports in the Western World.* Totowa, NJ: Rowman and Littlefield.

Betts, John. (1974) *America's Sporting Heritage: 1850–1950.* Reading, MA: Addison-Wesley.

Green, Harvey. (1986) *Fit for America: Health, Fitness, Sport and American Society.* New York: Pantheon.

Guttmann, Allen. (1994) *Games and Empires: Modern Sports and Cultural Imperialism.* New York: Columbia University Press.

Holt, Richard. (1981) *Sport and Society in Modern France.* London: Macmillan.

———. (1989) *Sport and the British: A Modern History.* Oxford: Clarendon.

Kirsch, George. (1989) *The Creation of American Team Sports: Baseball and Cricket, 1838–1872.* Urbana: University of Illinois Press.

Mrozek, Donald. (1983) *Sport, an American Mentality, 1880–1910.* Knoxville: University of Tennessee Press.

O'Hanlon, Timothy. (1982) "School Sports as Social Training: The Case of Athletics and the Crisis of World War I." *Journal of Sport History* 9 (Spring): 1–24.

Pope, Steven. (1995) "An Army of Athletes: Playing Fields, Battlefields, and the American Military Sporting Experience, 1890–1920." *Journal of Military History* 59 (July): 435–456.

Rader, Benjamin. (1990) *American Sports: From the Age of Folk Games to the Age of Televised Sports.* 2d ed. Englewood Cliffs, NJ: Prentice-Hall.

Thorpe, Jim, in collaboration with Thomas Collison. (1932) *Jim Thorpe's History of the Olympics.* Los Angeles: Wetzel.

Wythe, Major G., Captain Joseph Mills Hanson, and Captain C. V. Burger, eds. (1919) *The Inter-Allied Games of 1919.* New York: Games Committee.

Art

Sport in art is not an isolated area of study—it is intimately related to the study of history and cultures. Sport has a function in society that changes over time. One way to study a civilization is to study its art and its sports in addition to its politics and wars.

Normally when we think of art we envision a canvas painting on the wall of a museum. But art is much broader than painting alone, and it is not always in a museum. Sport can be depicted in art in many ways. Among the types of art to consider are the traditional canvas paintings in oil; graphic arts such as lithographs, posters, serigraphs, and offset; the medallic arts such as coins and medals; ceramic arts; sculptures in stone or metal; architecture and design of sports stadiums and facilities; film and photography; and philately.

Art is a way of permanently fixing an idea in some form for use again. A camera can be used to photograph a gymnast in action and the end result, a photograph, can be used in many ways. The photographer can use it for the next day's sports section as news or sell it for such commercial uses as an advertisement or sales brochure. The same photograph can be made into a poster and sold to gymnastics fans, used on the front jacket of a book, enlarged into a huge billboard sign to promote an event such as the Olympic Games, or reduced in size and made into a postage stamp. Each and every use is a form of art for this one image.

The variety is overwhelming and we are fortunate for that. We have been enriched as human beings with the art that has been left to us from different cultures over the centuries. Some examples of sports art are priceless treasures such as the statue of the Discus Thrower (Discobolus) by the ancient Greek artist Myron (fifth century B.C.E.). The original statue, made in bronze, no longer exists. Today we have only the replicas made by Roman artists in marble (see illustration page 54). But the statue is timeless and has been used over the centuries in paintings, desk-size and life-size replicas in marble and bronze, postage stamps, and posters. The image is unforgettable and is used frequently in different media.

The ancient civilizations of Egypt, Sumer, Greece, and Rome left numerous examples of sport art. Ancient paintings on the walls of tombs in Sumer and Egypt show in great detail the various types of sports and games that were used in their cultures, including over 400 wrestling scenes at the tombs of Beni Hasan. Greek ceramic vases with elaborate paintings of wrestling, boxing, running, jumping, and other sports fill whole rooms in dozens of museums from Athens to New York. Reliefs carved in stone show elaborate scenes of wrestlers, ball players, runners, and judges engaged in athletic performances, while statuary sculpted in marble honors ancient Olympic athletes from over 2,000 years ago.

The ancient Greeks did not invent art, but they perfected its techniques to such a fine degree that most art historians consider their creations unequaled to this day. The Egyptians built the incredible pyramids, but their statuary was rigid and lacking in form. Most statues looked alike, with bodies erect and one foot ahead of the other. It was the Greeks who learned to create a human form in solid stone and bronze so that an outstretched arm wouldn't fall off. The twisting, life-like motion depicted in so many Greek statues seems surrealistic to us today, but one has to imagine them as they were made, completely painted in color that did not survive to modern times.

The Greeks also created pottery of incredible beauty that was painted with the everyday scenes of daily life. The plates and vases were used in daily life to store foods, grains, oils, wine, and such, just as we use bottles, jugs, and refrigerators today. The scenes vary widely, of course, from religious rituals and festivals to scenes of sex orgies. The former are more well known, while the latter are rarely printed in books. There are, however, hundreds of ceramic scenes of sports illustrated in fine art books worldwide. But it is quite an experience to see hundreds of vases up close—several overflowing roomfuls can be seen at the Metropolitan Museum of Art in New York City, the British Museum in London, the National Gallery in Athens, the Louvre in Paris, and many others.

The Romans were not as artistically inclined with vases, but they copied Greek bronze statues in bronze or marble. These statues also fill museums around the world and show us chariot racers, boxers, wrestlers, pankratiasts (who practiced a combination of boxing and wrestling), runners, and athletes cleaning up after the competition.

The Greeks were unique among civilizations ancient and modern. They glorified the beautiful body and depicted their many gods in anthropomorphic style (as humans). Their statues and paintings of the gods reflected the image of the perfect body: lean, muscular, athletic, and naked. The Greeks did not consider nudity a problem, but they didn't run around naked either. For those who were not young or athletic it was a problem, and they kept their clothes on. But in the gymnasium, students and athletes trained naked, and outside, the statues honored the best of them, also naked. The beautiful bodies were the idols of the society, because the quest for Greek education was perfection. This attitude was common among many of the Greeks, but not all. The Spartans didn't care about art: almost

Luckily this famous fifth-century B.C.E. Greek representation of a discus thrower has been reproduced many times; the original has been lost.

nothing exists today from ancient Sparta. What we study is mostly of Athenian influence.

The Romans, however, were more inhibited. They though the Greeks were strange and in turn the Greeks thought the Romans were barbarians. When making replicas of Greek artworks, the Romans covered all genitals with fig leaves (which is one way to tell an original Greek piece from a Roman copy). But their differences went far beyond aesthetics. The Romans found no purpose to the meaningless sports of the Greeks and preferred the Etruscan sport of gladiatorial fighting. Whereas the Greeks educated their youths to seek perfection, the Romans educated theirs for warfare. As Rome conquered their neighbors, the gladiatorial combats grew in size and variety. Artworks that survived through the ages show us the bloody combats of armed men in mortal combat, men fighting against wild animals, and great naval combats in flooded arenas.

The Romans created artwork with their buildings, such as the Colosseum. Officially known as the Flavian Amphitheater, it was constructed in the first century C.E.. and was the scene of gladiatorial combats, animal hunts, and naval battles. Nearby was the Circus Maximus, an enormous site where great chariot races took place, also with bloody violence.

After the Roman empire crumbled almost 1,000 years passed in what we call the "Dark Ages." During this time sport changed as the nature of life changed, and a new activity appeared call the *tournement*. Emerging from France in the eleventh century, it spread throughout Europe. In this contest, two riders on horseback would race toward each other with long poles and try to knock each other off their horses. Eventually, it grew in stature and the magnificent suits of armor that we see in museums today are testimony to the skilled artwork of the craftsmen who made these suits and the equipment used in the contests. Many illustrations of *tournements* exist in fifteenth-century manuscripts.

After the fifteenth century books became more common and printed illustrations provide us with some very fine art on sport subjects. Engravings from these old books can be found today in galleries in every major city, illustrating everything from ancient statues of wrestlers and boxers to nineteenth century scenes of runners and rowers. The industrialization of printing processes allowed the price of books to drop; by the nineteenth century almost anyone could buy a book or penny magazine. Illustrations of famous riders and their horses proliferated in England. As boxing grew in popularity it appeared more frequently as well. By the late nineteenth century books were appearing on sport subjects, almost always with illustrations. By the twentieth century photography had become advanced enough that sports were being photographed and illustrated in daily newspapers.

Moving forward in time, photography led to moving pictures, and sport on film is another art form. The most famous filmmaker in this genre is Leni Riefenstahl, who created the film *Olympia* at the 1936 Berlin Olympic Games. Her use of slow motion, closeups, and editing created an unforgettable image of athletes in dramatic action. Since then, numerous films have been made with sport as a subject. Among the most famous films dealing with sports are *Chariots of Fire, Rocky* and its sequels, and *Requiem for a Heavyweight.*

Printing has greatly expanded the availability of art in general by allowing numerous copies to be made at a low cost. We can buy books and develop great collections of illustrations, but few could afford the originals, such as an ancient Greek vase or statue. One type of art that is collectable and affordable are coins and medals depicting sports themes and motifs. Since 1952 the Olympic Games have been commemorated on coins and today many dozens of such coins are produced by numerous nations. The medals presented to athletes at the Games are great pieces of art, designed by medallic artists and rendered into metal on huge presses that stamp blank pieces of bronze, silver, or gold-plated bronze into works of art.

Among the most common types of artwork is the poster. Readily available, thousands of sport scenes are depicted on posters for the admiring public, including baseball, football, basketball, ice hockey, tennis, and track and field stars. During the Olympic Games posters are produced by the millions. Whereas the 1912 Olympics in Stockholm had one single poster design, the 1980 Moscow Olympics had almost 1,000 designs.

The art of sport is voluminous and as varied as the nations on this earth. It is there for us to view, study, admire, and wonder that sport is so important that man immortalizes himself through permanent images.

—Harvey Abrams

See also Literature; Movies.

Bibliography: Bandy, Susan J., ed. (1988) *Coroebus Triumphs: The Alliance of Sport and the Arts.* San Diego, CA: San Diego State University Press.

Bergan, Ronald. (1982) *Sports in the Movies.* London and New York: Proteus Publishing.

Berlioux, Monique. (1983) *1896–1984: L'Olympisme par L'Affiche; Olympism through Posters.* Lausanne: International Olympic Committee.

Bura, Fabian. (1960) *Die Olympischen Spiele auf den Briefmarken der Welt.* Cologne: N. J. Hoffmann Verlag.

Danaher, Mary A. (1978) *The Commemorative Coinage of Modern Sports.* Cranbury, NJ: A. S. Barnes and Co.

Gordon, Barclay F. (1983) *Olympic Architecture: Building for the Summer Games.* New York: John Wiley & Sons.

Graham, Cooper C. (1986) *Leni Riefenstahl and Olympia.* Metuchen, NJ, and London: Scarecrow Press.

Kozar, Andrew J. (1992) *The Sport Sculpture of R. Tait McKenzie.* Champaign, IL: Human Kinetics.

Munson-Williams-Proctor Institute. (1980) *The Olympics in Art: An Exhibition of Works of Art Related to Olympic Sports.* Utica, NY: Munson-Williams-Proctor Institute.

Parrish Art Museum (1968) *A Salute to the Olympics—Sports in Art.* Southampton, NY: Parrish Art Museum.

Peak, Robert (1984) *Golden Moments: A Collection of United States 1984 Commemorative Olympic Issues.* Washington, DC: United States Postal Service.

Rhodes, Reilly, ed. (1990) *Sport in Art from American Museums.* New York: Universe Publishing.

Riger, Robert. (1967) *Man in Sport: An International Exhibition of Photography.* Baltimore: Baltimore Museum of Art.

Thompson, Brett, ed. (1980) *Olympiad: A Graphic Celebration.* San Diego, CA: A. S. Barnes & Co.

Yalouris, Nicolaos, ed. (1979) *The Eternal Olympics: The Art and History of Sport.* New Rochelle, NY: Caratzas Bros.

Yokohama, S. Sugahara. (1964) *Olympic Games Stamps.* Tokyo: Chuokoron Jigyo Shuppan.

Asian Games

The Asian Games were first held under the auspices of the International Amateur Athletic Federation and are now regulated by the Olympic Council of Asia. The first Asian Games were held in 1951, the same year as the first Pan-American Games, and may be considered part of the post-war reorganization of global sports culture. As the name suggests, the Asian Games are primarily Asian in terms of participation, although membership has fluctuated according to political and cultural criteria. Held every four years at the two-year midpoint between the Olympic Games, the Asian Games are important training and "filtering" events for Asian athletes, the best of whom generally go on to compete in the Olympics.

The first Asian Games were staged in India, which by 1951 was already an emerging leader in what came to be called the Third World, and were opened by Indian President Rajendra Prasad. Eleven Asian nations came to New Delhi to participate: Afghanistan, Burma (Myanmar), Ceylon (Sri Lanka), India, Indonesia, Iran, Japan, Nepal, the Philippines, Siam (Thailand), and Singapore. Six events were featured: track and field, basketball, cycling, football, swimming, and weight lifting. The fact that the games included no traditional Asian sports indicates how "western" international sport culture had become by the post-war period. Another sign of this Westernization was recently postcolonial India's heavy reliance for coaching advice on an American YMCA instructor, Ted Arnold, who had been working with a variety of athletes in Madras, India.

The Asian games have always been highly politicized, although perhaps no more than other international sports events. Israel attended the first games, but Syria did not. Iran attended but Iraq did not. Pakistan, only recently separated from India, refused to attend the first games. Communist China and Vietnam were also absent because India refused to recognize either government.

Athletes from 18 countries attended the second Asian Games, which were hosted in 1954 in Manila, the Philippine capital: Afghanistan, Burma, Cambodia, Ceylon, Nationalist China (Taiwan), Hong Kong, India, Indonesia, Israel, Japan, South Korea, Malaya, North Borneo (now Indonesia's Sabah State), Pakistan, Singapore, Thailand, Vietnam, and the Philippines. These nations represent a great part of Asia but by no means all of it. As has often been the case with the Asian Games, some absences were due to political disputes. For instance, the communist mainland Chinese refused to attend, seeing in the Taiwanese team a conspiracy to advance "the two-China plot." Israel, a founding member of the Asian Games Council, did attend, but none of its Arab neighbors recruited a team. No part of the Soviet Union sent athletes. Athletically, the Japanese dominated the second games, as they had the first.

Perhaps fittingly, Japan's Emperor Hirohito opened the third Asian Games in 1958, which were staged in Tokyo. His speech to athletes assembled from 20 countries was very short—three sentences—but no doubt meant much to a Japan so recently defeated by western forces. Japan was again triumphant on the field. There was some irony in the choice of Jakarta, Indonesia, as the site of the fourth Asian Games in 1962, since it was Japan that had created, during its occupation

Chinese and Korean women's handball teams compete in the 1994 Asian Games.

of the erstwhile Dutch East Indies, the basis for an organized Indonesian sports program.

Perhaps in reaction, Indonesian leader Sukarno used the fourth Asian Games to advance his self-appointed role as spokesperson for the emerging Third World. As a result, Israel and Taiwan were both barred from attending—being judged as western client states—and the politicization of the games became even more intense. Because an Indian sports official had objected to Sukarno's move, India itself was portrayed as hostile to Indonesia, and the Indian team was roundly booed by the Jakarta crowds on closing day.

Sukarno's conduct during the fourth Asian Games irritated the members of the International Olympic Committee (IOC), who felt that their authority was being challenged. Sukarno was unmoved and, in fact, immediately began to

experiment with a new international structure for sports in the "nonwestern" world, calling it "The Games of the Newly Emerging Forces" (GANEFO).

Insofar as GANEFO came into creation in clear opposition to the western powers, both the Soviet Union and communist China supplied money and sent athletes to the few GANEFO events that were staged. Indonesia also received enough support from emerging nations in Asia and Africa that the IOC felt obliged to back off from its threats of expulsion: most GANEFO states had athletes at the Tokyo Olympic games in 1964. In fact, although GANEFO did not survive long after Sukarno's ouster in 1965, the affair showed the West that Asian nations could indeed organize alternate games.

During the fifth Asian Games in Bangkok, Thailand in 1966, the government issued a special set of postage stamps featuring "modern" sports, that is to say, the western sports that were, and still are, featured at these events. At the next games in 1970, also in Bangkok, closing ceremonies featured a spectacular fireworks display and an entirely Asian assembly of contestants singing "Auld Lang Syne." These games, as before, were dominated by Japanese athletes.

The seventh Asian Games, held in Tehran, Iran, in 1974, were chiefly notable for the participation of mainland Chinese athletes for the first time. China's communist government had determined to send as many athletes and to compete in as many events as possible. The Chinese, in fact, took more top medals than any country other than the games' perennial Japanese champions. They also kept the tradition of political symbolism alive by refusing to play table tennis or fence with Israeli athletes, who were there only as a reflection of Iran's then pro-Western policy in contrast to the anti-Western or more neutral policies of other Middle East nations.

Israel, though, was barred from the next games, in Bangkok in 1978, six years after the infamous terrorist attack on Israeli athletes at the Olympics in Munich. One Thai organizer rationalized the expulsion with the comment, "Like a neighbor whose house is on fire, you want to move away from them." This was surely one of the low points in sports "internationalism."

In 1982, for the ninth games, the event moved back to its birthplace, New Delhi, where the government of Indira Gandhi is said to have spent nearly $1 billion for the construction of new facilities. With the threat of Sikh separatist action in New Delhi, the government felt compelled to deploy 15,000 soldiers and police throughout the city, but the games were held with little disruption. The mainland Chinese, having been legitimized by the IOC in 1979, put together a 400-member contingent for the New Delhi games. Chinese athletes took 61 gold medals, for the first time outperforming the Japanese.

The next games were staged in Seoul, South Korea, whose government believed Korea's international prestige would rise as a result. Considerable resources were poured into the tenth Asian Games and also into preparation for the 1988 Seoul Olympic Games. Even a new Cabinet-level sports ministry was organized to direct the preparations. Athletically, this effort paid off, in that South Korean athletes came in a close second to China in the achievement of medals.

However, there were domestic political problems during the Seoul games, and these sometimes threatened to crowd news of Korean sports victories off the front page. Most people noticed a heavy police presence, and five universities, hotbeds of opposition to the Korean government, were shut down during the course of the Games. While Korean students battled their government, Japanese Prime Minister Yasuhiro Nakasone took the occasion to apologize to the Korean people for the oppressive period of Japanese colonialism. The Chinese, for the second time, outdid their Japanese rivals.

In 1990, mainland China hosted the games. Prior to the commencement of the competition, the Olympic Council of Asia had voted to bar Iraq because of its part in events leading to the Persian Gulf War. This decision was not purely political but also personal: the President of the Council, Sheik Fahad al-Ahmad al-Sabah, had been killed during the Iraqi invasion of Kuwait. In spite of Iraq's expulsion, the Beijing Games featured virtually every eligible country. Beijing, determined to make the most of what was to be China's biggest-ever international gathering, directed massive resources to the games. Pan-Pan—an anthropomorphized cartoon panda—was declared mascot of the games, and the opening ceremonies featured the release of great numbers of panda balloons, a flight of 11,000 pigeons, and a spectac-

Southeast Asian Games

The Southeast Asian Games are biennial games, modeled on the Asian Games and the Olympics, designed to showcase competition between athletes from the Southeast Asian region. The games were established in 1959, and the founding members were Burma, Cambodia, Laos, Malaya (now Malaysia), Thailand, and Vietnam. Joining the games later were Brunei, Indonesia, the Philippines, and Singapore.

During the course of the third Asian Games (1958 in Tokyo), representatives from Thailand invited officials from Burma, Malaya, and Laos to consider the benefits of holding small regional events. These events, held more frequently than either the Asian Games or the Olympics, would allow athletes to hone their skills for the more global competitions and would also advance the cause of regional cultural interaction. This meeting resulted in the formation of the Southeast Asian Peninsular Games Federation, and the games have been held every two years since then.

The first games were held in 1959 in Bangkok, and the Thais took most of the gold and silver medals in the 12 featured sports, all of which were "Western" Olympic-style events.

As is the case with all international athletic bodies, the Southeast Asian Games have often been affected by sociopolitical factors. For instance, in 1965, Singapore became the seventh member of the federation—in the same year it became an independent republic. Pressed by political and economic concerns, some countries found it difficult to attend all of the games, so that, at the eighth games, held in Bangkok, only Thailand, Burma, Malaysia, and Singapore took part.

Partly in response to this instability, the games' organizers invited three other countries to join: Brunei, Indonesia, and the Philippines. All three accepted, the word "peninsular" was dropped from the federation's title, and the ninth Southeast Asian Games were held in Kuala Lumpur, Malaysia, in November 1977 with seven countries in attendance.

Thailand has tended to garner most of the medals throughout the games' history, but Indonesia has recently been close behind. At the eighteenth games (1995), with 10 countries participating, Thailand earned most of the gold, followed by Indonesia and the Philippines. The nineteenth Southeast Asian Games, scheduled for 1997 in Jakarta, Indonesia, will probably see fierce competition.

—Alan Trevithick

ular parachute display. A few traditional Asian games were featured in exhibition, notably kabbadi, the Indian game of team pursuit and capture, but most events were modern and western.

The 1994 games were hosted by Hiroshima, Japan, and signaled a new era in the life of that once-devastated city. The Hiroshima Games also featured something new: for the first time, an ex-Soviet Asian Republic, Kazakhstan, attended. Its athletes won two gold medals in wrestling and demonstrated anew that Asia is not a changeless geographical entity.

—Alan Trevithick

Bibliography: Kanin, D. (1982) *A Political History of the Olympic Games.* Boulder, CO: Westview Press.

Knuttgen, Howard G., Ma Qiwei, and Wu Zhonguan, eds. (1990) *Sport in China.* Champaign, IL: Human Kinetics Books.

Wagner, Eric A. (1989) *Sport in Asia and Africa: A Comparative Handbook.* New York: Greenwood Press.

Associations

The historical development of major sports associations and organizations has been examined by a number of sport historians. Peter McIntosh (1963) dramatically illustrates the prolific spread of sports, not just in Great Britain, but around the world from the middle of the eighteenth century to the beginning of the twentieth. For example, golf found its first home in St. Andrews, Scotland, in 1754 under the aegis of the Royal and Ancient Golf Club. When American John Daly won the 1995 British Open, he received his championship trophy at St. Andrews, under the shadow of that same club building.

After the founding of the first three sports organizations (for horse racing, golf, and cricket) there was a significant hiatus until the middle of the nineteenth century. Then, sports organizations mushroomed and multiplied. There was the Alpine Club (1857), the Football Association (1863), the Amateur Athletic Association (1880), the Amateur Metropolitan Swimming Association (1869), the Rugby Football Union (1871), the Yacht Racing Association (1875), the Bicyclists' Union (1878), the National Skating Association (1879), the Metropolitan Rowing Association (1879), the Amateur Boxing Association (1884), the Hockey Association (1886), the Lawn Tennis Association (1888), the Badminton Association (1895), and the Amateur Fencing Association (1898).

British sports organizations can be seen as being the "founding fathers" of modern sport. For example, swimming, in terms of its national sports associations, originated in Great Britain in 1869 and then emerged in the United States (1878), Germany (1887), and Sweden (1904). In the case of track and field athletics, the Amateur Athletic Association was founded in England in 1880, followed by similar organizations in the United States (1888), Sweden (1895), and Germany (1898). British sporting institutions subtly dominated their foreign offshoots.

The Marylebone Cricket Club and the Royal and Ancient Golf Club at St. Andrews, for example, became unofficial mediators frequently called on to settle disputes.

As a result of the extensive development and consolidation of sports associations and organizations in North America in the twentieth century, it too has shaped an extraordinary mosaic of sports. There is a clearly defined sport calendar that follows both the rhythm and seasons of the year. In the early fall, there is the U.S. Open in tennis and the World Series in baseball. As the fall moves into winter, college and professional football dominate sporting life. The year opens with the Super Bowl, and the National Collegiate Athletic Association basketball championship tournament is now known as "March Madness." With the coming of spring, there is the Masters golf tournament at Augusta. In May, with summer around the corner, there is the "Run for the Roses" at the Kentucky Derby and the roar of engines at the Indianapolis 500.

In terms of the creation of major sports associations in the twentieth century, a good case can be made for the leading role taken by the United States. The National Football League (NFL) was founded on 17 September 1920. Among the ten original teams were the Canton Bulldogs, the Cleveland Tigers, and the Rock Island Independents. The president of the organization was the celebrated athlete Jim Thorpe (1888–1953).

Professional football came of age in 1925 with the decision of collegiate star Red Grange (1903–1991) to sign for the Chicago Bears. On 6 December 1925, over 70,000 fans, lured in large mea-

The Association of Tennis Professionals

In 1877, a tennis tournament took place at a croquet club in a London suburb. By 1900 the All-England Wimbledon Championship, as it came to be called, had established itself as the world's premier tennis tournament. Just under a century later (in 1968), Wimbledon opened its doors to professional athletes. Many conservative factions, staunchly committed to the notion that "amateur" meant wholesome and good, while "professional" stood for plebeian and crassly pecuniary, lamented the decay of the All-England Championship. In actual fact the opening of Wimbledon revitalized tennis and made the All-England Championship a global sports spectacular in which all the world's leading tennis players participated.

The Association of Tennis Professionals (ATP) was founded in 1972 by four distinguished professional tennis players—Americans Arthur Ashe, Jack Kramer, and Stan Smith and one South African, Cliff Drysdale. Originally, the organization had members in two divisions based on world rankings in singles and doubles events. The ATP has played a key role in the development of professional tennis. In 1970, there were only 20 open tournaments around the world. By 1985, the Grand Prix circuit of tournaments numbered more than 80 with over $20 million in prize money. Perhaps of even more significance have been the ATP computer rankings used as a system of entry into Grand Prix events. A committee of ATP members works closely with ATP staff to provide an objective evaluation of all players' results. These weekly rankings are the basis for entries and seedings throughout the world for all Grand Prix events.

In its early years the ATP campaigned strenuously to raise the amount of prize money offered at Grand Prix tournaments. The organization has also assumed a quasi-union role in terms of protecting and preserving players' rights. As a result of the ATP presence all Grand Prix tournaments must have on-site trainers and physiotherapists to look after the players' health and fitness. Moreover, the ATP pension plan, a first for tennis, was set up to give some degree of financial security to players after retirement.

When the ATP began, Jack Kramer, its first executive director, ran the organization out of his business office in Los Angeles. Today the main office is at Ponte Verda Beach, Florida, and serves literally hundreds of professional players.

In 1990, the ATP changed its name to the Association of Tennis Professionals Tour. The European headquarters are in Monte Carlo, Monaco, and the International Group (including the Pacific Rim, Middle East, and Russia) is based in Sydney, Australia. In 1994, ATP Tour purses totaled $60.3 million. This was spread around 85 tournaments in 38 countries on six continents. In 1994-95, the sites of ATP Tour events signal an activity that is truly global in its distribution. These locations were Qatar, Dubai, Bucharest, Coral Springs, Atlanta, Milan, Stuttgart, Tokyo, Jakarta, Moscow, St. Petersburg (Russia), Bermuda, Oporto, and Nottingham.

—Scott A. G. M. Crawford

sure by the presence of the "Galloping Ghost," watched the Bears play the New York Giants.

In the 1960s, professional football began to rival baseball for the title of national pastime. Pete Rozelle (1926–) became NFL commissioner in 1960 and under his vigorous leadership the sport moved on to the central stage of U.S. sport theater. Rozelle tapped the NFL into lucrative television deals and made the three major networks (ABC, NBC, and CBS) compete with one another to acquire the sole rights for football coverage. Of even more importance was Rozelle's ability to merge the two leagues (the American Football League and the NFL) and get agreement that there should be an interleague championship game in 1967. It was this game that eventually came to be known as the Super Bowl. In the first official Super Bowl, the Kansas City Chiefs defeated the Minnesota Vikings by a score of 23–7.

In 1989, Paul Tagliabue (1940–) became the new NFL commissioner and in 1995 the league expanded from 28 to 30 teams with the addition of two new franchises called the Jacksonville Jaguars and the Carolina Panthers.

When Scottish-Canadian James Naismith created a recreational fitness activity to give students an indoor winter game in December 1891, he could not have conceived that "basketball" would emerge a century later as the fastest-growing global sport. In the fall of 1993, the National Basketball Association scheduled its first-ever game in Europe at Wembley Stadium, which is known as a mecca for soccer, rugby league, and pop concerts, but not basketball.

Allen Guttmann, in his 1994 book *Games and Empires: Modern Sports and Cultural Imperialism*, examines the many ways in which sports such as soccer, baseball, football, and basketball have spread from their Western origins to all corners of the globe. *Games and Empires* is a colorful tapestry.

It describes the introduction of cricket into the United States, although the sport would later be submerged by baseball, and India, where it would become a talisman in the struggle against the political might of Mother England. Guttmann tackles the emergence of soccer in South America and in Africa, chronicles the expansion of the Olympics to the furthest reaches of the world, and discusses the export of baseball to Japan and the Caribbean.

The internationalization of sport and its current global stage is a result of the growth and expansion of a variety of national sports associations. Who would have thought that the Super Bowl would reach 176 countries? Imagine the cultural significance of African American Doug Williams, the former Washington Redskins quarterback, who has worked as an assistant coach to the new World Football League's Scottish Claymores, in an athletic context where soccer once reigned supreme.

—Scott A. G. M. Crawford

Bibliography: Dunning, E., and K. Sheard. (1979) *Barbarians, Gentlemen and Players.* Oxford: Martin Robertson.

Guttmann, Allen. (1978) *From Ritual to Record: The Nature of Modern Sports.* New York: Columbia University Press.

———. (1994) *Games and Empires: Modern Sports and Cultural Imperialism.* New York: Columbia University Press.

Hickok, R. (1992). *The Encyclopedia of North American Sports History.* New York: Facts on File.

McIntosh, P. C. (1963). *Sport in Society.* London: C. A. Watts.

Auto Racing

See Drag Racing; Formula 1 Auto Racing; Indy Auto Racing; Karting; Stock Car Racing; Truck Racing; Vintage Auto Racing

Badminton

Badminton, which has been called the world's fastest racket sport, is played with rackets and shuttlecocks on a court divided by a net. First played as a recreational game, it has grown into an Olympic sport with an active professional tour.

Origins

Evidence of games similar to badminton can be found at least as early as the first century B.C.E. in China, where Ti Jian Zi, or shuttlecock kicking, became popular. The game of Ti Jian Zi involved hitting a shuttlecock with one's feet or hands, or occasionally with a bat. The game also was popular in Japan, India, and Siam, and spread to Sumeria and Greece.

In fourteenth-century England, the game of battledore shuttlecock, involving a racket or paddle and a shuttlecock, was widely played. This recreational game used no nets or boundaries and was primarily a means of testing two players' skill in keeping the shuttlecock in play as long as possible. By the late sixteenth century it had become a popular children's game, the object still being to hit the shuttlecock to each other, or to oneself, and to keep it in the air as long as possible. The ideas of using a net and of trying to prevent one's partner from returning the shuttlecock was still a century away.

During the seventeenth century, the social status of battledore shuttlecock rose as it became a pastime for British royalty and the leisured classes. Early English settlers in America also enjoyed the game at this time. In the 1800s, the seventh Duke of Beaufort and his family were avid players at his Gloucester estate, called Badminton House. At this estate, a "new game" of badminton battledore, involving a net and boundaries, evolved; thus, the name "badminton." By 1867, a formal game of badminton was being played in India by English officers and their families, who developed the first sets of rules.

Development

During the last three decades of the 1800s, badminton evolved into a competitive indoor sport, and clubs were formed throughout the British Isles to promote competition. The first tournaments were held there in the 1890s, and the first All-England Championships were held in 1899. Until the 1920s, the major badminton titles were contested by the English, Scots, and Irish. Rules varied from place to place until about 1905, when the Badminton Association of England adopted and promoted uniform new rules that are similar to the International Badminton Federation's official Laws of Badminton followed today.

Beginning in the 1920s, badminton spread from England to northern Europe (the sport was especially popular in Scandinavian countries) and North America. It also spread from India throughout the rest of Asia. In the latter half of the twentieth century, one Asian country after another has risen to the top of the world ranks: Thailand and Indonesia in the 1950s, Japan in the 1960s, China in the 1970s, and Korea in the 1980s.

The International Badminton Federation, which governs all international badminton competition throughout the world, was formed in 1934 with nine member countries. Currently there are more than 125 member nations. After World War II, several international competitions for teams and individual players were instituted, and by 1979 the game had become truly professional. A year-round international grand prix circuit worth $2 million a year in prize money currently attracts the top players to a touring career similar to that of other professional athletes.

The 1985 acceptance of badminton into the Olympic Games—and its debut at the 1992 Olympics in Barcelona—solidified the game's position as a major international sport. More recent accomplishments include a $20 million worldwide television agreement announced in June 1994, the biggest television deal in the history of badminton; and the inclusion of badminton in the Pan American Games for the first time in March 1995.

Rules of Play

Badminton is distinguished from other racket sports, all of which use a ball of some size, by two features: the use of a shuttlecock and the fact that the shuttlecock must not touch the ground. These factors make badminton a fast game requiring quick reflexes and strong conditioning. Indeed, when played by top athletes, it is considered to

Badminton

Although it is popular as backyard recreation, organized competitions in the fast-moving sport of badminton are always held indoors.

be the fastest racket sport in the world, with smashes of over 320 kilometers (200 miles) per hour having been recorded.

Although badminton may be played outdoors or indoors, all officially sanctioned competition around the world is played indoors. Competitive badminton is played in five events: men's singles, women's singles, men's doubles, women's doubles, and mixed doubles.

Scoring

A badminton game consists of 15 points, except for women's singles in which a game is 11 points. The best of three games constitutes a match. Points can be scored only by the serving side. A game does not need to be won by two points.

If the score becomes tied near the end of a game, the game may be lengthened by a procedure called "setting." For example, when the score becomes tied at 13-all in a 15-point game, the side that reached 13 first has the option of "setting" the game to 5 (a total of 18 points), so

that the side that scores 5 points first wins the game. The score may be set in the same manner at 14-all for 3 points (a total of 17 points). In women's singles, the 11-point game may total 12 points by setting at 9-all for 3 points or at 10-all for 2 points. Only the side that reached the tied score first has the option of setting or not setting the score; if the side elects not to set, the conventional number of points completes the game.

Side Changes

The sides change ends at the beginning of the second game and at the beginning of the third if a third game is necessary. In a 15-point game, ends are changed in the third game when the leading side reaches 8; in an 11-point third game, ends are changed when either side reaches 6. The side that wins a game serves first in the next game.

Strategy

In singles play, the goal is to move the opponent primarily up and back on the court, using deception and forcing errors by the opponent. In doubles play, a team's goal is to repeatedly hit the shuttlecock down to their opponents and force the opponents to hit defensive shots up in return. The offensive doubles formation is one player at the net and the other smashing from the backcourt. The defensive doubles formation is both players back, each defending his or her side of the court.

A typical rally in badminton singles consists of a serve and repeated high deep shots hit to the baseline (clears), interspersed with dropshots. If and when a short clear or other type of "set-up" is forced, a smash wins the point. More often than not, an error (where the shuttlecock is hit out-of-bounds or into the net) brings an end to a rally rather than a positive winning play. A player who is patient and commits few or no outright errors often wins by simply waiting for the opponent to err.

In doubles, there are fewer clears and more low serves, drives, and net play. Again, the smash often ends the point. As in singles, having patience and avoiding any unforced errors are important in winning doubles matches.

Basic Shots

Badminton's striking techniques and strokes vary greatly from relatively slow shots to quick and deceptive movements. Basic shots in badminton consist of underhand strokes (serve, underhand clear, underhand dropshot), overhead strokes (clear, dropshot, smash), a sidearm stroke (drive), and the hairpin drop at the net.

Unlike the serve in tennis, a player has only one attempt to put the shuttlecock into play in badminton. In badminton doubles, both players on a side have a turn at serve before the serve passes to the other side. A serve that hits the top of the net and goes into the correct service court is legal and "in play."

In addition, the badminton serve is a defensive shot—it must be underhand. The racket shaft must point downwards at the point of contact, so that the entire racket head is below the server's hand and fingers.

Faults

A fault is a violation of the playing rules, either in serving, receiving, or during play. If the receiving side faults, the serving side scores a point. If the serving side faults, no point is scored and the serve passes to the next appropriate server.

Equipment

The traditional feathered shuttlecock is used in all major badminton competitions. It must weigh between 4.74 and 5.50 grams (0.17 and 0.19 ounces) and have 14 to 16 feathers fixed in a cork base covered with a thin layer of leather or similar material. Shuttlecocks are humidified to prevent drying and brittleness. They are produced at different "speed" levels and weights to suit all playing environments. One shuttlecock usually lasts for only two games.

The badminton net stands 5 feet (1.524 meters) high at the center of the court and 5 feet, 1 inch (1.550 meters) at each end post.

Badminton rackets were made entirely of wood until the 1950s. Today's rackets are made of various blends of carbon, boron, aluminum, and steel. These rackets are very light (around 98 grams [3.5 ounces]) and can be strung very tightly with natural gut or synthetic string. Dimensions cannot exceed 27 inches by 9 inches (69 centimeters by 23 centimeters), and the head length cannot exceed 13 inches (33 centimeters).

The badminton court measures 17 feet by 44 feet (5.2 meters by 13.4 meters) for singles play and 20 feet (6.1 meters) by 44 feet for doubles play.

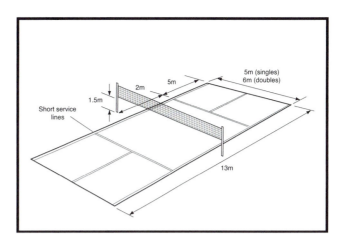

Major Events and Players

Major international badminton competitions include the Olympic Games, the Thomas Cup and the Uber Cup, the World Badminton Championships, and the Sudirman Cup.

Although badminton was included as a demonstration sport in Munich in 1972 and as an exhibition sport in Seoul in 1988, its Olympic debut as a full-medal sport came in 1992 in Barcelona. Four events were contested: men's singles, women's singles, men's doubles, and women's doubles. At the 1996 Olympic Games in Atlanta, the mixed doubles event was added to the program.

Thomas Cup and Uber Cup

The Thomas Cup is the Men's World Team Championship, similar to the Davis Cup in tennis. The event started in 1949 and was held every three years until 1984, after which it has been held every even year. The Uber Cup is the Women's World Team Championship, staged together with the Thomas Cup every even year. The event began in 1957.

In the competitions for the Thomas and Uber Cups, each "tie" between two countries consists of five matches—three singles and two doubles. Regional playoffs are held in several locations around the world, and the winners of these playoffs, along with the defending champion nations, gather in one location for the final rounds.

World Badminton Championships

The World Badminton Championships were initiated in 1977 to provide individual championships that would complement the above described team competitions. The World Championships

The 1930s Badminton Rage

Although the first badminton club in the United States was formed in 1878, it was during the 1930s that badminton became the fastest-growing sport in the United States. Americans' leisure time increase due to the shortened work weeks of the Depression, and many used this time to play badminton. Educational institutions, the Young Men's Christian Association, and hundreds of newly formed clubs offered badminton instruction. A New York beauty salon even installed a court on its rooftop to allow customers to get their exercise while their hair set.

Interest in badminton in the 1930s was also generated by professional players, well-known athletes who enjoyed the sport, and Hollywood movie stars who played the game for fun and fitness. Badminton professionals like George "Jess" Willard, Bill Hurley, Jack Purcell, Ken Davidson, and Hugh Forgie performed exhibitions in movie houses and staged badminton comedy shows and "badminton on ice" performances. Athletes from other sports who played badminton included tennis stars Sidney Wood and Hazel Wightman, Chicago Cubs slugger Larry French, Seattle Rainiers baseball player Freddie Hutchison, University of Southern California football coach Howard Jones, and Stanford football star Ernie Nevers. In Hollywood, Warner Bros. produced a short instructional film and Walt Disney visited the Pasadena Badminton Club to watch tournaments. Hollywood personalities who played badminton during the rage of the 1930s included Douglas Fairbanks, Joan Crawford, James Cagney, Claudette Colbert, Bette Davis, Boris Karloff, Dick Powell, and Ginger Rogers.

—Kathleen M. Spence

are currently held every odd-numbered year. Prior to 1977, the prestigious All-England Badminton Championships were considered the unofficial individual world championships for badminton. The All-England Championships were founded in 1899, and are still conducted annually. Since 1992, World Junior Badminton Championships have also been conducted.

Sudirman Cup

The Sudirman Cup is the World Mixed Team Championship, instituted in 1989. Held in conjunction with the World Badminton Championships in odd-numbered years, the tournament provides competition between teams consisting of men and women. In this contest, each "tie" between two contries consists of five matches—one men's singles, one women's singles, one men's doubles, one women's doubles, and one mixed doubles.

Both the World Badminton Championships and the Sudirman Cup attracted a record number of entries in 1995.

The record-holder for most individual world badminton titles (counting All-England titles [1947–present] and World Championships titles [1977–present]) is the legendary U.S. player Judy Devlin Hashman, with 17. By nation, players from Denmark have won more individual world titles (77) than any other country. Indonesia holds the most men's team world titles (9), and China and Japan are tied for the most women's team world titles (5).

Currently, Indonesian players dominate international badminton competition. In the World Player Rankings released 4 January 1996, Indonesians account for 6 of the world's top 10 men's singles players; the number three and six women's singles player; the number two, six, and seven men's doubles teams; and 2 of the top 10 women's doubles and mixed doubles teams. Indonesia took five Olympic medals in 1992 and four in 1996.

China is also near the top in international badminton competition. In the latest world top 10, the Chinese list 1 men's singles players, 4 women's singles player, 1 men's doubles team, 3 women's doubles teams, and 2 mixed doubles teams. Chinese players captured four medals at the 1996 Olympics; South Korea and Malaysia took four and two, respectively.

World Distribution

Badminton is truly a world sport. It is a major sport in most countries of northern Europe and southeast Asia, and virtually the national sport in Indonesia and several other countries. Denmark, Sweden, England, Holland, and Germany lead the European nations in their interest.

The International Badminton Federation lists the number of players registered with national badminton associations around the world at approximately 1.4 million. The federation estimates, however, that the actual number of people who play badminton is 10 times that figure.

The top five national badminton associations with the most registered players, according to the IBF list, are: Denmark (180,977); Germany (142,253); Japan (115,682); China (110,550); and the Netherlands (94,815).

—Kathleen M. Spence

Bibliography: Adams, Bernard. (1980) *The Badminton Story.* London: British Broadcasting Publications.

Bloss, Margaret Varner, and R. Stanton Hales. (1994) *Badminton.* Dubuque, IA: Brown & Benchmark.

Davis, Pat. (1983) *Guinness Book of Badminton.* London: Guinness Superlatives Ltd.

Grice, Tony. (1994) *Badminton for the College Student.* Boston: American Press.

Hales, Diane. (1979) *A History of Badminton in the United States from 1878–1939.* Pomona: California State Polytechnic University.

Hashman, Judy Devlin. (1984) *Winning Badminton.* London: Ward Lock.

International Badminton Federation. *World Badminton Magazine.* Cheltenham, UK: International Badminton Federation.

———. (1994) *IBF Statute Book.* Cheltenham, UK: International Badminton Federation.

United States Badminton Association. (1995) *Badminton '95* (USBA Official Media Guide). Colorado Springs, CO: United States Badminton Association.

———. (1996) *60 Years: 1936–1996, 60th Jubilee Fact Book.* Colorado Springs, CO: United States Badminton Association.

Ballooning

Ballooning is a sport of contrasts. While the balloon simply drifts with the wind, its pilot must thoroughly understand the complex micrometeorological conditions that cause that wind. A balloon in flight floats literally lighter than air; however, a typical four-place system can weigh as much as 363 kilograms (800 pounds). And, while the speed of the wind determines the distance of any given flight, too much wind means the pilot will probably elect not to fly at all.

Celebrating these contrasts, balloonists around the world rise in the pre-dawn hours to prepare their craft. They may launch from their own backyards or travel thousands of miles to participate in competition with others. They cruise the treetops looking for leaves, or soar to many thousands of feet to find wind directions with which to steer to a competitive goal or suitable landing site.

While some balloonists compete in championship events, fly paying passengers, or fly balloons as advertising billboards, most enter the sport for the sheer beauty of flight.

Origins

Ballooning marked the beginning of manned flight. Credit for inventing and developing lighter-than-air craft generally goes to the Montgolfier brothers. Sons of a paper manufacturer near Annonay, France, Joseph (1740–1810) and Jacques Etienne (1745–1799) began building model balloons out of paper laminated with tafetta. They thought the lifting power came from smoke, based on observations of cloth and paper floating up the chimney of their fireplace. So they powered their balloons with smoke from burning wet straw under the paper envelope. On 19 September 1783, the Montgolfiers launched a balloon carrying a sheep, a cock, and a duck.

That same year, J. A. C. Charles (1746–1823), working with Aîné and Cadet Robert, built an envelope out of silk coated with varnish. They filled it with hydrogen, made by pouring sulphuric acid over iron filings.

On 21 November 1783, the first manned balloon, built by the Montgolfiers, launched from the Bois de Boulogne. Pilâtre de Rozier (1756–1785) and copilot Marquis d'Arlandes (1742–1809) became the first live humans in recorded history to fly, and spent most of their time aloft putting out small fires in the balloon caused by the burning straw. Their aircraft would later become known as a hot air balloon.

Ten days later, on 1 December, Charles and Aîné Robert launched in a hydrogen-filled balloon from the Tuilleries Gardens, and gas ballooning grew in popularity in Europe and the United States.

It wasn't until 1960 that hot air ballooning again made its presence felt. On 10 October, Paul Edward Yost (1919–), an aeronautical engineer under contract to the U.S. Navy, launched a tiny aerostat from Bruning, Nebraska. Lift came from a small propane burner. Shortly thereafter, Yost

Balloon pilots, who undergo training similar to that of airplane pilots, may travel hundreds of miles to meet and compete with other enthusiasts.

began building hot air balloons for sport flying. His contribution resulted in the explosive growth ballooning has enjoyed since that time.

Practice

Both hot air and gas balloons operate on the same principle: gas of a lesser density will rise until it attains equilibrium, with lift somewhat diminished by the weight of the container holding the gas. The lifting gas in a balloon may be: air heated to make it less dense than the surrounding (ambient) air; hydrogen; helium; cooking gas; or, in recent years, ammonia gas.

In a hot air balloon, the pilot uses a propane burner to heat the air inside the envelope, making it less dense and providing lift. In a gas balloon,

the pilot releases weight, usually in the form of sand or water ballast, to allow the gas to lift the system. To come down, the hot air pilot allows the air in the envelope to cool, or vents hot air out the top. A gas-balloon pilot vents gas to descend.

In recent years, some manufacturers have been experimenting with a hybrid balloon called a Rozier, named for Pilâtre de Rozier. This is a gas-balloon sphere surrounded on the bottom half by a hot air balloon cone. The pilot uses a tiny propane burner to heat the air inside this cone, which then warms the helium, expanding it and increasing lift. Rozier balloons have proven useful for long-distance flights such as transoceanic and transglobal attempts.

Hot air ballooning is by far the most popular form of balloon flight today. Hot air systems cost a lot less to purchase than gas balloons and are less complex to rig. The propane, used to fuel the burner, costs just a tiny fraction of the price of gas to fill a gas balloon. In Europe, most gas ballooning uses hydrogen, while in the United States, helium is the gas of choice. A helium fill can cost up to $3,500 in 1996 dollars. Propane for a typical one-hour hot air balloon flight runs between $10 and $30. A gas-balloon flight, however, lasts many hours or even days, while a hot air balloon flight is usually about an hour.

A balloon joins the air mass within which it flies and goes wherever that air mass goes. So balloons are called "aerostats," that is, they are static within the air. The pilot can vary the direction of flight somewhat by adjusting the altitude of the aircraft—air currents at various levels can differ by as much as 90 degrees of the compass, depending on the prevailing weather conditions.

Flying with the wind, the aerostat can rarely fly back to its launch site. For that reason, a chase crew must follow the flight on the ground. Once the balloon lands, the pilot and crew pack the equipment onto a trailer or truck for the trip back to the launch site. A hot air balloon flight may cover 8 to 40 kilometers (5 to 25 miles) or more, depending on wind speed at the various altitudes chosen by the pilot. A gas flight may cover much greater distances.

Hot air balloons contain three components. The envelope is the fabric, "balloon" part of the system, which holds the hot air used for lift. The envelope is sewn together from panels of nylon or polyester cloth, usually coated with urethane or silicone to minimize porosity. The basket is the "cabin." It hangs from the envelope by aircraft cables connected to envelope cables. Most baskets are woven from wicker or rattan. The burner and fuel system are the "engine" of the hot air balloon. The burner is attached to a frame over the pilot's head, and is connected by fuel hoses to the tanks stored in each corner of the basket.

Balloon pilots are trained in much the same manner as pilots of any other aircraft. Instructors provide ground and flight training, covering equipment operation; weather; aviation regulations of the pilots' home country; emergencies; and launch, flight, and landing procedures. The student must complete a predetermined number of flight hours, and perform a solo flight and ascension to a given altitude (3,500 feet [1,067 meters] for a private pilot in the United States). Then the student takes a written exam, and upon passing it, an oral exam and flight test from a government-designated examiner.

Ideal weather for ballooning consists of high pressure, light surface winds, and moderate winds at higher elevations. While balloons can easily fly in the rain, packing away a wet envelope leads to mildew and premature degradation of the fabric and coating.

Balloons normally fly within three hours of sunrise or sunset, rather than in the middle of the day. The air near the ground is most stable at dawn and dusk, and the winds most predictable. As the sun heats the earth's surface, thermals and higher winds often develop, which are not conducive to ballooning. Balloons rarely fly in the middle of the day. A pilot has no brakes to slow the balloon's forward motion, so light winds make the most comfortable landings.

In addition to overall weather systems, the balloonist must learn to take advantage of various aspects of the terrain that may affect the flight. Winds flow differently in the wide, flat expanses of the plains than they do in wooded, mountainous areas. Yet both can be good areas for ballooning.

The worldwide sport aviation community falls under the overall direction of the Fédération Aéronautique Internationale (FAI), headquartered in Paris. The FAI governs all world aviation records and all international aviation competition, including world championships. The FAI has separate committees for each air sport, including one for ballooning.

Challenging the Winds

Since balloons can't accelerate or decelerate at will, balloon competition centers around the pilot's ability to observe minute weather phenomena, and to manipulate the controls of the balloon to take advantage of such. Championship tasks are based entirely on the concept of accuracy, with variations in tasks to accommodate different kinds of weather.

The one exception to this precept is the international Coupe Gordon Bennett gas balloon race, established in 1906 by newspaper magnate J. Gordon Bennett (1841–1918). In that race, the balloon which flies the farthest wins. Flights sometimes last three days or more, with each year's race beginning in the country of the previous year's winner.

In hot air ballooning, and in world championship gas ballooning, pilots are scored by their ability to fly to a target, and drop a marker on that target. The marker is usually a small sack filled with flour, weighing 70–100 grams (2.5–3.5 ounces). Attached to the sack is a tail of balloon fabric 168 centimeters (66 inches) long. Markers are often called "baggies."

Pilots may launch from a common site to fly to targets set by the officials, or choose their own launch site outside a given radius to fly back to the event location. In other tasks, the pilots choose their own targets and/or launch sites, declaring their targets to the officials before launch. It is not uncommon to combine several tasks in one flight.

At a competition briefing, pilots are given a detailed weather briefing, as well as the task or combination of tasks set for the flight, and the baggies to throw at their goals. They then return to their vehicles and crews, and release helium-filled party balloons to check the wind speed and direction at various altitudes. Surface winds often change a few degrees in direction and a few knots in speed from the time the briefing officer obtained his data.

Scoring is based on how many pilots threw their markers closest to the intended goal, with penalty points taken away for infractions such as launching too late, unauthorized ground contact before the end of the task, or dropping the wrong colored baggie in a multiple-task flight.

—Ruth P. Ludwig

Each FAI member country governs its own air sports through a National Aero Club (NAC), the National Aeronautic Association (NAA) in the United States. Within each NAC are separate air sport federations. So each country with an active ballooning community has its own balloon federation. The two most active are the British Balloon and Airship Club (BBAC) and the Balloon Federation of America (BFA). The BFA is the largest group of balloonists in the world.

Balloonists compete in local, regional, national, and world championship flying events, or to set world records. The FAI organizes balloon records into category (gas, hot air, or rozier) and size of balloon. Within these designations are records for altitude, distance and duration.

—Ruth P. Ludwig

Bibliography: Crouch, Tom. (1983). *The Eagle Aloft.* Washington, DC: Smithsonian Institutional Press.

Ludwig, Ruth. (1995). *Balloon Digest.* Indianola, IA: Balloon Federation of America

Wirth, Dick. (1982) *Ballooning, the Complete Guide to Riding the Winds.* New York: Random House.

Bandy

Bandy, sometimes known as "winter football," combines elements of soccer and ice hockey. Rules and tactics are similar to those found in soccer, but the game is played on ice and the skating players use wooden sticks, as in ice hockey, to strike and control a small ball. Organized and competitive bandy originated in England in the late nineteenth century, but the modern game has since proved more popular in the Scandinavian countries, Russia, and the Baltics. World championship bandy competition is administered by the International Bandy Federation, which was established in 1955. Bandy was played as a demonstration sport at the 1952 Oslo Olympics, but it has thus far not achieved the same level of global popularity as its closest rival, ice hockey.

Origins

Early references to "bandy" may designate any of a variety of games, some of which bear little resemblance to the modern sport. This is because the English word "bandy" originally meant simply to toss a ball back and forth, and referred to

no particular game. This use is seen, for instance, in a passage from Shakespeare, wherein Juliet employs a "bandying" metaphor while waiting for her maid to bring news of Romeo:

Had she affections, and warm youthful
    blood,
She'd be as swift in motion as a ball;
My words would bandy her to my sweet
    love,
And his to me. (*Romeo and Juliet*, II, v: 12–
    15)

Here, no specific ball game is invoked. Elsewhere, Shakespeare's use of the term may have indicated a form of tennis, as in "well bandied both; a set of wit well play'd" (*Love's Labor Lost*, V, ii: 29).

By whatever name, though, a game resembling modern bandy was being played in England long prior to Shakespeare's time, at least by the twelfth century. An illustration from that period, in an edition of Bede's "Life of St. Cuthbert," shows one of the saint's companions wielding a crooked stick in pursuit of a ball, and other sources show a similar game to have been popular in London. Also, a French bandy-like game was being played on the other side of the channel. Whether these games were called bandy is open to question: a later source, from the fifteenth century, refers to "bandy-ball," but has the players using straight sticks.

Certainly, though, games resembling modern bandy have been played in England for many years, sometimes known as bandy—or bandy-ball or bandy-cad—and sometimes as cambuca, hurley, or shinty. Played on frozen ponds, canals, or fields, particularly in East Anglia, teamed contestants fought to control either a flat puck-like object or a ball. A version of the game, known as "shinny," was popular for a time in America.

Practice

A National Bandy Association was formed in England in 1891, and the first international match was played the same year between the English Bury Fen team and a Dutch team from Haarlem. C. G. Tebbutt, the captain of Bury Fen, took the game to Sweden in 1894, providing equipment and guidance to the Stockholm Gymnastic Association. The

"Bandy-ball," a predecessor of the modern games of bandy and golf, sketched in an early manuscript.

growth of Swedish bandy was explosive: by 1926 there were almost 200 local bandy associations, and by 1990 there were 455. Organized bandy came to Russia in 1898, where it quickly became popular. Bandy was organized in Norway by 1903 and in Finland by 1908. The sport was played for a time in Denmark, Switzerland, and Austria, but it did not thrive and has now been all but abandoned.

For a time, the bandy "ball" was a wooden caster, much like the puck used in standard ice hockey, but in 1904 a wooden ball wrapped in leather was introduced. In 1907 a Russian team from St. Petersburg visited Sweden and introduced skating techniques and sticks that resemble those now used in bandy. In general the Swedes and the Russians are credited with developing bandy as a sophisticated and competitive sport. Bandy appears to have gone into something of a decline in Russia during the years just prior to and after the revolution, but it reemerged again strongly by 1923.

In all of the countries where bandy remains popular, the sport was originally associated with established soccer teams. In England, for instance, Sheffield United and other teams routinely fielded bandy squads during the winter season, as much for exercise as for any commitment to bandy itself. Until a Swedish Bandy Association was formed in 1925, bandy was administered by that country's Soccer Association. In Russia, top soccer stars from established teams such as Spartak and Central Army played "winter-football" during the off-season.

In Russia, bandy has never achieved the popularity of soccer, but matches drew crowds of thousands during World War II and retains loyal fans to the present. Early on, it was played with great enthusiasm and little regard for the rules. In fact, the Central Committee of the Konsomol felt obliged in 1940 to issue a resolution denouncing the roughness and near-anarchy of bandy: much drinking attended the games, putting the stick to the head of an opponent was normal, and referees were routinely abused by players if they dared to intervene.

The only form of bandy to reach American shores was also known, early on, for violence and general lack of discipline. "Shinny" was played from New England to Virginia during the latter half of the eighteenth century. The game pitted one team against another, and all players wielded crooked sticks with which they attempted to move a two- or three-inch diameter ball across a frozen field through the opponent's goal. Shinny was particularly popular on early college campuses until it was banned at Princeton in 1787 in light of the mayhem that generally accompanied it and heavily regulated at other schools.

Bandy's earlier reputation for violence is ironic in light of the fact that it has recently won praise from U.S. sports physicians for being relatively safe, particularly compared to regular ice hockey. By modern bandy rules, the stick cannot be used to hook or hold, and lighter and less extensive padding is required than in ice hockey. Modern bandy—not the wildly exuberant "shinny" of colonial times—has been played in the United States within the last fifteen years, particularly in Minnesota. Thus far, though, the United States has not achieved high marks in competitive play: at one bandy championship in 1987, the United States did put a team on the ice, only to be beaten by the Soviets 21–11, a record top score and point spread.

Bandy and bandy-like games were originally played on natural ice, or even on frozen fields. This may explain, in fact, why the game never developed more than it did in England itself: the unreliability of natural icing during English winters would not support a predictable competitive calendar. In Scandinavia, though, no such natural restrictions applied. With ample winter ice, Swedish bandy faced no shortage of playing areas. In fact, the first artificial bandy rink in Sweden was only built in 1956.

The modern bandy rink is 90 to 110 meters (98 to 120 yards) long and 45 to 65 meters (49 to 71

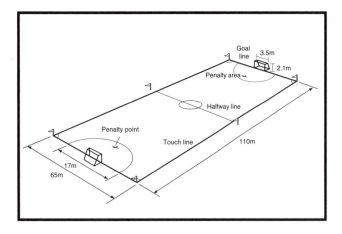

yards) wide. A short (15-centimeter [6-inch]) side-board runs along the side, and the goals at either end are 3.5 meters (11 1/2 feet) wide and 2.1 meters (7 feet) high. Each goal is situated within a penalty area, a half-circle 17 meters (18.5 yards) in radius from the mid-point of the goal line.

Each team has eleven players, including the goalkeeper. All players wear ice skates, and all but the goalkeeper hold crooked sticks. The stick can be no longer than 1.2 meters (4 feet) and has leather strapped around the crook to enhance ball control. The cork or plastic ball itself, usually red but always brightly colored, is 6 centimeters (2 ½ inches) in diameter and weighs between 58 and 62 grams (2.1 and 2.2 ounces).

The game is played in two 45-minute periods and teams trade after the first period. Tie scores are acceptable, except when championships are at stake, in which case two 15-minute periods are added, followed by "sudden death" if the game is still tied. Play begins with a "stroke-off" at the center of the field, after which both teams compete to control the ball and to drive it into the opponent's goal. A running player may kick the ball to his own stick but otherwise the ball may be hit only with the stick itself. The goalkeeper, within the penalty area, can use all parts of the body to block shots or to trap or catch the ball. Outside the penalty area, the goalkeeper is not allowed to use arms or hands, but may kick the ball. If he catches it, he has five seconds to put the ball back in play.

Dangerous play, defined as hitting or body-blocking with the stick, is strictly forbidden. The stick may not be raised above shoulder height or be used to strike another player's stick or to interfere with any player who does not control the ball. Such rules are apparently well observed by bandy players as statistics show the incidence of injury to be about half that encountered in ice hockey.

—Alan Trevithick

Bibliography: Aspin, Jehoshaphat. (1925) *A Picture of the Manners, Customs, Sports and Pastimes of the Inhabitants of England.* London: J. Harris.

Edelman, Robert. (1993) *Serious Fun: A History of Spectator Sports in the USSR.* New York and Oxford: Oxford University Press.

Gomme, Alice Bertha. (1898) *The Traditional Games of England, Scotland, and Ireland.* London: David Nutt.

Harste, Ann K. (1990) "Soccer on Ice." *The Physician and Sports Medicine* 18 (November): 32

Strutt, Joseph. (1876) *The Sports and Pastimes of the People of England.* London: Chatto and Windus.

Barrel Jumping

Types of skate jumping have been attempted throughout the history of skating. There is some evidence that long-distance skating competitions in nineteenth-century Holland incorporated natural obstacles such as fences, gates, and walls. The founding father of the modern sport of barrel jumping is Irving Jaffee, a former Olympic speed-skating champion. The first world championship was held at Grossinger, New York, in 1951. A major factor in establishing credibility for this tournament was that the organizers agreed to the use of a standardized barrel (40.6 centimeters in diameter and 76.2 centimeters in length [16 inches and 30 inches]). The winner of the first four titles was Terrence Browne of Detroit.

Competitive barrel jumping begins with 12 barrels. As with traditional jumping activities in track-and-field athletics, three attempts are allowed at each distance. Kenneth LeBel of the United States established a world record at his third world championship in 1965 by soaring 8.7 meters (28 feet, 8 inches) and clearing 17 barrels. Today, the world record is held by a Canadian, Yvon Jolin, who has jumped 18 barrels, 8.9 meters (29 feet, 5 inches). Since 1992 Patrick LeClerc of

Barrel Jumping

Richard Widmark, world barrel jumping champion in 1968 and 1971, in action.

St. Bruno, Canada, has held the world championship with a leap over 16 barrels.

Barrel jumping has been criticized for its daredevil element, having been compared to motorcycle jumping. Yet one needs to be in superior condition to successfully compete in the sport. One must develop incredible control as well as daring to succeed in this risky sport.

The basic premise of barrel jumping is that skaters work up a head of steam by skating around a rink and then attempt to leap over a series of 16-inch (41-centimeter) diameter barrels made out of composite materials such as fiberboard and cardboard. The barrels only seem to be like solid-steel fuel drums. Indeed, in barrel-jumping competitions the barrels provide a soft, cushioned landing as opposed to the severe impact of

clearing the barrels and landing on the ice. There are no scoring marks for style. There is no tariff of difficulty. The winner is the barrel jumper who goes the farthest distance.

Competitions in barrel jumping can be titanic encounters, as champion Richard Widmark has noted:

In the 1965 World Championship . . . Kenneth Le Bel and Jacques Favero were locked in a classic duel after both successfully negotiated 16 barrels. Favero led at that point, as he had taken less attempts to clear 16. Each contestant failed twice at 17 barrels, and Favero also missed his third attempt. As defending champion, Le Bel had the honor of last attempt, but to retain his title he would be forced to jump a distance never before negotiated. Adding to the tension was the presence of ABC sports television crews. It was late in the day and Le Bel was tired and sore, but like a true champion he vaulted over 17 barrels . . . the jump should be ranked among the greatest single efforts in sport.

World barrel jumping championship rules are simple and straightforward, very much in keeping with the nature of the sport itself. Many of the regulations are closely akin to those governing long jumping or highjumping in track and field. For example, "each contestant will be allowed a maximum of three (3) attempts to successfully negotiate a given number of barrels." Naturally there are a number of rules that are unique to barrel jumping. Two of the more unusual are these:

A balk will be charged if a contestant approaches the barrels, fails to take-off and passes between the flags placed (1) yard from either side of the take-off mark. Two such balks will be ruled as one official attempt. The contestant must remain on the ice and complete the attempt after the first balk.

The distance jumped will be determined from front of the first barrel to the point at which the rear skate touches the ice upon landing. The jump will be considered successful if the jumper lands on any other part of his body, however, the distance will be determined by the measurement of the last barrel plus one foot.

Safety is of paramount importance, so suspension type helmets, hip and spine protectors are mandatory. The majority of accidents result in sprains, torn muscles, and bruising. The most severe injuries are to the knee. Competitors normally sign a waiver releasing the organizing body from all liability.

The program for the twenty-seventh world championship (28 January 1978 at Northbrook, Illinois) sheds light on the sociocultural background of barrel jumping. Of the 12 competitors 6 were Canadian and 6 were Americans. The ages of the competitors ranged from 18 to 27 and the

Richard Widmark (1936–)

Richard Widmark vividly recalls learning to skate as a young boy and being a better than average speed skater by the time he was 12. He began barrel jumping in 1963, at the age of 27. In 1968 and 1971 Widmark took the world championship. With his 1968 performance he cleared 15 barrels and registered a distance of 25 feet, 1 inch (7.65 meters). In 1971 he again cleared 15 barrels but this time he upped his distance to 26 feet, 7 inches (8.1 meters).

Widmark recalls coming under the spell of Terrence Browne (world champion from 1951 to 1954), known as "The Flying Fireman." To watch Browne was to get a great sense of "energy and inspiration." Although Widmark enjoyed football and baseball as a teenager, speed skating, and subsequently barrel jumping, offered a greater athletic challenge. Added to the traditional thrill of competitive sports was a tremendous sense of personal accomplishment. In barrel jumping you "place yourself on the line," observed Widmark, "and the effort, as well as the performance is solitary, and, when it is successful, the feeling is one of profound satisfaction."

Against critics who dismiss barrel jumping as an Evel Knievel type of stunt, Widmark defends the activity as pure sport with a stark and spare arena highlighting a trained athlete being progressively challenged in jumping for distance.

In barrel jumping the technique in the air is remarkably similar to the "hang technique" in long jumping. The legs and lower back arch backward and are then drawn forward so that on landing there is a "leg shoot" position. Widmark stresses the importance of being a good speed skater ("at take off a barrel jumper needs to handle and harness a speed that may be in excess of 30 miles per hour") and likens the two-footed take off to the technique employed by a ski jumper. Great leg power is called for as well as a strong reaching and pulling action with the arms. In a 1987 interview, Widmark underscored the physical dangers of barrel jumping. "Everybody crashes and burns. . . . In this sport you know you're going to end up with a few bumps and bruises at the end of the day."

Today Richard Widmark is a painting contractor in Northwood, Illinois, now a major U.S. center for speed skating. Widmark continues to take a great interest in barrel jumping and has served as chief referee at world championships. His self-deprecating humor marks an athletic competitor who was appreciated for his sportsmanship and his good grace in victory and in defeat. He played and starred on the "Wildcats" Northwestern University football team and continues to enjoy the cut and thrust of athletic competition as a speed skater at the masters' level.

—Scott A. G. M. Crawford

occupations listed (barrel jumping is not a full-time or even part-time professional sport) were teacher (2), salesman, office clerk, traffic executive, students (5), engineer, and automobile mechanic. Competitors' weights went from a low of 68 kilograms (150 pounds) to a high of 82 kilograms (180 pounds). With an average weight of 75 kilograms (165 pounds), the body build and somatotype for barrel jumping resembles that of a track and field long jumper. While all competitors had a background in speed skating, a significant factor was the athleticism and variety of sporting pursuits followed by barrel jumpers. For the last decade Canadians have dominated the sport and they consistently win the Culligan World Cup, an international team award added for the first time at the 1978 world championships.

The Canadians have placed a great emphasis on age-range competitions to extend both the participatory base and longevity of barrel jumpers. They have instituted Pee Wee, Bantam, Midget, Juvenile, and Senior competitions as well as female divisions and have record lists of winning performances on natural as well as artificial surfaces. In 1971 the Canadian barrel jumping clubs regrouped to form the Fédération de Saut de Barils du Quebec Inc. Two years later Gilles Leclerc, a Canadian champion, opened a school for barrel jumpers at St. Bruno. It was a great success with over 100 young participants. The impact of Gilles Leclerc and his St. Bruno training academy is profound. The majority of Canadian barrel jumping records have been set by residents of St. Bruno.

—Scott A. G. M. Crawford

Bibliography: Anderson, Bob, ed. (1975) *Sportsource.* Mountain View, CA: World Publications.

Diagram Group. (1982) *Sports Comparisons.* New York: St. Martin's Press.

Sheffield, R., and R. Woodward. (1980) *The Ice Skating Book.* New York: Universe Books.

Stark, P. (1987) "Barrel Jumping," *Outside* (January): 55.

Tout sur le saut de barils. (1980) Courtesy of Gilles Leclerc, Association Canadienne de Saut de Barils, 1465 Place Louis Frechette, St. Bruno, Canada J3V2T8.

Widmark, R. (1996) Materials and items received and transcript of personal telephone interview (23 January).

Baseball, Finnish

Pesäpallo (Finnish baseball) is a good example of how aspects of a foreign game (in this case American baseball) can be assimilated into a popular pastime of another culture. With origins in an informal game played by villagers and country people in a rather free-for-all fashion, Finnish baseball has evolved into a more competitive and formal sport with organized clubs, standardized rules, uniforms, and modern equipment.

The development of Finnish baseball has clear connections to the industrialization of its native country in the twentieth century. The rules and organization of the game have evolved in keeping with the societal changes brought about by the migration of the population into towns and cities and by the increasing commercialism of contemporary life.

Origins

The modern game of Finnish baseball is based on the traditional game of "king's ball," in which a ball of birch bark (later a fist-sized leather ball) was pitched straight up in the air and hit by a player wielding a board or long racket. A similar game was played in German-speaking areas as *Schlagball*, in Nordic countries *as långboll*, and in Russia as *lapta* (Laitinen 1983, 36). All of these were peasant, or "folk" games, played outdoors, and in principle all could participate.

In the most commonly played form of king's ball, one for which Finnish language rules were developed in 1903, a "hitting line" was marked at the end of the playing field with a "running circle" close by. A mark at the other end of the field signified the "outgoal" or "running line" accompanied by another running circle. The players chose two "kings" who in turn selected their teams. One team batted while the other team's members distributed themselves around the field as catchers.

Batters hit in turn following a pre-set order. After a successful hit, the batter had to run to the farther circle or join the other batters in the hitting team's circle in order to wait for his or her next bat. If the batter ran to the farther circle, he

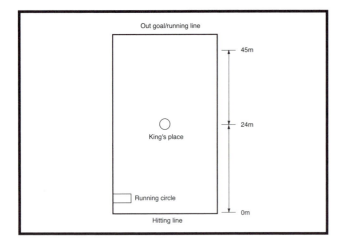

could return "home" following a successful hit by his teammate. The team in the field tried to "burn" the runners by hitting them with the ball. The circles at each end of the field were "safe" places in which players could not be burned. The basic idea of the game was that the batting team tried to stay "in" as long as they could, while the fielding team tried to get them "out" as quickly as possible (Laitinen 1983, 28–29, 50).

There was evidently a good deal of improvisation to this early game and something of a carnival atmosphere. There was no clear method for keeping score, players taunted each other freely and vigorously, and it was not unusual for a game to end in open quarrel and stone throwing. With minimal rules and rather vague boundaries there was always an element of surprise to a game of king's ball.

Development

Modern Finnish baseball was the brainchild of Professor Lauri "Tahko" Pihkala (1888–1981), a journalist, philosopher, sport historian, and critic of modern competitive sport. Pihkala's primary interests lay in national defense and in the educational possibilities of sports. At his initiative, Finland adopted as part of its official policy a system of sports badges, mass skiing treks, and a ski holiday for schoolchildren.

In 1914, at a time when agrarian Finland began to become more industrialized, and when competitive sport started to replace traditional forms of exercise, Pihkala initiated modifications to king's ball to create what he envisioned as a more functional, disciplined, and competitive game. Pihkala viewed the original game as a confused

"crowd game," which did not offer players sufficient scope for exercising responsibility and initiative. Additionally, since the game lacked a method for determining winners, it did not satisfy the criteria for a modern competitive sport.

As early as 1907, Pihkala had watched baseball games in the United States and sought to incorporate aspects of American baseball into his developing concept of Finnish baseball. Pihkala saw American baseball as a hitting and running game in which the rules produced more frequent exchanges of teams "at bat," speeding up the game. He viewed the American game as a form of "trench warfare" and proposed developing Finnish baseball into a "mobile war" between bases, in conformity with the basic Finnish military doctrine of forest warfare, which was to "fire and move" (i.e., shooting or throwing a hand grenade, and then plunging ahead) (Klemola 1963, 51–52, 237).

The geometry of the baseball field was crystallized for Pihkala in 1920. The running stretch zigzagged in a relatively small section of the infield and, as in American baseball, the runner had to reach the next base without being "burned" by a throw reaching the baseman before the runner touched it. There was no official out-of-bounds limit at the far end of the field, which maintained a little of the spontaneous spirit of king's ball. The new rules presupposed advancing from base to base by running. If a field player caught the ball in the air, the runner was "wounded"—lost the right to advance.

Pihkala's emphasis on the principles of military training in the game led to its being identified for

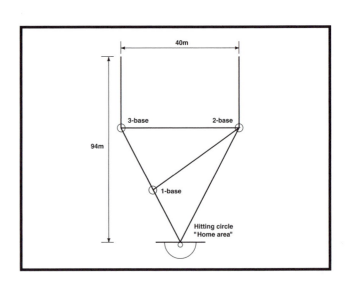

Originally a spontaneous "folk" game, Finnish baseball as a modern, organized sport has also been influenced by North American baseball. But there are differences—the American home run would be an "illegal strike" in the Finnish game.

a number of years with the paramilitary "protection league" of the political right and of the academic youth. The game was shunned by the Workers' Sport Federation as a bourgeois sport event; however, in addition to military training, Pihkala saw Finnish baseball as serving the educational goals of self-discipline and leadership. He associated these goals with those of English team sports as opposed to the aesthetic ideals of early Greek athletics. During Finland's struggle for independence in 1917, the ethos of the game was national unification; in the 1930s and early 1940s, it was military preparedness for national defense.

Practice

The contemporary game is guided by a set of conventional rules and tactics developed over the years since Pihkala's campaign to "modernize" the sport. Starting in the 1930s a far-end out-of-bounds line was marked on the field 84 meters

(276 feet) from the hitting circle. A legal hit had to land within the marked playing field, but after touching the ground there were no limits as to how far it could legally roll. In fact, the ball could roll into a river, as often happened at a well-known field (Vimpeli) in western Finland, a possibility now eliminated by the use of baseball stadiums. In the 1950s, the primary focus of the game was on hitting, with the players making individual tactical decisions. In the 1960s, a designated "play leader" was assigned responsibility for the team's strategy. In addition to demonstrating their hitting ability, players were expected to be able to run faster and to play according to the predetermined strategy (Karkkainen 1992).

The contemporary game is played on a field measuring 40 by 94 meters (131 by 308 feet) (somewhat smaller for women's teams). The bat can be as long as 100 centimeters (39 inches) and may weigh up to 700 grams (25 ounces). The ball has a circumference of 22 centimeters (8⅔ inches) and weighs 165 grams (5.8 ounces). Each fielder wears a leather glove designed with a large pouch to facilitate catching. The *syöttölautanen*, or pitching plate, has a diameter of 60 centimeters (2 feet).

Like American baseball, the Finnish game consists of nine innings, and each team fields nine players. Eight members of the fielding team are positioned around the field and the *lukkari* (pitcher) attempts to prevent the batter from getting a hit. Unlike the horizontal pitches in American baseball, Finnish pitches are vertical (straight up), which gives the pitcher greater tactical opportunities to mislead the batter and precludes power pitching. The ball must be pitched so that it falls on home plate if it is not struck.

A batter has three chances (strikes) to get on the field. Once he has gotten on base, succeeding players attempt to get on base themselves and advance the preceding players in the field. As in American baseball, a player is out if the ball reaches the base before he does. A run is scored when a player makes the circuit of three bases and reaches home plate. The batting team has at least nine attempts, plus one after each run, to get onto the field. When the batting team has burned three times, by failing to reach the base before the ball, the teams change places.

One major difference between American and Finnish baseball is the existence, on the Finnish ball field, of a rear boundary over which the batter may not hit the ball. Hitting the ball beyond the boundary is known as an "illegal strike." As a result of this limitation, players are less likely to advance more than one base at a time.

Ultimately Finnish baseball has become a game for all sections of the population and, since the 1920s, has been incorporated into the physical education program in the public schools. Team games are concentrated mainly in population centers, but there are also good teams in sparsely populated areas, where the game is even more popular than soccer. The national ranking of the teams reaches from the top—the *superpesis*—to the fourth division. The game is also played somewhat in Sweden, Estonia, and even Japan.

—Martti Silvennoinen

Bibliography: Karkkainen, P. (1992) "Pesäpallo—Finnish baseball: history and presentation of the national game." Presented at the first International Society of History in Sports and Physical Education seminar, "Sport and Cultural Minorities," 8–13 June, Turku, Finland.

Klemola, H. (1963) *Tahkon latu. Lauri Pihkala eilen ja tänään* [Tahko's trail: Lauri Pihkala in the past and present). 75-vuotispäivän juhlakirja. Helsinki: Otava.

Laitinen. E. (1983) *Pesäpallo: Kansallispeli 60 vuotta* [Pesäpallo: a national game in 60 years]. Saarijärvi, Saarijärven: Offset Ky.

Pihkala, L. (1932) *Pesäpallo itsekurin ja päällikk mielen kouluna* [Pesäpallo as a school self-discipline and commander-spirit]. Pesäpalloilijan vuosikirja.

Baseball, Japanese

Baseball was invented in the United States, so as a matter of course, Americans can claim that the sport is their national pastime. It is also true, however, that baseball has been played in Japan for more than a century and that many Japanese regard the sport as a part of their culture.

Over 4,000 Japanese high school teams compete for the national championship each year. Only about 50 teams can advance to the two major national championship tournaments, held in spring and summer at Koshien Stadium, the Mecca of high school baseball. The stadium, with a capacity of over 50,000, is packed with students, parents, and alumni who come from all over the country by chartered bus.

Professional baseball is popular in Japan, too. The annual total attendance for the two professional leagues is estimated at over 20 million. During the season, games are telecast live almost every night. Tabloid newspapers featuring scores and players' gossip sell millions of copies every day. Baseball players are national and local heroes for many Japanese. According to a survey conducted in 1996, the most popular choice of a future occupation among elementary school boys was professional baseball player.

Since baseball was introduced into Japan in the second half of nineteenth century, the sport developed a unique character to fit the Japanese social and cultural climate. Indeed, Japanese baseball is a completely different type of sport from the game North Americans are familiar with, although the rules and regulations are almost identical.

The Golden Age of Amateur Baseball

Baseball was first introduced to the Japanese in the early 1870s by Americans teaching English and Western culture at colleges in Tokyo. The game instantly became a popular extracurricular activity among college students. Baseball clubs were founded by students at prestigious colleges such as Ichiko (the First Higher School of Tokyo), Meiji Gakuin, Keio, and Waseda.

Ichiko, which later became a part of the University of Tokyo, dominated baseball from the late 1880s until the early 1900s. They not only went undefeated by any other college team, but they also beat U.S. teams in Japan. When the club beat a team of expatriate Americans from the Yokohama Country Athletic Club in 1896, their victory made newspaper headlines across the nation. For a country that had opened its doors to Western civilization only a few decades earlier, this triumph represented more than a small victory.

Baseball spread to high schools all over Japan as early as the late 1880s, thanks to college students who went back to their alma mater during school breaks and to college graduates who became high school teachers. Many high schools instituted interscholastic games with local rival schools as early as the 1890s. These games, fostering a sense of local identity among students and residents alike, soon became major sporting events.

The National High School Baseball Summer Tournament started in 1915, while the National High School Baseball Spring Tournament followed in 1924. These tournaments, both sponsored by major nationwide newspapers, have become symbols of high school baseball in Japan.

By the early twentieth century, intercollegiate games had become a major spectator phenomena. Colleges such as Keio, Waseda, and Meiji anxiously recruited high school graduates and soon began threatening Ichiko's dominance. The Keio-Waseda three-game series became one of the country's biggest baseball events. The rivalry was so heated that, lest their supporters fight each other and possibly cause riots, Keio and Waseda authorities decided to cancel the series in 1906. It was not resumed until 1925.

The first 30 years of the century were the golden age of amateur baseball. The Tokyo Six Universities League, whose members are Keio, Waseda, Meiji, Hosei, Rikyo, and Tokyo Universities, was organized in 1925. Thousands of spectators packed the stadium and millions of people all over Japan listened to the games on radio. Major college clubs toured the continental United States and brought the latest knowledge and equipment back to Japan. College and semiprofessional teams from the United States visited Japan. Major League All-Stars and All-American teams, including such legendary players as Babe Ruth, Jimmy Foxx, and Lou Gehrig, played exhibition games in Japan.

Semiprofessional teams were founded and sponsored by private corporations, as well as by public-sector organizations such as the Japan National Railways. Their national championship tournament started in 1927.

Social and Cultural Climate

Some attempts have been made to explain why baseball became so popular in such a relatively short period in a country where there was no tradition of Western sports.

Controlled by the feudal Tokugawa dynasty, Japan had closed its doors to the West until the 1850s. As information on advanced technologies, Western science, and culture flowed in after the Meiji Restoration of 1868, a sense of crisis deepened among the nation's leaders and spread to ordinary people. Adopting the goal of catching up with and getting ahead of the West, Japanese eagerly and industriously adopted Western civilization—including Western sports. Besides baseball, rowing, rugby football, soccer, and tennis were introduced into Japan. Like baseball, they first became popular at the college level, then at the high school level.

Although the Japanese were good pupils, their understanding of Western culture tended to be superficial. It was impossible, or at least difficult, for them to fully appreciate the internal meaning of the culture. Baseball was no exception, and the Japanese adapted the psychology of baseball to their own cultural norms: "The Japanese found the one-on-one battle between pitcher and batter similar in psychology to sumo and the martial arts. It involved split-second timing and a special harmony of mental and physical strength" (Whiting 1989, 28).

Ichiko College played a significant role in the early age of Japanese baseball. Most of the

The enormous popularity of baseball in Japan has made it an integral part of Japanese culture. Here teammates celebrate their victory in the 1995 Japan Series.

graduates of the school enrolled in the prestigious Imperial University of Tokyo and were expected to become national leaders, and their values, such as samurai spirit and Zen meditation, were strongly reflected in the game.

The organization and structure of Ichiko's baseball club were remarkably different from those of sports clubs commonly seen in Western societies. It was called Bu, which is closer to a military squad than a club. Bu was based on a rigid vertical hierarchy among students, and its members were required to be thoroughly loyal to the Bu. This version of baseball was spread widely, as Ichiko's graduates became instructors and coaches at other colleges and high schools.

Baseball's popularity was further increased by business interests and technological advancements. Major newspapers were competing for sponsorship of tournaments to increase their circulation when radio stations started live broadcasting in 1927. Meanwhile, private railroad companies built stadiums along their train lines.

The social environment did not always favor the development of baseball, however, as the exceedingly frenzied supporters started causing social problems. This climate was intensified as the militarism of the period and nationalism gradually took control of Japanese society from the mid-1920s. In 1932 the Ministry of Education issued the Baseball Control Act, whose aim was to promote "healthy development" of baseball among college and high school students.

The Advent of Professional Baseball and World War II

The Baseball Control Act ironically resulted in facilitating the birth of the first professional team in Japan. Since the act prohibited amateurs from playing with professionals, the *Yomiuri Shinbun*, a major national newspaper, which was planning to invite the Major League All-Stars in 1934, had to organize the All-Japan team, whose players were naturally regarded as professionals. The first professional team, established in 1934, was named the Tokyo Giants the next year.

Even though the Japan Professional Baseball Association was formed in 1936 by seven clubs, professional baseball gained support slowly in its early days. The average attendance was smaller than at college games. Major newspapers, except the *Yomiuri*, substantially ignored it. Many Japanese regarded earning money by playing sports as somewhat vulgar.

The fortunes of baseball were interrupted by World War II. Nationalists and militarists insisted that baseball should be banned because it came from the enemy, the United States. In 1941, the Ministry of Education suspended the national championship games of all sports at the high school level. In 1943, baseball terminology in English was prohibited and replaced by Japanese terms. Baseball, whether amateur or professional, was suspended altogether as the war intensified.

Baseball and the Media

The Japanese returned to baseball quite quickly after the World War II. The professional baseball league and the Tokyo Six Universities League resumed their activities in 1946. The National High School Baseball Summer Tournament was revived in the same year.

The Japan Professional Baseball League was split into two leagues in 1949. Eight clubs participated in the Central League; there were seven clubs in the Pacific League. (Although the franchises and sponsoring companies have changed many times since then, the number of clubs in each league has remained at six since 1958.)

In the 1950s professional baseball firmly established its status as the most popular spectator sport in Japan. The total annual attendance of both leagues jumped from 2.5 million in 1950 to 9 million in 1959. Stadiums installed lights and expanded seating capacity. Nationwide radio networks started broadcasting live games almost every night, and tabloid newspapers featuring professional baseball radically increased their circulation. Television, however, had the most decisive impact on professional baseball. A game between the Yomiuri Giants and the Hanshin Tigers in 1953 was the first game televised in Japan. It is no exaggeration to say that professional baseball has been televised every night during the season since then.

One of the unique characteristics of Japanese professional baseball is that every club, with the exception of Hiroshima Carp, has been financed by large corporations for promotional purposes. In the early age of professional baseball, most clubs were owned either by railroad companies or by multimedia conglomerates. For instance, the Yomiuri Giants, formerly the Tokyo Giants, are a subsidiary of the Yomiuri Shinbun Group, whose members include a major nationwide newspaper and a major television network. Other clubs, such as the Hanshin Tigers and Kintetsu Buffaloes, are owned by private railroad companies.

The 1960s and 1970s constituted the era of the Yomiuri Giants. With superstars like Sadaharu Oh (1940–) and Shigeo Nagashima (1936–), they won nine Japan Championships in a row from 1965 to 1973. The club drew the largest crowds in both leagues, and its annual home game attendance consistently exceeded 3 million. Yomiuri's television station televised all their home games, and other stations aired the away games. *Yomiuri Shinbun* and its subsidiary tabloid sports newspaper heavily promoted the team. With abundant

financial backing, the team could afford to acquire better-known U.S. players. They also had advantages in recruiting prospective amateur players. The Giants are "Japan's Team," and they were produced by the mass media.

Although the Giants remain the most popular team, they are no longer as dominant as they were in the 1960s and early 1970s. Circumstances surrounding professional baseball have changed the sport. An amateur players' draft started in 1965 gradually helped to disperse promising young talent to teams other than the Giants. As Japan's economy developed, parent corporations could afford to spend enormous amounts of money to lure active major league players from the United States. Clubs in financial difficulty were bought by corporations, including a supermarket chain, a land-development company, and a machine-lease company, that were in need of publicity. Their owners quickly moved the clubs to new ballparks and new home towns for better opportunities.

The Globalization of Japanese Baseball

Japanese baseball is now entering a new era of globalization. In the past, despite international exchanges in baseball, they were essentially one-way relations. Japanese baseball imported most of its knowledge and technology from the United States in the early days. International games, frequently held in the early twentieth century, dwindled after World War II. In professional baseball, exchange activities with U.S. major leagues were limited to importing players and hosting exhibition games. Japanese baseball was virtually isolated for quite a long period.

All this has changed since the mid-1980s. At the amateur level, international exchanges have been as active as ever, particularly since baseball was admitted to the Olympic Games in 1984. All-Japan national teams have participated in many international tournaments. At the professional level, satellite television channels, which started service in the mid-1980s, have been televising major league games from the United States, and cable television stations have a channel exclusively for U.S. sports. These changes in the mass media have made many Japanese feel closer than ever to major league baseball in the United States. This tendency was further intensified when

Hideo Nomo (1968–), ace pitcher of the Kintetsu Buffaloes, began playing with the Los Angeles Dodgers in 1995. More Japanese may play as professionals in the United States in the near future.

Baseball in Japan has a long history at both the amateur and professional levels. Professional baseball has established its status as the most popular spectator sport in the land, while amateur baseball, and high school games in particular, functions as both an educational and an entertainment activity. The social and cultural conditions surrounding Japanese baseball have helped to make it quite a different game from its counterpart in the United States. But as the globalization of the sport continues, baseball in Japan is likely to be reconstructed again in a worldwide framework.

—Hajime Hirai

Bibliography: Cromartie, Warren. (1991) *Slugging It Out in Japan: An American Major Leaguer in the Tokyo Outfield.* New York: Kodansha International.

Guttmann, Allen. (1986) *Sports Spectators.* New York: Columbia University Press.

Oh, Sadaharu. (1984) *Sadaharu Oh: A Zen Way of Baseball.* New York: Times Books.

Roden, Donald. (1980) "Baseball and the Quest for National Dignity in Meiji Japan." *American Historical Review* 85, 3: 511–534.

Whiting, Robert. (1989) *You Gotta Have Wa.* New York: Macmillan.

Baseball, Latin American

With the important exception of Japan, baseball has been restricted largely to the Western Hemisphere for much of its history. Although North Americans have contributed heavily to the game and tend to think of it as "theirs," it is as much a "national sport" in several Latin American countries as it is in the United States. Baseball is more popular than soccer in Cuba, Nicaragua, the Dominican Republic, Puerto Rico, and Panama and is important in Venezuela and Mexico. Good baseball is played also in Colombia, El Salvador,

Honduras, and Netherlands Antilles. Cuba's first professional league was founded in 1878, only two years later than the U.S. National League, and the game had been introduced in many areas of Latin America and the Caribbean before the start of the twentieth century.

Cubans learned baseball while attending school in the United States and brought the game back to Cuba as early as the 1860s. They in turn took the game to Puerto Rico, the Dominican Republic, the Yucatán Peninsula of Mexico, and Venezuela. In addition to Cuban influence in bringing baseball to the Yucatán, baseball interest in Mexico was strongly affected by that nation's close relations with the United States. Baseball was being played in Panama (still part of Colombia at the time) by people from Britain and the United States as early as 1882. An American introduced baseball at Bluefields on the Caribbean coast of Nicaragua in 1889, and Nicaraguans who had attended school in the U.S. initiated baseball in Granada and Managua two years later.

The professional game was established in Cuba in 1872 and during the twentieth century in the other countries. First held in 1949, the Caribbean World Series determined the professional championship of the Latin winter leagues, whose teams consisted of nationals plus imports from other Latin American countries and the United States. Cuba dominated the series through 1960, when they withdrew from professional play. Since that year the Dominican Republic and Puerto Rico have won the Caribbean championship most often.

Major international amateur baseball events include the World Amateur Championships, the Pan American Games, the Central American and Caribbean Games, the Central American Games, and the Olympic Games. Cuba has dominated the first three competitions named. After boycotting the 1984 and 1988 Olympic Games, Cuba won the Olympic baseball titles in Barcelona in 1992 and in Atlanta in 1996.

Cuba

In 1866 Nemesio Guillot, a young Cuban attending school in the United States, brought baseball equipment and enthusiasm for the game with him when he returned to his country. Shortly thereafter another Cuban, Esteban Bellán, played

Baseball quickly gained popularity across Latin America after its introduction to Cuba in the 1860s. Napolion Ray scores a run for the Cuban team against El Salvador during the 1941 amateur world series held in Havana.

baseball while attending Fordham University and then joined the Troy Haymakers, a charter member of the National Association, in 1871, the first year of professional league play in the United States. The Habana Baseball Club was founded in 1872 as Cuba's first professional team, and the Matanzas Club was established in 1873. Almost all of the players on these teams had attended schools and colleges in the United States. Bellán returned to Cuba and helped organize the first professional game, between Habana and Matanzas, in 1874. The Almandares Club was formed in 1878, and that year the three clubs organized themselves into Cuba's first professional league.

Soon baseball popularity spread throughout the island and Sunday afternoon games were being played in nearly every town. More than 200 teams were organized between the late 1870s and early 1890s. The Matanzas club played Cuba's first international baseball game in 1877 against the crew of a U.S. Navy ship. Additionally, Cuban immigrants organized baseball teams in the United States, and U.S. major league teams began to visit the island, the Philadelphia Athletics playing a series of exhibition games against Cuban professionals in 1886.

Baseball was felt to be a form of expression of Cuban national spirit, as opposition to Spanish colonialism grew through the later years of the nineteenth century, and colonial authorities viewed participation in the game with suspicion, even banning the sport for a year in 1873. Baseball was banned again by the Spaniards in 1895 when the war for independence began.

The popularity of the game and the competitive successes of Cubans and Cuban national teams grew throughout the twentieth century, one of the many high points being construction of Havana's Cerro Stadium in 1946. While opportunities in Cuban sport before 1959 were largely limited to a small and relatively wealthy elite, baseball (along with boxing) was available to all and even allowed players to earn a living through participation in the professional game. Professional play was dominated by two teams. Of the 73 national professional championships celebrated in Cuba between 1878–1879 and 1960–1961, Habana won 29, Almendares won 23, and these teams tied once. Other teams winning championships include Cienfuegos (5), Santa Clara (4), Marianao (4), Fe (4), and Matanzas, Orientales, and San Francisco, once each. During this period many Cuban players participated in summer baseball in the United States, and Cuban professionals were prominent on team rosters of Latin American countries. Black Cubans played in the U.S. Negro Leagues before major league baseball was integrated (and American Negro League players participated in winter play in Cuba and elsewhere in the Caribbean region and Mexico). Cuba hosted three of the first twelve Caribbean World Series and won the tournament seven times.

Cuba has dominated international amateur baseball competition. Through 1995, Cuba has won 9 of the 12 Pan American Games titles (including the first, in 1951, and the last seven), 12 of the 17 Central American and Caribbean Games titles, and 21 of the 24 World Amateur Championships they have participated in through 1994. Sport in revolutionary Cuba is an important political tool, and with the withdrawal of Cuba from professional baseball after 1961, the nation's best talent has been available for state-supported nonprofessional play.

Puerto Rico

Puerto Rico's first baseball game was played in 1896; a Spanish Army officer brought the sport from Cuba. U.S. soldiers stationed in Puerto Rico after the Spanish-American War (1898) helped popularize baseball. Government, company, and school teams were organized throughout the island, and players inducted into the military during World War I played the game in Army camps. Visits by U.S. and Cuban teams in the 1920s and 1930s increased interest in baseball, and professional play in the Puerto Rican Winter League began in 1938–1939. The league's original teams, which included U.S. and Latin American imports from the beginning, represented San Juan,

Mayagüez, Guayama, Ponce, Caguas, and Humacao. Between 1949 and 1992 the Caribbean (and Inter-American) World Series was held eight times in Puerto Rico and won twelve times by Puerto Rican teams.

In international amateur baseball Puerto Rico won the World Championship in 1951 and the Central American and Caribbean Games title in 1959. Puerto Rico has also won medals in the Pan American Games and the Olympic Games, including a bronze in 1988 Olympics.

Dominican Republic

Baseball was introduced in the Dominican Republic by Cubans who left their country after civil war began there in 1868. The game became popular all over the country, but first developed mainly in the area of sugar refineries in the southeastern part of the island, where there was no work during the sugarcane growing season and baseball filled the days of the "dead time." Important contributions to Dominican baseball were made by immigrants from the British Virgin Islands and other British colonies of the Caribbean, who settled in the area of San Pedro de Macorís. They came to cut and mill sugarcane and the game they brought was cricket, but by the 1930s cricket had given way to baseball.

In the early twentieth century, many amateur baseball teams existed, particularly around the cities of Santo Domingo, Santiago, and San Pedro de Macorís, and in 1907 the first professional team, Licey, was formed in Santo Domingo. Other professional teams surged and fell, but the most stable configuration has been four teams: Licey and Escogido in Santo Domingo, Estrellas Orientales in San Pedro, and Aguilas Cibaeñas of Santiago. International competition began in the 1920s, and in the 1920s and 1930s many Dominican ballplayers joined the professional teams of other Caribbean countries, while Dominican clubs hired players from Venezuela, Cuba, Puerto Rico, and even the United States. The presence of U.S. troops in the country from 1916–1924 favored the spread of baseball interest, as did the imposing influence of the country's most prominent fan, president Rafael Trujillo, during his 31 years of absolute political power. In the 1930s Negro League barnstormers toured the island each winter.

In 1937 Trujillo's agents bought the best talent that could be found in the U.S. Negro Leagues to assure a championship for the dictator's Ciudad Trujillo (as Santo Domingo was then called) Dragons, but this the high costs involved ended professional baseball in the Dominican Republic for thirteen years, until the lowering of the race barrier in the U.S. major leagues gave Dominican ballplayers a new opportunity to earn a living at their game and opened the Dominican Republic to another invasion, this time from American professional baseball interests.

From the mid-1950s onward there were ever-increasing connections between U.S. and Dominican baseball. Dominican professional league play was conducted in summer from 1951 through 1954, but with more and more of the top Dominicans playing summers in the U.S., the country adopted a winter schedule (in 1955), so that both their players and Americans could play the two seasons and thus augment their incomes. However, after free agency in the U.S. majors allowed salaries to rise to astronomical figures, the stars of both nationalities had second thoughts about risking injury by playing relatively low-paying winter ball, even if their U.S. teams would permit it.

With the loss in 1959 of Cuba as a source of players, U.S. professional teams stepped up scouting operations in the Dominican Republic and, beginning in 1977, established year-round rookie training camps, such as the Dodgers' academy, Campo Las Palmas.

Through 1972, Dominican Republic amateur teams had hosted the World Amateur Championship once and won the tournament in 1948. The national team also won the Pan American Games in 1955 and the Central American and Caribbean Games in 1962 and 1982.

Mexico

Cricket had been played by Englishmen in Mexico since 1827, but this sport did not catch on as did baseball with Mexicans. Games had been held by American sailors in Guaymas and American railroad construction workers in Nuevo Laredo in 1877, and several Mexican baseball clubs became active in the 1880s and 1890s, especially in Mexico City, Veracruz, and in northern Mexico where there were exchanges of matches with Texas teams. Also in the 1890s Cuban immigrants introduced baseball in Yucatán, where it expanded rapidly and took on a life almost independent from developments of the sport elsewhere in Mexico. By 1904 there were leagues for amateurs and also for semiprofessionals. The world champion Chicago White Sox visited Mexico City in the spring of 1907 and played the Mexican champions, and several Cuban baseball teams played in Mexico between 1919 and 1926. By 1926 there were more than 150 amateur baseball teams in the capital and an extensive schedule of games was played on Sundays. In the 1920s there were also several professional teams playing in the capital and elsewhere, and in 1925 the Mexican Professional League (summer) was organized. The Franco-Inglés field in Mexico City was the scene of most baseball action, and Ernesto Carmona was recognized as the foremost exponent of the sport. In the 1940s the Mexican League prospered under the leadership of Jorge Pasquel, who even brought U.S. major leaguers to Mexico for summer play. Alejo Peralta, owner of several teams, took over the league in 1955 and firmly established owner supremacy by suppressing player demands and attempts at establishing a rival league during the 1980s.

The Mexican Pacific Coast League (professional winter play) was organized in 1945, and teams of northwestern Mexico have won the Caribbean World Series twice since Mexico's first participation in the championship in 1971. Northwestern Mexican cities have hosted this tournament seven times (four in Hermosillo and three in Mazatlán).

Panama

In 1882, twenty years before the isthmus' independence from Colombia, Americans and British played baseball in Panama, and young Colombians attending school in the United States also played baseball when they returned to Panama City for their school vacations. In the 1890s the game was still mainly played by foreigners in Panama City, and when a club was established in Colón, on the Caribbean side of the isthmus, in 1892, players traveled by train to play inter-city matches. Around 1905–1906 teams of foreigners represented U.S. military forces and the Isthmian Canal Company, and purely Panamanian teams

Latin American Players in Major League Baseball

Players from Latin America have made important contributions to Major League and Negro League Baseball in the United States. Through 1992, Roberto Clemente, Martín Dihigo, Juan Marichal, Luis Aparicio, and Rod Carew have been elected to the Cooperstown Hall of Fame, and many other Latin players have achieved important baseball honors in the United States. Clemente (Puerto Rico; Pittsburgh Pirates) and Carew (Canal Zone of Panama; Minnesota Twins and California Angels) were batting champions. Marichal (Dominican Republic; San Francisco Giants and Boston Red Sox) and Aparicio (Venezuela; Chicago White Sox and Baltimore Orioles) were the best Latin American pitcher and shortstop, respectively, of their playing periods. Dihigo (Cuba; Negro Leagues) was an outstanding pitcher and hitter and could play all nine positions. He is also in the Cuban, Mexican, and Venezuelan Halls of Fame.

Before the landmark addition of Jackie Robinson to the Brooklyn Dodgers team in 1947, only light-complected Latin Americans had survived the racial test of aspirants to major league participation. In the earlier period many black Latins (especially Cubans) played in the U.S. Negro Leagues—and Negro Leaguers were welcome in the Latin winter leagues, as were white major league players. Since racial integration of the majors, Latin players have come to figure prominently on most team rosters, although black Latin players continue to face discrimination because of their race, and all Latin players have occasionally been stereotyped as being wild, lazy, or having other undesirable personal traits.

Listed below are the Latin American countries that have supplied players to the majors and a sampling of names of all-time great performers. The numbers in parentheses indicate: (number of players through 1992; year of first participation). Dominican Republic (166; 1956): Felipe and Matty Alou, Joaquín Andújar, George Bell, Pedro Borbón, César Cedeño, Tony Fernández, Pedro Guerrero, Juan Marichal, Manny Mota, Elías Sosa, Ozzie Virgil; Puerto Rico (147; 1942): Roberto Alomar, Luis Arroyo, Orlando Cepeda, Roberto Clemente, Willie Hernández, Luis Olmo, Juan Pizarro, Vic Power, Benito Santiago; Cuba (129; 1871): Sandy Amoros, José Canseco, Mike Cuéllar, Dolf Luque, Minnie Miñoso, Tony Oliva, Camilo Pascual, Tony Pérez, Tony Taylor, Luis Tiant, Jr.; Venezuela (64; 1939): Luis Aparicio, Tony Armas, Chico Carrasquel; Mexico (58; 1933): Roberto Avila, Aurelio Rodríguez, Fernando Valenzuela; Panama (23; 1955): Héctor López, Manny Sanguillén; Canal Zone (4; 1956): Rod Carew; Virgin Islands (8; 1959); Nicaragua (5; 1976): Denis Martínez; Colombia (3, 1902); Honduras (1; 1987); Netherlands Antilles (1; 1989); Belize (1; 1991).

—Richard V. McGehee

also existed, including school teams. In 1906 a baseball league was organized in the province of Bocas del Toro for employees of the United Fruit Company. Around 1913 baseball activity became clearly divided between Panamanian teams and those consisting mainly of foreigners in the Canal Zone. A few U.S. professional players were included in Canal Zone teams. In 1912 the New Orleans Pelicans came to the Canal Zone for a four-game series with an all-star team from the Canal Zone League. The racial segregation practices that existed in the Canal Zone led to the formation of Colored Leagues, whose players were largely Antillean men imported to work on the canal construction. Through 1925 baseball competition was generally separated into white and colored leagues in the Canal Zone, and Panamanian teams (with few colored players) elsewhere. The period from 1926 to 1935 saw firm establishment of the National League, which would become the future Professional League, and Amateur and Juvenile Leagues were also founded. By this time the social background of baseball players had changed considerably from the elites of the first clubs to largely a middle- and working-class composition. Panamanian teams played internationally in Costa Rica in 1926 and in Colombia in 1927, winning all games. Although the National League was integrated by this time, the teams playing internationally were not. However, the national team was integrated at the time of its first participation (third place finish) in the Central American Games of 1930 in Cuba. The national stadium was completed in 1929, and teams from Cuba and Nicaragua visited Panama in 1934–1935 to help prepare the Panamanian national team for their second place finish in the 1935 Central American Games.

The years 1935–1943 were dominated by semi-professional play, with black players making up 70 to 75 percent of the rosters (and 95 percent on the teams that won the national championships most years). Although professional players had been increasingly employed on Panamanian and

Canal Zone teams since 1932, the move toward professionalism was completed with establishment of the nation's Professional League in 1946. For the first year's play, 32 Panamanians were joined by 16 U.S. professionals, 20 Cubans, 3 Dominicans, 4 Mexicans, and 2 Nicaraguans. Several of the Americans, Cubans, and Dominicans were from the U.S. Negro Leagues. Also at this time a few Panamanian professionals were playing in the U.S. Negro Leagues and in Venezuela and Mexico. The high point of 1946 was a visit by the New York Yankees for exhibition games with professional all-star teams of Panama and the Canal Zone. The Brooklyn Dodgers and Montreal Royals visited in 1947.

In 1952 the Isthmian League of the Canal Zone disappeared and interest in Panamanian professional play decreased until 1962, when a short-lived experiment attempted to revitalize the Professional League by combining it with Nicaragua's. Under worsening economic conditions, the Professional League continued until its demise in 1972. The quality of amateur baseball also fell off during this period, as did the numbers of Panamanian players employed by minor and major league teams in the U.S.

Venezuela

Baseball was introduced in Venezuela in 1895 by the Cuban Emilio Cramer. However, the game developed more slowly there than in some other Caribbean nations. Venezuela first entered the World Amateur Championships in 1940 and won the tournament in 1941 and again in 1944 and 1945. A professional winter league was established in 1946, with four teams manned by Venezuelans and imports. The New York Yankees' appearance in Venezuela in 1947 added fire to local interest in professional baseball, and the Venezuelan Winter League has maintained its strong position in the country. Venezuela has hosted the Caribbean (and Inter-American) Series nine times and won the championship seven times.

Nicaragua

The introduction of baseball in Bluefields, on the northern coast of Nicaragua, in 1889 is attributed to an American resident of the area, who wanted to lure the locals away from the cricket they had been playing. David Arellano, a young Nicaraguan who played baseball while attending school in New York, brought the game to Granada two years later, and a series of games was begun in 1891 between Granada and the newly organized Recreation Society of Managua. Juan Deshón and other Nicaraguans studying in the United States introduced baseball in their hometowns in the early 1900s, and baseball rapidly became the most widely played sport in Nicaragua. The first organized league competition in Nicaragua was held in Managua in 1911–1912, with five local teams participating. Bóer, founded as a neighborhood club in Managua in 1905, was the winner, beginning a long tradition that would have its ups and downs, but continues to the present.

Military intervention in Nicaragua by the United States occurred occasionally in the late nineteenth and early twentieth centuries, and from 1912 to 1933 there was a nearly continuous Marine presence on Nicaraguan soil. Marines stationed in Managua fielded baseball teams and supplied officials for Nicaraguan baseball competitions. Probably the first international baseball game in Nicaragua occurred in 1914, when Bóer eked out a victory over the Marine's team, Denver.

In 1915 the first enclosed field went into operation and the first nationwide league play was held, featuring teams from Managua, Granada, Masaya, Chinandega, and León. Sunday baseball games were important social occasions and were often attended by the nation's president and high government and church officials. The Momotombo field belonged to and was administered by a benevolent association, and income from ticket sales for sporting events was distributed to the competing teams after a percentage was taken by the association to help run the Managua hospital. Prizes of a few centavos to one or two córdobas were paid by the association for triples, home runs, double plays, three successive strike-outs, etc., in order to encourage outstanding performances by players. Betting by fans and by the competing teams added interest to the games.

In the 1930s professional baseball was established in Nicaragua. Like his Dominican counterpart, Trujillo, Nicaragua's strongman, Anastasio Somoza, had his baseball team, Cinco Estrellas. The Nicaraguan professional Winter League functioned from 1956 to 1966, and Nicaragua (Cinco Estrellas) won the Inter-American Series title in 1964. During the Sandinista years more emphasis was placed on increasing mass participation in sport, but now professional caliber baseball is again a national passion. Bóer's win over San Fernando in the 1995 finals producing giant celebrations and regrettable hooliganism. In rematch, Bóer won again in 1996.

Nicaragua has participated in the World Amateur Championships since 1939 and hosted the tournament several times, first in 1948, upon completion of the National Stadium, and most recently in 1994. The national team won the Central American Games baseball competition in 1977, 1986, and 1994, but has finished no higher than second place in the more competitive amateur tournaments, including the Central American and Caribbean Games, the Pan American Games, and the World Amateur Championships.

International Amateur and Professional Competition

Latin American amateur baseball is important at all levels from juvenile to adult recreational and elite play. The highest level of international competition is the World Amateur Championships, but fiercely contested baseball also occurs in the Pan American Games and other regional games. Following the first World Amateur Championship, which was held in Britain in 1938 and with only Britain and the United States participating, most of the world championships have been held in Latin America and won by Cuba. Cuba has won 9 of the 12 Pan American Games baseball tournaments (the United States, Dominican Republic, and Venezuela winning one each). Nicaragua, Puerto Rico, Mexico, and Colombia have finished in the top three places, and Aruba, Netherlands Antilles, Brazil, El Salvador, Costa Rica, Bahamas, and Argentina have also competed.

In 1926 Mexico City hosted the first Central American Games, with official recognition of the International Olympic Committee. Cuba swept baseball three games to none against their Mexican hosts. The only other country participating was Guatemala, but although baseball had been played in Guatemala since the early 1900s, they did not bring a team to the 1926 festival. This regional event, known as Central American and

Caribbean Games since 1938, has continued to the present, and in its 17 editions, Cuba has won baseball 12 times, Dominican Republic twice, and Puerto Rico, Venezuela, and Colombia once each. Mexico, Panama, Nicaragua, and Netherlands Antilles have finished in the top three positions, and El Salvador, Guatemala, Honduras, Costa Rica, and Virgin Islands have also competed.

Baseball has been an Olympic demonstration sport seven times: 1912, 1936, 1952 (Finnish baseball), 1956, 1964, 1984, and 1988. It became a medal sport in 1992. At the 1984 Games, Nicaragua and the Dominican Republic (the latter a last-minute replacement for Cuba, which boycotted the Games) finished low in the eight-team tournament. Puerto Rico won the silver medal in 1988, again in the absence of a boycotting Cuba, and Cuba won the gold medal in 1992 and in 1996.

An international tournament, the Caribbean World Series, is used to determine the Latin American professional baseball regional champion each year. Dominated by Cuba before that country dropped professional sports in 1961, this tournament (including four years in the early 1960s when the competition was known as the Inter-American Series) has since been won most by teams from Puerto Rico (8) and Dominican Republic (8).

—Richard V. McGehee

Bibliography: Bjarkman, Peter C. (1994) *Baseball with a Latin Beat: A History of the Latin American Game.* Jefferson, NC: McFarland.

Klein, Alan M. (1991) *Sugarball: The American Game, the Dominican Dream.* New Haven, CT: Yale University Press.

LaFrance, David G. (1995) "Labor, the State, and Professional Baseball in Mexico in the 1980s." *Journal of Sport History* 22, 2: 111–134.

Oleksak, Michael M. (1991) *Beisbol: Latin Americans and the Grand Old Game.* Grand Rapids, MI: Masters Press.

Padura, Leonardo. (1989) *Estrellas del béisbol.* Ciudad de La Habana: Editora Abril.

Pérez, Louis A., Jr. (1994) "Between Baseball and Bullfighting: The Quest for Nationality in Cuba, 1868–1898." *Journal of American History* 81, 2: 493–517.

Pérez Medina, Ramón G. (1992) *Historia del baseball panameño.* Panamá: Dutigrafía.

Pettavino, Paula J., and Geralyn Pye. (1994) *Sport in Cuba: The Diamond in the Rough.* Pittsburgh: University of Pittsburgh Press.

Ruck, Rob. (1991) *The Tropic of Baseball: Baseball in the Dominican Republic.* Westport, CT: Meckler.

———. (1993) "Baseball in the Caribbean." In *Total Baseball,* 3d ed., edited by John Thorn and Pete Palmer. New York: HarperCollins.

Tijerino, Edgard. (1989) *Doble play.* Managua, Nicaragua: Editorial Vanguardia.

Torres, Angel. (1976) *La historia del béisbol cubano, 1878–1976.* Los Angeles: Torres.

Van Hyning, Thomas E. (1995) *Puerto Rico's Winter League: A History of Major League Baseball's Launching Pad.* Jefferson, NC: McFarland.

Zapata Cabañas, Gabriel. (1990) *Yucatán en torneos nacionales e internacionales de béisbol amateur.* Mérida, Yucatán, México: Maldonaldo.

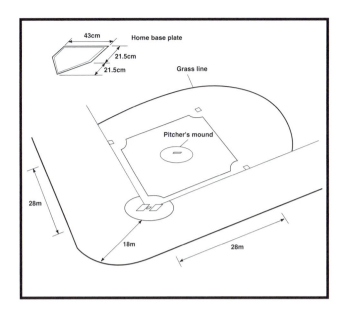

Baseball, North American

Baseball has long occupied a large place among North American sports. As early as the 1850s, sporting sheets began to argue that "base ball" was uniquely "America's game," and by the end of the nineteenth century it had become the most popular team sport in North America. Although millions of young men (and a few women) played an amateur or semiprofessional version of baseball, at the highest levels of play the professional game soon became ascendant. In 1903 the National and American leagues signed an agreement establishing the present structure of the professional game. Beginning in 1905, each season (except 1994 due to a players' strike) ended with a "World Series" between the championship teams of the two leagues.

Baseball's significance extended far beyond the playing field. Apart from sheer entertainment, references to baseball and the employment of baseball motifs abound in literature, music, painting, drama, politics, and religion, indeed in nearly every facet of American life. The game has given towns and cities, as well as occupational, ethnic, and racial groups, deeper emotional existences. Baseball's heroes have reflected some of America's most fundamental values. Finally, with its capacity for quantification and its slow, deliberate pace, both of which allow fans to collect and digest memories of the game's past, baseball has possessed a special power to connect past and present.

Origins

Modern baseball evolved from informal bat and ball games, the roots of which can be traced to seventeenth- and eighteenth-century England. In the early nineteenth century, boys played one or another of these games—called variously "old cat," "one-old-cat," "barn ball," "town," "rounders," "base," and even "base ball"—on empty lots, village greens, and cow pastures. During the 1840s and 1850s two styles of play, the Massachusetts (favored in New England and southern Ontario) and the New York games, competed for popularity.

A major turning point in baseball's evolution came in the 1850s, when New Yorkers, in particular clerks and artisans who were living away from home in impersonal boarding houses and who were experiencing profound changes in their lives and work, organized dozens of formal "base ball" clubs. Led by the Knickerbockers (formed in 1845), representatives of these clubs wrote and revised the rules of play, appointed game officials, scheduled matches, and in 1858 created the first national association.

Deriving its name from the four bases that form a diamond (the infield) around the pitcher's box (later called the mound), teams in the New York game consisted of nine players who used a leather-covered ball and wooden bats. Teams remained at bat until three outs were made; then the team that had been in the field took a turn at bat. An inning consisted of one turn at bat for each team and nine innings constituted a game. Each time a batter or "striker" touched all of the

Baseball great Joe DiMaggio in 1941, when baseball was still the national pastime and fans had fierce urban loyalties. Subsequent commercialization has helped to erode such allegiances.

bases without being put out a run scored. The team with the most runs after the completion of nine innings won the game.

New York's central place in commerce and communications helped its form of baseball spread rapidly. Tours by the famed Excelsiors of Brooklyn to upstate New York and to Philadelphia and Baltimore in 1860 attracted attention across the continent to New York's game. In 1863, New York area teams first contended for a self-proclaimed national championship, and, during the same year, the Young Canadians of Woodstock awarded themselves a silver ball for the first Canadian championship. The U.S. Civil War (1861–1865), by bringing together massive numbers of young men, also encouraged the growth

of the sport; after the war veterans of both the Union and Confederate armies returned home as enthusiasts of the game.

The early players comprised what contemporaries called a "fraternity," a term which implied that the ball players, regardless of divisions among them arising from their membership in distinct clubs, their ethnicity, social class, or religion, were members of a single brotherhood. The fraternity set itself apart from the urban masses by establishing a special body of customs and rituals and by donning colorful uniforms similar to the volunteer fire departments and militia units of the day. Off the diamond, the early players frequently shared such experiences as eating, drinking, wagering, talking, and even formal dancing.

League Formation

The early clubs initially charged no gate fees to watch their matches nor paid any of their players, but commercialism quickly entered the sport. In 1858 fans paid 50 cents each to watch a three-game championship series between all-star teams from New York and Brooklyn, and in 1862 an ambitious Brooklynite, William H. Cammeyer, built an enclosed field and charged fans a fee to watch games there. The "enclosure movement," as the drive to build fences around fields and charge an admission fee was called, introduced a new era of baseball history. To seize on the opportunities presented by gate fees, teams began to play more games, to embark upon long summer tours, to recruit athletes on the basis of their playing skills rather than their sociability, and even to pay outstanding players. It was, as the sportswriter Henry Chadwick declared several years later, "really the beginning of professional base ball playing" in the United States.

Professional baseball benefited from urban rivalries. The success in 1869 of Cincinnati's Red Stockings in winning 54 games without a single defeat provoked the envy of other cities. In both Canada and the United States, small businessmen, politicians, and civic boosters, among others, joined forces to form joint-stock company baseball clubs. Like most small businesses then and since, the clubs usually expired after a year or two, but out of the ruins of the old, new clubs frequently arose to replace them. From 1871 through the 1875 season, several of these professional clubs competed for a championship pennant sponsored by a loose confederation known as the National Association of Professional Base Ball Players.

Professional baseball entered a new era in 1876 when William A. Hulbert (1832–1882), president of a Chicago club, and Albert Spalding (1850–1915), player, manager, and soon-to-be sporting goods magnate, set about organizing a replacement for the National Association. Determined that the league would become the premier circuit of professional clubs representing only the larger cities, the National League prohibited clubs in cities with a population of less than 75,000 from joining, required any club wishing to join the circuit to have the approval of the existing clubs, and provided each team with a territorial monopoly.

By banning Sunday games, prohibiting the sale of liquor at ball parks, and charging a 50 cent admission fee, the league also sought without complete success to obtain the patronage of the middle class.

In the 1880s professional baseball shared in the nation's booming prosperity. No fewer than 18 leagues (including leagues with Canadian teams) appeared, although several expired after only a season or so. In 1882, the American Association, dubbed the "Beer Ball League" because brewery owners sat on the boards of directors of six of its clubs and it permitted beer to be sold at games, challenged the National League's hegemony over big league baseball. Beginning in 1884 and ending in 1890, the National League champions met those of the American Association in a post-season "World Championship" series.

Professional baseball reflected the changing ethnic composition of both Canada and the United States. Perhaps upon discovery that entrepreneurial opportunities in more respectable and less risky enterprises for recent ethnics were limited, a disproportionate number of Germans, German Jews, and later the Irish could be found among the ranks of the club owners. Likewise, an unusually large number of German and Irish names appeared on late nineteenth-century player rosters, suggesting that these ethnic groups may have found in professional baseball a means of upward social mobility. During the first half of the twentieth century, increasing numbers of old-stock players from the countryside and new ethnics from southern and eastern Europe, as well as a few Native Americans entered the big league ranks.

Opportunities for African Americans in professional baseball were another matter. Although blacks played amateur baseball from at least the 1860s on, as early as 1867 the National Association of Base Ball Players specifically excluded black clubs from membership, and the National League informally enforced a "color ban" against blacks from its founding in 1876. Yet a few blacks did play on racially integrated professional teams in other leagues; in 1884 Moses Fleetwood Walker and his brother Weldy played with Toledo in the American Association. In the late 1880s and in the 1890s, the era when racial segregation became the rule for much of the United States, white leagues ended racially integrated baseball.

The Doubleday-Cooperstown Myth

Until the early twentieth century, no one seemed much concerned about the origins of baseball. But then, for reasons that remain unclear, sporting goods magnate Albert Spalding decided to challenge octogenarian sportswriter Henry Chadwick's long-held claim that baseball had evolved from the English boys' game of rounders. To resolve the mystery of baseball's genesis, Spalding appointed a special committee of seven men (including two U.S. Senators) "of high repute and undoubted knowledge of Base Ball."

Rather than engage in research themselves or employ researchers to peruse newspapers, correspondence, and other early sources, the committee placed its faith in the recollections of oldtimers. One of the elderly respondents, Abner Graves (after some prodding and perhaps direction from Spalding), reconstructed from his memory the day in 1839 when Abner Doubleday is said to have invented baseball in Cooperstown, New York. Without bothering to take additional testimony from Graves or corroborate his account from other sources, the committee concluded in 1907 that the Graves's story was the "best evidence obtainable to date" of the game's origins. Doubleday, a Civil War hero who had written a two-volume memoir without once mentioning baseball, let alone seizing the opportunity to stake his claim as its creator, had died in 1893. Although Henry Chadwick described the committee's work as a "piece of special pleading which lets my dear old friend Albert escape a bad defeat," its conclusions were quickly accepted by nearly everyone as established truth.

During the 1930s, a group of businessmen in Cooperstown decided to offset some of the ravages of the Great Depression by promoting their village as the site for a national baseball hall of fame and museum. The plan won the endorsement of organized baseball, and in 1936 sportswriters chose as charter members to the Hall of Fame Ty Cobb, Babe Ruth, Honus Wagner, Christy Mathewson, and Walter Johnson. In 1939 the major leagues commemorated the "centennial" of baseball's creation with ceremonies at Cooperstown and the U.S. Post Office issued a commemorative stamp. The Baseball Hall of Fame and Museum has subsequently become something of a national shrine and is visited by thousands of fans annually.

Ironically, at the very time that the enterprising merchants succeeded in their campaign to locate the museum in Cooperstown, an equally industrious librarian in New York City began a reexamination of baseball's origins. In 1939, Robert Henderson discovered a little book of children's games authored by Robin Carver. The tiny tome, published in 1829, a full decade before Doubleday's alleged invention of baseball, included the rules for a game called "Base, or Goal Ball." Modern researchers (including those employed by the Hall of Fame) have added support to Henderson's evolutionary theory of baseball's early history. Nonetheless, the Doubleday-Cooperstown myth continues to enjoy wide acceptance in American popular culture.

—Benjamin G. Rader

In the 1880s conflicts between the National League franchise owners and the professional players escalated. They clashed in the first place over player drinking. The players resented restrictions on their personal behavior and the player reservation system that had been put into place in 1879. The reserve clause in contracts prevented players from offering their services to the highest bidders. The players also believed that they were not getting a fair share of baseball's additional earnings. Player grievances climaxed in the formation of a separate Players League in 1890. With three big leagues competing for the loyalties of fans and the superior leadership offered by Albert Spalding, the National League crushed the upstart league after only one season. In 1891, the American Association also collapsed, leaving only a twelve-team National League as a major league circuit.

The National League drifted aimlessly through the 1890s, confronted with the absence of the popular World Championship Series, the lack of superior teams in the largest cities, and an economic depression. In earlier times, the league had deliberately cultivated an image of Victorian propriety, but in the 1890s it acquired a notorious reputation for brawling, both on the field and in the stands. In1900, Byron Bancroft (Ban) Johnson (1863–1931), a former sportswriter and president of the Western League, mounted a challenge to the National League. Johnson renamed his loop the American League and began to raid National League teams for players.

In 1903, the leagues signed a peace pact in which they agreed to recognize each other's reserved players and established a three-man commission to oversee all of professional baseball. The agreement protected the reserved rights of minor league teams to their players, but provided that at the conclusion of each season the majors could "draft" players from the franchises of the minors at set prices. Although the National Agreement of 1903 did not provide for a championship series, in 1905 the leagues agreed upon a mandatory postseason World Series.

The Golden Age

The first half of the twentieth century may have been baseball's Golden Age. The game gained in acceptability among all social groups; in 1910 William Howard Taft established the tradition of the president of the United States opening each season by throwing out the first ball. "Take Me Out to the Ball Game," written by vaudevillian Jack Norworth in 1908, soon became the game's unofficial anthem. Between 1909 and 1923, the major league teams went on a stadium-building binge; great civic monuments of steel and concrete replaced shaky, wooden structures. Minor league baseball grew from 13 circuits in 1903 to 51 leagues in 1950.

Baseball exploded in popularity at all levels. Twilight leagues and Sunday School leagues sprang up across the continent. Vancouver, British Columbia, alone hosted 60 Sunday School league teams. Boys grew up reading baseball fiction, learning the rudiments of the game, and dreaming of one day becoming diamond heroes themselves. Newspapers carried detailed accounts of games, as well as stories about the game during the off season (Hot Stove League). Beginning in the 1920s, radio began to broadcast play-by-play descriptions of games.

In the meantime the game experienced fundamental changes on the playing field. Long ago, pitchers had stopped gently tossing the ball to the hitters with a straight arm and underhanded; a gradual relaxation of the rules permitted overhanded pitching in 1884 and in 1887 the hitters lost the privilege of asking for a pitch above or below the waist. In 1893 the league adopted the modern pitching distance of 60 feet, 6 inches (18.44 meters). Offensive and defensive tactics slowly grew more sophisticated.

Beginning in the 1860s, infielders gradually inched away from their respective bases and managers began to place their quickest man at shortstop. In the next decade, a few catchers donned masks and fielders put on gloves. At first, the skin-tight gloves (with the ends cut off to improve throwing) were used exclusively to protect the hands from the sting of the ball. In the 1890s with the extension of the pitching distance, teams turned more to bunting and the ingenious hit-and-run play.

The first two decades of the twentieth century came to be known as the "deadball era," or the "era of the pitcher." The adoption of rules providing for counting the first two foul balls as strikes (National League in 1901 and American League in 1903), increasing the width of home plate from a 12-inch (30 centimeters) square to a five-sided figure 17 inches (43 centimeters) across in 1900, and allowing the application of spit to the ball by pitchers, along with the appearance of big, strong-armed pitchers and the conservative tactics of managers resulted in an age of extraordinarily low offensive output. Except for John "Honus" Wagner (1874–1955) and Ty Cobb (1886–1961), the major stars of the day were such pitchers as Cy Young (1867–1955), Christy Mathewson (1880–1925), and Walter Johnson (1887–1946). Long-time field managers John J. McGraw (1873–1934) of the New York Giants and Connie Mack (1862–1956) of the Philadelphia Athletics also occupied much of baseball's public limelight.

For reasons that remain unclear, the 1920s witnessed a sudden reversal in offensive production. Traditionally, the surge in hitting has been attributed to the introduction of a more resilient ball, using more balls per game, outlawing the spit ball in 1920, and the growing popularity of "free swinging" by the hitters. Recent research emphasizes the importance of George Herman "Babe" Ruth (1895–1948). Led by the free-swinging Ruth, batting averages, scoring, and home runs soared. While repeatedly leading the league in home runs, Ruth himself became the game's preeminent hero. With Ruth's rise from lowly origins, his enthusiasm for the game, and his towering home runs, no other player in baseball history so won the awe and adoration of baseball fans.

During the Golden Age, great dynasties, mostly located in the larger cities, ruled major league play. From 1900 to 1969, when the leagues were divided into divisions, New York City franchises won 41 pennants. Beginning with Ruth's arrival in New York, the Yankees became synonymous with success; they won 29 flags in 39 years. In general, franchises located in larger cities drew more fans and commanded larger revenues; they were thus better able to purchase superior players from other big league clubs or minor league franchises. Only the St. Louis Cardinals, led by their astute general manager Wesley "Branch" Rickey (1881–1965), who created a system of developing new talent through the ownership of minor league teams (the farm system), seriously contended with the Yankee dynasty.

Ruth's Homeric feats during the 1920s helped to counter the negative effects of the Black Sox Scandal of 1919. Although a court acquitted eight Chicago White Sox players for fixing the 1919 World Series, Judge Kenesaw Mountain Landis (1866–1944), the newly appointed commissioner of baseball, banished them from organized baseball for life. The scandal also provided an impetus for reorganizing baseball in 1921. The new National Agreement gave sweeping powers to a single commissioner to suspend, fine, or banish any parties in baseball who had engaged in activities "detrimental to the best interests of the national game." Although Landis (who served until 1944) rarely used his vast powers to discipline the team owners, he employed them widely against the players. In 1922, the U.S. Supreme Court further strengthened major league baseball by exempting it from federal antitrust laws in *Federal Base Ball Club of Baltimore, Inc. v. National League of Professional B.B. Clubs and American League of Professional B.B. Clubs,* 259 U.S. 200.

The Great Depression and World War II dealt powerful blows to professional baseball. During the economic crisis of the 1930s, the establishment of an annual All-Star game between the best players in the two leagues (beginning in 1933), the introduction of night baseball with electric lighting at Cincinnati in 1935, and the founding of the Hall of Fame in Cooperstown, New York, in 1936, all failed to draw crowds to games. The big leagues even considered closing down during U.S. participation in World War II (1941–1945), but President Franklin D. Roosevelt, believing big league play would be good for morale, urged that baseball continue. With many of the best players drafted into the armed forces, the quality of play suffered.

Fearful that major league baseball might be discontinued during World War II and aware of the popularity of women's softball, Philip K. Wrigley (1894–1977), chewing gum magnate and owner of the Chicago Cubs, organized the All-American Girls Baseball League in 1943. While women had played versions of baseball and softball on college campuses and occasionally on barnstorming teams since the last quarter of the nineteenth century, ball-playing by women experienced a sharp growth in popularity during the 1930s and 1940s. Stressing a combination of feminine beauty and masculine playing skills, the league initially prospered in mid-sized, midwestern cities. Reflecting the post-war trend toward at-home diversions and the return to a more restrictive conception of femininity, the league folded in 1954.

Race Relations

The war years also represented a turning point in baseball's race relations. Having been excluded from white leagues since the 1880s and 1890s, African Americans carved out a separate baseball sphere. In the late 1880s the black barnstorming Cuban Giants (formed in 1885) booked some 150 games a season, but barnstorming reached its heyday in the first half of the twentieth century. Barnstorming black teams played other itinerant black teams, town teams scattered across North America and the Caribbean basin, and occasionally, during the off season, "all-star" big league white teams. While skill levels were high among the barnstormers, showmanship, which often entailed the employment of black stereotypes, was a fundamental part of the barnstorming game. The founding of the Negro National League in 1920 ushered in another era of professional black baseball, and teams frequently combined barnstorming with league play. League baseball reached the height of its popularity in the early 1940s. For more than two decades, Leroy "Satchel" Paige (1906–1982), a pitcher, was the star attraction of black baseball.

Despite substantial opposition from fellow club owners, in 1945 Branch Rickey, the general manager of the Brooklyn Dodgers, signed Jackie Robinson (1919–1972), a multi-sport African American star at the University of California at Los Angeles and a player in the Negro National League, to a contract to play with the Dodgers' Montreal farm club in 1946. The next year, amidst great fanfare, Robinson joined the parent team. Given baseball's distinction as the "national pastime" of the United States, the game's racial

Baseball, North American

"Casey at the Bat"

Written by Ernest L. Thayer for the *San Francisco Examiner* on 3 June 1888 and popularized by the innumerable presentations of DeWolf Hopper, the poem "Casey at the Bat" quickly became baseball's best-known piece of literature. The final stanzas follow:

There was ease in Casey's manner as he stepped into his
    place;
There was pride in Casey's bearing and a smile on
    Casey's face,
And when, responding to the cheers, he lightly doffed his
    hat,
No stranger in the crowd could doubt 'twas Casey at the
    bat.

Ten thousand eyes were on him as he rubbed his hands
    with dirt;
Five thousand tongues applauded when he wiped them
    on his shirt.
Then, while the writhing pitcher ground the ball into his
    hip,
Defiance gleamed in Casey's eye, a sneer curled Casey's
    lip.

And now the leather-covered sphere came hurtling
    through the air,
And Casey stood a-watching it in haughty grandeur
    there,
Close by the sturdy batsman the ball unheeded sped—
"That ain't my style," said Casey. "Strike one," the um-
    pire said.

From the benches, black with people, there went up a
    muffled roar,
Like the beating of the storm-waves on a stern and dis-
    tant shore,

"Kill him; kill the umpire!" shouted someone from the
    stand;—
And it's likely they'd have killed him had not Casey
    raised his hand,

With a smile of Christian charity great Casey's visage
    shone;
He stilled the rising tumult; he bade the game go on;
He signalled to the pitcher, and once more the spheroid
    flew;
But Casey still ignored it, and the umpire said, "Strike
    two."

"Fraud," cried the maddened thousands, and echo an-
    swered "Fraud,"
But one scornful look from Casey, and the multitude was
    awed.
They saw his face grow stern and cold; they saw his mus-
    cles strain,
And they knew that Casey wouldn't let the ball go by
    again.

The sneer is gone from Casey's lip; his teeth are clinched
    in hate;
He pounds with cruel violence his bat upon the plate.
And now the pitcher holds the ball, and now he lets it go,
And now the air is shattered by the force of Casey's blow.
…
Oh! somewhere in this favored land the sun is shining
    bright;
The band is playing somewhere, and somewhere hearts
    are light.
And somewhere men are laughing and somewhere chil-
    dren shout;
But there is no joy in Mudville—mighty Casey has Struck
    Out.

integration had vast symbolic importance. If the racial wall of the national game could be breached, it seemed manifest to many that other barriers to blacks should be removed as well.

Yet the entry of Robinson into the big leagues failed to herald the end of racial bigotry in baseball. Racial integration proceeded slowly; it was 12 years before the last big league club, the Boston Red Sox, finally employed a black player. Integration was also uneven. In 1959 the National League had twice as many blacks as the American League. Finally, studies consistently found that blacks had to outperform whites to make

team rosters and that blacks were commonly the victims of "stacking," that is, more frequent relegation than whites to "noncentral" playing positions such as the outfield or first base.

The Troubled Years

In the second half of the twentieth century, baseball entered more troubling times. After an initial resurgence of attendance in the late 1940s, crowds declined during the 1950s. The growth of sprawling independent suburbs and the appearance of television encouraged a larger trend away from inner-city and public forms of leisure to private, at-home diversions. Unlimited telecasts of big league games damaged minor league attendance and support for semiprofessional baseball. In the 1950s thousands of semipro teams folded and minor league baseball became a shell of its former self. The major leagues fared only somewhat better. Average game attendance remained below the 1948–1952 seasons until 1978, and even after that lagged behind the population growth of the metropolitan areas served by big league clubs. Baseball's television ratings were also weak, falling to about half that of regular season professional football games. Ironically, the rapid growth of Little League Baseball (founded in 1939 and composed of preadolescent boys) after World War II may have seriously damaged attendance at all other forms of baseball.

Big league baseball responded to the postwar woes in several ways. Reflecting changing population centers and the advantages of air travel, several franchises, led by the Boston Braves moving to Milwaukee in 1953, relocated and the number of franchises expanded from two 8-team loops in 1960 (the same as it had been since 1903) to 28 teams in two leagues of six divisions by 1994. Big league baseball became a truly international sport when it planted franchises in Montreal (1969) and Toronto (1977); both Montreal and Toronto had fielded teams for 55 and 78 years, respectively, in the powerful International League. Frequently abetted by subsidies from local governments, baseball also entered a new stadium building era. Efforts to capitalize on media, especially television, were only partly successful. Large disparities in media revenues between small and large city franchises endangered the game's financial stability.

The empowerment of the players added to the woes of the owners. With the appointment in 1966 of Marvin J. Miller as executive director of the Major League Baseball Players Association (which had been formed in 1956), the players won a series of victories over the owners. The right to salary arbitration (1972) and free agency (1976) triggered a cycle of escalating salaries; average annual salaries soared from $29,000 in 1970 to more than $1 million in 1992. Efforts by the owners to stem the effects of arbitration and free agency resulted in a seven-week strike in 1981 and a strike at the end of the 1994 season, closing

down the World Series and delaying the start of the 1995 season.

The Divisional Era

Baseball in the divisional era (1969–present) witnessed the demise of team dynasties. During the 1980s, only 3 of 26 clubs failed to capture at least one divisional flag, and teams in smaller cities won just as many, indeed overall more, flags than the cities in the largest metropolitan areas. The major leagues implemented an amateur draft in 1965, which allowed franchises to draft (in reverse order of their standings in the previous season) the rights to unsigned amateur players, thus reducing the advantages that richer franchises had long enjoyed in the procurement of promising college and high school players. In addition, women and men who commanded vast financial resources entered the ranks of the big league owners; they were less concerned than their more impoverished predecessors about earning profits from baseball. Finally, free agency—the right gained by veterans in 1976 to sign with any franchise—may have encouraged rather than discouraged competitive balance.

A new style of play also characterized the divisional era. The hitting revolution of the 1920s had encouraged an emphasis on the home run; in the 1940s and 1950s, the stolen base nearly disappeared as the game featured slugging at the expense of finesse, but in the divisional era dazzling speed and specialized pitching joined sheer brawn. Aided by the vast expansion of new talent by including players of African and Hispanic descent, the stolen base returned to baseball. All earlier stolen base records fell. As managers turned increasingly to relief pitchers, the number of complete games hurled by one pitcher dropped from about seven in ten at the beginning of the century to about one in ten in the divisional era.

Baseball Perseveres

Although baseball in the second half of the twentieth century no longer occupied the dominant position among North American sports that it had once enjoyed, it exhibited a remarkable perseverance. In particular, the game seemed to fulfill needs to establish connections with the past.

During the 1980s and 1990s, major and minor league attendance increased and an auxiliary culture of baseball memorabilia flourished. Baseball books, especially those of a historical nature, far outsold those on any other sport, and, in 1994, Ken Burns turned to baseball as the subject of the most monumental historical television documentary ever made.

—Benjamin G. Rader

See also Rounders.

Bibliography: Adelman, Melvin. (1986) *A Sporting Time: New York City and the Rise of Modern Athletics, 1820–70.* Urbana: University of Illinois Press.

Goldstein, Warren. (1989) *Playing for Keeps: A History of Early Baseball.* Ithaca, NY: Cornell University Press.

Humber, William. (1983) *Cheering for the Home Team: The Story of Baseball in Canada.* Toronto: Oxford University Press.

James, Bill. (1988) *The Bill James Historical Baseball Abstract.* New York: Villard Books.

Kirsch, George. (1989) *The Creation of American Team Sports: Baseball and Cricket, 1838–72.* Urbana: University of Illinois Press.

Levine, Peter. (1985) *A. G. Spalding and the Rise of Baseball: The Promise of American Sport.* New York: Oxford University Press.

Miller, James Edward. (1990) *The Baseball Business: Pennants and Profits in Baltimore.* Chapel Hill: University of North Carolina Press.

Porter, David L. (1987) *The Biographical Dictionary of American Sports: Baseball.* New York: Greenwood.

Rader, Benjamin G. (1992) *Baseball: A History of America's Game.* Urbana: University of Illinois Press.

Reichler, Joseph, ed. (1992) *The Complete and Official Record of Major League Baseball.* New York: Macmillan.

Riess, Steven A. (1980) *Touching Base: Professional Baseball and American Culture in the Progressive Era.* Westport, CT: Greenwood.

Seymour, Harold. (1960–1990) *Baseball.* 3 vols. New York: Oxford University Press.

Smith, Myron J., comp. (1986) *Baseball: A Comprehensive Bibliography.* Jefferson, NC: McFarland.

Spalding, Albert G. (1911; reprint, 1992) *America's National Game.* New York: American; Lincoln: University of Nebraska Press.

Sullivan, Dean A., comp. and ed. (1995) *Early Innings: A Documentary History of Baseball, 1825–1908.* Lincoln: University of Nebraska Press.

Thorn, John, and Peter Plamer, eds. (1993) *Total Baseball.* New York: Outlet Books.

Tygiel, Jules. (1983) *Baseball's Great Experiment: Jackie Robinson and His Legacy.* New York: Oxford University Press.

Voigt, David Quentin. (1983) *American Baseball,* 3 vols. University Park: Pennsylvania State University Press.

Basketball

Basketball's widespread appeal across age, gender, class, regional, and national lines reflects the game's broadly based origins and early development. Basketball was made in the United States, but by a Canadian. Devised by and for young white Protestant male competitors, it was quickly adopted by Catholics, Jews, African Americans, and females. Originally designed for exercise and the inculcation of moral values, it soon became a commercial pastime celebrated the world over.

Whatever the global appeal of soccer (association football), basketball is the game most played and most watched by people around the world. Hoops rattle throughout Asia, as well as Africa and South America. Professional leagues thrive in Europe, and even in distant Australia. In the United States, basketball attracts more participants and spectators than do football and baseball combined. In all, basketball is played by an estimated 200 million people on all continents. No other sport has enjoyed such recent increases in popularity, both in terms of those who play and the numbers of those who watch.

Some of basketball's appeal can be explained by its unique status as a team game that is relatively simple, inexpensive, and easy to produce. People happily play one-on-one. In its organized form, the game requires only five players at a time, half as many as a baseball or football team. Compared to most team sports, basketball needs little space and minimal equipment to play, and it leaves participants with few bruises and broken limbs. It can be played, and enjoyed, by female youths on a playground court or by an over-the-hill gang of businessmen on lunch break as well as by seasoned collegians and professionals.

The International Federation of Amateur Basketball has governed international play since the 1930s; the Olympics are the principal forum for competition. The United States, Soviet Union, and Yugoslavia have dominated international hoops since the 1950s. In recent years, televised competition has enhanced both the scope of basketball's global appeal and the quality of play.

Created as an indoor winter sport in a Massachusetts YMCA in 1891, basketball quickly spread through YMCAs and other physical education programs. In recent years women's basketball has made great strides, and basketball has spread to all regions of the world.

Origins

Unlike baseball, football, soccer, ice hockey, and all the other major team sports, basketball cannot claim a history of evolutionary development that began back in ancient or medieval times. Basketball was literally created overnight, the result of an assignment posed by a physical education teacher in December 1891 at a Young Men's Christian Association (YMCA) training college in Springfield, Massachusetts. A Canadian student, James Naismith (1861–1939), rose to the challenge of constructing an active indoor winter game that would prove attractive to young men. He typed up a rudimentary set of rules, had a janitor nail up peach baskets along the railing at each end of the Springfield gym, and invited his colleagues to toss a soccer ball into one of the two baskets.

Most of Naismith's original thirteen rules were designed to prevent players from running with the ball and tackling, blocking, tripping, or hitting each other, as they had learned to do in outdoor football. A "foul" sent a player momentarily to the sideline, and three consecutive fouls counted a goal. The first game consisted of two 15-minute halves, with 5 minutes' rest between. Naismith's physical education class numbered 18, so 9 men played on each team. Players had to pass the ball; no dribbling was allowed at first.

That inaugural game was hardly a spectacle that anyone would recognize today.

Development

Within its first decade basketball underwent dramatic change. Dribbling quickly became an acceptable means of moving the ball around the court. Standard team size was readjusted to seven, and finally set at five. The value of a field goal, originally set at three points, was changed to two points; foul shots, too, counted three at first, but were soon changed to one. Equipment also changed. By 1895 the old soccer ball was replaced by a slightly larger leather-covered basketball; peach baskets gave way to mesh-wire baskets with strings and pulleys that released the ball, and finally to a bottomless cord net fixed to an iron rim. Metal screens also made an early appearance behind baskets, in order to keep balcony spectators from guiding or deflecting shots. As more solid substance provided greater consistency for angled shots, wooden backboards became standard fare by the turn of the century.

This consolidation of basketball rules and style of play occurred despite several early changes of the administrative guard. For the game's first four years, James Naismith oversaw the development of his creation. In 1895, however, Naismith left Springfield for medical school and a YMCA job in Denver, largely leaving the supervision of basketball to his old Springfield colleague, Luther Gulick (1861–1918). Within the following year, Gulick and the YMCA passed the mantle of guardianship over to the Amateur Athletic Union (AAU). Committed to amateur ("gentlemanly") sport, the AAU required players and teams to pay a fee and "register" their intention to comply with the amateur code and to compete only against other registered teams.

This policy played havoc with the many teams sponsored by local YMCAs, athletic clubs, settlement houses, churches, schools, and colleges who not only competed with each other but also indiscriminately played against whatever local or touring professional teams they could schedule. Professional squads made their presence felt early in the history of basketball. In November 1896, a team in Trenton, New Jersey, rented the Masonic Temple, charged 25 cents for admission, and shared the profits after paying expenses.

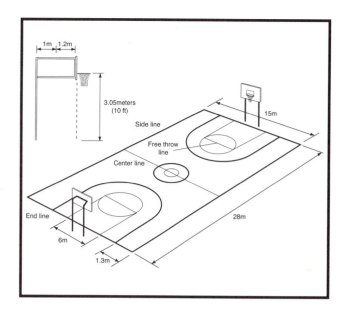

They also introduced a distinctive piece of equipment. A twelve-foot-high mesh-wire fence, presumably designed to keep the ball in play, separated players from spectators. For more than two decades, professionals played within a cage of mesh-wire or net, causing basketball to be called the "cage" game.

Never did the AAU register a majority of the basketball teams in the United States. In 1905 seven coaches of powerful college teams drew up their own set of rules. Three years later the newly formed National Collegiate Athletic Association (NCAA) assumed responsibility for the rules governing college basketball. Finally, in 1915 the NCAA, AAU, and YMCA joined forces in establishing a single rules committee to oversee any further changes in basketball throughout North America.

While refining its form and governance, James Naismith's new game expanded rapidly. Nearby colleges and athletic clubs embraced it as a competitive antidote to onerous gym exercises during New England's frigid winters. One of the first converts to the game was Senda Berenson (1861–1954), a gymnastics instructor at Smith College. Early in 1892 she introduced the game to her female students, but divided the court into three equal sections and kept players confined to a single section in order to avoid exhaustion. Within the following year this distinctive form of "women's basket ball" was being played not only at neighboring Mt. Holyoke College but also at distant Sophie Newcomb College in New Orleans,

Louisiana, and at the University of California in Berkeley.

For a time, though, basketball remained primarily a YMCA commodity. Its place of origin—an aggressive new training college for YMCA leaders—ensured immediate widespread exposure. Copies of Springfield's campus weekly, the *Triangle,* were mailed out regularly to every YMCA in North America. In the January 1892 issue of the *Triangle,* Naismith described his new game and heartily recommended it to YMCA leaders everywhere. Those leaders, in turn, wrote to the editor of the *Triangle* with news about the popularity of basketball as it was introduced to more than 200 YMCA gyms in the United States and Canada.

Many of those YMCA chapters and gyms were set on college campuses, especially in the Midwest and Pacific coast regions. Moreover, Springfield graduates—Naismith's old classmates and fellow athletes—found teaching and coaching jobs in college programs, where they eagerly introduced basketball. Amos Alonzo Stagg (1862–1965) at the University of Chicago, Richard Kallenberg at Iowa State University, and W. O. Black at Stanford University were merely three of many Springfield alumni who carried the muscular Christian gospel of basketball to the colleges.

High schools especially responded to that gospel, for the game proved useful for physical education classes as well as interscholastic competition. Most high schoolers first learned to play basketball in a local YMCA, but new high school gyms and equipment, not to mention the partisan spirit of high school play, soon became more attractive than the YMCA scene. The women's game was played with great passion, particularly in Iowa, Oklahoma, Missouri, and Texas high schools. By 1900 high school championship tournaments were held in conjunction with commercial exhibitions in Boston, Buffalo, and Chicago. In 1903 Gulick created a Public School Athletic League for New York City and supervised the construction of basketball courts in both elementary and high schools throughout the city. Within a decade, more than a dozen of the major cities in the United States sponsored similar city-wide leagues for public school athletes.

Basketball also thrived in rural and small-town schools. Hoops not only fed rural school and town pride; it also provided entertainment sorely lacking in places distant from the bright lights of the city. After 1909, when the agricultural colleges of Iowa and Montana produced the first high school state basketball tournaments, land-grant institutions from Maine State College to Washington State College fulfilled their public service purposes by providing space and publicity for annual high school championship playoffs. In the 1920s national tournaments for public and parochial (Catholic) high schools began; by 1925 more than 30 state championship teams were competing at the National Interscholastic Tournament at the University of Chicago.

Early professional leagues also held tournaments to close out their seasons, but barnstorming proved to be the more lucrative route. Around the turn of the century, the Buffalo "Germans" and the New York "Wanderers" emerged as the premier professional teams that traveled afar competing with the best local talent available in armories, dance halls, and high school gyms. Their successors included the Troy Trojans and "Globe Trotters" from upstate New York, but the most successful of all the early touring teams was the Original Celtics. Founded in Manhattan in 1914, the Original Celtics capitalized on the use of the automobile as a popular means of transportation. At their barnstorming pinnacle in the 1920s, they often appeared in southern and western towns previously unreached by the railway.

The loosely structured, theatrical character of professional basketball made the game uniquely attractive to ambitious first-generation Americans. Heroes of the cage game had names like Dehnert, Holman, Lapchick, Friedman, Borgmann, Husta, and Chismadia. All were of East European or Irish heritage; most were Catholic or Jewish. African Americans, too, laid early claims on professional basketball as a means of fun and success. Founded in 1922, the all-black Harlem Renaissance Five quickly became the strongest opposition to the dominance of the Original Celtics.

Most spectator sports took a beating during the economic troubles that began in 1929, but the Depression worked to the advantage of high school and college basketball in the United States. As unemployment mounted, families found themselves unable to spend freely on commercialized amusements, causing social life in the local college and school to take on more importance.

Basketball became one of the weekly social events. At the end of the decade of the 1930s, no less than 95 percent of all U.S. high schools sponsored varsity basketball teams.

A newly formed program, the Catholic Youth Organization (CYO), also made much of basketball's sociable and socially healthy potential. Begun in 1930 as an antidote to juvenile delinquency in Chicago, the CYO was the Catholic equivalent to the Protestant YMCA and the Jewish Young Men's Hebrew Association (YMHA). The CYO initially received most publicity for its sponsorship of interracial boxing tournaments, but basketball was always high on its agenda. Chicago's CYO and B'nai B'rith champions met annually on the basketball court.

Basketball also went visibly international in the 1930s. At the hands of YMCA enthusiasts, the game had been introduced all over the world shortly after its creation. By 1930, fifty nations had adopted the sport. Despite the economic hardships, representatives from Asia and Africa as well as Europe convened in 1932 to form the International Federation of Amateur Basketball (FIBA). Chinese and Japanese students who had learned the game from YMCA missionaries before World War I introduced basketball at the University of Berlin in the mid-1930s. Nazi propagandists overlooked the game's YMCA origins and gave it their stamp of approval on the grounds that basketball required not only speed and stamina but also an aggressive spirit that allegedly characterized the true German. At the Berlin Games of 1936, basketball became an official Olympic sport. Unfortunately, most of those games were played outdoors in a downpour of rain, with a U.S. squad beating a Canadian team, 19–8.

By the mid-1930s, American basketball was thriving at the college level, particularly in New York City where promoter Ned Irish (1905–1982) arranged doubleheaders at Madison Square Garden featuring the best western teams against eastern powers St. John's University, New York University, and Long Island University. One of those western stars, Frank Luisetti of Stanford University, dazzled spectators with a running one-handed shot. In both 1937 and 1938 he was honored as the collegiate player of the year.

Building on the foundation of these intersectional doubleheaders, the National Invitational Tournament (NIT) was created in 1938 as the first intercollegiate championship playoff. Some 16,000 spectators turned out to see Temple University win the first NIT. Impressed with that successful event, college coaches in 1939 created the NCAA tournament. Their first playoffs, at Northwestern University, suffered from inadequate publicity. The NCAA tournament remained second fiddle until 1951, when scandals discredited the NIT.

Despite the game's growth during the 1930s, it was perceived by the American public as a second-rate sport. Not only did it lack the cachet of a major professional organization until the late 1940s, it had modest national media coverage save the minuscule game summaries of YMCA, professional barnstorming teams, or amateur contests in local daily newspapers. The most significant watershed in basketball's rise to international stature came during World War II. U.S. servicemen introduced the game to people the world over and government-sponsored cultural exchange tours fueled a steady flow of U.S. teams and coaches to all parts of the globe.

The Post–World War II Era

The American collegiate game enjoyed the national and international limelight until the early 1950s. Coached by the winningest coach in basketball history—Adolph Rupp (1901–1977)—Kentucky was the biggest winner of the period. Apart from a few tournament appearances by Southern schools, basketball languished in football's shadows in part because the region's most talented black players were racially excluded from the leading teams and national tournaments. Formidable black college teams (for example, 1950s power Tennessee A&I coached by African American John McLendon, a Naismith student from Kansas) were forced to compete exclusively against each other in relative obscurity. Gamblers wagered millions of dollars per week on the major games, triggering a national controversy in 1950–1951 when several New York City teams were implicated in a point-shaving scandal.

By the time of this well-publicized scandal, the previously unpopular professional game was in the midst of a fundamental transformation. The pros were renowned for their physical, pushing, grabbing, and defensively oriented style played by a tough, beer-drinking, ethnically diverse group of industrial workers, many of whom had served stints in the military. Respectability came in 1946 when 11 businessmen—skilled in hockey and entertainment promotion—organized the Basketball Association of America (BAA) and brought a cleaner brand of basketball to a mainstream, middle-class audience. The newly formed BAA competed with a less profit-oriented and more knowledgeable, civic-minded National Basketball League (formed in 1937)—located in smaller midwestern, industrial cities. The two struggling leagues merged and formed the National Basketball Association (NBA) in 1949. The number of NBA franchises shrank to eight teams in 1954 as the well-financed, large-city franchises forced the smaller ones to relocate or fold. By the end of its first decade, the young NBA unquestionably showcased the best basketball in the world.

The African American Influence

The transformation of the professional game into its elegant, fast-paced, high-scoring contemporary mode derived from an increasingly innovative style of play centered around big men and an emergent generation of innovative African American players. The conservative horizontal offenses of the 1940s became more daring and vertical in the 1950s when quick forwards like "Jumping" Joe Fulks (1921–1976) and Kenny Sailors (1922–) popularized the jumpshot, and coaches developed tall players and built teams around them. As late as 1947, only 25 players on the 12 NBL teams were 6 feet, 6 inches (1.98 meters) tall or taller, reflecting the popular wisdom that large players were too clumsy and ill suited to the game's demands. Those stereotypes were forever shattered by George Mikan (1924–) (6 feet, 10 inches [2.08 meters]), Bob Kurland (1924–) (7 feet [2.13 meters]) and Ed Macauley (1928–) (6 feet, 8 inches [2.03 meters), whose dominance near the basket prompted the young NBA to widen the free throw lane and penalize goal tending. The most revolutionary rule change in the professional game, however, was the introduction of the 24-second clock in 1954, which prevented deliberate offensive stalling and thereby increased scoring by 30 percent over the following five years.

The influence of a black basketball aesthetic was just as revolutionary. Derived from the faster, louder, stop-and-go play of the cement, urban (particularly Harlem) courts, young black players learned that the game was not just about weaves and standard patterns, but also about explosive speed, deception, and slam dunks. Like improvisational jazz music of the 1950s, the emergent black style of play defied the established standards of traditional "white" performance. The Harlem Globetrotters was the most innovative team of the era, whose stars Reece "Goose" Tatum (1921–1967) and Marques Haynes (1926–) integrated improvisational bits from professional comedians and circus clowns into their performance. Organized in 1927 by a Jewish immigrant, Chicagoan Abe Saperstein, the barnstorming 'Trotters took their exciting court antics to the farthest reaches of the globe.

Despite the stellar quality of black basketball, the American professional ranks remained racially segregated until the early 1950s. Earl Lloyd (1928–), Chuck Cooper (1926–), and Nat "Sweetwater" Clifton (1922–) were the first African Americans to play in the NBA in 1950, but the league remained 80 percent white as late as 1960. Though the way was opened up by the Harlem Renaissance, Globetrotters, and several collegiate teams, it was in the NCAA's Division I that the African American style burst through the locked doors of integrated national competition. Black collegians Bill Russell (1934–), Wilt Chamberlain (1936–), Elgin Baylor (1934–), Oscar Robertson (1938–), and Connie Hawkins (1942–) elevated the game to new levels in the 1950s and 1960s.

At the height of the civil rights movement in the United States, two white coaches devised systems that made black style integral to their teams' personas and became the two longest running dynasties in basketball history. Arnold "Red" Auerbach (1917–), a feisty street-smart strategist born in Brooklyn to Russian Jewish immigrants, became coach of the Boston Celtics in 1950 and assembled a superb, balanced team around center Bill Russell. They won 11 NBA championships between 1959 and 1969. John Wooden (1910–), a devout Muscular Christian from small-town Indiana, built powerhouse teams at the University of California at Los Angeles (UCLA) around stellar centers such as Lew Alcindor (1947–) (later Kareem Abdul-Jabbar) and won nine national titles between 1964 and 1975.

Basketball

Women's Basketball

Between the late 1940s and early 1960s, U.S. women's basketball became a bona fide varsity sport. Teams had six players and the court was divided so that the three forwards did the scoring and the three guards covered the backcourt. In 1971 the U.S. Congress passed Title IX legislation, which prohibited sex discrimination at federally funded academic institutions. Thereafter, teams were reduced to five and women were freed from the limits imposed by the halfcourt game. Increased funds to women's athletics attracted first-rate coaches such as former collegian and Olympic star Pat Head Summitt (1952–) of Tennessee, who recruited players from a growing pool of quality high school talent. When the NCAA took control of women's basketball in the late 1970s the large universities with strong programs (such as UCLA, Tennessee, Virginia, Texas, and USC) eclipsed traditional small college powerhouses and shifted the production of women's basketball from New England and the Midwest to southern and western states. The NCAA's prestigious Final Four tournament conferred the truly national scope of women's basketball in 1982 and through increased network television coverage, expanded attendance 90 percent during the decade by the early 1990s.

The Olympics embraced women's basketball in the 1976 Montreal Games. The Soviets won the gold medal in the 1976 and 1980 Games against an impressive field that included strong Chinese and Korean teams. In the aftermath of the 1976 Games, collegiate All-American stars Ann Meyers (1955–) of UCLA and Nancy Lieberman (1958–) of Old Dominion dominated U.S. women's basketball. Both played in the 1976 Olympics, but their influence came later when they became the first women to be drafted by men's professional teams, and then led the short-lived Women's Professional League in 1979–1980. Four years later the United States, led by African American stars Cheryl Miller and Lynette Woodard (the first female member of the Harlem Globetrotters), defeated the Soviets 83–60 in the 1984 Games. In 1988 they repeated by defeating Yugoslavia for another gold medal which firmly established them as the world power of women's basketball. In recent years, the women's traditional "finesse" game has increasingly come to resemble the speedier, powerful, vertical male version.

The Modern Era

The era of stalwart professional dynasties ended with the creation of a rival professional league—the American Basketball Association (ABA)—in 1967, which shifted the NBA's balance of power. By 1976, when the NBA absorbed four ABA teams, professional salaries averaged $110,000—more than twice what baseball and football players made. Moreover, the NBA Players' Association won a collective-bargaining agreement, severance pay, first-class airfare, disability, medical insurance, and pensions. Despite the improvement in players' salaries and overall play, however, the NBA limped along in television ratings and profitability throughout the 1970s. For the first time since the advent of the 24-second clock, the NBA enhanced the drama by adopting the three-point shot (from 23 feet, 9 inches [7.23 meters]).

The American professional game continues to provide the model for global competition. A U.S. "Dream Team" took advantage of revised FIBA eligibility rules that permitted professional athletes' participation in the Olympics, to trounce all their opponents at the 1992 Barcelona Games by unprecedented margins. The Dream Team's success propelled the game into the most geographically diffused and commercially lucrative phase of any sport in history. Even in places without a strong basketball tradition, like Britain, attendance for England's National Basketball League has soared from an early 1970s' average of 7,500 to 330,000 in 1985. The game's popularity since the 1970s continues untrammeled in Latin America, and now China claims more players than the entire population of Europe. Efforts are currently under way to establish a professional league in Asia, with likely locations for teams in Tokyo, South Korea, Taiwan, and the Philippines.

Basketball has enjoyed even greater success on the European continent where NBA stars are celebrated in Italian, Spanish, and French newspapers and glossy magazines. Since 1987, basketball has been Italy's second most popular sport. More than half the members of the national Spanish junior team are currently playing college ball in the U.S. Moreover, of the 21 foreign players on NBA rosters in 1995, 14 had attended U.S. universities.

The renaissance of big-time college basketball came in the 1979 NCAA title game when the two of the three dominant players of the 1980s—Earvin "Magic" Johnson (1959–) and Larry Bird

(1956–)—were pitted against each other for the first time. The 6 foot, 9 inch "Magic" destroyed the stereotypical notions of how size dictated positions and, along with Bird, elevated creative passing and teamwork. Magic's dexterity and court vision brought the brilliance of the black aesthetic to new heights. The Magic-Bird rivalry catapulted the month-long NCAA tournament atop the pinnacle of international sport just beneath the Olympics and World Cup competitions. Gross receipts for the NCAA tournament have increased from eight million dollars in 1979 to over 184 million dollars in 1995. The rivalry also sparked unprecedented interest in both the game and the basketball player as a marketable celebrity. Buoyed by the advertising agency's success in marketing athletic shoes and sportswear (e.g., Nike, Reebok, and Converse) with superstar endorsers, basketball stars, especially Michael Jordan (1963–) have become some of the world's highest paid athletes and most recognizable personalities.

The game's hold on the American imagination is reflected in the emergence of a cadre of successful basketball films. Unlike baseball, football, and boxing, basketball was largely ignored by filmmakers until the late 1970s, but recently has become part of a pervasive sports, media, and entertainment enterprise. Since the 1970s filmmakers have moved away from silly, frivolous scripts to ones that dramatize the contradictory nature of basketball in contemporary society. The commercial success of *White Men Can't Jump* (1991) and the artistic recognition conferred upon the documentary *Hoop Dreams* (1995) illuminate the importance of urban playgrounds as breeding grounds of big-time talent, the centrality of the black aesthetic, and the game's promise of social mobility for millions of young people throughout the world.

—William J. Baker and S. W. Pope

Bibliography: Applin, Albert G. (1982) "From Muscular Christianity to the Marketplace: The History of Men's and Boy's Basketball in the United States, 1891–1957." Ph.D. dissertation, University of Massachusetts.

Fox, Stephen. (1994) *Big Leagues: Professional Baseball, Football, and Basketball in National Memory.* New York: Morrow.

George, Nelson. (1992) *Elevating the Game: Black Men and Basketball.* New York: HarperCollins.

Hollander, Zander, ed. (1979) *The Modern Encyclopedia of Basketball.* Garden City, NY: Dolphin Books.

Hult, Joan S., and Marianna Trekel, eds. (1991) *A Century of Women's Basketball: From Frailty to Final Four.* Reston, VA: National Association for Girls and Women in Sport.

Isaacs, Neil D. (1975) *All the Moves: A History of College Basketball.* Philadelphia: Lippincott.

Koppett, Leonard. (1968) *24 Seconds to Shoot: An Informal History of the National Basketball Association.* New York: Macmillan.

Levine, Peter. (1992) *Ellis Island to Ebbets Field: Sport and the American Jewish Experience.* New York: Oxford University Press.

Naismith, James. (1941) *Basketball: Its Origin and Development.* New York: Association Press.

Neft, David S., and Richard M. Cohen. (1991) *The Sports Encyclopedia: Pro Basketball.* New York: Grosset & Dunlap.

Peterson, Robert W. (1990) *Cages to Jump Shots: Pro Basketball's Early Years.* New York: Oxford University Press.

Rooney, John F., and Richard Pillsbury. (1992) *Atlas of American Sport.* New York: Macmillan.

Rosen, Charles. (1978) *The Scandals of '51: How Gamblers Almost Killed College Basketball.* New York: Holt, Rinehart, and Winston.

Vincent, Ted. (1981) *Mudville's Revenge: The Rise and Fall of American Sport.* New York: Seaview Press.

Biathlon

Biathlon is a challenging combination of cross-country skiing and target shooting. The competitor skis a designated loop with a specially adapted .22 rifle harnessed on his or her back, pausing to shoot at a specified number of ranges along the route. At each shooting range the biathlete must switch gears from the exertions of skiing to the quiet concentration required for target shooting. Thus biathlon requires athletes to master the physical and mental demands of two somewhat conflicting disciplines. Physical strength and stamina are needed to ski a course that can run as long as 20 kilometers (12.5 miles) for the individual event, yet the athlete needs great self control to quiet the body and concentrate the mind on arriving at the shooting range in order to aim the rifle and fire with accuracy.

Biathlon has been an Olympic event for men since 1960. Today, there are Olympic events for both men and women, as individuals and on

Believed to have originated with Norwegian hunters 4,000 years ago, the modern biathlon has military origins in Scandinavia. The earliest recorded biathlon event took place in 1767.

Modern biathlon has military origins in Scandinavia, where the terrain and climate required troops to be trained and equipped for combat in winter conditions. The earliest recorded biathlon event occurred in 1767 between "ski-runner companies" who guarded the border between Norway and Sweden. The world's first known ski club, the "Trysil Rifle and Ski Club" was founded in Trysil, Norway, in 1861 to promote national defense at the local level. In the late 1930s, the Finnish Army, outnumbered ten to one but outfitted with skis, routed the Russians from their border.

The first international biathlon competition was held as a demonstration event at the 1924 Winter Olympics in Chamonix, France, and was continued at the Winter Olympics of 1928, 1936, and 1948. After 1948, biathlon was dropped from the Olympic program in response to the antimilitary sentiment that followed World War II.

In 1948, the Union Internationale de Pentathlon Moderne et Biathlon (UIPMB) was founded to promote the development of both sports as Olympic events. The UIPMB instituted annual World Championships for biathlon in 1957 and it was included as an individual event for male athletes for the first time at the Winter Olympics in Squaw Valley, California, in 1960. In 1966 the biathlon relay was introduced at the World Biathlon Championships and added to the Olympic program in 1968. The first Women's World Championships were held in Chamonix, France, in 1984, and women's biathlon events were included at the 1992 Winter Olympics in Albertville, France.

relay teams, and national and international competitions for junior athletes as well.

Origins

The ancient origins of biathlon may be revealed in rock carvings found in Norway that date from about 2000 B.C.E., which show two hunters on skis stalking animals. Biathlon, like many of the other activities we now regard as sport, may very well have evolved from things our ancestors learned to do in order to survive, in this case travel across deep snow and hunt for food. Skill in such activities was essential; great prowess was cause for admiration. It is easy to imagine early contests on primitive skis, using spears instead of rifles, as a precursor to the contemporary form of the sport.

Events

There are three race events in biathlon—individual, sprint, and relay—each with different distances, rules, and penalties. Competitors ski a set number of loops of the course depending on the event, taking four stops for shooting.

The five metal targets at each stop are set at a distance of 50 meters (164 feet). The targets can be reset mechanically after each shooting bout and can be set for prone or standing shooting positions. A hit is registered immediately by a white plate which flips up to cover the black target. For prone shooting the hit must strike a 45-millimeter (1.76-inch) diameter circle in the center of the target. A standing shot can hit anywhere in the 115 millimeter (4.5 inch) diameter circle. Missed shots require the competitor to ski penalty loops, which add to the overall time and lower the competitor's score.

At biathlon events, references to something called "range time" are often heard. This term refers to the time it takes to enter the firing range, unsling the rifle, shoot five rounds, re-sling the rifle, and exit the range. Cross-country skiing requires intense physical effort; while on the course, competitors' heart rates rise to between 170–190 beats per minute. Thus, when they approach each shooting range, athletes must reduce skiing speed to slow their breathing in preparation for shooting. World-class range times average about 30–40 seconds for the prone position and 25–30 for the standing position.

The individual competition demands more endurance during skiing and greater body control at the range than in the shorter distances of the other events. In the individual competition, men ski a total of 20 kilometers and women ski 15 kilometers (9.4 miles). The athletes start at one-minute intervals and ski five loops ranging from 2.5 kilometers (1.6 miles) to 5 kilometers (3.1 miles), shooting five shots at each of four stages for a total of 20 shots. There is a one-minute penalty for every missed shot that is added to the competitor's ski time at the end of the race, for a total of 20 possible penalty minutes if all shots were missed. The winner is the athlete with the lowest combined ski time and penalty minutes.

In sprint competition, men ski a total of 10 kilometers (6.2 miles) and women ski 7.5 kilometers (4.7 miles), starting at one-minute intervals. Athletes ski one loop, shoot five rounds in the prone position, ski a 150-meter (164-yard) penalty loop for each missed shot, and then ski another loop. They then shoot five rounds in the standing position, ski a 150 meter penalty for each shot missed, and ski a final loop to the finish. They thus ski a total of three loops ranging from 1.75 kilometers (1.09 miles) to 3.75 kilometers (2.3 miles) and shoot two shooting stages for a total of ten shots. All penalties are skied during the race, so penalty time (about 30 seconds for each penalty) is already included in the time when the athlete crosses the finish line.

In the relay competition all teams start simultaneously in a mass start and ski the same course.

Ski-Arc

As another example of transformation from survival activity to sport, consider the emerging sport of ski archery, known as ski-arc. The early Scandinavian ski-shod hunters must have used spears and, later, bows and arrows to stalk their prey. Norse legends tell of Ullr, the God of Winter, an expert skier and archer who could not be matched by any of the other Norse gods.

In 1208, the Norwegian Birkebeiner, or "birch-leg warriors," skied 55 kilometers (34 miles) to rescue their kidnapped prince during the Norwegian civil war. The Birkebeiner, a cross-country ski race held annually in Norway, is named for these heroes and draws thousands of competitors.

Modern ski archery competition is similar to biathlon. A typical race covers an 8–12 kilometer (5–10 mile) course with two or three shooting stops. One stop requires the archer to shoot from a kneeling position. The four targets at each stop measure 180 millimeters (7 inches) and are set at 18 meters (19.7 yards) distance.

The ski archer carries the bow on the back while skiing; arrows are stored at the assigned shooting position at each target area. As in biathlon events, scoring is determined by a combination of ski time and shooting points scored. There is national and international competition in the sport and enthusiasts look forward to ski-arc eventually becoming an official Olympic event.

—Bonnie Dyer-Bennet

Both men's and women's courses are 4 x 7.5 kilometers, that is, each member of a four-person team skis a 7.5-kilometer leg of the race. Each leg is run in the same way as the sprint race except that racers get to use "extra rounds" at the range. Each competitor has eight bullets to hit five targets at both the prone and standing stages. When racers ski into the range they place three extra rounds from their magazines into a small cup before they begin shooting. They then attempt to hit all five targets with five shots. If they miss any, they then load rounds from the cup into the firing chamber until they have hit all five targets or used up all three extra rounds, whichever comes first. If, after shooting all eight rounds, the competitors still have not hit all five targets, they must ski a penalty loop for each missed target.

There is a tag zone where each skier, on completion of his or her leg of the relay, touches the next teammate, who then starts out on the course. The winning team is the one whose last competitor crosses the finish line first.

Athletes generally arrive several hours ahead of their starting time to prepare for competition. Prevailing snow conditions may require changes in the wax used on the running surfaces of skis and the competitors are also permitted to take practice shots at paper targets on the range so that they can make adjustments to their rifle sights according to sun and wind conditions.

Equipment

There have been several changes in the equipment used in biathlon competition over the years. From 1958 to 1965, competitors used NATO caliber rifles, first 3.08 and then large bore .223. In 1978 the .22 caliber was adopted as the official rifle. The biathlon rifle is single-loading, must weigh not less than 7.5 pounds (3.4 kilograms), and is equipped with nonoptical sights. Biathlon modifications to the .22 rifle include lightweight stocks, carrying harnesses, quick-release shooting slings, snow covers on the sights, five-round magazines, magazine holders in the stock, and bolt modifications to speed up the bolting action. Athletes are required to pass a rifle safety certification course before being allowed to compete in biathlon events.

The ski equipment used in biathlon has also undergone some changes. Traditionally racers used the classic, diagonal cross-country stride. However, in 1985 the "skating" technique was introduced to biathlon, which revolutionized the physical techniques of the sport as well as demanding new equipment. The skating technique uses explosive propelling motions of the arms and legs for which longer ski poles and shorter, stiffer skis are needed in order to take full advantage of the athlete's motions. The introduction of skating has also reduced race times. It is not uncommon for World Cup winners to "clean" every set of targets and finish a 20-kilometer race in under one hour.

—Bonnie Dyer-Bennet

Bibliography: *United States Biathlon Association Bulletin.* (1994) 14, 2.

Biathlon (Cycling and Running)

See Duathlon

Billiards

Billiards refers to a group of games played on a rectangular table with a predetermined number of balls. In one general form of the game (carom billiards) players score points when they propel one of the balls (the cue ball) into others, thus scoring a *carom*. In the other general form, players score when they drive object balls into any of six pockets on some types of tables by first hitting them with the cue ball. The cue ball is propelled by striking it with the small end of a long, tapered stick known as a cue. Games played on pocket billiards tables include English billiards, which is played with 3 balls; snooker, which is played with 21 object balls and a cue ball; and pocket billiards, which is also known as pool. Each game, especially pool and carom billiards, has variants that tend to be associated with certain countries or areas of the world. Local differences in rules and game etiquette are common.

Origins

Billiards probably developed from one of the late-fourteenth- or early-fifteenth-century outdoor lawn games in which balls were propelled at other balls or at targets by a stick, cudgel, mace, staff, or mast. In addition to billiards, other modern games such as hockey, golf, croquet, and shuffleboard also evolved from these games during the period between about 1350 and the late 1600s (Hendricks 1974). Billiards was first played on the ground, often on plots that were measured and sunken in order to provide boundaries, before it

Like many sports, billiards was carried by the British throughout their empire. These early twentieth-century African billiard players have donned collar and monocle for the game.

developed into a table game. The earliest mention of pool as an indoor table game is in a 1470 inventory list of the accounts of King Louis XI of France, who reigned from 1461 to 1483 (Hendricks 1974). The king's table had a stone playing bed covered with green cloth (apparently to simulate grass) and a hole in the middle into which the balls were guided. Early billiards tables in both France and England commonly used a "port" and a "king" (a hoop and a pin, as in croquet) at opposite ends of the table, as had the earlier ground billiards. It was played by two individuals, each of whom had one ball. Points could be scored by "passing" (propelling one's ball through the port before one's opponent did), by touching the king without knocking it over, or by "hazarding" (driving the opponent's ball into

a pocket). The term *billiards* may have developed from the medieval Latin *billa*, which, in turn, came from the Latin *pila*, meaning "ball." In his authoritative survey of the history of the game, *William Hendricks' History of Billiards*, the author indicates that the modern word probably descends from Latin terms that refer to the ball and from the Old French word *bille* (a piece of wood), which refers to the stick. The modern reference to the stick as a "cue" is derived from the French *queue,* meaning "tail," and probably refers to the practice of striking a ball with the small, or tail, end of the billiard mace. Because the mace had a wide, flat-faced head it was difficult to use for shots in which the cue ball rested near or against the table rail. Hence, players turned the mace around and shot the ball with the handle, or tail.

France's Louis XIII (reigned 1610–1643) and Louis XIV (reigned 1643–1710) were avid pool players. The latter is generally credited with spreading the game through Europe, although it seems more likely that Louis XIII actually did so (Hendricks 1974). Mary Stuart, queen of Scotland, was one of the earliest patrons of billiards in the British Isles. In 1586, during her arrest in the castle at Fotheringay, her playing table was taken away, apparently as part of her punishment. A few months later she was beheaded and, according to some sources, her body was wrapped in the cloth stripped from the table (Hendricks 1974). Later, a form of billiards was played at the court of James I of England, who reigned from 1603 through 1625.

It is not known when billiards first arrived in the Americas, although reliable information indicates that William Byrd II was playing billiards at his Virginia plantation by 1709, while Thomas Jefferson and Alexander Hamilton later played with Lafayette (Hendricks 1974). The game flourished in eighteenth-century America, and most towns had public billiards tables. By 1764 the game had moved west of the Appalachians: one of the first buildings erected in the newly founded French town of St. Louis, Missouri, was a billiard parlor (Hendricks 1974). By the mid-1830s, billiard tables were to be found as far west as the Bent's Fort outpost on the Santa Fe Trail in Colorado.

Development of Billiards

Equipment

Tables

A standard pocket billiards table is half as wide as it is long. Tables range between 1.8 and 3 meters (6 and 10 feet) long. The playing area of a table is called the "bed" and should be between 74.3 and 76.2 centimeters (29 1/4 and 30 1/4 inches) from the floor. The best tables have beds made of slate that are from 1.3 to 5.1 centimeters (1/2 inch to 2 inches) thick and rest on wooden supports. The bed is covered with cloth and bordered by cushioned rails.

Modern billiards games are played on three basic table types: the pocketless carom table, the English table, and the pocket billiards, or pool, table. On all tables, the short rail at one end of the table where the manufacturer's name plate is usually affixed is known as the "head rail." This is the end from which play is normally initiated. The opposite end is known as the "foot rail" and is where balls are usually "spotted" or racked for play. The long sides of the table are known as "side rails." The "center spot" is located at the geometric center of the table. On carom and pocket billiards tables, spots are also placed at the center of each half of the table, i.e., on the long axis of the table and halfway between the center spot and the end cushions. The spot nearest the table head is called the "head spot" and the spot nearest the foot of the table is the "foot spot." The "head string" is an imaginary line running through the head spot parallel to the head rail. Similarly, the "foot string" runs through the foot spot and parallels the foot rail. The "center string" connects the midpoints of the long rails and the "long string" bisects the table along its length. The foot spot is located at the intersection of the foot string and the long string. Tables normally have a visible foot spot because when balls are racked for play, the first ball of the group is placed on the foot spot. Tables are further divided by the placement of "diamonds" (inlays or markings) along the rails. The head and foot of a table have three diamonds each, dividing the width of the table into fourths, while the long rails have either six or seven diamonds (depending on whether the table has pockets), dividing the length of the table into eighths. These not only help locate the various strings but also assist players in determining angles for shots that are banked off the cushions.

Carom tables are typically 2.7 or 3.0 meters long (9 or 10 feet) by 1.4 or 1.5 meters (4 1/2 or 5 feet) wide and the same height as pocket billiards tables, but they have no pockets. English tables, used for English billiards and snooker, are large, usually 3.7 by 1.8 meters (12 feet by 6 feet, 1 1/2 inches), and are 87.6 centimeters (34 1/2 inches) tall. They have six pockets and have four spots along the center string, but other than the center spot, these are located by measured distances from the head and foot cushions, rather than by the geometry of the table. The "balk line," which runs parallel to the short rail at the head of the table, is 73.7 centimeters (29 inches) from the rail. In the early days of the carom game, good players could "gather" the three balls in a small area and score literally hundreds of points while moving the balls very short distances. Balk lines and rule changes were added to prevent this. After the introduction of balk lines, players were permitted to score only a limited number of points within the "balk area" (from the end of the table to the line) before moving the balls to other parts of the table. A balk-line spot is located at the middle of the balk line and the "D," a 29.2-centimeter-radius (11-1/2-inch) semicircle with the balk spot at its center and the balk line as its diameter, is formed with its curved side toward the rail. The spot (also known as the "billiard spot") is located in the middle of the table, 32.4 centimeters (12 3/4 inches) from the short rail at the other end of the table. The "center spot" is in the geometric center of the table and the "pyramid spot" is located between the center spot and the spot, 89 centimeters (35 1/8 inches) from the cushion. American snooker tables are smaller (3 by 1.5 meters [10 feet by 5 feet]) and spot measurements are correspondingly shorter.

The first billiards tables were constructed entirely of wood and were nonuniform in size and sometimes in shape. Thus, the long boards used for the bed were subject to warping, regardless of the sturdiness of the frame or trestles that supported them. Hence, the single most important improvement in tables resulted from the substitution of slate for the wooden bed. Slate is heavy, will not warp if properly supported, and can be easily worked to the required smoothness. Its greatest virtue, however, is the fact that it occurs naturally in flat layers, making it ideal for table beds. By 1840 in England, slate had replaced wood for the construction of the best tables. Slate was adopted in America by the 1850s but not until the 1880s in France. There have been various efforts to use other materials for billiard table beds, including cast iron, glass, marble, and cement, but none of these were successful and slate remains the material of choice.

The rails around tables posed a second problem. Early tables had flat, vertical walls that prevented balls from falling off the table. These were often called "banks" due to their resemblance to river banks. Players soon discovered that they could bounce balls off the banks to execute shots—these came to be known as "bank shots." Later, rails were padded with cushions, but in order to assure that balls would rebound at the desired angle and speed, the cushions had to be made uniformly resilient. A variety of stuffings were used to try to achieve this uniformity, including narrow strips of felt or other cloth, hair, curled hair, horsehair, wool, and Russian duck. In 1835, English table manufacturer John Thurston hit upon the idea of making cushions of pure native rubber, cut into sheets and affixed to the rail in layers (Hendricks 1974). Rubber was not without its drawbacks, however. Natural rubber strips could break in time or after extended play and their resiliency varied according to how much they were stretched. More important, natural rubber was affected by temperature, becoming hard and inelastic in the cold—an important consideration in the days before central heating (Hendricks 1974). These problems were solved with Goodyear's discovery of vulcanizing in 1839. Vulcanized rubber was resistant to temperature changes and provided accurate angles of reflection. It came into general use for cushions after 1845.

The character of the cloth that covers billiard tables is also essential to skilled play. Early tables were covered by coarse wool (known as baize) that not only lacked a fine texture but also contained numerous knots. Both of these features affected the course of balls. Fine cloths were expensive in the early 1800s, but by the middle of the nineteenth century textile technology had improved to the point that good cloths, often felted to mask the weave, were universally available.

Balls

Billiard balls were initially turned from wood and some were later molded from clay, but by the early nineteenth century ivory was the preferred material. However, elephant tusks had to have a diameter of approximately 6.4 centimeters (2 1/2 inches) in order to produce billiard balls. No more than five balls could be made from one tusk and only three of those would be of high quality. It would thus require four elephants to provide the ivory needed for one set of good snooker balls (Hendricks 1974). During peak years early in the nineteenth century, as many as 12,000 elephants were slaughtered and their tusks shipped to Liverpool or London to make billiard balls (Hendricks 1974).

As might be expected, ivory billiard balls were extremely expensive. Moreover, neither wood nor ivory is uniform in density and both are subject to warping and cracking due to moisture and temperature changes. Hence, substitute materials were sought throughout the nineteenth century. In 1878, after unsuccessful trials with other materials, chemist John Wesley Hyatt discovered that collodion, a solution composed of nitrocellulose, camphor, and alcohol, formed a durable substance when allowed to dry and harden. This material could easily be molded to near-perfect roundness and was not affected by temperature or moisture. Hyatt and his brother Isaac patented their process for making the substance in 1870 and called it celluloid, the world's first commercial plastic. Unfortunately, early billiard balls made of celluloid were not only highly flammable but if struck too hard could explode (Everton 1979). However, this problem was eventually solved and Hyatt's discovery led directly to the modern technique for making billiard balls of cast phenolic resin, sparing countless elephants and founding the plastics industry in the process (Hendricks 1974).

Modern balls range in diameter from $2\frac{1}{16}$ to $2\frac{27}{64}$ inches (roughly 5 centimeters), depending on the game. Larger balls are used in carom games while snooker and English billiards utilize small balls. Pocket billiards balls are 5.7 centimeters ($2\frac{1}{4}$ inches) in diameter (Billiard Congress of America 1995). Balls used in any particular game are always of the same size and weight, except on coin-operated tables, where the cue ball differs in size, weight, or both so it can be distinguished from the other balls and returned to players after being pocketed.

Cues
While late-seventeenth-century billiards made the transformation from a ground to a table game, it was still played with a mace—a stick with a wide face that resembled a cross between a miniature hockey stick and a golf wood. According to Hendricks (1974), "The mace stroke was accomplished by resting the flat side of the head of the mace on the table, then pushing the ball with the shaft of the mace held at shoulder height between the thumb and first two fingers of one hand." Hence, players stood upright when using the mace—a stance that permitted play by ladies who might otherwise risk exposure of an ankle if they bent over the table. The ball was pushed or shoved with the mace, not struck. In

modern versions of billiards, pushing the ball or striking it more than once with the cue is usually regarded as a foul. A major transformation of the game occurred when players began to the use the small end of the stick (the handle of the mace) to strike a ball that was close to a rail. Since the rails of the day were as high or higher than the balls, the head of the mace was all but useless when the ball rested against a rail. The first cues, which were little more than maces without heads, introduced a new level of skill to the game, although the mace continued to be used by women and for long or difficult shots. No precise date or place exists for the introduction of the cue, but Hendricks (1974) indicates they probably appeared between 1679 and 1734 and had superseded the mace by the second half of the eighteenth century. Maces were still manufactured during the first years of the twentieth century, but by then were rarely used and were sometimes rather contemptuously referred to as "ladies' cues."

The first cues were made of various woods, including oak and mahogany, but ash, hickory, and maple eventually became the most popular. Players who used the first cues took pains to strike the ball at dead center for two reasons. First, striking the ball off-center frequently resulted in a miscue: that is, the tip of the cue skidded off-center when the ball was struck, imparting a glancing blow and propelling the ball in an unintended direction. Second, if the cue did not skid due to an off-center strike, it imparted spin to the ball. This spin caused the ball to rebound off either the cushion or other balls at angles or in ways that were, at the time, uncontrollable. Around 1790, the "Jeffrey" cue was introduced. This cue had a tip that was obliquely cut, rather than square. With this angled tip, the ball could be struck slightly below center, imparting back spin that skilled players could use to their advantage. Players also roughened the tips of their cues so they would grip the balls better when struck, resulting in fewer miscues. About the same time, players began to apply chalk to the tips of cues, also in order to prevent them from slipping when the ball was struck. The techniques of striking the ball below and, later, above center permitted skilled players to control the actions of the balls in ways that were impossible with the mace, which was designed to contact the center of the ball only.

It is not known where or when the use of horizontal spin of the ball came into use, although it is commonly attributed to one Captain Mingaud, a French infantry officer who was a political prisoner around the turn of the nineteenth century. Mingaud had access to a billiards table in prison and studied the game intensely. In order to get additional traction, he allegedly put a leather tip on his cue, allowing him to apply various sorts of spin to the ball. Whether Mingaud actually developed the cue tip or spins is debatable, but special tips were clearly in existence by 1818 (Hendricks 1974). Regardless of its origin, side spin, which is imparted to the ball by striking it slightly to either the right or left of center, is commonly called "English" in the United States, although the English refer to it as "side." The use of "draw" (cueing low to impart backspin), "follow" (cueing high to impart topspin), and combinations of English, draw, and follow are now part of every skilled player's repertoire.

Modern cues are tapered, wooden rods about 1.4 meters (57 inches) long and weighing between 397 and 624 grams (14 and 22 ounces). Sometimes other materials, such as aluminum or fiberglass, are used. The end of the cue, to which is affixed a rounded leather tip, is generally about 1.3 centimeters ($\frac{1}{2}$ inch) in diameter. The handle, or butt end, of the cue may be decorated with inlays and is often covered with linen or other material for a comfortable grip. The diameters of the shaft near the tip end of the handle vary on different cues according to player preferences. Some cues come in two pieces, making them easier to transport.

The Games

Early billiard games varied greatly, i.e., they were played with or without kings and ports, with or without pockets, or with two or more balls. The modern game has settled into essentially four types: carom, or French billiards; English billiards; snooker; and pocket billiards, or pool.

Carom Billiards

Carom billiards, or French billiards, is played on a table with no pockets and with three balls: one red, one white, and one distinguished by two or three red or black spots. A point, or carom, is scored when a player's cue ball is propelled into the two object balls, the red ball, and the opponent's cue ball in succession. In some versions of the game, the shooter's cue ball must contact a cushion one or more times during a successful carom. A success entitles the player to continue his or her turn (known as an "inning") until he or she fails to score.

Scoring and rules of carom billiards differ regionally, as in other games. Generally, when a player misses a carom, a point is deducted from his or her total and the turn goes over to the other player. A point and turn are also lost due to general billiards rule infractions, such as playing out of turn, jumping a ball off the table, making a shot while any of the balls are still moving, pushing or shoving a cue ball rather than cleanly striking it, double-striking the cue ball (hitting the cue ball a second time with the cue tip after the cue ball has struck an object ball), touching or moving any ball with the cue prior to shooting, or not having at least one foot on the floor while shooting. Nonshooting players can also lose a point by interfering with the shooter. The "safety" shot permits a player to end his or her turn without incurring a point penalty. A safety is executed by causing the cue ball either to strike a cushion after contacting an object ball or to drive an object ball into a cushion. Players must attempt to score on the first shot of their inning after hitting a safety. Failing to do so results in a point penalty.

The most popular form of carom billiards is three-cushion billiards. The determination of who has first turn, if there are two players or two teams, is done by "lagging." To lag, the red ball is first placed on the head spot. Then each player places a cue ball behind the head string—one to the right and the other to the left of the head spot. Simultaneously, the players shoot their cue balls against the foot cushion of the table in an attempt to bring it to rest as close as possible to the head cushion. The player whose ball ends up nearest the head cushion, without hitting either the red ball or the opponent's cue ball, gets choice of turn and choice of cue ball: either the white or the spot white. If more than two players are involved, turn may be decided by lot. After turn is determined, the red ball is placed on the foot spot and the white object ball (the nonshooter's cue ball) is placed on the head spot. The shooter's cue ball is placed on the head string within 6 inches to the right or left of the white object ball. To initiate the game, the first player drives the cue ball into the red object ball in an effort to score a carom. After the break shot, either the red or the white object ball may be struck first. In order to score, the cue ball must strike the first object ball and at least three cushions, in any order, before hitting the second object ball. In straight-rail billiards, the cue ball must hit the object balls in succession, but no cushion contact is required. The winner in either game is the first player to reach a predetermined number of points, usually 50.

Balkline, a form of straight-rail billiards, was the most important billiard game for U.S. professional players in the early part of the twentieth century, but it was replaced by three-cushion in the late 1920s (Mizerak 1990). Willie Hoppe (1887–1959) was the dominant straight-rail and three-cushion player in America for most of the first half of the twentieth century and is regarded by many as the greatest all-around billiards player in history. By the late 1940s in the United States, pocket billiards games surpassed carom billiards in popularity. Carom billiards tables are now rare in comparison to pocket billiards tables, but carom billiards continues to be popular on the European continent.

English Billiards
English billiards combines attributes of the carom game with those of the pocket game. It is played with three balls: a red, a white, and a spot white. Because of the large size of the standard English billiards table, players sometimes use 2.7-meter (9-foot) long-butt and 2.1-meter (7-foot) half-butt cues.

To determine the order of play, players "string" by shooting a cue ball up the table from the D. The player whose ball stops nearest the opposite cushion gets choice. For the start of the game, the red ball is placed on the spot and the shooter places his or her cue ball anywhere within the D and shoots at the red. The shooter continues his or her turn until he or she fails to score, whereupon the turn goes to the other player. A "break" comprises the shots constituting a player's turn. When the first player's break ends, the second player puts his or her cue ball into play. However, the player may not shoot at a ball within the area behind the balk line when his or her cue ball is brought into play. Instead, the cue ball must be shot off a cushion outside the balk area before it can strike a ball within the balk

area. Points are scored by the "winning hazard" (or "pot"), the "losing hazard" (or "loser"), and the "cannon." A winning hazard is worth two points when the cue ball propels the other white ball into a pocket or three points when the cue ball makes the red ball go into a pocket. A losing hazard occurs when the shooter's cue ball is pocketed after striking another ball. This is worth two points if the cue ball hits the other white and three points if it hits the red. If the nonshooter's cue ball is pocketed during a break, it remains in the pocket until his or her turn. The cue is then placed in the D for play. If the red ball is pocketed during play, it is immediately retrieved and placed on the spot. The red may only be pocketed five times in succession, while only 15 consecutive hazards—winning, losing, or both—may be scored. Hence, players must also be skilled in the cannon, which is when a player's cue ball hits both of the other balls on the table. This maneuver is worth two points. An additional two points are scored if the shooter's cue ball is pocketed after striking the white ball and three points after striking the red ball. Shooters may score no more than 75 consecutive cannons. The nonshooter may score points as well: one if the shooter's cue ball fails to hit another ball and three if the shooter pockets the cue ball without hitting another ball. Players concede points to opponents for some fouls and lose a turn and any points scored for others. English billiards is popular in Great Britain and former members of the British Empire but is essentially unknown in the United States.

Snooker
Snooker may be played on any pocket billiards table, although it is normally played on the same table and with the same size balls as English billiards. Snooker is played with 22 balls, including the white cue ball, 15 red balls, and 6 numbered balls. The numbered balls include a yellow (worth two points), a green (worth three points), a brown (worth four points), a blue (worth five points), a pink (worth six points), and a black (worth seven points). The red balls are worth one point each. Turn is decided by a coin flip or by stringing. The balls are placed on the table in a particular formation. The yellow ball is placed on the balk line where it intersects the D to the left of the balk-line spot, the brown ball is placed on the

balk-line spot, and the green ball is placed on the intersection of the D and the balk line to the right of the balk-line spot. The blue ball is placed on the center spot, the pink on the pyramid spot, and the black on the spot. The red balls are racked in a triangle behind, but not touching, the pink ball.

Play is initiated by shooting the cue ball from within the D and striking any of the red balls. If a player succeeds in pocketing a red ball, he or she then must attempt to pocket any of the nonred balls. Players must designate which nonred ball they intend to pocket and the value of that ball is added to his or her score. Failure to hit the designated ball is a foul and the value of the designated ball is deducted from the player's total. After a nonred ball is pocketed it is respotted, but red balls remain in the pockets. A player's turn continues, alternately shooting reds and nonreds, until he or she misses a shot. The second player shoots the cue ball from where it rests after the first player's last shot unless it has been pocketed. In that case, it is played from within the D. Play continues until all of the red balls have been pocketed. The player who pockets the last red ball may attempt to pocket any one of the remaining balls and, if he or she is successful, that ball is respotted. At this point, the nonred balls must be struck by the cue ball and pocketed in order of value, i.e., beginning with the yellow and ending with the black. At this stage of the game, pocketed balls are not respotted. The player with the highest total score after all of the balls have been pocketed is the winner.

During the game, the object ball next in line to be shot is termed "on." The term "snooker" refers to the situation in which an on ball is obstructed by one that the player must not hit with the cue ball. Thus, the player is "snookered." Snookered players must attempt to hit the on ball (by banking the cue ball off a cushion, for example), because failing to hit it or hitting another ball first is a foul and results in loss of turn and a penalty worth the value of the on ball.

Snooker was developed in British colonial India in the mid-1870s (Everton 1979) and is extremely popular in Great Britain and former British colonies, including Canada. Large billiard rooms in the United States sometimes have snooker tables, but its popularity is minimal in comparison to pocket billiards.

The Drama of Billiards

Billiards has often provided a backdrop for both drama and comedy. The first dramatic mention of the game appears in Shakespeare's play *Antony and Cleopatra*, written around 1609. In Act II, scene v, Cleopatra suggests to her handmaiden Charmian, "Let's to billiards." Although history indicates that the game did not exist in ancient Egypt, Shakespeare's mention suggests that he regarded billiards as a suitable diversion for royalty in his own time (Hendricks 1974). With respect to comedy, pocket billiards often provided slapstick material for early Hollywood short films starring the likes of Laurel and Hardy, the Three Stooges, and W. C. Fields. In addition to being one of the world's great jugglers, Fields was an expert pool player.

The dark side of the game was suggested in Meredith Wilson's Broadway musical *The Music Man* when con artist Professor Harold Hill, played by Robert Preston, declared, "There's trouble in River City," in reference to a pool parlor. Billiards play has also been featured in several films, including *From Here to Eternity*, *Irma la Douce*, and *Sleuth*, as well as numerous television shows (Mizerak 1990). Pool and pool players have been the focus of at least two significant films. The first of these, the 1961 film *The Hustler*, starred Paul Newman and Jackie Gleason as the legendary player Minnesota Fats. The movie is based on a novel by Walter Tevis and depicts the seamy life of a pool hustler, "Fast Eddie" Felson (Newman). Newman reprised this role in the 1986 film *The Color of Money*, for which he received an Oscar. In that film, Newman's character mentors a young pool hustler played by Tom Cruise. When *The Hustler* appeared, pocket billiards in the United States was suffering from a steep post–World War II decline in popularity. The film is credited with reviving interest in the game during the 1960s and 1970s (Mizerak 1990; Shamos 1995). By the mid-1980s, interest in pool had again waned. This time, *The Color of Money* and its two handsome stars stimulated a resurgence of the game, resulting in the opening of "upscale" pool rooms across the country that bear little resemblance to the dark and dissolute pool parlors of the 1920s and 1930s (Shamos 1995).

—Garry Chick

Pocket Billiards

Pocket billiards, more commonly known as pool, is played with a cue ball and up to 15 object balls. Each ball is numbered and has a distinctive color. Numbers 1 though 8 are solid-colored and numbers 9 through 15 are white with a wide stripe of a distinctive color. Pocket billiards games probably come in more variety than any of the other general game types described above (the Billiards Congress of America rules and records book lists 26, but local variations in these make the actual number much larger). Rules for each of the varieties and the popularity of the games themselves depend on regional variation and the tables in use (i.e., regulation versus coin-operated). Currently, the three most popular pocket billiards games, which are played in officially sanctioned tournaments, are straight pool, also known as 14.1 continuous; eight ball; and nine ball.

Straight Pool

In straight pool, the 15 numbered balls are grouped with a triangular plastic or wood rack, the apex of the triangular group toward the head of the table. The ball at the apex is put on the foot spot. Balls are racked at random. The balls' numbers are not important, since each is worth one point when pocketed. Players lag to determine turn, but unlike most other games, the player who wins the lag usually chooses to go second. Each match consists of a number of "blocks" agreed upon by the players. Each block consists of an agreed-upon number of points—usually 150 in tournament play. Players must "call," or designate, each shot before shooting. As long as the called ball goes into the correct pocket, all other balls pocketed (in any pocket) as a result of the shot are worth one point.

Play is initiated with the break shot. The first player may place the cue ball anywhere behind the head string and must pocket a designated ball into a called pocket. Alternatively, due to the difficulty of calling a shot on the break, the player may choose a "safe" break. For a safe break, the player must cause at least two object balls to hit a cushion. The cue ball must also hit a cushion after contacting the object balls. Failure to do either of these results in a two-point penalty. The opposing player may either play the balls as they are on the table or have them reracked and broken again by the first player. If the first player fouls on the break shot by either pocketing the cue ball ("scratching") or knocking it off the table, he or she loses a point. If the player breaking the rack fails to pocket a called ball in the intended pocket or plays safe, the turn goes to the opponent. From this point on, all shots must be called. Shots that involve a combination of balls, caroms off other

balls, or banks off the cushions are legal as long as the called ball is sunk in the designated pocket. Balls that are pocketed illegally are spotted on the long string, beginning as close as possible to the foot spot.

After the fourteenth ball is pocketed, the fifteenth ball is left on the table as the "break ball" and the remaining balls are reracked minus the ball at the foot spot apex of the triangle. The player who pocketed the fourteenth ball then continues play (hence the name 14.1 continuous). The player may attempt to call and pocket one of the racked object balls or shoot safe. Or, if the break ball is in a good position, the player may attempt to sink the break ball in a designated pocket and carom the cue ball off the break ball or a cushion into the racked balls, thus scattering them and permitting additional shots. A player's turn continues until he or she misses, fouls, or scores the requisite number of points to terminate a block.

Straight pool was the game of choice for tournament play in the United States for most of the twentieth century. Many of the legends of pocket billiards derive from "runs"—the number of balls pocketed consecutively without losing turn—that skilled straight pool players can produce. Willie Mosconi (1913–1993) holds the officially recognized run record of 526 balls, made on a 2.4-meter (8-foot) table at a 1954 exhibition. On another occasion, Mosconi pocketed 356 balls in succession on a 3.0-meter (10-foot) table in perhaps an even more impressive feat (Mizerak 1990). In tournaments, however, runs tend to be much shorter and average about 15 balls per turn, although the players are capable of much longer runs (Mizerak 1990). The reason for shorter runs is that straight pool players do not usually attempt to make difficult shots because if they miss, their opponent may well run out the table, the block, or even the match. Hence, safe play is developed to a high level in straight pool.

Nine Ball

In recent years, nine ball has supplanted straight pool as the primary tournament game (Mizerak 1990). Nine ball is played with the balls numbered 1 through 9, which are racked in a diamond shape with the 1 ball at the head of the diamond and located on the foot spot. The 9 ball must be in the center of the rack and the remaining balls may be located randomly. Nine ball is termed a "rotation" game in that the balls must be shot in consecutive numerical order. However, they need not be pocketed in numerical order. While the lowest-numbered ball on the table must be contacted first by the cue ball, any pocketed ball counts and shots need not be called. For a shot to be legal after the break, an object ball must be pocketed or the cue ball or any object ball must contact a cushion. The game is won by the player who legally pockets the 9 ball. The number of balls pocketed is not important. The break is executed by shooting the cue ball into the racked balls from anywhere behind the head string. The 1 ball must be struck first. A legal break requires that either one or more object balls be pocketed or that at least four object balls be driven to a cushion. If a player sinks one or more balls, he or she continues play. If the 9 ball is pocketed on any legal shot, including the break, the shooter wins the game. If the shooter scratches, any balls pocketed on that shot are spotted at the foot spot and the opponent may place and shoot the cue ball from anywhere on the table.

Tournament play has embraced nine ball due to its fast pace, unpredictability, spectacular shot making, and clever safety play. Since shots need not be called, there is always some element of luck involved—especially on the break. Because of this, weaker players can often defeat stronger ones. Tournaments require players to win the majority of a designated number of games, typically best of nine.

Nine ball also has the reputation of being a gambling game and for that reason has been banned in some billiards parlors and taverns from time to time. Some variants of nine ball are designed specifically with gambling in mind. For example, players may choose to wager not only on the 9 ball but also on the 5. In this game, the balls are racked in a standard diamond shape with the 1 ball on the foot spot, the 9 in the middle, and the 5 at the apex of the diamond opposite the 1 ball. Typically, half the sum wagered on the 9 is bet on the 5. The rules are otherwise the same as described above. The game ends when the 9 is pocketed, regardless of the status of the 5 ball.

Eight Ball
While straight pool is the sternest test of skill and nine ball is the current favorite in tournament play, the most popular form of pocket billiards is eight ball (Mizerak 1990). The object of eight ball is not to score points, as in straight pool, but to pocket a set of the object balls, either those numbered 1 through 7 (termed "solids" or "low") or those numbered 9 through 15 (termed "stripes" or "high"), followed by the 8 ball. For eight ball, the 15 object balls are racked in a triangular formation with the 8 ball in the center. A solid-color ball and a striped ball must occupy opposite corners at the foot of the rack. The other balls are placed at random in the group and the ball at the apex of the triangle is located on the foot spot. Players lag to determine turn. The opening player places the cue ball anywhere behind the head string and breaks the racked balls. If an object ball, either solids or stripes, is pocketed on the break, the player has the option of choosing which group to shoot and then continues to shoot at the balls in that group. (This part of the game is commonly subject to "house rules." Frequently, the player must continue to shoot balls from the same group pocketed on the break. The player may choose the group he or she wants to shoot only if one or more balls from each group is pocketed on the break.) If no ball is pocketed on the break, the next player shoots at a ball of his or her choice. If the ball is pocketed, the player must thereafter shoot balls from that group. As long as players fail to pocket an object ball, they alternate turns until a ball is legally pocketed and the assignment of balls is determined.

For a legal break, the shooter must either pocket an object ball or drive at least four balls to a cushion. If a player legally pockets a ball on the break, his or her turn continues until a foul or a missed shot occurs. If a player scratches or commits another foul, the turn is lost and any of his or her balls pocketed on that shot are spotted. If an opponent's ball is pocketed on any shot, it remains in the pocket. If the 8 ball is accidentally pocketed before a player has pocketed all of the balls in his or her designated group, the game is lost. When a player has pocketed all of his or her balls, he or she may then attempt to pocket the 8 ball and thereby win the game. The shot on the 8 ball must be called. The player legally shooting the 8 ball loses the game if (1) the 8 ball is missed and either the 8 ball or the cue ball is not driven to a cushion, (2) the 8 ball is pocketed in other than the designated pocket, (3) a scratch or other foul occurs, or (4) the cue ball strikes a ball from the opponent's group prior to hitting the 8 ball.

House rules are probably more common in eight ball than in any of the other billiards games (Mizerak 1990; see Roberts and Chick [1979] for an extensive description of a local variant of eight ball). Depending on local rules, pocketing the 8 ball on the break may win the game, lose the game, or, at the shooter's discretion, either require it to be spotted on the foot spot for continued play or have the balls reracked for a new break. Some house rules are specific to coin-operated tables such as those commonly found in bars. Since only the cue ball is returned to the table after being pocketed, rules for spotting object balls, except for when a ball is propelled off the table, are countermanded.

Outlook

Billiards in one form or another is played in nearly every country around the world. World championship tournaments are held for both amateurs and professionals in three-cushion billiards, snooker, and various pocket billiards games. In addition, women are making inroads into a game long dominated by men. National- and international-level championships have been held for women since the mid-1970s.

Billiards has often been a game on the edge of respectability. Pool rooms in the 1920s were commonly regarded, often with good reason, as dens of inequity where men congregated to loiter, smoke, fight, gamble, and play (Shamos 1995). The term *pool* has long had a negative connotation and, realizing this, the billiard industry has struggled to rid itself of the word. In 1921, the Brunswick-Balke-Collender Company, a major manufacturer of tables in America, insisted that the game be referred to only as "pocket billiards" and that the term *pool* was "meaningless and obnoxious" (Mizerak 1990, 58). In 1922, a New York law prohibited the use of the terms *pool* and *pool parlor* in public view and individuals under 18 were prohibited from entering "billiard parlors" (Mizerak 1990). However, the game is now largely stigma-free and in recent years has enjoyed a surge of popularity.

—Garry Chick

Bibliography: Billiard Congress of America. (1995) *Billiards: The Official Rules & Records Book.* Iowa City, IA: Billiard Congress of America.

Everton, Clive. (1979) *The Story of Billiards and Snooker.* London: Cassell.

Hendricks, William. (1974) *William Hendricks' History of Billiards.* Roxana, IL: William Hendricks.

Mizerak, Steve, with Michael E. Panozzo. (1990) *Steve Mizerak's Complete Book of Pool.* Chicago: Contemporary Books.

Roberts, John M., and Garry E. Chick. (1979) "Butler County Eight Ball: A Behavioral Space Analysis." In *Sports, Games, and Play: Social and Psychological Viewpoints,* edited by J. H. Goldstein. Hillsdale, NJ: Erlbaum, 65–99.

Shamos, Mike. (1995) "A Brief History of the Noble Game of Billiards." In *Billiards: The Official Rules & Records Book.* Iowa City, IA: Billiard Congress of America, 1–5.

Biodynamics

See Physical Education

Boating

See Ice Boating; Motor Boating; Sailing; Yachting

Bobsledding

The history of bobsledding as an organized and identifiable sport stretches back for over 100 years. Emerging from the alpine areas of Europe, the sport now has a regular worldwide platform as an event of the Winter Olympics. Bobsledding, despite being very expensive, requiring specific climatic conditions, and with facilities available in only a small number of countries, has an increasingly global appeal. At present over 30 different nations are affiliated with the International

Bobsledding

Bobsleigh and Tobogganing Federation (IBTF). The spectacle of two or four men traveling down a 1,600-meter (1,744-yard) course at speeds approaching 130 kilometers (78 miles) per hour, thereby suffering a centrifugal force of up to 4g's as they approach a bend, makes bobsledding in particular one of the most fascinating winter sports for participant and spectator alike. While other sports may be in decline, bobsledding is growing and increasing in popularity, especially, and in many ways surprisingly, in countries where snow is seldom, if ever, seen.

Origins

The sled and the luge were a common sight in the mountainous regions of Europe and North America throughout the nineteenth century. Developing from local transport forms, the sled and the luge had increasingly been used as part of the pursuit of leisure by visitors to mountain areas as they sought new thrills and new ways of traveling down mountainsides at great speed.

At the forefront of this search for new thrills were the British, and in 1875 a group of tourists were responsible for the invention of the Skeleton. The Skeleton took the basic form of a sled with the addition of a sliding seat that would enable the rider to travel down a slope while lying on his or her stomach. The Skeleton could be controlled by shifting the rider's weight on the seat. The Skeleton took the old sled and luge to new speeds while opening minds to the possibility of new and future forms of downhill travel that would be used primarily for sport.

The first identifiable bobsled was designed in 1886 by Wilson Smith, an Englishman. This idea was advanced by Christian Mathias, a St. Moritz, Switzerland, blacksmith. The bobsled was taking on definite form. Count Renaud de la Fregeoliere (1886–1981), who was president of the IBTF from 1923 until 1960, described the first bobsled:

A rustic plank, with at least half a dozen crude bits of wood across it, was laid over two long sledges. These pieces of wood were for the passengers feet. The front sled, mounted on a pivot, provided the steering by means of two strings. At the back, a primitive harrow acted as a brake.

In the early days those brave enough to board these early contraptions had to restrict their runs to the high frozen banks of roads in the Alpine regions. Foremost amongst these were the Swiss areas surrounding Davos, St. Moritz, Les-Avants-sur-Montreux, Leysin, Murren, and Engelberg. As the bobsled became a more frequent sight, and specific roads were used on a more regular basis, organized clubs grew up in the locality. The first of these was founded in 1896 by Lord Francis Helmsley of Britain at St. Moritz, the spiritual home of the bobsled.

The use of roads as bobsled runs was far from ideal, and the clubs began to think in terms of purpose-built runs. The first was built by the St. Moritz club in 1903. This first run was 1,600 meters (1,750 yards) long and linked le Parc Badrutt with Celerina. A second run, the Schatzalp, was built in Davos in 1907 and included 51 bends. The first national championships were held in Germany at Oberhof, also in 1907, with the winning team receiving a trophy donated by Crown Prince William of Prussia. From these beginnings bobsled clubs grew up in Germany, Romania, and France, as well as Switzerland.

With the increasing spread of bobsled as a sport across the Alpine regions of Europe and the increasing number of clubs this spread encouraged, it was decided that some attempt at standardization was required. As Count Renaud de la Fregeoliere noted:

Up until 1924 I spent nine winters in the mountains and used a dozen types of bob, wooden ones, iron ones, bobs with steering wheels, with strings, bobs from 41 or 43 centimeters or 67 centimeters wide, weighing from 30 to 250 kilograms, for two to five team members, on ten different runs. There were as many clubs as there were rules.

During the early 1920s there were international moves to organize a winter sports week recognized by the International Olympic Committee as the Winter Olympics. These first Winter Olympics were held at Chamonix in France in 1924 and played host to the first four-man bobsled event. The staging of the games were of vital importance to bobsled as a sport; the International Olympic Committee was the catalyst for the formation of the IBTF, which in turn introduced standardized

Begun by daredevil Alpine tourists, bobsledding is slowly but steadily gaining popularity; even such climatically unlikely countries as Jamaica and Venezuela have Olympic teams.

rules and regulations for bobsledding. The meeting in Chamonix on 31 January 1924, attended by six delegates from six countries, is central to the history of bobsled as it heralded the birth of a modern, regulated, and centrally organized sport. Since that time, bobsled has flourished, gaining ever more support and interest from around the world.

Practice

The basic origins of bobsledding as an organized sport are centrally important to understanding the cultural context of bobsled. Essentially bobsled emerged from the thrill-seeking Alpine tourists who were searching for a new form of amusement in the snow. This group of people was comprised primarily of those wealthy enough to spend part of the winter in places such as St. Moritz. This shows up in the background of those key figures who established bobsled clubs, who brought about the standardization of rules, and established the IBTF. The fact that Count Renaud de la Fregeoliere, Lord Francis Helmsey, and Crown Prince William of Prussia are key figures in the evolution of the sport demonstrates its origins as the pastime of the aristocratic and the wealthy. Equally the distribution of the seven founding nations of the IBTF—Austria, Belgium, Canada, France, Great Britain, Switzerland, and the United States—says much about its cultural context. These are nations with the social groups who have traditionally wintered in Alpine regions, or they are nations with a tradition of Alpine sports and access to snow, thereby able to host bobsled events. Until the Second World War the adoption of bobsled by other nations followed a similar pattern. The nations joining the IBTF were either those with traveling wealthy elites or those with snow. By 1945 only Argentina, Spain, Italy, Japan, Liechtenstein, Holland, Poland, Romania, and Czechoslovakia had been added to the list of members, and the active participation of some of these nations was at best limited.

Bobsledding as a competitive sport has been dominated by the Winter Olympics. For most spectators who enjoy the sport, the Olympics has been the only time it has entered their consciousness. Although the IBTF has held World Bobsled Championships every year since 1930, these do not reach the same global audience as the Olympics. In many ways this reliance on the Winter Olympics has stunted the growth of bobsledding by comparison to other winter sports such as skiing or ice skating, as both of these receive regular media coverage annually through their national and international championships. The more fundamental problems that have held back any wider growth of bobsledding have continued to be the high cost of participation and the limited availability of runs. By 1988 the IBTF recognized 19 official runs, only 3 of which, Calgary (Canada), Lake Placid, New York (United States), and Sapporo (Japan) were outside the European Alpine area.

The limited number of bobsled runs, which obviously restricts the chances of training for those competitors who do not have a national run, adds further to the cost of the sport. At present even a second-hand bobsled will cost up to $15,000. For these reasons the development and spread of the sport has been slowed. In the post–World War II period, the coverage of bobsled events has improved as the media coverage of the Winter Olympics has grown, and it is a highly popular event when it is screened due to the combination of speed, ice, and danger. Despite this popularity, it is not a sport that the viewer or spectator can then go out and try. Therefore the nations that have joined the IBTF and who have competed in the Winter Olympics over the last 50 years are, in the main, those nations with access to snow who have come late to the event, or those with a political agenda. Nations such as Andorra, Bulgaria, Sweden, Chinese Taipei, Venezuela, and the former Yugoslavia have joined the ranks of bobsled nations as a result of their wider cultural and sporting links with Alpine sports events. The participation of the former German Democratic Republic since 1973, the former Soviet Union since 1980, and China since 1984 has its roots in the sporting agenda of the communist nations. The competitors from these nations were usually members of the armed forces, and success was seen as the glorification of a communist regime. A quirkier spread of bobsled has taken place in the last ten years among nations supporting the Olympic movement but with no background in winter sports. This has included the involvement of Australia, Mexico, and Jamaica in recent winter games. These nations have been reliant on private

Cool Runnings

Many different sports have been used by Hollywood as the backdrop for a film. The essential elements usually include a heroic struggle against the odds, the raw excitement of the sport in question, and some deep soul searching for one of the main characters. In 1993 the film *Cool Runnings* centered on the experience of the Jamaican bobsled team and its struggle to get into, and be accepted at, the 1988 Winter Olympics in Calgary.

Cool Runnings charts the experience of a group of track-and-field athletes who failed to qualify for the Jamaican team going to the Seoul Summer Olympics. In a desperate search for Olympic glory, they discover a former U.S. bobsledder and coach living on the island who had once dreamt of taking Jamaican sprinters and transforming them into a bobsled team. Although he is a disillusioned drunk, the coach, played by the late John Candy, is convinced of the Jamaicans' desire for Olympic glory and sets about training them. Although lacking funding, official support, training facilities, and a bobsled, and with only three months to go before the start of the Games, the Jamaicans make it to Calgary. The film depicts their attempts to raise money, their first experience of winter weather, and their dogged attempts to learn how to bobsled. Despite the odds being stacked against them and opposition from the bobsledding fraternity, the Jamaicans qualify for the Olympic finals. By embracing their Jamaican identity and by sledding brilliantly in the second round, the team wins over their fellow bobsledders and the Jamaican Olympic officials and capture the world's imagination. The final run meets with disaster and the Jamaican sled crashes. From adversity however, springs success. All the conflicts in the film are resolved and the Jamaicans are heralded as the true sporting winners.

The film did much to promote bobsledding. Although based on real events, the film is largely fictional. The romance, however, was real. The Jamaicans who went to Calgary had never seen snow before; their first-ever run on ice was only days before their final qualifying run, and they really did raise their funding from such strange sources as T-shirt sales and the release of a reggae record. As Tal Stokes, the driver in 1988, noted, "Walt Disney is a business, they did a good job, they captured the spirit of the athletes involved." The film gave bobsledding a higher profile and ensured the successful continuation of Jamaican bobsledding. Some of the profits from the film were put back into the sport and the interest encouraged the Red Stripe beer company to sponsor the team. At the 1994 Winter Olympics in Albertville the Jamaicans finished fourteenth and ahead of traditional bobsled nations such as the United States, France, and Italy. This serves as a mark of Jamaican bobsledding development, their acceptance by the rest of the bobsledding world, and the fulfillment of the dreams portrayed in the film.

—Mike Cronin

funding, foreign coaches, and huge amounts of travel, as there are no domestic training facilities.

The sport of bobsledding is still dominated by those nations with a wider cultural background in winter sports. Although the sport has spread and its basic principles are understood worldwide, the bulk of competing nations are still drawn from Western and Central Europe and North America, essentially those nations responsible for the early development of the sport. The picture is much the same with respect to Olympic medals. Of the seven leading medal-winning nations to date, four—Switzerland, the United States, Italy, and Britain—can date their membership in the IBTF to within three years of its foundation. Of the other three—the German Democratic Republic, the Federal Republic of Germany and the Soviet Union—political considerations become more important than a cultural context. This said, however, the pre–World War II Germany joined the IBTF in 1926. Bobsledding should thus be seen as a sport that does, through the Winter Olympics and in terms of recently recruited nations, operate in a global context, yet has its central core support and its real roots in the original areas of its evolution.

Along with its cultural background and its current spread of support, bobsledding, from an organizational perspective, has been equally dominated by its traditional member nations. Since the foundation of the IBTF in 1923, all the rule changes and sled design alterations have been centrally controlled and agreed.

The meeting in 1923 to formulate commonly agreed standards formed the basis on which bobsled would operate as a competitive sport. In the first instance, the standard international rules were based on those used by the St. Moritz club and were aimed solely at a four-man bobsled. The four-man bobsled was abandoned in 1928 and increased to five man. This experiment only lasted for two years, and the four-man bobsled has existed ever since. The two-man bobsled competition was introduced in 1932, and with the four-man bobsled forms the basis of all bobsled competitions. Over the years the rules changed to include new technological developments and to encourage greater safety. These included the adoption of amateur status in 1927, the banning of women from competing in 1933, the introduction of maximum weight limits for bobsled teams in 1939, 1952, 1966, and 1978, and the introduction of a uniform and standard bobsled for all competitors in 1984. As the IBTF was an all powerful body that completely controlled the rules of bobsledding since the sport's earliest days, there has been a near total absence of different rules or strategies springing from local cultural or national conditions. All nations that have ever attempted to develop bobsledding as a sport in their own locality have always done so under the aegis of the IBTF. Even those nations (e.g., the United States, Romania, and Italy) that did not have the natural climatic conditions to develop a run, and thus had to turn to artificial runs, did so only after consultation with the IBTF. Likewise, in 1979 when the French Federation was seeking to encourage the growth of bobsledding by going back to the nineteenth-century idea of racing on the road, thereby avoiding the heavy cost of building a run, it did so with the full knowledge and approval of the IBTF.

The first bobsled competition at the Winter Olympics was staged in 1924. This took the form of a four-man competition. In 1932 a two-man competition was added. The format of the competition has always remained the same. Each bobsled team makes four runs down the course. The course is a chute of packed ice which twists and turns down an incline. The team with the lowest aggregate time is the winner. All internationally recognized runs are between 1,200 and 1,600 meters (1,313 and 1,750 yards) long and the journey to the finish line will be down a gradient of between 8 and 15 percent. The first section of the run lasts for 50 meters and allows team members to push the bob from the start to build up momentum before jumping in. Once in the bob, the frontman will take control and will attempt to keep the bob on the straightest course. The other members will sit as low as possible in the bob to offer the least wind resistance, thereby increasing the speed of the bob.

Since the 1950s the weight limits for both competition have been standardized. The four-man bob must not weigh in excess of 630 kilograms (1,389 pounds), and the two-man bob no more than 375 kilograms (827 pounds). By making the weights standard, the rules removed the unfair advantage that heavy teams were having over their lighter competitors. The bob itself is a sectionalized steel structure that is positioned on four blades. The front of the bob is covered with a streamlined plastic cowling, and the whole machine is steered by cables attached to the blades. In 1988 the winning bobsled team at the Winter Olympics covered the four runs over the 1,600-meter course in an aggregate time of 3 minutes, 47.51 seconds. Since the introduction of the bobsled to the Olympics, teams from Germany have won the most medals (25), followed by Switzerland (21) and the United States (14).

Outlook

Bobsledding is an excellent example of a sport that grew from a rudimentary form of travel and leisure, the sled and the luge. Its growth was initially inspired by specific climatic conditions and patronized by a wealthy elite searching for new forms of entertainment. Once it had taken a definable form, the organization, regulation, and growth of the sport was centrally controlled by a single international body that has never been challenged by other cultural practices or traditions. The sport, due to its expense and its climatic requirements has, despite some global growth, remained dominated by the original areas where the sport was taken up and by a similar class of athlete as its inventors. The only changes to this have been in the last three decades as political concerns led the former Soviet bloc nations to take to the sport by entering athletes drawn from the armed services and with the participation of some non-Alpine nations. The spectator base for bobsledding is still primarily drawn from those who have an interest in Alpine sports, but because of the thrill of the sport, the high speeds, the potential for accidents, and the romance of snow and ice, bobsledding, especially during the Winter Olympics, always attracts a large television audience.

—Mike Cronin

Bodybuilding

Bibliography: "Bobsleigh and Olympism." (1984) *Olympic Review* 206 (December): 1003–1030.

Kotter, K. (1984) "Le bobsleigh et la federation internationale de bobsleigh et de tobogganing." *Message-Olympique* (June): 59–66.

Mallon, B. (1992) "On Two Blades and a Few Prayers." *Olympian* 18, 6: 54–55.

O'Brien, A., and M. O'Bryan. (1976) *Bobsled and Luge.* Canada: Colban.

Bocce

See Bowls and Bowling

Bodybuilding

Competitive bodybuilding is an unusual sport in that the majority of the athletic component—lifting weights, the bedrock of a contestant's muscularity—is not presented but is re-presented through a display of poses. Rigorous training, a strategy for continual improvement in muscle development including size, shape, proportion and body symmetry, disciplined dieting and nutrition, posing practice, and the preparation of a choreographed posing routine are integral components of bodybuilding competition. Bodybuilding is defined as working out with weights to reshape the physique by adding muscle mass and increasing separation and definition of the various muscle groups. Bodybuilding may be contrasted with various resistance training approaches (e.g., bodyshaping, bodysculpting, and fitness training), which aim at toning muscles not at developing larger muscles.

Gyms, health clubs, and other exercise facilities are filled with men who bodybuild for a variety of motives. Of these only a small proportion actually lift weights for competitive purposes; however, women who lift weights to build larger muscles are a group unto themselves. In the majority of cases these women are either active com-

petitors or have aspirations to compete. In a study of 205 women bodybuilders registered with the International Federation of Bodybuilding (IFBB) (one of several bodybuilding organizations), 74 percent were active competitors, while many of the others were either anticipating their first competition or were temporarily sidelined due to injury (Duff and Hong 1984, 375).

Competitive bodybuilding is organized formally at both the amateur and professional levels through a number of associations, each with a bureaucracy, by-laws, agendas, membership fees, contests, promotions, and personnel consisting of judges, promoters, competitors, and fans. The soul of bodybuilding is encountered in the informal sector of the gym, where relationships with other bodybuilders articulate a subculture of bodybuilding. The ethos of the sport is expressed through rituals and symbols of belonging, identity, and meaning. A calendrical cycle based on anticipated bodybuilding competitions, which cluster in the spring and summer months, charges the atmosphere of the gym and thickens the subcultural rituals. The competitions themselves are ceremonial markers that coalesce the populations of competitive bodybuilders. The subculture of bodybuilding is experienced and expressed in the mundane of day-to-day training and its sacred and ritual aspects.

The traditions of competitive bodybuilding summon elements from its origins in the early twentieth century, which have become intertwined with the post-modern era. Bodybuilding, like other sports, has endorsed the new age in multiple ways, incorporating the most recent technologies for diet, nutrition, and training. Yet bodybuilding, which centers on the body, occupies a somewhat liminal position in an age that privileges the mental over the physical. Historically, bodybuilding for men has been associated with the working classes and blue-collar professions where physical efficacy is viable as a component of work, thus perpetuating a mind-body dichotomy and class distinction. Today's bodybuilders, however, cross-cut all the professions. The influx of white-collar men entering the subculture began in the 1980s (Klein 1993, 186).

Bodybuilding incorporates central themes of Euro-American society, including a focus on individuality (it is not a team sport), the protestant work ethic, and the spirit of capitalism. The

Most bodybuilders focus on conditioning rather than competition. Traditionally bodybuilding has been associated with masculinity, but the recent entry of women into the sport has provided an alternative focus.

philosophies of bodybuilding have paid and continue to pay homage to "superior" genetics, but the adage "work hard and you will succeed" is more important for achievement in the sport. Bodybuilding endorses the priority of "hard work" over good genetics by valuing consistent and serious training. Genetic predisposition without an achievement orientation and systematic training are meaningless.

Bodybuilding from its inception has also represented masculinity. The male bodybuilder is engaged in a sport that exaggerates Western notions of gender difference—muscles denoting masculinity and signifying "biological" disparity between the genders.

Competitive women's bodybuilding has a different cultural venue, however. The female bodybuilder is in a position to contribute to the ongoing wider social redefinition of womanhood and femininity. This redefinition challenges the

ideology of the gender dichotomy in which muscularity embodies power and privilege as the "natural" purview of men.

Origins and Development

Aside from its derivation from the ancient Greek and Roman emphasis on physiques and athletics, the roots of American physical culture descended from mid-nineteenth-century health reform movements with their emphasis on exercise (Bolin 1992, 84). In 1893, Eugene Sandow stepped onto the American stage of a growing physical culture movement and gave impetus to it. Modern bodybuilding can be traced to this strongman and physique showman who sustained great public appeal for Europeans and Americans alike (Todd 1991, 4). He represented a new ideal of muscular manhood whose ground had been cleared not only by health reform but also by the muscular Christianity movement beginning in the mid-nineteenth century in England and the United States. Strength and stoicism replaced passivity and turning the other cheek in a cultural form that linked athleticism and religion. According to author David Chapman,

> [m]any mid-Victorian religious men had been alarmed at the encouragement of "feminine" virtues in the church. . . . What was needed was a more active role for robust members of the community. Many men of the cloth strove to become more physical and aggressive. . . . Aggression and strength were man's portion. . . . (1994, 112)

By the end of the nineteenth century a cult of manliness was embraced through exercise, athletics, and weight training, and Sandow became an international icon of this new masculinity. In the United States, this dovetailed with other early twentieth-century cultural trends such as the association of strenuousness/exercise with the moral order à la Roosevelt (Rader 1990, 125).

In the context of the late nineteenth century when Sandow entered the scene, these trends can be linked to an emerging middle class and increasing urbanism in the United States (Klein 1992, 35). As the population became more sedentary, the concern for public health began to escalate and was manifested by the portrayal of athletic and healthy images in the popular media. Masculinity became idealized in a somatotype that harked back to the Greeks, replacing the prevalent masculine models of the thin, wan intellectual and the corpulent businessman of the 1800s (Banner 1983, 227, 231, 286; Chapman 1990, 127, 191). For women, the Gibson Girl dominated the scene from the late 1800s to World War I. "The Gibson Girl was a healthy, strong, athletic, albeit corsetted ideal" (Bolin 1992a, 85).

Eugene Sandow rode the wave of the strongman era that infused subsequent U.S. and Western European interests in fitness and health. By the time Prussian-born Sandow had met his tutor, former strongman Professor Attila while in Brussels, an industry had developed supporting the Euro-American social theme and trend of physical culture. This included the invention of resistance training machines, the use of various types of weights, and the widespread availability of training/exercise programs. Attila, who had his own school of physical culture, guided Sandow in adding muscle mass to his already beautifully proportioned physique through his theory of progressive resistance training (systematically increasing the amount of weight lifted). At this time, musclemen, strongmen, and other athletes presented their "acts" in music halls and theaters. Consequently, charisma and stage skills were a prerequisite for success in the business. Attila schooled Sandow in these techniques, and he became a consummate performer (Chapman 1994, 8–10).

Having already gained British acclaim, Sandow was introduced to the American public at the Chicago World's Fair in 1893 (Chapman 1994, 59–60; Rader 1990, 127). He soon became the masculine ideal for American men. Upon his return to England, Sandow built on his reputation and brokered it into a prosperous career in physical culture. Not only did he make a living through displays of his strength and physique, but he also built a thriving business that included mail-order training programs, equipment he invented, and athletic studios. In addition, he capitalized on the health and clinical aspects of weightlifting. He transformed the concept of the gymnasium into a posh health facility, targeted the health needs of women, promoted women's exercise programs challenging dominant notions of femininity at the time, and denounced the corset. He is credited with publishing one of the first bodybuilding magazines *Physical Culture* in 1898 (changed to *Sandow's Physical Culture* in 1899). King George V of England honored him with the title Professor of Scientific and Physical Culture to the King (Chapman 1994, 70–129, 175).

Sandow had a profound influence on U.S. physical culture entrepreneurs such as his contemporary Bernarr MacFadden. MacFadden similarly deployed physical culture into a successful business with a series of magazines initiated with *Physical Development* in 1898, and with books, promotions of strength and physique exhibitions, healthatoriums, and home exercise equipment and programs (Chapman 1994, 175; Todd 1991, 4). Perhaps MacFadden's greatest contribution to contemporary bodybuilding was his sponsorship of the first major U.S. bodybuilding contest in 1903. This contest was unprecedented because the physique competition was the focus of the show, with the athletic feats and strength displays relegated to a supporting position. MacFadden's 1903 competition followed on the heels of the world's first major bodybuilding contest held in Britain in 1901 by Sandow. Undoubtedly Sandow's "Great Competition," as it was called, served as a model for MacFadden's contest for the "most perfect specimen of physical manhood."

Following Sandow's lead, MacFadden's contest was prefaced by a series of local and regional contests that qualified competitors for the final tournament to select the most perfect man in the United States. MacFadden emulated Sandow's judging criteria, which sounded remarkably modern and included general muscular development, symmetry, muscle tone, overall health, and appearance of the skin. Balanced muscular development took priority over simply having the biggest muscles (Chapman 1994, 129–135). MacFadden's contest became an annual event. This same contest hosted what is possibly the world's first women's bodybuilding contest, the Women's Physical Culture Competition (Todd 1991, 3).

MacFadden's 1921 physique contest spawned one of the best-known U.S. bodybuilders, Angelo Siciliano, who later changed his name to Charles Atlas and claimed the title of the Most Perfectly Developed Man in America (Klein 1993, 36; Schwarzenegger 1985, 36). Atlas perpetuated the ideal of a muscular masculinity through his mail-order courses on physical development. He embodied the industrial self-made man, who, through hard work (i.e., Atlas's program of exercise), could overcome hardship (i.e., being weak).

All of these early physique men, who combined strength and beauty, impacted American images and standards of masculinity by providing a trajectory for the idealization of mesomorphic masculinity (Mishkind et al. 1987, 41). While these physique competitions (such as MacFadden's) placed bodybuilding in center stage, athletic demonstrations and strength feats still dominated the public imagination. Well into the 1920s and 1930s, strength and athletic performances continued to be the focus of competitions, with the physique component relegated to sideshow status. The public admired the mesomorphic ideal of muscular beauty *along with* strength.

In the 1930s, physique contests began to gain in popularity. Charles Atlas may have prodded

the subsequent growth of physique contests during the latter part of the decade (Gaines and Butler 1974, 130–131). The Amateur Athletic Union (AAU) inaugurated its first Mr. America Contest in 1939. Other national contests followed, facilitating the promotion of local and regional bodybuilding contests as qualifying events, thereby boosting the sport economically and socially. While strength competitions continued to thrive, physique competitions attracted their own kind of disciple.

Joe Weider, along with his brother Ben, is regarded as a driving force in the modern history of bodybuilding and remains a major promoter of bodybuilding as a sport and way of life in the 1990s. He got his business start in 1940 with a newsletter, *Your Physique.* Like his predecessors, he was a former competitive bodybuilder whose entrepreneurial interests exceeded his competitive ones. In 1946, Joe and his brother founded the International Federation of Bodybuilding (IFBB), which today is the sixth largest sports federation in the world with 134 member countries. Their goal was to make bodybuilding into a bona fide sport. (They continue a longstanding effort to win International Olympic Committee recognition of bodybuilding as a sport, although the subjectivity in judging still remains problematic.) At that time bodybuilding was still an afterthought, an exhibition that was tacked on after weightlifting competitions (Klein 1993, 97, 37). Bodybuilding made the jump from exhibition to competition by the latter part of the 1940s.

The distinction between training for strength and power and training for bodybuilding was beginning to be made (Hilsen 1991, 19; Schwarzenegger 1985, 40–45). This is not to suggest that strength is not a core cultural feature of the bodybuilding experience, but that training for a bodybuilding contest requires a very different strategy (see below). The physique competition was gaining in popularity in terms of its own unique enterprise.

The era of bodybuilding spanning the 1940s and 1950s continued to incorporate the health concerns of the physical culture movement and to provide opportunities for physique competitors through contests such as Mr. America and Mr. Universe. Steve Reeves became a public figure in bodybuilding via his subsequent career in Hollywood's Hercules movies. Bodybuilding developed as its own distinct genre of competition that would eventually become a mega business as consumer culture and capitalism expanded in the late twentieth century.

In the 1960s, bodybuilding included a number of amateur and professional contests at the national and international levels in the United States as well as Europe. European bodybuilding was dominated by the Mr. Universe competition. In 1965, the Mr. Olympia bodybuilding championship was created by the IFBB. By the 1990s it would become the highest award possible in international bodybuilding competition. The 1960s can be regarded as the beginning of the Arnold Schwarzenegger era in the United States. After winning many international contests in Europe, Arnold, at the invitation of Joe Weider, came to America to become a "big star" in bodybuilding and in Hollywood. California became the national mecca of professional bodybuilding at the time, and it still remains so (although Venice Beach as a cultural center for bodybuilders has been around since the early days, circa 1939) (Klein 1993, 37). In the 1970s, Gold's Gym dominated professional bodybuilding and situated a subculture of training and competition. A majority of the big names in bodybuilding of this era trained there, including Arnold Schwarzenegger, Franco Columbo, Frank Zane, Dave Draper, and Ken Waller (Gaines and Butler 1974, 24).

The 1970s were punctuated by the publication of Charles Gaines and George Butler's book *Pumping Iron* (1974), followed by the movie of the same name, which helped popularize the sport and gain it greater national recognition (Todd 1995, 17). They educated the public by providing a backstage glimpse of the sport and its key players and places. Bodybuilding was becoming more competitive and the standards of perfection demanded greater expertise in the knowledge of dieting, nutrition, and training.

Through the 1980s and 1990s, bodybuilding has continued to grow as a big business. The competitors have achieved, over the course of time, degrees of muscularity, proportion, and leanness not thought humanly possible.

The transition from the remnants of physical culture occurred during the 1960s and 1970s, when bodybuilding really exploded into an industry. Factors affecting bodybuilding's economic expansion include a general growth in the fitness industry in the 1970s and the aging of the large babyboom population, who wanted to stay in shape (Klein 1993, 41). Arthur Jones invented his Nautilus equipment and began manufacturing it in 1970 (Darden 1982, 8), and Gold's Gym evolved from a one-owner gym into a franchise, along with World Gym (Douglas 1990, 10).

The old days of bodybuilding's barbell clubs were challenged by this general growth in the fitness industry. Health spa and fitness clubs came to replace the older barbell clubs dominated by free weights. By the 1980s, bodybuilding had been reborn. The professional bodybuilders and the gyms they trained in were transformed into elite clubs with a variety of resistance machines along with aerobic classes, stair climbers, stationary bikes, tanning beds, computerized diets, and personal trainers. Professional bodybuilders had the opportunity to earn money through personal training, endorsements of fitness commodities, guest performances, and seminars. Health clubs expanded and became co-ed during this time. The popularization of bodybuilding ultimately converged health spas with the development of elite gyms and led to the decline, but not disappearance, of barbell clubs and hardcore gyms. The elite gyms are often expansive facilities catering to the public at large as well as providing a setting for the professional, but these elite centers have lost some of the sense of camaraderie and family forged by the subculture of bodybuilding in its earlier days (Klein 1993, 73). By the end of the 1980s the single-owner, hardcore gyms were on the verge of extinction as a cultural species, although outcroppings of these gyms still remain at the local level of competition in various parts of the United States.

Several factors have contributed to the transformation of the physical culture phenomenon into contemporary bodybuilding. One factor was the introduction of anabolic steroids in the late 1950s. Athletes and their coaches in a variety of sports from the national to the Olympic level experimented with the drugs to enhance athletic performance. Another factor was the changing face of the nation: technology continued to advance, sports became a scientific endeavor (which propelled the research into anabolic steroids to begin with), and sports grew into industries, as capitalism and consumerism also expanded. These trends were expressed through a focus on competition and winning rather than on sport participation. These factors shifted physical culture, with its concern for health, into today's arena where athletes risk penalties, legal reprisal, and imprisonment to win by ingesting anabolic steroids. (The use of anabolic steroids in sports is a socio-cultural problem embedded in a society where winning at all costs has emerged as a central value.)

Women and Bodybuilding

Women's bodybuilding has a shorter history than men's, as well as its own trajectories. Although modern bodybuilding competitions for women began in 1975, antecedents can be found in the physique exhibitions of the music halls of an earlier era. Health reform in the mid-nineteenth century conjoined with early feminism touted the innovative idea that exercise was healthful for women and that women's muscles could be beautiful. This flew in the face of the dominant view of middle-class femininity as frail and ethereal, which continued through the turn of the century (Bolin 1992a, 83–84). In fact, even today female bodybuilders continue to wage the war against societal standards of femininity.

Eugene Sandow began to incorporate women into his physical culture enterprises very early in the twentieth century. Although strongwomen such as Sandwina (whose name was modeled on Sandow) continued to perform feats of strength in music halls and circuses, Sandow wanted to normalize and democratize female strength and exercise, as well as to continue to promote physical culture as curative. Bernarr MacFadden also saw an opportunity to expand his market. In the second issue of his *Physical Culture* the first articles on women appeared (Todd 1991, 5). MacFadden argued strenuously for the health and beauty benefits of exercise and muscle development for women. In 1900, he founded the first women's physique magazine, *Women's Physical Development* (changed in 1903 to *Beauty and Health: Women's Physical Development*).

According to Jan Todd (1991), MacFadden may be counted as one of the first to promote the ancestor of modern women's bodybuilding contests. From 1903 to 1905, MacFadden staged a series of local and regional physique competitions culminating in a grand competition with a prize for the "best and most perfectly formed woman" (Todd 1991, 3, 6). His financial success in the physical culture business for women may have paradoxically placed the development of women's physical culture back in the closet for some time. In 1905, he hosted the Madison Square Garden Mammoth Physical Culture Exhibition, which included the finale of MacFadden's women's competition. Shortly before the competition was to take place, Anthony Comstock of the Society for the Suppression of Vice, had MacFadden's offices raided for the spreading of pornography. The offensive items were posters of the finalists of the women's physique competition, who were dressed in white formfitting, leotard-like exercise wear, along with a photo of one of the men's winners in a leopard-skin loincloth and other items (Todd 1991, 3–8). MacFadden was arrested and found guilty of dissemination of pornography, although the trial's publicity served to promote his physique extravaganza even more (the exhibition boasted 20,000 spectators; an additional 5,000 had to be turned away [Todd 1991, 3]). Nevertheless, as a result of his litigation, MacFadden ceased all publication and promotion of women's physiques. Thus, just as MacFadden had been an impetus in women's physique development, his withdrawal and the public awareness of the outcome of his court case, seriously impeded the development of women's participation in physical culture exhibitions and competitions (Derwald and Derwald 1991, 44, 45, 95). The history of women's physique exhibitions continued to be relegated to sideshow strength performances through the early decades of the 1900s of women like Sandwina, who displayed her strong and beautiful figure at the Barnum and Bailey Circus in 1910. Although women's strength performances embodied some elements of modern bodybuilding in that their well-developed physiques were part of their acts, these strength demonstrations may just as easily be claimed by the related weight training sports of Olympic weightlifting and powerlifting.

Weight training for female athletes was introduced in the 1950s, and women's competitive bodybuilding emerged as a sport about 20 years later. Competitions began in 1975 just prior to the first competitive powerlifting contests for women in 1977 (Holloway et al. 1989, 43–49). The social movements for gender equality in the

Bodybuilding

1960s were a major influence in bringing women into the sports arena. Feminism, subsequently buttressed by the passing of Title IX (which prohibited sex discrimination in education policy) in 1972, provided an added impetus for women to participate in athletics of all kinds. Women's bodybuilding found a home in the hardcore gyms where men trained, and it moved, along with male bodybuilding, from these gyms into scientific and contemporary pavillions of nutrition and training, which opened their doors to the public and became part of the modern fitness industry of the 1980s. The first Miss (now Ms.) Olympia was held in 1980, establishing the zenith of women's international titles.

The sport of women's bodybuilding evolved dramatically from its inception in the late 1970s, when women wore high heels and the bodybuilding contests were not much more than beauty pageants (Douglas 1990, 9). It was not until the 1980s that women's bodybuilding contests were recognized as bona fide events in their own right, not just as sideshows for male competitions.

Practice

The question of whether bodybuilding is a sport continues to be debated among sports researchers and within organizations. For example, bodybuilding is yet to be considered an Olympic sport, despite lobbying efforts of its promoters. The generally accepted definitional criteria among researchers for an activity to qualify as a sport are (1) physical activity, (2) a competitive element, and (3) organizational support. The detractors of the bodybuilding-as-sport position, claim physical exertion does not actually occur in the competition itself, which is limited to posing displays of muscularity. Those who support the view that bodybuilding is a sport maintain that posing and presenting choreographed routines is indeed a physically demanding and gruelling activity.

Bodybuilding was born in hardcore gyms (the term *hardcore* is usually used in reference to gyms where weightlifting is marked by intensity, commitment, and seriousness), and, at the amateur level, hardcore gyms are still the site of choice for competition training. They provide an atmosphere that cannot be replicated in the social milieu of the modern health club. As much as *hardcore* describes a form of training, it also de-

notes a particular kind of sociocultural and physical ambiance. A hardcore gym offers a number of advantages for the competitively inclined, including the presence of mentors—former competitors and active competitors—to help the novice bodybuilder learn all aspects of the sport as well as a pool of other serious lifters from which to find a training partner. There is camaraderie in such gyms, but also subcultural rules of respect and the sanctity of training, which discourage unnecessary interruption and distraction from workouts. There is a no-nonsense atmosphere, embellished with pictures of professional bodybuilders and local competitors.

Although there is undoubtedly variation in these features of hardcore gym subculture, there are cultural patterns that have a national continuity spanning amateur and professional interests. A particular kind of clothing has come to be associated with hardcore bodybuilding: tank tops, tee shirts, sweatshirts, sweatpants, and "baggies" designed for the workouts. Bodybuilding attire testifies to the subcultural value of training as a priority; it is functional, comfortable, and allows movement.

Preparation for bodybuilding contests may be divided into a contest phase and an off-season phase. While competitive bodybuilders train toward their competitions throughout the entire year, their training and diet vary as their selected contest draws nearer. Off-season preparation is characterized by rigorous, systematic, and regular training in order to acquire as much muscle as possible. Several months before a competition the athletes' training may be altered. There appears to be generalized agreement that one will not attain much, if any, muscle growth in the several months just prior to a contest. This is, in part, a result of the altering of the diet, which affects energy levels and, consequently, how much weight an athlete can lift. Although there is a great deal of variation in pre-contest training, there generally is a move to lighter weights and more repetitions, and super sets (two exercises performed back-to-back without rest in between) are usually incorporated in the training. Simultaneously bodybuilders tend to add or increase aerobic activity in their workouts in order to acquire the necessary leanness.

Contestants usually begin their contest diet two to four months "out" from (before) a competition, or even earlier depending on their metabolism. A number of dietary strategies are available. Bodybuilding is one of only a few sports where a rigorous diet is such a central feature in training and preparing for a contest. Participants have estimated that diet is 90 to 98 percent of pre-contest preparation. Since success for the competitor demands a lean body coupled with significant muscle mass in a symmetrical form, fat is considered the somatic enemy of the competitive physique; diet, training with weights, and aerobic activity compose the antidote.

For bodybuilders diet has a unique definition. It does not necessarily include drastic reduction of calories but rather entails modifying the relative proportion of carbohydrates, protein, and fats in the calories consumed. Quality calories and good nutrition are necessary in order to train intensively and to spare muscle while losing fat. A bodybuilder's diet typically consists of five to seven small meals a day. It has been recommended in bodybuilding literature and in subcultural discourse that no more than 10 to 20 percent of the diet should be composed of fats. The ultimate goal of the competitive diet is to reduce body fat to a very low percentage, preferably 7 percent or lower for men (Kennedy 1983, 60) and 10 to 12 percent or lower for women (McLish 1984, 171). The ultimate assessment of body fat is visual, which is apparent in the subcultural saying of "let the mirror be your guide."

This precontest preparation phase may be characterized as a sacred period in the competitors' lives. In the local gym there is an overall expectation that they may be tired and irritable from the diet and training. Their colleagues and mentors offer support and encouragement.

For the day of the competition, bodybuilders strive to have a physique that has "peaked"—one that has achieved its potential in terms of maximum leanness, muscularity, vascularity, striations, and skin thinness and tautness. Fluids under the skin can obscure the muscles and can be avoided through the manipulation of diet. A peak may be missed, sometimes by a few hours or several weeks, because the diet strategy did not work or it was not followed closely enough.

At the local, state, and national levels, competitions usually consist of two segments: (1) the morning, or pre-judging, portion in which the majority of the judging decisions are made and (2) the evening contest or show, in which the finalists and winners are announced and awarded. A judges meeting will occur prior to the competition in the morning contest. It is here that the judges discuss guidelines and criteria for judging that are endorsed by the sponsoring national organization.

The day of the competition includes a back stage "pumping up" through exercise and lifting light weights, wherein blood is brought to the surface resulting in vascularity and muscle fullness. Sometimes a training partner is allowed backstage to help in this process. The competitor's body is stained with a temporary tanning agent, and posing oil is applied to give shine and enhance the visibility of the muscle. Sometimes an oil that causes the skin to feel hot and appear vascular may also be used.

The competitors are stripped of all identifying attributes in the contest. Both males and females wear competition posing suits identified only by a number, and they are prohibited jewelry except wedding bands. During the morning judging the competitors are ranked for each class—usually by weight at the amateur level—and the winners are selected but not announced. After the pre-judging, the competitors rest the remainder of the day in preparation for the evening contest when they will pump up again and present a posing routine to music. In the evening show the winners of each class are given trophies, usually through third place, and the first place winners from each class compete for an overall trophy. The contest culminates with an overall men's and women's winner.

Judging occurs as the competitors display their physiques through mandatory poses and the presentation of a short choreographed routine set to music. The somatic standard of excellence for bodybuilders can be configured as an "X." The lower portion of the "X" signifies the ideal of large flaring thighs, with a thin waist and wide shoulders and back (latissimus dorsi). Contestants are evaluated in terms of their symmetry or proportions, muscular development, vascularity, skin tightness and tone, leanness, muscle fullness, muscle shape, and the overall configuration of their physiques.

While in nonprofessional competitions weight classes dominate, height classes are used by some organizations. Other additional classes include novice classes, teen classes, and masters classes

Bodybuilding

that may be further subdivided by age. In the professional competitions, there are no class divisions. Professionals in the International Federation of Bodybuilders (IFBB) contests are typically judged in three rounds based on symmetry, muscularity, and posing ability, including the choreographed routine. The latter is not a factor in amateur contests.

The pre-judging contest begins with a symmetry round. In this round the bodybuilders must stand feet together facing the judges, semi-flexed but looking relaxed. By taking quarter turns to the right the competitors present the judges with a left side view, a back view, and a right side view. Generally this is followed by a short posing routine, less than one minute in length, without music. Subsequently, the competitors are brought out in a line and requested to do a series of mandatory poses that usually include a front double biceps pose, a side chest pose, a triceps pose, a rear deltoid pose, a rear "lat" (latissimus dorsi) pose, a calf pose, a "most muscular" pose, and sometimes a front "lat" pose and an abdominal/leg pose. These poses may vary depending on the sponsoring organization. In the evening, the competitors, depending on their placing, will have an opportunity to present their choreographed routine. After presentations of the routines, each class of competitors will engage in a posedown. Hard rock-and-roll music is usually played and the audience cheers on their favorite contenders, who engage in a drama of comparison. Men and women in their classes move around the stage and may stand next to an arch competitor in a symbolic duel of muscles and body parts.

Contemporary bodybuilding owes its modern form to the Weider brothers. Joe Weider is the driving force behind the National Physique Committee, which organizes amateur and professional bodybuilding on the local, state, regional, and national levels. For a number of years, the only other organization for competitive bodybuilders was the Amateur Athletic Union; however, a number of "natural" contests and bodybuilding organizations (those that drug test, using polygraph and/or urine testing methods) began emerging in the late 1980s. This burgeoning of natural organizations has occurred in part as a result of a generalized increase in public awareness of anabolic steroid use among athletes.

Natural organizations include the World Natural Bodybuilding Federation (WNBF), which sponsors professional bodybuilding and the National Gym Association (NGA), a WNBF-affiliated amateur organization.

The use of anabolic steroids among competitive bodybuilders is cause for concern. Anabolic steroids first became available for medical treatment in the 1940s. By the 1950s, athletes in many different sports began using them as legal performance enhancers. Eventually they were banned, but their use continued. Throughout the 1980s there was a public outcry against the use of these substances. Concern centered on the unfair advantage anabolic steroids gave athletes in national and international sports events as well as on the health risks posed. As a result, widespread drug testing became routine in many professional sports, including some bodybuilding organizations and within the Olympics. The recent growth of "natural" (drug-free) bodybuilding organizations and their increasing popularity is a positive sign for the sport.

Steroid use also inflamed the already-existing debate over what constitutes femininity, as some female bodybuilders were using the drugs to increase their muscle mass too. Demand for muscularity has challenged an essential dichotomy in the Western paradigm of gender wherein femininity is somatically associated with curvaceousness and softness, while masculinity is associated with muscularity and hardness. The competitive woman's muscular morphology contests this formula as it must in order to meet judging criteria that demands striated visible muscles.

While bodybuilding as a sport symbolically sustains traditional images of masculinity as associated with strength and power, the addition of competitive women's bodybuilding diminishes gender differences. This occurs not only through the muscularity of the competitive women bodybuilders, but also in the subculture of bodybuilding itself. In the less public sphere of the gym, however, serious athletes are serious athletes regardless of gender and are treated equally.

—Anne Bolin

Bibliography: Banner, Lois. (1983) *American Beauty.* Chicago: University of Chicago Press.

Boff, Vic. (1990) "The President's Message." *Iron Game History* 1, 1: 12–13.

Bolin, Anne. (1992a) "Vandalized Vanity: Feminine Physiques Betrayed and Portrayed." In *Tatoo, Torture, Adornment and Disfigurement: The Denaturalization of the Body in Culture and Text,* edited by F. Mascia-Lees. Albany: State University of New York Press, 79–90.

———. (1992b) "Flex Appeal, Food and Fat: Competitive Bodybuilding, Gender and Diet." *Play and Culture* 5, 4: 378–400. Reprinted in *Building Bodies* (1996), edited by P. Moore. New Brunswick, NJ: Rutgers University Press.

———. (Forthcoming) "Beauty or the Beast: The Subversive Soma." In *Athletic Intruders: Women, Culture and Sport,* edited by A. Bolin and J. Granskog. Albany: State University of New York Press.

Chapman, David L. (1994) *Sandow the Magnificent: Eugene Sandow and the Beginnings of Bodybuilding.* Urbana: University of Illinois Press.

Cohn, Nik. (1981) *Women of Iron.* Wideview Books.

Darden, Ellington. (1982) *The Nautilus Bodybuilding Book.* Chicago: Contemporary Books.

Del Rey, Pat. (1977) "Apologetics and Androgyny: The Past and the Future." *Frontiers* 3: 8–10.

———. (1978) "The Apologetic and Women in Sport." In *Women and Sport: From Myth to Reality,* edited by C. A. Oglesby. Philadelphia: Lea and Febiger, 107–111.

Derwald, Richard, and Kathy Derwald. (1990) "The Night Women's Bodybuilding Died." *Natural Physique* 4, 3: 44–45, 95.

Douglas, S. (1990) "Muscle Go Round." *Muscle Magazine International* 95: 9–13.

Duff, Robert W., and Lawrence K. Hong. (1984) "Self Images of Women Bodybuilders." *Sociology of Sport Journal* 1: 374–380.

Duquin, Mary E. (1982) "The Importance of Sport in Building Women's Potential." *Journal of Physical Education, Recreation, and Dance* 53: 18–20, 36.

Gaines, Charles, and George Butler. (1974) *Pumping Iron.* New York, NY: Simon and Schuster.

———. (1983) "Iron Sisters." *Psychology Today* 17: 65–69.

Guttman, Allen. (1991) *Women's Sports: A History.* New York, NY: Columbia University Press.

Hart, M. (1976) "Stigma or Prestige: The All American Choice." In *Sport in the Sociological Process,* edited by M. Hart. Dubuque, IA: William C. Brown, 176–182.

Hilsen, Herbert. (1991) "Letter to the Editor." *Iron Game History* 1, 4/5: 19–20.

Holloway, Jean Barrett, Denise Gater, Meg Ritchie, et al. (1994) "Strength Training for Female Athletes: A Position Paper: Part I." *National Strength and Conditioning Association Journal* 11, 4: 43–55.

Klein, Alan. (1986) "Pumping Irony: Crisis and Contradiction in Bodybuilding." *Sociology of Sport Journal* 3, 2: 112–133.

———. (1993) *Little Big Men: Gender Construction and Bodybuilding Subculture.* Albany: State University of New York Press.

McLish, Rachel. (1984) *Flex Appeal.* New York, NY: Warner Books.

Messner, Michael A. (1993) "Theorizing Gendered Bodies: Beyond the Subject/Object Dichotomy." In *Exercising Power: The Making and Remaking of the Body,* edited by Cheryl Cole, John Loy, and Michael Messner. Albany: State University of New York Press.

Mishkind, Marc E., Judith Rodin, Lisa Silberstein, and Ruth Striegel-Moore. (1987) "The Embodiment of Masculinity: Cultural, Psychological and Behavioral Dimensions." In *Changing Men: New Directions in Research on Men and Masculinity,* edited by Michael S. Kimmel. Newbury Park, CA: Sage Publications, 37–52.

Rader, Benjamin G. (1990) *American Sports: From the Age of Folk Games to the Age of Televised Sports.* Englewood Cliffs, NJ: Prentice-Hall.

Sabo, Don. (1985) "Sport, Patriarchy, and Male Identity: New Questions about Men and Sport." *Arena Review* 9, 2: 1–30.

Schwarzenegger, Arnold. (1985) *Encyclopedia of Modern Bodybuilding.* New York: Simon and Schuster.

Snyder, E., and S. Kivlin. (1975) "Women Athletes and Aspects of Psychological Well-Being and Body Imagery." *Research Quarterly* 46: 191–199.

Snyder, E., and E. Spreitzer. (1976) "Correlates of Sport Participation among Adolescent Girls." *Research Quarterly* 47: 804–809.

Snyder, Eldon, and Elmer Spreitzer. (1978) *Social Aspects of Sport.* Englewood Cliffs, NJ: Prentice-Hall.

Todd, Jan. (1991) "Bernarr MacFadden: Reformer of Feminine Form." *Iron Game History* 1, 4/5: 3–8.

Todd, Terry. (1995) "Mac and Jan." *Iron Game History* 3, 6: 17–19.

Vertinsky, Patricia. (1990) *The Eternally Wounded Woman: Women, Doctors and Exercise in the Late Nineteenth Century.* Manchester: Manchester University Press.

Weider, Betty, and Joe Weider. (1981) *The Weider Book of Bodybuilding for Women.* Chicago: Contemporary Books.

Boomerang Throwing

While the boomerang has existed for nearly 15,000 years in Australia, boomerang throwing as an organized sport began in the 1970s in Australia and the United States. A national fellowship of throwers in Australia formed the Boomerang Association of Australia in 1970. In the United States, the boomerang movement was triggered in part by a milestone article on boomerangs in a 1968 issue of *Scientific American* and was nurtured by the Smithsonian Institution, which sponsored yearly educational workshops on the making and throwing of boomerangs. The United States Boomerang Association was formed in 1981. Now the sport is practiced

The boomerang is believed to be about 15,000 years old, but boomerang throwing as an organized sport is a twentieth-century phenomenon. Boomerangs are popularly associated with Australia, but they were probably known in many parts of the world.

worldwide, with International Team Cup Challenges and World Team and Individual championships held every two years.

Origins

The specific origins of the boomerang are lost in time. While traditionally thought of as an Australian artifact, boomerangs and their cousins, nonreturning throw sticks, have been discovered throughout the world. The oldest wooden boomerangs are from Wyrie Swamp in South Australia. They were discovered by archaeologist Roger Luebbers in 1974 and appear to be 8,000 to 10,000 years old. Depictions of boomerangs also appear in Arnhem Land rock paintings believed to be more than 15,000 years old. With no written history, the Australian Aborigines relied on stories to pass information from generation to generation. Thus, most accounts of the origin of the

returning boomerang are anecdotal. Whether created by accident or design, the lifting forces that cause a boomerang to return also cause it to swoop high in the air when thrown sidearm, making it an efficient weapon for birding. The nonreturning, low-flying throw stick was used for hunting ground game.

Recent research has stunned the boomerang world with discoveries that the oldest boomerang might not be Australian. A boomerang made from a mammoth's tusk was discovered in southern Poland in 1987 and has been dated at 23,000 years old. A replica reportedly returned when thrown. Egyptian throw sticks and returning boomerangs were discovered in King Tutankhamun's tomb (1350 B.C.E.) in 1927 by Howard Carter. In his book, *The Boomerangs of a Pharaoh*, Jacques Thomas recounts his studies of these Egyptian artworks, concluding that several of them are indeed returning boomerangs. In prehistoric times, the throw stick and returning boomerang were apparently known in many parts of the world.

Competition

Surprisingly, it is not Australia but the United States that has dominated international competition since its outset. In November 1981, a U.S. team of 10 boomerang throwers went to Australia to challenge the Australians at their native sport. It was the first such international competition in history. To the surprise of many, the Americans came away victors by sweeping the three-test series. The Australians came to the United States in 1984 and evened the score, winning the Lands' End Boomerang Cup.

While Australia has had its share of "world champions" dating back to the 1940s, the first Individual World Championship featuring an international cast of competitors was held in Paris, France, in 1985. The United States sent a four-man team, with Chet Snouffer (1956–) emerging as champion ahead of teammate Eric Darnell (1946–). A promotional tour of the beach resorts of France ensued, introducing thousands of the French to the sport.

International Team Championships began in 1987, with five U.S. teams and two European teams competing in the United States. In May 1988 a three-man World Cup Team from the United States won the Australian Bicentennial Boomerang Cup. In August 1988 the United States won the second International Team Championships in France, Germany, and Switzerland. Ensuing international team events have been held in Washington, D.C. (1989); Perth, Australia (1991); Hamburg, Germany (1992); and Tokyo, Japan (1994). The United States has won each of these team events. In addition, four of six Individual world champions have been from the United States: Chet Snouffer, who won in 1985, 1989, and 1994, and John Koehler, who won in 1991. Other world champions have included an Australian, Rob Croll, in 1988 and Fridolin Frost of Germany in 1992. World Championships are scheduled for Christchurch, New Zealand (1996), St. Louis, Missouri (1998), and Sydney, Australia (2000).

Competitions are held worldwide, with local, regional, national, and international events filling the calendar. Nearly three dozen tournaments are now held annually in the United States, and the

Seventeen-Minute Boomerang Flight Sets World Mark

On 8 August 1993, John Gorski (1969–), age 24, of Westlake, Ohio, established a new world feat in Maximum Time Aloft with a single throw that hovered for over 17 minutes before descending for the catch. On a sunny Sunday afternoon at Mingo Park in Delaware, Ohio, Gorski launched his boomerang. Seventeen minutes and six seconds later, he caught it within 40 meters of the launch point. The boomerang was made by Jonas Romblad (1970–), age 23, of Stockholm, Sweden, who was in attendance when the flight occurred. Romblad, a student of aeronautical engineering at the Royal Institute of Technology in Stockholm, designed the boomerang from a composite made of high-tech materials, including Kevlar and carbon fiber. While the specialized boomerang was designed to climb and hover in the air for the Maximum Time Aloft event, normal flight times would be 30 to 40 seconds without some form of thermal assist. The World Record in competition is 2 minutes, 59 seconds by Dennis Joyce (1956–) of Newport News, Virginia. The previously recognized feat was a 14-minute throw in Sydney, Australia, which disappeared out over Sydney Harbor.

Gorski threw the boomerang on the soccer fields at Mingo Park at 3:10:08 p.m. EDT. The boomerang settled into a thermal and rose dramatically, soaring to over 200 meters in the air before beginning a gradual descent back down onto the field. All told, the boomerang drifted 150 meters to the north, hovering over the Olentangy River for several minutes before reversing course and drifting back almost due south for another 225 meters. It then turned and, descending, headed north once again, and was caught less then 40 meters from the launch point at 3:27:14 P.M.

"I couldn't believe I got it back," an elated Gorski recounted later. "I thought, 'I'm never going to see this boomerang again,' but then it stopped drifting and just hung there." However, no one dreamed that the boomerang, which seemed destined for the town of Marion, 20 miles [32 kilometers] north, would actually reverse course and be caught in the park. Tournament director Chet Snouffer summed it up as, "An unbelievable, once-in-a-lifetime experience! He caught the perfect wave and surfed it right into the record books!"

—Chet Snouffer

sport continues its international growth. National boomerang clubs are springing up from New Zealand to the Netherlands, Japan to Brazil, and throughout Europe, Russia, and Asia. While the United States Boomerang Association lists over

500 members, it is estimated that there are now hundreds of thousands of recreational boomerang throwers in the country, based upon sales estimates by the many cottage industry manufacturers of boomerangs and witnessed by the recent involvement of national team sponsors and boomerang distributors.

Rules

The rulebooks of the U.S. Boomerang Association and the Boomerang Association of Australia are the two standards after which most countries pattern their contests. The layout of a standard boomerang field consists of a circle 100 meters (109 yards) in diameter lined on the grass. At its center lie five concentric circles resembling a large archery target. The bull's-eye is a 2-meter (2.2-yard) radius circle and is worth 10 points for a boomerang that lands or is caught there on return. Each subsequent circle is at 4, 6, 8, and 10 meters (4.4, 6.6, 8.8, and 10.9 yards) radius and is worth decreasing points of 8, 6, 4, 2 respectively. Circles for measuring range are drawn at 20-, 30-, and 40-, and 50-meter (22-, 33-, 44-, and 55-yard) radii from the center. The 50-meter radius also defines the 100-meter circle.

There are eight standard events in boomerang competition. They include Accuracy, Trick Catch, Australian Round, Fast Catch, Maximum Time Aloft, Endurance, Doubling, and Juggling. With the exception of Maximum Time Aloft, every boomerang must fly a minimum of 20 meters out to register a score.

Accuracy is similar in concept to darts, except the competitor throws from the bull's-eye on the ground. Each player takes five throws in turn and totals the points. A perfect score is 50. The boomerang cannot be touched after its release until it comes to a complete stop.

An exciting spectator event is Trick Catching. Catches are made with one hand, behind the back, under the leg, and with the feet. In the United States, each catch receives points based upon increasing difficulty. In other countries, each catch receives a point.

Australian Round tests distance, accuracy, and catching ability. A 50-meter throw earns the maximum distance points with six, while a bull's-eye scores ten points. Four points are awarded for a catch.

The Legendary Boomerang

In the early days of the Dreamtime, people had to crawl on their hands and knees because the sky was nearly touching the ground. An old chief came to a magic pool and he stooped down to drink. As he did so, he saw a beautiful straight stick in the water and he reached in and picked it up. Then he suddenly thought, "I can push the sky with this stick and we'll be able to stand up." So he pushed and pushed until he pushed the sky to where it is today and the trees began to grow and the possums ran about in the branches and the kangaroos started hopping for joy. Then he looked at his stick and saw it was terribly bent. Thinking it was no longer good, he threw it away but it came back to him. He tried again and it came back again. So he kept the stick and called it the boomerang.

—Australian legend as told by Les and Arthur Janetski, in *Boomerang: How To Throw, Catch, and Make It*, by Eric Darnell and Benjamin Ruhe (New York: Workman Press, 1985).

Fast Catch involves making five throws and catches as quickly as possible with the same boomerang. The current world record is 15 seconds for five throws!

Maximum Time Aloft times the longest of five throws to stay in the air. The world record during sanctioned competition is just shy of 3 minutes for one throw. However, in practice, boomerangs have hovered for 10 minutes or more with an incredible 17-minute flight recorded in 1993.

With its roots in Europe, the Endurance event tests fast-catching ability over a five-minute period.

The final two events are further challenges requiring specialized boomerangs. Doubling involves throwing two boomerangs at the same time, catching both upon return. Juggling takes two identical boomerangs. They are kept alternating in the air for as many throws as possible without a drop. The current world record is 502 catches.

Long-distance throwing is a separate event, held when the space is available. Man's obsession with seeing how far he could throw a boomerang and have it return probably dates back to the first stick. Australian Frank Donellan popularized the distance event in the 1930s and 1940s with claims of throws over 140 meters (153 yards) out and back. As late as the 1980s those claims seemed suspect as the modern record was only 125 meters (137 yards) using state-of-the-art materials and measuring devices. However, the current world record now stands at a certified 149 meters (163 yards) out and back by Frenchman Michel Dufayard. One cannot help but wonder if Donellan wasn't actually throwing boomerangs the length of one and one-half football fields over 50 years ago.

Boomerang Throwing around the World

It is interesting to note how different cultures value different aspects of the boomerang. There is a distinct conservative bent in Australia toward preserving the purity of the shape, materials, and competitive events of boomerang throwing. In France, where extreme sports are in vogue, throwers value world record performances and hold tournaments designed specifically for world record attempts. Radical shapes and bright colors hallmark the French creations. The French teams are renowned for their aggressive, flamboyant style in competition. On the other hand, German craftsmen typically value the boomerang's craftsmanship at least as much as its performance. German and Swedish engineers go to great lengths to craft intricate strip-laminated and inlaid boomerangs as well as boomerangs made from high-tech materials like carbon fiber, fiberglass, and Kevlar. While craftsmanship and design are important to the Americans, they seem more pragmatic in their approach to the sport. Performance is the bottom line, and winning the tournament can be more important than setting a record or having the best-looking boomerang. Radical designs, use of a variety of materials, and the addition of weights and flaps with duct tape and holes drilled for wind resistance characterize the U.S. scene. It may be this free-wheeling, anything-goes philosophy that has enabled the United States to stay just ahead of her counterparts in boomerang competition.

In the United States, the boomerang's greatest popularity seems to be the heartland, from Kansas and Missouri through Illinois, Indiana, Ohio, and Pennsylvania. The inside joke is that it is the lack of good surf that contributes to the Midwest's obsession with the boomerang. However, it may well be the prevalence of open fields and flatlands, which are ideal boomerang throwing areas, as well as a number of active boomerang clubs in the area.

With open space the sole requirement for boomerang throwing, it may come as a surprise to learn that the Japanese are importing and selling hundreds of thousands of boomerangs every year. Open space is at a premium in this island nation; consequently, it is the indoor boomerang made of foam plastic that accounts for the bulk of sales.

Regardless of the appeal, the boomerang has stood the test of time. Its popularity continues to grow exponentially in these increasingly complex times, perhaps due to its inherent simplicity. Thrown here, it lands here. The boomerang represents the cycle of life and reminds us of one great universal truth—what you throw out does indeed come back to you.

—Chet Snouffer

Bibliography: Aepli, Beat, (1988) *Bumerang.* Zell, Switzerland: ZKM.

Darnell, Eric, and Ruhe, Benjamin. (1985*). Boomerang: How To Throw, Catch, and Make It.* New York: Workman Press.

Hawes, Lorin L. (1975) *All about Boomerangs.* Sydney: Hamlyn Group.

Hess, Felix. (1975). *Boomerangs: Aerodynamics and Motion.* Groningen, Netherlands: Privately printed.

———. (1968) "The Aerodynamics of Boomerangs." *Scientific American* (November): 124–136.

Mason, Bernard. (1974) *Boomerangs: How To Make and Throw Them.* New York: Dover.

Porquet, Jean-Luc, and Dominique Pouillet. (1987) *Le boomerang: Son histoire, sa fabrication, ses techniques.* Bourges, France: Editions Hoebecke.

Ruhe, Benjamin. (1977) *Many Happy Returns.* New York: Viking Press.

Smith, Herb A. (1975) *Boomerangs: Making and Throwing Them.* Littlehampton, UK: Gemstar.

Snouffer, Chet. (1994) *The Leading Edge.* Newsletter of the Free Throwers Boomerang Society, 1980–1994. Delaware, OH: Leading Edge Boomerangs.

Thomas, Jacques. (1985) *Magie du boomerang.* Lyon, France: L'imprimerie des Beaux-Arts.

———. (1991) *The Boomerangs of a Pharaoh.* Lyon, France: Jacques Thomas.

Many Happy Returns. (1981–) Newsletter of the United States Boomerang Association. Delaware, OH: United States Boomerang Association.

Bowls and Bowling

The terms "bowling" and "bowls" refer to a series of loosely related sports that have been adapted and refined to such an extent that many of their common origins have been submerged. The games' most common element is the use of a heavy ball that is tossed or rolled underarm to reach its target. That is the "bowl" itself—it is the action that is "bowling." Success is measured either by the bowl's proximity to a target, which has itself been bowled into place (the "jack," derived from a Latin phrase meaning a "thrown stone"), or by knocking standing targets over ("skittles" or pins placed on fixed marks). These sports come from all over the world and have been shaped by much transplanting and adaptation. In some areas, several types of bowling now exist side by side, with seasonal overlaps.

Origins

As with so many other ball games, the origins of bowling have been traced to ancient Egypt, where tombs of circa 500 B.C.E. were found to contain simple bowling implements. There are scattered classical references, but the game's key developments go back to late-medieval Europe where folk play was used as part of seasonal rituals both to reinforce social bonds and occasionally to emphasize distinctions of rank. For instance, although Henry VIII of England built bowling alleys in some of his palaces, he tried to forbid popular participation because he was afraid it would distract his subjects from more warlike sports.

Generally, it was the later impact of industrialization and urban life that prompted the emergence of many modern bowling games. Traditional folk activities were then refined, changed, and codified as they were selected to meet the leisure needs of the new bourgeoisie. The games also came to be used as tools to assert national identity and international cultural dominance. Some local forms of bowling spread to new areas and eventually found their way back in much more sophisticated forms. These games exploited new technologies and offered opportunities for investment.

The process of bowling's modernization has been largely dominated by Europe and North America, although many less well-recorded ethnic versions probably survive outside those areas. They occur in three main broad categories: thrown bowls with Latin-European origins; rolled bowls from the British tradition; and skittle/pin games adapted by North Americans from older European models. Each variety also uses a different playing surface—in thrown balls, sand or gravel; in British bowls, grass or artificial copies; in pin games, wooden lanes.

Practice

The Latin-European Tradition: Bocce and Pétanque/Boule

Italy and France have produced two main games, codified relatively recently, with broad similarities. They began and remain predominantly open-air activities, played on long, rectangular pitches originally improvised from rough village spaces during hot, dry summers. These have surfaces of raked sand or gravel on which the tossed balls fall and stick, rather than roll. Both games are still often played informally in the village and cafe tradition by men of all ages, but they have now acquired national and international competitive networks and, in many cases, dedicated indoor facilities that allow for year-round play in urban areas and participation by women and children.

Bocce (literally "bowls") is the Italian variant of bowling. Almost inevitably it is claimed to go at least as far back as classical Rome, with Emperor Augustus and others cited as keen players. By the Middle Ages bowling had become rather more popular and intensely localized, with many regional variations in style and rules. Since about 1900 it has paralleled the industrialization of Italy with organization and partial standardization, which has transformed a game "of humble origins . . . into authentic sport" (Marchiavo 1983, 7).

Bowling uses an "alley" or "rink" approximately 18.3 meters long by 2.4 meters wide (60 feet by 8 feet). Increasingly, common indoor facilities usually provide several of these side by side, as do dedicated areas found in many public parks. There are foul areas at each end of the alley and a short regulator peg in the center. The small target ball, the *pallino*, is then tossed from one end

Bowls and Bowling

This seventeenth-century lithograph shows bowling at New York's famous Bowling Green, reputedly the first sporting field in the American colonies.

and must land at least 1 ¼ meters (5 feet) beyond the peg. Each player then aims to throw his bowl, which is heavier than the *pallino*, as close as possible to the target. This is usually done after a walk-up of several steps within the foul area. The throw is complicated by variations on the way the target is approached, according to regional practices. Competitors comprise two players with two shots each or teams of three to six people using fours shots each. If a bowl displaces others already in place it is disqualified. The winner of a game is the first to score 15 points in pairs, or 18 in a team competition.

Bowls themselves were probably originally stone, which gave way to heavy woods. The bowls may have shared with pétanque the practice of having heavy nails knocked into them to increase their throwing weight. Now they are usually made of bronze or titanium, but there has been an increasing use of synthetics since 1929.

The twentieth century has seen organization and codification whose variations represent some of the minor rivalries of the Italian state tradition. The Unione Bocciofila Italiana (UBI) was founded in Turin in 1919 and reorganized in 1956.

Two other groups eventually joined the UBI in 1978—the Federazione Italiano Sport Bocce and the Federazione Italiana Gioco Bocce. Between them, they claim almost 4,000 societies and 165,000 affiliated members, but this does not include the huge numbers who play locally on a casual basis. The UBI is subdivided into three groups representing different approaches to the game. The largest, La Sezione Rafa , accounts for two-thirds of the clubs and their members and uses synthetic bowls only. The next, La Sezione Volo, uses only metal bowls and accounts for most of the remaining affiliates. Much smaller is La Sezione Petanca, which covers variations closer to the French model. All are linked with the Fédération Internationale de Boule (FIB) and the International Olympic Committee. In 1963 the Comitato Olympico Nazionale Italiano accepted bocce's rules, but the game's appeal is too localized for major international events.

Italy stages a number of regional competitions, reinforcing the country's strong regional rivalries. International play is largely limited to Italy and France, which occasionally compete at adult and juvenile levels in grandly titled tournaments.

There is a cup provided by the prince of Monaco, whose territory lies between the two main contenders, and the results have long been dominated by Italy. Although it now has the superstructures of a modern sport, bocce is still largely local and recreational in its appeal. Given its peasant origins, it is hardly surprising that it remains male-dominated, although a small number of women play. Despite its growing complexity, its appeal lies in its being a *"sport simpatico e popolare,"* in the words of a recent enthusiast—something essentially part of an Italian summer.

Pétanque, or boule, has many similarities to bocce. It grew out of regional peasant cultures and was adapted for the needs of a cafe society. The game has been codified and organized, although it is probably more widely followed for recreational rather than competitive purposes. Although quintessentially French, it has attracted a significantly wider international following than bocce has achieved.

Pétanque's origins lie in southern France, where it emerged as "jeu provençal"; it has much in common with that game, which still survives as a minority interest. However, boule players throw from a stationary position without the short run-up common to jeu and bocce. Most scholars see the pétanque variation as a very recent development, emerging as late as the early twentieth century. Strictly speaking, the word *pétanque* is an amalgam of two French words meaning "feet tied together"—a fanciful description of the standing throw. The game is said to have been codified near Marseilles around 1910 and reportedly spread rapidly northward thereafter, overtaking jeu provençal in popularity as well as another related game, la Lyonnaise. Originally, pétanque used wooden balls with a surface made of hammered nails, but these have been replaced by steel balls invented in 1930 by a village mechanic, Jean Blanc, whose factory still ranks as the balls' key producer.

Pétanque may be played by singles, doubles, or triples. Game balls are up to 8 centimeters ($3\frac{1}{8}$ inches) in diameter and weigh up to 800 grams (28 ounces). Any surface except grass may be used, but there is a strong preference for the uneven and rough playing area. Full play requires a minimum area of 1.5 meters wide ($5\frac{1}{2}$ feet) by 12 meters (40 feet) long. A small wooden target, the *cochonnet*, is thrown about 6 to 10 meters (20 to 33

feet), after which players throw their balls so they come to rest as close to the target as possible. Skill in bypassing an opponent is highly regarded. Scoring is simply based on points related to proximity, and games can be won by an agreed total of between 13 and 21 points. A full pétanque match consists of three games.

Outdoors, like bocce, pétanque's season lasts from April to October, but the game has found a growing winter popularity in France where it is often played in covered equestrian centers whose rough riding surfaces offer ideal playing fields. Although its popularity depends very heavily on a warm and relaxed French cafe and village image, pétanque has grown considerably both as an urban and an exported activity in recent decades. It remains male-dominated in France, but women and children play in some of the countries in which it has been enthusiastically adopted. The French created a Fédération Française de Pétanque et Jeu Provençal in 1945 and an international federation later. Returning holiday-makers introduced it to England as an ideal garden game in the 1960s and its spread was fostered further when a British Pétanque Association was formed in 1974, eventually attracting about 250 clubs. These clubs are often linked with public houses that encourage local teams and provide the rinks. The various associations have agreed on a standard 39 rules, the last of which demands reasonable dress. The sport eventually spread to other parts of mainland Europe, including Belgium, Switzerland, and Spain, and to North Africa, the United States, and China. World championships have been organized since 1959, with France dominating them. The British started a national Open Championship in 1986. For all this, it remains a relatively informal pursuit for francophiles, as well as for the thousands who now play using the full rules and proper metal bowls. There are many more enthusiasts who play in their gardens or at campsites and beaches using cheap, plastic, sand-filled sets bought from garden centers, supermarkets, and filling stations with rules unique to their own families and friends. Simplicity and informality have done much to enhance the growth of pétanque.

Bowls: The British Contribution

Rolling wooden bowls toward a jack has been practiced in Britain since the early Middle Ages.

Bowls and Bowling

Southampton claims to have the oldest continually played-over greens, dating from the 1290s. Most early British games took place on fairly rough surfaces, well-grassed but unevenly contoured, and the players were usually gentry or prosperous urban tradespeople. One such who played was the eighteenth-century radical Tom Paine, who bowled on the castle green in Lewes, Sussex. His society, re-formed in 1753, still survives. However, between the sixteenth century and the later Victorian period, such clubs were few in England, where the game had largely fallen into oblivion. It was the lowland Scots who kept up and refined the tradition of bowls, playing on flat, seaside turf adjoining their golf links, and it was a Scot, W. W. Mitchell of Glasgow, who codified the rules for the first time in 1849. Thereafter, the game was reintroduced to England and began a spate of growth that took it overseas as well.

In England, bowls was soon divided into two main types, excluding the handful of followers of the traditional game. Both variants use specially prepared grass greens, although one is now much influenced by artificial and indoor facilities. They came essentially to match wider regional differences within England, both in terms of the social tone of membership and in attitudes to tension between amateurs and professionals. The culturally dominant form, and the most adaptable to overseas and indoor play, has been the Lawn, or Flat, Green code. This appealed most to the emergent Victorian southern bourgeoisie and its imitators, with its strong commitment to amateur play and quest for social exclusiveness. The other variant, Crown Green, uses a deliberately contoured area that is difficult to replicate with indoor artificial surfaces. Crown Green play was largely restricted to the northern parts of England and appealed more to lower-class players. It had a strong semiprofessional element that made it suspect to the more purist Lawn Green followers.

Lawn Green is played on a flat square of between 31 and 41 meters (33 and 44 yards) that is usually divided into rinks up to 5½ meters (18–19 feet) wide, so that several matches can go on side by side. The green is surrounded by a shallow ditch and a bank at least 23 centimeters (9 inches) high. The Crown Green may be either square or rectangular, but must be a minimum of 25 meters (30 yards) wide. It usually rises to a

central crown up to 35 centimeters (14 inches) high and the surface may be irregular. The Lawn jack (target) is white and some 6.4 centimeters (2 $^{17}/_{32}$) inches in diameter; the Crown jack is marginally smaller. Both variations use bowls that were originally turned from heavy woods, but rubber and then synthetic composites became much more common in the twentieth century. These "woods," a description still often used despite the dominance of artificial materials, have a built-in bias to one side, originally produced by inserting metal weights, that causes the bowls' trajectory to curve in the direction of the bias. Bowling in a straight line is virtually impossible, increasing the demand for skill and also allowing a player to bypass an opponent's bowls. Players normally have a set of four bowls each and scoring depends on proximity to the jack. As the game has become more formalized, strict dress codes have appeared. What was once a sign of class distinction still serves to differentiate between the casual bowler playing on a municipally owned green and membership in a private club.

As bowls' popularity grew, so did the complexity of its organization. A web of regulatory bodies emerged, reflecting both rival games and tensions within them. Essentially, for the two codes of play, there are three governing organizations: two for the Lawn game and one for Crown. When Lawn bowls spread rapidly in England around 1900 it attracted considerable southern support and a desire for wider competition than the average club afforded. The result was the English Bowling Association (EBA), founded in 1903. For a while this was dominated by the aging and irascible cricket hero W. G. Grace, who claimed with a characteristic lack of modesty to have founded the English game. He was eventually ousted, and the EBA settled down to a more restful and productive role in clarifying the rules and overseeing tournaments. It came to represent 35 of 38 English counties and remains the arbiter of Lawn bowls. It has never, however, enjoyed an absolute hegemony, since an older, simpler version of the game remained alongside the newer development in many northern and eastern English counties, where the EBA was regarded as too elaborately middle-class in its approach. Players in those areas unwilling to adapt to EBA standards formed a separate organization, the English Bowling Federation (EBF), in 1926. Initially, most of their competitions were organized in pairs that played shorter games with two woods each. Their lawns were smaller, usually lacking the mandatory surrounding ditch of EBA play. Since the 1960s, though, the EBF has allowed three- and foursome competition matches, which have proved more attractive to competitors. Both organizations have long arranged a series of regional tournaments leading to parallel national championships. The EBA provides one in southern England, at the socially prestigious Worthing Club, whose lawns are to bowls what Wimbledon is to lawn tennis. The EBF's series centers on Skegness, in the east Midlands. It is no accident that the venues of both national competitions are seaside resorts, emphasizing the link between the game and middle-class leisure patterns as they had emerged by the end of the nineteenth century.

Crown bowls has developed similarly, but in ways that reflect its strong regional roots in the north of England and the major role played in its development by professionals and semiprofessionals. (By comparison, the Lawn game has emphasized its amateur purity, although many of its star players in recent decades have had commercial links with the production and retailing of bowls services and products.) In 1878, an annual prize tournament began in Blackpool, a northern English seaside resort catering principally to the industrial working classes. From 1907, the tournament was formalized as the annual Waterloo Cup, which remains the peak of Crown Green competitions. A British Crown Green Amateur Association was founded in 1903, eventually formulating 41 rules; it reappeared as the British Crown Green Bowling Association in 1932. Sunday play was forbidden until 1962.

A gambling element has always accompanied Crown Green matches. This has centered on a small group of about 100 professional players whose exhibition matches represent the peak of playing skills. Crown Green still claims to be the older version of the English game, closer to the Tudor model than the softer formality of the revised Scottish import, but its general following has remained more regionally restricted. There are more likely to be Lawn clubs in Crown strongholds than vice versa. Crown matches were the first to be televised, which did much to boost popular interest and foster a widening age range of participation in what had come to be mistakenly regarded as a relatively undemanding pastime for middle-aged and retired men. There have always been claims that modern bowls is a gentlemanly outlet for aggression—perhaps too much so for some observers. The maleness of both varieties of bowls was taken for granted in the early years of its popularity, and the role of women was restricted to making refreshments at tournaments. By the end of World War I, however, female interest in the game had grown, at least among the middle classes, and a parallel women's game emerged. This has been largely restricted to the Lawn code, although there is a small number of female Crown players. In turn, this led to two national organizations matching the men's. The English Women's Bowling Association was founded in 1931, to be followed by the English Women's Bowling Federation. The regional differences parallel the masculine ones. Both organize national tournaments. Women's play still tends to be largely segregated, but this is exacerbated in the eyes of many by dress codes that seem archaic at the end of the twentieth century—particularly regarding the shape of the hats the women invariably wear. It has, however, appealed much more readily to all ages than the men's games did originally and there is a strong juvenile element as well as a number of mother-daughter tournament teams. Both men's and women's associations now have links with a body that unites the representative groups from the four nations of the British Isles (England, Scotland, Wales, and Ireland) in the British Isles Bowls Council, formed in 1962.

Lawn Green in particular served another purpose. It became another of the bonding agencies that spread throughout the British Empire and the Commonwealth. Expatriates took it with them to Australia, New Zealand, Canada, Africa, and onward. It was the playing of bowls in England as a sideshow by visiting Australian cricketers in 1899 that did much to revive the game's popularity there. Australia's New South Wales Bowling Association, founded in 1880, claims to be the oldest. It and others joined the Australian Bowling Council, formed in 1911, that combined with a parallel female organization is estimated to represent almost half a million players. New Zealand formed an association in 1886 and has over 50,000 male players. South Africa has a similar number, linked in the South African Bowling

Association, formed in 1904. All these groups play internationally through the Commonwealth Games. A few anglophiles (possibly 7,000) play in the United States under the auspices of the American Lawn Bowls Association, founded in 1915, and there are some similar organizations in Argentina and parts of Europe. All the governing bodies are linked by the International Bowling Board, formed in 1905, which oversees the game throughout the world. One other phenomenon that has extended world participation in bowls has been the growth in British middle-class overseas holiday-making in the warmer parts of Europe. Many of the more ambitious resorts in Spain and Portugal have encouraged the development of bowls facilities, often linked with package tours, to attract tourists escaping the British winter and expatriates settling in retirement for the same reason.

Bowls' greatest limitation has been its role as a seasonal game. While that may have fit the requirements of preindustrial society, its seasonal nature has been at odds with growing urban demands for year-round participation. The answers have been the significant growth of indoor play, benefiting from artificial light and protection from the weather, and sharing facilities with other games. The first step in this direction was taken by a Scot, William Macrae, in 1888. Carpets were often used in the early years to cover boarded-over swimming pools. Play was informal and uneven until the first specifically indoor club was formed in London's Maida Vale by the Paddington Club in 1935. It remained a distinctly eccentric pursuit until the 1960s when a boom started that has continued since, but the phenomenon was largely confined to the south of England until the later 1980s. Television has played a major role in increasing bowls' popularity by enhancing the sense of competition. This has accompanied a steady rise in the number of local leisure center buildings with multiuse halls. The development of portable artificial surfaces using plastic-based "grasses" has made it possible to produce indoor rinks with varying characteristics suitable to the level of play. It has proved easier for Lawn than Crown play to be replicated indoors. Most indoor players are over 45, it is often less formal than the outdoor game, and has proved particularly attractive to women, but it shares most of the rules and scoring patterns developed for open-air play. In England, indoor play was largely overseen by the EBA until the early 1970s, but a National Indoor Bowls Council, formed in 1964, gradually took control of the game. There is also an International Bowling Board, which emerged as the fashion spread; an international championship began in 1979 that largely catered to British players. The normal indoor game uses a 46-meter (50-yard) carpet divided into rinks. There are well over 250 British clubs with this equipment. However, greens on this scale have proved too much for many places with smaller facilities, so a derivation, the Short Mat game, has emerged, using 12 to 15 meter (40 to 50 foot) carpets. That began in Ireland, but it has also proved popular in mainland Britain and many parts of the Commonwealth, although not on the scale of the outdoor game.

Ten-Pin Bowling and the Americanization of Skittles

Skittles shares similar claims of antiquity as other forms of bowls, but is said to have emerged fully in the late Middle Ages when German parishioners were persuaded to roll stones against wooden clubs set up to represent the forces of evil. Martin Luther is said to have played and to have fixed the number of skittles at nine. Variants were played in England, one version of which used a wooden disk, the "cheese," instead of stones or balls. As it developed, European skittles became closely identified with recreational drinking, and was often played in alleys erected alongside inns. These playing "lanes" were usually floored with wooden planks: it was this surface that later became the norm, although outdoor versions have remained. Most of the games used nine skittles or pins set in a diamond shape. Ten-pin has survived in this form as a widely played but relatively informal game throughout Europe. It accompanied European settlers to the New World, with Dutch, German, and British migrants playing their own regional versions. Outdoor games in places such as New York City's Battery Park were increasingly superceded by indoor play, but there was also a great deal of gambling, which led many state authorities to ban the pin games. There is a compelling but unproven legend that the change from nine to ten pins was a cunning way around that prohibition. Whatever the case, the new game achieved growing popularity throughout the United States, including the antebellum South.

The Most Famous Game of Bowls

The most famous game of bowls in history, if it ever actually took place, was played by Sir Francis Drake and other captains of the English fleet as they waited for the appearance of the Spanish Armada, the large fleet assembled to invade England, on 19 July 1588. The story claims that Drake and the captains were playing after dinner on the green of the Pelican Inn, at Plymouth Hoe in southwest England, when news was brought that the enemy navy had been sighted. Drake is said to have replied, "We have time enough to finish the game and beat the Spaniards, too," which he duly did. They would have been playing the game in its early English form, with two woods each on an uneven ground. Historians have argued about the actual event ever since, because the story did not appear in print for another 40 years or so. Some have claimed that Drake would have been far too anxious to fight to have wasted time playing a game. Others have surmised that since the tide was running against the English fleet that afternoon, it would have been better to occupy the time in play until it turned. Drake's comment was also seen as a means of reassuring the men and boosting morale. Whatever the truth, the story has become a mainstay of English naval heroism and was a favorite among artists trying to portray the roots of Victorian imperialism. It is also supposed to represent the calm, phlegmatic approach to life and its priorities that bowls is claimed to engender—the natural sense of English superiority that has proved so arrogant in its treatment of foreigners ever since.

—John Lowerson

Bowling became an essential activity in many new suburban neighborhoods but often suffered from its strong association with blue-collar males, and its appeal was still limited. Much of that changed in the 1950s, when the game was mechanized with automated clearing and restacking for the fallen pins. The spread of the automobile and high levels of plant investment in suburban alleys along with refreshment facilities made it attractive to a new sector of participants. Bowling soon acquired an image of clean play, suitable for teenagers of both sexes and for wholesome family participation—an impression that has remained intact despite the growth of competitive leagues and professionalization. By then, bowling had become just as important for pleasure as for organized competition. It also became a symbol of exportable American culture to other parts of the world, especially where U.S. forces had bases during the cold war decades. The game was exported to Britain by the 1960s, and a British Ten-Pin Bowling Association was formed in 1961, although many over-ambitious developments failed. It has enjoyed a steady resurgence there since the 1980s, linked with the growth of car ownership among younger fans, and there are now some 40,000 players. Some European cities have also acquired bowling alleys, but perhaps the greatest growth spurt has been in Japan, where a 504-lane Tokyo site was long claimed to be the world's largest.

Most facilities are smaller than that, but the main game is now standardized throughout the world. Individuals or small teams (the most popular for competitive play is five) play on two of the single lanes into which the building is divided. These have a highly polished wooden floor that requires special shoes and offers least resistance to the moving bowls. Each lane is 18.3 meters (60 feet) long by 1.1 meter (3 feet, 6 inches) wide. A foul line is marked about 4.9 meters (16 feet) along the lane and the player bowls from there after a short walking approach. At the other end stand the ten bottle-shaped pins, 38.1 centimeters (15 inches) tall and weighing between 1.53 and 1.65 kilograms (3 pounds, 6 ounces and 3 pounds, 10 ounces). They are usually made of maple and are placed on marks in a three-foot triangle with its apex toward the player. The bowls vary in size, according to the skills and physique of the player. Fashioned initially from heavy wood, then from rubber, bowling balls are now usually made from various plastic composites and may be multicolored. The maximum circumference is 68.5 centimeters ($27\frac{1}{2}$ inches) and the maximum weight 7.3 kilograms (16 pounds). Each ball also has two finger holes and a thumb hole—occasionally there are more—and these can be custom-drilled to fit the player.

Each player's hope is to knock down all ten pins with one ball, but this requires considerable skill or luck. Each player has a frame of two balls, and a game consists of ten frames. The winner is the one whose score is highest when all the frames are completed. If ten pins are knocked down with one ball, that is a "strike," if two, a "spare." Scoring is done almost always electronically as part of the automated system that collects the fallen pins, restacks them on the marks, and returns the balls to players along a narrow, elevated alley between the lanes.

Many players compete only with friends, but most rinks have locally sponsored leagues representing various community and commercial associations. Bowling rules were standardized by the American Bowling Congress (ABC) formed in 1895. A Women's International Bowling Congress (WIBC) appeared in 1916. Both were linked until 1939 with the International Bowling Association (IBA) but are now governed by the Fédération Internationale des Quilleurs (FIQ), founded in 1951. Between 1923 and 1936, the IBA organized world championships. These were revived by the FIQ in 1956 and since 1963 have been held every four years, women having also been admitted since that date. Unlike some other aspects of bowls, the games' variations have been genuinely international—many winners in the various team events have come from outside the United States. The WIBC has also organized annual championships since it was founded, and these have attracted around 80,000 entrants in recent decades. In 1961 the WIBC inaugurated the Queen's Tournament and offered prize money. In addition, a male professional circuit emerged with some 2,000 players, forming a Professional Bowler's Association in 1958. That body organized an annual Tournament of Champions in Akron, Ohio, that was originally sponsored by Firestone. A Professional Women's Bowling Association appeared in 1959. Frequently televised, professional matches indicate the commercial importance of a game that is said to attract some 7 million bowlers in organized U.S. leagues alone. These leagues have been linked since 1943 by the National Bowling Council, which represents commercial interests as well as players. This, in turn, has fostered various juvenile organizations, such as the Young American Bowling Alliance, formed in 1982, which encourages competitive collegiate bowling. Beyond these associations, at least 80 million Americans are said to play at least once a year.

Ten-pin has come to dominate the North American bowling scene, but there are other developments of the older immigrant import that frequently share the standard facilities. Candlepin, popular in the eastern United States, uses cylindrical pins that taper at both ends and are 38 centime-

ters (15 inches) tall and a ball that is $11\frac{1}{4}$ centimeters ($4\frac{1}{2}$ inches) in diameter and weighing 1.1 kilograms (2 pounds, 7 ounces). A frame consists of three balls. Another variant, duckpins, was developed by two professional baseball players, Wilbert Robinson and John J. McGraw, at a bowling alley they owned jointly. It uses pins 23.3 centimeters ($9\frac{1}{2}$ inches) high and a ball up to $12\frac{1}{2}$ centimeters (5 inches) in diameter with finger holes and weighing 1.7 kilograms (3 pounds, 12 ounces). Duckpins also has a three-ball frame. In the United States—especially in its stronghold, New England—duckpins is organized by the National Duck Pin Bowling Congress, founded in 1927.

The most important of the alternatives to tenpin appeared just across the U.S. border in Canada before World War I, when Thomas J. Ryan, a Toronto businessperson, developed a less-demanding and faster version of the game. His version, called Canadian Fivepin, uses five smaller pins in a standard alley. The pins are 31.8 centimeters ($12\frac{1}{2}$ inches) tall and have a thick rubber band around the middle to make them easier targets. The ball is 12.7 centimeters (5 inches) in diameter. The game caught on rapidly in Canada among leagues and both sexes. Rules were formalized after the foundation of a Canadian Bowling Congress in 1926 that today presides over 20,000 leagues with more than 600,000 players. Two individuals or teams may play, and the layout and rules are similar to those of tenpin. Its continued popularity represents both Canadian originality and the nation's steadfast determination to keep an identity distinct from its powerful southern neighbor.

More recently, many bowling games have received heavy media attention. Television's sharp focus on the games' intimacy and restricted playing space has given them a new role in the world of sports and more fans than their previously localized nature had attracted. This has also done a great deal to increase participation in games whose equipment and space requirements are relatively simple.

—John Lowerson

Bibliography: Collins, M. F., and C. S. Logue. (1976) *Indoor Bowls*. London: Sports Council.

English Bowling Association and British Crown Green Association. (1992) *Know the Game: Bowls*. London: A. and C. Black.

Freeman, Garth. (1987) *Petanque: The French Game of Bowls*. Leatherhead,UK: Carreau Press.

Harrison, Henry. (1988) *Play the Game: Ten Pin Bowling*. London: Ward Lock.

Holt, Richard. (1981) *Sport and Society in Modern France*. London: Macmillan.

Lowerson, John. (1993) *Sport and the English Middle Classes, 1870–1914*. Manchester: Manchester University Press.

Marchiano, Armando. (1983) *Bocce, che passione!* Padua, Italy: Casa Editrice MEB.

Martin, Joan L., Ruth E. Tandy, and Charlene Agne-Traub. (1994) *Bowling*. Madison, WI: William C. Brown and Benchmark.

Phillips, Keith, ed. (1990) *The New BBC of Bowls*. London: BBC.

Boxing

"Boxing" is an Old English term that 600 years ago meant fighting with the fists. Until the end of the nineteenth century the real sport was prizefighting, using bare knuckles, for money. What distinguishes both prizefighting and modern boxing from unarmed fighting intended to maim is a code of rules under which no blows may be inflicted below the waistline and none after the opponent has gone down. Precepts from the sport have affected cultural practice in a way few sports have: fights between enemies, fights between boys, have tended to follow prizefighting rules.

The traditional boxing stance consists of the fighter turning his or her left side toward the opponent with both fists raised, the left fist advanced and the right covering the chin. To move around the "ring," the roped, canvas-surfaced square in which the fight takes place, the boxer steps forward with the left foot. The right foot follows without overtaking the left, thus preserving the original, highly stable stance. To move back, the boxer simply reverses this order. The body should be bent slightly forward from the hips. Boxers around the world use the same rules, positions, and movements, except for a minority of left-handers called "southpaws," who box right side first.

Very occasionally, the sport produces a great champion. These fighters are able to withstand, mentally and physically, blows to the head and stomach; move like a ballet dancer; and lash out with the speed of a cornered cat.

Origins and Development

The first written rules of prizefighting were published by Jack Broughton (1704–1789) in London in 1743. Broughton taught gentlemen to box using the "mufflers" (gloves) he is said to have invented, although earlier boxing academies existed in nearby streets. Most people, however, would not have learned the rules of boxing from Broughton, but from participation in the sport itself. The weekly newspaper *Bell's Life in London and Sporting Chronicle* dominated and directed the sport from 1822 until the 1870s. Starting in 1841 the editors also published a boxing yearbook called *Fistiana*, which soon modified Broughton's Rules. While still requiring "a fair 'stand-up' fight," the new rules allowed fighting "in close," which was basically upright wrestling, until either or both men went down. Thus, a "round" (period of fighting) continued until a fighter punched or threw his opponent to the ground. A round might last a few seconds or 40 minutes. The rest between rounds was 30 seconds, after which contestants had to be "at the scratch" (ready to fight) or lose the match. The fight continued until one contestant gave in or his second gave in for him. If a second had to step in, this usually meant his fighter could not stand unaided. Fighters invariably bled, and spectators commonly laid bets on "first blood." Contestants occasionally died, but local authorities usually turned a blind eye.

Weight and bulk counted most when fighters were in close, so the notion of science, which became part of the sport in the late eighteenth century, was mainly concerned with punching or stopping a punch. Champion prizefighters like Daniel Mendoza (1764–1836) gained acclaim as "scientific" boxers, since they used their foot speed to stay out of the reach of bigger men. Movement of the feet, advance and retreat, linked skill to manliness, and international matches soon followed.

Thomas Molineaux, a black man from Virginia, fought the best men in Britain between 1810 and 1815, and his two losing battles with Tom Cribb (1781–1848) for the English championship

Boxers pose for an instructional picture circa 1900. Rules governing boxing—known as the Queensberry Rules after their publisher, the Marquis of Queensberry—first appeared in 1867.

attracted unprecedented public attention. Molineaux died in poverty in Galway 4 August 1818. The Anglo-American contest rated most highly in the annals of prizefighting took place at Farnborough in Hampshire in 1860 when Tom Sayers (1826–1865) and John C. Heenan (1833–1873), from New York State, fought for 2 hours and 20 minutes, before the ropes were broken during crowd disorder and the match abandoned when Heenan could hardly see and Sayers had lost the use of his right arm. In the following month a debate in the House of Commons initiated by critics of prizefighting drew a strong speech in defense of the sport from Lord Palmerston, the prime minister, and Sayers's burial at Highgate Cemetery was as grand as a state occasion.

Another city to adopt boxing was Paris. The country already enjoyed savate, which had national and regional championships and allowed blows with the feet (see Cudgeling), but boxing swept France in a few years immediately before World War I. British boxers started crossing the English Channel, and a cluster of African American fighters, including the world heavyweight champion, Jack Johnson (1878–1946), stayed to ply their trade. The first major French fighter was Georges Carpentier (1894–1975). He switched from the older sport in 1908 and boxed through the weights, winning all the way up to heavyweight. At that level he lost to Jack Dempsey (1895–1983) at Jersey City, New Jersey, before 90,000 spectators on 2 July 1921.

Boxing, as opposed to prizefighting, used rules written by a Cambridge University athlete, John Graham Chambers (1843–1883) and published by Sir John Sholto Douglas (1844–1900), a contemporary scholar who was the eighth Marquis of Queensberry. These brief rules, which appeared in 1867 and came to be known as the Queensberry Rules, distinguished between boxing competitions and contests. According to these rules, competitions were for amateurs as well as professionals. These bouts were limited to three rounds in about ten minutes and were usually decided on points. Contests, on the other hand, were tests of endurance that continued until one man could no longer fight; they were confined strictly to professionals. Only in the latter code was it specified that new gloves of fair size and best quality be used, so Queensberry Rules assumed the superiority of contests over competitions. Amateurs sparred, professionals fought, and both boxed sportingly according to Queensberry. Common to both codes were timed rounds and one-minute rests between rounds; gloves were to be used, and wrestling was not allowed. The ten-second count ending a contest was not referred to under competitions, and attempting to knock the opponent out in an amateur match or while sparring was frowned upon in amateur competitions.

There is a dichotomy in boxing between the amateur and the professional. Amateur boxing organizations will not tolerate boxers competing for money, but modern professional boxers were invariably introduced to the sport as amateurs. The professional level of the sport has always attracted greater public interest.

Between the two world wars, the sport of boxing expanded in two ways. First, professional boxing made unheard-of profits, and second, both amateur and professional boxing became popular in Europe and the United States. Meanwhile, the ubiquitous color bar in professional rings began to be relaxed. When Joe Louis (1914–1981), an African American, won the world heavyweight title in Chicago in 1937 the sport's desegregation process had just started. Black men were not permitted to win British professional championships until 1948. (The amateur ranks had dropped their social class barrier back in 1880 and never seem to have bothered with a racial one.)

Professional Boxing

Britain and the United States traded domination in the early days of organized professional boxing. In the 1880s bare-knuckles prizefighting had refused to give way to boxing with gloves, but the contest between the new and old styles was decided in 1891, when English-born Bob Fitzsimmons (1862–1917) knocked out Kildare-born "Nonpareil" Jack Dempsey (1862–1895) under Queensberry Rules in New Orleans for the world middleweight championship. Prizefighting was English, boxing became North American.

Initially, immigrants from countries with a boxing culture brought the sport with them to the United States. England, Ireland, Australia, New Zealand, and South Africa all contributed their customs to the sport in this way. In fact, Irish-American John L. Sullivan (1858–1918), the "Boston Strong Boy," is one of the most famous boxers of all time. More input into U.S. boxing, from the earliest days until after World War II, came from Central European Jewish immigrants. One of the most famous boxers from this background was Benjamin Leiner, who as Benny Leonard fought over 200 contests and reigned as world lightweight champion from 1917 to 1925. Italian immigrants contributed the legendary Rocky Marciano (1923–1969), the heavyweight who never lost a professional fight. African Americans have done equally well in the professional fighting arena, dominating the weights since Louis's 1937 victory.

Poverty was (and still is) the common denominator that impelled many athletes into professional boxing. Boxing generally thrives where the living is not easy. From the mid-twentieth century, boxers from less-developed countries began to re-

place white men, whose generally improved living conditions allowed them to choose less painful work and pastimes. From Mexico to South Korea, poorer countries have produced more and more boxers, especially at the lighter weights.

Promoting prizefighting was never a safe business proposition. The ropes and stakes and the rest of the paraphernalia had to be transported to an unadvertised, and often remote, place to avoid interference from hooligans or police. A prizefight was a breach of the peace. The fewer people who knew where and when the match was on, the better able were the organizers to give the slip to magistrates and to collect the spectators' money. By contrast, boxing under Queensberry Rules, usually an indoor sport, was controllable. The public house, music hall, or people's palace had a door at which everyone was obliged to pay to gain admission, and the enormous industrial boom that started in the 1880s allowed male workers to join the queue for leisure time and sport especially. The leading promoter in the history of boxing was George L. "Tex" Rickard (1871–1929), who between 1906 (Joe Gans versus Battling Nelson) and 1927 (Gene Tunney versus Dempsey) pushed gate money from $70,000 to $2.7 million by speculating hugely and titillating the press. Over 100,000 people watched Tunney beat Dempsey, first in Philadelphia and then in Chicago—attendance that has never been matched again anywhere in the world. (Audiences in the boxing arena have become increasingly redundant since the 1950s because of television payments to promoters.)

In later years, cinema and radio increased the popularity of boxing even more without commanding great sums of money from advertising. With the advent of television, particularly during the reign of heavyweight Muhammad Ali (born Cassius Clay in 1942, he rejected this name on his conversion to Islam in the early 1960s), the rewards for successful professional boxers (except fly and bantamweight) have skyrocketed. Ironically, the quality of much televised boxing, in which the focus on knockouts has driven the artistry out of the sport, has declined.

Amateur Boxing

The first championships for amateurs were contested at three weights (light—under 140 pounds [52 kilograms, or 10 stone in the older British

"The Fight"

Reader, have you ever seen a fight? If not, you have a pleasure to come, at least if it is a fight like that between the Gas-man and Bill Neate. The crowd was very great when we arrived; open carriages were coming up, with streamers flying and music playing; and the country people were pouring in over hedge and ditch in all directions, to see their hero beat or be beaten. The odds were still on Gas, but only about five to four. About two hundred thousand pounds were pending. The Gas says he has lost 3000£ which were promised him by different gentlemen if he had won. This spirited and formidable young fellow seems to have taken for his motto the old maxim, that "there are three things necessary to success in life—*Impudence, Impudence, Impudence!*"

The *swells* were parading in their white box-coats, the outer ring was cleared with some bruises on the heads and shins of the rustic assembly (for the *cockneys* had been distanced by the sixty-six miles); the time drew near; a bustle, a buzz, ran through the crowd, and from the opposite side entered Neate, between his second and bottle-holder. He rolled along, swathed in his loose greatcoat, his knock-knees bending under his huge bulk; and with a modest, cheerful air, threw his hat into the ring. He then began quietly to undress; when from the other side there was a similar rush and an opening made, and the Gas-man [Tom Hickman] came forward with a conscious air of anticipated triumph, too much like the cock-of-the-walk. He strutted about more than became a hero, sucked oranges with a supercilious air, and threw away the skin with a toss of his head, and went up and looked at Neate, which was an act of supererogation. The only sensible thing he did was, as he strode away from the modern Ajax, to fling out his arms, as if he wanted to try whether they would do their work that day. By this time they had stripped, and presented a strong contrast in appearance. If Neate was like Ajax, "with Atlantean shoulders, fit to bear" the pugilistic reputation of all Bristol, Hickman, might be compared to Diomed, light, vigorous, elastic, and his back glistened in the sun, as he moved about, like a panther's hide. They tossed up for the sun, and the Gas-man won. They were led up to the *scratch*—shook hands, and went at it.

In the first round every one thought it was all over. After making play a short time, the Gas-man flew at his adversary like a tiger, struck five blows in as many seconds, three first, and then following him as he staggered back, two more, right and left, and down he fell, a mighty ruin. Neate seemed like a lifeless lump of flesh and bone, round which the Gas-man's blows played with the rapidity of electricity or lightening. It was as if Hickman held a sword or a fire in that right hand of his, and directed it against an unarmed body. They met again, and Neate seemed, not cowed, but particularly cautious. I saw his teeth clenched together and his brows knit close against the sun. He held out both his arms at full length straight before him, like two sledge-hammers, and raised his left an inch or two higher. The Gas-man could not get over this guard—they struck mutually and fell, but without advantage on either side. No one could tell how it would end. This was the only moment in which opinion was divided; for, in the next, the Gas-man aiming a mortal blow at his adversary's neck, with his right hand, and failing from the length he had to reach, the other returned it with his left at full swing, planted a tremendous blow on his cheek-bone and eyebrow, and made a red ruin of that side of his face. The Gas-man went down, and there was a roar of triumph as the waves of fortune rolled tumultuously from side to side. This was a settler. Hickman got up, and "grinned horrible a ghastly smile," yet he was evidently dashed in his opinion of himself; it was the first time he had ever been so punished; all one side of his face was perfect scarlet, and his right eye was closed in dingy blackness, as he advanced to the fight, less confident but still determined. After one or two rounds, not receiving another such remembrancer, he rallied and went at it with his former impetuosity. But in vain. His strength had been weakened,—his blows could not tell at such a distance,—and he was obliged to fling himself at his adversary, and could not strike from his feet; and almost as regularly as he flew at him with his right hand, Neate warded the blow, or drew back out of its reach, and felled him with the return of his left.

To see two men smashed to the ground, smeared with gore, stunned, senseless, the breath beaten out of their bodies; and then, to see them rise up with new strength and courage, stand ready to inflict or receive mortal offense, and rush upon each other "like two clouds over the Caspian":—this is the high and heroic state of man! About the twelfth round it seemed as if it must have been over. Neate just then made a tremendous lunge, and hit Hickman full in the face. He hung suspended for a second or two, and then fell back, throwing his hands in the air, and with his face lifted up to the sky. All traces of life, of natural expression, were gone from him. His face was like a human skull, a death's head, spouting blood. The eyes were filled with blood, the nose streamed with blood, the mouth gaped blood. He was like one of the figures in Dante's *Inferno.* Yet he fought on after this for several rounds, still striking the first desperate blow, and Neate standing on the defensive, and using the same cautious guard to the last, as if he had still all his work to do; and it was not until the Gas-man was so stunned in the seventeenth or eighteenth round that his sense forsook him and he could not come to in time, that the battle was declared over. When the Gas-man came to himself the first words he uttered were, "Where am I? What is the matter?" "Nothing is the matter, Tom,—you have lost the battle, but you are the bravest man alive." Neate instantly went up and shook him cordially by the hand, and seeing some old acquaintance, began to flourish with his fists, "Ah, you always said I couldn't fight—What do you think now?" But all in good humor, and without any appearance of arrogance; only it was evident that Bill Neate was pleased that he had won the fight. One of the carrier pigeons flew with the news of her husband's victory to the bosom of Mrs. Neate. Alas for Mrs. Hickman!

—Condensed from "The Fight" by William Hazlitt.
In *The Round Table: A Collection of Essays on Literature, Men, and Manners*. Edinburgh: Archibald Constable and Co., 1817.

system of weight}; middle—under 158 pounds [59 kilograms]; and heavy) in 1867 at Lillie Bridge, a sports stadium in western London. The Queensberry Rules were written for this occasion, but boxing was only part of a two-day open-air program of general athletics, bicycling, and wrestling for gentlemen from newly formed London sports clubs and the universities of Oxford and Cambridge. The organizing committee reviewed all entries to exclude "riffraff," so laborers, artisans, and tradesmen were not able to compete. However, it became apparent that members of the Lillie Bridge set were not the best at several sports—especially boxing. So, six of the boxers and the editor of a weekly newspaper, the *Referee*, met to form the Amateur Boxing Association (ABA), which allowed blue-collar workers to enter its annual championships each spring. The ABA competitions, held first in 1881 with an extra weight division (the "feather" class at 126 pounds [47 kilograms, or 9 stone]), proved such an attraction for spectators that the Lillie Bridge event was soon discontinued. The real amateur sport developed, not among the comfortably off, but in boys' clubs in the uglier parts of cities, near factories, docks, and railway arches.

In the United States the social integration of wealthy clubs with the *hoi polloi* came much later. The Golden Gloves tournament was started by a newspaper, the *Chicago Tribune*, in 1926 and became annual a few years later. However, the spread of the sport to the rest of the world was erratic. The Olympic Games program first included boxing at St. Louis in 1904, when U.S. boxers won all seven titles (the British made a clean sweep at the London Games four years later). Boxing was dropped for the 1912 Games, but returned in 1920 and has been retained ever since.

The organization of international amateur boxing began in 1920 with the formation in Paris of the Fédération Internationale de Boxe Amateur. Only five countries were represented, and the elected president was an Essex man, John Herbert Douglas (185?–1930). Douglas was a wealthy businessman who had won the middleweight Queensberry Cup three years running, had refereed much professional boxing, and since 1907, had been the president of the ABA. The new body ran European championships irregularly, often using the Olympic Games, and most curiously counting a non-European venue, Los An-

geles, in 1932. The results say much about the internationalization of amateur boxing. The Olympic titles were won by boxers from Hungary, Canada, and Argentina (two), South Africa (two), and the United States (two). The European titles (awarded to the European who placed best at the Olympics) went to men from Hungary (the same flyweight, Istvan Enekes), Sweden, France, Italy (two), and Germany (three). Boxing was no longer confined to English- and French-speaking territory.

World War II ended the introductory phase of international amateur boxing. When the sport resumed after the war, countries were split into two hostile camps: capitalist and communist. The communists eschewed the whole of professional sport as degrading and subsidized their amateurs with state funds. Amateur boxing in capitalist countries largely lacked government support, but compensated with television fees and sponsorship from industry and business. In both systems excellence at sport was considered vital for national prestige. In market economies, professional boxing siphoned off gifted amateurs. For example, "Smoking" Joe Frazier, professional boxing's champion from 1970 to 1973, was an Olympic heavyweight champion in 1964. Thus, nations like Poland, the Soviet Union, and Cuba had an advantage in building up an amateur sport with charisma.

The Olympic Games were not to be staged in a communist country until 1980, even though boxers from these countries entered and won gold medals at the first postwar Games in London in 1948. Laszlo Papp of Hungary won boxing gold medals at three successive Olympic Games (London, 1948; Helsinki, 1952; Melbourne, 1956), and he remained the sole holder of this remarkable boxing record until Teofilo Stevenson, the Cuban, did the same at Munich (1972), Montreal (1976), and Moscow (1980).

Africa, Asia, and the Middle East became involved in boxing through the amateur version of the sport. The International Amateur Boxing Association was formed in London in 1946. Its congresses, held every four years, indicate the widening interest in boxing: the first congress outside Europe was held in Tanzania in 1974, followed by Madrid, Spain; Colorado Springs, Colorado; and Bangkok, Thailand. At the Dar es Salaam Congress, Professor Anwar Chowdhry of

Pakistan was elected general secretary by this increasingly important ruling body in world sport, and Stephen Muchoki of Kenya was reckoned to be the best boxer at the International Amateur Boxing Association World Amateur Boxing Championships held in Belgrade in 1978. In 1986, bantamweight Moon Sung-Kil of South Korea won a gold medal in the fourth world championships, held in Reno, Nevada. Between these games and the Olympics, boxing produced winners worldwide. Tournaments organized by the Arab Boxing Union involve associations from Iraq to Algeria; and the Oceanic Federation, which includes Australia, has successfully staged its championships in the tiny mid-Pacific Island of Tahiti.

The World Amateur Boxing Championships were first held in Havana, Cuba, in 1974. They bridged the four-year gap between Olympics and tapped the huge television fees available for supposedly amateur athletics. Boxing was, and still is, genuinely amateur. Boxers get medals, pride, and satisfaction, but no cash unless they turn professional. The sport was, however, disgraced at the 1988 Olympics, held in Seoul, South Korea, by chauvinistic judging and some crowd misbehavior. This led directly to changes in the scoring at all major international tournaments. Five ringside judges, equipped with computers for the first time, had to register points as they saw them scored, but only those points signified by a majority within a second of each other were counted toward the final result. The new system, hated at first, has rapidly gained devotees since it was tried at the Barcelona Olympics in 1992, and the increased impartiality, with its low, measured scores is adjudged a triumph in the management of amateur boxing.

The physical dangers of boxing have long been known. At the National Sporting Club in London, the self-styled home of modern boxing, four boxers died within 41 months at the turn of the century. Amateur fights have produced far fewer fatalities, presumably because their bouts are shorter. Boxing's governing bodies and medical associations inevitably disagree about whether punches to the head cause cumulative brain damage. This debate has become more urgent as the focus of the sport leans more toward raw power. Even so, the headguards in amateur fights, obligatory since the late 1980s, are generally unpopular with both boxers and spectators. Argument rages about the guards' value in reducing concussions, but they have lessened the number of cut eyes and detached retinas.

Despite these dangers, boxing is unsurpassed at developing and maintaining physical fitness. In recent years some women have appreciated this and taken to the sport. In addition, boxing can provide a test of character, determination, and valor. Boxing feints, the movement of the feet, the skill in a rally, are all elements that can be appreciated by the aesthete, inside or outside the ring. According to the ABA rules published in the *Referee* on 15 February 1880:

> . . . decisions shall be given in favour of the competitor who displays the best style and obtains the greatest number of points. The points shall be for "attack," direct clean hits with the knuckles of either hand on any part of the front or sides of the head, or body above the belt; [for] "defence," guarding, slipping, ducking, counter-hitting, or getting away. Where points are otherwise equal, consideration to be given the man who does most of the leading off.

Many boxing fans believe that the sport should heed the spirit of these rules and remember that the goal is not to maim, but to hit, stop blows, and avoid being hit. In order for boxing to prosper, the slide from artistry toward power must be reversed in the ring and appreciated by those outside.

—Stan Shipley

Bibliography: Doherty, W. J. (1931) *In the Days of the Giants.* London: Harrap.

Fleischer, Nat. (1929) *Jack Dempsey: The Idol of Fistiana.* New York: Ring Athletic Library.

———. (1960) *50 Years at Ringside.* London: Corgi.

——— and Sam Andre. (1980) *A Pictorial History of Boxing.* London: Hamlyn.

Gorn, Elliott J. (1986) *The Manly Art: Bare-Knuckle Prize Fighting in America.* Ithaca, NY: Cornell University Press.

Hartley, R. A. (1988) *History & Bibliography of Boxing Books.* Alton, Hampshire, UK: Nimrod Press.

Heller, Peter. (1974) *"In This Corner!": Forty World Champions Tell Their Stories.* New York: Dell.

Johnson, Jack. (1977) *Jack Johnson: In the Ring and Out.* London: Proteus.

Magriel, Paul, ed. (1951) *Memoirs of the Life of Daniel Mendoza.* London: Batsford.

Mason, Tony, ed. (1989) *Sport in Britain: A Social History.* Cambridge: Cambridge University Press.

Miles, Henry Downes. (1906) *Pugilistica.* 3 vols. Edinburgh: John Grant.

Reid, J. C. (1971) *Bucks and Bruisers: Pierce Egan and Regency England.* London: Routledge.

Roberts, Randy. (1979) *Jack Dempsey: The Manassa Mauler.* Baton Rouge: Louisiana State University Press.

Shipley, Stan. (1993) *Bombardier Billy Wells: The Life and Times of a Boxing Hero.* Tyne and Wear, UK: Bewick.

Bullfighting

Bullfighting is practiced primarily in Spain and to a lesser extent in Mexico, Central America, South America, southern France, and Portugal. Its existence depends on (1) a large and constant supply of "noble" or "brave" bulls (i.e., bulls specially bred to charge aggressively in a straight line); (2) a large and constant supply of young poor men; (3) large numbers of hero-worshipping people addicted to thrilling displays of raw physical courage; (4) a smaller number of aficionados obsessed with technical and historical details; and (5) generations of taurine writers and intellectuals who consider bullfighting a fine art rather than a sport. In any given year, approximately 10,000 bullfights are held worldwide, usually in the context of a local religious fiesta that may also include running bulls or brave cows through the town streets, as in the famous festival of Pamplona.

Although bullfighting possesses many ritualistic aspects, it is misleading to call it a ritual. In a true ritual, such as the Catholic Mass, the officiate and communicants are engaged in deliberately symbolic activity; their every word and action has an agreed-on spiritual referent; everything is rigidly predetermined, nothing is left to chance. None of these qualities can be found in a bullfight. There is no deliberately symbolic activity, only simple signals such as handkerchief waving and clarion calls. The bullfighter's actions do not "stand for" anything beyond themselves, and the spectators are always entitled to disagree about them. A great deal is left to chance as it is impossible to predict the behavior of bulls, crowds, or matadors beforehand. There is always a fair chance that the performance will turn sour and anticlimactic, or tragic and ugly.

The rules of a typical bullfight call for a four- or five-year-old bull to be "picced" in his withers with a long lance, further weakened by *banderillas* and risky or flashy cape passes, then killed with a sword thrust by a man wearing decorative rather than protective clothing. Since picadors' (mounted riders who pierce the bull with lances during the first stage of the fight) horses now wear thick padding, the element of cruelty to animals is incidental rather than central to the actual mechanics of the bullfight, more apparent than real. Bullfighting has been a de facto ecological preserve for the Iberian *toro bravo*, a species as rare and unique as the American buffalo, cherished and pampered by ranchers. For another, the archaic concept of manhood that animates the spectacle requires a worthy opponent at all times (women toreros exist but they are still regarded as anomalies, as are midget and comic bullfighters). That is why Hispanic publics always shout out their disapproval if they perceive that a bull is being mishandled and mistreated. Nevertheless, the psychology of both bullfight performers and spectators is thoroughly sadomasochistic, as could hardly be otherwise in a show that features public killing and needless risk of human life. For the thoughtful student of world sports, bullfighting raises questions of a moral or ethical nature much more serious than the ones raised by overwrought animal-rights activists.

Origins

A predatory species of mammal known as *Homo sapiens* and a herbivorous mammal species known as *bos taurus* had gone forth and multiplied with particular success in the Iberian peninsula. Mythology tells us that when Hercules had to steal bulls, he went to what is now the province of Cádiz in southern Spain. Apart from being used as food, the bull was in all likelihood a totemic figure and/or sacrificial victim for the races that populated Iberia during the Bronze Age. Local cults were later blended with beliefs and practices common to the entire Mediterranean area—chief among them the cult of Tauromorphic Bacchus, or Dionysus, firmly entrenched in the Hispania of

Steeped in mythology and a curious blend of psychology and economics, both the bullfight and the matador have become romantic symbols of male honor and national pride.

Roman days. But the Visigothic barbarians who occupied Hispania when Rome fell had no interest in animal-baiting, and the grand amphitheaters were abandoned and never used again.

In the hinterlands, however, the bull continued to play the role of magical agent of sexual fertility, especially in wedding customs that called for the bride and groom to stick darts into a bull tied to a rope. The object was not to fight the beast—certainly not to kill him—but to evoke his fecundating power by "arousing" him, then ritually staining their garments with his blood. This nuptial custom evolved into the rural *capea*, or bull-baiting fiesta, which in turn led to grandiose urban spectacles organized to celebrate military victories or royal weddings. The common people were permitted to crowd into gaily decorated plazas (one in Madrid had room for 60,000 spectators) and watch their lords, mounted on gallant steeds, lancing bulls.

Until the eighteenth century, vast herds of aggressive Iberian bulls roamed freely and bred themselves with no interference from the human species. When knightly bullfighting was in flower, the elite sent their peons into the wilds to round up as many bulls as they could. But not every wild bull had the right amount of *bravura* (focused aggressiveness) to make the aristocrat look good with his lance; thus, large numbers of bulls were supplied in the hope that enough of them would act out their roles convincingly.

As bullfighting on foot became more popular in the 1700s, the demand for bulls increased accordingly, specifically for bulls that could be counted on to charge and not to flee. So the landed blue bloods did the same thing with the bulls that they had done with themselves in earlier epochs: They developed techniques for testing *bravura*, then perpetuated the blood of the bravest through consanguineous mating. Whether or not we think that aristocrats were a superior species, it is unquestionable that the animals they bred were and are amazingly consistent in their power, size, and aggressiveness. Hundreds of brave cattle ranches are now in existence to supply the roughly 25,000 bulls killed every year by Spanish matadors. The many brands of brave bulls that constitute the indispensable raw material for today's *corridas* (program of bull fights for one day, usually six) descend from only five different *castas* or bloodlines, all developed in the eighteenth century. The prestige of a particular brand of bulls was traditionally based on the number of horses, toreros, or innocent bystanders they had killed or maimed. On several occasions, bulls being shipped to a bullfight by train escaped from their railroad crates to wreak havoc. Cossío's taurine encyclopedia lists hundreds of notorious bulls.

Practice

In a rural fiesta, no one is in a hurry to see the bull dead; when the time comes to kill him, any method will do, from a shotgun to a mass assault with knives. In the urban *corrida*, however, it is crucial to show efficiency and know-how; the bull is to be dispatched cleanly (at least in theory) and in three timed *suertes*, or acts—picador, *banderillas*, and matador. Daily experience in the slaughterhouse gave certain ambitious plebeians the necessary knowledge and skill, and the boldest discovered they could earn more money by doing their jobs in public in the manner of a duel: man against monster. The guild system then dominant in the workaday world served as the model for turning bullfighting into a true profession with rules, regulations, hierarchism, apprenticeship, and seniority.

The first professional bullfighters were men completely immersed in the ethos of the eighteenth-century urban slum. They detested the effeminate aristocratic fashions imported from France and proudly affirmed "pure" native concepts of male honor, along with bold and insolent styles of dressing, walking, talking, and killing. Among the rank and file of the down and outs, the readiness to kill or die with a maximum of nonchalance was the only route to prestige. Bullfighting on foot appealed chiefly to violent men

who had nothing to lose and something to prove. Ironically, the sport has always enjoyed enthusiastic support among the same poor masses who would never have chosen bullfighting as a way to escape poverty; masses who, in other words, were either resigned to their lowly fate or hopeful that through hard work and daily sacrifice they could somehow find a better life, but who were willing, all the same, to deify those few who were neither resigned nor inclined to hard work. Bullfighters were rebels in a rigidly stratified society, violators of the general law of submission to circumstances. But the violation of one value system implies adherence to another.

The code matadors lived by was called *vergüenza torera* or *pundonor*. Both terms possess a certain connotation of "touchiness" that descends quite directly from the oldest, most benighted tradition of Spanish honor obsessions. Simply put, *vergüenza torera* is a bullfighter's willingness to place his reputation ahead of his own life. This is not a mythical or romantic notion but a genuine code of conduct. Flashy flirtation with death has both financial and psychological rewards: By all accounts, the heady delusion of omnipotence and heroism that matadors experience is quite addictive. A retired bullfighter is like a reformed alcoholic, always on the verge of a relapse into his favorite vice. Sometimes death is the only sure cure. Those bullfighters who best embody the imprudent honor code receive positive reinforcement from the crowds—rewarded, as it were, for their appetite for punishment. Toreros who stray from the code are negatively reinforced in the form of jeers, taunts, thrown objects, and malicious reviews. Readers of *Death in the Afternoon* may recall Ernest Hemingway's witty, catty, and often vicious disparagement of the bullfighters of his day.

Throughout the nineteenth century, the popular concept of bullfighting was that of a martial art. Matadors were considered to be warriors; their "suits of light" were a kind of super-uniform, and their performances were so many episodes of a grandiose national saga. Unlike other European nations during this period, Spain saw its colonial possessions shrinking instead of expanding. For many Spaniards, the *corrida* may have been a gratifying fantasy of national potency to make up for the less-than-glorious reality.

The military origins of bullfight music have been firmly established by scholars. Every change of *suerte,* or scene, in a bullfight was, and is, signaled by a bugle call; the melodies are much the same as those used in infantry and cavalry barracks. The *pasodoble,* the stirring music played even today by bullring bands, descends directly from the military march. Over 500 of them were composed, and the band was always on hand to set the right tone of militancy. Following the loss of Spain's colonies to the United States in 1898, numerous bullfights were organized in which people wore the national colors and bullfighters made inflammatory speeches. During the Spanish Civil War (1936–1939), both sides sponsored *corridas;* bullfighters would parade with clenched fists or fascist salutes, whichever was appropriate. And in the darkest days of their country's isolation under Franco, Spaniards flocked to bullrings to reaffirm their identity with something they knew was their own and which they took to represent their finest qualities. However barbarous its origins, however sordid some of its practices, the *fiesta de toros* had truly become Spain's *Fiesta Nacional.*

For every successful matador paraded around the bullring on the shoulders of ecstatic fans, there is an invisible army of forgotten young men who tried and failed. Like certain marine species that give birth to thousands of young in the hopes that a few will reach maturity, the overwhelming majority of would-be matadors have been eliminated by environmental factors, each harsher than the last. The bull's horns are the most basic, physical agent of this process of natural selection. For many Spanish youth, the beginning was the end. From 1747 to 1995, at least 170 young aspirants were killed by goring, along with 142 *banderilleros,* 70 picadors, 59 full matadors, and 4 comic bullfighters. These statistics do not include toreros killed during ranch tests or private parties, nor do they include *capeas* (amateur bullfights), which have arguably been festal Spain's major device for maiming young bodies and crushing hopes. Doctors specializing in *taurotraumatología,* or horn-wound surgery, are accustomed to working on the pierced thighs, ruptured rectums, and eviscerated scrota of bullfighters. When an apprentice torero recovers from his first goring and reappears in the ring, his manager anxiously watches for any sign that his valor or his determination have been compromised. The all-powerful element of luck will still

preside over his career. To be successful, a man must meet a noble and cooperative bull at the right moment; he must also have *padrinos,* or godfathers, a good manager, opportunities, a crowd-pleasing personality, grace, flair, and a whole series of other qualities that are difficult to isolate but nevertheless mean the difference between glory and mediocrity.

In view of this brutal selection process, it might well be asked why any young man in his right mind would want to be a bullfighter. Poverty is the answer most often given to this question. Many portions of the Spanish populace have been condemned to misery, illiteracy, and lack of opportunity. Harsh as they have been, however, these social conditions are not sufficient in themselves to explain matador motivation. They obviously do not tell us why bullfighters who were already immensely wealthy—such as Espartero or Belmonte or Paquirri—remained in the plazas, or why so many men who had actually found good jobs wanted only to fight bulls. Additional motivational factors include self-destructive tendencies and unusually powerful oedipal conflicts. With an activity that has been one of the only means of advancement in a rigidly stratified society, whose wellspring is passion and whose lifeblood is the ritual combat between two animal species, where a lucky and skillful few succeed where so many hundreds fail, where so many frustrated men hound their sons into bullrings to avenge their own defeats, where critics dip their pens in poison and crowds go from adulation to mockery in a second, we cannot help but find sadomasochistic behavior patterns. In general, matadors are men obsessed with insurmountable violent masculine role models and rivals; their ambition is directly correlated with the obstacles placed in their path. Violence becomes identified with fullness of being; winning or losing, brutalizing or arranging to be brutalized, the bullfighter keeps his buried fantasies of omnipotence alive. Hemingway idolized masochistic matadors with adolescent enthusiasm, but in many ways they are like compulsive gamblers who throw caution to the winds and unconsciously play to lose all. Unlike gamblers, bullfighters go for broke in front of huge crowds of people egging them on; so in the last analysis, the taurine honor code is a matter of mass cultural psychology. Countless bullfighters have confessed to fearing the crowd's reactions more than the bulls themselves. Mass desire is as potentially sadomasochistic as individual desire: It will polarize around any expert manipulator of violence, seemingly autosufficient and untouchable in his charisma. The dramatic death of a matador in the line of duty (caused most often by his socially sanctioned suicidal honor), and his subsequent deification in popular lore, simply carry the whole idolatrous process to its logical conclusion.

From a historical point of view, bullfighting has been nothing less than a microcosm of Spain, a nation built not on individuals but on quasi-familial factions, where a "strong man" ultimately derived his strength from the debility of his supporters and the weak got nowhere without patriarchs, *caudillos*, godfathers, political bosses, and other men who bestowed rewards and punishments in accordance with their mood swings. Until recently, the Spanish political system served to keep most Spaniards out of politics altogether, instilling in them a fatalistic attitude vis-à-vis the whims of authority. The office of *presidente* of a bullfight still represents this legacy of arbitrary despotism. Fraud and influence peddling were once endemic on the "planet of the bulls." Horns were shaved, half-ton sandbags were dropped on bulls' shoulders, critics were bribed. (One of the cruel ironies of bullfighting is that the most honest and reputable critics are also the ones most determined to preserve the authentic risk of human life upon which the whole enterprise is founded.) Beyond tricks and venality, we can see that bullfighting's personalistic patronage system mirrors that of the larger society. The provincial *fiesta de toros* was a cautionary tale about what could happen to people without connections or friends; small-town mayors anxious to please their supporters had no qualms about acquiring the largest, most fearsome bulls for penniless apprentice toreros to struggle with and occasionally succumb to. Sooner or later a would-be bullfighter must find protectors/exploiters, the more the better, or he will get nowhere. El Cordobés wandered for years without such connections, and when he finally found them they were desperate gambling types much like himself who were willing to take a chance on a brash newcomer. The other side of this coin of unfair exclusion is unfair inclusion, young men from the right families, prodigies favored from the beginning by cattle breeders, impresarios, and critics. Traditionally, the whole point of a matador's career was to go from being a dependent, a client, a receiver of favors in a more-or-less corrupt system of personalistic patronage, to being a dispenser of favors and patronage—the boss of his *cuadrilla*, or team, a landowner, a big man in his community, a pillar of the status quo, idolized by impoverished and oppressed people. A whole web of complicities make bullfighting possible—including local religious belief systems. The *fiesta de toros* is always held in honor of a patron saint, a kind of supernatural protector in touch with an arbitrary central authority that can be cajoled into doing favors for his "clients."

Like old-fashioned Spanish political oratory, bullfighting can be seen as a series of dramatic public gestures. Every bullfighter is a potential demagogue, a man who stirs up the emotions of a crowd to become a leader and to achieve his own ends. A bullfighter gains power and wealth only when he learns how to sway the masses, to mesmerize them, to harness their passion for his private profit. The matador rides to the top of society on the backs of mass enthusiasm. But no bullfighter could sway the masses if they were not disposed to be swayed. As soon as we become spectators of the spectators, we find their mobile and emotional disposition to be intimately related to popular concepts of power, authority, justice, and masculinity. Without heed to experts or critics, bullfight spectators evaluate artistic merit or bravery on their own and express their views instantly and unselfconsciously. The downside of this refreshing spontaneity, however, is that popular value judgments tend to be arbitrary, impulsive, and irreflexive. The impulsive evaluations of bullfight crowds rattle and unnerve bullfighters, sometimes leading them to commit acts that result in serious injury or death. At the Almería Fair in 1981, for example, the normally cautious Curro Romero was gored in an attempt to appease a hastily judgmental crowd. Afterwards the public was very sorry, of course, as sorry as it had been in 1920 after hounding Joselito into fatal temerity at Talavera and in 1947 when it drove Manolete to impale himself on the horns of Islero. *Blood and Sand,* the famous bullfighting novel by Blasco Ibáñez, ends with this description of the public: "The beast roared: the real one, the only one."

Bullfighting

At the very least, the public judges the taurine performance in an arbitrary, capricious, and personalistic manner. Since the decisions of the bullring *presidente* form part of the entire affair, they too fall under the scrutiny—and often the vociferous condemnation—of the spectators. Like old Spain itself, the bullfight is a *mise en scène* of an authoritarian power in an uneasy relationship with a blasphemous and rebellious underclass. For many Spanish writers, the crowd's impulsive style of reacting to duly constituted authority was the worst evil of bullfighting, one that reconfirmed Spaniards in their submission to the despotic whims of the powerful. As the very embodiment of arbitrary might, the *presidente* possesses total immunity and his decisions cannot be appealed. The public's only recourse is to whistle, hoot, or insult. Thus, in much the same manner as the old African monarchies described by anthropologists, the *corrida de toros* permits a ritualistic contestation of power that is momentarily gratifying but essentially without consequence. In his own way, of course, the matador polarizes the crowd's criteria of dominance and submission: Whatever power he has must be seen in terms of popular concepts of power (who deserves to have it and who doesn't) worked out long ago during Spain's traumatic history of civil conflicts. According to one Spanish sociologist, "The bullfight spectator believes in certain qualities inherent in a man that constitute manliness, and precisely because he believes in them he goes to see bullfights." It would be correct to picture the bullfight as a dramatization of machismo, as long as we remember that machismo is primarily a psychological mechanism of compensation that provides a fantasy image of superiority in the absence of real sociopolitical power. Perhaps a bullfighter's manly hyperbole serves to mediate between personal and national inferiority complexes. In any event, the evidence would seem to be on the side of those who argue that bullfighting is the legacy of obscurantism, that it is emblematic of the manipulability of the people, their gullibility, their irrational hero-worship, their civic immaturity. It would surely be an exaggeration to see bullfighting as the "cause" of Spain's former political backwardness, but it was certainly no cure.

The bullfight is a spectacle of killing and gratuitous risk of life. It is extremely difficult for human beings to gaze upon such transgression without being aroused in some way. Even reactions of horror and nausea confirm that violent spectacle is inherently erotic. Properly defined, disgust is nothing but negative arousal, caused by the fear of degradation that accompanies the desire to give way to the instincts and violate all taboos. In reality, most people do not transgress one taboo after another and set off on the primrose path to ruin. Culture (whether in the form of Spanish bullfighting or American "slasher" movies) is there to provide official fantasy gratification as a safe substitute for the real thing. Order must be preserved even as desire requires some sort of release. The majority of Spaniards and many foreigners enjoy the titillating taurine spectacle without guilt or moral qualms of any kind. The group norms that hold sway at a bullfight enable each spectator to feel his or her physiological arousal as entirely appropriate. Intense stimulation actually increases commitment to the group's rationalization of it. This is the sociopsychological mechanism that has permitted Spaniards to experience titillation at bullfights and associate it, at a conscious level, with patriotism, manly ideals, integrity, honor, art, and so on. What happens to this happy group consensus when a goring occurs and the transgressive nature of bullfighting is fully manifested? Community norms are already in place that will provide cognitions appropriate to the intense arousal spectators experience. These stand-by norms quickly forge a new group consensus whose conscious elements are pity, grief, forbearance, resignation, and ultimately, reaffirmation of all the heroic qualities that led the matador to risk his life in the first place. The normative emotionality that takes shape around the fallen bullfighter goes far beyond the bullring in its sociocultural implications and lasts for many years after the tragedy. There is still plenty of cultural debris left over from the emotional explosions that accompanied the deaths of star matadors.

—Timothy Mitchell

Bibliography: Araúz de Robles, Santiago. (1974) *Sociología del toreo.* Madrid: Prensa Española.

Arévalo, José Carlos, and José Antonio del Moral. (1985) *Nacido para morir.* Madrid: Espasa-Calpe.

Bergamín, José. (1981) *La música callada del toreo.* Madrid: Turner.

Blasco Ibáñez, Vicente. (1911) *The Blood of the Arena.* Chicago: McClurg.

Cambria, Rosario. (1974) *Los toros: Tema polémico en el ensayo español del siglo XX.* Madrid: Gredos.

Chaves Nogales, Manuel. (1937) *Juan Belmonte, Killer of Bulls.* New York: Doubleday.

Claramunt, Fernando (1989). *Historia ilustrada de la tauromaquia.* Madrid: Espasa-Calpe.

Collins, Larry, and Dominique Lapierre. *Or I'll Dress You in Mourning.* New York: Simon & Schuster.

Conrad, Jack Randolph. (1957) *The Horn and the Sword: The History of the Bull as a Symbol of Power and Fertility.* New York: E. P. Dutton.

Cossío, José María de. (1961) *Los toros. Tratado técnico e histórico.* 4 vols. Madrid: Espasa-Calpe.

Delgado Ruiz, Manuel. (1986) *De la muerte de un Dios: La fiesta de los toros en el universo simbólico de la cultura popular.* Barcelona: Nexos.

Fernández Suárez, Alvaro. (1961) *España, arbol vivo.* Madrid: Aguilar.

Hemingway, Ernest. (1932) *Death in the Afternoon.* New York: Charles Scribner's Sons.

Levers de Miranda, Angel. (1962) *Ritos y juegos del toro.* Madrid: Taurus.

Mitchell, Timothy. (1991) *Blood Sport. A Social History of Spanish Bullfighting.* Philadelphia and London: University of Pennsylvania Press.

Noel, Eugenio. (1914) *Escritos antitaurinos.* Madrid: Taurus.

Tynan, Kenneth. (1955) *Bull Fever.* New York: Harper & Bros.

Buzkashi

Buzkashi (goat dragging) is a spectacular, volatile, and often violent equestrian game played primarily by Turkic peoples in northern Afghanistan. Central Asian in origin, buzkashi also occurs, for the most part as a self-conscious folkloristic survival, in the Muslim republics of the former Soviet Union north of the Oxus River and in China's Xinjiang Province. During the 1980s and early 1990s, buzkashi was played among Afghan refugees near Chitral and Peshawar in Pakistan where, however, it bears no cultural relationship to Pakistani polo. In both its principal forms—i.e., traditional-grassroots game (*tudabarai*) and modern-governmental sport (*qarajai*)—the central action is much the same: riders on powerful horses congregate above the carcass of a goat or calf, lean from their saddles, struggle with each other to grab the carcass off the ground, and then try to keep sole control of it while riding away at full speed. While regarded primarily as playful fun, both forms of buzkashi also exist as an implicitly political arena in which patron/sponsors seek to demonstrate and thus enhance their capacity for controlling events.

Origins and Development

As with most folk games, the origins of buzkashi are impossible to trace precisely, but it doubtless sprang from nomadic forebearers of the same Turkic peoples (Uzbek, Turkomen, Kazakh, Kirghiz) who are its core players today. Equestrian nomads, these groups spread westwards from China and Mongolia between the tenth and fifteenth centuries. The game quite likely developed, in much the same way as American rodeo, as a recreational variant of everyday herding or raiding activity. There is no evidence to support the lurid notion, advanced for touristic purposes during the 1960s and 1970s, that the game was originally played with live human prisoners instead of dead livestock.

In recent generations other ethnic groups in northern Afghanistan have entered the culture of buzkashi: Tajiks, Hazaras, and even Pushtun migrants from south of the Hindu Kush whose new prominence in the north was supported by central government policy. Another key development dates from 1955 when the central government, based in Kabul, hosted its first tournament on the birthday anniversary of King Mohammed Zahir. From the mid-1950s to the early 1980s, successive national regimes hosted similar buzkashi competitions in Kabul. With the collapse of the authority of the central government during the Afghan-Soviet War (1979–1989), the tournament fell apart. In the 1990s, as political chaos continued, buzkashi has largely reverted to its original status as a locally based pastime north of the Hindu Kush.

Practice

Whatever its form and occasion, buzkashi depends on sponsorship of both the champion horses and riders and of the ceremonial event in which buzkashi is played. In the traditional, rural context of northern Afghanistan, both types of sponsorship are exercised by *khans,* men of social, economic, and political importance who constitute the informal and ever-shifting power elite of local life. The *khans* breed, raise, and own the special horses whose bloodlines are proudly chronicled and whose success in buzkashi contributes to owner status. *Khans* likewise employ specialist riders (*chapandazan*) for their prize horses. Most important of all is their sponsorship of the celebratory events called *toois* at which buzkashi is traditionally played. These are scheduled for winter, both because it is the agricultural slack season and because horses and riders can play then without overheating.

Khans stage *toois* to celebrate ritual events such as a son's circumcision or marriage. While the ritual itself is generally a private, family affair, it provides the occasion for much wider gatherings whose centerpiece is a day or several days of buzkashi. It also represents a status-oriented initiative in which the social, economic, and political resources of the sponsor (*tooi-wala*) are publicly tested. If those resources prove sufficient and the *tooi* is a success, its sponsor's "name will rise." If not, the *tooi-walla*'s reputation can be ruined. Preparations include the amassing of funds for food and prize money and the recruitment of nearby hosts for the hundreds of invited guests who, the sponsor hopes, will accept invitations to attend. Equally hopeful but likewise problematic is the expectation that the guests will present the sponsor with cash gifts to help defray the costs of the *tooi.*

After a ceremonial first day's lunch, everyone mounts and rides to the buzkashi field: sponsor, closest associates, invited *khans,* their sizable entourages (including prize horses, *chapandazan,* and assorted associates who have come in the name of "friendship" but can be quickly mobilized in case of serious conflict), and the local populace. The field itself typically consists of a barren plain, unbounded and undemarcated, on the village periphery. A goat or calf carcass lies in the middle. (While the term buzkashi specifically refers to "goat," calf carcasses are often used because, it is said, they last longer.) Without ceremony but in accordance with Muslim law (*hallal*), the animal has been bled to death, decapitated, and dehooved to protect contestants' hands. An eviscerated carcass makes for faster play, but purists tend to favor a

Buzkashi plays an important part in both traditional and modern Afghan culture.

heavier, ungutted animal so that only real power, rather than mere quickness, will prevail.

Most traditional buzkashis begin without fanfare and gather intensity as more and more participants arrive. Any number may take part, and some games involve hundreds of riders at once. A morning or afternoon session consists of several dozen play cycles, each of which starts with the riders forming an equestrian scrum over the dead calf. With their horses lurching, rearing, and trying to hold position, riders lean down from the saddle and grab at the carcass. More horses and riders batter their way toward the center of an ever-growing, ever more fiercely contested mass of wild movement. Lunging half-blind in the melee, one rider manages to grab hold of the carcass briefly, but, as a saying goes, "Every calf has four legs," and other riders quickly wrench it away. The calf is trampled, dragged, tugged, lifted, and lost again as one competitor after another seeks to gain sole control. There are no teams although friendly riders (or the riders of friendly *khans*) may sometimes assist each other. Everyone has the right to try, but play is monopolized in practice by the *chapandazan* in their distinctive fur-trimmed headgear. Meanwhile the "town crier" (*jorchi*) shouts the amount of prize money offered. The longer a given play cycle is contested, the greater that amount grows and the fiercer the competition.

Finally one horse and rider emerge from the mass (*tudabarai*), take the calf free and clear, and drop it in uncontested triumph. Play stops for a brief moment while the town crier launches into a stylized praise chant for the rider, the horse, and most of all the horse owner:

Oh, the horse of Hajji Ali,
On him rode Ahmad Gul.
He leapt like a deer.
He glared like a leopard.

How he took it away.
How he showed what he is.
How the name of Hajji Ali rose.
How we all hear his name.
How his pride is complete.

Prizes for the victorious rider once took the form of carpets, rifles, and even horses. Now almost all are cash, with amounts depending on *tooi* sponsor liberality and sometimes exceeding $100. The horse owner's sole reward is prestige or "name," that amorphous but most important currency of traditional Afghan life.

Barely has the chant finished before the next play cycle starts. Cycle follows cycle with no sense of cumulative score. The last cycle each day, typically played with a carcass in shreds, has special value, and the winning rider proudly departs with the tattered calf dangling across his saddle. The visiting *khans* and their entourages then retire for dinner and sleep at one or another of the nearby host houses where every event of the past day is reviewed in conversation: whose horse did well, whether the prize money was sufficient, and—most of all—what happened in case of serious dispute. Disputes and the issue of who can control them represent the darker, less readily admitted core of interest in buzkashi.

Buzkashi in the Movies

While never yet played outside its Central Asian homeland, buzkashi has been featured in several Western films and popular publications. Joseph Kessel's 1967 novel *Les Cavaliers* (The Horsemen) deals exclusively with the game and its protagonists. Set at the time of the first Kabul tournament, the story features a father-son Oedipal dynamic that some readers find belabored, but the depictions of buzkashi within traditional Afghan culture are colorful, engaging, and mostly accurate. A movie version, also entitled *The Horsemen*, was produced by Columbia in 1971. Starring Jack Palance and Omar Sharif in the father-son *chapandaz* roles, it represents one of Hollywood's rare attempts at creating a film without any Western characters; it failed, perhaps for that reason, at the box office. The actual buzkashi footage is, however, superb.

Jacob Bronowski's 1974 magnum opus *The Ascent of Man* describes buzkashi as a surviving example of the terrifying impact that the ancient Scythian and, later, Mongol equestrians must have had on settled communities. More broadly (and more dubiously), buzkashi is made to symbolize "the monomaniac culture of conquest." The film series based on Bronowski's book includes some excellent clips of buzkashi.

—G. Whitney Azoy

Three factors contribute to dispute in traditional buzkashi. First, the play activity itself is already full of physically brutal contact. Second, the question of being sufficiently "free and clear" for a score is notoriously subjective and difficult to adjudicate. And third, the horse-owner *khans*, whose horses and riders compete, are very often rivals of each other in the real-life game of local politics. Indeed it is during buzkashi that such rivalries and alliances, otherwise hidden by the diplomatic niceties of day-to-day existence, are revealed in all their disruptive potential.

It takes little to trigger a dispute. Had a victory claimant really gotten the carcass "free and clear" before dropping it? Was one rider guilty of grabbing another's bridle or whipping him in the face? Did the *chapandaz* of Mujib Khan have a rope secreted in his sleeve in order to enhance his grasp of the carcass? Suddenly the violent pushing and shoving, hitherto "for fun," now becomes "for real." Each *khan's* entourage coalesces around him. The current play cycle is abandoned and the air is full of angry shouts as everyone tries to gain control of an increasingly uncontrollable situation.

While outright fighting is rare, an aggrieved group may leave the buzkashi and go home rather than suffer perceived injustice. Such defection tarnishes the reputation of a *tooi* and thus of its *tooi-wala*. More typically the shouting and jostling gradually subside as one or another of the *khans* makes himself heard and emerges in the role of peacemaker. Much prestige thereby attaches to him. He has, after all, demonstrated an ability to control volatile events, to impress his will on a dynamic that had shifted from playful to political. Now his "name will rise" in the countless tellings and retellings of this buzkashi. Such reputational gain can then be of considerable importance as potential followers calculate the benefits of attaching themselves to a patron or of taking sides in a real-world dispute over land, water, livestock, or women.

Beginning in the mid-1950s, Afghanistan's central government likewise began to enlist buzkashi in its efforts at political impression management. The Afghan National Olympic Committee was charged with staging a "national tournament" in Kabul each year on the birthday of King Mohammed Zahir. Provincial contingents were organized in the north (as yet unlinked by all-weather roads to the rest of the country), and the game itself was transformed into a more or less codified sport (*qarajai*) with uniformed teams, authorized referees, a demarcated field of play (the *qarajai*), a cumulative scoring system, and severe penalties (including arrest) for any form of dispute during play. Only the players (typically 10 or 12 per team) and the referees (usually military officers) were allowed on the field. Horse-owner *khans*, their *tooi*-sponsorship role now co-opted by the government, had to sit on the sidelines. And instead of having the vague "free-and-clear" objective of *tudabarai*, players now had to carry the calf around a flag and drop it in clearly marked circle (the *daiwra*). The king assumed the role of national *tooi-wala*, hosting the tournament banquet and presented the championship medals. The tournament allowed Kabul residents to rub elbows with rustic horsemen from the distant north. And the northerners returned home each year with fresh tales of a broader Afghanistan and potent impressions of the central government's capacity for control.

By the time of the king's fall from power in 1973, the Kabul buzkashi tournament had become a fixture in the national calendar. Subsequent nonroyalist regimes retained the October timing but shifted the occasion first (under President Mohammed Daoud, 1973–77) to United Nations Day and then (under communist rule) to the anniversary of the 1917 Bolshevik Revolution. Always presented in the name of sheer play and fun, Kabul buzkashi tournaments continued to serve as a symbol both of Afghan national unity and of governmental capacity for dispute-free control. The nationwide collapse of Afghan government control in the early 1980s was reflected in the year-by-year disintegration of Kabul buzkashi. In Daoud's era, the tournament had lasted 12 days and featured ten provincial teams in a precisely orchestrated round-robin. From 1980 onwards, fewer teams came each year. By 1983 the Soviet puppet government had abandoned all pretense of staging buzkashi.

During the Afghan-Soviet War (1979–1989), buzkashi was played in Pakistan's North West Frontier province by refugees based in Peshawar and Chitral. Many of the same *khans* and riders who had dominated the game in prewar Afghanistan now formed the core of competitions played on Fridays in the winter months. Now, however, the principal *tooi-wala* role shifted to several men whose newly developed renown rested on their leadership of local refugee relief efforts. As usual, all was done in the name of fun, but soon the new breed of sponsor-entrepreneurs were competing to attract resource-rich spectators from the fast-growing expatriate community: diplomats, United Nations personnel, and directors of nongovernmental aid organizations. Thus ingratiated with their "guests," these *tooi-walas* in exile promoted themselves as conduits for international aid to the refugee community.

By the mid-1990s, the central government in post-Soviet Afghanistan was still too weak to resume the national tournament and the main locus of buzkashi had reverted to the northern provinces. Some traditional *khans* still sponsored *toois*, but local warlords and militia commanders were replacing them in the primary sponsorship role.

—G. Whitney Azoy

Buzkashi

Bibliography: Azoy, G. Whitney. (1982) *Buzkashi: Game and Power in Afghanistan.* Philadelphia: University of Pennsylvania Press.

Balikci, Asen. (1978a) "Buzkashi." *Natural History* 87, 2: 54–63.

———. (1978b) "Village Buzkashi." *Afghanistan Journal* 5, 1: 11–21.

Dupree, Louis. (1970) "Sports and Games in Afghanistan." *American Universities Field Staff Reports.* South Asia Series XIV (1).

Michaud, Roland, and Sabrina Michaud. (1988) *Horsemen of Afghanistan.* London: Thames and Hudson.

Camogie

A modified form of hurling with 12 players per team, camogie is Ireland's national field sport for women. The game is very similar to hurling, although physical contact is more restricted.

Origins

Camogie was first played in 1904. Opportunities for women to participate in sport were very limited in Ireland until the early twentieth century. It was female members of the Gaelic League, the national language movement, who decided to found a game that was both distinctly Gaelic and strictly female. In developing camogie in and around Dublin, they modified the Irish national field game but maintained use of the stick, which had come to symbolize Irish nationalism and Gaelic culture. The Camogie Association of Ireland, founded in 1904, is still the governing body for the sport.

Development

In the early days, the game did not catch on or spread much beyond Dublin itself. It was with the development of competition in the universities that the game took hold, with women from Dublin, Belfast, Cork, and Galway competing in the annual intervarsity competition, the Ashbourne Cup, first held in 1915. Freedom to pursue a sport while simultaneously promoting the ideals of the Gaelic League made university women ideal candidates for furthering camogie. However, while subscribing to the ideals of the Gaelic Athletic Association (GAA), the Camogie Association remained a distinct organization, thereby giving Irish women their own voice in the process of fostering nationalism, feminism, and Gaelic sport.

In the 1930s, the Camogie Association tried to increase its sphere of influence beyond the major Irish cities. It reorganized on a national basis and founded an All-Ireland championship for county teams, mirroring the organization of hurling. The game has continued to spread since that time. Now its areas of strength, like its rules and style of play, parallel even more closely those of its brother game, hurling.

The camog or stick used in camogie, Ireland's national field sport for women, is just a smaller version of the hurling caman, *which has become a symbol of Irish nationalism and Gaelic culture. Camogie is very similar to hurling, but physical contact is more restricted.*

Practice

The field for camogie is smaller than for hurling, at a maximum of 110 meters (120 yards) long and 68 meters (75 yards) wide. The stick (*camog*) is shorter and lighter than hurling's "hurley" (*caman*) and the ball is also lighter than the "slitter" (*sliothar*). The rules of camogie are also very similar to those of hurling, although the "H"-shaped goal posts of hurling have been modified by the addition of a second crossbar. One point is scored when the ball passes between the crossbars, and three points are scored when the ball is driven below the lower crossbar and into the goal. The goals posts are 6.1 meters (20 feet) tall and 4.6 meters (15 feet) apart, and the lower crossbar is 2.1 meters (7 feet) high.

—Timothy J. L. Chandler

See also Hurling.

Bibliography: Arlott, John, ed. (1975) *The Oxford Companion to Sports and Games.* London: Oxford University Press.

Camogie Association of Ireland. (1990) *Playing Rules and Constitution.* Dublin: Camogie Association.

Carroll, Noel. (1979) *Sport in Ireland.* Dublin: Department of Foreign Affairs.

Canoeing and Kayaking

Canoeing is the use of a popular and versatile category of small craft for transportation and recreation on the water. Canoes are lightweight and have a narrow shape and shallow bottom. This allows them to move very efficiently in both shallow and deep water. They are usually powered and steered by paddles held by the canoeist, unlike rowboats or rafts that have oars connected to the boat.

The canoe is a very diverse category of vessel. Contemporary canoes are generally divided into two basic styles, known as Canadian canoes and kayaks. Canadian canoes usually have an open deck, while kayaks are enclosed with a small passenger cockpit. Canadian-canoe paddles have a blade (the wide section placed in the water) at one end. Kayak paddles have blades at both ends. In a literal sense, the word canoeing refers specifically to the use of Canadian-style canoes, while the use of kayaks is called kayaking. However, both are frequently referred to as canoes when discussed together, because of their common characteristics. Competitive canoe races, for example, often include divisions for kayaks. They also have interchangeable features. A Canadian canoe used in white-water rapids may have an enclosed deck like a kayak.

Canoes and kayaks are among the oldest and most basic forms of transportation in the world. While they still serve as practical transportation, they are most often used today for recreation. Many people enjoy paddling in them on lakes or slow rivers for relaxation or exercise. Hunters, fishermen, hikers, and campers use canoes and kayaks to reach remote areas by water. Canoe racing is an established competitive sport that is featured in the Olympics. An especially challenging form of canoeing and kayaking is white-water paddling on the fast-moving rapids of rivers or on oceans and bays with strong currents and surf.

Origins

Canoes had a vital role in many early cultures. They made it possible for people to travel on open seas or in regions with many rivers and lakes. Canoes were used by individuals or tribes to migrate from one region to another, to carry warriors into battle, or for fishing and hunting.

The canoe's history began in primitive times, when people first rode logs to travel over the water. This idea was refined by various cultures throughout the world. In addition to canoes and kayaks, these primitive craft also evolved into rowboats, sailboats, and rafts. The name "canoe" is based on an early word for boats used in the Caribbean. The term was later adapted and broadened to describe similar vessels used in many societies. Some early canoes were small boats for one or two people. Others were very large and capable of carrying many people and substantial cargo over long distances.

One original form of canoe is known as a dugout because it was made by burning and hollowing out the center of large logs to create an open space for passengers and cargo. Dugouts were used in many regions, including the Pacific South Sea islands, the Caribbean, Africa, and the Pacific Northwest coast of North America, among others. The largest dugouts were made from the trunks of immense trees, and the boats were as long as 18 meters (60 feet) or more. The exterior hulls were also shaped. Dugouts were either low in the water, or they were larger and had a large bow that rose to a point. In some cultures, they were often decorated with carvings and other designs. Some dugouts, called outriggers, had pontoons on either side for stability.

A direct ancestor of the modern Canadian canoe was the bark canoe developed by Native Americans. These boats had frameworks constructed of individual pieces of wood covered by strips of bark. The white, papery bark of the birch tree was frequently used, so these canoes are often called birchbark canoes. The lightweight canoes could be carried (portaged) over the land and they could be easily repaired.

The pointed kayak was developed by the Aleuts and other inhabitants of the far northern Arctic regions of America and Greenland. Kayaks were made by wrapping animal skins over a frame of wood or bone. These kayaks were very fast and maneuverable. Their covered, watertight decks provided protection for the kayaker in turbulent, cold waters. If a kayak capsized, the passenger could turn the boat upright again by shifting his weight and maneuvering the paddle

Britain's Hilary Peacock and Douglas Parnham train twice daily on the Thames in 1975 as they attempt to capture Olympic medals.

while he was underwater, a move now called an Eskimo roll. A related boat in the north was called a *umiak*, which was larger and more open and carried women and supplies.

When European explorers and settlers arrived in the Americas, they used the designs of native canoes to create their own vessels. The bark canoe was especially popular among fur trappers and other European explorers who traveled into the continent's remote interior. The canoe gained a romantic image associated with adventure. In some instances, they were also used against the native cultures who had originally developed them. In the Arctic, foreign traders enslaved the native inhabitants and forced them to participate in large hunting parties in specially designed kayaks called *baidarkas*.

Other methods of water and land transportation gradually took over the primary role of the canoe. In the mid-nineteenth century, the emphasis for canoes began to shift to recreational paddling and competitive sport. In North America, people on wilderness vacations rode in canoes operated by expert guides. Recreational canoes also were used at resorts and other sites. Early interest in canoe sports was particularly strong in Europe. John McGregor, a lawyer, was an important early booster of the canoe in England and Europe. In Britain McGregor founded the Canoe Club in the 1860s (which became the Royal Canoe Club) as one of the earliest recreational canoe associations. He was particularly interested in a vessel called the Rob Roy canoe. McGregor made many trips in his canoe, and he wrote about these voyages to promote interest in it. Although McGregor called the Rob Roy a canoe, it was actually a kayak. Because of this, the distinctions between canoes and kayaks became less distinct in Europe than in America. The Rob Roy also had a sail. For a time, the most popular European canoe sport was sailing. Canoeing gradually focused more on paddling, while recreational sailing became a separate sport (although people still sail in canoes today).

In the late nineteenth and early twentieth centuries, recreational canoeing continued to gain popularity throughout the world. Specialized canoes and kayaks were developed, along with new competitive racing sports. Numerous organizations were formed to promote sport canoeing, including the American Canoe Association in 1880. In 1924, an international canoeing organization, the Internationella Representantskapet for Kanotidrott (IRK) was formed in Europe. A movement to make canoeing an Olympic sport also began at this time. Canoe racing was officially included in the Olympics for the first time in the 1936 games in Berlin. After World War II, the IRK was succeeded by a new organization, the International Canoe Federation.

In the middle and latter twentieth century, canoeing benefited from the increasing emphasis on physical fitness and the popularity of outdoor activities like hiking and camping. New local and national canoeing associations were formed, including the United States Canoe Association and the American White-Water Affiliation. Canoes and kayaks became very sophisticated and specialized. New materials and mass-production methods made canoes and kayaks widely affordable. A particularly inexpensive form of paddle boating developed in the late 1960s with very small molded-plastic boats and rafts that cost under $100. In the 1970s, white-water sports in rapidly running rivers became popular.

Practice

The early canoes, kayaks, and dugouts have been modified in many ways, but most modern versions of them continue to be based on the original designs. The specific design of an individual canoe or kayak is based on a combination of factors. Because the canoe is such a diverse category, there are many variations, and some canoes differ in specific ways from the basic guideline in their shape, size, or other characteristics. Some canoes, for example, have deeper hulls or are powered by motors or sails.

Modern canoes range from 3 to 8 meters (10 to 25 feet) or more in length. Most are between 3.3 and 6.1 meters (11 and 20 feet) long. When viewed from above, they are somewhat wider in the center (amidships) and narrower or pointed at the front (bow) and rear (stern).

Open Canadian canoes can carry one or more people comfortably, and usually they have room for cargo. Kayaks are designed to be watertight, so they are usually covered, and the only opening is a small cockpit for the passenger. Some kayaks have a seat on top of a completely enclosed hull.

The exact length, weight, and shape of the bow, stern, hull, and keel line (bottom) will determine how a canoe or kayak handles in the water. These qualities include how fast the craft can be paddled, how stable and balanced it is, and how quickly it can be turned. Other considerations include comfort, the number of passengers and amount of cargo a canoe can hold, and how portable it is.

Some of these qualities are contradictory. Longer canoes are generally faster, but they cannot be turned as easily or quickly. Those that are shorter are more responsive to turns, but they are more difficult to paddle in a straight line. The most important consideration in canoe design is the situation that the particular boat will be used in. Some boats made for very specific purposes emphasize certain characteristics while sacrificing others. General-purpose canoes are a compromise of various features. A recreational canoe designed for leisurely use on calm lakes or long-distance touring will likely emphasize comfort, stability, and ease of paddling. A boat used for flat-water racing is built to attain maximum speed, so they tend to place less emphasis on comfort. A canoe or kayak built for use in white-water rapids or narrow channels will be shorter and have other features that make it more responsive for fast turning. A white-water vessel also bobs in and out of the water, so a covered hull is necessary to keep water out and allow the boat to be easily turned upright if it capsizes.

Some canoes and kayaks have very shallow hulls so they can be maneuvered quickly in water of various depths. Others have deeper hulls or a keel, rudder, or centerboard of solid material extending below for greater stability. The extent that the bottom of a boat's hull curves up at the bow and stern when viewed from the side is one important measurement, which is called *rocker*.

When a canoe has more rocker, the bow and stern curve up noticeably from the hull's center. Another important variable is the difference between the width amidships (the center section) and at the bow and stern when looked at from above or below. Some are wider in the center and come to a distinct point at the bow and stern, while others are narrow all along the hull or somewhat blunter at the bow and stern.

The material a canoe is built with also affects its performance. The original canoes and kayaks were constructed with wood, animal skins, reeds, and other natural materials. Later, canoes and kayaks were manufactured using wood frames covered with wooden planks or canvas. Contemporary canoes are often made of aluminum, fiberglass, carbon fiber, or other modern materials. Each material has advantages or disadvantages. Aluminum canoes, for example, are durable and versatile, but they also tend to be cooler to ride in because they conduct heat and cold.

In addition to the design and construction of the canoe itself, performance is affected by the placement of people and cargo in the craft. Weight should be evenly distributed in the canoe so it will have a satisfactory balance in the water, called *trim*. If these are too unbalanced, the boat will be higher and lower in different sections, which make it difficult to handle.

Paddling is the basic skill of canoeing. Each individual movement of the paddle through the water is called a stroke. There are many styles and combinations of strokes. The skillful canoeist learns which to use for specific purposes. People develop personal paddling styles, and canoe enthusiasts often debate the merits and disadvantages of specific strokes.

Canadian-canoe and kayak paddling are both based on similar basic strokes and principles, but there are also differences. Because canoe paddles have only one blade, it is somewhat awkward to shift from one side to the other, so canoeists usually paddle primarily on one side of the boat (although some do alternate sides in races and other circumstances). In open Canadian canoes, kneeling is considered the most efficient position for paddling in many situations. Canoeists also paddle from an upright sitting position, especially in calm waters. In kayaks, the paddler is usually seated in the cockpit, or on top of the hull, with legs extended in front. Kayakers can also more easily shift their strokes from one side to the other because they hold their paddles in the center with the two blades extending over the hull.

There are three basic categories of stroke for both canoes and kayaks. Power strokes propel the canoe forward, stop it, or push it backward. Turning strokes exert force on one side to either change the canoe's direction or to correct its course. The third basic category is the stabilizing, or bracing, stroke, which is used to keep the craft level and upright.

The most basic power stroke is the forward, or bow, stroke. The paddler places the blade of the paddle in front of him on one side of the boat, lowers it into the water and pulls it back toward the stern in a movement that is approximately parallel to the center-line of the canoe. Then he raises the paddle out of the water and starts the cycle again.

Among the basic turning strokes are the pry and draw strokes, in which the paddle is pushed away from the boat or pulled towards it at a perpendicular angle to make it turn quickly. A sweep stroke is a large circular motion. Turning strokes are also used to keep the canoe on a straight course. This is necessary because basic forward strokes tend to push the canoe's bow to the opposite direction. The craft would ultimately go in a circle if the paddler did not compensate by steering the canoe back toward a straight line. These correction strokes are especially important in Canadian canoes, where the paddle is used on one side of the boat most frequently. In kayaks, it is more common to regularly alternate strokes on both sides to stay on course.

Bracing strokes steady the canoe if it is leaning too far to one side or is in danger of capsizing. The canoeist extends his paddle and upper body towards the other side, which shifts the weight back towards the center. Bracing strokes also are used to steer the craft.

There are many variations and combinations of these basic strokes. A single stroke may combine the actions of a power, turning, or stabilizing stroke. The J-stroke, for example, is a basic movement that simultaneously propels the canoe and keeps it on a straight course by combining a forward stroke with a turning movement. The strokes also depend on the number of paddlers in a vessel. A solo paddler must concentrate both on steering and powering the boat. When two or more people are paddling, these responsibilities are shared. One paddler might focus on power strokes while the other emphasizes strokes that steer the canoe.

Paddles have differing sizes, shapes, and weights that also determine the strokes that are used. One paddle might be lightweight or have a narrow blade to make it easier to use, while another paddle may be larger and heavier to provide more power. The blades and handles are often angled or shaped to make specific types of paddling more efficient.

People sometimes paddle while standing up, or they use a style called poling, in which the canoeist powers and steers the craft with a single long pole dropped to the bed of earth below the water. While used in a variety of situations, poling is especially suited to swamps, shallow water, or other situations where weedy vegetation or other conditions make other forms of paddling difficult.

White-water sports are a special category of boating. (People also use rafts with attached oars in white-water sports. White-water rafting has basic similarities to white-water canoeing. It is also different because oars are used and rafts are often larger and may hold more people.) White-water paddling and rafting require specialized skills and fast reflexes, because the vessels move very quickly in turbulent water, among rocks, and other obstacles. In contrast to calm-water canoeing, where paddling is necessary to move the vessel forward, fast-moving currents naturally propel white-water craft. So the ability to slow down, stop, and turn quickly become the priorities. In addition to riding the crest of the fast-moving currents to go forward, white-water paddlers also steer into quieter eddies to slow down, to rest, and to aim their boats for the next stage of the run. In rapids, the white-water canoeist must also paddle across or against the currents when necessary, which can require great skill and strength.

Strategy is another important aspect of white-water sport. Canoeists and rafters usually plan their runs in advance. Boating organizations and publications issue maps and guidebooks. They rate individual rivers by categories of difficulty, so people can choose sites that are within their level of ability. While individual ratings methods may vary, rivers are generally designated as Class I to Class VI. A Class I river is considered easiest to navigate because the waters are calmer and there are fewer obstacles, while a Class VI river is considered the most difficult, or to be avoided, because of extreme turbulence, waterfalls and other hazards.

White-water paddlers and rafters also study the water on the site before making an actual run, to judge water levels and other changeable conditions. They figure out exactly where to go and they look for hazards to avoid. In addition to rocks, they survey the currents and look for falls or other sharp changes in the elevation of the water. This is called *reading the river.* These advance precautions are also advised for those who are using canoes and kayaks on water that appears calm, to avoid being caught in unexpected stretches of rapids or other hazards.

Safety is an important consideration in all forms of canoeing and kayaking. The canoe should be equipped with life jackets for passengers, and with other flotation devices and features to make it easier to turn the boat upright if it capsizes or is swamped. Warm clothing is also advised when the air and water are cold. In white-water boating and other situations where there is a risk of physical injury, boaters wear helmets and other protective equipment.

Often canoes must be carried, or portaged, between bodies of water or to bypass especially dangerous stretches of river. In early times, when canoes were used on long journeys, portaging was especially important. Today, portaging may be confined to carrying a boat a short distance from a cartop rack or a storage site on land into the nearby water. However, more extensive portaging is common when canoes are used for hiking, camping, and other long trips. For short distances, pairs of canoeists often hold the boat parallel to the ground at the bow and stern with their arms straight down. For longer distances, a common method of portaging is to carry the boat upside down over the head. Boaters often use padded crossbars built into the boat or attached to it, which brace and cushion their heads and shoulders. When canoes and kayaks are used in traveling over longer distances, canoeists also must determine in advance the amount of gear they can carry along with the canoe while portaging.

People also use canoes and kayaks for hunting and fishing. They use the boats to travel to a destination, or they may actually hunt or fish from the craft itself. In addition to boat-handling skills, these sports requires the ability to keep the craft stabilized while casting or pulling in fishing lines or while firing a gun. In some instances this may be more difficult in a canoe than in a wider, more stable rowboat or motorboat.

Competition

The sport of canoeing encompasses many competitive events. Prominent canoeing sports include wild-water racing, slalom white-water events, and sprint or marathon racing on flat water. Many canoeing sports include divisions for both canoes and kayaks. In these sports, canoes are designated as C (or OC for open canoes), and kayaks are designated as K. Classifications also include the number of people the boat can hold. A two-person Canadian canoe, for example, is classified as a C2, while a one-person kayak is a K1. Canoe races are held in many venues. In addition to the Olympics, formal events with strict criterion sanctioned by a canoeing organization are held in many localities and on a national and international level. The specific race categories and rules may vary, depending on the guidelines of the sponsoring organization. Informal races are also popular.

Slalom canoe races are held either on rapidly running rivers or on artificial courses with simulated rapids, rocks, and other obstacles. The slalom racers must follow a specific course marked by a series of approximately 20 to 30 gates, which are two poles hanging down from either end of a narrow crossbar over the water. Slalom canoeing is a very challenging and exciting sport that requires a combination of speed, accuracy, and stamina. Scoring is based on the time it takes to complete the run plus the racer's ability to accurately follow the specific course and make the required maneuvers. Penalty points are given when the racer misses or bumps into a gate. Slalom races often include events for individuals and teams, and such divisions as one-person kayaks and one- or two-person canoes. A canoe used in slalom racing has a covered deck.

Wild-water races also take place on running rivers. However, the object in wild-water racing is to complete the course as quickly as possible, with no defined course of gates (except to mark dangerous sections). These courses tend to be

longer, often three kilometers (4.8 miles) or more. Runs are timed, and the fastest paddler is the winner. Sanctioned wild-water races often include divisions for one-man kayaks and one- or two-person canoes.

Other types of canoe racing take place on calmer, open lakes, rivers or artificial pools. These include long-distance marathon races or short sprints. Here, endurance and the ability to paddle fast are the required skills. Sprint courses are often 500 meters (547 yards), 1,000 meters (1,094 yards), or as long as 10,000 meters (10,940 yards) or more. Marathon courses may be much longer. A short course might be straight from start to finish, while longer courses may include at least one turn that the racers must navigate. Competitors start simultaneously in different lanes from starting gates. Winners are determined by the first paddlers to cross a finish line. Boats generally include K1 to K4 kayaks and C1 to C4 canoes. Craft built for this type of racing are generally very long and narrow. Kayaks may have a rudder to add stability.

Canoe polo is a fast-paced water sport in which teams of players in small one-person kayaks attempt to score points by maneuvering passing a ball into the opponent's goal. Official teams often have five players.

Other canoe and kayaking sports include mass-races, which are informal events with a large number of canoeists racing on open water. Competitions are also held in poling, sailing and other specialized canoe sports. In some instances, canoeing is also incorporated with other activities into multifaceted endurance sports. A triathlon that also includes activities like cycling or running, for example, may include a section where the participants paddle a canoe.

—John Townes

Bibliography: Harrison, David. (1993) *Sea Kayaking Basics.* New York: Hearst Marine Books.

Ray, Slim. (1992) *The Canoe Handbook.* Harrisburg, PA: Stackpoole Books.

Riviere, Bill. (1985) *The Open Canoe.* Boston and Toronto: Little, Brown & Co.

Roth, Bernhard A. (1977) *The Complete Beginner's Guide to Canoeing.* Garden City, NY: Doubleday.

Roberts, Kenneth G., and Philip Shackelton. (1983) *The Canoe: A History of the Craft from Panama to the Arctic.* Toronto: Macmillan of Canada and Camden, ME: International Marine Publishing.

Carom Billiards

See Billiards

Carriage Driving

The horse was domesticated at least 5,000 years ago, and equines served as a major source of transport for both humans and cargo until the end of World War I. Horse-drawn vehicles were particularly important from the time the Aryans invaded what is now western and central Europe with their chariots during the second century B.C.E. to the early twentieth century. Since that time, primarily due to the advent of the internal combustion engine, the importance of the horse in civilization has been gradually reduced to its current role in sport and recreation.

Origins

The creation of equestrian sports incorporating vehicles lagged far behind those in which the horse is ridden under saddle, such as flat racing, polo, and hunting. The amount of equipment required for carriage sports and the additional personnel necessary for harnessing and handling restricted their development to the most affluent of horsemen. The creation of breeds suitable for carriage sports was likewise slower than those for flat racing and polo. Cold-blooded draft horse breeds, which are heavier, sturdier and more powerful, were bred to include lines from the faster, lighter-boned, and more high-strung hot-blooded breeds such as the Thoroughbred to produce "warmbloods" ideal for driving. The result was carriage horses with the power of cold bloods and the speed and competitiveness of hot bloods.

Two critical elements fused together at the beginning of the nineteenth century to lay the foundation of coaching as an important "wagered" sports competition from 1800 until 1890 in northern Europe and the United States. First, the construction of roads became scientific and uniform, providing a safe and stable surface for carriages. Second, suspension systems for carriages came into vogue, and carriage design and workmanship altered the tenor of carriage travel. Gradually, uncertain, uncomfortable, slow transportation by coach yielded to secure, pleasant, and relatively fast travel and also improved mail transportation.

Driving clubs were first instituted in England. Among the more famous ones were the Benson Driving Club (1807–1854), The Whip (founded 1808), and the Richmond Driving Club (1838–1845). There was a Four-in-Hand Driving Club from 1850 to 1926. Since 1958 there has been a British Driving Society, and the Coaching Club has been in existence for over 125 years. A traditional feature of the Ascot race meeting is an enclosure for coaching club members. There was a similar area set up at Lords Cricket Ground for the Eton-Harrow and Oxford-Cambridge cricket matches from 1872 to 1914.

Organized carriage driving competitions have existed in central Europe and Germany for a hundred years, primarily due to the efforts of German Benno von Achenbach (1861–1936). He had been trained by an Englishman named Edwin Howlett, who is considered the father of modern four-in-hand driving (four horses under harness, two in front and two behind). What was previously the vocation of coachmen became a hobby for the leisure class.

Four-in-hand driving as a sporting hobby contracted sharply after World War I. Organized contests for carriage drivers did not develop until after World War II, and multinational European contests were initiated in the 1950s. Driving contests of the time generally included two phases: dressage and marathon. As a formally recognized international sport with uniform rules, however, combined driving has only recently passed the quarter-century mark.

A ridden version of three standard military tests for horses (dressage, cross-country, and stadium jumping, known collectively as three-day eventing because each phase was tested on a different day) had been an Olympic sport since 1912. Adaptations were dictated by the presence of the carriage and the fact that a driver's only control over the horses is through the reins that

Carriage driving is a sport limited to those affluent enough to afford the necessary horses and equipment. It has a wider following in Europe but is growing in popularity in the United States.

attach to each side of a metal bit through the horse's mouth, the voice, and the whip. Where use of the voice is not permitted in ridden dressage, it is allowed for driven dressage. Jumps used in the cross-country phase of a ridden three-day competition are replaced by a marathon section with hazards—narrow gates or water-filled ditches—and, in place of stadium jumping, a precision driving test known as the cones phase.

Dressage is an equestrian discipline based on military training wherein a horse must demonstrate obedience, strength, and flexibility as its driver directs it through a prescribed routine of movements. Ridden dressage has been a staple of classical equestrian training since the seventeenth century. Ridden dressage movements form the basis of the driven dressage test.

Marathon driving, also based on schooling for the battlefield, required the horse to be driven across open country, through water and to negotiate obstacles such as an orchard of narrowly spaced trees or a combination of gates. Such a test demonstrated a horse's stamina, courage, and athleticism.

Practice

In 1969, Prince Philip of Britain was serving as president of the Fédération Equestre Internationale (FEI), the governing body for show jumping, dressage, three-day eventing, and other international equestrian competitions. At an FEI meeting, Polish delegate Eric Brabec suggested to Prince Philip that the FEI draft a set of standardized rules for carriage driving competitions. Brabec's suggestion was acted on almost immediately. With the aid of Sir Michael Ansell of Great Britain, a meeting of European drivers was convened in Bern, Switzerland, which shortly produced a set of rules based on ridden three-day tests. The first test, dressage, includes two parts: presentation and the driven dressage test. Presentation requires that horses, equipment, driver, and grooms be cleanly turned out and correctly outfitted. Hours are spent to groom horses to a high sheen, polish vehicles and harness to a high gloss, and outfit driver and grooms to shine.

The rules for this competition are based primarily on nineteenth-century driving standards. Much discussion has been made of whether such a "beauty" contest ought to be included in a combined driving event. Proponents suggest that it adds to the appeal of the sport and underscores the need for attention to detail the sport requires. Critics decry presentation as outdated and elitist.

Dressage tests take place in a large, rectangular arena with at least three judges (five for important international contests) scoring the test from different vantage points. Scores are based on the accuracy of the driven test and the quality of the horses' performance of the required movements. The test is driven at two gaits, the walk and trot, with halts and backing included. Movements include circles and serpentines down the length of the arena.

Scoring is based on how close a driver and team come to achieving perfection; penalties are incurred for deviation from the ideal, based on a high score of 10 points per movement. Thus, the lowest dressage score wins. Scores in the 30s are considered excellent.

The second phase of a combined driving event is known as the marathon, although the distance covered is usually about 17 miles (27 kilometers). This phase tests the fitness and stamina of the team and the ability of the driver to maneuver the team through obstacles and complete the distances within a prescribed pace. Three to five sections are included, with the obstacles course as the final section. A full, five-sectioned marathon would run as follows: section A, to be driven at a trot; section B, a walk section at the end of which is a compulsory 10-minute halt where horses are inspected for fitness to continue; section C, to be driven at a fast trot; section D, a second walk phase with a compulsory 10-minute halt; and section E, the obstacles course to be driven at a trot. Usually eight obstacles are included in this course. Obstacles may be, for example, a series of gates to maneuver through, a sloped, wooded area to be driven through, or a shallow pool of water to be negotiated.

The greatest spectator appeal to the sport is during the final phase of the marathon. Drivers, belted onto their carriage seats, must drive with enough speed not to incur penalty points, as their grooms—acting as navigators—shout reminders from their posts on the backs of the marathon vehicles. They prompt drivers when needed to keep them on course through the confusing maze of gates, and they often throw their weight to one side or the other around a turn to shift the cart on the track, freeing a wheel or avoiding its entrapment on a gatepost or tree. As in dressage, penalties are scored and the low score wins. Time penalties are scored on each phase and through each individual obstacle in the final section.

A veterinary check before the final competition, the obstacles competition (colloquially known as the cones competition), verifies that the horses are fit to compete in the concluding contest, which tests the driver's ability to negotiate a technical course, as well as the horse's fitness after a grueling cross-country test the previous day.

The obstacle phase is usually held in the same arena as the first day's events—presentation and dressage. The course consists of gates, which are pairs of plastic cones similar to traffic cones, with a tennislike ball atop each. The object is to drive one's horses and carriage between each set of cones without dislodging any balls. The cones are spaced just a few inches wider apart than the wheels of the carriage passing between them, and courses are complicated, twisting back and forth across the arena. Precision driving is required, as is careful attention to the prescribed pace. Penalties are scored for dislodging balls and exceeding the allowed time for the course. Courses generally include 18 or 20 gates.

The first international competition driven under the new FEI-created rules was held in 1970 in Lucerne. The following year, Hungary inaugurated the European Championships. These competitions were exclusively for four-in-hands, four horses hitched by pairs pulling one vehicle. As carriage driving has gained in popularity both in Europe and the United States, however, competitions for pairs and single-horse driving developed.

In Europe, driving is a sport enjoyed by all ages, whereas in the United States it is primarily an adult sport. Most of the top drivers traditionally have been men. That has been changing, however, as the ranks of experienced women drivers have grown. The 1995 World Pairs Driving Championship was won by Mieke van Tergouw of the Netherlands. The 1995 pairs driving champion was Pennsylvanian Lisa Singer.

Throughout the world, carriage driving is an amateur sport. Prize money is minimal, and there are virtually no sponsorships of drivers or horses. Despite its amateur status, however, competitions, especially in Europe, draw sizable numbers of spectators. The 1995 European Driving Championship for pony four-in-hands was seen by an estimated 25,000 spectators and received television coverage.

Eastern European countries, traditionally preeminent in driving competitions, have had difficulty maintaining their state-owned stud farms and training centers as their economies change to a free-enterprise system. Following the 1993 World Pairs Driving Championship in Gladstone, New Jersey, the pair driven to the individual silver medal by Vilmos Lazar of Hungary had to be auctioned at the end of the event to help defray the costs of competition.

Despite the loss of state funding in Eastern European nations, carriage driving remains a popular sport throughout Europe and is gaining popularity in North America and elsewhere around the world. During the 1995 World Pairs Driving Championship in Poznan, Poland, a record number of countries competed.

—Kate Lincoln

Bibliography: The Duke of Edinburgh. (1982) *Competition Carriage Horse Driving.* Macclesfield, UK: Horse Drawn Carriages Limited.

Jung, Emil Bernard. (1980) *Combined Driving.* New York: Publisher.

Pape, Max. (1982) *The Art of Driving.* New York: J. A. Allen.

Rogers, Fairman. (1900) *Manual of Coaching.* Philadelphia: J. B. Lippincott.

Von Achenbach, Benno. *Anspannen und Fahren.* Germany.

Watney, Mrs. B. M. I. (1981) *The British Driving Society Book of Driving.* London: British Driving Society.

Chariot Racing

Although the present state of historical and archeological knowledge is insufficient for us to know precisely the origins of chariot racing, we can be sure that races were possible only after the invention of the two-wheeled horse-drawn chariot in the second millennium B.C.E. A second prerequisite was the existence of land level enough for the chariots to reach high speeds. It is tempting to conjecture that chariot races began in eastern Anatolia, Mesopotamia, among the Hittites, or in ancient Egypt (where the "royal dogma" made the pharaohs ineligible as contestants), but the oldest depictions of chariot races come from late Mycenean Greece (Tiryns, thirteenth century B.C.E.). In Greece, the sport experienced its first great flowering. In Book XXIII of Homer's *Iliad* (eighth century B.C.E., the chariot race is the high point of the funeral games held in honor of Patroclus, and it continued to enjoy this status at the great panhellenic athletic festivals celebrated at Olympia, at Delphi (where one can still see the famed bronze *Charioteer*), and at many local competitions. Chariot races also appear in Etruscan funeral art.

Chariot races reached the apogee of their popularity in Roman times, in Rome's huge *Circus Maximus.* (The Latin *circus*, from which we take our word, referred to the circular track of the chariot race.) The races were, in fact, *the* Roman sport, organized to perfection and passionately followed throughout the *Imperium Romanum* (Roman Empire). The satirical poet Juvenal's famous reference to *panem et circenses* ("bread and circuses") expressed his dismay at a public depoliticized and deprived of its rights by the ancient equivalent of food stamps and football games. The *Imperium Romanum* had no fewer than 74 "circuses" where racing societies known as *factiones* (factions) outfitted their teams with expensive equipment and administered the contests. Victorious charioteers enjoyed great fame and received immense sums in prize money. Their careers were comparable to those of today's superstar athletes.

After the fall of Rome, the passion for chariot races survived in the Hippodrome at Constantinople, the capital of the Byzantine Empire,

Chariot Racing

One of the most ancient sports, chariot racing is depicted at its height in Roman times in this bas-relief. Roman charioteers enjoyed fame and fortune not unlike today's sports superstars.

where they became a part of official state ceremony. The success of the C.E. sixth-century charioteer Porphyrios was so great that he was all but deified by the public. Although the seizure of the city by Crusaders, in 1204, briefly interrupted the races, they resumed after the intruders were expelled and continued until the conquest of Constantinople by the Ottoman Turks in 1453.

Origins

Chariot races—which survive today only in the form of harness racing, a worthy relic within the world of modern sports—have a lively history that offers insights into many different cultures. The preconditions for the emergence of the sport were the domestication of horses and the invention of the two-wheeled light chariot. In addition, the horses had to become accustomed to a harness and to run with as well as against one another. These difficult preconditions were fulfilled at the beginning of the second millennium B.C.E., but there is no scholarly consensus about where the first races took place. Lack of an adequate supply of wood and of land level enough for a race eliminates a number of areas from consideration. Archeological evidence suggests that eastern

Anatolia played a leading role in the first phase of horse-taming and chariot-making. It is certain that the invention of the horse-drawn chariot was a great success. By the middle of the second millennium B.C.E., it was known not only in Egypt and the ancient Near East but also in India and among the Mycenean Greeks. (Somewhat later, chariots appeared in China as well.) Some scholars speak of the "world of the war-chariot," but it is doubtful that chariots were particularly well adapted for military use. Chariots were, however, culturally important as status symbols, which gave the chariot race a certain aristocratic flair.

Where did chariot racing begin? The question is as difficult to answer as the question about the place of the chariot's invention. We can assume that the use of the chariot for transportation stimulated the desire to use it for sport. This assumption is supported by the comments on the experience of speed that are found on the Sphinx-stele of Thutmosis IV (1412–1402 B.C.E.). Unfortunately, although the preconditions for chariot racing were present and although there are extraordinarily good sources to document the use of chariots in second-millennium Egypt, the "royal dogma" that prevented the pharoah from man-to-man sports competition (lest he be defeated) severely limited Egyptian references to chariot racing. References to kings such as Amenophis II (1438–1412 B.C.E.) and Ramses III (1184–1153 B.C.E.) as trainers of horses cannot be taken as proof of their participation in chariot races. B. J. Kemp was certainly mistaken, some years ago, when he described a Theban site at Kom el'Abd as a race track. From the tomb of Tutankhamen (1347–1338 B.C.E.), however, archeologists *have* recovered six well-preserved chariots. These, along with two found at other Egyptian sites, are the only ones to survive from antiquity. Their method of construction was not only elegant and efficient; it reveals the chariot-makers' technical sophistication. The surprisingly ingenious construction of the wheels from six V-shaped spokes gave the vehicle the solidity that was needed if the chariot was to be employed by warriors, by hunters, and— theoretically—by sportsmen.

The fourteenth-century B.C.E. writings of Kikkuli, in the Hittite cuneiform script, contain the Hittites' impressive instructions for the training of horses. Details are given for a 184-day training program. They are proof of the highly sophisticated breeding and care of horses and of a systematic awareness of techniques to increase their speed. Although the Hittite word *uasanna* (a firm track) appears numerous times, it cannot be taken as indisputable proof of chariot racing, especially in light of the fact that daily training often began at night. Accustoming horses to draw chariots before the break of day strongly suggests military rather than sporting use of the vehicles.

If one turns away from the search for chariot racing in other cultures that *might* have known the sport, if one looks for unambiguous evidence, one finds the first depiction of a chariot race on a late Mycenean amphora from the city Tiryns in southern Greece. On this thirteenth-century B.C.E. vase, as in later sources, chariot racing appears in conjunction with a funeral ritual. The most vividly detailed account appears in Book XXIII of Homer's *Iliad* (lines 262–652). Homer describes the chariot race as the most splendid sporting event in the funeral games held in honor of Achilles' friend Patroclus, slain by the Trojan hero Hector. The race, which takes place on the Trojan coast, is contested by the leaders of the Greek army that is besieging the city. They are eager to win the valuable prizes offered by Achilles. In picturing the dramatic scene, the poet demonstrates how well he understood the subtleties of the sport. He describes the determining of starting positions by lot, tactical and technical measures, an accident, a suspected violation of the rules, betting, the awarding of prizes, and a protest against the initial announcement of the results. Homer's account of the race is more than twice as long as his report on the other seven athletic events, which says something about the importance of chariot racing.

Development

After the Homeric age, the chariot lost most of its military importance, replaced by armored infantry and by cavalry, but chariot racing continued for centuries to enjoy popularity as a sport. No important athletic meet was complete without a chariot race, and the chariot race was often the high point of an athletic festival. Until the very end of the race's Greek history it remained an aristocratic—at times even a royal—property, which is no surprise when one considers the expense of a stable of horses and the costs of sending a four-horse chariot to Olympia. If the owner lived on one of the Greek world's many islands or on the coast of Anatolia or North Africa, his equipage had to be transported by boat, which meant—in addition to the initial cost of the steeds, their alternates (in case of injury or sickness), the chariot itself, and its equipment—the travel expenses for the men and animals. The entourage was large. Aside from the charioteer and the trainers, there were woodworkers and leatherworkers, a veterinarian (or his equivalent), cooks, and miscellaneous servants. Once the ship had docked at Pheia, some 30 kilometers (18.6 miles) from Olympia, freight wagons were required. At Olympia, the chariot owner needed tents, beds and blankets, and all the other necessities for camping out (because Olympia had no accommodations for visitors). So great was the expense of participation that there was a secondary contest, which must have had its own special excitement, to see whose entourage made the most splendid appearance at the games.

The victors' lists from the Olympic Games sparkle with the names of the high and mighty. There were tyrants from the archaic period (like Cleisthenes of Sikyon), kings like Damaratos of

Sparta and Philip II of Macedon, Roman emperors like Tiberius and Nero. The poets Pindar and Bacchylides celebrated the numerous charioteering victories of their aristocratic patrons. Costly memorials to the victors were also erected at the site of the panhellenic games. The bronze statue of the *Charioteer of Delphi* is one of the few extant examples of this nearly forgotten genre. Commemorative coins were another way to publicize a victory; they spread the victor's fame throughout the entire Greek world. Victories sometimes had direct political consequences. The Athenian adventurer Alcibiades, who sent no fewer than seven four-horse chariots to compete in the Olympic Games of 416 B.C.E., made political capital from his victory. He used it to claim the leadership of the foredoomed Athenian expedition sent to conquer the island of Sicily. No less a figure than the tragic dramatist Euripides composed the victor's ode to the unscrupulous Alcibiades.

Thanks to the rule that declared the owner of the chariot to be the victor, rather than the charioteer, women who were otherwise excluded from the Olympic Games could become Olympic victors. The first of them was the Spartan princess Cynisca, whose victor's inscription proudly testifies to her lineage. Among the later victors was Queen Berenice, the wife of Ptolemy III of Egypt.

For chariot races and for simple horse races, the Greeks constructed hippodromes, but none of them has yet been archeologically attested. The demarcations of the lanes, like the stands erected for spectators, were of perishable materials. Not even the hippodrome at Olympia, whose starting gates were described in detail by the C.E. second-century traveler Pausanias in Book VI of his *Description of Greece*, has left a trace behind. The peculiarity of the starting gates lay in their form, like that of a ship's prow, so that the boxes might be opened in sequence, like a chain-reaction. The spectacle of the boxes opening one after another, seen from close-up, must have been quite dramatic. At any rate, the inventor of the starting gates, the Athenian Cleoitas, was so proud of his invention that he referred to it in the inscription on the base of his statue.

The track at Olympia lay parallel to the stadium but extended much farther to the east. Recent research by Joachim Ebert has compared its dimensions to those of a Roman "circus." According to

Grave Inscription for Crescens

Crescens, charioteer for the "Blues," of moorish birth, 22 years old.

With the four-horse chariot he won his first victory when L. Vipstanius and Messalla were the consuls [ca. C.E. 115–116] on the day of the races in honor of the birthday of the divine Nerva in the twenty-fourth race with the following horses: Circius, Acceptor, Delicatus, Cotynus. From the consulship of Messalla to the races for the birthday of the divine Claudius in the consulship of Glabrio [ca. C.E. 124–125] he started 686 times and won 47 times. In single races, he was victorious 19 times, in double races 23 times, in triple races 5 times. Once he overtook the entire field from behind. 8 times he won with a lead. 38 times he won by means of a final spurt. He won 130 second places and 111 third places. In prize money, he took in 1,558,346 sesterces.

the report of a messenger in Sophocles' play *Elektra* (lines 698ff), there cannot have been room for more than ten chariots to compete at any one time. The earlier assumption that more than forty raced simultaneously was based on Pindar's fifth Pythian Ode. Ebert believes that Pindar's number is the result of poetic exaggeration. The *taraxippos* (horses' fright) remains a mystery. It seems to have been an altar placed near the first curve of the track; perhaps, as Pausanias suggests in the sixth book of his travels, the altar was blamed for the accidents that were liable to occur there. At the altar, priests sought by means of sacrifices to pacify the demons responsible for the accidents.

Chariot races figure frequently in the visual arts of Etruscan civilization, especially in the first half of the fifth century B.C.E. In eleven different tombs—four in Chiusi and seven in Tarquinia—chariot races can be seen in frescoes of the highest quality. The races are also a motif in ceramics and in stone and bronze reliefs. There can be no question about the significant place occupied by chariot racing in Etruscan culture. The depictions of chariot races—and other sports—in tomb frescoes strongly suggest that they were a part of funeral games in honor of the deceased. Although the frescoes show only two-horse chariots, the earliest form, there is reason to believe that three-horse chariots were also used (but none drawn by four horses). In contrast to Greek charioteers, who wore a knee-length *chiton*, the Etruscans were clothed in a shirt that normally reached no lower than mid-thigh. The spur (*kentron*) used by the Etruscans was also shorter than its Greek counterpart. On the basis of Etruscan evidence, we have become aware of characteristics of the sport that are unknown in Greek iconography—such as the use of a crash helmet and the custom of knotting the reins tightly at the charioteer's back. In short, Etruscan chariot races seem to have had some unique elements (although we cannot completely ignore the possibility of influences from Greek colonies in southern Italy).

These influences do seem to have played an important role in Lucania in the fourth century B.C.E. Grave paintings of high quality decorated a number of tombs, especially those in the vicinity of the Greek town of Paestum. In these paintings, two-horse chariot races are dramatically depicted. Here, too, the races appear in conjunction with other sporting events, often boxing matches.

The Roman historian Livy correctly summed up the sports preferences of the Etruscans when he wrote, in Book I, of their *pugiles et equi* (boxing matches and chariot races). The Romans, who acted on their own even if they did not entirely escape the influence of Greek and Etruscan traditions, raised the sport of chariot racing to its zenith—if one judges on the basis of technical and organizational perfection and the effects of the sport on the masses. Unlike the peoples who came before them, the Romans left us monumental material evidence of their passion for chariot racing. From the *Imperium Romanum* 74 large-format structures have survived, some of them in excellent condition. Outside of Rome itself, the chief geographical centers of chariot racing were southern Spain, North Africa (especially in what is now Tunisia), and the Near East (Syria, Palestine, Egypt). The northernmost "circus" was constructed in what is now the German city of Trier (*Augusta Treverorum*).

The great model of all subsequent "circuses" was Rome's *Circus Maximus*, a hair-pin shaped facility which had room for some 150,000 spectators. The exterior measurements of the *Circus Maximus* were approximately 620 meters by 140 meters (678 yards by 153 yards); the space framed by the seats measured approximately 580 meters by 80 meters (635 yards by 88 yards). The track itself was divided down the middle by a barrier 11

meters (12 yards) wide, known as the *spina* or *euripus*. At each end of the barrier stood the *metae* (turning columns). The starting line was slightly off-center and there was a corresponding shift, hardly noticeable to the naked eye, of that segment of the right-hand stands that stood between the starting line and the barrier. This was the distance the chariots had to travel before they could begin to jockey for the innermost lane. This breakpoint was marked by a chalk line (*linea alba* or *calx*). The chariots started at the signal given by the sponsor of the races, the *editor ludi*, who was positioned directly over the starting gates. The signal consisted of a white cloth (*mappa*), which he dropped. At the same time, a mechanical device opened the gates of the starting boxes (*carceres*), which were staggered across the width of the stadium in order to give every chariot an equal opportunity to reach the breakpoint.

Since there were four "circus factions"—the Whites, the Reds, the Blues, and the Greens—it was customary for races to consist of eight or twelve chariots. That allowed each faction to field teams of at least two chariots per race even in smaller stadiums. One can easily imagine that a field of only four chariots (*singularum*) called for tactics very different from those required when each faction had two or three chariots racing at once (*binarum* and *ternarum*, respectively). When a faction had two or three chariots in the race, the drivers were able to work together for their advantage and to disadvantage the chariots of rival factions. The usual distance for a race was seven rounds, which corresponds to approximately 4 kilometers (2.5 miles). Since roughly 15 minutes were required to complete a race, it may have been possible to offer the crowd as many as 24 races in a single day. Between races it was customary to keep the spectators entertained with running, jumping, and throwing events or with other "pause fillers." If the organizers wanted to run more than 24 races a day, they shortened each race from seven laps to five. The standings of the factions were indicated by means of a movable "scoreboard" consisting of seven artificial dolphins or seven oversized eggs (*ovaria*).

As for the charioteers (*agitatores* or *aurigae*), they came for the most part from the lower social strata. If they were successful, which sometimes meant frequent changes in team membership, they were able to achieve not only great fame but also a substantial income. Charioteers like Crescens, P. Aelius Gutta Calpurnianus, and C. Appuleius Diocles can easily be compared with modern superstars. Roman chariot races are best understood, from a sports-historical perspective, if one compares them with modern soccer (association football) games.

Roman chariot races were so well organized that quantified records were kept with every conceivable sort of statistic. In that sense, too, one is tempted to compare chariot racing to modern sports events. Chariot races were a very common motif in the visual arts of ancient Rome. In this connection, North African mosaics demonstrate the marvelous artistry of the men who produced them. The frequency of the chariot-race motif can be explained in part by the popularity of the sport and in part by commissions from the victorious charioteers and their enthusiastic public and private patrons. At any rate, images of the immortalized victors were enticing enough to be exploited ideologically.

Professional charioteers lived dangerous lives. As one sees in the iconography of the sport, a spill could all too easily take a driver's life. In an attempt to safeguard the charioteer from an accidental death, protective gear was developed; there were leather pads for the thighs and chest, and a leather crash helmet too. In addition, the charioteer carried a sharp knife with which, in the event of a crash, he could cut himself free from entangling reins.

That successful charioteers were treated like modern sports heroes is attested by written as well as by visual evidence. Antiquity's fanatical sports spectators had a tried and true method of helping their idols to victory. They fabricated curse-tablets with magical texts intended to disable the horses and charioteers of the opposing teams. Most of these magical lead tablets with their formulaic texts derive from the domain of the North African "circus," such as Hadrumetum (Sousse) and Carthage.

The last chariot races held in the city of Rome took place in 549 C.E. under Totila, king of the conquering Ostrogoths. When the seat of empire was shifted to Byzantium (renamed Constantinople), chariot races continued until the Crusaders, whose ostensible purpose was the liberation of the Holy Land from the Saracens, seized the city in 1204. (During their occupation, the Crusaders

Curse-Tablet from Carthage

I swear, whoever you are, invisible spirit . . . [horses' names]. Bewitch their gait, their feet, the victory, the start, the life, their speed. Take away their victory, hobble their feet, trip them up, slice their sinews, cripple them, so that they can't get to the circus tomorrow. They shouldn't run or move about or win or make it out of the starting gates . . . nor should they round the turning column. They should crash together with their charioteers Dionysios of the "Blues" and Lamarus and Restituanus.

introduced the knightly tournament.) Before and after this intrusion from the west, Byzantine chariot races, like many other aspects of Byzantine public life, were strictly regulated. The races were occasions for the ceremonial public appearance of the emperor.

Like the *Circus Maximus,* which fulfilled part of the Roman populace's desire for "bread and circuses," the Byzantine hippodrome was an intensely political venue, a stage for imperial diplomacy. As a site of public congregation and a barometer of the political climate, the hippodrome was the scene of frequent riots, the most horrific of which occurred in 532 B.C.E. Before the tumults ended, quelled by Justinian's general, Belisarius, 30,000 people had died. This bloody event was known as the "Nika Rebellion" because of the cry *"Nika!"* ("May he be victorious"), which one shouted as an inspiration to one's favorite charioteer. This "factional" riot was the worst of the many violent conflicts between the "Blues" and the "Greens" of Constantinople, Thessalonika, Antioch, and other Byzantine cities.

From the decorations of Constantinople's hippodrome (known today in modern Istanbul as the *atmeydani* or "place of horses") we have an Egyptian obelisk and a fragment of the famed "snake column" with which the Greeks celebrated their victory, in 479 B.C.E., over the invading Persians. (The column, originally dedicated at Delphi, commemorates the battle fought near Plataea, north of Athens.) The base of the obelisk has not only hippodrome scenes from the Byzantine state cult but also a depiction of the raising of the immense obelisk after its successful transportation from Egypt during the reign of Theodosius the Great (C.E. 379–395). Compared to what we know of Roman charioteers, information on the lives of Byzantine charioteers is sparse. Porphyrius, the supremely successful sixth-century charioteer, is an exception; we have not only his graven image but also a number of poems in his honor.

When Renaissance scholars rediscovered Greek and Roman sports, they were inspired to imitate the ancients. In Florence and elsewhere, they staged chariot races. They were not very successful.

—Wolfgang Decker

Bibliography: Cameron, Alan. (1976) *Circus Factions: Blues and Greens at Rome and Byzantium*. Oxford: Clarendon Press.

Cameron, Alan. (1973) *Porphyrius the Charioteer*. Oxford: Clarendon Press.

Decker, Wolfgang. (1992) *Sports and Games of Ancient Egypt*, transl. by Allen Guttmann. New Haven, CT: Yale University Press.

———. (1995) *Sport in der Griechischen Autike*. Munich: C. H. Beck.

Harris, H. A. (1972) *Sport in Greece and Rome*. Ithaca, NY: Cornell University Press.

Humphrey, John H. (1986) *Roman Circuses: Arenas for Chariot Racing*. London: B. T. Batsford.

Hyland, Anne. (1990) *Equus: The Horse in the Roman World*. New Haven, CT: Yale University Press.

Littauer, M. A., and J. H. Crouwel. (1985) *Chariots and Related Equipment of the Tomb of Tut'ankhamun*. Oxford: Griffith Institute.

———. (1979) *Wheeled Vehicles and Ridden Animals in the Ancient Near East*. Leiden: E. J. Brill.

Climbing

See Mountain Climbing; Rock Climbing

Coaches and Coaching

Coaching has increasingly emerged as a critical profession across the twentieth-century sport world. A coach plays a key role in an athlete's success. He or she influences not only athlete performance but also the athlete's sense of personal fulfillment and, in the case of team sports, team culture and cohesion. A coach must possess integrity, athlete trust and acceptance, technical knowledge, and good organizational skills.

Origins

Variants of coaching roles existed in early civilizations. In ancient Greece and Rome, there was informal training for such activities as running, archery, and gladiatorial skills. The term *coach*, however, did not enter our vernacular until the latter part of the nineteenth century, when "trainers" worked with teams or individual athletes through private clubs, or "masters" undertook coaching and instructional activities at private schools or colleges. These informal roles remained prominent throughout the first half of the twentieth century. *Professional* coaching positions did not become common until the mid-1900s, with a few notable exceptions, such as John Madden's coaching of the Slavia soccer club in 1905 Czechoslovakia.

Several factors are associated with the rise in coaching roles on both the amateur and professional levels: the status of sport in particular societies, the rise of international and national competition, the development of specialized knowledge and equipment, the organization of formal coaching schemes, the inclusion of physical education programs in educational institutions, and the ever-growing popularity of professional sport.

Coach Education and the Practice of Coaching

Formal coach education programs and accreditation have evolved since World War II, and they often cross national borders. Examples of internationally recognized coaching courses that develop common philosophies or areas of content across hemispherical boundaries are those of Canada and Australia. Such contemporary courses include the disciplines of communication, teaching skills, athletic technique, biomechanics, sport psychology, leadership and management, nutrition, training, and group dynamics. Usually each of

Brazilian head basketball coach Maria Helena Cardoso exhorts her team during a time out in the 1987 Pan American Games final against the U.S. women's team.

these courses is taught by a specialist in the field (e.g., nutrition is taught by an expert nutritionist).

Expert advisers may be called upon to optimize the coaching role, rendering the coach's qualifications more beneficial to the athlete and/or team. At least one international team (the New Zealand field hockey team) has employed an adviser to facilitate the coach's role and coaching practices. In the 1990s, there is a trend toward increasing collaboration between coaches and sport psychologists, recognizing that the mental aspect is as critical as the physical. They are getting together in the interest of the athlete's well-being as well as optimal performance. The sport psychologist places emphasis on goal setting, relaxation skills, visualization, motivation, and coping and concentration skills. This union is still developing toward a full and complementary partnership on all levels, including the international level.

Professional associations for coaches, both sport specific and generic, are abundant, and programs,

conferences, and journals are readily accessible to coaches for advice and information on new philosophies and technologies. Coaches have been the subject of assessment scales, such as the CBAS SCP, which have been utilized to provide insights from observers and athletes on coach personalities and practices.

Coaches have many responsibilities, to themselves, their athletes, and the public. They must respond favorably to the numerous pressures resulting from public expectation, parental concern, athlete diversity, ethical issues, constant technological and physiological advances, and staffing issues. In the face of these multiple pressures, a coach must maintain personal satisfaction, self-esteem, and positive relationships in both the personal and professional spheres in order to function successfully. Since a coach is held liable by others for team/athlete performance results, outstanding coaches usually receive considerable public recognition and media

A Coach's Cigar for the Sultan

Sunday bleachers are bare
where a dissolute eddy of wind
lifts a lone chip bag
into a slow waltz
along front row seats
to settle on the fringe
of yesterday's contested turf,
but tomorrow night they come again
drawn by ritual
to a sudden death semi-final
where a new world starts
with the gut aching slash of perfection
the coach calls a play
and the eyes call a miracle,
when the hammer of God delivers
a 5 oz. leather missile rising
up and over Babe's own Stand
along with Monday's moon
and twenty thousand home run hearts.

—Robin McConnell

attention for their coaching triumphs. They often become part of a virtual sport folklore that includes well-known figures such as Vince Lombardi (1913–1970) in American football, Fred Allen (1920–) in rugby, John Wooden (1910–) in basketball, and Joyce Brown in netball.

A fundamental element of athlete success lies in an athlete's complete acceptance of the coach's philosophies and actions. Young athletes' positive sport experiences are influenced by their coaches. Although the athletes may become more self-determining and self-directed in their learning and development, they still value the athlete-coach relationship to the highest levels. R. C. McConnell's (1996) research findings reflect this, suggesting six distinct stages, with a cycle that begins and ends with a form of self-coaching that is accompanied by a positive coaching relationship.

Women and members of certain ethnic groups have been markedly underrepresented in coaching. This fact reflects the prevailing white male's dominance in the realm of sport. The processes of coach selection may utilize informal networks that are currently oriented toward males. This situation is further compounded by the female's dependency on male coaches. Nancy Theberge of the University of Waterloo (1988) notes the need for women to shape their own career hopes,

preferences, and achievements, rather than relying on male-oriented culture and structures to determine their athletic future. There is a growing body of international research investigating the issue of women and coaching. The Black Coaches Association (BCA) in the United States has suggested that African Americans held a disproportionately small number of coaching positions in the early 1990s. Given the cultural diversity of athletic groups, gender and ethnic sensitivity would most likely enhance coach-athlete relationships and team dynamics, in addition to fostering player self-esteem.

Regardless of gender or ethnic background, a coach's primary responsibility remains the athlete. Rainer Martens of the American Coaching Effectiveness Program endorses the philosophical ethos of the American Alliance for Health, Physical Education, Recreation and Dance (AAHPERD) Bill of Rights for Young Athletes, drawn up in 1979: coaches place athletes first and winning second. In the overall world of sport there seems to be consensus that the ethical guidelines of the Australian Coaching Council (ACC) apply to coaches in all settings.

Respect the talent of all athletes and seek to develop their potential

Treat each athlete as a unique individual

Learn as much as you can about your sport and the disciplines which contribute to athlete excellence

Make sure that the the period of time with you is a positive experience and self-enhancing for the athlete

Never deceive or mislead the athlete

Be fair and considerate

Be dignified and controlled and teach athletes to be likewise

Actively discourage the use of ergogenic or behavior-modifying drugs (Pyke 1991, 13–14)

—Robin McConnell

Bibliography: Chelladurai, P. (1984) "Discrepancy between Preferences and Perceptions of Leadership Behavior and Satisfaction of Athletes in Varying Sports." *Journal of Sport Psychology* 6: 27–41.

Cote, J., J. H. Salmela, and S. Russell. (1995) "The Knowledge of High-Performance Gymnastic Coaches: Methodological Framework." *Sport Psychologist* 9: 67–75.

Grusky, O. (1963). "The Effects of Formal Structure on

Managerial Recruitment : A Study of Baseball Organization," *Sociometry* 26: 345–353.

McConnell, R. C. (1996). *Sport Team Leadership*. Unpublished doctoral thesis. Massey University, Albany, Auckland.

McKee, S. (1994) *Coach*. Mechanicsburg, PA: Stackpole Books.

Maclean, J. C., and P. Chelladurai. (1994) "Dimensions of Coaching Performance: Development of a Scale." *Journal of Sport Management* 9, 2 (May): 194–207.

Martens, R. (1991). *Successful Coaching*. Champaign, IL: Leisure Press.

Pyke, F. S. (1991) *Better Coaching*. Canberra: Australian Coaching Council.

Theberge, N. (1988) "Making a Career in a Man's World: The Experiences and Orientations of Women in Coaching." *Arena Review* 12 (2): 116–127.

Tutko, T. A., and J. W. Richards. (1971) *Psychology of Coaching*. Ottawa: Coaching Association of Canada.

Walton, G. M. (1992) *Beyond Winning: The Timeless Wisdom of Great Philosopher Coaches*. Champaign, IL: Leisure Press.

Coaching (Four-in-Hand)

See Carriage Driving

Cockfighting

Cockfighting, the contesting of specially bred male chickens, is just one of a range of blood sports. Blood sports comprise that subportion of all sports that depend largely on the likelihood of injury, bloodletting, or death.

In cockfighting, throughout all its many variations, the bird acts as a surrogate for the owner or handler. Just as skillful playing of most sports can garner real prestige for the participant, involvement in a blood sport imbues participation with a special status. While there may be wagers riding on the performance of a particular rooster, the communal display of virile zeal is more important.

From this perspective, the human participant in a cockfight, in spite of the obvious violence involved, views him or herself as taking part in a sport, not engaging in animal cruelty. In his well-known study of Balinese cockfighting, Clifford Geertz explores the notion that cockfighting reflects the basest component of humanity. Yet, he shows that cockfighting is multifaceted and contains elements that extend beyond the gory spectacle.

Origins

The chicken entered our food chain via a ritual past. According to Marvin Harris, "chickens were domesticated in the jungles of Southeast Asia and were never part of the basic Indo-European, pastoral-farming complex" (1985, 128). *Gallus domesticus* has a history rooted in the leafy wilds of India as well as Myanmar, Thailand, Cambodia, and Indonesia.

This original chicken was tough, robust, and easily agitated. The noisy Red Jungle Fowl, typically weighing in at about 1 kilogram (2.2 pounds), was claimed by Charles Darwin to be the progenitor of contemporary chickens (Smith and Daniel 1982, 10). Within the Red Jungle Fowl's lineage lies a legacy of magic and ritual. Over the years a fantastic array of domestic fowl were developed from this dominant line. Several types were bred expressly for their pugilistic talent.

The small domestic fowl was apparently unimportant in the human diet until Roman times, at which point they were still bred for sport or religious reasons. Virtually wherever chickens exist, they are associated with mythology, magic, or symbolic utility.

The male *Gallus* doesn't take incursions into his turf lightly. Neither can Homer's "rosie-fingered dawn" creep soundlessly over the horizon while a cock remains vital. His capacity for morning racket and raw, unyielding courage have earned the fowl a special niche in human civilization.

Thought to be prophetic, the bird was pampered, cultivated, and desired both for its special relationship with the sun and as a provider of magic-laden plumes. In part because of this, the habit of keeping chickens, though not necessarily for food, spread through much of Africa, up through Iran, and through many Pacific islands. Long-ago Aryan invaders of India learned to

Handlers restrain fighting cocks in Bali.

enjoy cockfights and held the birds in great esteem. By 1000 B.C.E. they forbade any peoples under their control to eat chicken. The Persians incorporated the cock into their sacred domain because they felt he had a unique relationship with fire and light. Crowing, it was believed, struck a chord of fear into the belly of darkness and evil. Worshipers of the dawn (the Persians ritually bathed every sunrise) regarded the advent of cocks as a match made in heaven. According to their beliefs, without the feisty, loud-mouthed rooster god Bashyacta, the yellow demon creature of sleep would overcome all.

Evidence shows that the birds were raised, presumably for sport and ritual, by the Celts, Gauls, and ancient Britons. Chickens were reportedly introduced into Greece in the time of Themistocles (circa 524–460 B.C.E.) with the associated sport spreading throughout Asia Minor and Sicily. From Rome, the pastime moved northward and became popular throughout Italy, Germany, Spain and its eventual colonies, and through England, Wales, and Scotland. In some areas, especially among maritime nations quick to see the advantages, fowl were reared for food. Chickens could well endure the life at sea and provided fresh meat and eggs, but were also used to forecast the future and for entertainment.

The Romans, as did many fowl-rearing nations, believed in chicken divination. Casting grain among a sacred flock, observers watched to see if the birds exhibited vigor and greedily gobbled down the meal. This augured well, but lack of appetite suggested to any Roman general an

Bath Prophecy

On the 30th of March 1809, the destruction of the city of Bath was to have been effected by a convulsion of the earth, which should cause "Beacon-hill to meet Beechen Cliff." This inauspicious junction was said to have been foretold by an old woman, who had derived her information from an angel. This reported prophecy rendered many of the inhabitants truly unhappy, and instigated crowds of visitors to quit the city. The portentous hour, 12 o'clock, passed, and the believers were ashamed of their former fears. The alarm is said to have originated with two noted cock-feeders, who lived near the aforementioned hills; they had been at a public house, and, after much boasting on both sides, made a match to fight their favorite cocks on Good Friday, which fell on this day; but fearing the magistrates might interfere, if it became public, they named the cocks after their respective walks, and in the agreement it was specified that "Mount Beacon would meet Beechen Cliff, precisely at twelve o'clock on Good Friday." The match was mentioned with cautions of secrecy to their sporting friends, who repeated it in the same terms, and with equal caution, until it came to the ears of some credulous beings, who took the words in their plain sense; and, as stories seldom lose by being repeated, each added what fear or fancy framed, until the report became a marvelous prophecy, which in its intended sense was fulfilled; for the cocks of Mount Beacon and Beechen Cliff met and fought, and left their hills behind them on their ancient sites, to the comfort and joy of multitudes, who had been infected by the epidemical prediction.

—From William Hone, ed., *The Year Book of Daily Recreation and Information*, 1832.

words "cock's egg," meaning a malformed egg, and "cockney," a "malformed" variation of the English accent. Because of roosters' image of pugnacity and courage, an insouciant fellow may be called a "coxcomb" and an overconfident person "cocky" or "cocksure." A disappointed person may be described as "crestfallen." Cowards are said to "chicken out" and to suffer from being "chicken-livered" or "chicken-hearted." Other words associated with the bird are the proverbial "chanticleer," meaning a wondrous lover, or the jaunty "cock of the walk." Someone called "Sir cockalorum" is a small but ornery, self-important man.

The magic quality of the cock greeting the dawn is evidenced by the rooster-shaped windvanes and weathervanes that grace so many churches and homes. But avoid the mythical cock-born "cockatrice" that kills instantly with a passing glance. Since antiquity, images and language using the cock motif have been commonplace when trying to convey ideas related to courage, durability, magic, robustness, patriotism, and aggressiveness.

In the same vein, the image of the game cock is routinely associated with people, places, and products. The cock is virtually the national symbol of France, and is frequently used on clothing and other advertising. Sports figures have frequently been called game cocks. Products from opium to snow skis carry the cock mark, including Cockspur, a Barbados rum, and Fighting Cock, "Kentucky's finest," straight bourbon.

ill-boded time or location for battle. In fact, as the story goes, during the First Punic War an exasperated Roman admiral, P. Claudius Pulcher, badly wanted to attack the Carthaginians even though the sacred chickens had refused their feed. However, the admiral foreswore his faith in divination and seized the flock, throwing them overboard. "If they will not eat," he cried, "let them drink!" Of course, the Romans lost that particular battle.

Cocks in Culture

Cockfighting is so old and widely distributed that examples of its imprint on language, design, and decoration are easy to find. In today's English language, examples of this influence include the

Practice

Cockfighting is very widespread and exists in several variant forms. Depending on geography, cocks fight "bare-heeled," with attached blades, or with "spurs," "harpoons," or "gaffs." Tools attached to the fowl for the fight may be fabricated from a large pool of materials that includes ivory, tortoise shell, bone, specially prepared chicken spurs (superimposed over the bird's normal one), plastic, brass, and even alloy cut from jet turbine engine blades. There are "boxing" events in which the fowl's real spur is covered by padded "gloves" to keep from severely injuring his opponent. These sessions may be to help train the combatant or because the owners do not want any blood shed.

Cockfighting

Geertz, in his benchmark essay on cockfighting in Bali, routinely comments on the poise, calm, and cool character of the Balinese people. "In the normal course of things," he explains, "the Balinese are shy to the point of obsessiveness of open conflict. Oblique, cautious, subdued, controlled, masters of indirection and dissimulation—what they call *alus*, 'polished,' 'smooth'—they rarely face what they can turn away from, rarely resist what they can evade" (1972, 25). The anthropologist believes the cockfight provides an opportunity for the Balinese to roughhouse. Yet, because of the thorough distribution of the sport, cockfighting is as likely to be a staple among the loud and passionate as among the calm and reflective.

The Fight

Cockfighting is still an important part of the panoply of pastimes available across America, Europe, and elsewhere. A number of magazines cater to the enthusiast, and several craftspeople, like specialist jewelers, fabricate the blades, gaffs, and harpoons used in the bouts. Though certainly part of a fringe entertainment in most of the West, cockfighting provides a sound enough infrastructure to support a number of businesses. In some areas of the world the sport is fully engaged in the economy, much as baseball is in the United States.

Text descriptions of cock fights the world over exhibit a good deal of agreement regardless of the host culture. The competitions described here were observed in southern Louisiana (Louisiana is one of only four U.S. states that has not formally forbidden the sport). The locations are clearly—in keeping with rural standards—marked as "cockpits." According to authorities in Louisiana, statutes exist that could suppress the sport. But apparently there is no particular law to regulate the pits as there is in the case of dog fighting. In any event, an integral part of the sport is wagering, which is certainly unlawful. Massachusetts outlawed cockfighting in 1836 and now, presumably, every community has some sort of provision, based on everything from nuisance to noise to business license regulation, that works to control the activity. The sport is still quite common in the coastal regions of Texas, southern Louisiana, Mississippi, and most of Florida. Police in Louisiana say they are loath to suppress cockfighting because of its status as a "traditional" pastime. In this case, as Esmas (1984) so clearly points out, the role of tourism has had some effect. Although cockfighting is not one of the well-publicized features of Louisiana, it does exist thanks to a certain attitude: participants are aware that most "outsiders" view the sport as somewhat barbaric, but claim not to care and say "outsiders should keep to themselves."

Cock fights in Bali described by Geertz (1972) and other fights observed in Louisiana shared the following structure:

1. Different fights were assigned different values
2. Regional membership was a significant factor in wagering
3. Wagering was an integral part of virtually every fight
4. A protocol was enforced regarding the wagering and the performance of the cock handlers
5. An attempt was usually made to match fowl in some reasonable way (usually by size)

The following series of events typically takes place both in the recorded Balinese and the observed "cajun" fights:

1. Bout preliminaries include picking competitors, prepping the birds, and showing each to the crowd and to the competition.
2. Wagering business is dealt with. In Geertz's description, a very clearly drawn line exists in the betting procedure. He describes the behaviors as a text in which are embedded design elements of Balinese society. He views the wild excitement typical of the fight as a foil to the routine reserve of the people.
3. The pair of fowl are placed together and conflict almost invariably results. The cockfight usually continues until one of the birds is killed or rendered disabled. It seems that the goal is *not* to kill the bird but to exhibit "heart" or gameness.
4. Wagers are resolved. Money is exchanged very quickly.
5. The next bout period is initiated.

Among breeders and aficionados, winning is a good way to gain enhanced prestige. However, this attitude is largely balanced by a subtle feeling that cockfighting is part of the "old" ways. Many nonparticipants call the sport barbaric and primitive.

Details of a Cock Fight

The southern Louisiana cockfights described here took place in a very new cockpit that had been purpose-built near a small, rural complex containing a horse track, bars, and small restaurants. The contemporary-style metal quick-fab building featured basic bleachers, built by the owner from sheet plywood, and a simple bar. The pit building fronted a large parking area and boasted an attractive, well-lit sign with its name and the word "cockpit" prominently displayed. Nothing about the situation seemed furtive, although the pits are frequently in out-of-the-way locations.

The pit itself was assembled from metal reinforcing-bar and hardware cloth. The ring or pit was raised slightly above than the surrounding earth. Concrete covered most of the area, but not the pit or a small rectangular area into which dead chickens were tossed and in which the heel attachments were put on. There were both a main pit and a "drag" pit available where long or unusual fights could be finished.

The birds, which are lavished with attention and generally fed special meals as part of the preparation period, were kept in custom-built individual carriers that looked like large portable typewriter cases. Matches were made among the breeders and owners. The game cocks were informally presented to the crowd.

If wagering takes place, as is likely, much of it occurs at this point. During the southern Louisiana cockfighting episodes, wagering was clearly an important part of the event. According to Geertz, betting on cockfights has special significance for the Balinese. For them, it reaffirms social boundary areas, maintains social position, and echoes notions central to their society. Similar features are apparent in Louisiana pits, where there seems to be no wagering just for fun. Bets may be for something as trivial as buying the next round of drinks, but overall the event conformed in a general way to "serious play" (Huizinga 1950). The fights between evenly matched birds are straightforward, but are also part of a variety of competition patterns. Each region offers particular styles of organizing the matches, including informal pairs, derbies, melees, and other increasingly complex forms.

Before each fight, the contestants were examined by an "official." In the sample from southern Louisiana, this person looked under the wings and into the eyes, shook the game cock, and thrust a lemon down over each spur to verify that the weapon was well attached and sturdy. Last, the official wet a cotton ball and wiped down the metal weapons. He squeezed the remaining water into the cock's mouth and discarded the ball. The cocks were then paired by weight and weapon. Their attachments are designed to be uniform for a fair event, not to be more brutal, as is sometimes claimed. In Bali and in a number of other regions, including Louisiana, the weapons may be edged so they can both slash and pierce. In Louisiana these competitors are called "slashers." Gaff cockers claim the slashers are less sophisticated and more brutal.

Once in the pit area, the fighting cocks assume their combat positions in a flash, with feathers out and chest forward. Beady eyes glinting, the competitors clash after a few cackled threats. Their strikes are extraordinarily fast. The target is clearly the opponent's head, which involves leaping up, twisting around, and stabbing backward with the metal spurs or other heel appliance. Often the exchange continues until one bird is dead. Of course, at that point the winner may also be in poor condition, possibly having been gouged in the eyes or repeatedly stabbed in the head, body, and wings. Sometimes if a bird is "chicken" the match is ceded and the appropriate neck wrung. Most fights are fast, but long bouts are not unusual. These involve lengthy periods of one of the birds chasing his opponent around and around the ring—a standoff resolved either by one bird's sudden action or by an owner stopping the match. As their courage ebbs and flows, the birds fluff up for the attack or smooth down to try to escape.

Almost certainly, simple notions of violence and morality are inadequate when trying to understand blood sports such as cockfighting. Participants in cockfighting events often openly show adoration for their birds, fondling, petting, and cooing soothingly to them. Because the game fowl's *raison d'etre* is to seek dominance among his kind, cockfighters see their role as a positive one of support, not a negative one of predatory delight in the fights. Cockfighters believe their birds are happiest when allowed to exhibit prowess in the fight, contesting the ground with a fairly matched opponent.

Perhaps it is true, as F. F. Hawley pointed out in his insightful *Cockfight in the Cotton*, that "as the United States grows yet more urban, rural folkways are viewed with less nostalgia and sympathy" (1989, 10). Hawley, in his *Cockfighting in the Piney Woods* (1987), also describes the idea of the cocker as an outsider. According to Hawley, the cocker is not a rebel but a traditionalist. For the nonparticipant, the blood sport habitué is a compelling indicator that other world views, while quite different, may be equally attractive. The modern cocker, considered pariah in many circles, is subjected to increasing pressure to conform to the different, though not necessarily more salubrious, values and behaviors of his or her antagonists. When opponents of cockfighting call participants barbarians, villains, scofflaws, and so on, they valorize the pursuit in some people's minds. Such categorization is also common among cockers, to be sure. The journals serving the fraternity are saturated with descriptions of participants as "good men," "the best sort of man," "a man's man," and so on. It is easy to get the implication about nonparticipants. Regular discourse among cockers routinely deals with the outsider as effete, inappropriately nosy, or otherwise suspect.

—Jon Griffin Donlon

Bibliography: Donlon, J. G. (1990) "Fighting Cocks, Feathered Warriors, and Little Heroes." *Play & Culture* 3, 4: 273–285.

————. (1990) "Gamecock Imagery in Contemporary Discourse." *Aethlon: The Journal of Sports Literature* 8, 1: 157–162.

————. (1992) "Fightin' Cocks in Words and Pictures: Some Notes on Roosters and Symbolic Representation." *Centaur: The Journal of Human/Animal Interface* 1: 55–63.

————. (1993) "Cajun Cockpits." *Journal of Material Culture* 2: 25–36.

Dulles, Foster Rhea. (1965) *A History of Recreation: America Learns To Play.* New York: Appleton-Century-Crofts.

Dundes, Alan. (1994) *The Cockfight: A Casebook.* Madison: University of Wisconsin Press.

Esmas, Marjorie R. (1984) "Tourism as Ethnic Preservation: The Cajuns of Louisiana." *Annals of Tourism Research* 11.

Geertz, Clifford. (1972) "Deep Play: Notes on the Balinese Cockfight." *Daedalus, The Journal of the American Academy* 101 (Winter): 1–37.

Gunter, Charles R. (1978) "Cockfighting in East Tennessee and Western North Carolina." *Tennessee Folklore Bulletin* 44 (December): 160–169.

Harris, Marvin. (1985) *Good To Eat: Riddles of Food and Culture.* New York: Simon and Schuster.

Hawley, F. Frederick. (1987) "Cockfighting in the Piney Woods: Gameness in the New South." *Sport Place* (Fall).

————. (1989) "Cockfight in the Cotton: A Moral Crusade in Microcosm." *Contemporary Crises.*

Herzog, H. (1988) "Cockfighting and Violence in the South." In *The Encyclopedia of Southern Culture,* edited by W. Ferris. Chapel Hill: University of North Carolina Press.

————. (1985) "Cockfighting in Southern Appalachia." *Appalachian Journal* 12: 114–148.

Huizinga, J. (1950) *Homo Ludens.* London: Roy Publishers.

McCagy, Charles, and Arthur Neal. (1974) "The Fraternity of Cockfighters: Ethical Embellishments of an Illegal Sport." *Journal of Popular Culture* 8: 557–569.

Pridgen, T. (1938) *Courage: The Story of Modern Cockfighting.* Boston: Little, Brown.

Smith, Page, and Charles Daniel. (1975) *The Chicken Book.* Boston: Little, Brown.

Commercialization

The commercialization of sports is the act of subjecting sports "to the conditions of commerce . . . to cause (something having only a potential income-producing value [in this case, sport]) to be sold, displayed or utilized so as to yield income" (Gove 1976, 456). Many use the term "commodification of sport" as a synonym.

Although the terms and the concepts they represent have existed for several decades, it is only in the last half of the twentieth century that more than a handful of persons have taken the phenomenon seriously. Initially, most of the interest came from a small group of critical, mostly leftist writers. However, people from all political and social perspectives took up the topic. In fact, there currently appears to be a waning interest in the topic of commercialization of sport because of the overwhelming evidence of the phenomenon. Sociologist T. R. Young (1986, 120) noted, "The most significant structural change in modern sports is the gradual and continuing commodification of sports. This means that the social, psychological, physical, and cultural uses of sports are assimilated to the commercial needs of advanced monopoly capital." It is difficult to argue that sport has not become thoroughly entwined with economic transactions of all sorts in some cultures. The ramifications of this involvement with economics, however, is open to discussion.

The commercialization of sport is not a cultural universal. It is a product of unique technical, social, and economic circumstances. Sports in many contemporary cultures do not exhibit the characteristics of commercialization found in modern industrial-capitalist (Western) societies. Moreover, Western societies have not always been commercialized as they currently appear to be. Some argue that sports in contemporary Western cultures are the epitome of commercialization, and they contend that there are virtually no sports activities that do not require some type of cash transaction.

No discussion of the phenomenon can be divorced from the primary institutions that contributed to its rise. Sports in the colonial United States were most often unstructured, spontaneous activities. Early sports participants initiated, coordinated, and managed their own activities. For the most part they made the objects used in their pursuits. It was not until the latter part of the nineteenth century that organized sport crossed the ocean from Great Britain and arrived in America (Dulles 1965). While it took nearly a century to reach full fruition, the seeds of sports commercialization were being planted as early as the 1860s and 1870s. Urbanization forced a large number of people to live in new settings and to abandon traditional leisure activities, which included drinking, carousing, and gambling. Moreover, the dominant class sought to discourage these unproductive activities in which workers participated during their free time. They encouraged participation in and watching such activities as baseball, horseracing, and boxing (Sage 1990).

Not only was there a perceived need for organized sports in early industrialized countries, there was also a growing ability for workers to participate—both as spectators and as participants. Labor became increasingly routinized with regularly scheduled days and hours of work. Time in the evenings and on the weekends was available for pursuits other than paid labor and subsistence. For an increasing number of people, sports filled the bill.

Industry moved to meet the burgeoning desire for organized sports. The most prominent producer of sports equipment was Albert Spaulding.

In 1876, after completing a lackluster career as a pitcher in the emerging professional baseball league, he opened the A. G. Spaulding and Brothers Company. Spaulding's ability to influence the organizers of the various professional sports leagues allowed him to sell his goods and to capture a virtual monopoly on sporting goods by the latter part of the nineteenth century. But others recognized a good thing when they saw it, and by the beginning of the twentieth century, they began producing their own lines of sports equipment. Large numbers of American males were willing to purchase tickets, equipment, and services from large and small distributors of sporting goods and services (Sage 1990).

The first two decades of the twentieth century have been called the golden age of sport. The growth in sales of sporting goods and services certainly glittered brighter than ever. Commercial spectator sports captured the interest of a large proportion of the population. It appeared that American males could not get enough of such famous athletes as Babe Ruth, Knute Rockne, Jack Dempsey, Bill Tilden, and Bobby Jones. Commercialized sports was one of several male bastions. However, the 1920s found women beginning to take an interest not only in watching sports but in participating in them as well. Although the commercialization of sports slowed during the Great Depression and World War II, by the early 1950s it had solidly established itself as a significant phenomenon of modern Western culture.

Professional Sports

Professional sports may represent the epitome of the commercialization of sports. The consequences go far beyond merely its own personnel. The influence of professional sports is felt at all levels—Olympic, college, high school, and youth. Professional sports is a big business that has made impressive growth over the last three decades. Athletes, support personnel (managers, coaches, officials, media persons, lawyers, and agents), and sports team owners benefit handsomely from the willingness of sports fans to pay to watch their favorite sports and to purchase the commodities endorsed by sports personalities. Hundreds of professional athletes earn well over $1 million a year. This is a relatively recent occurrence. Before 1977, $1 million contracts did not

Commercialization

Some cultural critics argue that sports in the contemporary industrialized West are the epitome of commercialization—and professional sports are the most commercialized of all.

exist. Five years later, 23 professional athletes earned over $1 million a year. By 1988, that number had risen to 118, and by 1994 there were well over 200 professional athletes who earned salaries in excess of $1 million (McPherson, Curtis, and Loy 1989). Sage (1990) reported the average 1989 salaries for athletes in four different professional sports: $577,200 in the National Basketball Association, $490,000 in the national baseball leagues, $212,000 in the National Football League, and $156,000 in the National Hockey League. *Forbes*'s 1994 list of the top-earning athletes included basketball stars Michael Jordan at $30 million and Shaquille O'Neal at $17 million, golfers Jack Nicklaus at $15 million and Arnold Palmer at $14 million, and boxers Micheal Moore and Evander Holyfield at $12 million each. In most cases, athletes' endorsements make up over 90 percent of their earnings (Lane 1994).

Owners of professional sports franchises are some of the wealthiest people in the world. They continue to make large profits from their sports teams. In the United States there are about 110 professional sports franchises, including football, basketball, baseball, and hockey. The combined revenues of the four previously mentioned sports leagues equaled $5.1 billion in 1993 (Ozanian 1995). In addition to the money from gate receipts and television revenues, owners realize profits through the buying and selling of franchises. Sports franchises are very profitable short- and long-term investments. For example, the Dallas Cowboys football team was purchased for $600,000 in 1960. In 1989 the team sold for $140 million. In baseball, the Toronto Blue Jays sold for $7 million in 1976. Ten years later the team brought $45 million (McPherson, Curtis, and Loy 1989).

The profits for the players, owners, and other associates of professional sports come from various sources. One source, the fares paid at the gates for the opportunity to see one's favorite professional players or teams, continues to increase. By 1995 it was no longer possible to take a family of four to a major professional sporting event for less than $100. In fact, with good seats, $3 hot dogs, and $15 parking fares, it costs over $200 for a family of four to go to National League Football and National Basketball Association games (Kasky 1994). Although fans decry the high price of attending sporting events, the seats continue to fill at stadiums in most cities. The one exception may be baseball, in which attendance in 1995 was down considerably, possibly due to an extended work stoppage in 1994 and 1995.

Olympic Games

The ideal of the modern Olympic Games stands in stark opposition to the commercialism of sports. However, many commentators have argued that this idealism has been compromised to the point that the Olympics is currently the epitome of commercialism. In the early part of the twentieth century 98 percent of the games' amateur competitors made no money from their participation. In contrast, today's Olympic athletes are far from amateurs. The International Olympic Committee recognized the inevitable creep of commercialism and professionalism, and instead of requiring participants to be amateurs they merely ask that participants have an "amateur spirit." At the 1992 Barcelona Olympics, professionals competed more visibly than ever. Contestants included professional tennis stars, professional track and field stars, and a U.S. basketball team that collectively earned about $33 million a year. One U.S. sprinter summed up the attitude of many competitors when he said, "We're not in this sport because we like it or we want to earn our way through school. We're in it to make money" (Benjamin 1992, 65).

The games have also come under criticism because of the movement toward corporate sponsorship. While most Olympic administrators recognize the need for support from the private sector, there is concern about how much help and control should be exchanged. One Olympic executive warned, "it is marketing's role to support the Olympic movement financially and materially and not vice versa" (Lucas 1992, 120). Private enterprises that range from soft drink producers to automobile companies compete for the purpose of being an official sponsor of the games. The fees paid are quite large. For example Coca Cola paid $22 million for the guarantee that no competitive soft drinks be allowed to display the Olympic symbol for the Seoul games (Lucas 1992).

Intercollegiate Sports

Intercollegiate sports are not immune to the criticism of sport's commercialism. Sports at the university and college level, many argue, are big-time entertainment businesses, not collections of students striving merely to achieve physical, mental, and moral health. College sports have come a long way since their meager beginnings in the Ivy League schools when student associations, unassisted by coaches, administration, and private enterprise managed and controlled events. Over the past 140 years, student control has been replaced, and the commercial aspect of the activities has grown immensely. Sage (1990) reports that many universities have athletic budgets in excess of $12 million, football bowl games generate $30 million for the teams, teams for the men's intercollegiate basketball championships earn $1.37 million, and the National Collegiate Athletic Association has annual profits of approximately $9 million a year. Commenting on college sports, a former athletic director at a Big Ten university commented, "This is a business, a big business. Anyone who hasn't figured that out by now is a damned fool" (Denlinger and Shapiro 1975, 252).

Mass Media

The mass media, in a variety of forms, have been linked to the commercialization of sports. They exist in a symbiotic relationship with sports, each benefiting greatly from the other. The media is the twentieth-century umbilical cord for sports. In turn, the media and those who advertise through the media profit enormously from the presentation of sports programming.

Sports employs all forms of the mass media. Books and magazines that specialize in particular sports are published regularly. Newspapers often devote up to one-third of their nonadvertising space to sports coverage. Radio stations all over the country have changed their menu to include 24-hour coverage of sports.

However, it has been television, the popular culprit of many societal woes, that has affected sports most profoundly. Speaking about television's transforming power, Rader (1990) noted, "Eventually, no sporting entrepreneur, no matter how rich or imaginative, dared buy a team, stage a sporting spectacle, or even set a date or a starting time for a game without first consulting the chiefs of television" (245). Television and sports are involved in a relationship in which the economic stakes are very high. Television contracts for the coverage of professional, Olympic, and college events reach billions of dollars. The return on the investment by the major television networks is just as impressive.

Television has altered individual sports in the effort to accommodate larger viewing audiences. In some sports, additional time-outs have been implemented to allow for more commercials. In tennis, the rules regarding play-offs have been changed to allow matches to fit into prescribed schedules. The scheduling of events in the Olympic Games has been modified not to provide athletes with the optimum conditions for peak athletic performances, but to allow large audiences in the United States to view events at more convenient times.

Gambling

An indirect consequence of the mass media and an adjunct to the commercialization of sport is an increase of gambling on sporting events. Some betting on sports is legal in Great Britain and Las Vegas. However, it is likely that more money is bet on sports illegally. McPherson, Curtis, and Loy (1989) report that Americans lose over $200 million on sports bets each year. In addition, they note that more than 25 million Americans confess to betting on college sports at least once in their lives. The link between sports and gambling is complex. For example, the profits from legalized gambling are often used to build sports facilities and to operate many youth sports programs.

Social Consequences

While most agree that sport is more intertwined with commerce than ever, there is considerable disagreement about the meaning of the phenomenon. Even if sport is commercialized, how does this affect the individual and society? Proponents of modern sport argue that capitalist systems have made more sports available to a greater number of people. Whereas sports were once reserved for the upper class, they are now increasingly enjoyed by the middle and lower classes. Moreover, they contend that the owners, producers, and distributors of sports are simply responding to the demands of sports consumers.

Kelly and Godbey (1992) provide a two-stage response to the previous questions. The first critique has to do with the availability of commercialized sports. They argue that purchasing power in modern Western cultures is unequally distributed with a small proportion of people controlling a large potion of the nation's wealth. On the other end of the social spectrum, a significant portion of the population has little discretionary income with which to purchase any type of sport experience. Some may benefit, but not everyone.

Kelly and Godbey's second critique is more profound. They question the nature of commercialized sports and the power of "the market system to do more than distribute goods. Does it also alter and shape human consciousness?" (340). When sport becomes commercialized (i.e., when it becomes a commodity), its power to positively transform the individual and society may be truncated. Instead, sport is just one more means of passive entertainment. Furthermore, sport becomes a symbol of social status. Sports has been heralded as one of the primary means of bringing society together. However, commercialized sports, when used to display social status, effectively divides society. Finally, commercialized sport is another way of defining life in terms of the purchase price rather than an inner sense of meaning and achievement.

—Daniel G. Yoder

See also Gambling; Management and Marketing.

Bibliography: Benjamin, D. (1992) "Pro vs. Amateur." *Time* (July 27): 64–65.

Denlinger, K., and L. Shapiro. (1975) *Athletes for Sale.* New York: Thomas Y. Crowell.

Dulles, F. R. (1965) *A History of Recreation: America Learns To Play.* New York: Appleton-Century-Crofts.

Gove, P. (1976) *Webster's Third New International Dictionary of the English Language.* Springfield, MA: G. & C. Merriam Co.

Kasky, J. (1994) "America's Best Sports Buys." *Money* (October): 158–170.

Kelly, J. R., and G. Godbey. (1992) *The Sociology of Leisure.* State College, PA: Venture.

Lane, R. (1994). "The Forbes All-Stars." *Forbes* (December): 266–278.

Lucas, J. A. (1992) *Future of the Olympic Games.* Champaign, IL: Human Kinetics.

McPherson, B. D., J. E Curtis, and J. W. Loy. (1989) *The Social Significance of Sport: An Introduction to the Sociology of Sport.* Champaign, IL: Human Kinetics.

Ozanian, M. K. (1995) "Following the Money." *Financial World* (February 14): 27–31.

Rader, B. G. (1990) *American Sports: From the Age of Folk Games to the Age of Televised Sports.* 2d ed. Englewood Cliffs, NJ: Prentice-Hall.

Sage, G. H. (1990) *Power and Ideology in American Sport: A Critical Perspective.* Champaign, IL: Human Kinetics.

Young, T. R. (1986) "The Sociology of Sport: Structural Marxist and Cultural Marxist Approaches." *Sociological Perspectives:* 3–28.

Commonwealth Games

The Commonwealth Games were inaugurated as the British Empire Games in Hamilton, Ontario (Canada), in 1930, with 400 competitors representing 11 countries. Since then they have been celebrated on 14 other occasions and grown considerably in status, second only to the Olympic Games as an international multisport festival. Sixty-three of the 67 Commonwealth nations participated in the XV Commonwealth Games at Victoria, British Columbia (Canada), in 1994, represented by 2,557 competitors, and attended to by an international television and radio audience of more than 500 million. The festival has undergone name changes that reflect the growing political maturity of member countries, and the changing relationship of Great Britain to its former Empire. From 1930 to 1950 (no games were held in 1942 and 1946), the games were known as the British Empire Games; from 1954 to 1962 as the British Empire and Commonwealth Games; from 1966 to 1974 as the British Commonwealth Games; and since 1978 as the Commonwealth Games.

Despite encountering some of the inevitable problems associated with multisport festivals today, particularly those involving finance and politics, the Commonwealth Games have enjoyed and deserved the commonly applied label of "The Friendly Games," bestowed because of the spirit that has generally prevailed.

In 1891, five years before the modern Olympic Games, founded by Frenchman Pierre de Coubertin (1863–1937), began at Athens, an Englishman named John Astley Cooper (1858–1930) proposed an "Anglo-Saxon Olympiad" and/or "Pan-Britannic Gathering" to celebrate industry, culture, and athletic achievements among the English-speaking nations of the world (including the United States). His rather convoluted ideas stimulated some interest and debate, but foundered in the wake of Coubertin's more energetic progress. Then in 1911, as part of the "Festival of Empire" coronation celebrations for George V (1865–1936), an "Inter-Empire Sports Meeting" was held in London. Teams representing Australia, Canada, New Zealand, South Africa, and the United Kingdom competed, with the Canadian team emerging victorious, an auspicious omen. In his farewell address to the Amateur Athletic Union of Canada in 1924, National Secretary Norton H. Crowe urged the initiation of British Empire Games. The next president of the Union, John H. Crocker, enlisted sportswriter M. M. (Bobby) Robinson to implement Crowe's proposal; and Robinson successfully presented a proposal at meetings in Amsterdam (host of the 1928 Olympic Games) and later in London, for the First British Empire Games to be held at Hamilton in 1930. Canada has now hosted these Games on four occasions, more than any other Commonwealth country.

By 1930, there was some disenchantment at the perceived lack of sportsmanship demonstrated at the Olympic Games and resentment at the domination of U.S. athletes. The empire, too, was less of a force in international affairs. The prospect of some more "private" competition was therefore appealing, and perhaps a way of partly restoring some prestige. Owing to the collapse of the U.S. stock market in 1929, however, finance was a major problem. Bobby Robinson only succeeded in his quest largely because of the financial support provided by the City of Hamilton. Travel grants were awarded to invited countries, and free accommodation was promised to teams while in Hamilton, thus making their participation possible. Also, liberal use was made of volunteer labor

Commonwealth Games

A. Issajenko (214), hoping to bring home a medal at the 1986 Commonwealth Games.

to plan, organize, and run these inaugural games. These provisions by the first host city set unique precedents that were followed in future celebrations; otherwise, the ceremonies and pageantry were modeled closely on the example provided by the Olympic Games.

Hamilton celebrated the opening day with a civic holiday for its 155,000 inhabitants. The teams paraded past the Governor-General's box in their uniforms; Prime Minister R. B. Bennett (1870–1947) read goodwill messages from King George V and other notables; and Lord Willingdon formally declared the games open after praising the sporting traditions of the empire. Percy Williams (1908–1982) of Canada (winner of the 100 meter and 200 meter sprints at the 1928 Olympic Games) proclaimed the oath of allegiance on behalf of all competitors. The crowd then sang "God Save the King," followed by a 21-gun salute, the releasing of pigeons, and a fireworks display. Six sports only were featured at these first games: track and field athletics, lawn

bowls, boxing, rowing, swimming and diving, and wrestling. Women competed only in the swimming events. Canada had the first victory when Gordon Smallcombe won the hop, step, and jump event. Although the six original sports remained the "core" of the program, other sports were added over the years, as follows: cycling (first held in 1934); weightlifting and fencing (1950); badminton and shooting (1966); gymnastics (1978); archery (1982); and judo (1990).

Sixteen countries were represented at London in 1934, but Ireland was not among them as the republican government two years earlier had abolished the oath of allegiance to the king. The games at Sydney in 1938 provided a happy event that contrasted sharply with the "Nazi Olympics" in Berlin only 18 months earlier. Australia had been granted the games "in honor of the 150th anniversary of the founding of the first white settlement on her shores." Because of World War II a dozen years would pass before athletes of the empire could meet again in friendly competition, across the Tasman Sea in neighboring New Zealand. There the star of the Auckland track in 1950 was 18-year old Australian sprinter Marjorie Jackson (1931–), who won four gold medals and equaled two world records.

The games at Vancouver in 1954 produced the Bannister-Landy "mile of the century," one of most dramatic moments in sports history, and heralded the larger and more sophisticated spectacles of the modern era, now aided by air travel and television in particular. Cardiff, in 1958, attracted the largest assembly to date: 35 nations sent more than 1,100 athletes, ten world records were broken and the games' record book was almost rewritten. But there were protest demonstrations because South Africa's team was believed to be selected "on the basis of color rather than ability"; and these were the last games in which South Africa competed (until 1994), and it withdrew from the Commonwealth in 1961. The apartheid issue was to plague Commonwealth and world sport in future years. The closing ceremonies were highlighted by a message from Queen Elizabeth, who had chosen the occasion "to create my son Charles Prince of Wales today," and by the spontaneous intermingling of competitors at the very end in a mass gesture of common friendship, a happy sight common to succeeding games. At the conclusion of the next successful games in Perth, for example, Welsh boxer Rocky James led the choir and crowd in a moving rendition of "Waltzing Matilda."

No fewer than 15 world records were set in swimming alone at the 1966 games in Kingston, as this quadrennial festival continued to provide Olympic-caliber competition for Commonwealth athletes. More world records were set at Edinburgh four years later, when the queen attended the games for the first time. In Christchurch, New Zealand, in 1974, perhaps the greatest excitement came when Filbert Bayi of Tanzania defeated New Zealander John Walker in the 1,500 meters (1,640 yards) in the new world record time of 3 minutes, 22.2 seconds. The games at Edmonton, Alberta (Canada) in 1978 were threatened with a boycott by African nations over the simmering issue of sporting contacts with South Africa, particularly the rugby rivalry between New Zealand and South Africa. The Commonwealth nations were committed to the Gleneagles Agreement of 1977, which prohibited sporting contacts with the

The Miracle Mile Games

During their history, the Commonwealth Games have featured some of the greatest champions of sport in their most memorable performances, providing some of the most dramatic moments in sports history. This was illustrated most vividly, perhaps, at the British Empire and Commonwealth Games in Vancouver in 1954 in two events alone.

In the list of "The 6 Most Dramatic Events in Sports History" drawn up for the best-selling *The Book of Lists* (1977), the No. 1 choice is "The Bannister-Landy 1-Mile Duel (1954), "which took place at the V British Empire and Commonwealth Games, and was billed as 'the Mile of the Century.' " Three months earlier, Roger Bannister (1929–) of England had been the first person to break the 4-minute mile. John Landy of Australia was the only other person to have covered a mile in under 4 minutes, and was the world-record holder. At the start, Landy got off to a fast lead with Bannister running third, then second, behind him. As the bell sounded for the last lap, the final 440 yards, Landy was still in front, with Bannister at his heels. Coming into the stretch around the bend, Landy looked back over his left shoulder as Bannister passed him on his right-hand side. Bannister went on to win the historic race in 3 minutes, 58.8 seconds against his rival's time of 3 minutes, 59.6 seconds. The dramatic moment in which Bannister took the lead was preserved for posterity by the erection of a statue of both runners outside the Empire Stadium in Vancouver, scene of what are sometimes referred to as the "Miracle Mile Games."

The marathon event at the same games provided drama of a different sort, when Jim Peters, the 35-year-old captain of the England team, lurched into the stadium after running 26 miles, with only a lap to complete for the gold medal. But spectators then witnessed the agony of this brave, exhausted runner falling down eleven times, staggering and crawling in a vain attempt to reach the finishing line, in what has been described as the most heroic athletic display ever. No statue commemorates his courage, but the Jim Peters Fund to assist underprivileged children was established in his honor.

—Gerald Redmond

Republic of South Africa. Although Nigeria still did not participate at Edmonton, diplomacy won the day and allowed other African nations to compete in what has been described as one of the finest Commonwealth celebrations. Another boycott "was staved off after early ominous rumblings" at Brisbane, Australia, in 1982, and these games also went ahead in wonderful new facilities accompanied by glorious sunshine.

Through no fault of the Scottish hosts, the 1986 Games in Edinburgh were the unhappiest of all, plagued by a boycott of virtually all African and Caribbean nations, as well as the most populous in the Commonwealth, India, over the issue of the British Government's refusal to implement sanctions against South Africa. In the words of Cleve Dheensaw, "the 1986 Games were left as the playpen of the largely Anglo-Saxon nations." In fact, more nations boycotted than took part. Inclement weather and severe financial problems added to the difficulties. Although the 1990 games in Auckland, New Zealand, finished with a large deficit also, the celebration itself was a great success. Boycott threats were not realized, and the opening ceremonies were regarded as the greatest ever staged. After the setbacks of the 1986 games, the 1990 games helped to restore the prestige of the Commonwealth's major festival. This process of renewal continued at the 1994 games in Victoria, aided by the return of South Africa to the competition, the republic having rejoined the Commonwealth less than three months before the games. The 1998 games are scheduled to be held in Kuala Lumpur, Malaysia.

—Gerald Redmond

Bibliography: Agbogun, Jacob B. (1970) *A History of the British Commonwealth Games.* M.A. thesis, University of Alberta, Canada.

Bateman, Derek, and Derek Douglas. (1986) *Unfriendly Games: Boycotted and Broke, The Inside Story of the 1986 Commonwealth Games.* Glasgow: Mainstream Publishing Projects and Glasgow Herald.

Dheensaw, Cleve. (1994) *The Commonwealth Games.* Victoria, British Columbia: Orca Book Publishers.

Harris, Peter B. (1975). *The Commonwealth.* London: Longman.

Judd, Dennis, and Peter Slinn. (1982) *The Evolution of the Modern Commonwealth 1902–80.* London: Macmillan Press.

Mathews, Peter, ed. (1986) *The Official Commonwealth Games Book.* Preston, UK: Opax Publishing and the Commonwealth Games Consortium.

McIntyre, W. David. (1977) *The Commonwealth of Nations: Origins and Impact, 1869–1971.* Minneapolis: University of Minnesota Press.

Moore, Katharine Elizabeth. (1986) *The Concept of British Empire Games: An Analysis of Its Origin and Evolution from 1891 to 1930.* Ph.D. dissertation, University of Queensland, Australia.

———. (1989) " 'The Warmth of Comradeship' ": The First British Empire Games and Imperial Solidarity," *International Journal of the History of Sport* 6, 2 (September): 242–251.

Redmond, Gerald, ed. (1978) *Edmonton '78: The Official Pictorial Record of the XI Commonwealth Games.* Edmonton, Alberta: Executive Sport Publications.

Victoria Commonwealth Games Society. (1994) *Let the Spirit Live On: XV Commonwealth Games.* Victoria, British Columbia: Victoria Commonwealth Games Society.

Wallenchinsky, D., I. Wallace, and A. Wallace. (1977) *The Book of Lists.* New York: William Morrow.

Conditioning

The idea of conditioning refers to the physical or mental preparation for a sport or competitive event. Increased performance, which is any mental or physical effort subjected to psychological or physiological measurement or assessment, is usually considered a goal of conditioning. Some components of conditioning are muscular strength and endurance, flexibility, cardiorespiratory fitness, and body composition. Another important aspect of physical conditioning for sport is injury prevention.

In its earliest form, conditioning was a part of everyday life. Physical labor for the maintenance of life inherently meant physical conditioning. The other major antecedent for physical conditioning was in preparation for battles or war. There is evidence of this type of preparation in prehistoric drawings of warlike dances and games. Strength conditioning seemed to be the major component of physical training as warriors prepared for battle. Ancient myth and folklore include accounts of strong men such as Samson, Hercules, and the Greek warrior Milo, who was said to have carried a calf up to a hayloft each night and then retrieved it each morning. As the calf gained weight Milo gained strength, until he was carrying a full-grown cow up and down a ladder daily.

The early Greeks have had a profound and lasting effect on conditioning for sport and competitive events. The Greek Spartans were motivated and conditioned by a strong spirit of militarism. Physical conditioning was preparation for life as a soldier. Every boy went through vigorous training that involved tremendous

One of the early manifestations of conditioning was military training. Soviet soldiers perform conditioning exercises in the mid-1960s.

physical hardships. Young men spent the greatest part of their youths in training for the army. The Romans also believed in physical training to prepare young men for the rigors of battle. Military exercises and games took precedence over any other form of exercise. The Greek Athenians, however, believed in conditioning for sport and for the welfare of the whole body. The Athenians

were very active in the development of sport and athletic events.

A vase dated 1250 B.C.E. depicts the first-known athletic event in Cyprus, and in 776 B.C.E. the Greeks instituted the first Olympic Games. The first known association of professional athletes came into existence in 50 B.C.E. in Greece. With the appearance of professional athletes in Greek society, the *gymnastes* came into existence. These men helped to condition the athletes and prepare them for their specific sport. They used their knowledge of anatomy, physiology, and nutrition to keep the athletes in good competitive shape. Later, the medical *gymnastai* became important to the development of conditioning. Their concern was conditioning the athlete and maintaining him at a high peak of physical efficiency. The greatest of all Greek trainers was Herodicus of Megara. This man was a doctor as well as an athletic trainer and was the mentor to Hippocrates.

For many centuries after the fall of the Roman Empire there was a lack of interest in sport and conditioning. During medieval times, however, the practice of chivalry included intense physical conditioning. The idea of chivalric conditioning was to train the young men to be strong in mind and in body and to defend their holy religion. Jousting and tournaments between knights became competitive events during this time.

With the rise of modern nationalism came the need for more organized and directed physical conditioning. Individual nations needed to have strong and healthy soldiers to defend their national borders. Communist countries have been particularly strong in their pursuit of strength and conditioning as a nation. East Germany required fitness training for everyone. Mao Zedong (1893–1976) of China said that "the youth of China are encouraged to get fit, keep fit, and spur on the revolution."

Russia has been an extremely important influence in the development and promotion of conditioning for the strength of the nation and preparation for sport. After the Russian Revolution of 1917 the Communist party recognized physical exercise as a means of improving the strength of the country and its people. From this idea of increasing military strength came the birth of Soviet athletics in 1918. By 1921, more than 150 sports clubs had been formed and 6,000 physical education instructors had been trained. During World War II, the Soviet Union credited the physical fitness of its soldiers and the general public with helping its people withstand months of hunger and fatigue. In 1952 the Soviets participated in their first Olympic Games and they, along with the United States, have dominated ever since. In addition, the Soviets have the largest body of scientific research on the training of athletes.

England, France, and the United States have also influenced the development of conditioning in relation to performance and sport. During the last decades of the nineteenth century and the early decades of the twentieth century physiological investigations of human performance began. In 1893, Dr. Philippe Tissue conducted studies of performance and fatigue of the athletes in a 24-hour bike race, which made him a pioneer in performance research. In the late nineteenth century, British philosopher Herbert Spencer began some of the first physiological research, which looked at muscular energy. This helped to create the surge of physiological research into conditioning and sport that has continued today. The United States has been at the forefront of much of modern performance research. Biological sciences like anatomy, physiology, biomechanics, kinesiology, and nutrition, as well has chemistry, have provided vast quantities of knowledge that have served to broaden the scope of conditioning and sport. Technology and technological devices have now become the ultimate tools in the measurement of performance.

Physical conditioning for sports participation prepares athletes for high-level performance and protects against injury. Improper conditioning is a major contributor to athletic injuries. Muscular imbalance, improper timing, inadequate muscular or tendinous strength, inadequate muscular or cardiovascular strength, problems related to flexibility, and problems related to body composition are some of the causes of sports injuries and poor performance.

Conditioning can be defined as a systematic process of repetitive, progressive exercise or work, involving the learning process and acclimatization to the workload. S. E. Bilik, a sports medicine pioneer, stated in 1917 that the primary objective of sports conditioning and training is "to put the body with extreme and exceptional care under the influence of all agents which promote its health and strength in order to enable it to meet extreme and exceptional demands upon it." Logan and Wallis (1960) identified a foundation of conditioning the SAID (specific adaptation to imposed demands) principle, which indicates that conditioning and training should be directed to the specific demands of a given sport.

Four components of conditioning must be addressed to properly train an athlete. The first is cardiorespiratory conditioning. Through aerobic conditioning the cardiorespiratory system, which includes the heart, lungs, and circulation, functions more efficiently. With proper cardiovascular training the heart becomes a bigger, stronger, more efficient pump capable of doing more work with less effort. The lungs also benefit by becoming more efficient at passing air through the lungs, thus increasing vital capacity. Circulation improves by increasing blood flow, meaning that more oxygen and fuel are delivered to the muscles. This type of conditioning is particularly important for sports such as track, tennis, basketball, and cycling, which require efficient and well-conditioned heart and lung functioning.

The second component of conditioning is muscular strength and endurance. Increases in muscular strength are associated with increases in muscle mass and productivity. Increases in muscular endurance are associated with improved blood flow to the working muscles. Resistance training, which increases the tension on the muscle, is the primary mode used to increase muscular strength and endurance. There is a wide selection of strength training equipment used for this type of conditioning. Strength training in some form is used in almost every sport for increased performance and particularly for the prevention of injuries.

Flexibility, the third component of conditioning, helps to increase the range of motion around a joint by lengthening the muscles, tendons, and ligaments connected to the bone, thus allowing for increased freedom of movement. Static stretching exercises, which are done by holding a stretched position for 30 to 60 seconds, are the most effective way of increasing flexibility. Flexibility is important for all sports; however, it is particularly important in gymnastics, dance, and figure skating.

Body composition, or the percentage of body fat, is the fourth component of conditioning. It is important for athletes to maintain a lean body mass for optimal performance as well as to avoid injuries. Excess weight can limit athletic performance by putting too much stress on the body, especially the joints. Body fat can be controlled by proper conditioning combined with proper nutrition.

There are six principles of conditioning that also need to be considered for optimal performance.

Muscles and Femininity

And, ladies, when some jealous and false prophet arises to decry your noble efforts by drawing a forbidding picture of your great-great-grandchildren as huge, muscular amazons divested of sweet womanly charms by too steady encroachment on the field where men alone are fitted to excel, believe him not! By some happy provision of kind Nature, no matter if the woman's biceps grow as firm as steel, the member remains as softly rounded, as tenderly curved, as though no greater strain than the weight of jeweled ornaments had been laid upon them. This is a comforting assurance, and one that may induce many hitherto prudent ladies to lay aside old fashioned prejudice and join the growing host of womankind in the bowling alley.

—Margaret Bisland, "Bowling for Women,"
Outing 16 (April 1890): 33–36.

1. *Specificity* is training the specific component that is primarily utilized in competition. If an athlete needs a particularly large amount of muscular strength, then heavy weight training is essential to proper preparation for the event. Specificity relates to the following principles.
2. *Intensity* refers to the percentage of one's maximum capacity that is being used while training. This intensity level is pertinent to cardiorespiratory training as well as muscular strength and endurance. The higher the intensity of training, the greater the training effect.
3. *Duration* refers to the amount of time the exercise or conditioning bout continues. As with intensity, the greater the duration of training, the greater the training effect. However, there is a maximum training threshold that must be considered; the point of diminishing returns is reached if training is too long or hard, and the chance of injury will increase. A competitive marathon runner, for example, must consider duration while conditioning for the race; running 26 miles a day would cause the body to break down.
4. *Frequency* refers to the number of times per week an athlete trains. Although the noncompetitive or recreational athlete may train three to five times a week, the competitive

athlete needs to train six to seven times a week and sometimes more than once a day. Although increased frequency of training tends to promote increased performance, it is also necessary to allow the body proper rest to avoid overtraining.

5. *Progression* is the gradual increase in intensity and duration of conditioning. As the body adapts to training modes the exercise load can be increased.

6. The *overload* principle is related to progression. Overload means that to improve any aspect of physical conditioning the athlete must continually increase the demands placed on the appropriate body systems. Power lifters continually increase the amount of weight they lift to increase their strength.

There has been much progress in the field of physical training and conditioning. Physical conditioning has evolved from conditioning for military strength to a highly technological aspect of performance in sport. It has been determined that certain components and principles of conditioning should be adhered to for optimal performance and prevention of injuries. The study of conditioning and performance has become an important and highly researched academic pursuit. Most universities now have some sort of human performance laboratory that studies many varied but related aspects of sport and conditioning, such as exercise physiology, exercise science, biomechanics, kinesiology, athletic training, and sport psychology. As this ever-changing field continues to grow there will be new and exciting concepts investigated to continually test the peaks of human performance.

—Sally Crawford

See also Aerobics; Exercise; Medicine.

Bibliography: American College of Sports Medicine. (1992) *ACSM Fitness Book.* Champaign, IL: Leisure Press.

Arnheim, Daniel D. (1989) *Modern Principles of Athletic Training.* St. Louis, MO: Times Mirror/Mosby College Publishing.

Bilik, S. E. (1956) *The Trainers Bible.* New York: TJ Reed and Co. (originally published in 1917).

Durant, Will. (1939) *The Life of Greece.* New York: Simon and Schuster.

Harris, Harold A. (1964) *Greek Athletes and Athletics.* London: Hutchinson and Company.

Logan, G. A., and Wallis, E. L. (1960) "Recent Findings in Learning and Performance." Paper presented at the Southern Section meeting, California Association for Health, Physical Education and Recreation, Pasadena.

Sharkey, B. J. (1984) *Physiology of Fitness.* Champaign, IL: Human Kinetics Publishers.

Snook, G. A. (1984) "The History of Sportsmedicine, Part 1." *American Journal of Sports Medicine* 12, 252 (July/August).

Tuer, David F., and Howard F. Hunt. (1986) *Encyclopedic Dictionary of Sports Medicine.* New York and London, Chapman and Hall.

Coursing

Coursing—the development, breeding, and preparation of racing dogs, as well as the competition itself—is one of the world's oldest sports. The greyhound eventually came to the fore as the swiftest animal that could be domesticated and trained to run at breathtaking speeds over a variety of distances.

Origins

While coursing qualified as a popular blood sport in Victorian England (along with boxing and foxhunting), some groups came to rail against it because the dogs usually killed the live hare that was released to encourage them to run. The invention of the mechanical hare and, later, an electrified hare on a circular track saved the sport, and by the early 1930s, greyhound racing was thriving in the United States. Meanwhile, in certain regions of Britain greyhound racing became hugely popular and attracted wildly enthusiastic crowds made up mostly of working-class men eager to drink ale and wager on a succession of closely contested races. The first newspaper report of a coursing meet, in Lancaster, England, in 1840.

Dog racing has evolved over millennia; the trained dog held an important place in ancient Egypt and Assyria and in the Mayan civilization. Unlike many breeds that have been transformed over the centuries—for example, such bull-baiting types as the boxer, bulldog, and mastiff—the greyhound has remained virtually unchanged.

Coursing

In the time-honored sport of coursing, greyhounds came to the fore as the fastest breed of dog that could be trained to run at breakneck speed over a variety of distances. Greyhound racing is now a highly lucrative sport; here greyhounds raise money in a benefit for the March of Dimes.

The dog most favored in coursing almost from the very beginning was the greyhound. . . . Its characteristics have always been a slender body and long legs but, above all, superlative vision, acute sense of hearing, and swiftness. . . . The greyhound followed the quarry not by scent but by sight, which differentiates it from most other dogs (Brasch 1971).

The Roman poet Ovid compared Apollo's pursuit of Daphne to the greyhound's headlong chase of a hare. In the reign of Queen Elizabeth I, the fourth Duke of Norfolk drew up the first code of conduct for coursing: the hare had to be given a head start of (219 meters) 240 yards, and the race was "not necessarily won by the dog that made the kill, but by the one most instrumental in achieving it" (Brasch).

Lord Oxford is credited with founding the first coursing club in Swaffham in 1776. Its eccentric organization, restricted membership to 26 (the letters in the alphabet), and each member was assigned a distinct racing color. Other clubs were formed in Britain, and in 1836 an unofficial national championship came into being, called the Waterloo Cup after Liverpool's Waterloo Hotel. Hotel proprietors and publicans frequently found themselves promoting greyhound race meetings, since the taproom and the racetrack seemed to complement each other. Conducted in a climate of unlimited gambling, these meetings brought together crowds of spectators eager to speculate and make merry.

Development

In 1858 a National Coursing Club was set up to monitor the sport in England. Even more than horse racing, coursing lent itself to chicanery and deception. Most often there was the subterfuge of substituting one greyhound for another, so careful scrutiny was critical if the sport's reputation was to be maintained.

The first attempt at creating a mechanical hare took place at Welsh Harp, Mendon, in 1876. The "hare" was mounted on a rail and moved by means of a rope and pulley system. The major drawbacks of the system, and the reason this innovative gadget was unsuccessful, was that it was set up on a straight track of 411 meters (450 yards). This meant that the quickest greyhound would win again and again, thus all but eliminating the important gambling elements of luck, tactics, lane draw, and guile. Moreover, the nature of the course meant that spectators had to choose between being either at the starting line or the finish line. To counter these difficulties, the shape of the track was changed to a circular or oval track.

Although the mechanical hare's prototypes were tried out in England, it was an American, Owen Patrick Smith, who shaped greyhound racing as it exists today. In 1907 in South Dakota, Smith successfully tested a mechanical hare (otherwise known as a mechanical lure), and two years later used it on a greyhound racing track that he established in Tucson, Arizona. Much fine tuning had to take place until Smith finally came up with a trouble-free, reliable mechanical hare that sped smoothly along an electric rail set on an oval track. The first recorded race with the electric hare took place in 1919 at Emeryville, Canada. By the time he died in 1927, Smith had organized the International Greyhound Racing Association.

Ironically, it was also an American, Charles Munn, who introduced the now-electrified form of greyhound racing to its native England in 1925. Despite early indifference, Munn eventually found a partner for his venture, Gen. A. C. Critchley, and set up an experimental track in 1926 at Belle Vue, Manchester. They could not have selected a better site, since the area was primarily populated by working-class people who were excited by the sport and who wagered passionately on the outcome.

Tracks sprang up in most of the major cities of Great Britain in the late 1920s, offering cheap gambling and a night out for ordinary working people who found it difficult to go to horse-racing. Sixty-two companies with a total capital of 7 million pounds were registered for greyhound-racing in 1927 alone. Britain was "going to the dogs" and by 1932 the annual attendance at licensed tracks in London had risen to 6.5 million. Several of the leading tracks drew 200 to 300 bookmakers (Holt 1989).

In the pre–World War II era, greyhound racing became Scotland's second-most-popular spectator sport after soccer (association football). In Fife, Scotland, in the 1950s it was common to see coal miners walking their race dogs on common land around the slag heaps and pit towers of the coalfields. Greyhounds could be housed, fed, and exercised on a relatively meager income compared to the costs of other animals, such as racehorses.

Sports historian Richard Holt describes the "rich tradition of potions and tricks" that was part and parcel of the greyhound racing culture. The common practices of concealing a dog's true form and cloaking the champion performer created an atmosphere in which deception and guile posed no moral or ethical dilemma, but rather were integral elements in an unpredictable, unfolding drama. "Champion dogs were greatly prized, even given the best chair beside the fire and, in some accounts, their trophies displayed alongside family heirlooms" (Holt 1990).

The history of British greyhound racing in the late 1920s and throughout the 1930s illustrates the democratization of the sport, which in 1932 had 187 tracks and was attracting an average annual attendance of over 20 million people. Nevertheless, just as with boxing and horseracing, public figures were concerned about whether the sport was "good" for Britain. J. H. Thomas, a Labour member of Parliament, declared in 1928 that greyhound racing upset the family structure. But race promoters had their own set of family values, and in 1934 two Scottish tracks set up children's nurseries and a London track built a playground (Jones).

In 1925, the advent of night racing played a key role in popularizing greyhound racing as a spectator sport in the United States. During its early years the sport was plagued by criminal elements who took advantage of the quick profits that could be make by "doctoring" a dog or bribing an untrustworthy dog handler. Eventually, dog owners and racetrack promoters saw to it that the sport was regulated and closely supervised. This helped establish credibility and integrity in the sport. In 1932, with the legalization of greyhound racing gambling at on- and off-course locations in Florida (parimutuel betting), the sport's future was assured. Two years later, greyhound racing and parimutuel betting were enjoying success at U.S. tracks as far north as Massachusetts.

Practice

Greyhound racing continues to be an exhibition of pure speed. Races tend to be no more than 550 meters (601 yards), but 950-meter (1,039-yard) marathons do occur. The British Greyhound Derby is 480 meters (535 yards), the U.S. Greyhound Derby is 603 meters (660 yards), and Britain's Greyhound Cesarewitch is 805 meters (880 yards). At these distances the greyhound maintains an average speed of 60 kilometers (37 miles) per hour—faster than harness horseracing (48 kilometers [30 miles] per hour), but slightly slower than flat horseracing over similar distances (62 kilometers [39 miles] per hour).

Before a race, the participating dogs are paraded before the audience, weighed, fitted with plastic muzzles, and placed in a cage-like starting gate. At the starting bell, the mechanical lure is set in motion around the track and the greyhounds are released. The most common distances for a greyhound race are $5/16$ mile (503 meters [1,650 feet]), $3/8$ mile (604 meters [1,980 feet]) and $7/16$ mile (704 meters [2,310 feet]). The first dog to cross the finish line (or "wire") in the final lap is the winner. The other dogs are placed in their order of finish.

Betting is an important element of the sport for many fans. The wagers at tracks are handled on a parimutuel basis, which means the money bet on a particular race is pooled and a majority of the proceeds divided among the winners. The track association also takes a percentage to cover operating costs and as profit. Other portions go to purses for the owners of the winning dogs and as taxes to the appropriate government bodies. Track operators also earn money on admission tickets, food sales, and other concessions.

People attending greyhound races receive charts that list the physical characteristics and performance records of the dogs in each race. Some people bet casually, based on hunches.

"Heeded lyke a snake"

In a short history of greyhound racing, *Roots of the Greyhound*, published by the Greyhound Hall of Fame and Museum in Abilene, Kansas, appears one of the earliest descriptions of a perfectly contoured greyhound. The words still apply to a champion Hall of Famer today. The poetic description was written by Dame Juliana Berners in the *Boke of St. Albans* (1486):

> A greyhound should be heeded lyke a snake,
> And neckyd lyke a drake,
> Backed lyke a bream,
> Footed lyke a catte,
> Taylled lyke a ratte.

—Scott A. G. M. Crawford

Others are more methodical, carefully studying the statistics and careers of individual dogs. Winnings are based on the bettor's ability to predict which individual greyhound will win as the first-place finisher, "place" in second, or "show" in third. There are many options for wagers, which are made at the track's betting windows before each race. A "quiniela" is a bet on which dogs will be the top two winners in no particular order, while a "perfecta" pays off if the bettor predicts their exact order of finishing. A "trifecta" is a bet on the top three winners in exact order. The payoffs for wagers depend on the type of wager and the betting patterns, odds, and overall amounts bet on the individual race.

Nighttime greyhound racing has a singular ambiance and setting. The configuration of the track; the darkened backdrop and brightly illuminated track; the lean, lithe dogs with their becoated dog handlers; and the intense involvement of wagering spectators all come together to create a kind of working man's theater. Nevertheless, greyhound racing continues to find it difficult to compete with the mystique of horseracing and the tradition of the Kentucky Derby. As J. E. Vader says, "There are no manes and tails blowing, no bright silks, no sweat, no bloodlines going back centuries, no 'My Old Kentucky Home.'"

Greyhound racing is established in 18 U.S. states. Florida leads the way with 15 of the 51 tracks, closely followed by southern New England, which has 6 tracks in 5 states. However, it is clearly an international sport. In the mid-1940s in Australia, record crowds of 17,000 people watched a champion dog named Chief Havoc (winner in 26 of 35 starts) attempt to set timed records at various distances. In some Australian history books the greyhound was known as the Kangaroo Dog because in the early years of the settlements they were used for hunting kangaroos.

Greyhound racing today is a small part of the rich mosaic that is "communicated" contemporary sport. In the *Chicago Tribune* of 10 September 1995, a listing of sports events either with television or radio coverage included auto racing, baseball, football, golf, soccer, tennis, track and field, harness racing, polo, and thoroughbred racing. Included in the list was a greyhound racing program at Dairlyland, Illinois, and Geneva Lakes, Illinois. The sport continues to expand, and among spectator sports in the United States is ranked sixth. In 1988, the revenue from the 51 U.S. dog tracks generated $225 million in tax dollars. In Great Britain, the sport continues to be associated with working-class communities. A 1995 *Economist* obituary on union leader Sam McCluskie opened with the comment, "There are leaders of British trade unions whom one could still imagine owning a racing greyhound."

Within the United States the sport is controlled by the American Greyhound Track Operators Association, with headquarters in Miami, Florida.

—Scott A. G. M. Crawford

Bibliography: Brasch, R. (1971) *How Did Sports Begin?* New York: David McKay.

Cummings, P., ed. (1949) *Dictionary of Sports.* New York: A. S. Barnes.

Diagram Group. (1982) *Sports Comparisons.* New York: St. Martin's Press.

Grimsley, W., ed. (1971) *Great Moments in Sport.* New York: Plimpton Press.

Hall of Fame Souvenir Issue (1987) Abilene, KS: Greyhound Hall of Fame.

Hickok, R. (1992) *The Encyclopedia of North American Sports History.* New York: Facts on File.

Holt, R. (1989) *Sport and the British: A Modern History.* Oxford: Oxford University Press.

Jones, S. G. (1988) *Sport, Politics and the Working Class—Organized Labour and Sport in Inter-War Britain.* Manchester: Manchester University Press.

"Obituary—Sam McCluskie" (1995) *Economist* 336,7933 (23 September).

Raitz, K. B., ed. (1995) *The Theater of Sport.* Baltimore: Johns Hopkins University Press

Rooney, J. F., Jr., and R. Pillsbury. (1992) *Atlas of American Sport.* New York: Macmillan

Roots of the Greyhound (1990) Abilene, KS: Greyhound Hall of Fame.

Speak, M. A. (1998) "Social Stratification and Participation in Sport in Mid-Victorian England with Particular Reference to Lancaster, 1840–70." In *Pleasure, Profit, Proselytism: British Culture and Sport at Home and Abroad,* edited by J. A. Mangan. London: Frank Cass and Co.

Vamplew, W., and K. Moore, J. O'Hara, R. Cashman, and I. Jobling. (1992) *Oxford Companion to Australian Sport.* Melbourne: Oxford University Press.

Vader, J. E. (1989) "Paws." *Sports Illustrated* 70 (26 June).

Zucker, H. M., and L. J. Babich. (1987) *Sports Film: A Complete Reference.* Jefferson, NC: McFarland.

Cricket

Cricket, a bat and ball game, has long been regarded as the archetypal English game, and its complex and even archaic rules are often baffling to people who have not grown up in cricket-playing countries. The core rules of the game were formulated in the eighteenth century by wealthy landowners who loved to gamble and favored codification of the rules to safeguard their bets. By that time cricket had been established as a game between two sides of 11 that took turns batting. An innings was completed when 10 of the 11 players had been dismissed—caught, bowled, stumped, run out, and leg before wicket were the chief means of dismissal. Play occurs at both ends of rectangular-shaped areas, with wickets consisting of three stumps at each end of a 22-yard (20-meter) grass pitch in the center of an oval or field. An over (now six balls) is bowled from one end to one batsman, followed by an over at the other end, by another bowler, to the second batsman. A batsman can hit the ball (on the full or the bounce) to any part of the field and a run or runs are scored when both batsmen safely reach the other end. If the ball reaches the boundary, four runs are scored; if the ball crosses the boundary without bouncing, six runs. A unique feature of cricket is that batsmen do not have to run when they hit the ball: they can continue to bat for hours and, in international cricket, for days on end.

Underarm bowling was the norm initially, but the laws were altered in the nineteenth century to allow round arm and eventually overarm bowling. The laws of cricket dictate that the ball should be bowled (with a straight arm) and not thrown. New traditions developed as the game became more popular in the nineteenth century: the English three-day county game was instituted in 1864, and international contests known as Test matches began in 1877, which came to be played over five days. An abbreviated form of cricket, limited overs, was introduced in 1963 and soon became popular.

The leisurely pace of cricket has inspired much reflection and literature. Neville Cardus, a notable writer, regarded cricket as akin to the arts and depicts it in theatrical and romantic terms. Others make lofty claims for the game as a moral and healthy pastime; one Australian clergyman even claimed that had Adolf Hitler played cricket World War II would not have occurred.

Cricket boasts a rich language of fielding positions such as "fine leg," "gully," "silly mid on," as well as terms for specialist balls that include "bosie," "googly," "wrong-un," "Chinaman," and "zuter." Phrases such as "sticky wicket" and "it's not cricket" have assumed many broader meanings outside cricket. Cricket has faced a series of crises in the twentieth century but has been able to reinvent itself to suit a changing society and media. Ironically, it is now more popular in many Commonwealth countries than it is in Britain itself.

Origins

The origins of cricket are obscure. Even the name is shrouded in mystery: it is still not clear whether the word cricket refers to the target that is defended (the three stumps that make up the wicket) or the implement used to defend this target, the bat. The derivation of the word cricket is also uncertain. Some scholars argue that the word is related to the Flemish or Low German *krick-stoel*, a low stool similar to the earliest types of wicket. Others contend that cricket derives from the Old English *crycc* or Middle Flemish *crick*, literally a staff for leaning on. Uncertainty about cricket's prehistory has encouraged fanciful attempts to establish its ancient antecedents. Some writers have attempted to link cricket with bat-and-ball folk games such as stool-ball, trap-ball, tip-cat, cat-and-dog, and club-ball, suggesting that they were the acorn from which the mighty oak cricket

sprang. Others have posited a connection between cricket and folk games such as *creag*, a game played by the Prince of Wales in 1299–1300. There is no evidence, however, that any of these games bore any resemblance to cricket.

The first authentic reference to cricket dates to 1598, and it seems clear that cricket was played in the south of England in the sixteenth century. Increased references to the game in the seventeenth century suggest that the game was becoming more popular in both city and country. The involvement of wealthy landowners who patronized the game from the late seventeenth century helped transform an informal intervillage pastime to a more organized sport. Aristocrats with time and money to lavish on leisure played an important role in establishing and codifying the rules of the game; one reason consistent rules were desirable was the substantial bets (up to £10,000) placed on matches. From 1711 articles of agreement were often drawn up for individual matches. These articles set out the core rules of the game and were later incorporated into the versions of the "laws" drafted in 1744, 1771, 1774, and 1788. By the end of the eighteenth century, rules covered the form of the bat, ball, stumps, and bails; the size of the wicket; methods of batting and bowling and methods of dismissal. The essential rules of the game were completed by the next century with the evolution from underarm to roundarm bowling in 1835 and the legalization of overarm (over the shoulder) bowling in 1864. Many refinements of the rules have followed, but the major changes in the game in the nineteenth and twentieth centuries relate to improvements in facilities, technology, and equipment and changes in the form of competition and styles of play: the introduction of three- and four-day competition, the beginning of five-day test (international) matches, and limited overs contests.

Development

Eighteenth Century

Cricket was transformed in the eighteenth century largely because it fired the imagination of a number of aristocrats. The Prince of Wales, who was a keen cricketer in the 1730s, became a leading patron of the game in Kent and died young, possibly as the result of a cricket injury, in 1751. Another patron, the Duke of Richmond, brought

A cricket match in progress, Simla, India, in 1865. Taken to India by British colonialists in the nineteenth century, cricket is now a major sport in both India and Pakistan.

his well-credentialed team from Slindon Parish, Sussex, to London in the 1740s. Sir Horatio Mann created a cricket ground at his Bishopbourne Estate in Kent and was eager to include good cricketers on his estate staff.

Cricket appealed to English aristocrats because it was a complex and leisurely game amenable to subtle distinctions of class. The aristocrat could lead the side and bat, leaving the more physically taxing fast bowling to the estate laborer. Cricket paintings that adorn the walls of many a country house from this century suggest another aspect of the game's appeal: at a time when England was undergoing rapid urban and industrial change, cricket conjured a romantic vision of bucolic bliss and class cooperation on rustic swards on sunlit afternoons.

Village cricket clubs also flourished; 1,000 were reported in England and Wales in this century. Competition grew more demanding in the 1740s, and matches were played between teams representing counties. Teams designated as "All England" also took the field. Hambledon Cricket Club, which existed from 1756 to 1791 at Broadhalfpenny Down in Hampshire, with its headquarters at the Bat and Ball Inn, was the most famous club. Including aristocrats, yeoman farmers, respectable tradesmen, and plebeian players—a blend of aristocratic patronage and local enthusiasm—the club founded a tradition of success. The ethos of the club inspired its historian John Nyren to publish one of the first classics of cricket, expressing, as John Arlott put it, "authentic peasant portraits in their [own] language." It

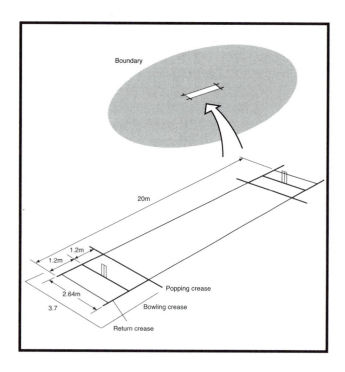

Boundary

20m

1.2m
1.2m
2.64m
3.7
Popping crease
Bowling crease
Return crease

suggestions that women cricketers achieved greater acceptance in the eighteenth century than in later centuries. Their matches were advertised in the press, gate-entry was charged, and large crowds watched.

Nineteenth Century

Cricket continued to grow in popularity in the nineteenth century with many new clubs and competitions. Matches between Eton and Harrow were first introduced to Lord's in 1805, followed by contests between the Gentlemen and Players (that is, amateurs and professionals) in 1806 and Oxford and Cambridge universities in 1827. Star players emerged, such as Alfred Mynn (1807–1861) and Fuller Pilch (1804–1870), who fired the public imagination. The game was sufficiently popular by 1836 to be featured in *The Pickwick Papers*. Charles Dickens included therein a match between Dingley Dell and All-Muggleton.

The responsibility for the second great transformation in cricket—the spread of the game throughout England and abroad and its growth into a highly profitable mass spectator sport—was not so much the achievement of the gentlemen of the MCC at Lord's but of the working-class professionals whose role has not been properly acknowledged until recently. William Clarke, a bricklayer from Nottingham, formed a lucrative All England XI in 1846. It became a successful professional troupe that traveled around England in pursuit of profit. The professionals, or teams made up predominantly of professionals, took the game overseas to Canada and the United States in 1859, to Australia in 1862, and to Australia and New Zealand in 1864. Their tours overseas proved immensely profitable and did much to stimulate interest in overseas cricket. The professional John Wisden (1826–1884) published his annual cricket almanac for first time in 1864; it soon became the bible of cricket collectors. A complete set of *Wisden* is the cornerstone of any reputable cricket library. The professionals also played an important role in establishing international cricket. The first such match was played in 1877 at Melbourne between an English team made up entirely of professionals and an Australian eleven.

Professional tours inspired colonial sides to organize tours of England. The success of the Australians, who in 1878 performed very creditably against the best English sides, helped install

was the beginning of a very rich tradition, for cricket has inspired more literature than almost any other sport.

From the 1730s to the 1770s, cricket found a London home at the Artillery Ground, Finsbury, the grounds of the Honourable Artillery Company, which was partly enclosed, enabling gate entry charges. London cricket was controlled by the London Club, which dated from the 1730s. A coterie of influential aristocrats headed by the Prince of Wales established this club, which functioned as the administrative hub of the game. The London Club was a forerunner of the powerful Marylebone Cricket Club (MCC), which was founded in 1787 and became cricket's governing authority. Lord's cricket ground was established at the same time. The ground took its name from a shrewd businessman, Thomas Lord (1755–1832), who was engaged to develop a cricket ground for his patrons, the gentlemen of the MCC. Lord recognized the commercial potential of cricket and enclosed Lord's. It was later relocated twice, finally, in 1814, at St. John's Wood, London, where it became the spiritual mecca of world cricket.

From the 1740s there were intervillage cricket games for women, particularly in the counties of Surrey and Sussex. The rise of more organized cricket for women paralleled that of the men's game. Some of the games were robust and boisterous and involved gambling. There are many cricket as an international game, and indigenous traditions soon developed. International matches, which were played regularly from 1877, came to be known as tests. Contests between England and Australia were for the "Ashes." The Ashes was a potent symbol, developed after England suffered its first defeat on home soil against Australia in 1882. An advertisement in the press a few days later declared that English cricket died on that day, that its body would be cremated, and that the ashes would be taken to Australia. What started as a joke escalated in the next decades into a serious metaphor of Anglo-Australian contest—a life-and-death struggle. From the mid-1860s many amateur cricketers believed that the professionals had become too influential, and there was a concerted attempt to limit their role in cricket and to reassert gentlemanly (amateur) control of the game. Amateurs linked cricket with the ideals of amateurism, athleticism, and muscular Christianity and sought to purify the game of its gambling associations. In the new forms of competition, such as the county championship from the 1860s, the role of the professional was defined as subsidiary.

Class distinctions were incorporated into all facets of the game: the amateur was segregated from the professional in terms of accommodation and dining, and he even entered the field from a different gate. The amateur had his name and initials recorded in the schoolbook, the professional was identified by surname only. It was also thought proper that England should be captained by an amateur; not until 1953, when the Yorkshireman Len Hutton became captain, was England captained by a professional.

W. G. Grace (1848–1915), the doctor who dominated the cricket world for the last four decades of the nineteenth century, was a superstar who helped popularize cricket. Bearded, solidly built, and ebullient—an archetypal John Bull—he became one of most recognizable Englishmen of his era. He was such a popular figure that the public overlooked his "sharp practice," which bordered on cheating, and his mercenary attitude (he demanded £1,500 to tour Australia). Grace received 10 times what the professionals were paid. The era before World War I has been called the Golden Age of cricket, a period when the game itself was seen as a form of imperial cement that bound the British Empire together. An Indian prince, K. S. Ranjitsinhji, who was selected to play for England in the 1890s, became a potent symbol of empire. "Ranji" declared that cricket was one of the most powerful links of empire and "one of the greatest contributions which the British people have been made to the cause of humanity." Similarly lofty claims were made for cricket as character building. One Australian official was convinced that cricket encouraged "cleanliness of mind and thought."

By the nineteenth century, cricket was elevated to become a manly game, played in many British public schools, and despite the earlier popularity of informal village cricket for women, women who took up the game in the late nineteenth century were viewed with suspicion as trespassers on male territory. Women formed cricket clubs from the 1880s but battled to gain public acceptance: crowds attended initially because women's cricket was regarded as a novelty event. Once the novelty had worn off women cricketers were either treated with a monumental lack of interest or with ridicule.

Twentieth Century

The twentieth century has seen significant growth in international cricket competition and an ever-expanding program of international tours and contests. Many new competitors have been accorded test status, including South Africa (1889), West Indies (1928), New Zealand (1930), India (1932), Pakistan (1952), Sri Lanka (1981), and Zimbabwe (1992). Many other nations have acquired associate status, including Bangladesh, the Netherlands, Canada, Kenya, and the United Arab Emirates. The expansion of international competition led to the creation of a world cricket authority, the Imperial Cricket Conference (later the International Cricket Conference) in 1909.

International cricket for women dates from the 1930s, when England toured Australia in 1934–1935 and played three tests. Since then a number of other women's teams have played test cricket, including New Zealand, India, and teams from the West Indies. For much of the century women's cricket has struggled to gain acceptance and, although women's cricket was popular in the 1930s, there were many low periods until it was established on a surer basis in the 1970s. The staging of a World Cup for women's cricket—two years before the men—was an inspired idea that helped to revive interest in the game. Since cricket is still regarded as a man's game, there remains an onus on women who play cricket to prove their femininity. It is odd that women in some countries, such as Australia and England, play in a culotte (a divided skirt)—to promote a suitably feminine image—whereas women in India and the West Indies compete in trousers.

The twentieth century has been notable for major controversies that have rocked the cricket world and altered the character of the game. The first to arouse great passion was the infamous Bodyline series of 1932–1933. There was much debate about the tactics employed by the English captain, Douglas Jardine, to curb the Australian run-machine, Sir Donald Bradman. Bradman's status had become legendary in Australia because he had rewritten the record books on the previous tour of England in 1930 and appeared invincible. Jardine instructed his chief bowler to bowl *at* the batsmen in an intimidating fashion and in a manner many considered unfair and not in the spirit of the game. The series strained relations between Australia and England until a cricket solution, a change in the rules, was devised. The tour aroused enormous interest because it coincided with the introduction of national ball-to-ball radio commentary.

With its long broadcast periods of play (six hours a day) and extended breaks the game has attracted articulate and erudite commentators, such as poet John Arlott, with his rich Hampshire accent; Australian Allan McGilvray, whose mellow voice had been familiar to Australians for decades; and Brian Johnston, "Johnners," whose Etonian humor enlivened many broadcasting hours from the 1960s to the 1980s.

The introduction of a new form of cricket, limited overs, in English domestic cricket in 1963 had wide ramifications. The experiment resulted from dwindling interest in three-day domestic cricket. A limited overs match could be completed in a day and a result was always achieved, eliminating the draw. The abbreviated format, which encouraged innovative play, proved an instant success. Although it took some time for officials to fully comprehend the potential of the abbreviated game, limited overs internationals were played from 1971, and the 1975 World Cup in England—exclusively composed of limited overs matches—proved a huge success. An epic final between the West Indies and Australia was watched by a substantial worldwide audience.

Advances in television also greatly extended the popularity of cricket in the 1970s. The game translated well on television, for from the mid-1970s slow-motion replays helped unravel some of the intricacies of the game. This television-related boom in cricket made the game attractive to Australian media tycoon Kerry Packer, who virtually hijacked world cricket after he was denied exclusive Australian television rights. In a daring raid, Packer signed up the majority of the world's best cricketers—offering players far more generous payment—and established a rival cricket circuit. For two seasons Establishment cricket and World Series were locked in deadly combat, and a number of court cases ensued before a truce was worked out in May 1979. Packer's great innovation in this period of crisis was to popularize limited overs cricket and night play, which proved commercially attractive. One result of the truce was that the limited overs internationals took priority over more traditional cricket in terms of securing the preferred times and days. Many had feared that the days of test cricket were numbered; a Packer offsider declared in 1982 that Test cricket was a dinosaur awaiting extinction. Although interest in Test matches has declined on the subcontinent, major series still draw well in England and Australia.

The issue of South Africa and its apartheid regime dogged world cricket from the 1970s to the 1990s, and tours to the area were suspended during this period. The boycott of South Africa spawned a succession of "rebel" tours from various countries and resulted in suspensions for players who had accepted "blood money." Although many South Africans worked for multiracial cricket, progress was, of necessity, slow. South Africa reentered world cricket in the 1990s with the ending of apartheid.

The question of gambling and corruption surfaced in the 1995 when it was alleged that some Pakistani cricketers had been in league with bookmakers and may have thrown matches. Although the administrators failed to take any decisive action, the issue declined in importance in 1996 when the allegations could not be proved.

Spread of the Game

Although the game became popular in the south and north of England, it has been relatively weak in the more outlying regions of Britain, including

Scotland, Wales, and Cornwall, and has never achieved great popularity in Ireland. The spread of the game in England was perhaps restricted because cricket was a middle-class game, whereas soccer established itself as the "people's game." English middle-class administrators of cricket did not, it has been argued, seek out a working-class constituency but preferred the game to be the privileged preserve of the comfortable classes. The major cricket grounds of England are far smaller than equivalent soccer grounds. Cricket nonetheless enjoyed strong working-class support in the midlands and north of England.

The British took cricket with them to all parts of their empire, though they made very limited attempts to encourage the indigenes of Asia and Africa to play the game. Indeed, the original ethnocentrism of the sport is enshrined in its language: a "French" or "Chinese" cut—an incorrectly played mishit—reflects the one-time view that non-Anglo-Saxons had limited aptitude for the game. For almost a century in India (from the time of the first cricket club at Calcutta in 1792) cricket was a game for European soldiers, merchants, educators, and missionaries, and the local population were not encouraged to play. Indian teams were not formed until the mid-nineteenth century and it was not until the late nineteenth century that they played against European teams. In the twentieth century, however, cricket became the most popular sport on the subcontinent, India, Pakistan, and Sri Lanka. The support of cricket by comprador communities, such as the Parsis of Bombay, and by many Indian princes endowed the game with glamour and status. Cricket on the subcontinent was able to reinvent itself to fit in with local culture and society. It has its own particular forms and rhythms, including Hindi broadcasts, passionate and noisy crowds, and wickets that have encouraged slow bowling.

In the West Indies, too, cricket was initially a white man's game. C. L. R. James, in the cricket classic *Beyond a Boundary*, shows how West Indian cricket, although part of colonial oppression, was domesticated and transformed into a vehicle for the liberation struggle. Creolized West Indian cricket developed its own rich traditions—including cricket as carnival—and produced outstanding teams that dominated world cricket from the mid-1970s to the 1990s.

British settlers established cricket clubs at an early stage of European settlement in Australia and New Zealand. For Europeans living in remote parts of the empire playing cricket was a way to maintain their culture in remote and exotic locations. Cricket received a further boost in the late nineteenth century when Test matches gave colonial teams an enjoyable opportunity to thrash the motherland. Cricket comes close to being the national game of Australia, and it is also popular in New Zealand and South Africa, where it ranks second to rugby. Each of these countries reinvented cricket to suit its particular climate, culture, and society. The hard and firm wickets of Australia encouraged fast and leg spin bowling and more certain shot making. Australia developed its distinctive forms of barracking, language, and culture.

Although cricket was exported at an earlier period than soccer, it spread far less, remaining confined to the former British Empire. Allen Guttmann has claimed that this limited spread was probably due not to intrinsic factors, such as the greater complexity of the rules, but to the fact that by the time soccer was exported, in the later period of the empire, Manchester's economic influence was paramount and soccer was the favorite sport of Manchester. It is likely that cricket's failure to spread, for example, from local elites of Philadelphia and other social bastions to the broader population in North America was because these elites preferred to maintain cricket as an exclusive game. Cricket also failed to find a niche in Ireland, though rugby was played there, possibly because cricket was the archetypal English game.

Cricket as a sport has been a great survivor in that it has been able to reinvent itself many times over. It has evolved from the era of gentlemen who loved to gamble, to the time of the professional, to the amateur era, to the more commercial and professional era following World Series Cricket. In the 1980s and 1990s the balance of cricket has shifted away from England. It is ironic that the game is now more genuinely popular on the subcontinent, in Australia, and in the West Indies than it is in Britain and even England.

The Caribbean dominance of the game from 1975 to the early 1990s may be threatened in future by encroaching Americanization (basketball in particular).The greater media penetration of American sport is likely to encourage more West

Indians to pursue lucrative careers in American basketball. However, the global future of cricket seems to be secure in that it has become the sport of the Indian subcontinent, has a growing base in Africa (South Africa, Zimbabwe, and Kenya), and remains popular in Australia and New Zealand.

—Richard Cashman

Bibliography: Altham, H. S., and E. W. Swanton. (1962) *A History of Cricket*. 2 vols. 5th ed. London: Allen and Unwin.

Birley, Derek. (1979) *The Willow Wand: Some Cricket Myths Explored.* London: Queen Anne Press.

Bose, Mihir. (1990) *A History of Indian Cricket.* London: Deutsch.

Bowen, Rowland. (1970) *Cricket: A History of Its Growth and Development throughout the World.* London: Eyre and Spottiswoode.

Brookes, Christopher. (1978) *English Cricket: The Game and Its Players through the Ages.* London: Weidenfeld and Nicolson.

Cashman, Richard, et al., eds. (1996) *The Oxford Companion to Australian Cricket.* Melbourne: Oxford University Press.

Flint, Rachel Heyhoe, and Netta Rheinberg. (1976) *Fair Play: The Story of Women's Cricket.* London: Angus and Robertson.

Frith, David. (1987) *Pageant of Cricket.* Melbourne: Macmillan.

Haigh, Gideon. (1993) *The Cricket War: The Inside Story of Kerry Packer's World Series Cricket.* Melbourne: Text Publishing.

Harte, Chris. (1993) *A History of Australian Cricket.* London: Deutsch.

Howat, Gerald. (1980) *Village Cricket.* London: David and Charles.

Moorhouse, Geoffrey. (1983) *Lord's.* London: Hodder and Stoughton.

James, C. L. R. (1963) *Beyond the Boundary.* London: Hutchinson.

McPhee, Hilary, and Brian Stoddart. (1995) *Liberation Cricket: West Indies Cricket Culture.* Manchester: Manchester University Press.

Manley, Michael A. (1988) *History of West Indian Cricket.* London: Deutsch.

Rundell, Michael. (1985) *The Dictionary of Cricket.* London: Allen and Unwin.

Sandiford, K. (1994) *Cricket in the Victorian Age.* Aldershot, UK: Scolar Press.

Sissons, Ric. (1988) *The Players: A Social History of the Professional Cricketer.* Sydney: Pluto Press.

Wisden Cricket Almanac (annual from 1864).

Croquet

Croquet very likely evolved from a game called *palle mall* in which players hit a ball (*palla*) with a mallet (*maglio*) through a series of iron rings. An account of a variation on this theme appeared in a May 1663 diary entry by the famous English essayist Samuel Pepys. The modern form of croquet originated in France in the early years of the nineteenth century and was immediately recognizable by its unique mallet. This mallet, in its French peasant form, had a broomstick as a handle. The word "croquet" is derived from the French word *croc*, meaning something shaped like a hook or a crook.

Origins

The sport of croquet was transplanted from France to Ireland, where there are records of its being played regularly after 1852. Once the sport was introduced to England it flourished. Walter James Whitmore promoted and publicized the sport in England. The game's stellar figure both as player and tactician, Whitmore became the unofficial world champion with his 1867 victory in the Moreton-on-Marsh, England, Croquet Open Championship. A year later he published a pioneering volume entitled *Croquet Tactics*. Also in 1868, the All England Croquet Club was formed. Tennis historian E. Digby Baltzell, describing this period in the 1860s, was trying to be humorous but may have hit on the truth when he observed:

> In spite of this mild emancipation, as there were more than half a million more women than men in England, most of them, with the help of their mothers, were basically engaged in hunting husbands. On the smooth croquet lawns, as well as in the surrounding shrubbery looking for lost balls, proper, crinoline-clad Victorian ladies, more or less cunning, sought to capture the hearts of clean-cut English gentlemen.

Croquet might have come to rival cricket as a major outdoor English sport if it had not been for the arrival of another new sport that quickly

Croquet

*Croquet was one of the first sports in which it was socially acceptable for middle- and upper-middle-class women to partic-
ipate—doubtless for the same reasons that have limited its popularity in a less genteel age.*

became a public passion. Tennis was so popular that players took up all available grass space. Not surprisingly, by 1875, the All England Croquet Club had to add the words "and Lawn Tennis Club" to its title. Five years later the demise of croquet was spelled out when the Wimbledon-based croquet club changed its name to the All England Lawn Tennis Club. Croquet suffered from having neither the popular appeal of cricket nor the physical dash and style of tennis. One sports historian comments, "even the ladies grew bored and impatient with croquet's leisurely lack of vigor." By the turn of the century, croquet was no longer played at Wimbledon, and the game's headquarters was moved to Roehampton and then Hurlingham.

Croquet's international expansion was led by the American National Croquet League, founded in 1880, and the first Australian croquet club, founded at Kyneton, Victoria, in 1866. The Australian Croquet Council was founded in 1950. (Australia now leads the world with over 6,000 registered players.) In 1896 the Croquet Association was founded. The major impetus to the sport

at the turn of the century was neither organizational nor regulatory. It was the arrival of stellar croquet players from Ireland who transformed the recreational game into a national sport.

In the nineteenth century croquet provided an important vehicle for women to move beyond the traditional boundaries of home, church, and school and to seek a role in some quasi-athletic pursuit. Writer Janet Woolum makes the argument that a milestone in women's sports was the 13 June 1877 founding of the Ladies Club for Outdoor Sports at New Brighton in Staten Island, New York. Club members took part in archery, lawn tennis, and croquet. Author Jennifer Hargreaves, however, says that although croquet was "a highly sociable and fashionable pastime," women's entrance into athletics saw them stereotyped as the weaker sex capable of "doing" only gentle and respectable games. In other words, it was only acceptable for women to perform "the smallest and meanest of movements." Even with croquet, it was felt that it might be more appropriate for women to play croquet's indoor variations—Parlor Croquet, Table Croquet, and

An Anglo-American Match

It was not far to Longmeadow, but the tent was pitched and the wickets down by the time they arrived. A pleasant green field, with three wide-spreading oaks in the middle and a smooth strip of turf for croquet.

"Welcome to Camp Laurence!" said the young host, as they landed with exclamations of delight.

"Brooke is commander in chief, I am commissary general, the other fellows are staff officers, and you, ladies, are company. The tent is for your especial benefit and that oak is your drawing room, this is the messroom and third is the camp kitchen. Now, let's have a game before it gets hot, and then we'll see about dinner."

Frank, Beth, Amy, and Grace sat down to watch the game played by the other eight. Mr. Brooke chose Meg, Kate, and Fred; Laurie took Sallie, Jo, and Ned. The English played well, but the Americans played better, and contested every inch of the ground as strongly as if the spirit of '76 inspired them. Jo and Fred had several skirmishes and once narrowly escaped high words. Jo was through the last wicket and had missed the stroke, which failure ruffled her a good deal. Fred was close behind her and his turn came before hers, he gave a stroke, his ball hit the wicket, and stopped an inch on the wrong side. No one was very near, and running up to examine, he gave it a sly nudge with his toe, which put it just an inch on the right side.

"I'm through! Now, Miss Jo, I'll settle you, and get in first," cried the young gentleman, swinging his mallet for another blow.

"You pushed it; I saw you; it's my turn now," said Jo sharply.

"Upon my word, I didn't move it; it rolled a bit, perhaps, but that is allowed; so stand off, please, and let me have a go at the stake."

"We don't cheat in America, but you can, if you choose," said Jo angrily.

"Yankees are a deal the most tricky, everybody knows. There you go!" returned Fred, croqueting her ball far away.

Jo opened her lips to say something rude, but checked herself in time, colored up to her forehead and stood a minute, hammering down a wicket with all her might, while Fred hit the stake and declared himself out with much exultation. She went off to get her ball, and was a long time finding it among the bushes, but she came back, looking cool and quiet, and waited her turn patiently. It took several strokes to regain the place she had lost, and when she got there, the other side had nearly won, for Kate's ball was the last but one and lay near the stake.

"By George, it's all up with us! Good-by Kate, Miss Jo owes me one, so you are finished," cried Fred excitedly, as they all drew near the finish.

"Yankees have a trick of being generous to their enemies," said Jo, with a look that made the lad redden, "especially when they beat them," she added, as, leaving Kate's ball untouched, she won the game by a clever stroke.

—Louisa May Alcott, *Little Women* (1869).

Carpet Croquet—instead of the outdoor variety.

John Lucas and Ron Smith speak of a croquet craze sweeping the United States in the 1860s (in Australia it was described as "most infectious"). They describe town club competitions and affirm the importance of croquet for advancing women's rights:

Here was sporting activity in which it was socially acceptable for women to participate. The lackadaisical nature of the game allowed women to participate in full hoop skirts dragging on the ground and required no more physical effort than that needed to push a stroller from the nursery to the park.

Nevertheless, during the 1860s, 1870s, and 1880s there were conservative groups in Britain and the United States who feared the downfall of women who let themselves be carried away by the excesses of such sports as bicycling and croquet. An article in the *American Christian Review* in 1878 described the consequences of such involvement:

1. A social party.
2. Social and play party.
3. Croquet party.
4. Picnic and croquet party.
5. Picnic, croquet, and dance.
6. Absence from church.
7. Imprudent or immoral conduct.
8. Exclusion from the church
9. A runaway match.
10. Poverty and discontent.
11. Shame and disgrace.
12. Ruin.

Despite such gloomy pronouncements, croquet flourished as a women's sport. In America, long before women took part in competitive tennis or basketball tournaments their first venture into competition sport was with croquet in the 1860s.

Practice

At the first championship in England in 1867 the playing area consisted of nine hoops and two pegs. The court's dimensions were 20 meters (66 feet) by 15 meters (48 feet). The hoops had a maximum width of 20 centimeters (8 inches) and the balls measured 9 centimeters (3 ½ inches) in diameter. Three years later the court size was increased to 46 meters (150 feet) by 32 meters (105 feet) and the hoops' width reduced to 10 centimeters (4 inches). In 1871, the number of hoops was reduced from nine to six. This configuration, called the Hale setting, lasted from 1871 to 1922.

Croquet was originally played with the balls struck in a particular sequence (blue, red, black, and yellow), as in snooker. In 1914, this strategy and style of play were changed forever by the introduction of the "either-ball game," in which "the opponent could now play either of his balls[. This] meant that no easy break could be left for the next turn, for the opponent would remove the most useful ball to a safe position" (Arlott 1975). Simultaneous with the introduction of the either-ball game was the introduction of a 9.4-centimeter (3 ¾ inches) hoop. With a ball diameter of 9.2 centimeters (3 ⅝ inch), the margin of error became minute, thus magnifying the importance of accurate ball striking. Perhaps only golf's "putting" attaches the same premium to precision striking and placement of the ball.

Advocates of croquet sought to make the game more competitive and attractive for the skilled player. In 1922 the Willis setting was adopted. This distanced the two center hoops, transforming certain "easy" shots into difficult ones. Six years later the "lift" shot was introduced to combat the manner in which croquet lent itself to one player's domination:

The introduction of the rule by which a player, at the end of his opponent's first break, was able to lift either of his balls and play from the baulk line, reduced the length of shot from over 30 yards to a maximum of 19, with an alternative though slightly more risky, shot of only 13 yards (Arlott 1975).

Croquet is unusual in that it is not a team sport. Almost without exception, croquet consists of one individual challenging another. Many of the descriptions of croquet make it seem as complex and cerebral as chess. However, the essence of the game is its simplicity. The object of the sport is to score points by striking the ball through each of the hoops in the proper order and hitting the stake. Each player, in turn, tries to make a point or to *roquet*. This means to hit an opponent's ball with one's own. If a competitor scores a point he or she is entitled to another stroke. If not, the next player takes a turn.

In virtually every individual sport, the structure of the competition allows a degree of involvement by even an outplayed player. In croquet, matters can be different. During a Washington, D.C., challenge tournament in the late 1980s a competition took place in which a competitor started and continued playing at such a level of excellence that he completed the whole course without yielding his turn. It was a dazzling, bravura performance in which his competitor's only physical action was to doff his hat and shake the winner's hand.

Croquet was and continues to be an elitist activity. In the early days of the sport, croquet hoops on a lawn showed the house owner to be on the cutting edge of fashion (Betts 1974). Today, club memberships still tend to be expensive and exclusive. Not surprisingly, the world's oldest "name" universities, Oxford and Cambridge, encourage the sport. In the United States Croquet clubs are found in resort areas with an exclusive appeal, such as Greenbrier in West Virginia. The oldest university teams are at Harvard, Yale, and the University of Virginia. There are only a handful of clubs in the Midwest, 22 in California, and more than that around the coastal resort townships of central and southern Florida. The largest cluster of croquet clubs is in the wealthy suburbs of such larger northeastern cities as Philadelphia, New York, and Boston. If it is to flourish into the twenty-first century, croquet will have to become more attractive to the younger player. *The Oxford Companion* makes the point that in the two decades after World War II, the champions were always younger players. In 1965 an 18 year old won the President's Cup.

Just as tennis has its Davis Cup, yachting its America's Cup, and golf its Ryder Cup, croquet has its MacRobertson International Shield. The Croquet Association, with its headquarters at the Hurlingham Club, organizes all of the major championship events. In England these consist of the open championship (singles and doubles), the men's, women's, and mixed-doubles championships, and four invitation events. The most highly regarded of this latter group is the President's Cup. Interclub competition is not part of the croquet scene in the United Kingdom. In the United States croquet has been organized since 1976 by the United States Croquet Association. This organization recognizes six types of club membership: private, country and sports, resorts and hotels, real estate developments, college teams, and retirement communities. But without any Olympic recognition and the absence of any college, professional, or television off-shoots, croquet continues to languish on the periphery of sport.

Croquet has caught on in the British Commonwealth and is played today in Australia, New Zealand, and South Africa.

—Scott A. G. M. Crawford

Bibliography: Arlott, J., ed. (1975) *Oxford Companion to World Sports and Games.* London: Oxford University Press.

Baltzell, E. D. (1995) *Sporting Gentlemen.* New York: Free Press.

Barnett, S. (1990) *Games and Sets: The Changing Face of Sport on Television.* London: British Film Institute.

Betts, J. R. (1974) *America's Sporting Heritage: 1850–1950.* Reading, MA: Addison-Wesley Publishing.

Blanchard, K., and A. Cheska. (1985) *The Anthropology of Sport.* South Hadley, MA: Bergin and Garvey.

Brasch, R. (1971) *How Did Sport Begin?* New York: David McKay.

Brownfoot, J. N. (1992) "Emancipation Exercise and Imperialism: Girls and Games Ethnic in Colonial Malaya." In *The Cultural Bond—Sport, Empire, Society,* edited by J. A. Mangan. London: Frank Cass.

Daly, J. A. (1988) "A New Britannia in the Antipodes: Sport, Class and Community in South Australia." In *Pleasure, Profit, Proselytism: British Culture and Sport at Home and Abroad,* edited by J. A. Mangan. London: Frank Cass.

Diagram Group. (1982) *Sports Comparisons.* New York: St. Martin's Press.

Gorn, E. J., and W. Goldstein. (1993) *A Brief History of American Sports.* New York: Hill and Wang.

Hargreaves, J. (1993) "The Victorian Cult of the Family and the Early Years of Female Sport." In *The Sport Process,* edited by E. G. Dunning, J. A. Maguire, and R. E. Pearton. Champaign, IL: Human Kinetics.

Holt, R. (1990) *Sport and the British.* Oxford: Oxford University Press.

Kilian, M. (1995) "Homespun Gold." *Chicago Tribune* (5 November).

Lewis, R. M. (1991) "American Croquet in the 1860s: Playing the Game and Winning." *Journal of Sport History* 18, 3 (Winter): 365–386.

Lidz, F. (1995) "Mallets Aforethought." *Sports Illustrated* 83, 10 (14 September).

Lucas, J. A., and R. A. Smith. (1978) *Saga of American Sport.* Philadelphia: Lea and Febiger.

Michener, J. (1976) *Sports in America.* New York: Random House.

Rooney, J. F., Jr., and R. Pillsbury. (1992) *Atlas of American Sport.* New York: Macmillan.

Woolum, J. (1992) *Outstanding Women Athletes.* Phoenix: Oryx Press.

Cross-Country Running

Origins

Cross-country running is described from the earliest times of foot messengers to boys' games of hunt the hare or fox. Around the world there appear to have been various types of cross-country races. In Kazakstan, Uzbekistan, and Tajikistan, for example, day-long races across country were held. In Europe, at least as early as the middle of the fourteenth century, the sport of cross-country running emanated from hunting. Writer Jean Froissart played *au chace-lievre* at Valenciennes about 1350. A poem written sometime around 1560 records "when we play hunt the fox, I out run all the boyes in the schoole." Shakespeare says in *Hamlet* "hide fox, and all after." And in the latter half of the seventeenth century Randle Holme speaks of youths "playing hare and hound."

An important development in northern England and southern Scotland was the adaptation of the eighteenth-century sport of steeplechasing (a race to a church steeple on horseback) to foot racing. As early as 1828 men of the Six Feet Club of Edinburgh were running a foot steeplechase. In 1835, the Six Feet Club had a membership of 135 and held races in both May and November. Their uniform was a scarlet coat with club buttons. Throughout the 1830s, there were many foot steeplechases, particularly in the lowlands of

Cross-Country Running

Scotland, where it first took hold, fewer in the north and midlands of England, and very few in the south and west of England or Wales. In Ireland there were races at Cavan and Tipperary in the early 1840s. The courses included fences, hurdles, ditches, brooks, and even the swimming of rivers. The distance commonly run was 1,207 meters (3/4 mile) to 2,414 meters (1 1/2 miles).

Development

By the beginning of the nineteenth century, the sport had become established as a pastime at many English schools. At Shrewsbury School cross country was first mentioned in 1828 and four years later was said to be of "old standing." At Harrow School in 1834, the boys secretly organized a 4-mile (6.4-kilometer) run to nearby Baily Hill, run in 24 minutes. By 1839, Rugby School had 11 different courses established, ranging in distance from 5 to 8 1/4 miles (8 to 13 kilometers) and a longer run of 12 1/4 miles (20 kilometers) for pupils who had proved themselves with shorter distances. The longest at Shrewsbury School was 12 miles (19 kilometers). By the 1840s, the sport appeared to have reached Oxford University where two clubs, the Kangaroo Club and the Charitable Grinders, organized steeplechase runs.

The paper-chase stems from at least 1856 when it is mentioned in the journal *Household Words.* Paper-chasing consisted of laying of a trail of paper by two runners called the hares, one of whom would lay false trails. They were followed after an interval of 10 minutes by runners called hounds. On 7 December 1867, runners from the Thames Rowing Club and the London Athletic Club organized the first regular steeplechase. Enthusiast Walter Rye organized a club called the Thames Hare and Hounds on 3 October 1868 which conducted the paper-chase form of cross-country running.

In 1876 an attempt was made to institute an English Championship race at Epping Forest, but the effort was poorly supported. The following year a championship race of 11 3/4 miles (22 kilometers) was run, although longer distances of up to 24 1/2 miles (39 kilometers) were recorded for a club run. Competitors, wearing canvas shoes with India-rubber soles, known as *plimsoles,* ran over fields and plowed ground, and jumped five-

The agony shows on Paula Radcliffe's face as she crosses the finish line in the 1992 World Cross-Country Championships, winning the title for Great Britain.

barred gates, ditches, and brooks. Although few clubs competed in the early championships, by 1890, 27 teams participated. It was not long before cross-country runners replaced the old flat-soled shoes with plated-type of running spikes. Paper-chases became less popular except by the older established clubs where they had limited survival until about 1930.

Cross-country running was quickly taken up by several other countries. In Canada, Toronto University held foot steeplechases in the 1860s and later cross-country races known as harrier races. There was a national championship by 1882. On the east coast of the United States, a number of hare and hound clubs appeared in the

219

Boston, New York, and Philadelphia areas in the late 1870s—e.g., the Westchester Hare and Hounds, Germantown Hunt Club Hare & Hounds, and Harvard University Hare & Hounds. In 1883 the New York Athletic Club organized the first cross-country championship in the United States over a 5-mile (8-kilometer) course marked with red flags. There were 24 entries. The distance was increased to 9 miles (14.5 kilometers) in 1886, although championships were not run in a number of years up to 1904, since the sport was not yet fully organized. In Australia, there were several clubs in Melbourne and Sydney in the late 1880s. In the latter, the English runner Bernard Wise played a leading part. An Australasian championship began in 1910, but cross country in New Zealand did not develop until after 1917. In South Africa, there were paper-chases in Durban as early as 1883 over a course of earth banks and hurdles, and a year earlier in Pietermaritzburg. National championships did not begin until 1948, but provincial races were held in Western Province over 10 miles (16 kilometers) in 1907 and also in Natal in 1909.

In northwest Europe there was an interest in cross-country running. Championship races commenced in France in 1889, and between 1896 and 1925 there were even professional cross-country championships in France. Neighboring Belgium ran its field race in 1896; Denmark held a 15-kilometer (9.4-mile) race in 1901 (the distance was reduced to 8 kilometers in 1918). Sweden began its championships in 1907 with 8-kilometer races. Finland entered the scene in 1913 and Paavo Nurmi, one of the greatest runners of all time, clocked up seven victories. In the same year, Germany ran the *Waldlauf* (forest run) over 7,500 meters (4.7 miles), increasing the distance to 10,000 meters (6.2 miles) by 1920. The Dutch championships began in 1919 with 5-kilometer (3.1-mile) races, but within five years the distance became 10 kilometers.

In 1898 a team of eight English runners went to Paris and took the first eight places in front of the French team over a 9-mile course. They returned home with a very large trophy. In the United Kingdom, Ireland had been running championships since 1880, Scotland since 1886, and the Welsh since 1894. It was the Welsh who took the initiative and interested the Irish, Scottish, and

English in a "home international" race, the first of which took place at Hamilton Park racecourse in Glasgow in 1903. Teams of six scored. In 1907 France joined in and in 1923 Belgium. England invariably won the team race, but France carried off the title six times by 1928. Outstanding runner was the Jean Bouin of France, who died in World War I.

Cross-country running was introduced in the Olympics at the Stockholm Games in 1912. It was suggested by the Swedish organizers in 1910 and consisted of an 8,000-meter (5-mile) team race of three runners with an unusual race arrangement. It started in the stadium and returned to the stadium track after 4,000 meters before a second lap was run to finish within the stadium. The course was marked with red cloth attached to bushes and a trail of red paper. A large number of runners dropped out after only one lap. Sweden won the team race from Finland and Great Britain; Norway and Denmark did well but did not finish in the top three. The United States, South Africa, France, Austria, and Germany were also represented. The 1920 race was held at Antwerp over a one-lap course that started and finished in the stadium. Forty-eight ran with Finland winning, beating Great Britain and Sweden. The U.S., French, Belgian, and Danish teams finished, in that order. The race at Paris in 1924 was a disaster. It was run over 10,650 meters (6.6 miles) from and to the stadium on a very hot day (36 degrees Celsius [97 degrees Fahrenheit]). Forty runners started, but only teams from Finland, the United States, and France finished, in that order. Only 15 runners finished the race; the remainder were taken to the hospital. After this disaster, cross country was dropped from the Olympics; it has since been considered but not readopted.

The International CC race between 1929 and 1972 saw various other countries competing on an irregular basis. Spain, Italy, Switzerland, and Luxembourg competed in Paris in 1929. The 1950s and 1960s saw interest from the North African countries of Tunisia, Morocco, and Algeria. The 1960s were also notable for other English-speaking countries such as South Africa, New Zealand, Canada, and the United States taking part. Outstanding individuals for this period were England's Jack Holden, who won four times, in 1933, 1934, 1935, and 1939, and Mimoun of France, who won four times between 1949 and

1956. In 1961 a men's junior race was established. About this time both Belgium and France were inviting runners from other countries to compete at international cross-country meetings, such as Hannut and Dieppe.

The Balkan states introduced the Balkan championships in 1957. The following year the International Amateur Athletic Federation agreed with the International Cross Country Union (CCU) that the latter's championships be an IAAF-permitted competition. At the Congress of the International CCU at San Sebastian, Spain, in 1971, a motion was passed to ask the IAAF to organize in the future the world cross-country championships. This was duly accepted at the 1972 IAAF Congress in Munich. The first IAAF race took place at Waregem, near Ghent, Belgium, over 12,000 meters (7.5 miles) in 1973; the home team won. The Belgian team continued to win medals as one of the top three teams until 1977. Belgium's renowned runner, Gaston Rolelants, won the race three times between 1962 and 1972. In 1981, Ethiopia took possession of the team title for five years, but since 1986 Kenya has won on every occasion, with usually Ethiopia or Morocco being runners up. John Ngugi of Kenya won the race five times between 1986 and 1992. In pre-IAAF days, 15 was the largest number of teams competing; however, since 1981 the average has been 26, with a peak of 39 in 1986 when the competition was held at Neuchâtel, Switzerland. Teams now compete from all continents. Other competitions now in existence include the Maghrebin championships for North Africa, which began in 1967, and the African, Asian, and South American championships. In 1990 the IAAF introduced the IAAF Cross-Country Challenge, which consists of 11 races in which runners could take part and score points, if 8 or more nations took part, with prizes for the first 12 for both men and women.

Women's cross country can be traced back to the late 1870s, when middle-class women in the London and Dublin areas ran hare and hound races. There was an interesting experiment in the Toronto area in November 1910 when 200 girls of Harboard Collegiate were invited to compete in a paper-chase. France was the first country to organize a national championship, which began in 1919. In England cross-country running began in 1923, with national championships following in 1930, while Belgian women were competing in the 1920s. The first women's international was at Brussels when France beat Belgium on 23 March 1930. At Douai, Belgium, in 1931 there was a three-cornered match between France, Belgium, and England won by the latter. A return match was held in England the following year and another in 1938.

The English Cross Country Union (ECCU) instituted a women's 4-kilometer (2.5-mile) international championship in 1967 at Barry, South Wales, in conjunction with the men's event. England won the team prize and Doris Brown of the United States the individual title, which she retained over the next four years. Up to 1975 the United States and England vied for team honors; the Soviet Union then became dominant. The following year the course was lengthened to approximately 5 kilometers (cross-country courses are not measured as accurately as formal running tracks). Norwegian Grete Waitz won five titles in six years between 1978 and 1983; Lynn Jennings of the United States captured three victories in the period 1990 to 1992, when 6 kilometers (3.75 miles) was the usual distance. In 1990 the first under-20 junior competition was held, and since that time either the Ethiopians or Kenyans have usually taken the team prize.

—David Terry

Bibliography: *1903–1980 67e International de Cross Country, Courir.* (1980) Saint Maur, France.

Bloom, M. (1977) *Cross Country Running.* Mountain View, CA: World Publications.

Fraser, I. (1968) *The Annals of Thames Hare and Hounds.* London: Thames & Hudson.

IAAF Bulletin (1973–1986). In French and English.

Richardson, L. N. (1965) *International Cross Country Union 1903–1953.* Ambergate, UK: ICCU.

———. (1953) *Jubilee History of the International Cross-country Union 1903–1953.* Ambergate, UK: ICCU.

Cross-Country Skiing

See Skiing, Nordic

Cudgeling

Fencing with sticks for sport is probably as old as warfare. The Egyptians have the oldest known record of a fencing match in the form of a temple relief from 1200 B.C.E. It depicts two fencers with blunted sticks and masks, one of whom says: "On guard, and admire, what my valiant hands shall do!"—an old but always popular way of boasting. This form of fencing survives in the southern highlands of Egypt as a martial art system called *Tahteeb* practiced by members of the Ikhwaan-al-Muslimeen (Muslim Brotherhood). In Europe the cudgel, or singlestick, was the training weapon for the single-handed sword. Until the end of the nineteenth century, each European country seems to have had its own types of stick fighting. However, few styles remain from a long tradition of European fencing that reaches back to the roots of Western civilization and has parallels throughout the world.

Asia

The Indian art of *silambam* emphasizes the use of a 1.2-meter (4-foot) staff. After seven years' training, practitioners advance to other weapons and may use their bare hands. *Gatka* is a stick- and knife-based martial art from India and Pakistan. Gatka is practiced today in the worldwide by members of the 3H Foundation, the followers of Yogi Bhajan, a Sikh leader and teacher. The International Gatka Federation is based in the Netherlands and teaches the traditional fighting art of the Sikhs, a religious group in the Punjab, neither Muslim nor Hindu. They have traditionally filled rolls of military and police in India. British influence is seen in the use of a singlestick (a meter-long piece of bamboo with a leather handle) in place of the sword for the lower levels of training. The techniques are practiced to drumbeats and performed with a high stepping movement that is taught with a chanted mantra. Both single and double sticks are used as well as other weapons. Horseback techniques are still taught. The system is closely tied to the kundalini yoga used by the Sikh and is taught at the 3H Foundation's biannual yoga training in New Mexico. The grip in photos of women practicing staff is the reverse grip (with the thumb inward), rather than the normal open grip.

Kalaripayattu, based in the southern Indian state of Kerala, is a composite martial art. After two phases of weaponless training, the third phase of Kalaripayattu training is training in the use of various weapons, which begins with the short staff and quarterstaff and progresses to weapons such as the spear and shield, sword and shield, daggers, knives, battle axes, and so on.

In the Philippines, when Fernando Magellan was killed by the sharpened stick of a local chief during a failed landing attempt on his round-the-world voyage in 1521, the Spaniards had made their first bloody experience with 'arnis.' Arnis, kali, and escrima are the national weapon arts of the Philippines. All three have in common the use of the stick in combat, either as itself or as a replacement for or representative of the sword or knife. They have had full contact events with stick that is much like old cudgeling or backswording in eighteenth century Europe. After conquering the island group, the Spanish tried to root out this art. It was passed on for centuries only in secrecy or family circles. But with Philippine independence after World War II arnis appeared in public again, now as a stick fencing sport with 0.76-meter (30-inch) long rattan sticks. Nowadays arnis teaches a number of techniques and principles using sticks, but they can be applied equally well to rolled-up papers, pens, ties, and bare hands, which makes arnis a most versatile form of self-defense. This may well be the most popular stick fencing in North America today. Arnis uses single and double sticks extensively, as well as stick and dagger, knives, and quarterstaff. There are major stylistic differences including stick length, blocking, and body-work. A lot of the techniques are really designed for blades, and some European influence is highly visible especially in the sword and dagger techniques. Locks, throws, and strikes are also used.

Europe

The cudgel or singlestick was the practice weapon for military sword, broadsword, or saber. The singlestick or cudgel was the training weapon for the single-handed sword as well as a weapon in its own right. Depending on the time

These French contestants in 1993 bout of boxe française, a sport developed from the traditional savate, which employed a formalized version of what were originally street stick-fighting techniques.

and place, it ranged from a clublike affair (Talhoffer's colb or the cudgel described in Herbert Berry's *Masters of Defence*—a teardrop-shaped weapon an ell (an old measure of length equivalent to 45 inches or 1.44 meters) long to that used to train military swordsmen in the nineteenth century, approximately 1 meter (3 feet) long by about 2.5 centimeters (1 inch) in width. The earliest known manual of European fencing, an anonymous sword and buckler manual currently in the collection of the Tower of London, delineates techniques that are illustrated in other medieval documents depicting the training of knights or squires and entertainments conducted with stick or sword indiscriminately. Talhoffer's *Fechtbuch* of 1467, for example, has some 20–30 plates of combat with cudgel and shield.

In England, from the Middle Ages, the common man had to train at cudgel and buckler. In the seventeenth century the famous Scottish mercenary Captain Sinclair wrote his treatise 'CUDGEL

PLAYING Modernized and Improved or, the Science of Defence Exemplified in a few Short and Easy Lessons for the Practice of the Broadsword or Single Stick on Foot Illustrated with 14 Positions'. This was to instruct the common fighting man in the use of weapons such as the "Sinclair sword," a cutlass-like weapon. Prizefights in restoration times would begin with several bouts at cudgels to warm up the crowd prior to combats with more lethal weapons.

Singlestick and cudgel play was a bulwark of rugged English manliness in the nineteenth century, according to *Tom Brown's School Days*, in which a backswording event that involves two men trying to draw blood from each others' scalps with cudgels is recounted with relish. "The weapon is a good stout ash stick," author Hughes tell us, "the players are called old gamesters . . . and their object is to break one another's heads." The game is over when the blood flows "an inch anywhere above the eyebrow." As recently as

Village Sports

[To Mr. Hone.] You may know, perhaps, that the inhabitants of many of the villages in the western counties, not having a fair or other merry-making to collect a fun-seeking money-spending crowd, and being willing to have one day of mirth in the year, have some time in the summer what are called *feasts;* when they are generally visited by their friends, whom they treat with the old English fare of beef and plumb pudding, followed by the sports of single-stick playing, cudgelling, or wrestling: and sometimes by those delectable inventions of merry Comus, and mirthful spectacles of the village green, jumping in the sack, grinning through the horse-collar, or the running of blushing damsels for that indispensable article of female dress—the plain English name of which rhymes with a *frock.*

Single-stick playing is so called to distinguish it from cudgelling, in which two sticks are used: the single-stick player having the left hand tied down, and using only one stick both to defend himself and strike his antagonist. The object of each gamester in this play, as in cudgelling, is to guard himself, and to fetch blood from the other's head; whether by taking a little skin from his pericranium, drawing a stream from his nose, or knocking out a few of those early inventions for grinding—the teeth. They are both *sanguine* in their hope of victory, and, as many other ambitious fighters have done, they both aim at the *crown.*

In cudgelling, as the name implies, the weapon is a stout cudgel; and the player defends himself with another having a large hemisphere of wicker-work upon it. This is called the *pot,* either from its likeness in shape to that kitchen article, or else in commemoration of some ancient warfare, when the "rude forefathers of the hamlet," being suddenly surrounded with their foes, sallied forth against them, armed with the *pot* and *ladle.*

Single-stick playing, and cudgelling, would be more useful to a man as an art of self-defense, if he were sure that his enemy would always use the same mode of fighting: but the worst of it is, if a Somersetshire single-stick player quarrel with a Devonshire wrestler, the latter, not thinking himself bound to crack the stickler's head by the rules of the game, will probably run in and throw him off his legs, giving such a violent shock to his system that the only use he will be able to make of his stick will be that of hobbling home with it.

—W. Barnes, letter to the editor, Mr Hone, of *The Year Book of Daily Recreation and Information*, 1832.

1886, the British Army used singlestick drill to train recruits for combat.

The quarterstaff, a stick 1.8 meters by 3 centimeters (6 feet by 1¼ inches), was also a medieval weapon that survived to modern times. Developed from a common peasant weapon, it was mentioned in training manuals of many countries. It formed the basis of training with two-handed weapons. It was used for physical training by non-commissioned officers in the British military, and official quarterstaff bouts continued into the 1960s. At some time, it was adopted by the British Boy Scouts and transferred to the U.S. Scouts. World Scout Jamborees after World War II included occasional bouts with padded scout staffs on a log. The object, as in the Robin Hood legends, was to topple the opponent. The pugil stick fights that the U.S. Marines were force to drop from training in 1985 for reasons of safety appear to be from the same set of techniques. Quarterstaff was still taught in the Boy Scouts into the 1970s, through it was dying out at that time. The technique used an alternate grip, like in baton, where the thumbs were toward each other. (The normal grip is like that used for a sword, thumb away from the pro-ponent. The alternate grip—thumb toward the proponent—is like the grip you use to hold a hammer when you are using the claw.) Strikes were made with either end and also with the center. A favorite technique was to slide along the staff to crush the opponent's fingers and then hit him. One handed and some spinning techniques called 'moulinet' were also used. Very old Scout manuals show some of these techniques.

Stick fighting remained popular until Italian masters formalized saber fencing into a nonfatal sporting/training form with metal weapons in the late nineteenth century. Few of these "extinct" fencing styles remain from a long tradition of European fencing. Those that survive in the main are subsumed with the styles studied in association with savate, a French form of unarmed combat.

Modern Sport and Combat

The survival of European stick fighting is associated with savate—French footfighting. The earliest beginnings of savate may be with pancration, a sport in the original Olympics that combined wrestling, boxing, and other techniques. Roman legions carried it and cestus, an armored glove for punching, along with them. Many local styles existed; and some, like Cornish wrestling and *lutte breton,* still survive.

The link between the French *stic* and foot fighting systems began in the early 1700s with chausaun (from the name of the deck shoe worn by sailors), a combat system that includes the use of the belaying pin (a shipboard tool shaped something like a bowling pin and used to manage the rigging), along with kicks and hand strikes practiced by sailors on ships. In other parts of France foot fighting systems were called savate, for shoe. In Basque country, these were called zipota. Around the middle of the seventeenth century, King Louis XIV was painted kicking a knife from an opponent's hand.

Savate itself was established in the 1800s. It started as a unification of many of the different foot fighting styles across the various provinces of France, along with various hand defense techniques. Hubert Lecour opened the first school and taught both savate and la canne et baton. Canne is the use of one or more short sticks, each held in one hand. The baton is the use of a longer stick, held in both hands. Michael Casseux was one of the most notable in the foundation of savate. From his studies, Casseux came up with 15 divisions of boot techniques and 15 divisions of cane or stick fighting techniques. Many people walked with canes at the time because to prevent dueling, nobles had been forbidden to carry swords. Hence there were many street-fighting techniques based around canes. In the 1830s savate (and la canne) was adopted by the army as part of training. Later, Hubert Lebroucher introduced the techniques of lutte parisienne to savate. Developing along with freestyle wrestling, lutte parisienne was a very dirty and efficient street form of grappling. Joseph Charlemont in the 1870s codified the grading and exported savate to the world. His son, Charles, fought Joe Driscoll in the Bout of the Century, which he won by a groin kick. His brother, Charles, developed boxe française from English boxing and savate. This technique added the fist strikes to the slaps and pokes of savate.

Many of these stick fighting arts did not survive the transition to the saber foil and the end of carrying canes in public and the sword in war. Its end was sudden. Singlestick last appeared in the 1904 Olympic Games. Le canne et baton, and lutte parisienne survived, but just barely. During the 40-year period from the beginning of World War I to the end of World War II, savate went from 50,000 players to 33. Comte Pierre Baruzy, who earned his Silver Glove and Maitre ranks under Charles Charlemont, was responsible for rebuilding savate with these few. A lot was almost lost, but due to the Count's level of skill and dedication, and written records of the masters, the art was recovered.

La canne de combat is still practiced by about 10,000 people in France as well as a few hundred in Belgium, the Netherlands, Spain, Italy, and the United States. The Association Française de Boxe Française, Savate et Disciplines Assimilés has a committee dealing with the sport. World championships are held yearly and attract players from all over Europe. La canne de combat is basically fencing using a small (tapered) stick, 95 centimeters (37.4 inches) long and about 15 to 20 millimeters (0.6 to 0.8 inches) wide; it is handled with one hand. Each attack has to be armed, that is, the weapon must make a full swing before it hits the target. Valid target areas are the top and the sides of the head, the torso, and the legs between knees and ankles. Response to an attack can either be a "parade" (block) or an "esquive" (moving the target beyond reach). It is done in a circular "piste" 6 meters (6 ½ yards) in diameter. Although the basic movements are quite easy to learn, getting the high-speed action seen in the spectacular bouts calls for many years of training. Scoring is similar to that in boxing. Rounds last 2 minutes, and to score a hit must start behind the shoulder. There is a fair bit of force behind it, and torn muscles and cracked ribs are common.

Baton, a 127 by 2.5 centimeter (50 inch by 1 inch) stick, is taught as an exercise and timing drill. This uses an opposing hand grip about a foot wide. The stance and grip is very similar to the greatsword stances illustrated in German woodcuts and to the halberd guard position of Swiss woodcuts. It is slower than la canne but the strikes are very powerful. A good baton strike overhead must be deflected as a standing block will cause the defending baton to snap.

The current French association has attempted to suppress or limit the influence of the combative lines to make savate popular as a sport and reduce the danger of training. This involved limiting both kicks and strikes, separating la canne, and dropping the study of lutte parisienne, baton, fouette, knife, and panache. These changes came at the cost of much of the old tradition, although a few enthusiasts still teach the combative form. In the 1980s several of these formed a group dedicated to preserving combative style of savate, which they called Savate Danse Du Rue. In Marseilles a school of chaussoun preserves the art as a cultural activity and a rough sport called chaussoun Marseilles rather than as a functional fighting system. The Academy of French Martial Arts in Dallas continues the French fighting tradition in the United States.

—Steve Hick

See also Fencing; Martial Arts, Philippines.

Bibliography: Allanson-Winn, R. G., and C. E. Walker. (1903) *English Cane, Staff and Single Stick*.
Aylward, J. D. (1956) *The English Master of Arms from the Twelfth to the Twentieth Century*. Notes and Queries no. 198.
———. (1953) *The English Master at Arms Notes and Queries no. 198*. London: Routledge and Kegan Paul.
Berry, Herbert. (1991) *The Noble Science: A Study and Transcription of Sloane MS. 2530, Papers of the Masters of Defence of London, Temp. Henry VIII to 1590*. Cranbury, NJ: University of Delaware Press.
Scout Manual. (1913) New York: Boy Scouts of America.
Castle, Egerton. (1969) *Schools and Masters of Fence: From the Middle Ages to the Eighteenth Century*. London: Arms and Armour Press.
———. (1897) *Bibliotheca Artis Dimicatroi*. London.
D'Amoric, Georges. (1898) *French Cane Fighting*. London.
Delahaye, M. (1986) *Savate, Chaussoun, et Boxe-Française*. Paris: Editions Française Reder.
———. (1986) *La Boxe-Française*. Paris: Editions Française Reder.
Flos duellatorum in armis, sine armis, equester, pedester; il fior di battaglia di maestro Fiore dei Liberi da Premariacco. Testo inedito del MCCCX publicato ed illustrato a cura di Francesco Novati. (1902) Bergamo: Istituto Italiano d'Arti Grafiche (original 1410).
France, Ministre de l'Education Nationale. (1989) *L'Education physique et sportive à l'école:Les sports de combat les jeux d'opposition à l'école elementaire*. Paris: Ministre de l'Education Nationale.
Great Britain, War Office. (1886) *Manual of Instruction for Single Stick Drill*. London: Harrison and Sons.
Khalsa, Nanak Dev Singh. (1991) *Gatka: As Taught by Nanak Dev Singh Khalsa, bk. 1. Dance of the Sword : Beginner Levels I, II & III*. 2d ed. Amsterdam: GT International.
Lebroucher, H. (1910) *Manuel de la Boxe Française*. Paris: Libraire de Jules Tanull.
Fechtbuch, Tower of London I-33 (Ms membr. I 115).
Reed, P., and R. Muggerridge. (1984) *Savate, the Martial Art of France*. Phoenix, AZ: Paladin Press.
Riboni, Guiseppe. (1862) *Broadsword and Quarter-Staff without a Master*. Chicago: E. B. Myers.
Schaer, Alfred. (1901) *Die Altdeutschen Fechter und Spielleute*. Strassburg: K. J. Trubner.
Silver, George. (1972) "Paradoxes of Defense and Brief Instructions." In *Three Elizabethan Fencing Manuals, Scholars Facsilimars and Reprints*, edited by J. L. Jackson. New York: Delmar, 489–634.
Talhoffer, Hans. (1887) *Fechtbuch aus dem Jahre 1467. Gerichtliche und andere Zweikampfe darstellend*. Edited by Gustav Hergsell and J. G. Calve. Prague: By the editors.
Thimm, Carl, A. (1968) *A Complete Bibliography of Fencing & Dueling*. New York: Benjamin Blom.
Turner, C., and T. Soper. (1990) *Methods and Practice of Elizabethan Swordplay*. Carbondale: Southern Illinois University Press.

Curling

Curling is a sport in which participants slide "rocks" or "stones" (see the glossary of curling terms in the sidebar) along a sheet of ice toward a "house." The competition is between two teams or "rinks." There are four players on a team (sometimes a fifth player is named who acts as a substitute). Each player throws two rocks in each "end"; nowadays a game normally lasts ten ends. The objective is to score more points than the other team. Points are awarded at the completion of each end to the team with rocks closest to the "tee." A team counts one point for each rock closer to the tee than *any* of the opposing team's rocks. In order to count, a rock must be in the house. If the end terminates with no rocks in the house, the end is "blank."

The dimensions of the sheet of ice or "rink" on which a game occurs may vary slightly from jurisdiction to jurisdiction. In Canada the sheet is almost always 44.5 meters (146 feet) long and 4.3 meters (14 feet, 2 inches) wide; for international competitions the sheet is the same length but 4.75 meters (15 feet, 7 inches) wide. Some of the most important rules of curling may be identified by referring to the lines drawn on the ice.

A "center line" runs down the ice for 42.1 meters (138 feet); it begins 1.2 meters (4 feet) from one backboard and terminates 1.2 meters from the other. At each end of the center line a "hack line" or "foot line" is drawn at right angles.

Curling, an indoor game that combines elements of lawn bowling and shuffleboard on ice, will be included in the 1998 Olympics.

"Hacks" are placed at each hack line; rocks are thrown from a hack. A "back line" is drawn across the ice 1.8 meters (6 feet) from each hack line; the back line marks the farthest point a rock may travel down the sheet and still remain in play. A "tee line" is drawn 1.8 meters out from each back line. Each tee line passes through the middle of a house; in each house, the point where the tee line intersects with the center line is the "tee." "Sweepers" may assist a rock from tee line to tee line. At a point 6.4 meters (21 feet) out from each tee line a "hog line" goes across the ice. When delivering a rock, a player must release the stone before it reaches the near hog line (10 meters [33 feet] from the hack); at the other end, the rock must stop beyond the hog line (but before the back line) in order to remain in play. The area between the hog line and the tee line, not including the house, has become in very recent years a "free guard zone." With its first two shots, a team may establish "guards" in this zone. The opposing team may not remove these guards with its first shot in some jurisdictions or with either of its first two shots in other jurisdictions.

The attractions of curling are similar to those of golf. At the highest competitive levels of play, the sport represents a fascinating test of skill and strategy, and it particularly highlights players' capacity to perform well under pressure. The game can also be enjoyed by recreational players, however, because almost anyone can make a shot occasionally, and there is very little chance that serious injuries will occur. Moreover, players and spectators can appreciate the interval between shots, when there are a few seconds to reflect upon the significance of the shot just played, to identify the strategy that might now be used, or just to share a friendly remark. In years gone by, it was not uncommon for players to use the natural break between shots to take a few puffs on a cigar or a pipe or to pass around a bottle of whisky.

Origins

For nearly two hundred years, students of the history of curling have argued over whether or not the sport was "invented" in Scotland or in continental Europe. There is evidence dating from the fifteenth to the seventeenth centuries, in the form of paintings, printed documents, and old curling stones, that can be used to support either point of view. The argument is essentially hypothetical because it proceeds from the groundless assumption that a "new" game appeared some 400–500 years ago either in Scotland or in continental Europe. The idea in curling is to score points by sliding objects that stop and then remain closer to a target than do those of an opponent. Games such as quoits, lawn bowling, and shuffleboard incorporate the same principle, although, of course, the object used to play the game may be thrown or rolled or shoved. Games like these have been played for hundreds, even thousands, of years in various parts of the world.

Development

Although it can not be said that the Scots "invented" curling, it can be asserted that curling as we know it today was developed primarily in Scotland. From early in the sixteenth century until early in the nineteenth century, the Scots played according to local rules that dictated varying numbers of players per team and shots per player and that suggested or required rinks of assorted dimensions as well as stones of diverse shapes and sizes. Then, early in the nineteenth century, when improved means of transportation made it possible for curlers to compete against distant opponents, uniformity of rules became desirable. This uniformity was accomplished in large part through the formation in 1838 of the Grand Caledonian Curling Club (it became the Royal Caledonian Curling Club in 1843, after it received royal patronage). The Royal Canadian Curling Club was not so much a club as an association of clubs, and it adopted or promoted the most important rules that have marked the sport to the present day: a team consists of four players; each player throws two rocks per end; the sheet of ice on which a match occurs should be 42 meters (138 feet) from "foot-score to foot-score" (hack to hack); only circular stones should be used. This last stipulation was very important, because a circular stone with a handle can be given an "in turn" or an "out turn" on delivery that will cause it to move *across* the ice at the same time as it travels *down* the ice.

While Scots were developing the modern game of curling, they were also exporting it. Between the mid-eighteenth and early twentieth centuries they introduced curling into several countries. Usually they did this by emigrating, but sometimes they did it simply by visiting foreign lands. Thus, over the course of about 150 years, from the 1760s to the 1910s, curling began in England, Sweden, New Zealand, Switzerland, Norway, Austria, Italy, France, and the United States. It was played for a time in Ireland, Russia, and even China. Most important, curling began in Canada. By early in the twentieth century, the sport was more popular and more skillfully played in Canada than it ever had been anywhere.

The hotbed of curling in Canada was the prairie region (the southern and central parts of the current provinces of Manitoba, Saskatchewan, and Alberta). The prairies were settled between the 1870s and the 1920s. Although no statistics are available to prove it, curling was probably the region's most popular winter participant sport. There were several reasons. First, among the immigrants to the region were a significant number

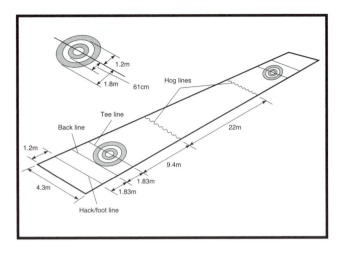

of Scottish people who came either from Scotland itself or from eastern Canada. Second, the driving force of the prairie economy was commercial agriculture; in summer many people were extremely busy, but in winter they had plenty of leisure time. Finally, excellent natural ice could be maintained inside covered rinks for three or four months in a year on the prairies, much longer than in Scotland, eastern Canada, or other parts of the world in which curling had gained a following.

The indoor natural ice curling rink, soon ubiquitous on the prairies, was a facility that had origins in both Scotland and eastern Canada. The prepared sheet of natural ice, made by placing low boards around the edges of a hard, flat surface (compacted clay or sand, or perhaps even wood or cement) and then flooding this surface with water that eventually froze, had been introduced in Scotland in the 1820s. In the 1830s and 1840s, eastern Canadians had begun building sheds over these kinds of sheets. As settlement proceeded on the prairies, little two- or three-sheet curling sheds or "rinks" were built almost as quickly as churches and schools, and in the cities much larger structures with perhaps a dozen sheets were constructed.

Prairie Canadians not only curled more often than other people did, they also curled better. From the 1880s to the 1950s, they introduced and promoted most of the techniques and strategies that gradually made curling a more impressive and demanding athletic contest. They especially developed the sliding delivery, which resulted from—and at the same time encouraged—a style of play based on "hits" rather than "draws." Although every curler was an amateur, the top players on the prairies became as serious about

Glossary

artificial ice   Ice made by "artificial" means, usually on a floor made of cement. The floor is cooled by pumping cold brine through pipes buried under the surface. Water sprayed on the floor will freeze. The ice remains in place even though the temperature in the building is well above the freezing point.

back line   Line at the back of the house. There is one at each end, 1.8 meters (6 feet) out from the hack line. To remain in play, a rock thrown from one end must not go beyond the back line at the far end.

blank end   An end in which no points are counted.

bonspiel   A curling tournament, usually held over several days.

center line   A line drawn down the ice, from hack line to hack line. The center line meets the tee line at the tee.

crampit   Portable foothold used when throwing a rock. In the twentieth century, replaced by hacks. Early crampits normally were iron spikes strapped to the foot. Later types were flat iron sheets with short pegs on the bottom to grab the ice.

draw   A shot thrown with weight sufficient to come to rest in the house.

end   A distinct segment of the game in which each team plays eight shots in one direction. Points are then counted and play begins in the opposite direction. At present, ten ends normally constitute a game. If the game is tied at the finish of ten ends, an "extra end" is played.

free guard zone   The area between the hog line and the tee line, not including the house. There is a free guard zone at each end of the rink. In this zone certain kinds of "guard" shots may not be removed from play by the opposition. The precise rules vary slightly. The normal regulations are that if the first or second shot played by a team comes to rest in this zone, the other team may not knock these stones out of play with either of its first two shots.

guard   A rock situated in front of another, making it difficult for the opponent to take out the latter. A guard almost always sits in front of the house. It protects either a stone already in the house or one that will be placed there as the end progresses.

hack   The foothold used when delivering a rock. At one time the hack was just a small hole cut into the ice. Now it is a rubber-surfaced metal or wooden plate that is screwed or sunk into the ice. There are two hacks at each end, one used by right-handed players, the other by left-handed players.

hack line   A line drawn 1.2 meters (4 feet) out from the backboards. There is one at each end of the rink. The front of each hack touches the hack line.

hit   A shot that moves an opponent's stone and probably knocks it out of play.

hog line   A line on the ice 10 meters (33 feet) out from the hack. There is a hog line at each end. A rock must pass the far hog line to be in play. When delivering a rock, a curler must release it before it touches the near hog line.

house   A series of four concentric circles. There is a house at each end of the rink. The center point of each house is a tee, located 3.7 meters (12 feet) out from the hack line, in the middle of the sheet (on the centre line). The concentric circles are 0.3 meters, 1.2 meters; 2.4 meters; and 3.7 meters (1 foot, 4 feet, 8 feet, and 12 feet) in diameter. The smallest circle is usually called the "button."

in turn   The turn or twist applied to a rock by a player who turns the elbow in at release. In turns thrown by a right-handed player turn clockwise, and they work their way from left to right as they go down the ice. The opposite holds true if a left-handed player throws an in turn.

out turn   The turn or twist applied to a rock by a player who turns the elbow out at release. Out turns thrown by a right- handed player turn counter-clockwise, and they work their way from right to left as they go down the ice. The opposite holds true if a left-handed player throws an out turn.

rink   1) A team of curlers. (2) The sheet of ice on which curling occurs. (3) The building that encloses one or more sheets of ice.

rock   The item with which curling is played, like the puck in hockey or the ball in baseball. Nowadays, rocks are made almost always of "granite" (actually, this is not quite accurate, petrologically). Until the twentieth century, rocks were sometimes made of wood; and until the 1940s rocks made of iron were used in the Canadian province of Quebec, as well as in eastern Ontario.

skip   The player who directs play for the team, who sets up the strategy, and who usually throws the last two rocks on each end for the team. Therefore, the skip is the most important player. The other players are the lead (throws the first two rocks), the second (throws the third and fourth rocks), the third or the vice-skip (throws the fifth and sixth rocks, and acts as skip when the skip is throwing).

slide   The action of a player while delivering a rock. A right- handed player slides on the left foot, a left-handed player on the right foot.

stone   Synonym for "rock."

sweeper   A person who uses a broom or brush to sweep a rock. Sweeping removes debris from the path of the rock, and smooths the surface of the ice in front of the rock so that it slows down more gradually than it would if left on its own. The lead and the second on a team do more sweeping than the other two members. Normally, two sweepers work on a rock at the same time.

take-out   A shot that knocks an opponent's stone out of play.

tee   The exact midpoint of the house. In Scotland, formerly called the "cock."

tee line   A line drawn across the middle of the house, 3.7 meters (12 feet) out from the hack line. There is a tee line at each end of the rink.

—Morris Mott

their sport as any professional athlete. Beginning in the 1880s, players arranged "bonspiels" from which winners took home very valuable pieces of merchandise. In the 1920s they promoted a Canadian (men's) national championship event. The event (called The Brier) was first held in 1927, and it is still the most prestigious national championship tournament in the sport.

In the latter part of the nineteenth century and the first part of the twentieth, then, Canadians took the Scottish game of curling and nurtured it to new heights of popularity and skill. Meanwhile, although the game had been introduced in several countries, curling was not yet popular around the world. It did not become so until after World War I and especially after World War II.

Between the 1920s and the 1990s, the sport became truly an international one. The rise in popularity was due partly to the examples of athletic excellence provided by top curlers, especially after the 1960s when important competitions began to be televised. The greater popularity was due, as well, to the work of curling missionaries such as Ray Turnbull (1939–) of Canada, who promoted the sport in northern Europe and Japan. The biggest reason curling gained an international following, however, was the availability of "artificial ice."

Artificial ice had been invented in England late in the nineteenth century. Before World War II a few artificial ice rinks were built in England, Scotland, the United States, and Canada. However, most curlers could not afford to join clubs that installed artificial ice. This situation changed only in the prosperous 1940s, 1950s and 1960s. Artificial ice rinks were built in many cities in the four countries just mentioned and appeared also in warm countries where the natural ice game had not been well established. Curlers now had consistent ice, and they had it, theoretically at least, 12 months of the year.

The results in different countries of all these post–World War I developments may be outlined briefly. In Canada, the prairies remained the most important curling region, but clubs sprung up in every province and territory. Women started to participate in significant numbers early in the twentieth century, and by the 1980s there were nearly as many females as males on the ice. By the 1990s there were over a million curlers in Canada, far more than anywhere else.

Hacks, Shoes, and the Delivery of the Rock

Early Scottish curling took place on frozen rivers, streams, and lakes. The curlers had to carry with them a portable foot grip, usually called a "crampit." The crampit encouraged a delivery from a sideways position.

In Canada, in the last half of the nineteenth century, curling moved indoors. Permanent holes or "hacks" were cut in the ice, and as time went on leather or rubber was inserted in the holes. The hack allowed a curler to keep the shoulders square to the target and therefore to be a more efficient athlete. In particular, the hack allowed a curler to be much more accurate with "take-out" shots.

The "slide" developed as a follow-through from the face-the-target delivery. Early in the twentieth century the slide evolved, especially in the prairies of Canada, where curlers played a knock-out style that often required heavy weight. The momentum from delivering a fast rock carried the curler a few feet forward out of the hack.

In the 1930s and 1940s, Ken Watson (1904–1986) of Winnipeg, Manitoba, was the world's best curler; he was the leading exponent of the slide. He and other curlers of his day simply slipped off one toe rubber and slid on leather-soled shoes. In the 1950s and 1960s, in order to cut down on friction, some curlers began to apply liquid solder to the leather sole or perhaps they glued a piece of Teflon to it. Since the 1960s special curling shoes have been manufactured. They have featured brick, stainless steel, or some other sliding material.

Nowadays a top male or female curler in the act of throwing a rock is a beautiful athletic sight. He or she is using footwear that allows for the kind of smooth, balanced delivery that curlers a century ago could not even have imagined.

—Morris Mott

Meanwhile, in the United States, where curling had achieved a reasonable degree of popularity by the turn of the twentieth century, the sport lost appeal until after World War II. Then, with the gradual adoption of artificial ice rinks, curling developed a large following. By the 1990s the United States Curling Association oversaw men's and women's curling in 27 states in the union. There were some 15,000 registered curlers.

In Scandinavia, curling became an important sport in Norway and Sweden and recently it has gained a foothold in Denmark, Finland, and Iceland. In Norway, curling was a minor sport from the 1880s to the 1950s. In the 1960s and 1970s, the game became very popular, especially because Norwegian teams did well in international competitions. By the 1980s, Norway had over 1,000 curlers. In Sweden, the home of the first European curling club established outside the United Kingdom (it was founded in 1852), curling remained a rather insignificant sport until the 1960s. By the 1990s there were 5,000 curlers.

In continental western and southern Europe, curling first gained prominence at the turn of the twentieth century as an outdoor sport played at resort hotels in the Alps. The hotels catered to Scottish and English tourists who wanted to play the sport. During the interwar period the continental Europeans started to curl in significant numbers. By the 1990s in Europe, curling had its largest following in Alpine countries: Switzerland, France, and Germany. Each had a few thousand curlers. Smaller numbers of aficionados resided in Austria, Italy, the Netherlands, Belgium, Liechtenstein, Luxembourg, Andorra, Bulgaria, Hungary, the Czech Republic, Romania, and Russia.

In Britain, as well, curling gained adherents. In the 1970s the sport caught on in Wales; by the 1980s there were about 60 Welsh curlers. In England by 1914 there were 37 curling clubs, but the sport nearly disappeared between the two world wars, and when men or women from England curled they usually did so in Scotland or at a resort hotel in the Alps. In the 1960s English curling revived somewhat, and by the late 1980s there were some 200 curlers. Finally, in Scotland, the home of the sport, curling was given a boost early in the twentieth century by the construction of indoor rinks. In the interwar period several indoor artificial ice rinks were designed to accommodate both curling and ice-hockey. After World War II, ice hockey declined in popularity and curling benefited from the greater availability of ice. It was further stimulated after the 1950s by the Scots' desire to match the skill of Canadians in international matches. By the 1980s Scotland had some 30,000 curlers.

Curling was introduced in a number of other countries after the 1960s, including such unlikely ones (given their climates) as Mexico, South Africa, and Côte d'Ivoire. The next spurt in popularity seems likely to occur in the Pacific Rim. In the 1980s and 1990s curling associations were formed in Japan, Australia, New Zealand, and Korea to serve a steadily growing number of participants.

Since the 1960s the highlights of the curling year have been the world championship events. A men's world championship (unofficial) began in 1959; a women's in 1979; a junior men's and junior women's in 1975 and 1988, respectively (a "junior" curler must be 21 or younger). These championship events are administered by the World Curling Federation, made up of 31 curling associations. This federation was founded in 1966 (as the International Curling Association) in part to oversee the unofficial world men's championship event that the Scotch Whisky Association had arranged annually since 1959. It was also founded in order to apply for status for curling as an official sport at the Winter Olympic Games. The International Olympic Committee granted this status in 1992; the first Olympic Games at which curling will be an official medal sport (rather than a demonstration sport) will be held in Japan in 1998.

When international competition became an important part of the curling scene, the Richardson rink of Regina, Saskatchewan, was in its prime. This team (the "skip" was Ernie Richardson [1931–], and the other members of the rink were a brother and two cousins, all named Richardson) was probably the finest in curling history; certainly the skill and dedication of the Richardsons were a revelation to the Scots, Americans, and others who played against them. Until the 1970s the Canadians dominated international play. Thereafter, other countries became more competitive. At world championship events of the 1990s, the Canadians almost always supply the team to beat, but the events are exciting because teams from several countries have reason to expect they can do it.

The future of curling seems very promising. It is now an Olympic sport, which means it will soon receive a lot of exposure around the world. It is now almost always played on artificial ice, and the outside climate no longer determines who can participate. It can be enjoyed by young as well as old, by males as well as females and, as thousands of Scots, Canadians, and others can attest, by serious athletes as well as those who just want an opportunity to visit and laugh with their friends.

—Morris Mott

Bibliography: Creelman, William A. (1950) *Curling Past and Present: Including an Analysis of the Art of Curling by H. E. Wyman.* Toronto: McClelland and Stewart.

Kerr, John. (1890) *History of Curling, Scotland's Ain' Game and Fifty Years of the Royal Caledonian Curling Club.* Edinburgh: David Douglas.

————. (1904) *Curling in Canada and the United States, a Record of the Tour of the Scottish Team, 1902–1903, and the Game in the Dominion and the Republic.* Edinburgh: George A. Morton.

Lukowich, Ed, Eigil Ramsfjell, and Bud Sumerville. (1990) *The Joy of Curling: A Celebration.* Toronto: McGraw-Hill Ryerson.

Maxwell, Doug, et al. (1980) *The First Fifty. A Nostalgic Look at the Brier.* Toronto: Maxcurl Publications.

Mitchell, W. O. (1993) *The Black Bonspiel of Willie MacCrimmon.* Toronto: McClelland and Stewart.

Mott, Morris, and John Allardyce. (1989) *Curling Capital: Winnipeg and the Roarin' Game, 1876 to 1988.* Winnipeg: University of Manitoba Press.

Murray, W.H. (1981) *The Curling Companion.* Glasgow: Richard Drew Publishing.

Richardson, Ernie, Joyce McKee, and Doug Maxwell. (1962) *Curling, An Authoritative Handbook of the Techniques and Strategy of the Ancient Game of Curling.* Toronto: Thomas Allen.

Sautter, Erwin A. (1993) *Curling—Vademecum.* Zumikon, Switzerland: Erwin A. Sautter-Hewitt.

Smith, David B. (1981). *Curling: An Illustrated History.* Edinburgh: John Donald Publishers.

Watson, Ken (1950). *Ken Watson on Curling.* Toronto: Copp Clark Publishing.

Weeks, Bob (1995). *The Brier: The History of Canada's Most Celebrated Curling Championship.* Toronto: Macmillan Canada.

Welsh, Robin (1969). *A Beginner's Guide to Curling.* London: Pelham Books.

————. (1985) *International Guide to Curling.* London: Pelham Books.

Cycling

Cycling is the fastest form of human-powered motion. A bicycle enables a person to travel short distances twice as fast as by running. Over long distances a bicycle is more than three times as fast as running. Consequently, bicycles are used for transportation, recreation, and sport. Throughout the world, the main use of bicycles is for everyday travel. However, in affluent regions, especially North America, Europe, and Australasia, bicycles are used extensively for recreation, whether for a gentle ride in a nearby park or on an international tour. The speed of cycling also invites competition.

A wide variety of cycle sports has developed in many countries. For more than 100 years, bicycles have been raced on roads and both indoor and outdoor tracks. As each form of cycle sport has arisen, it has developed specific rules and conventions that control the venues and types of events, who may compete, and the design of bicycle used. A new sport often spreads to other countries, and international controls and a hierarchy of events leading to world championships emerge to guide it.

Bicycles are the most efficient vehicles ever invented. At competitive speeds most of a cyclist's power is used to push aside the air through which he or she passes. This fact has a great influence on the various ways cycle racing is conducted. For example, racing cyclists crouch to reduce their air resistance. This can be lessened by a further 20–30 percent when a cyclist "drafts" behind another, so riding in groups plays a major part in the tactics of cycling. At higher altitudes the atmosphere is less dense and air resistance is lower than at sea level. Consequently, some cycling records have been set at high-altitude venues despite it being more difficult for riders to breathe.

Origins

Cycle competition probably began with races between riders of "hobby horses" (early bicycles without pedals) in the 1820s. However, cycling first became a significant sport in the 1860s with the mass production of France's "velocipedes," two-wheeled machines with cranks and pedals attached to the front axle. The world's first recorded bicycle race was held in 1868 over a distance of 1,200 meters (1,313 yards) on a track at Saint-Cloud, a suburb of Paris. In the same year, track races for women were held in France. The first recorded cycling road race was between Paris and Rouen, a distance of 123 kilometers (76 miles), in 1869. Both men and women competed in this race. At about the same time, races were held in other countries, including Australia, England, and the United States.

The early bicycles were so uncomfortable that they were known as "boneshakers." They had to

A picnicking French family cheers on weary participants in the 1954 Tour de France. The cyclists were on their seventeenth lap, near St. Veraud.

be pedaled furiously to achieve a speed as fast as running. However, they represented a completely new form of transportation and were enthusiastically accepted in France, the United States, and Britain.

In the 1870s bicycles became much lighter and got larger front wheels to increase their speed. The classic "high bicycle" was the fastest thing on the road and could outdistance a galloping horse. High bicycles were used for traveling long distances and for competitive sport. As early as 1873, riders on high bicycles completed a 1,300-kilome-

ter (808 miles) ride across Britain in 14 days. Riders competed on tracks and roads, over distances from 1 kilometer (0.6 miles) to 100 kilometers (62.1 miles) or more. In 1882 Herbert Cortis became the first person to ride more than 32 kilometers (20 miles) in an hour. By 1886 Thomas Stevens had ridden and wheeled a high bicycle around the world in the first-ever overland circuit of the planet.

However, by 1890 the dangerous high bicycle had begun to be replaced by "safety" bicycles with smaller, equal-sized wheels. These new bicycles also had pneumatic tires and a chain drive,

Race Across America

The Race Across America (RAAM) is a grueling annual bicycle marathon from California to the East Coast. It is considered one of the world's most challenging endurance events. The race was founded in 1982 to bring greater recognition to ultramarathon cycling, a sport that pushes human limits. During the race, the participants cycle almost continuously, taking only very short rest breaks. In addition to extreme physical challenges, participants must contend with monotony, frustration, and other psychological barriers. In some instances, riders experience hallucinations during the race.

John Marino, the event's founder, broke the transcontinental bicycling record in 1978 by riding from Santa Monica, California, to New York City in 13 days, 1 hour, and 20 minutes. He later decided to organize a transcontinental race and recruited three other top ultramarathon cyclists to help: John Howard, who had won six national cycling championships; Lon Haldeman, who in 1981 broke Marino's transcontinental record; and Michael Shermer, who in 1981 established a north-south cycling record. They were the only participants in the first race, which was originally named the Great American Bike Race. They started at 10:06 A.M. on 4 August 1982. Haldeman won by completing the 4,791-kilometer (2,976-mile) route from California's Santa Monica Pier to New York City's Empire State Building in 9 days, 20 hours, and 2 minutes. Serious cyclists and casual observers were impressed by the drama of the nationally televised race. Shermer, Haldeman, and Marino formed a business, Ultra-Marathon Cycling Inc., to organize an annual event with the new name "Race Across America."

The routes and specific distances of the RAAM change yearly, but they always average around 4,800 kilometers (3,000 miles) and have so far always started in California. Routes have ended in Atlantic City, New Jersey; Savannah, Georgia; and other East Coast cities. The average speed of the participants is an important measurement because of the variations in routes. In ultramarathon cycling's first decade, the fastest average speed was attained by Pete Penseyers in 1987. He averaged 24.8 kilometers (15.4 miles) per hour, completing 5,002 kilometers (3,107 miles) in 8 days, 9 hours, and 47 minutes.

Racers qualify for RAAM in earlier, shorter marathon races. The typical field for the actual RAAM ranges from 20 to 40 racers, not all of whom finish. In 1986, only 7 of 26 starters completed the race. However, this average has increased markedly—by 1989, 14 of 28 starters finished. Since the race began, new divisions have been added to accommodate more RAAM competitors. The inaugural year for the women's division, 1984, was marked by a dramatic finish-line sprint between Shelby Hayden-Clifton and Pat Hines, who tied at 12 days, 20 hours, and 57 minutes. In 1989 the race was opened to teams, with four-person relay and tandem divisions added. This aspect was expanded in 1992 with a new race called Team RAAM. Four-person team races tend to be faster and have more competitive sprints because each racer cycles for shorter distances and can rest while his or her teammates take over the lead. In 1995, for example, Rob Kish won the solo RAAM in 8 days, 19 hours, and 59 minutes. In contrast, Team Kern-Wheelman, the Team RAAM winners, crossed the same route in only 5 days, 17 hours, and 5 minutes.

—John Townes

Bibliography: Shermer, Michael. (1993) *Race Across America: The Agonies and Glories of the World's Longest and Cruelest Bicycle Race.* Waco, TX: WRS Publishing.

Zukowski, Stan. (1995). "ScRAAMbled Legs." *Bicycling Magazine* (October).

making them considerably faster. While a champion rider could reach 40 kilometers per hour (25 miles per hour) in a sprint on a high bicycle, a safety bicycle rider could achieve 50 kilometers per hour (31 miles per hour). In 1894 the world distance record for 24 hours was an impressive 502 kilometers (312 miles) on a high bicycle, but 685 kilometers (426 miles) on a safety bicycle.

Cycle sport first became organized in the 1870s in England, which at that time was the leading country in the production of bicycles. Class differences were reflected in the establishment of separate amateur and professional cycling events. Amateurs were "gentlemen" who competed for enjoyment and did not accept financially valuable prizes. On the other hand, professional riders were paid and provided entertainment for the working classes. Cycle sport was essentially a male pastime in England, and most people opposed strenuous cycling by women. Nevertheless, there were some female competitors in France and the United States. In the 1880s organized cycle sport at a national level quickly spread to other European countries and the United States. The international control body, the Union Cycliste Internationale (UCI), was established in 1896.

Development

Track Racing in the Nineteenth Century

By confining cyclists to tracks, there is greater opportunity for spectators to see the races and for promoters to charge for admission. In the 1890s, cycling on specially constructed tracks with steeply banked sides became enormously popular throughout Europe, North America, and Australia. Almost every city had a cycle track, whether surfaced with dirt, wood, asphalt, or concrete. Sprint and handicap races were held over a variety of distances. Track bicycles had a fixed drive and no brakes or gears—a tradition that continues today. In 1893 Arthur Zimmerman won the first World Cycling Championship in Chicago, Illinois. Another famous racer was Marshall "Major" Taylor, an African American who broke through barriers of racial prejudice in the early 1900s. Endurance races lasting for six days began in Birmingham, England, in 1875. These were popular and rowdy affairs at New York City's Madison Square Garden in the 1890s. In one of these events, Charlie Miller completed a record 3,360 kilometers (2,088 miles).

Road Racing in the Nineteenth Century

In the 1890s cycle racing on roads thrived throughout the world. Professional road racing flourished in France and Belgium with the establishment of such place-to-place races as the Paris-Brest-Paris, Bordeaux-Paris, Paris-Brussels, Liège-Bastogne-Liège, Paris-Roubaix, and in 1903 the most famous of all, the Tour de France. The early races were grueling events over bad roads with single "stages" (non-stop distances) up to 500 kilometers (311 miles) in length.

There were many road races in the United States, the most popular of which was the annual Pullman Race in Chicago, Illinois. In Australia, the first Warrnambool-Melbourne cycle race was held in 1895. However, in England there was concern about the dangers of cycle racing on public roads. Consequently, "massed-start" racing, in which cyclists raced beside each other, was banned. The only form of road racing permitted was time trialing.

Speed Contests

In the pre-automobile era there was enormous interest in the speed of cycling. Contests were held between cyclists and horses, and even between cyclists and trains. In 1899 American Charles Murphy became a national hero when he pedaled a mile in a minute, reaching 97 kilometers an hour (60 miles an hour). Murphy rode on a specially constructed track between railway lines on Long Island and was paced by a steam train with a shield at the back of the rear carriage that allowed him to draft efficiently.

Motor Pacing

In the nineteenth century, records were often set by cyclists behind other cyclists who took turns to make the pace. In special track races in the 1890s cyclists were paced by several teams of four, five, or even six riders on tandem bicycles. From 1898 onward, the pacing was done by motorbikes. The world one-hour paced record was broken 80 times between the turn of the century and 1937. The UCI now approves an official hour paced record, which currently stands at 91 kilometers (56.54 miles). On the other hand, unofficial paced bicycle records have been set behind racing cars. The fastest of these is Fred Rompelberg's 269 kilometers an hour (167.16 miles an hour) at Utah's Bonneville Salt Flats in 1995. Speeds of up to 200 kilometers an hour (125 miles an hour) have been achieved by riding bicycles down steep ski runs.

Cyclocross

At the start of this century, the prospect of using bicycles for maneuvers and dispatch in warfare led to the formation of cyclist divisions in armies around the world. Some French soldiers enjoyed riding through fields and forests, leading to the first cyclocross contests. Cyclocross was taken up by European road racers as a way of maintaining fitness during winter, when roads were often icy and dangerous. Cyclocross events are held over many laps of short courses (up to 3 kilometers [1.9 miles] long) with obstacles that oblige riders to dismount and shoulder their bicycles. Nowadays, riders use lightweight bicycles with wide clearance around knobby, tubular tires. Some riders have several bikes scattered around the course so that if one is damaged or disabled, they can continue riding on another. Helpers repair or clean the abandoned bikes. In the 1970s cyclocross extended into the United States, where both men's and women's championships were established.

Touring Events

There is a long tradition of touring rides (*randonées*) conducted under specified conditions. In 1877 the concept of *Audax* ("bold") events was formulated in Italy. Participants had to swim, run, walk, or cycle a set distance in 14 hours,

Tour de France

The Tour de France cycle race is the largest annual sporting event in the world. Stretching to approximately 4,000 kilometers (2,500 miles)—the precise itinerary and distance vary from year to year—but always including a voyage round France taking in the Pyrenees and the Alps, it lasts for three weeks in July. Coinciding with the start of the school vacation and Bastille Day on 14 July, the Tour is deeply French in both its customs and its culture. It is also very popular in the Benelux countries, Switzerland, Italy, and Spain. The success of Irish and Colombian riders and of American Greg LeMond as well as several Australians and East Europeans has recently given the Tour a remarkable global appeal, enhanced by live television film taken mostly by camerapersons perched on the back of motorcycles close to the riders. The best riders must be able to sprint, race against the clock, and climb, day after day, week after week. The greatest of them have become probably the most widely known sporting heroes in twentieth-century continental Europe.

The development of the modern bicycle in the 1890s led to classic races, such as the Paris-Bordeaux and the Paris-Roubaix. These were promoted by the new sporting press, especially the daily sports and cycling paper, *Le Vélo,* which alienated one of its main backers, the conservative Baron de Dion. He founded a rival paper, *L'Auto,* whose first editor, Henri Desgranges, backed an idea to organize a race around France. The magnitude and daring of the project captured public attention.

The first Tour was only two-thirds the length of later races and was run day and night in six stages. Maurice Garin, nicknamed "the Bulldog," a former chimney sweep, won the first Tour. The next year the leaders were set upon by a mob during one of the night stages and four, including Garin, later disqualified because of allegations of cheating. Desgranges decided to abandon the night stages and lengthen the race itself to go round the whole country, taking in Alpine passes and what were little more than rough tracks in the high Pyrenees.

L'Auto reveled in the terrible demands of the Tour. For it was more than a race; it was an epic, a kind of heroic story through which France would come to know itself. The "giants of the road," as they were known, passed through historic sites and scenes of great deeds in the French past. As many as a third of the country would actually see the race go by, organizing local festivities to coincide with it. Perhaps more than any other great sporting event, the Tour is rooted in the landscape and culture of its host country. As a showcase for France it is superb, and tourist towns now pay vast sums to feature in the race.

The Tour is run in teams. The teams were originally sponsored by bicycle manufacturers but are becoming increasingly beverage- and fashion-based. National teams were introduced in 1930 because manufacturers' teams were abolished (so as to promote the idea of the best rider, not simply the best bike). National teams were dropped after 1939 when the Germans, Italians, and Spanish absented themselves because of the international situation. Despite complex deals within and between teams, the Tour is primarily about individual achievement. The main riding group *(le peleton)* is preceded by a massive advertising caravan. The winner, supported by his "servants" (the *domestiques* or supporting riders), is the best overall performer with the lowest aggregate time. There is a prize for the best climber (the "King of the Mountains") and a coveted points prize for the best sprinter as well as a host of other minor awards.

The great riders have become household names, men possessed of seemingly miraculous powers of endurance. (The Tour is limited to men, although a women's Tour de France was launched in 1984.) The epithets attached to their names, as French literary critic Roland Barthes in a famous essay "Le Tour de France comme épopée" in *Mythologies* (1957) has remarked, seemed to derive "from an earlier age when the nation reverberated to the image of a handful of ethnic heroes: Brankart le Franc, Bobet le Francien, Robic le Celte" and so on.

The race is run over a period of just over three weeks with 21 stages (in 1996); a stage is a single day with designated starting and finishing point (usually a town or mountain resort called an 'étape,' which pays handsomely for the privilege). Hence the tour is both a single cumulative race and a series of one-day races. Victory even in a single stage is considered a significant achievement, especially in the mountains. A special prize for the best climber was introduced in 1934. (Three years later the derailleur gear was officially recognized and climbing became easier and faster; before then riders had to complete the Tour without gears.)

Heroic feats are part of the popular mythology of the Tour. As riders pass over the great mountain passes—the Tourmalet, the Galibier, the Alpe d'Huez—the deeds of past champions are recalled. Men like the tall, graceful Italian, Fausto Coppi, the "champion of champions," setting out alone across the Alps in 1952 to win a magnificent stage or Bartali, "Gino the Pious," praised by the Pope, who first won in 1938 and then again after a gap of 10 years, a feat never repeated since.

Belgians have played a great part in the Tour, especially those from Flanders, who dominated around World War I. The greatest of all was a rider who devoured four successive titles from 1969 to 1972 and another in 1974: Eddy Merckx (1945–), the "Cannibal," who also won an unprecedented number of other classics.

Two French riders who have won the Tour five times. Jacques Anquetil (1934–1987), the winner in 1957 and again in four successive years from 1961, was a specialist in racing against the clock. His rivalry with the unfortunate Raymond Poulidor (1936–), seemingly destined to be second, caught the attention of even the austere General Charles de Gaulle. Next came "the Badger," Bernard Hinault (1954–), a Breton, like Poulidor from a peasant family, who took charge of the Tour in the 1980s. After a bad fall close to the end of the fourteenth stage of the Tour in 1985, he remounted, blood streaming from a broken nose, to ride across the line on the way to his fifth title.

Hinault's record sixth title was denied him in 1986 by the first American to win the race, Greg LeMond, who repeated his success in 1989. Lemond's success delighted the sponsors of the race. For the Tour has its eye firmly on the global marketplace and is becoming less French in the process despite the guiding hand of Jacques Goddet, who ruled the race for so long since the Desgranges era. Recent winners have been Irish and Spanish, most notably the remarkable Spaniard Miguel Indurain (1964–), whose amazing lung capacity and quiet authority made the Tour his from 1991 to 1995.

Unlike its rivals the Tour of Italy (the Giro) and the Tour of Spain (the Vuelta), the Tour de France is now a world phenomenon. Eastern Europe, Russia, and Australia as well as North and South America are represented. This explains the interest of global companies, such as Coca-Cola, and the new importance attached to controlling drug use by riders, which had hitherto been more or less accepted because of the almost superhuman demands of the event. As it approaches its centenary mark, the Tour goes from strength to strength, eclipsed only by the Olympics and the World Cup as a popular sporting spectacle.

—Richard Holt

Bibliography: Abt, S. (1991) *Tour de France: Three Weeks to Glory.* New York: Bicycle Books.

Blondin, A. (1977) *Sur le Tour de France.* Paris: Mazarine.

Chany, Pierre. (1985) *La fabuleuse histoire du Tour de France.* Paris: O.D.I.L.

Holt, R. (1981) *Sport and Society in Modern France.* London: Macmillan.

Laget, S. (1990) *La saga du Tour de France.* Paris: Gallimard.

Ligget, P. (1988) *The Tour de France.* London: Harrap.

Nicholson, G. (1977) *The Great Bike Race.* London: Methuen.

Watson, G. (1990) *The Tour de France and Its Heroes.* London: Stanley Paul.

which was approximately the time between sunrise and sunset. The distance to be covered by cycling was 200 kilometers (125 miles). This still holds today despite better roads and machines. *Audax* rides were adopted in France in 1904, and are today conducted in 18 countries. Events are also held over distances of 300, 400, 600, and 1,000 kilometers (186, 249, 373, and 621 miles). In the Paris-Brest-Paris race, from 1901 onward, and in the early years of the Tour de France, there was a separate touring category called *touristes routiers*. The 1,200-kilometer (746-mile) Paris-Brest-Paris ride is no longer conducted as a race, but continues every four years as an *Audax* ride. All bicycles must be fitted with lights. Until 1995 bicycles were also required to have fenders. The maximum time allowed is 90 hours, although some riders complete the ride in less than 50.

Time Trialing

Unpaced time trialing, called *contre la montre* (against the clock) in France, has also been called "the race of truth." Individual trials over standard distances and times were the main form of road racing in England for the first half of this century. Amateur riders competed over distances of 16 kilometers (10 miles), 40 kilometers (25 miles), 80 kilometers (50 miles), and 161 kilometers (100 miles), and on rides of 12 and 24 hours. Individual riders were sent off at one-minute intervals. Trials were usually held at secret locations on quiet, country roads starting early on Sunday mornings. On flat, windless courses, variable gearing offered little advantage. The first ride "under the hour" for the popular 40-kilometer distance was done in 1939 by Ralph Dougherty on a bicycle with a single fixed gear.

Since World War II, time trialing has continued in England despite the reappearance of massed-start road races. Women also compete in time trials. Notable postwar riders, many of whose records still stand, include Eileen Sheridan and Beryl Burton. With better streamlining and training, times continue to fall, and the 40-kilometer record now stands at 45 minutes. The British 24-hour road record is 816 kilometers (507 miles).

Despite their theoretically greater speed, tandem cyclists record remarkably similar times to solo cyclists in trials over distances greater than 16 kilometers. In the United Kingdom, tricycles are raced, with times 10–15 percent slower than for bicycles.

Time trials are also held on cycling tracks. Champion cyclists can cover 200 meters (219 yards) at 70 kilometers (43 miles) per hour. The world unpaced hour record is highly coveted, and has been attempted by many road cycling champions. The distance traveled in an hour has gradually increased from the 25 kilometers (15 miles) covered by F. L. Dodds in England on a high bicycle in 1876 to 55 kilometers (34 miles), the current record held by Swiss rider Tony Rominger. The world unpaced 24-hour record is held by Australian Rod Evans, who rode 853 kilometers (530 miles).

Many time records are set from place to place, notably in England. In the United States, the annual Race Across America (RAAM) covers almost 5,000 kilometers (3,000 miles), from the Pacific coast to the Atlantic, and has been completed in eight days. In 1985 British rider Nick Saunders rode around the world in 78 days. The most extreme cycling record is for an entire year: in England, Tommy Godwin covered over 120,000 kilometers (75,000 miles) during 1939.

Time trials are also incorporated into stages of European road races. A team time trial over 100 kilometers (62 miles) is an Olympic event.

Track Cycling

The popularity of track cycling has gradually declined during this century. The famous Newark, New Jersey, track in the United States closed in the 1930s, and even the Parc des Princes track in Paris closed in the 1970s. Track cycling is still held in Europe and other countries, culminating in the annual world championships. Track cycling is the major element of the Olympic cycling program. Track races include the following events:

- The 1,000-meter sprint. This is contested between two cyclists who usually start slowly seeking a tactical advantage. Riders may even stop still, balancing on their pedals for several minutes. The final 200 meters is ridden flat out.
- The 1-kilometer individual time trial. From a standing start, the distance is covered in just over one minute.
- Pursuit races, in which two cyclists or teams of cyclists start off on opposite sides of the track. If one cyclist or team of cyclists catches the other, the race is over. Otherwise, the winner is the first one to cross the finish line.
- A special form of track racing, called *keirin*, that originated in Japan in 1948. Nine riders start from separate stalls and follow a motorbike, which gradually increases the pace before pulling out with about a lap and a half

to go, leaving the riders to contest the final sprint. *Keirin* is dangerous but extremely popular in Japan and has now been included in the world championships.

Road Racing

Road racing is held in countries throughout the world, but the most popular series of races form the professional European road-racing circuit. This consists of classic, one-day place-to-place races and stage races, including the three-week Giro d'Italia (Tour of Italy), Vuelta de España (Tour of Spain), and the most famous of all, the Tour de France. The Tour de France is one of the world's greatest sporting events, with an estimated 20 million spectators lining the route each July. The race covers many areas of France and usually includes parts of neighboring countries. The route climbs mountain passes over the Alps and the Pyrenees. Road-racing bikes are rugged and light, with thin tires and 16 gears. Cyclists race in commercially sponsored teams that provide support for their top riders. Professional road cyclists are the fittest of all endurance athletes, with a phenomenal energy expenditure of 25–30 megajoules per day. There have been many famous professional road cyclists, but special mention should be made of those who have each won the Tour de France on five occasions: Jacques Anquetil (1957, 1961–1964), Eddie Merckx (1969–1972, 1974), Bernard Hinault (1978– 1979, 1981–1982, 1985), and Miguel Indurain (1991–1995). Recently, English-speaking riders from Ireland, England, Australia, and the United States have made an impression on the European circuit. American Greg LeMond has won the Tour de France three times (1986, 1989–1990).

Olympic Games

Track and road cycling have been included in all Olympic Games of the modern era, starting in Athens in 1896. The top cycling nations at the Olympic Games have been France, Germany, Italy, and Great Britain. Other strong cycling nations, in descending order of the number of medals won, have been the Netherlands, the former Soviet Union, Belgium, Australia, and Denmark. Olympic cycling events consist of track and road events for men and women, and include both individual and team events. The types of Olympic cycling event have varied over the years. Tandem races were part of the program from 1906 to 1972. Women's events were included for the first time in 1984. Mountain bike races were introduced in 1996 and triathlons will be introduced at the Sydney Olympics in 2000.

Unrestricted Bicycles

The International Human Powered Vehicle Association (IHPVA) was established in the mid-1970s to promote innovative cycle designs. It sanctions record attempts by streamlined vehicles not permitted by the UCI. With reduced air resistance, remarkable speeds have been achieved when compared with the world records mentioned above. The 200-meter sprint record, in effect the fastest any human has ever traveled under human-generated power, is 110 kilometers (68 miles) per hour achieved by Chris Huber aboard the *Cheetah* in Colorado in 1992. A streamlined bicycle has covered 77 kilometers (48 miles) in one hour. Over 24 hours, the unrestricted record is 1,021 kilometers (634 miles).

BMX

BMX (bicycle motocross) is a competition over a short dirt track (typically 300 meters [328 yards]) with humps and banked corners. BMX competitors ride small, single-geared bicycles with 50-centimeter (20-inch) wheels, and wear helmets and other protective clothing. BMX is a family sport. Competitors range in age from 4 to over 45, with separate races for males and females. However, it is most popular with boys of ages 11–12. BMX originated in Santa Monica, California, in 1969 and quickly spread to other countries. National championships are held in more than 30 countries, and world championships occur each year under the control of the UCI. Another form of riding, "freestyle," consists of acrobatic stunts done on a BMX bicycle. "Observed trials" is a contest in which riders traverse extremely difficult terrain on a special low-geared BMX bicycle. By balancing on the pedals and hopping their bicycles, riders can jump over logs and rocks or even climb waterfalls. The objective is to complete the course without putting a foot to the ground ("dabbing").

Triathlons

Triathlons and other multisport events introduced a wide range of athletes to road cycling.

The first triathlons were held in California in the 1970s, leading to the establishment of the Hawaiian Ironman Triathlon in 1978. Every triathlon consists of a swim, a bike ride, and a run. The bike ride is over distances from 20 kilometers (12 miles) for sprint events up to 180 kilometers (112 miles) for "ultra" events. All riders must wear helmets for the bicycle portion of the competition. The International Triathlon Union (ITU), established in 1979, now coordinates the sport in more than 100 countries. World championships are held each year, and triathlons will be included in the Sydney Olympics in 2000. Triathlons impose design restrictions similar to other forms of cycle racing. However, disc wheels and handlebars that permit a more streamlined riding position were introduced by triathletes and have since been adopted by other cyclists.

Mountain Bike Racing

Mountain bike racing also began in California in the 1970s. Tough, versatile bicycles were developed for racing down fire trails, and then wide-range gears were added for riding up them. Races were held throughout the United States and the first national championships were organized in 1983. Many male and female riders with backgrounds in cyclocross and road racing have taken up mountain biking. Although it involves rugged terrain similar to that popular with cyclocross riders, techniques differ. Mountain bikes have wide, wire-beaded tires, and usually have suspension (shock absorbers), at least on the front wheel. The bicycles weigh several kilograms (pounds) more than their cyclocross counterparts. Mountain bikes can be pedaled over an entire course or, if necessary, be pushed instead of carried.

The sport of mountain biking was enthusiastically adopted in Europe and Australia, and the first world championships were held in 1987. Races were originally over long, cross-country courses, and the riders had to be entirely self-sufficient. Commercial sponsorship has led to pressure for shorter courses with several laps so spectators and television cameras can watch the racers more easily. World championships now consist of cross-country races of about two hours' duration, and downhill races in which competitors wear full-face helmets and body armor. Separate men's and women's events are held. Mountain biking has been incorporated under the UCI and was included in the 1996 Atlanta Olympics.

Women's Cycling

Women have competed in cycling events from the earliest times, but were often excluded during the first part of this century. More recently, the number of women competing in cycling has increased at all levels and in all types of cycle sport. In 1984 women's cycling events were introduced at the Olympic Games, and in the same year the first Tour de France Féminin (Women's Tour of France) was held. Separate record categories have been established for women that broadly match those for men.

Amateur and Professional Cycling

The existence of parallel structures for amateur and professional cycling has at times caused complication, confusion, and some corruption. The Olympic movement clung to the amateur ideal and, as a result, in 1965 the UCI established separate federations. However, the payment of expenses in many sports has led to the breakdown of the distinction between amateur and professional, and since 1993 the UCI has abolished the two federations, replacing them with advisory boards. The UCI now recognizes only open-track records. From 1996 all Olympic cycling events will be open.

—Ron Shepherd

See also Duathlon; Triathlon.

Bibliography: Abt, Samuel. (1989) *In High Gear*. Mill Valley, CA: Bicycle Books.

Alderson, Frederick. (1972) *Bicycling: A History*. Newton Abbott, UK: David and Charles.

Cripps, Cecil. (1990) *Racing the Wind!* Melbourne: Vetsport Promotions.

Henderson, Noel. (1989) *European Cycling: The 20 Classic Races*. Brattleboro, VT: Vitesse Press.

Liggett, Phil. (1992) *The Complete Book of Performance Cycling*. London: Collins Willow.

McGurn, James. (1987) *On Your Bicycle*. London: John Murray.

Nye, Peter. (1988) *Hearts of Lions: The History of American Bicycle Racing*. New York: W. W. Norton.

Ritchie, Andrew. (1975) *King of the Road: An Illustrated History of Cycling*. London: Wildwood Press.

RTTC 1995 Handbook. Ashford, Kent, UK: Geerings.

Smith, Robert A. (1972) *A Social History of the Bicycle*. New York: American Heritage Press.

Wallechinsky, David. (1992) *The Complete Book of the Olympics*. Boston: Little, Brown.

Watson, Roderick, and Martin Gray. (1978) *The Penguin Book of the Bicycle*. Harmondsworth, UK: Penguin Books.

Darts

The sport of darts is a fine example of an activity that has evolved from military training and a historic legacy of soldiering, combat, and armed engagement. Other activities with a similar ancient tradition are javelin and discus throwing, archery, and cross-staves. A modern example might be the Olympic pentathlon, which was developed out of military roots in the Napoleonic era.

Origins

Darts appeared in a variety of historical sources. Darts or "dartes" were in use as early as the Middle Ages. Archers used heavily weighted hand arrows in close combat and even threw them at archery targets for recreation. Anne Boleyn gave a set of darts to her husband Henry VIII and, in the sixteenth century, a popular children's game was "blow-point," in which a type of arrow was forced through a pipe and directed at a numbered target. Amongst the "cultural baggage" transported to the New World, the Pilgrims shipped darts on board the Mayflower.

Due to the concentric rings, medullary rays, and central core displayed in the cross-section, Cuddon (1980) sees the ends of tree trunks as the probable origin of dart boards. The nineteenth-century game of "puff darts" had darts that measured 25 millimeters (1 inch), and they were fired through a pipe or tube measuring 91.5 centimeters (3 feet). The board had a diameter of 177 to 203 millimeters (7 to 8 inches) and was marked out with 20 sectors (just like the modern dart board). The major change, however, is in the numbering sequence on the board.

Development

Darts is primarily a modern and twentieth-century activity. The sport took off as a result of one of the most celebrated cases in "sports law." In 1908 at Leeds Magistrates' Court, England, the judicial system focused on the nature and function of darts. Was it a game of chance or skill? If it was the former it would be prohibited from the domain of licensed premises. However, if it could be proved that the key ingredient was skill then it would be legally admitted into the pub recreational environment. In what must have been a moment of Perry Mason–like drama "Foot" Anakin, the errant publican (he had allowed games of darts to take place inside his pub), turned in a bravura performance. He put three darts in the single 20 and followed this up by throwing three double 20s. For an encore, he repeated this feat by achieving another three double 20s. Not surprisingly the case against Anakin was dismissed and darts in British pubs became legal. More than any other sport—billiards and snooker included—darts has come to be known as *the* premier pub sport.

Darts is played by 6 million people on a regular basis in Great Britain, making it the country's leading participation sporting pastime. In the current world of darts there are pub and club competitions, and tournaments at league, super league, and professional levels. Today, darts are played virtually all over the world. The World Darts Federation World Cup was inaugurated in 1977. A year later that same body instituted the Europe Cup. Both of these championships are held biennially.

The mass media provided a key role in developing darts within Great Britain. Newspapers such as *The People* (now the *Sunday People*) and the *News of the World* sponsored various tournaments that came to be recognized as unofficial regional and national championships. The *News of the World* Individual Championship came to be known as the championship of England and Wales (1947–1948). Scotland did not join this tournament until the 1971–1972 season.

The National Darts Association of Great Britain (NDA) was founded in 1953. The country's first major competition was inaugurated in 1938–1939 and players sought the Lord Lonsdale Trophy. Since 1962 the NDA has supervised this trophy competition as well as three pairs championships (men's, women's, and mixed) and two individual championships (one open, the other for women).

Some idea of the mass grassroots of pub darts can be gained by examining the Lord's Taverners Seven Darts Tourney organized for the Lord's Taverners in 1966–1967. Over 40,000 pubs took part representing a participation force of over one million players. Popular British television series such as *Coronation Street* and *The East Enders*

Known as the premier pub sport, darts is more than a casual pastime; televised tournaments can be as intense as in any other professional sport. Here Dennis Priestly concentrates during the 1996 World Darts Championship.

were, of course, set within the walls of the pub, and dartboards and dartplayers were regularly seen to be a part of the televised cultural mosaic.

Practice

Dart boards are normally made up from bristle, cork, or elm wood. The standard match board is numbered 1 to 20 in the following clockwise sequence: 1, 18, 4, 13, 6, 10, 15, 2, 17, 3, 19, 7, 16, 8, 11, 14, 9, 12, 5 and 20. The board is split into 20 triangular sections which meet two center rings. The outer ring scores 25, and the inner ring (the bulls-eye) scores 50.

The outer ring is divided into 8 millimeter ($\frac{1}{5}$ inch) wide sections which are known as "doubles." A dart landing in one of these sections scores exactly double the value of the respective triangular section. This is also the traditional manner to finish a game of darts. Each player must finish on an exact double of the number required to

win the game. The only exception is if 50 is required to win the game. In that case a "bulls-eye" counts as double 25.

The inner ring (8 millimeters in width) is known as the "treble." All darts landing in this section score three times the value of the respective triangular section. All the other areas of the triangular sections of the dart board, between the double segment and the treble segment, and between the treble segment and the outer ring score the relevant number.

A standard dart board has a diameter of 45.7 centimeters (18 inches). Each player is allocated three darts. The average length of a dart is 15.3 centimeters (6 inches) long. While the point is made of steel, the barrel or midsection of the dart is plastic, wood, or brass. The tail portion is of feathers, paper, or plastic. Professional players and champion amateur players seem fastidious as they search to find the perfect amalgamation of weight and balance in a dart. Unlike shooting and archery, in which fine-tuning can be done throughout a competition (for example, adjusting a sight or tightening a string), the dart remains constant and unchanged throughout the competition. At the end of a round (three darts to be thrown) a high-scoring series of scores would merit the accolade of "good arrows."

In competitions the board is hung in such a way that the center is 1.72 meters (5 feet, 8 inches) above the floor. The darts are flighted in, and fired from, a distance of 2.43 meters (8 feet), 2.59 meters (8 feet, 6 inches) or 2.74 meters (9 feet). The throwing line is called the toe line or the "hockey."

Games begin with a high number and go to zero with competitions opening (and closing) with a double. Standard starting totals are 1001, 501 and 301.

Variations on the standard game include "Darts Baseball," "Fives," "Halve It," "Closing," "Scram," and "Shanghai." A traditional pub favorite and one that lends itself to an informal recreational activity rather than a "serious" sport is "Around the Clock." It is a game with no limit to the number of players. Players take turns, after scoring a double, trying to place a dart in each sector beginning at 20 and working their way down to 1.

The traditional setting of darts—a closed space in which alcohol flows freely and smoking is not discouraged—has created several misconceptions about the sport and its participants. Simon Barnes of the London *Times* observed:

One look at the faces of the contestants tells you all. This is no afternoon jolly, no amateur lash-up. For the players, this is not a sideshow in life: this is life. It is real, it is serious, it is emphatically not a laughing matter. It is career, reputation, ambition and mortgage: darts is as intense as any other professional sport.

Barnes interviewed Rod Harrington, the number 5 seed and the winner of the 1991 World Masters, known as "The Prince of Style" because he plays darts wearing a tie! While Harrington does not require the linear, sculpted body of the triathlete or the cardiovascular system of a distance runner, he does need to be alert, fit, and physically prepared for the competition. Harrington revealed that as a result of the stress of this particular com-

Maori Darts

Darts straddles the ancient and the modern world by means of a cultural conduit. This connection is the concept of darts throwing as a display and performance of a fine motor movement in front of a discerning group of onlookers.

Games-and-play folklorist Elsdon Best established that dart throwing, as a sport, was a traditional Maori activity that was discontinued following European settlement in New Zealand. According to Best, the dart was tossed underhand and the criterion for success was distance, not accuracy. Best is quoted as saying, "Dart-throwing contests were sometimes quite large meetings, social gatherings of the people. Prior to casting his dart, a player would expectorate upon it and recite over it a charm to cause it to make a good flight."

Dart competitions were much more than Maori recreational pastimes. They were a significant episode in Maori storytelling and myth making. In a similar fashion the dart match dominated Samoan sport. Contests were intervillage. They might last for days and include "feasting, drinking, gift exchange, speeches, and ceremony."

—Scott A. G. M. Crawford

petition he had lost 7 pounds (3 kilograms) in body weight. To stay in shape he swims 8 kilometers (5 miles) a week, covering 1,609 meters (1,760 yards) of breaststroke in 40 minutes, a pace equivalent to "a sub-three-hour marathon."

The fastest time for a match of three games of 301 (start with a "double" and end with a "double") was set by Jim Pike (1903–1960) at Broadcasting House, Broad Street, Birmingham, in 1952 with a time of 2 minutes, 30 seconds. The record time for going round the board in "doubles" at the standard 2.7-meter (9-foot) throwing line (recovering his own darts) was set by Bill Duddy at the Plough, Hornsey Road, London, on 29 October 1972. His time was 2 minutes, 13 seconds. Duddy won the "News of the World" Championship in 1968. The shortest recorded time to score 1,000,001 up on one board was 7 hours, 36 minutes set by a team of eight players from the Fox and Grapes Inn, Wakefield, West Yorkshire. As for the marathon record, it once stood at 554 hours, set at the Great Western Hotel, Orange, New South Wales, Australia, during October 1974. The record for a score of 100,001 was achieved in 3,732 darts by Alan Downie of Stornoway, Scotland, on 21 November 1986.

A significant number of players are in agreement about the elusive key element in achieving darts success. The recipe is rhythm and confidence. The returns for such success are modest in comparison to the major sports such as tennis, golf, boxing, tennis, and auto racing. Nevertheless, Rod Harrington spoke of making a profit of £16,000 (approximately $24,000). Darts followers still talk in hushed tones about John Lowe's televised tour de force in winning £100,000 (approximately $150,000) in a knock-out darts tournament.

Organizations

An organizational schism has affected the world of contemporary darts. The British Darts Organization (BDO—25,000 players in 64 countries) and the World Darts Federation (500,000 players in over 50 countries are faced by a breakaway group called the World Darts Council. The BDO has staged the Embassy World Professional Darts Championship and the Winmau World Masters tournament since 1974, and in 1995 it launched the Unipart European Darts Masters. The Skol World Championship was run by the World Darts Council (WDC) while the rival championship was sponsored by the BDO. The WDC felt that, after the momentum of the 1980s, when darts carved out a significant niche in British television, complacency set in, resulting in reduced television exposure and shrinking sponsorship. The real difference between the WDC and the BDO is a philosophical one.

The schism continued to be felt in 1994 as the BDO promoted the Embassy world darts championship at Frimley Green, Surrey, and the WDC launched the Proton Cars world darts championship. The latter offered a purse of £55,000 (approximately $82,500) with the winner receiving £12,000 ($18,000), only about one-third the purse for the Embassy championship.

Phil Taylor, formerly a loyal member of the BDO, won the 1995 Proton Cars world darts championship. The contest claimed to feature the 24 highest-ranked players in the world with 17 Britons, 6 Americans, and 1 Irishman. However, all were members of the WDC. Nevertheless, the Embassy world darts championship, sponsored by the BDO, remains the premier prize in darts—

equivalent of Wimbledon in tennis, the Indy 500 in auto racing, and the Tour de France in cycling. The 1995 Embassy tournament attracted 32 players, 7 of whom are full-time professionals. Of this number 21 were Britons, 6 were Europeans, and 5 were from the British Commonwealth. The total purse was £143,400 (approximately $215,000), with £34,000 ($51,000) going to the winner.

While darts remains primarily a British sport, it enjoys a degree of cosmopolitan exposure, especially in Commonwealth countries. For example, the Australian Darts Council was founded in 1927. The Darts Federation of Australia was created in 1976 to facilitate Australia's entry to the World Darts Federation, which had been set up the previous year. Australia hosted the World Cup in 1985 and has won the Pacific Cup (primarily contested with New Zealand) on four occasions.

There are over 100,000 "darters" in the United States, Puerto Rico, and Guam. The American Darts Organization hosted the 1979 World Cup (the first time that a major championship was held outside of the United Kingdom), and controls a circuit of professional tournaments worth over $1 million a year in purse money.

Darts organizations such as the BDO continue to lobby for acceptance of darts as an Olympic sport—so far without success. Perhaps there is still a question whether darts is truly a sport or merely a pastime.

—Scott A. G. M. Crawford

Bibliography: Barnes, S. (1994) "Mortgage Money Rides on Point of a Dart." *Times* (London), 3 January.

Barnett, S. (1990) *Games and Sets—The Changing Face of Sport on Television.* London: British Film Institute.

Blanchard, K., and A. Cheska. (1985) *The Anthropology of Sport.* South Hadley, MA: Bergin and Garvey.

Cuddon, J. A. (1980). *International Dictionary of Sports and Games.* New York: Schocken Books.

Hickok, R. (1992) *The Encyclopedia of North American Sports History.* New York: Facts on File.

Holmes, R. (1995) Communication from Public Relations Officer, British Darts Organization.

Hunn, D. (1995) "Croft Repels Arrows of Outrageous Fortune," *Times* (London), 8 January.

Levenson, S. (1994) "At the Double," *Times* (London), 9 January.

McWhirter, N., and R. McWhirter. (1995) *Guinness Book of Records.* Enfield, Middlesex: Guinness Superlatives.

Vamplew, W., K. Moore, J. O'Hara, R. Cashman, and I. Jobling. (1992) *Oxford Companion to Australian Sport.* Melbourne: Oxford University Press.

Young, M. ed. (1992) *The Guinness Book of Sports Records, 1992.* New York: Facts on File.

Decathlon

See Track and Field, Decathlon

Definitions

Play, games, and sports are commonly thought to be closely related. Games and sports are usually regarded as forms of contests, although "cooperative games" lack competition, and certain activities, such as rock climbing, swimming, or bicycling, are referred to as sports even when they are noncompetitive. Participation in games, sports, and contests is usually termed "play" even when it does not seem playful or is done professionally. Hence, definitions of play, games, sports, or contests that are applicable in all situations have yet to be devised. The definitions in this discussion represent necessary compromises between inclusivity and exclusivity, that is, what is to be encompassed by the term or concept and what is not.

The Concept of Play

The term "play" is used to describe a variety of activities engaged in by both animals and humans. Play occurs among many species of mammals, a few birds, and possibly some reptiles and fish (e.g., Fagen 1981; Smith 1982). Among playful species, play is normally much more common among juveniles than adults although adult humans are much more playful than adults of any of their feral counterparts. However, some domestic species, such as certain breeds of dogs (e.g., Labrador retrievers) have been bred to retain juvenile playfulness into adulthood.

Among nonhuman mammals, play commonly has the appearance of adult survival-related activities, including fighting, fleeing, mating, and predation. Play rarely occurs under stressful conditions and many observers hold that the play of juvenile animals is part of the process through which requisite adult skills are learned. However, the play of both juvenile and adult humans is much more complicated than that of animals and the attribution of functions to it, such as the practice of adult survival skills, is highly problematic. Indeed, the most formal definitions of human play emphasize that it is nonutilitarian and intrinsically motivated (see, e.g., Huizinga 1955; Caillois 1961; Loy 1968; Guttmann 1978).

The Dutch historian Johan Huizinga defined play as

> a free activity standing quite consciously outside "ordinary" life as being "not serious," but at the same time absorbing the player intensely and utterly. It is an activity connected with no material interest, and no profit can be gained by it. It proceeds within its own proper boundaries of time and space according to fixed rules and in an orderly manner (1955, 13).

Roger Caillois, a French sociologist and literary critic, while simultaneously summarizing and critiquing Huizinga's work, defined play as an activity "which is essentially free, separate, uncertain, unproductive, governed by rules, and make-believe" (1961, 9–10). Susan Birrell (1978, 283–285) argued that if one deleted the redundant attributes ascribed to play by both Huizinga and Caillois, then play is an activity that is "free," "separate," and "fun."

The Concept of Game

Caillois (1961), in criticizing Huizinga's conception of play, contended that Huizinga ignored the unique, irreducible characteristics of different forms of games. Caillois offered a four-fold classification of games based on what he called the player's fundamental attitude. His categories of games included: (1) agon, or competition, such as chess and basketball; (2) alea, or chance, such as craps and roulette; (3) mimicry, or simulation, such as mime and disguise; and (4) ilinx, or vertigo, such as skiing and mountain climbing. Although his game classification has proved useful in analyzing the social functions and corruption of game forms in society at large (Caillois 1961; Loy 1969), Caillois' classification has a number of weaknesses. For example, many activities not usually thought of as games can be classified under one or more of his categories. Further, the same activity can fall into more than one category, thus confounding comparisons among game categories.

One of the most theoretically significant and empirically sound game classifications is that developed by anthropologists John M. Roberts and Malcolm J. Arth and mathematician Robert R. Bush. They defined a game as "a recreational activity characterized by: (1) organized play, (2) competition, (3) two or more sides, (4) criteria for determining the winner, and (5) agreed-upon rules" (1959, 597). They categorized games in terms of how outcomes are usually determined, that is, through physical skill, strategy, chance, or some combination of these. They indicated that (1) games of physical skill must involve the use of physical skill but may also involve strategy and/or chance, (2) games of strategy must involve strategy and may also involve chance but physical skill must be absent, and (3) games of chance must involve chance but both physical skill and strategy must be absent. Most games involve combinations of either physical skill and strategy, such as the various ball games found around the world, or strategy and chance, such as card games. Like Caillois (1961), Roberts, Arth, and Bush illustrated how predominant societal game forms are models of important cultural activities.

Allen Guttmann (1978) contended that the definition of Roberts, Arth, and Bush (1959) does not distinguish between competitive and noncompetitive games, leading to the conclusion that societies without games exist or have existed in the past. Actually, Roberts, Arth, and Bush (1959) distinguish competitive from noncompetitive activities and refer to what some might call noncompetitive games as "pastimes." Of their initial crosscultural sample of 50 societies, 5 were found to lack games by their definition. Later, Roberts and Barry (1976) noted that it was likely no human societies lacked games of physical skill and that the societies reported as lacking games in Roberts, Arth, and Bush (1959) likely either once had games and had lost them or the reports indicating they had no games were simply in error. The separation of competitive games from noncompetitive organized play permits a definition of games that is inclusive, exclusive, and exhaustive. Any activity that fits Roberts, Arth, and

Bush's definition of a game can be classified within the categories of physical skill, strategy, or chance. Since these are outcome determinants, they are not useful in classifying noncompetitive activities that, by definition, have no outcomes.

The Concept of Sport

Games are often thought of as a subset of play, that is, play with rules or organization. In turn, sport is often considered a subset of games (e.g., Guttmann 1978; Sutton-Smith and Roberts 1980; Loy, McPherson, and Kenyon 1978). Guttmann (1978), for example, defines sport as (a) a physical contest (as opposed to an intellectual contest), (b) a type of competitive game (as opposed to a noncompetitive game), and in turn, (c) a type of organized play (as opposed to spontaneous play). Although this is a lucid and appealing delineation of play, game, sport, and contest, McPherson, Curtis, and Loy (1989) point out that (a) not all sport is play (e.g., professional athletes are employed in work); (b) not all sports are games (e.g., competitive swimming or Olympic figure skating are not described as games); and (c) not all contests are playful (e.g., duels and wars constitute contests but not playful ones).

McPherson, Curtis, and Loy (1989, 15) define sport as "a structured, goal-oriented, competitive, contest-based, ludic physical activity." Most sports are played in a circumscribed space designed expressly for the activity and have guidelines that demarcate the duration of the event. Further, many sports are institutionalized and governed by large, complex organizations that delineate objectives, sanction, and administer the sport. Sport is goal-oriented in that clear criteria are usually established to determine success, failure, and standards of achievement. There are three types of competition in sport. First, competition may be direct—opponents (teams or individuals) confront each other. Second, competition may be parallel—opponents take turns or compete in separate areas, such as in track and field events or golf. Third, competition may be against a standard, as in archery, diving, or figure skating. Contest-based means that sport usually involves the demonstration of individual or team superiority in the areas of "speed, endurance, strength, accuracy and coordination" (Weiss 1969, 100). Finally, it is stressed that sport involves physical prowess, although strategy is commonly involved and chance influences all sport outcomes in varying degrees.

In summary, various definitions of play, games, sport, and contest support Birrell's (1978) contention that "sport is a specific form of both play and contest, being a playful contest which may or may not occur in game form and whose outcome is primarily determined through the demonstration of superior physical skill" (307–308). Salter (1980) implies that the degree of "emphasis on victory" represents the continuum of ludic activities ranging from play to games, to sport, to athletics, to, finally, what he calls "terminal contests." Specifically, he suggests that play has no emphasis on victory, games have some emphasis, sport has substantial emphasis, athletics have great emphasis, and terminal contests, such as duels and wars, have total emphasis on victory. Further, as emphasis on winning increases, the element of playfulness in such activities decreases.

—Garry Chick and John W. Loy

Bibliography: Birrell, Susan J. (1978) "Sporting Encounters: An Examination of the Work of Erving Goffman and Its Application to Sport." Ph.D. dissertation, University of Massachusetts, Amherst.

Caillois, Roger (1961) *Man, Play, and Games.* New York: Free Press of Glencoe.

Fagen, Robert M. (1981) *Animal Play Behavior.* New York: Oxford University Press.

Guttmann, Allen (1978) *From Ritual to Record: The Nature of Modern Sports.* New York: Columbia University Press.

Huizinga, Johan (1955) *Homo Ludens.* Boston: Beacon Press.

Loy, John W. (1968) "The Nature of Sport: A Definitional Effort." *Quest* 10: 1–15.

———. (1969) "Game Forms, Social Structure, and Anomie." In *New Perspectives of Man in Action,* edited by R. C. Brown and B. J. Cratty. Englewood Cliffs, NJ: Prentice-Hall, 181–199.

Loy, John W., Barry D. McPherson, and Gerald Kenyon. (1978) *Sport and Social Systems.* Reading, MA: Addison-Wesley.

McPherson, Barry D., James E. Curtis, and John W. Loy. (1989) *The Social Significance of Sport.* Champaign, IL: Human Kinetics Publishers.

Roberts, John M., and Herbert Barry III. (1976) "Inculcated Traits and Game-Type Combinations: A Cross-Cultural View." In *The Humanistic and Mental Health Aspects of Sport, Exercise, and Recreation,* edited by Timothy T. Craig. Chicago: American Medical Association, 5–11.

Roberts, John M., Malcolm J. Arth, and, Robert R. Bush. (1959) "Games in Culture." *American Anthropologist* 61: 597–605.

Salter, Michael A. (1980) "Play in Ritual: An Ethnohistorical Overview of Native North America." In *Play and Culture,* edited by Helen B. Schwartzman. West Point, NY: Leisure Press, 70–82.

Smith, Peter K. (1982) "Does Play Matter? Functional and Evolutionary Aspects of Animal and Human Play." *Behavioral and Brain Sciences* 5: 139–184.

Sutton-Smith, Brian, and John M. Roberts. (1980) "Play, Games, and Sports." In *Handbook of Cross-Cultural Psychology, Volume 4: Developmental Psychology,* edited by Harry C. Triandis and Alastair Heron. Boston: Allyn and Bacon, 425–471.

Weiss, Paul. (1969) *Sport: A Philosophic Inquiry.* Carbondale: Southern Illinois University Press.

Diffusion

Why is it that the young men of Munich, Rio de Janeiro, and Nairobi play soccer while their counterparts in Madras prefer cricket? Why do the Japanese and the Cubans, two peoples who .differ greatly in politics, economics, and culture, share a love of baseball? How, in other words, can we explain national differences in preferences for sports? A German authority, writing in 1989, observed that Africans have taken to soccer because they are "fascinated by everything that is round and can bounce," but this kind of genetic explanation for ludic (from *ludus,* Latin for game) difference is clearly absurd. Closer to the mark is the notion of a "cultural fit" between a sport and a nation. Baseball, wrote Charles Peverelly in 1866, "is a game which is peculiarly suited to the American temperament and disposition." The trouble with this explanation is obvious; it implies that Danes and Brazilians, equally addicted to soccer, share a common "temperament and disposition."

If neither the intrinsic properties of a sport nor the match between those properties and some alleged "national character" is sufficient to account for the popularity of a sport, what does? The diffusion within a country from one social class or geographical region to another is a complicated matter, but the pattern of ludic diffusion from one country to another is relatively clear. The key, quite simply, is the relative political, economic, military, and cultural power of the nations involved. A nation that exercises political or economic or military power usually, but not always, exercises cultural power as well.

The reason that cricket and soccer are among the world's most widely diffused team games is that both of these sports received their modern form at a time when Great Britain, where both sports originated, was unquestionably the world's most powerful nation. Britannia ruled the waves and British ships carried cricket bats and soccer balls to the ends of the earth. Enthusiasm for the Tour de France and similar races in Belgium, Spain, and Italy proves that the French, too, had their sphere of cultural influence. In the late nineteenth century, when the United States began to challenge Great Britain's global hegemony, baseball became popular in Japan and in the Caribbean. After World War II, from which the United States emerged as the dominant actor on the global stage, Europeans suddenly discovered the joys of basketball and volleyball, sports invented 50 years earlier in Springfield and Holyoke, Massachusetts, respectively.

Cricket was the first modern ball game. Its rules were codified in 1744 and the Marylebone Cricket Club—the game's most authoritative institution—was founded in 1787. Between these two dates, the British decisively defeated the French in a series of imperial conflicts fought principally in Asia and North America. By the time Nelson's victory at Trafalgar in 1805 and Wellington's at Waterloo in 1815 confirmed British hegemony, men (and occasionally women) of British birth or ancestry were playing cricket in Philadelphia and New York as well as in Toronto, Kingston, Adelaide, and Cape Town. As part of the British effort to pacify and to administer the Indian subcontinent, viceroys like Lord Curzon and missionary educators like C. E. Tyndale-Biscoe taught cricket to the sons of Indian princes. (It was not always easy. Hindu boys were horrified when their teachers admitted that cricket balls were made of leather, a material that was "jutha" or "unclean.")

Cricket continues to be popular throughout the Commonwealth, but it has never been widely played elsewhere except among men and women claiming British birth or descent. Soccer, not cricket, was destined to become the world's most popular sport. In 1848, a century after the birth of

This basketball game between Mexico and the Philippines at the 1936 Olympics is an example of the cultural influence of the United States in the twentieth century.

modern cricket, fourteen collegians who had played a number of different ball games at Eton, Harrow, Rugby, Winchester, and several other schools, met in Cambridge and agreed upon a common set of rules that enabled them to play together. When the Football Association was formed in 1863, soccer got its name (derived from "association football"). Great Britain was then near the zenith of its imperial power.

The year that the Football Association was founded, Cyril Bernard Morrogh, an Irish pupil from Killarney, introduced soccer to his Belgian classmates at the Maison de Melle, which catered to scions of the nobility and the upper middle class. Konrad Koch, an eighteen-year-old anglophile student at Braunschweig's Gymnasium Martino-Katharineum brought the game to Germany in 1874. Pim Mulier, a Dutch boy who had studied at an English boarding school, founded the Haarlemsche Football Club in 1879. Although Englishmen living in France had been playing soccer as early as 1864, it was not until twenty years later that boys from the Ecole Monge and other Parisian schools began to imitate them. By 1896, soccer had reached Hungary. It was introduced by Charles Loewenrosen, a schoolboy whose parents had emigrated to England, when he returned to Budapest on a holiday visit.

In Italy, schoolboys played less of a role than they did in France, Germany, Hungary, and the Low Countries. British sailors introduced soccer in the 1880s when they docked and went ashore in Genoa, Leghorn, Naples, and other peninsular ports, but it was Britons "in trade" in Turin and Milan, the industrial and financial centers of northern Italy, who first organized viable teams. Initially, the teams were composed entirely of Britons. Then, in 1887, Edoardo Bosio, a businessman from Turin, visited England and discovered the game, which he promptly introduced to the employees of his firm. By 1898, there was a Federazione Italiana del Football.

British merchants, bankers, railroad manufacturers, and educators diffused soccer throughout Latin America, an area that well into the twentieth century was dominated by British capital and entrepreneurial expertise. The Argentine story is typical of Latin America. The wool trade brought Thomas Hogg, owner of a Yorkshire textile factory, to Buenos Aires. The energetic merchant helped to found a British commercial center, a British library, a British college—and a cricket club (in 1819). His sons Tomas and James created the Dreadnought Swimming Club (1863) and the Buenos Aires Athletic Society (1866). Then, on 20 June 1867, the Hogg brothers were the mainstay of Argentina's first soccer team. The game received another important impulse when Alexander Watson Hutton arrived from Scotland in 1881 to join the faculty of St. Andrews College (in Buenos Aires). It was not long before the sons of the anglophile Argentine elite began to play the game, which they learned while studying in England or at the several English secondary schools in their own country. By 1901, there was an Argentine Association Football League.

In Mexico, British mine owners and other businessmen established a cricket club in 1827. By the time that U.S. investors in the Mexican economy

surpassed British entrepreneurs in the value of their holdings, which occurred in 1890, baseball had already made an appearance. As British influence waned, U.S. influence waxed, and baseball became Mexico's most popular sport. The game had already spread to Cuba. Among upper-class Cuban youths sent to study in the United States was Nemesio Guillot, who is said to have introduced baseball to Havana when he came home in 1864. The first historically attested game was reported in *El Artista* on 31 December 1874. (Havana beat Matanzas by a score of 51–9.) Cuban patriots who fled their homes after the failure of their first war for independence (1868–1878) sought solace in baseball during their exile in Santo Domingo. They sowed the seeds from which today's crop of Dominican major leaguers was grown.

The 1870s were also the years when Japan, closed for centuries to Western influence, opened its ports and began to modernize. After the Meiji Restoration (1868) that returned political power from the Tokugawa family to the emperor, U.S. educators were invited to reform the Japanese educational system. Horace Wilson, teaching at what is now Tokyo University, introduced baseball in 1873. The game spread relatively slowly, but three prestigious universities—Meiji, Keio, and Waseda—formed an intercollegiate league in 1914. In 1936, two years after a memorable tour by a U.S. team that included George Herman "Babe" Ruth, a professional league was launched.

Basketball, invented in 1891 by James Naismith at Springfield's YMCA Training School, reached the Far East a mere four years later when Willard Lyon established the first Chinese YMCA at Tientsin. Lyon's colleagues carried the game to the Philippines and to Japan. Their efforts to propagate basketball bore early fruit. When Elwood Brown, a boundlessly energetic exemplar of "muscular Christianity," staged the first Far Eastern Championship Games, in Manila in 1913, basketball was part of the program.

Other YMCA workers attempted to interest Europeans in the newly invented game, but they made little headway until World War I, when the United States became a military ally of Britain, France, and Italy. Elwood Brown was among the YMCA workers who accompanied the American Expeditionary Force sent to do battle against the Germans. He suggested that the military victory achieved in 1918 be celebrated by Inter-Allied

Games. General John Pershing agreed. The basketball tournament that was part of the program concluded when U.S. servicemen defeated a team of French soldiers, who had just learned the game, by a score of 93–8.

Between 1918 and 1939, the most important development in the global diffusion of modern sports was the progress of the Olympic Games. When Pierre de Coubertin, a French aristocrat, revived the ancient games at Athens in 1896, all but 2 of the approximately 300 athletes were Europeans or North Americans. Among the Olympians, there was 1 Chilean and 1 Australian. The 3 Africans who sailed to London for the 1908 games were white, as were 19 of the 21 Africans who competed in Stockholm in 1912. The other 2 were an Egyptian fencer and an Algerian marathon runner. That year, female swimmers and divers were allowed to strive for Olympic glory (most of which went to the Australians). In 1928, at Amsterdam, women competed in gymnastics and in track-and-field sports. The Los Angeles games of 1932 were another breakthrough, from the point of view of ludic diffusion. An Argentine, Juan Zabala, won the marathon—Latin America's second gold—and Japanese swimmers astonished the world by winning 11 of a possible 16 medals in their events. It was not until after World War II that Kenyans and other representatives of sub-Saharan Africa began to play a prominent role at the Olympics. The International Olympic Committee itself began, in 1894, with twelve European members, an American, an Argentinian, and a New Zealander. Asian members were added in 1908 (Turkey) and 1909 (Japan). The first Africans, both of European descent, were elected in 1910 and 1913. It was not until 1981 that the first women were elected to the International Olympic Committee.

Among the more startling developments of the postwar period has been the penetration of typically American games into areas that were once dominated by sports of British, French, or German origin. In Spain, Italy, Belgium, and Turkey, basketball is the second or third most popular sport (after soccer). The 32 teams of Italy's professional league draw two million fans a year to their games. The French still prefer soccer, rugby, and cycling, but they have become increasingly fascinated by surfboards, rollerblades, hanggliders, and other artifacts of *les sports californiens.*

In Australia, Japanese sponsors (who control a significant number of the nation's golf courses) have joined the Cincinnati Reds, the California Angels, and six other U.S. clubs in establishing an eight-team professional baseball league (1989).

The most intriguing sign of a further shift in the global balance of ludic power is the popularity in Great Britain of American football (a game derived, ironically, from British rugby). Two years after the birth of the London Ravens in 1983, a 38-team British American Football League was formed. Anheuser-Busch, which has underwritten Channel 4's production costs for telecasts of National Football League games, organized a semiprofessional Budweiser League that grew to nearly 200 teams by 1988. The next step in the march of conquest took the NFL to the European continent, where Trans World Sport has arranged for television coverage of nascent football leagues in France, Germany, Italy, Spain, and a number of other countries. In 1991, the NFL launched a World League of American Football that included teams representing London, Barcelona, Frankfurt, and several U.S. cities. The venture faltered and was suspended but has now been revived as a purely European league.

Will the London Monarchs ever be the equal of the San Francisco Forty-Niners? Perhaps not, but other teams have turned the ludic tables and "beaten them at their own game." When Australian cricketers vanquished the English at the London's Oval in 1882, they simultaneously affirmed their membership in the British Empire and their claim to a national identity of their own. When a team of schoolboys from Tokyo challenged and defeated the overconfident U.S. baseball players at the Yokohama Athletic Club, in 1896, the joyful news was telegraphed the length and breadth of Japan. Similar scenes have been enacted countless times.

Despite the pleasure to be obtained from "beating them at their own game," the global diffusion of modern sports from Great Britain and the United States (and, to a lesser degree, from France) has not been universally acclaimed. In parts of the Islamic world, fundamentalists have attempted to stop the spread of women's sports and other manifestations of Western influence. European defenders of traditional sports have formed organizations, like the Vlaamse Volkssport Centrale (1980), to preserve and revive folk games. Radical scholars writing from a Marxist perspective had condemned the displacement of older ludic forms as "cultural imperialism" or as "cultural genocide."

The radical critique of ludic diffusion tends to overlook the fact that there is probably no such thing as an "authentic" traditional culture. All but the most remote and isolated cultures borrow and adapt from one another. While it is true that the more powerful nations have what might be termed a favorable balance of ludic trade, they too import sports from abroad. The popularity of Asian martial arts among the middle classes of Europe and the United States is a case in point. It is also true that those who have adopted a foreign sport have usually adapted it (which is exactly what Americans did when transforming rounders into baseball and rugby into gridiron football). Even when adopters are not adapters, they come to feel that the sport they have borrowed is their very own, an authentic expression of who they are. People follow the fortunes of their team at the World Cup because they believe that soccer is *their* game and the players are representatives of them as a nation. It is doubtful, when Brazilians celebrated their World Cup triumph in 1994, that many of them worried about Charles Miller's role, a hundred years earlier, in bringing the game to São Paulo from England. Soccer is, in the words of Pele, "the greatest joy of the people." And something similar can be said about modern sports wherever they are played.

—Allen Guttmann

Bibliography: Arbena, Joseph L., ed. (1988) *Sport and Society in Latin America: Diffusion, Dependency, and Mass Culture.* Westport, CT: Greenwood Press.

Baker, William J., and J. A. Mangan, eds. (1987) *Sport in Africa.* New York: Africana.

Bale, John, and Joseph Maguire, eds. (1993) *The Global Sports Arena.* London: Frank Cass.

Bottenburg, Maarten van. (1992) "The Differential Popularization of Sports in Continental Europe." *Netherlands Journal of Social Science* 28, 1 (April): 3–30.

Bottenburg, Maarten van. (1994) *Verborgen Competitie.* Amsterdam: Bert Bakker.

Guttmann, Allen. (1994) *Games and Empires: Modern Sports and Cultural Imperialism.* New York: Columbia University Press.

Hick, Daniel, ed. (1992) *L'empire du sport.* Aix-en-Provence, France: Centre des Archives d'Outre Mer.

Lanfranchi, Pierre, ed. (1992) *Il calcio e il suo pubblico.* Naples: Edizioni Scientifiche Italiane.

Mangan, J. A. (1986) *The Games Ethic and Imperialism.* New York: Viking.

Mangan, J. A., ed. (1992) *The Cultural Bond: Sport, Empire and Society.* London: Frank Cass.

Olivera, Eduardo A. (1932) *Origenes de los deportes britanicos en el Rio de la Plata.* Buenos Aires: L. J. Rosso.

Roden, Donald. (1980) "Baseball and the Quest for National Dignity in Meiji Japan." *American Historical Review* 85, 3 (June): 511–534.

Rummelt, Peter. (1986) *Sport im Kolonialismus, Kolonialismus im Sport.* Cologne: Pahl-Rugenstein.

Stokvis, Ruud. (1989) "De Populariteit van Sporten," *Amsterdams Sociologisch Tijdschrift* 15, 4 (March): 673–696.

Wagner, Eric A., ed. (1989) *Sport in Asia and Africa.* Westport, CT: Greenwood Press.

Disabled Sports

The evolution of sports for persons with disabilities began after World War II, when service-connected injuries such as paraplegia, quadriplegia, and amputation increased significantly. Sports and recreation were recognized as important components of the rehabilitation process. Therapists and physicians in many countries use participation in vigorous physical and recreational activities as an integral part of rehabilitation. Sport integrates the individual into society and helps to enhance self-esteem. In today's world, sport for the disabled is much more than therapy. It is a means by which athletes with disabilities can attain a high level of physical fitness and compete with fellow athletes from all over the world. Today the athlete with disabilities is an athlete, not a patient.

In contrast to the Special Olympics, which serve mentally retarded youth and adults, the Paralympics are for athletes with physical and sensorial disabilities. Physical disabilities in the sports and disabled athletes movement include spinal cord injuries, amputations, blindness, cerebral palsy, and les autres conditions (the others), such as arthritis, osteogenesis imperfecta, and dwarfism. Many countries have national research and training centers to provide the environment, facilities, and equipment that allow athletes with disabilities the optimal setting for training and conditioning for their specific sports.

Many countries discriminate against persons with disabilities and treat them as social outcasts. Crowds at sport competitions for athletes with disabilities are often sparse, with spectators limited to family, friends, and fellow athletes. Numerous sport-minded societies may view the athlete with a disability as not being a "real" athlete. In contrast, in 1984 Claudine Sherrill wrote, "The ultimate athlete can be anyone, disabled or able-bodied, who demonstrates the capacity to dream, the unwavering intent to be the best, and the willingness to pay the price of long, hard and strenuous training."

Jim Mastro, a gold medalist in swimming at the 1984 International Games for the Disabled with impaired vision, compared the status of athletes with disabilities with that of women athletes in the late nineteenth century; Baron de Coubertin, organizer of the first modern Olympic Games in 1896, did not approve of "women perspiring in public, assuming positions he deemed ungainly, and appearing in public riding horses, skiing, or playing soccer." During the years when women were denied inclusion in the Olympics (1886–1928), the female gender was ideally characterized as modest, chaste, obedient, and submissive. The idea of women publicly competing in sport not only repulsed much of the general public but was contrary to the Olympic philosophy. Accepting ancient Greek thought that only the male body could be both athletic and beautiful and that only the movement of males could meet the Olympic criterion of an aesthetically pleasant image to watch, women were denied the right to compete. As recently as 1981, the International Olympic Committee (IOC) was described as neither fostering nor assisting in the expansion of women's sports, at least in comparison with men's sports. It was not until the 1984 Olympics that women were finally allowed to compete in a marathon; previously, the IOC had been fearful that the physical strain of such a grueling event would be too much for the delicate female body.

The Greeks did not recognize beauty in any physical form unless it was healthy and whole. Confucian traditions put inordinate stress on outward appearances. Often persons with disabilities have been shunned and viewed as inferior. Will the sophisticated and often spoiled sports fan ever view the performance of a paraplegic, blind, or cerebral palsied athlete as skilled and graceful and worthy of inclusion in the Olympics? Spectator attendance at modern-day Paralympics and Special Olympics support the idea that athletes with physical and mental disabilities are indeed worthy of watching.

Sport shifts the focus from the athlete's disability to his or her ability. Helen Keller said, "It is not enough to give the handicapped life; they must be given lives worth living." Thousands of athletes with disabilities will support and verify the role of sport in making their lives fulfilling and worth living.

Origins and Development

The oldest of international organizations on sport for persons with disabilities is the Comité International des Sports des Sourds (Committee International on Silent Sports) (CISS). It was founded in 1924 in conjunction with the first international competition for athletes with disabilities, the World Games for the Deaf in Paris. In conjunction with this event, CISS has conducted Summer World Games every four years since 1924 and Winter World Games since 1949.

In 1944 the National Spinal Injuries Centre of the Stoke Mandeville Hospital in Aylesbury, England, was founded. Wheelchair sports were included as part of the rehabilitation process of war veterans. Ludwig Guttmann introduced England's first organized wheelchair sports program on the front lawn of the Stoke Mandeville Hospital in 1948. Those activities are known as the Stoke Mandeville Games. Guttmann expanded these games to include bowling, table tennis, and field events in which wheelchair athletes competed. After 1960, weightlifting, fencing, and swimming were added. Not only were these games successful in terms of athletic participation, but it became increasingly apparent that many psychological benefits, such as an increase of self-confidence, began to surface in the participants.

The first Stoke Mandeville Games for the Paralyzed included 16 former servicemen and women. In 1952 the first annual international sports festival for those spinally paralyzed was conducted, with the Netherlands bringing a team of ex-servicemen to Stoke Mandeville. For over 40 years, the Stoke Mandeville Games have provided opportunities for athletes with physical disabilities—especially those with spinal cord injuries who must participate in wheelchairs—to compete against each other.

Dr. Guttmann traveled to the United States to meet Benjamin H. Lipton in the 1950s. Lipton was the director of the Joseph Bulova School of Watchmaking, a school where individuals with disabilities were trained as watchmakers and technicians, and coach of the school's athletic team. Guttmann and Lipton discussed the future of wheelchair athletics in the United States. Lipton is recognized as the father of wheelchair athletics in the United States.

In 1958, as a result of the first National Wheelchair Games held in the United States, the National Wheelchair Association (now called Wheelchair Sports, USA) was organized. Its function was the establishment of rules and regulations governing all wheelchair sports, with the exception of basketball, which was governed by the National Wheelchair Basketball Association, founded in 1949. During this same time period Guttmann founded the International Stoke Mandeville Games Federation (ISMGF), which governed the international games.

In 1960 the First International Games for Disabled that were of an Olympic nature were held in Rome for spinally paralyzed athletes under the auspices of the International Stoke Mandeville Games Federation. This marked the beginning of the Olympics for the Disabled, which were held every fourth year in the same country (if possible) as the Olympic Games from 1960 through 1980. After 1980, the International Olympic Committee requested that disabled athletes no longer use the term Olympics, and the games continued under the name Paralympics. Twenty-three countries sent 400 athletes to Rome to compete in traditional sports such as basketball, tennis, fencing, track and field, as well as some newly invented sports such as dartchery. Ironically the Olympic village was completely inaccessible and wheelchair athletes had to be carried up a flight of stairs to enter the accommodations. Pope John XXIII granted a private audience to all participants and exclaimed, "You are the de Coubertin of the paralyzed."

The 1968 Olympics for the Disabled were hosted by Ramat Gan, Israel, while Mexico City hosted the Olympics. Twenty-nine countries sent a total of 750 competitors to this second Olympics for the Disabled competition. Wheelchair basketball was a popular sport with the spectators, and 5,000 people attended the finals to watch the host country defeat the United States 49–40 for the gold medal. General Moshe Dayan presented the awards.

Meanwhile, Eunice Kennedy Shriver founded Special Olympics in 1968 to help erase misconceptions about people with mental retardation. After a fact-finding tour of the United States she learned that the people with the greatest unmet needs in the nation's health care system were those with mental retardation. When she opened her Rockville, Maryland, backyard to 100 mentally retarded children and adults in 1963, little did she realize how far it would evolve.

Special Olympics was established to provide year-round sports training and athletic competition in a variety of Olympic-type sports for children and adults with mental retardation. It is founded on the belief that people with mental retardation can, with proper instruction and encouragement, learn, enjoy, and benefit from participation in individual and team sports, adapted as necessary to meet the needs of the participants. Sports training and competition is offered in 23 Olympic-type sports (summer sports, winter sports, and demonstration sports) open to anyone ages eight and up.

Toronto, Canada, hosted the 1976 Olympiad for the Physically Disabled (following the Montreal Olympics) with 38 countries officially participating and 100,000 spectators paying to attend. For the first time in history, blind and amputee athletes were invited to compete, in addition to the spinally paralyzed.

In 1980 the Olympics for the Disabled was held in Arnhem, the Netherlands, with 2,000 athletes from 42 countries competing. Moscow hosted the 1980 Olympics that many countries boycotted, including the United States. For the first time in international competition for athletes with disabilities, cerebral palsied athletes were invited to participate, but the invitation was limited to those who were ambulatory. Inclusion of all the disability groups not only increased the visibility of wheelchair sports by increasing athletic participation, it also accelerated public support through expansion of local, regional, national, and international competitions.

Over the years the increase in the number of sports for the disabled was not without growing pains. It was not until after the 1980 Olympics for the Disabled that the sport technical and medical committees permitted certain classes of spinal cord–injured athletes to race in distances over 400 meters. Similarly, quadriplegics, until 1981, could not compete internationally in track events longer than 200 meters. While basketball, swimming, and archery have been practiced by athletes with disabilities for a number of years, only recently have such sports as tennis, wheelchair rugby (murder ball), volleyball, and winter skiing become popular. These changes came about as a result of pressure from athletes, coaches, and scientists.

The United States and International Olympic Committees issued a formal statement in 1981, rejecting the use of the term Olympics to describe competition by disabled athletes with the exception of Special Olympics, Inc., which is exclusively for mentally retarded persons. Subsequently, Paralympics was the term of choice to replace the term Olympics.

The United Nations declared 1981 as the International Year for Disabled Persons. As a result of the Universal Declaration of Human Rights, Declaration of the Rights of the Child, Declaration on the Rights of Disabled Persons, and the Nils-lvar Sundberg Declaration, all aspects of the lives of persons with handicapping conditions have been greatly enhanced. It is the responsibility of all persons to assure that the education of individuals with handicapping conditions becomes an integral part of cultural development and that equal access to leisure activities becomes inseparable from social integration.

For the first time in Olympic history in 1984, at the Los Angeles Olympics, two wheelchair races were included as demonstration events. Sixteen wheelchair athletes representing eight countries competed. The women's wheelchair 800-meter (875-yard) race was won by Sharon Rahn Hedrick of the United States with a time of 2:15.50. The men's wheelchair 1500-meter (1604-yard) race was won by Paul Van Winkle of Belgium with a time of 3:58.50. There was no paucity of spectators as over 90,000 cheering fans yelled their appreciation for the astounding physical performance of the elite male and female wheelchair racers who competed. The television audience numbered over 1.5 billion viewers. The underlying purpose of hosting demonstration events at the Olympics

Moussetapha Badid of France crosses the finish line in the Wheelchair Division of the 1988 Boston Marathon.

is to seek the integration of sports for athletes with disabilities into the international sports movement for able-bodied athletes while preserving the identity of sports for disabled athletes.

Many Americans involved in the sports for athletes with disabilities movement were bitterly disappointed and deeply embarrassed that the United States could not work out the logistics and funding for the host city of the Olympics to sponsor and stage the first Paralympics held in the United States. Because Los Angeles was unable to host the 1984 Paralympics, the International Games for the Disabled was held on Long Island, New York.

Following the Seoul Olympics in 1988 the Paralympics were held in Seoul, Korea. The credo of the games focused on several themes: challenge and overcoming; peace and friendship; participation and equality. Security was extremely tight to guard the safety of the athletes. Despite organizing the best and largest Paralympics up to this point, South Korea is one of numerous countries that has discriminated against its handicapped in very determined ways. Government officials have acknowledged that the more than one million disabled South Koreans rarely have been seen or heard over the past few decades, isolated from society and treated as embarrassing social outcasts who are a burden to their country. Byun Jae Il, a top official of the Seoul Paralympic Organizing Committee stated, "To be a democratic society all of the isolated people must be included in the society."

The 1988 Seoul Paralympics were an important step in gaining worthy recognition of their disabled. Over 70,000 spectators witnessed the opening ceremonies. A grand festival of art and culture was an integral part of Paralympic activities. The growing importance of the Paralympic Games was further underlined when various events were broadcast with great success by television channels from all over the world. A budget of $26 million was required to stage the Seoul Paralympics.

Over 4,000 athletes from 60 countries participated in the Seoul Paralympics. Three hundred and seventy world records were set, in addition to over 600 Paralympic records. For the first time in the history of disabled sports, athletes with disabilities were selected for participation in IOC drug testing. Athletes were screened under the same procedures in place for able-bodied competitors.

Special sports included Goalball (for blind and visually impaired athletes), which uses a 5-pound (2.3-kilogram) ball with bells in it hurled by three members of each team into the opponent's goal. Guide runners assisted blind and visually impaired runners in competing in track events. Tandem biking allowed blind and visually impaired athletes to team with sighted riders to compete in cycling. Other sports included judo, swimming, table tennis, wheelchair tennis, weight lifting, wheelchair basketball, sitting and standing volleyball for athletes with amputations, boccia, fencing, and equestrian events.

Since the Amateur Sports Act was passed in the United States in 1978, athletes with disabilities have been integrated into a variety of national and international sports events generally reserved for athletes without disabilities. The

U.S. Olympic Festival has provided impetus to the sports for disabled athletes movement by inclusion of a variety of events for athletes with disabilities. Participation by athletes with disabilities has been an integral part of these games since 1985. Demonstration events in 1985 included swimming for blind and visually impaired athletes and for spinally paralyzed athletes; weight lifting for the spinally paralyzed and for athletes with cerebral palsy, and wheelchair basketball. In 1986 cycling for amputee athletes and for athletes with cerebral palsy were added along with gymnastics for mentally impaired athletes. In track and field, spinally paralyzed, blind, and deaf athletes competed. Additions in 1987 were wrestling for blind and deaf athletes, standing volleyball for amputee athletes, and wheelchair tennis. Each year the U.S. Olympic Festival expands the inclusion of sports for athletes with disabilities.

At the 1990 Olympic Festival athletes from the Special Olympics took part in two demonstration events in swimming. As the athletes entered the University of Minnesota Aquatics Center they were greeted by a standing ovation and television cameras. Sellout crowds of over 3,000 people attended the aquatic events. Integration with able-bodied athletes is perhaps the greatest benefit for athletes with disabilities.

The culmination of the hard work and perseverance of the athletes, coaches, and support staff associated with wheelchair athletics was displayed at the 1992 Paralympics in Barcelona, Spain. The 1992 Paralympic logo, "Sports Without Limits," was designed to express the effort to create full social integration of people with disabilities through participation in sporting events. Improved access and independence were the anticipated results of a positive public impact that the display of world class athleticism would showcase through the Games.

An estimated 60,000 spectators and millions of television viewers witnessed the opening ceremony; which was similar to the one at the Olympics. At both events, Paralympic archer Spaniard Antonio Rebollo shot a flaming arrow across the length of the stadium and lit the Olympic flame. Sixty-two countries were represented by approximately 3,000 athletes competing in 16 sports over a 14-day period. Numbers such as these are a true representation of the progression of athletes with disabilities through-

Disabled Sport in Film

Traditionally sports movies highlight greater, rather than lesser, champions. However, there are other movies that deserve attention because they highlight the role of the handicapped in our society and the ways in which the disadvantaged can be allowed to succeed.

In the history of cinema, there have been many controversial films. One early movie that achieved notoriety was Todd Browning's bizarre 1932 story entitled *Freaks*, about a traveling circus sideshow. Browning assembled a real-life cast of handicapped, deformed, and disfigured performers. Film historian Ephraim Katz, described the film thus: "Midgets, dwarfs, armless and legless living beings, sword swallowers and bearded ladies provided some of the most ghastly and grotesque sights in film history."

Hollywood, in its early years, highlighted the macabre aspects of the handicapped, whether it was Charles Laughton as the hunchback Quasimodo in *The Hunchback of Notre Dame* (1939), or the facially scarred Lon Chaney in *The Phantom of the Opera* (1925). A strong case can be made that in the early years of cinema handicapped people were ignored, portrayed in melodramatic and exploitative scenarios, or treated condescendingly as minor figures.

In the last two decades there has been a remarkable cultural renaissance for the handicapped. The following short list of films shows the extent to which handicapped people can succeed in quite extraordinary ways. These movies may not necessarily examine sporting themes, but in each of them are a series of cameos, vignettes, or subplots in which sport (or physical activity or athletic competition) occupies center stage.

One Flew Over the Cuckoo's Nest (1975). A story about the institutional trauma of living in a mental hospital. A basketball game orchestrated by Jack Nicholson and starring Native American Will Sampson is brilliantly conceived as both radical protest and social catalyst.

The Other Side of the Mountain, Parts I and II (1975 and 1977). The story of the rehabilitation of U.S. skier Jill Kilmont, who was paralyzed in a racing accident.

The Eleanor and Lou Gehrig Story (1978). The moving story of Lou Gehrig's amazing baseball career and the courage that he displayed in coming to terms with amyothrophic lateral sclerosis, the illness that eventually killed him.

The Terry Fox Story (1983). Based on the true-life story of an amputee who, in his celebrated "Marathon of Hope," very nearly ran the 3,000 miles across Canada. Fox is enshrined in Canada's National Sporting Hall of Fame.

Champions (1984). An account of English steeplechase jockey Bob Champion (John Hurt) and his fight to keep riding horses in the face of the onslaught of cancer.

My Left Foot (1989). Daniel Day-Lewis played the part of Christy Brown, who became a recognized artist and writer despite severe cerebral palsy. The film has nothing to do with sport yet sport provides a moment of cinematic excellence. As film critic Roger Ebert wrote: "There is an early scene in which Christy's brothers and other neighbor kids are playing soccer in the street, and crippled Christy, playing goalie, defends the ball by deflecting the ball with his head. There is great laughter and cheering all round, but the heart of the scene is secure: This child is not being protected in some sort of cocoon of sympathy, but is being raised in the middle of life, hard knocks and all."

—Scott A. G. M. Crawford

out the world. The Honorary President of the Paralympic Games was Her Majesty the Queen of Spain.

The United States won a total of 176 medals (76 gold), with Germany second (171 total; 61 gold), followed by Great Britain. The same sports venues used in the Olympic Games were used in the Paralympic Games. The opening and closing ceremonies for both events were held in the Estadi Olimpic de Montjuic. The mascot (Petra) for the Paralympics was created by avant-garde artist Javier Mariscal, one of Spain's leading designers. Petra is an armless yet cheerful, daring, friendly girl, full of strength and a bit stubborn.

Shooting took place at the $70 million Catalunya Police Academy. Shooters fired at targets containing an electronic sensing system, which transmitted the shot's position and point value to a television monitor that was visible to the shooter and the audience. In weightlifting, Kim Brownfield of the United States set a Paralympic record in winning the gold with a lift of 551 pounds (250 kilograms), which was below his world record of 606 pounds (275 kilograms). Basketball teams played before sellout crowds of over 12,000 screaming fans. With its exciting, rough and tumble nature, wheelchair basketball is a popular spectator sports in the world. It is also a sport whose rules and strategies are well understood by the world at large. The Canadian women won the gold medal game over the Americans. The United States won the men's gold medal 39–36 over the Netherlands, only to have their gold medals taken away from them when one of the players tested positive for a banned substance. The controversy continues as drugs rules that were developed for Olympic athletes are applied to athletes with physical disabilities, many of whom require a multitude of medications to control a variety of problems not encountered by able-bodied athletes.

Over 7,000 athletes representing 140 countries converged on New Haven, Connecticut, to participate in the 1995 Special Olympics World Games. The Olympic torch was delivered from Athens, Greece, to the opening ceremonies at the Yale Bowl. U.S. President Bill Clinton took part in the ceremony and ABC's *Wide World of Sports* provided coverage of the games, along with other networks. For the first time the World Games included a marathon, along with a variety of sports such as badminton, cycling, equestrian events, roller skating, softball, and volleyball.

Outlook

The 1995 Special Olympics World Games left a legacy that stretches far beyond the usual. That legacy consists of the record number of individuals with mental retardation competing, the millions of spectators who witnessed the event on television and in person, and the number of sports and competitions featured. Perhaps most significantly, these games showcased the abundance of sports and recreation opportunities now available for individuals with mental retardation.

One of the most notable of these new opportunities is Special Olympics Unified Sports, a program that combines, on the same team, athletes with and without mental retardation. The aim of Special Olympics Unified Sports is to provide Special Olympics athletes the opportunity for meaningful training and competition with teammates who do not have disabilities. The careful selection of teammates who are similar in age and ability ensures that Unified Sports participants play important and valued roles on the team. The program provides a forum for positive social interaction among teammates that often

leads to long-lasting friendships. "What 'Games of Inclusion' really means is that more Special Olympics athletes than ever before are being accepted as individuals in every aspect of our program," said Dr. Tom Songster, director of sports and recreation at Special Olympics International (SOI). "The exciting part is watching them take their Unified Sports experiences into other areas of their lives, such as school, work and their communities. Sports is simply the vehicle."

First introduced at the 1991 International Special Olympics Summer Games in Minneapolis, Special Olympics Unified Sports began with just three sports and 100 athletes. Only four years later, eleven sports, including for the first time golf, sailing, basketball, tennis, and the marathon, will feature Unified competition. More than 1,000 Unified athletes and partners will compete together, and the numbers continue to grow.

Unified Sports has been especially successful in schools, where teachers and administrators have struggled for years to find a way to bridge the gap between students without disabilities and their special education peers. George Smith, director of sports training and education at Special Olympics, says Unified Sports is one answer, noting that the program "provides an opportunity for people to have a common ground, and what better common ground than sports?"

Currently there is a growing movement toward Unified Sports in both Special Olympics and organizations governing sports for athletes with physical disabilities, whereby both athletes with disabilities and able-bodied individuals can participate together. It is apparent that inclusion of athletes with disabilities serves to display the true meaning of sport and that all should be provided equal opportunity to participate.

The 1996 Atlanta Paralympics on 16–25 August 1996, held immediately after the 1996 Summer Olympics, may have been to the disabled sports movement what Los Angeles 1984 was to the Olympic movement in the United States—bringing media attention, awareness, and sponsorship to the Games and providing a funding base for disabled sports. The theme was "The Triumph of the Human Spirit." A four-year plan to prepare for the Atlanta gamess included workshops, clinics, training camps, junior programs, coaching certification programs, and research conducted at the national and international level. The Atlanta

Paralympics brought together nearly 4,000 elite athletes with physical or visual impairments, representing over 100 nations. Athletes competed in 19 sports, 14 of which were Olympic sports. Most of the venues used in the Olympics were also used for Paralympic competition. New Paralympic sports include wheelchair racquetball and quad rugby. Other sports included the Olympic sports of athletics, basketball, cycling, swimming, judo, shooting, equestrian, fencing, table tennis, archery, soccer, and tennis. Sports unique to the Paralympics include boccia, powerlifting, goalball, and lawn bowling.

—Mary E. Ridgway

Bibliography: Adams, R. C., and J. A. McCubbine. (1991) *Games, Sports, and Exercises for the Physically Disabled.* 4th ed. Philadelphia: Lea and Febiger.

Alger, S. L. (1992) "Sports without Limits: Barcelona '92." *Sports 'N Spokes* 18, 4: 12–33.

Allen, A. (1981) *Sports for the Handicapped.* New York: Walker and Company.

Daniels, J. L. (1981) "World of Work in Disability Conditions." In *Rehabilitation Counseling,* edited by R. M. Parker and C. E. Hansen. Boston: Allyn and Bacon, 169–199.

DePauw, K. P. (1984) "Commitment and Challenges: Sports Opportunities for Athletes with Disabilities." *Journal of Physical Education, Recreation and Dance* (February): 34–35.

———. (1990) "PE and Sports for Disabled Individuals in the United States." *Journal of Physical Education, Recreation and Dance* (February): 53–57.

Hopper, C. A. (1984) "Socialization of Wheelchair Athletes." In *Sports and Disabled Athletes,* edited by C. Sherrill. Champaign, IL: Human Kinetics, 197–202.

Janes, M. (1995) "Special Olympics." *Exceptional Parent* (May): 56–57.

Labanowich, S. (1987) "The Physically Disabled in Sports." *Sports 'N Spokes* 12, 6: 33–42.

Mastro, J. (1985) "Psychological Characteristics of Elite Male Visually Impaired and Sighted Athletes." Ph.D. dissertation, Texas Woman's University.

Monnazzi, G. (1982) "Paraplegics and Sports: A Psychological Survey." *International Journal of Sports Psychology* 13: 85–95.

Ryckman, R. M., M. A. Robbins, B. Thornton, J. A. Gold, and R. H. Kuehnel. (1985) "Physical Self-Efficacy and Actualization." *Journal of Research in Personality* 19: 288–298.

Sherrill, C. (1984) "Social and Psychological Dimensions of Sports for Disabled Athletes." In *Sports and Disabled Athletes,* edited by C. Sherrill. Champaign, IL: Human Kinetics, 21–33.

———. (1986) *Adapted Physical Educational and Recreation.* 3d ed. Dubuque, IA: Wm. C. Brown Publishers.

Sherrill, C., B. Gench, M. Hinson, T. Gilstrap, K. Richir, and J. Mastro. (1990) "Self-Actualization of Elite Blind Athletes: An Exploratory Study." *Journal of Visual Impairment and Blindness* (February): 55–60.

Sherrill, C., T. Gilstrap, K. Richir, B. Gench, and M. Hinson. (1988) "Use of the Personal Orientation Inventory with Disabled Athletes." *Perceptual and Motor Skill* 67: 262–266.

Spears, B. (1981) "Tryhosa, Melpomene, and Nadia: The IOC and Women's Sport." In *Olympism,* edited by J. Segrave and D. Chu. Champaign, IL: Human Kinetics, 81–88.

Steadward, R., and C. Walsh, (1984) "Training and Fitness Programs for Disabled Athletes: Past, Present, and Future." In *Sports and Disabled Athletes,* edited by C. Sherrill. Champaign, IL: Human Kinetics, 3–17.

Stein, J. U. (1982) "New Vistas in Competitive Sports for Athletes with Handicapping Conditions." *Exceptional Educational Quarterly* (May): 28–34.

Warehime, R. G., D. K. Routh, and M. L. Foulds. (1974) "Knowledge about Self-Actualization and the Presentation of Self as Self-Actualized." *Journal of Personality and Social Psychology* 30, 1: 155–162.

Diving

J. A. Cuddon indicates that in classical literature, there were references to diving, especially in the spheres of fishing and warfare. In the eighteenth and nineteenth centuries, diving was popularized by the Germans and the Swedes, who, because of their affection for gymnastics, took various pieces of apparatus (for example, the swinging trapeze) to the beach and used these to perform gymnastic stunts prior to entering the water.

Competitive diving began in Great Britain in 1883 with the Amateur Swimming Association setting up the first plunging competition. The plunge was a headfirst crouching dive, rather after the fashion of the modern racing dive off starting blocks at the start of a swim race. "The idea was to travel (float) motionless and face-downwards as far up the pool as possible within a minute. Large, heavy and fat men were particularly successful" (Cuddon 1979).

The first actual diving competition took place in Scotland in 1889. Six years later the Royal Life Saving Society held the inaugural National Graceful Diving Competition. Springboard and platform diving was admitted in 1904 to the Olympic program as a men's event. Women took part, for the first time, at the 1912 Stockholm Olympics.

Diving has flourished throughout the twentieth century and is now an integral part of swimming competitions held at all manner of international sports festivals. It is on the program at the European and World Championships, the Commonwealth Games, and the Pan-American Games. During the 1970s and 1980s the most successful divers (men's and women's events) were from the United States, Italy, Germany, and the then Soviet Union. In recent years, young Chinese divers have come to threaten seriously the U.S. domination of this activity.

English swimming authority Pat Besford articulates an apt and evocative definition of what constitutes diving: "This complicated sport demands acrobatic ability, the grace of a ballet dancer, iron nerve, and a liking for heights."

Origins

One of the earliest historical remnants indicating the existence of diving is dated 480 B.C.E. Called "Tomba del Tuffatore" (the "tomb of the diver"), it is a huge burial chamber to the south of Naples, Italy, that houses, high up on a roof slab, a painting of a male athlete diving from a small elevated platform.

It is generally accepted that the first book on diving was written by a German, H. O. Kluge, and published in Germany in 1843. While this comprehensive guide listed and described a wide variety of dives, it did not provide either teaching tips or a series of skill progressions for the diver. However, the former Yale diving coach Phil Moriarty, in an introduction to his coaching text *Springboard Diving*, describes a much earlier reference to diving in a 1595 book entitled *Master Digbie's Book of the Art of Swimming*. This manual gave the would-be diver an explanation of how to dive underneath the water:

> He must, if he be in a place where he may stand upon the ground, with as much force as he can, leap up, and bending his head toward his breast, fall forwards downe into the water. . . . His hands he must hold before his head, with their backs together (Moriarty 1959).

The Swedish divers Johannson, Hagberg, and Mauritzi came to London during the late nineteenth century and entertained crowds with exhibitions of what was called "fancy diving" from a 10-meter (11-yard) platform erected at Highgate

One of the earliest portrayals of diving, "Tomba del Tuffatore" (Tomb of the Diver), was found in a fifth-century B.C.E. burial chamber in Naples, Italy.

Ponds. These exhibitions inspired the 1901 formation of the world's first official diving organization, called the Amateur Diving Association.

Springboard diving was on the program for the first time at the 1904 St. Louis Olympics and platform diving was introduced at the 1906 Athens Olympics. It should come as no surprise that when the sport first became an Olympic event, it was called "fancy diving" because of the wide range of shapes, body positions, and aerial movements maintained by the divers.

Practice

Today the Fédération Internationale de Natation Amateur—the world governing body for aquatics—lists nearly 90 different types of dives that may be performed at various levels of difficulty. Some of the basic dive types, as outlined in *Olympic Gold 84* (Barber 1984), are as follows: forward dives with the body facing the water and the dive made forward; backward dives with the back to the water and rotating away from the board or platform; reverse dives with the diver facing forward, but the rotation of the body back towards the board; inward dives with the back to the water and rotating inward towards the board or platform; twisting dives made from either starting position with the body twisting in the air; armstand dives made from the platform only—the diver begins the movement sequence from a motionless handstand on the platform's edge.

There are, according to *Olympic Gold 84*, a series of body positions: tuck, pike, straight, and free. Tuck means that the body is bent at the knees and at the hips, with the knees held together and drawn to the chest; pike means that the body is bent at the waist with the legs straight; straight means that the body is not bent; and free refers to a combination of two or more of these body positions. The springboard is 4.9 meters (16 feet) long and 51 centimeters (20 inches) wide. Springboards are balanced on moveable fulcrums that can be adjusted, altered, and calibrated until they are at a perfect level of tension. In watching springboard divers as they warm up on their board, doing a series of preliminary steps, jumps, and bounces, the analogy that comes to mind is of string instruments being fine-tuned for a symphony orchestra performance.

A key element in the art and science of diving is a sports characteristic that it shares with gymnastics—that is, a degree of difficulty as a scoring factor. The standard Olympic Diving Table rates the toughness of dives from a low of 1.2 to a high of 3.5. For example, the reverse three-and-one-half somersault is rated a 3.5 degree of difficulty, the highest for any springboard dive. The degree of difficulty factor means that an uncomplicated dive done flawlessly may score as well as the most advanced of dives performed poorly.

As indicated, the judging of gymnastics and diving employ similar criteria. In diving, a panel of seven judges awards points according to the following highly subjective formula:

- Failed dive—0 points;
- Unsatisfactory dive—.5--2 points
- Deficient dive—2.5–4.5 points
- Satisfactory dive—5–6 points
- Good dive—6.5–8 points
- Very good dive—8.5–10 points

After the score numbers have been displayed on cards, the high and low scores are discarded. The remaining scores are then multiplied by a factor of three-fifths and by the degree of difficulty of the particular dive. Greg Louganis retained his platform Olympic title in 1988 by performing an excellently executed dive that also had a listed superior degree of difficulty (see sidebar). The judges on that occasion gave the American one 9.0, five 8.5's, and one 8.0.

Diving is a bruising activity. Platform divers are more missile than body as they hurtle through the air to hit the water at speeds of as much as 80 kilometers (50 miles) per hour. Micki King of the United States won a gold medal at the 1972 Munich Olympics. However, four years earlier at Mexico, she had broken her left forearm when she smashed into the board, ending up out of the medals. America's premier female diver and a four-time Olympic winner, Pat McCormick, dived her way through a career interrupted by broken fingers, cracked ribs, and an assortment of serious cuts and bruises.

Leigh Montville examined the diving-related health problems of the U.S. diver Mary Ellen Clark, who won a bronze medal at the 1992 Olympics. Her coach, Ron O'Brien (who also coached Greg Louganis), speaks of divers in reverential tones. He likens divers to people who are not afraid to jump out of planes:

The platform divers are simply the ones who don't need parachutes. The impact of diving from the tower is so substantial that most platform divers practice no more than 30 dives in a day and then stay away from the platform for two days to let their bodies heal. Joints become stiff. Shoulders separate. This is not a sport for the timid (Montville 1995).

Mary Ellen Clark happens to suffer from vertigo, a form of dizziness accompanied by extreme anxiety that has seriously disturbed her life and training for several years. It threatened to prevent the 32-year-old from being a U.S. trialist for the 1996 Atlanta Olympics. She has tried acupuncture, homeopathic remedies, and antiseizure medicines, all to no avail. O'Brien, her coach, in conversation with other coaches, learned of three other lower-level divers with the same ailment. They did not return to diving. Clark remains determined to conquer the vertigo, as evidenced by her interview with Montville: "I want to get back. I'll try anything. I'll try them all at once. I'm giving this the

Diving

Greg Louganis

The greatest American diver of all time is Greg Louganis. He won both the springboard and the platform diving events at the 1984 Olympics in Los Angeles. Four years later at the age of 28 he repeated this feat at the Seoul Olympics. While he was expected to do well at the 1988 Olympics—indeed he was the pre-meet favorite—he will always be remembered for how he coped with adversity. With only a few dives remaining in the competition, Louganis set out to do a demanding dive (a reverse two-and-one-half somersault in the tucked position), but one that was well within his range of ability.

It wasn't routine this time. As he spun backward the second time, it became apparent he hadn't jumped far enough off the board. It became particularly apparent to his head, which struck the board. The symmetrical dive suddenly turned into one you see all the time at the local plunge, arms and legs out of sync as the diver . . . enters the water (United States Olympic Committee 1988).

Despite being badly shaken, Louganis had his head gash sealed with four stitches. He was able to continue competing but found himself engaged in a neck-and-neck tussle with Tan Liangde, a diminutive young man from China, who had defeated Louganis twice in the 1988 swim season. Liangde finished his final dive sequence with an excellently executed inward three-and-one-half somersault in the tuck position.

The pressure on Louganis was tremendous. Nevertheless, he responded magnificently and was greatly helped by the fact that his concluding dive was classified, by the judges, as the most difficult dive of the platform competition. The final combined score differential of 2.14 points gives a clear picture of the narrow margin of victory and the closeness of the competition. Louganis won the gold medal with a score of 638.61, Liangde took the silver with 637.47. Louganis became the first diver to win the springboard and platform diving event at back-to-back Olympics.

In the official United States Olympic Committee report, writer Frank Litsky penned a most insightful and moving account of the life of Louganis, underscoring the picture of a boy growing up in the face of not one but many personal and social problems. He was the illegitimate son of two fifteen-year-olds in California and was adopted when eight months old. In his elementary school years he enjoyed dance, gymnastics, and drama and began diving as a nine-year-old.

As a young teenager he stuttered, was a poor reader (it was eventually determined that he was dyslexic), and was ridiculed because of his Samoan heritage. Diving afforded him a forum to show what he could accomplish. Apart from his four Olympic gold medals, Louganis won five world championships (1978, 1982, 1986) and collected a total of forty-seven indoors and outdoors U.S. titles.

Litsky quotes Louganis describing what he felt was his finest achievement, which was to give up smoking:

When I was 23, I saw a 12 year old diver smoking at poolside. I asked him why he was smoking, and he said "I want to be just like you." It really had an impact. It finally hit me that I have a responsibility to other people. So, I stopped smoking right then (United States Olympic Committee 1988).

Following the 1988 Olympics Louganis attempted to launch himself on an acting career with mixed results. The 1994 revelation that like the basketball great "Magic" Johnson, he was HIV-positive, and that he had been aware of his condition at the time of his head injury at Seoul, created considerable comment and controversy. The opening sentences of Litsky's biographical sketch of Louganis are even more poignant in light of his HIV-positive status: "His early life was a nightmare. His later life made athletic history." His coach, Ron O'Brien, is quoted as saying, "We'll never see another like him in our lifetime" (United States Olympic Committee 1988).

—Scott A. G. M. Crawford

best shot, as far as it goes" (Montville 1995). She won the bronze medal at the 1996 Olympics.

Men's springboard diving (the 3-meter [10-foot] board) has been marked by the enduring presence and depth of U.S. diving. For example, at both the 1932 and 1964 Olympics the three medal winners were from the United States. This can be traced primarily to the impact of well-funded and strongly supported university- and community-based swim programs in states such as California and Florida.

In a similar fashion, in platform diving (from a 10-meter-high fixed platform), the United States has been enormously successful. Nevertheless, the most brilliant diver prior to the Louganis era was the Italian Klaus Dibiasi. He won gold at three Olympics (Mexico City, Munich, and Montreal). He missed out on a gold medal at the Tokyo Olympics by the narrow margin of 1.04 points. The Italian was a hard-working perfectionist with a six-day-a-week training regimen and 130 to 150 dives per day.

In women's diving, while the United States has been a consistent medal winner, the 1970s, 1980s, and 1990s have illustrated the strength of women's diving in the Germanys, the various Soviet republics, Cuba, and China. The 1950s were blue-ribbon years for the United States, with the national team taking a clean sweep of the platform diving medals at the Helsinki and Melbourne Olympics.

Wallechinsky (1984), in his commentaries on women's springboard diving, gives a number of colorful cameos on the stories "behind the scenes." Such evocative writing enables the reader to see beyond the statistical boundaries of competition and get some sense of the athletic subculture, the social milieu of a given period, and the human dynamics—including interpersonal relationships—in the world of competition diving. For example, Wallechinsky describes 28-year-old air force captain Micki King taking two hours to produce a urine sample for the drug-testing process and then quaffing wine with three Australian weight lifters during her post-tournament celebration. Concerning the 1920 Antwerp Olympics, the commentary is concise yet full of fascinating material, such as this biographical sketch of Aileen Riggin:

> Tiny Aileen Riggin of Newport, Rhode Island, was only 14 years old when she won her Olympic gold medal. In 1922 she was the subject of the first underwater and slow motion swimming films. She returned to the Olympics in 1924 and won a silver medal for springboard diving and a bronze in the 100-meter (109-yard) backstroke. Later she turned professional, acted in movies, and starred in Billy Rose's first Aquacade (Wallechinsky 1984).

Pat McCormick dominated women's diving in the 1950s. The *New York Times*, describing her brilliant form at the 1952 Helsinki Games in the springboard event, spoke of "the petite blond wife of the Washington Senators outfielder, Jackie Jensen" shaking off the upset of the theft of $300 in cash and a diamond wristwatch from her room on the eve of the final round of dives" (Brown 1979). Four years later Pat McCormick, the mother of an infant son, regained her springboard title at the Melbourne Olympics.

Mrs. McCormick gave her finest demonstration of her mastery of the board on her final effort, which brought a roar of approval from the delighted crowd. Her back one-and-a-half with a one-and-a-half twist was executed flawlessly and she cut the water with scarcely a splash (Brown 1979).

Diving competitions, as with gymnastics and figure skating events, have a history plagued by acrimonious exchanges over accusations of unfair scoring. At the 1956 Olympics in Melbourne the head coach of the U.S. men's diving team, Karl Michael, accused the Russian and Hungarian judges of colluding. Michael felt that this bias allowed Joaquin Capilla of Mexico to win the gold medal. Capilla agreed with the view and was quoted as saying that the diving was a competition between the judges and not the divers. As a result of this controversy, new rules were introduced that dictated that (1) scoring would be done electronically (judges would no longer hold up cards), (2) no national coaches would serve as judges, and (3) if judges were deemed incompetent they could be removed from the panel during the judging.

While divers of Greg Louganis's caliber make a career out of cloaking complex diving routines in a mantle of effortlessness, the sport is incredibly technical. In *Diving: The Mechanics of Springboard and Firmboard Techniques* (1969), physicist George Eaves endeavors to simplify the mechanical and kinesiological intricacies of diving. The title of Appendix VII shows that this is no easy matter: "The motion of a free falling body, neglecting air resistance, can be regarded as two independent motions, being the accelerated motion of the center of gravity and the rotations about axes through the center of gravity."

The world record high dive of 53.9 meters (176 feet, 10 inches) was performed by Oliver Favre of Switzerland in France on 30 August 1987. The women's record is 36.8 meters (120 feet, 9 inches), by American Lucy Waidle in Hong Kong on 6 April 1985.

Since 1960, ABC's television program *Wide World of Sports* has established itself as a leader in spotlighting unusual and especially daring physical activities. It was this program that brought the high divers of Acapulco into the living rooms of millions of Americans. At La Quebrada (The

Break in the Rocks) outside of Acapulco, Mexico, divers plunge 26.7 meters (87 feet) into the water. But there are two caveats. The water that they land in is only 3.7 meters (12 feet) deep. Moreover, the base of the rocks sticks out 6.4 meters (21 feet), forcing the divers to leap out at least 8.2 meters (27 feet) (the distance leaped by an Olympic finalist in the men's long jump event!) to avoid maiming themselves. Timing the dive with the ebb and flow of the ocean wave plays a key role in achieving a successful dive.

In terms of awesome human feats, nothing can match the soaring bodies on Pentecost Island (part of the New Hebrides chain in the South Pacific). There the Melanesian inhabitants do land diving from heights of 7 to 24 meters (25 to 80 feet), assisted by long lanai ropes tied around their ankles and securely fastened to the diving platform.

> The ceremony and pageantry do not overshadow the fact that land diving is also a sport. A man's proficiency in diving off the platform is a measure of his courage and manliness; he competes against himself, the forces of nature and his fellow tribesmen (Blanchard 1995).

—Scott A. G. M. Crawford

Bibliography: "Another Day, Another Dive." (1995) *Economist* 337 (28 October): 7938.

Arlott, J., ed. (1975) *The Oxford Companion to World Sports and Games.* London: Oxford University Press.

Barber, G., ed. (1984) *Olympic Gold 84.* Kensington, New South Wales: Bay Books.

Blanchard, K. (1995) *The Anthropology of Sport.* Westport, CT: Berain and Garvey.

Brown, G., ed. (1979) *New York Times Encyclopedia of Sports: Volume 12.* Danbury, CT: Grolier Education Corporation.

Carlson, L. H., and J. J. Fogarty. (1987) *Tales of Gold: An Oral History of the Summer Olympic Games.* New York: Contemporary Books.

Cuddon, J. A. (1979). *The International Dictionary of Sports and Games.* New York: Schocken Books.

Eaves, G. (1969) *Diving: The Mechanics of Springboard and Firmboard Techniques.* New York: A. S. Baines and Company.

Froboess, F. (1956) *Fell's Official Guide to Diving.* New York: Frederick Fell.

Montville, L. (1995) "Vexed by Vertigo." *Sports Illustrated* 83, 6 (7 August).

Moriarty, P., with C. Sparks (1959). *Springboard Diving.* New York: Ronald Press Company.

Rooney, J. F., Jr., and R. Pillsbury. (1992) *Atlas of American Sport.* New York: Macmillan.

Smith, D., with J. H. Bender. (1973) *Inside Diving.* Chicago: Henry Regnery Company.

United States Olympic Committee. (1988). *Seoul-Calgary 1988.* Sandy, UT: Commemorative Publications.

Wallechinsky, D. (1984) *The Complete Book of the Olympics.* New York: Viking Press.

Zucker, H. M., and L. J. Babich. (1987) *Sports Films.* Jefferson, NC: McFarland.

Drag Racing

During the 1930s, in the early days of the Great Depression, in Southern California, before cars had become a national obsession but after they had become commonplace, the idea of playing with the power of old Model A and Model T Fords was born. Southern California was a natural place for this birth, being the coast that had ended migration westward (thereby forcing those inclined to find limits to do so in new ways), and having both terrain and climate conducive to testing a car's ability to accelerate.

Young men began beefing up old junkers and testing them. Two guys, their cars side by side, waiting for the light to change at an intersection, revved their engines, challenging each other to a duel: who could get away quickest? Unable to catch up to the cars they pursued, the police could not stop the game. The threat of restrictive legislation led to a search for suitable, and safe, venues for races. This led to races on the bed of Muroc Dry Lake, and then to being officially timed in 1937 by the Southern California Timing Association (SCTA), which imposed strict penalties on members found guilty of drag racing on streets.

Development

In 1950 the SCTA ran a hot rod-versus-motorcycle race at a former naval air field near Santa Ana, California. The success of this event led to more local air-strips becoming available as drag strips. In 1951 *Hot Rod* magazine proposed a much needed National Hot Rod Association (NHRA), whose regulations would ensure nationwide con-

Drag Racing

The stereotypical hotrodders racing from a red light were the forerunners of today's professional drag racers. This "slingshot" is just one of many styles of racing vehicle.

formity of requirements. Thus the NHRA was born and oversaw the booming development of the sport through the 1950s. Over a period of 25 years, drag racing became, under the auspices of the NHRA, a regionally popular spectator sport, a lucrative sport for the winners, and a highly organized motor sport with very strict safety regulations devised in conjunction with the Specialty Equipment Manufacturers Association (SEMA). International recognition was granted to the sport in 1965 when it was finally accepted by the Fédération Internationale de l'Automobile. Drag racing also exists in somewhat more restricted form in Australia, Canada, England, Germany, Italy, Japan, New Zealand, and Sweden, but it has never achieved the professionalism nor the popularity internationally that it has in the United States. Americans do not just love the cars available to wealthy people; we love that which replaced the horse in providing mobility, access,

and independence. Whether or not it is a matter of survival in any given situation, it is often in our best interest or perhaps in the very nature of living things to be able to be bigger than, better than, stronger than, or faster than our competition. Drag racing is the marriage of our fondness for our "wheels" and our instinctive drive to win.

Everything from street cars to motorcycles to highly engineered race cars are used for drag racing. The most highly engineered cars produce up to 1,500 horsepower. In U.S. drag racing, engine capacity is limited to 800 cubic inches. There are several different competition classes, divided for example by the type of fuel used into "gas" (ordinary pump gas) and "fuel" (methanol or nitromethane [top fuel]), or categorized by the type of car driven, e.g., an unmodified car off the assembly line or a modified version.

What has evolved into the pure dragster (also called a "rail" or a "slingshot"), is a long chassis built of metal tubing, with two small bicycle-like tires in front and two massive, treadless tires in the rear, all of which support a 1,000–1,300 pound (455–591 kilogram) motor, mounted in this era, behind the driver and between the rear wheels. A "funny car" (or "flopper") is basically a "rail" with a fiberglass body—made to resemble a flashy passenger car—that lowers over the cockpit, driver, and engine. The faster cars have at least one attached parachute that the drivers open at the end of each run to assist the brakes in stopping the vehicles. Cars must meet exacting technical standards for their competition class and go through a technical inspection prior to each race. Drivers are licensed by the NHRA and must wear SEMA-approved safety equipment, including fireproof suits, gloves, boots, and helmets with face shields.

Practice

The race track itself consists of a two-lane paved strip one-quarter mile (402 meters [440 yards]) in length (plus a "shut-down" area of at least 200 meters [220 yards]), and at least 15 meters (50 feet) in width. There is a separate road for cars returning from the track to the pits. Some drag strips have elaborate, banked turn-outs at the finish end of the track for getting cars off the track quickly at the end of a race, and some have gigantic nets at the end of the track for catching the occasional runaway car whose brakes have failed or whose parachute has not opened.

At the start of a race, two competitors line up side by side on the starting line. A "Christmas Tree" (a pole with a vertical series of lights) stands 20 feet down the course from the drivers, dividing the lanes. The top light is red, the next five are yellow, the sixth green, and the seventh red. The drivers start their engines, spin their rear tires until they are hot and tacky, and maneuver their cars so that the front wheels break an infrared light beam—part of a timing device that is connected to another set of lights at the finish—ensuring that neither driver has a distance or time advantage. The lights descend the Christmas Tree blinking on and off at half second intervals. When the green bulb lights up, the cars leave from a standing start attempting to beat each other, or sometimes the clock, to the finish line. Starting before the green light is on illuminates the bottom red light and disqualifies the driver. Straying out-

side one's marked lane also disqualifies the driver. As each car crosses the finish line it breaks another light beam stopping the clock and recording the elapsed time (ET) for that car. The car then passes through another light beam connected to the finish line, recording the car's peak speed. The first car to break the timing light beam on the finish line, wins. In amateur categories the ET is occasionally modified by a time handicap system in which the ET is adjusted to include the time advantages given to the slower cars within the class. Racers compete in a series of elimination rounds against other cars in their class, ultimately resulting in one winner.

Getting off the starting line quickly is essential and cannot be done without the superb reflexes of the driver. If the driver "pops" the clutch, the car's front end can rise right off the ground, which is a showy but aerodynamically poor move. If the driver accelerates too slowly, the competition will never be caught. Much of this ability to "launch" depends on the drivers' skills, but drivers are dependent upon the abilities of the mechanics who work constantly on the cars in the pits between rounds, fine-tuning clutches and transmissions and sometimes replacing an entire engine in less than an hour.

Although the goal of the race is to cross the finish line first, records are kept of the peak speeds reached in an area beginning 66 feet (20 meters) before the finish line and ending 66 feet after it. It is possible to lose a race but capture an event's speed record.

Professional drag racers are people who support themselves by drag racing; by often receiving expense money and appearance money as well as by sometimes winning the prize money. The professionals are, as a group, intense, competitive, and agile, exhibiting on the starting line the ability to contain what must be an explosive amount of adrenaline as the lights descend the Christmas Tree, and on the track Zen-like concentration, sheer guts, and physical strength. Professional classes of drag racing have become so expensive to compete in, due to the costs of high-tech equipment and spare parts necessary to remain competitive, that from year to year there are dozens, not thousands, of competitors in the elite levels. These cars usually have either one major sponsor—such as "The Hawaiian," Don "The Snake" Prudhomme's car, sponsored for years by the U.S. Army—or a number of sponsors whose decals or logos ornament the cars.

However, one of the reasons for the sport's popularity is that spectators tend to identify with the participants and can also race themselves, if licensed to, even in the family car. Thus, the highest percentage of racers competes in the "sportsman" classes, made up of people who earn their living doing something else, but who compete, sometimes against the professionals, for the prize money.

The average drag racer is a male between the ages of 20 and 40. But an increasing number of drivers are women, including superstar Shirley "Cha Cha" Muldowny (1940–) who set the women's world record for the lowest elapsed time—4.974 seconds—at the NHRA Keystone Nationals at Reading, Pennsylvania, on 17 September 1989.

Among the most famous U.S. drag racers is Don "Big Daddy" Garlits (1932–)—the first to exceed 200 miles per hour—who has broken his back and been badly burned in a variety of engine explosions. The lowest elapsed time (ET) recorded by a piston-engined dragster from a standing start to 440 yards (402 meters) and the NHRA record is 4.799 seconds by Cory McClenathan (1963–) at the NHRA Keystone Nationals at Reading, Pennsylvania, on 26 September 1992. The first terminal speed over 300 miles per hour (483 kilometers per hour) was achieved by Kenny Bernstein (1944–) who hit 301.70 miles per hour (485.44 kilometers per hour) in a qualifying round at Gainesville, Florida, on 20 March 1992.

Drivers collect points in a series of races throughout North America culminating in the Winston Finals. The NHRA obtains its major ET (elapsed time) and terminal speed (miles per hour) records from the NHRA Winston Series races and other specified record meets. The NHRA continually updates the records in these classes: Top Fuel Eliminator, Funny Car Eliminator, Pro Stock Eliminator, Pro Comp Eliminator, Modified Eliminator, Super Stock Eliminator (both standard shift and automatic transmissions), Stock Eliminator (standard and automatic), and one-eighth mile. Since 1960 when the NHRA began record-keeping, the speed with which the records are surpassed has itself increased.

For the spectator, drag racing events are exciting even in the pits—which are accessible to the

The Pits

Leading up to and between racing events the pit crew working on a fuel dragster might be found scouring junk yards for school bus engine blocks, or preparing the dragster trailer for the next racing event by stocking it with everything from compressed air to head gaskets. At a race the pit crew is responsible for making the car run perfectly; for towing the car to the starting line and starting it, because these cars have been stripped to the bare bones for weight and have no starters; for pushing the car back to the starting line, because, again to save weight, most of the cars have no reverse gear; for towing the car from the finish end of the track back to the pits; and for doing anything to the car that needs doing between runs. Since the driver knows how the car is running, how the clutch feels, and so on, the driver and pit crew work together to improve on the car's performance. When there is no problem to attend to, the pit crew does routine maintenance; changing the oil and filter, refueling, putting in new spark plugs, adjusting the tire pressure, and always refolding and repacking the parachute, which will not open if it has been folded or packed improperly. Sometimes a blower (equivalent of a carburetor), an engine block, or heads must be changed. As the racing event progresses, contestants are eliminated, quickening the time between elimination rounds. If a major engine job needs to be done under this kind of time pressure, the pit crews work feverishly against the clock in order to get their car back on the starting line in time for the next run. An interesting aspect of drag racing is that a good deal of camaraderie exists between the racers, and an eliminated driver and crew can often be found helping another crew get their car back on the starting line, ready to race.

—Brooke Dyer-Bennet

public—where one can get a close-up view of famous drivers and their highly skilled crews hard at work between rounds. Spectating at a drag race includes experiencing the thunderous sound waves of powerful engines, watching quick, colorful elimination rounds, and inhaling the aromas of hot rubber and fuel. Drag racing is a sprint rather than a marathon and appeals to people who are thrilled by a combination of mechanical ability, lightning reflexes, power, and courage.

—Brooke Dyer-Bennet

Bibliography: Arlott, John. (1975) *The Oxford Companion to Sports and Games.* London: Oxford University Press.

Hickok, Ralph. (1995) *A Who's Who of Sports Champions: Their Stories and Records.* Boston and New York: Houghton Mifflin.

Menke, Frank G. (1975) *The Encyclopedia of Sport.* 5th ed. South Brunswick, NJ, and New York: A. S. Barnes and Co.

National Dragster. (1960–) Glendora, CA: National Hot Rod Association.

Dressage

See Horseback Riding, Dressage

Drugs and Drug Testing

The use of performance-enhancing drugs in sport attracted wide public interest when Ben Johnson's moment of glory after winning a gold medal and setting a new world record in the 100 meters (109 yards) at the 1988 Seoul Olympics was followed by the ignominy of a positive drug test. The sudden emergence of Chinese swimmers in 1994 and their rapid decline in 1996 startled many and once again focused media attention on possible drug use.

Drug use, commonly referred to as "doping," is defined by the International Olympic Committee (IOC) as "the administration of or use by a competitive athlete of any substance foreign to the body or any physiological substance taken in abnormal quantity or taken by an abnormal route of entry into the body with the sole intention of increasing in an artificial and unfair manner his/her performance in competition." The word *dope* is either derived from the French *du* (to dip or layer) or, more likely, from the Dutch *dop,* a spirit made from grape skins. The phrase *Dutch courage* refers to the taking of an alcoholic beverage or drug (or a *dop*) before undertaking a difficult or unpleasant task. This practice is what we consider doping today.

Of what benefit is doping? In broad terms doping measures are either ergogenic (work enhancing) or anabolic (growth stimulating). Short-term effects are generated by taking drugs such as stimulants or by undergoing blood transfusions just prior to the sporting event to enhance performance. In certain events such as shooting or archery, (beta) blockers are taken to slow down the heart rate and reduce hand tremors. Diuretics may be used to lose weight and so enable competitors to participate in lower weight categories in sports such as wrestling, or they may be used to help mask the use of drugs. Effects of drugs may be sustained over the longer term, by administering the drugs during training on a regular basis. These are usually hormones such as anabolic steroids and growth hormones (or their derivatives or analogues) or hormones that induce natural anabolic steroid production. The effect of such anabolic drugs combined with rigorous strength training programs is to cause an increase in lean muscle mass, and apparently greater physical strength. Similarly, the hormone erythropoeitin may be used during the buildup to the competition phase of training to increase the number of circulating red blood cells, which improves endurance.

What drives doping in sport? The spectrum of answers ranges from individual prestige in being the best to merely wanting to improve personal appearance. Prestige encompasses national and personal esteem and that of the coach and or institution that produces the successful athlete. There is also the matter of keeping up with those competitors who are *already* doing better through doping. The underlying reason for doping in competitive sport can usually be traced to monetary and personal gain. The aspiring U.S. high school football player can look forward to a university scholarship with free education and the possibility of a lucrative professional career, while the athlete from a Third World country may get to travel and see the world and at the same time provide for a better standard of living for less fortunate family members back home.

The list of banned substances varies from sport to sport, but those that are prohibited generally include anabolic agents, amphetamines, corticosteroids, peptide hormones and their analogues, stimulants, narcotic analgesics, and (beta) blockers. The use of blood transfusion and the use of certain drugs to mask the presence of illegal substances in the urine are also banned.

In one of the most famous cases of drug use in sports, Canadian sprinter Ben Johnson was stripped of his gold medal and world record in the 100 meters after testing positive for steroids at the 1988 Olympics in Seoul.

History of Drug Use in Sport

Doping probably has a history as long as that of organized contest, with competitors in the ancient Olympics fortifying themselves with strychnine-laced alcohol or mushroom potions, possibly hallucinogenic, to mask fatigue and pain. Nineteenth-century endurance athletes were known to take heroin, cocaine, caffeine, strychnine, and alcohol in their attempts to improve performance. The third Olympic Games held in St. Louis in 1904 produced an early doping scare when a U.S. entrant in the marathon took ill after consuming a mixture of strychnine and egg white. As new drugs with anabolic (growth-potentiating) or ergogenic (performance-enhancing) capabilities have evolved and as natural hormones have been successfully isolated, they have rapidly been assimilated into the sporting sphere. Examples of these are the amphetamines used after World War II, testosterone in the 1950s, and more recently erythropoeitin,

human growth hormone, and recombinant DNA synthesized growth hormone in the 1980s.

The Drug Debate

Central to the debate on the use of drugs in sport is whether indeed measures should be taken to limit and or prohibit the use of drugs of any form in sport. There are those who would argue that it is the right of the individual to choose whatsoever they wish to eat, drink, inhale, inject, or catheterize themselves with and that whether or not there are adverse consequences to their actions, either immediate or delayed, the individual is free to choose. Freedom of choice is of paramount importance. Proponents pose questions such as "What real harm is there in allowing people to improve their performance with drugs?" and "What legal right does a sporting body have to insist that an athlete provide a sample of their urine or blood on demand, is this not an invasion of privacy?" Surely, unlike the alcoholic or the crack or cocaine addict, the athlete who uses performance-enhancing drugs is unlikely to pose a threat to society. There is little doubt that postgame alcohol ingestion coupled with the use of a motorcar causes more damage to athletes than all known doping practices, yet alcohol use is not banned outright.

The counterargument is based largely on two principles: (1) that of fair play and (2) that of the medical dictum of *primum non nocere*—in the first instance, do no harm (to the patient). The concept of fair play is inherent in most sports where rules have evolved to ensure both equality and safe participation. The victor should ideally be the best athlete, whose success has been achieved through inherited natural endowment and the hard work of training. The successful participation of a single athlete whose performance is pharmaceutically enhanced immediately places all other competitors in the invidious situation of having to make the decision to either follow suit and "do drugs" or remain content with their unenhanced performances. The concept of fairness held by most opponents to drug enhancement is evident in the International Olympic Committee (IOC) definition, "increasing in an *artificial* and *unfair* manner his/her performance in competition" [emphasis added].

The second principle is that a physician should do no harm to the patient. The prescription and administration of hormonal supplementation, stimulants, narcotic analgesics, diuretics, (beta) blockers, and blood transfusions is, by statute in most countries, the function of physicians. The medical dilemma now arises. How, for example, can the transfusion of blood to a perfectly healthy individual be justified medically? While the additional red blood cells may provide the aerobic edge to ensure victory in a world championship cycle race, there are risks of transfusion reactions. Similarly, there are several known long-term effects of prolonged anabolic steroid use, such as hepatic tumors, acromegaly (abnormal bone and soft tissue growth), and diabetes. Opponents argue that a physician should not be party to the possible production of pathology in a normal individual. Yet, if a physician is not supervising the administration of these drugs or procedures, who then will do it, and who will monitor the athlete for problems as they arise? Thus, based on med-

ical ethics, a physician should not administer performance-enhancing drugs, and neither should those who are not medically qualified, because of the potential for disaster.

This concept of *primum non nocere* is alluded to in the preface to the International Amateur Athletic Federation's *Procedural Guidelines for Doping Control*, in which it is stated, "It must be understood that the primary purpose of the anti doping programme is not to catch and punish but to protect the innocent and to educate the young."

Changing Attitudes toward Doping

The present attitude of the international administrating bodies of most sports is that doping is wrong and that the practice should cease. The relative conviction of the various sporting codes in support of this stance can be assessed by the difference in the severity of the punishment meted out to offenders. The approach to doping has changed over the years, though. At the 1956 World Games in Moscow, it became apparent that the Soviet athletes' performances had been improved by the use of the male anabolic steroid hormone testosterone. The initial response was not one of outrage; there was no introduction of rules to outlaw the practice. Instead, there was an attempt by a U.S. physician to produce a safer anabolic steroid so that U.S. athletes would be able to compete at an equal level—equity through abuse. Aided by a major pharmaceutical company, he sought an anabolic steroid that would enhance muscle growth but reduce the unwanted side effects of testosterone, such as testicular shrinkage, prostatic enlargement, acne, and hair loss (a goal which has yet to be achieved). The final product was methandrostenolone, or Dianabol, and the birth of a new culture of drug abuse in gymnasiums. Forty years later, there are reports in the medical literature of anabolic steroid use among U.S. high school seniors, ranging from 7 to 18 percent, with over one-third of the users in one study not even involved in organized school sports programs (Buckley et al. 1988).

Anti-doping investigation, with its associated punitive measures, was first introduced into the Olympic movement at the Mexico City Olympic Games in 1968. The tests used, however, were relatively primitive, with little legal certainty that

Hero for a Day—Ben Johnson and the Steroid Scandal of the 1988 Seoul Olympics

It was the best of times, it was the worst of times. On Saturday, 24 September 1988, Canadian sprinter Ben Johnson set a world record in the 100-meter event at the 1988 Seoul Olympic Games before an on-site crowd of 70,000 and with an estimated 2 billion others watching via television. His time of 9.79 seconds was 0.04 seconds faster than his previous world record of 9.83 seconds set in Rome in 1987. By nightfall on Monday, 26 September 1988, Ben Johnson had been disqualified because of his use of anabolic steroids, specifically stanozolol, in what was to become the most controversial event of the Games—indeed, some say, in the history of the Olympics.

The international impact of Johnson's disqualification was evident in newspaper headlines around the world. "Fastest Junkie on Earth" (*London Daily Star*), "Drugs turn Johnson's medal into a piece of fool's gold" (*Baltimore Sun*), "CHEAT!" (London *Daily Mirror*), and "The fastest man in the world—a doping sinner" (Germany's *Abendzeitung*). The impact of the Johnson affair was particularly dramatic in Canada. This may have been due not only to the nation's historical lack of success at the Olympics but, perhaps more importantly, the event had tarnished Canada's reputation as an honest, moral, fair-playing nation. Arguably, Ben Johnson had become the watershed of modern steroid use. Almost every subsequent scandal uses Johnson as the marker by which to measure its nature and significance.

An intriguing question emerges concerning why Ben Johnson became the focal point even though he was only one of at least 10 athletes disqualified for drug use at Seoul and the total number of disqualifications there were less than the 1984 Los Angeles Games. In addition to Canada's national embarrassment, it may have been the fact that the IOC had publicly stated its intention to crack down on cheating; it may have been the fact that the 100-meter final is traditionally one of the most prestigious events in the Olympics; it may have been the fact that Ben Johnson had broken a world record, beating his much more recognized U.S. rival, Carl Lewis; and perhaps it was due to the fact that the world had been deceived—a global audience had witnessed human history in the making only to have their collective memory betrayed.

From the very beginning Johnson maintained his innocence and there were various conspiratorial theories put forth by coaches and administrators. However, in the end Johnson told his story, admitting his long history of steroid use and that an injury prior to the Seoul Olympics had put additional pressure on him to speed up the rehabilitation process. The Dubin Inquiry established by the Canadian government to investigate the nature and extent of banned substance abuse involved 122 witnesses, culminated in 15,000 pages of testimony, cost millions of dollars, and revealed that the problem was endemic in elite sport. Sadly, after Johnson's two-year ban by the International Amateur Athletic Federation had expired, he returned to competitive track and field only to test positive a second time. He officially retired on 7 March 1993 amid a lifetime ban. Technically, Ben Johnson remains the fastest man in history and he was certainly a hero for a day. But he will forever be remembered as the man who shamed a nation and sold his soul for a piece of gold.

—Steven J. Jackson

the results obtained were valid. A few less fortunate people were exposed, while the majority of suspected doping cases were never confirmed because of false negative tests or successful appeal against the test procedures. A major advance in the confirmation of doping occurred in 1983 with the introduction of gas chromatography and mass spectrometry, scientific methods used to screen for and identify various drugs and their metabolites in urine. Further refinements in 1995 have increased the sensitivity of these tests and will result in a greater yield of positive results.

Detection is based on the presence in the athlete's urine of substances that are not normally produced by the body. These metabolites are analyzed and categorized according to their ana-bolic or ergogenic properties. Athletes are deemed to have supplemented their body's normal hormone production or to have induced excessive hormone production if the concentration found in the urine exceeds the normal range of the healthy population at large, or if the ratio of one naturally occurring hormone to another is outside the normal, or nonpathological, range. What constitutes normality is at present weighted in favor of the errant athlete; for example, the normal ratio of testosterone to epitestosterone found in urine is 1:1, whereas an athlete is only deemed to be positive for testosterone use if the ratio is greater than 6:1.

Unfortunately, urine analysis is not suitable for the detection of either blood transfusion or the abuse of peptide hormones. Blood sample analysis is required. The provision of a blood sample involves a physically and emotionally invasive procedure, requiring the consent of the individual to what would otherwise be deemed unlawful assault. Recent changes in drug testing rules now make provision for blood sampling.

Drug testing has developed into a large industry, which requires not only testing of competitors at athletic competitions but also worldwide random, out-of-season testing. In-competition testing is done primarily in an attempt to identify those who are using short-term ergogenics, usually stimulants. The chance identification of evidence of anabolic substance use is in effect a bonus. Out-of-competition testing looks to eradicate the use of anabolic agents such as anabolic steroids and the peptide hormones that increase natural production of the body's anabolic hormones, the use of erythropoeitin, as well as the practice of blood doping. Any attempt to impede the detection (by taking other drugs that alter the rate of excretion of the banned substances from the body or by introducing uncontaminated urine into the bladder by catheterization) is also considered an offense. The presence of stimulants or any of the remaining in-competition banned substances is not considered an offense if they are detected in an out-of-competition test.

Drug-Testing Procedure

In-competition testing procedure involves the identification of the athletes to be tested, the collection of a specimen from the athlete, the safe transmission of the sample to an accredited laboratory, the subsequent analysis of the sample, and finally notification of the governing authority and the athlete of the results. The protocol for each of these steps has developed with experience both in the field and in the courts of law, and each is governed by a set of procedures designed to minimize reprieve based on a legal loophole. First, the identity of the athlete must be confirmed to ensure that the appropriate athlete is tested. Once identified, the athlete signs a document confirming notification and the time of notification. The athlete then has one hour in which to present for the test, and the athlete must be chaperoned to prevent the opportunity to substitute clean urine by catheterization or by insertion

of a condom filled with urine into the vagina. To prevent any allegations that the sample was contaminated by substances ingested *after* the event, the athlete is allowed to drink from only sealed bottles or cans provided by the sampling officers. Once in the sampling area, the athlete must declare the use of all medications during the preceding three weeks, and this information is recorded. The athlete then chooses a sampling kit from a range of kits, and must be satisfied that the kit is adequately sealed and that it has not been tampered with in any way. The sampling officer must witness the urine being excreted by the athlete and must be satisfied that urine has not been transferred from some other source such as a bag under the armpit with a tube running down the inside of a sleeve of a track suit. The specimen is divided between two containers, the first being for initial testing and the second being for retesting on appeal by the athlete. The serial numbers on the bottles and the containers in which they are placed are recorded, and the bottles containing the urine samples are placed in tamper-proof containers for dispatch to the accredited laboratory. If the athlete is dissatisfied in any way with the procedure, his or her objections are recorded. Copies of the documentation containing the athletes name, the serial numbers of the specimen bottles and the outer containers, and the history of medication use, go to the athlete, the international governing body, and the sampling officer; a copy without the athlete's name is sent to the laboratory. On receipt of the sample at the laboratory the outer containers and their seals are checked for evidence of tampering, and the first sample is tested. Failure to present for testing after notification carries the same penalty as a positive test.

The process for random unannounced out-of-season testing is similar. Once again the athlete may not refuse to be tested. Who chooses the athlete, and how is secrecy maintained so that the athlete does not receive advance notice of the test? While there is general acceptance of the rules of the international governing bodies, the risk exists that national sporting authorities may tip off an athlete under their jurisdiction of an impending out-of-season test. This may be done either to avoid the associated bad publicity or to ensure, through avoidance of the test, the continued success of the athlete and the nation. Several major sports have sought to minimize this problem by handing over the task of out-of-season testing to independent drug testing companies with established networks of sampling officers around the world. A list of athletes to be subjected to such testing is submitted to the testing company by the international governing body of a sport, and the company then randomly conducts the tests.

The impact of doping on sport is profound, and those involved in the medical care of athletes cannot be ambivalent on the issue. There are some, like Dr. R. Voy, former chief medical officer of the United States Olympic Committee, who believe that doping has severely damaged the fabric of the sporting movement. Voy has stated, "Instead of being a competition and celebration of the body human, the Olympics have in some ways become a mere proving ground for scientists, chemists, and unethical physicians. In my opinion, despite renewed concern about drug use in sports, the Olympic ideal will never fully recover from the impact of this problem until it is absolutely, verifiably eliminated" (1991, xv).

—Maurice Mars

Bibliography: Buckley, W. E., C. E. Yesalis, K. E. Friedl, W. A. Anderson, A. L. Streit, and J. E. Wright. (1988) "Estimated Prevalence of Anabolic Steroid Use among Male High School Seniors." *Journal of the American Medical Association* 260, 23: 3441–3445.

Goldman, B., P. Bush, and R. Klatz. (1984) *Death in the Locker* Room. South Bend, IN: Icarus Press.

Killip, S., and R. Stennett. (1990) *Use of Performance Enhancing Substances by London Secondary School Students, Report 90-03.* London and Ontario, Canada: Board of Education for the City of London.

Strauss, R. (1987) *Drugs and Performance in Sports.* Philadelphia: W. B. Saunders.

Voy, R. (1991) *Drugs, Sport, and Politics.* Champaign, IL: Leisure Press.

Wadler, G. I., and B. Hainline. (1989) *Drugs and the Athlete.* Philadelphia: F. A. Davis.

Duathlon

The term *duathlon* (originally biathlon) describes a multisport endurance race that combines competition in two distinct disciplines. The most typical form of duathlon involves having participants bike and run in some combination for specified distances. The objective is for the athletes to complete the component events of the race (running, biking, and the transition between the two) as rapidly as possible. The fastest contestant wins. Top performers earn awards by either winning the races outright or by doing well within their specified five-year age (and gender) group.

Duathlon and triathlon are like distinct trees with common roots. Although duathlon receives less media attention, both events lie at the heart of the multisport movement. Because of their synergy (examples appear below), it might be useful to those who would understand multisports to read the entries for *both* triathlon and duathlon in these volumes. The analysis of cultural factors related to triathlon is also applicable to duathlon. Because duathlon usually incorporates some subset of triathlon sports, the analyses below will use illustrations from triathlon and duathlon.

Origins

The earliest forms of multisport races were dual-discipline events (Tinley 1986) that often involved swimming and running. The form persisted for some time and there have been duathlons that involve all combinations of swimming, biking, and running. Additionally, other sport "disciplines" such as in-line skating have appeared in the mix.

In tracing the early development of multisport events, veteran triathlete Scott Tinley noted the compatibility of the California lifestyle with swimming, biking, and running (Tinley 1986). Many children there frequently do all three in the same day. Early impetus seems to have come from distance runners who would dive in for a swim following a long run. According to Tinley, David Pain organized the earliest quasi-formalized multisport event in 1972. He threw himself a birthday party that had attendees race a 10-kilometer (6.2-mile) run followed by a 0.8-kilometer (one-half-mile) swim. He called his race a biathlon. Two years later Don Shannahan and Jack Johnstone, friends of Pain (pun intended), assembled the first triathlon that involved the two disciplines from the biathlon plus biking.

In the late 1970s and early 1980s, triathlon received a good deal of publicity. Adherents flocked to the sport. The Triathlon Federation of

Duathlon

The most common form of duathlon, a combination of two endurance disciplines, involves running and biking. Swimming and in-line skating are among other possible components of these events.

the United States, which came to be known as Tri-Fed U.S.A., emerged as the national governing board (NGB) for multisport endurance events (triathlon and duathlon) in 1982. (In 1996 the name was changed to U.S.A. Triathlon to bring it into conformity with other U.S. regulatory bodies for Olympic sports. Seven years later the International Triathlon Union (ITU) appeared as a confederation of NGBs. They sought to gain Olympic status for triathlon and to enhance professional competition. These significant political events in the multisport movement signaled an implicit diminution in the status of duathlon—now a poor relation in the multisport world. For example, the name of the sport is in no way included in the names of the major national or international organization. Still, the world has embraced the sport. Its popularity reflects several factors. In some parts of the world there is a scarcity of competitive swimmers. Additionally, several countries have

climates that make for a short outdoor season and others have too high a level of water pollution to permit safe competitive swimming.

Until the advent of the ITU with its avowed purpose of gaining Olympic status for triathlon, most dual-sport athletes called their sport biathlon. ITU president Les McDonald suggested that the name of dual-sport events be changed to duathlon. The thinking was that multisporters should not offend the ski-shoot participants in biathlon, an Olympic sport of long duration, at a time when triathlon sought admission to the games. Moreover, McDonald noted that the international federation of the athletes who ski and shoot had formally requested that endurance multisporters not usurp their name. For a brief period, the awkward term cyruthon (CYcling, RUnning) strained the wit of those concerned with the sport. Eventually the federations adopted the term *duathlon* as suggested by the Europeans and

McDonald. Interestingly, many nonsanctioned local events still use the term *biathlon.*

Practice

Although technically the term *duathlon* covers any combination of two endurance disciplines, typical events come in one of two primary forms. Most duathlons are run-bike-run affairs. Of the remainder, many consist of a run of specified length followed immediately by biking another distance. People involved in the sport regard the prevalent form as both more triathlonlike and more difficult because it is usually more problematic to run immediately after biking.

The Powerman Duathlon series boasts among the richest of multisport purses in the world. The original Powerman race was held in Zofingen, Switzerland, in 1989. It has expanded into a worldwide series. Although many pro triathletes compete in these events, there are also duathlon specialists such as Ken Souza.

Analysis

Blanchard and Cheska (1985) regard the institution of sport as both universal and reflecting, in individual forms, the evolutionary state of the particular culture. In their evolutionary model, they specify eight dimensions along which sport can be distinguished as more or less modern. Progression through their model implies increasing levels of secularity (i.e., less ritual in the sport), bureaucracy (e.g., more and more formal organizations governing the sport), diversity in social identity among participants so that the sport is more inclusive, categories of social distance among participants indicating a wider range of interpersonal relations among participants, role specialization within the sport, elaboration of sports equipment, vagueness of adaptive or ecological meaning of the sport (i.e., its day-to-day utility to the participants), and record-keeping or quantification of performance.

Several of the Blanchard and Cheska axes are useful for understanding multisports. The bureaucratization of multisports has been alluded to earlier and is amplified in the article on triathlon in this encyclopedia.

Role specialization may be regarded (wryly) as the antithesis of multisport. The point of duathlon and triathlon is to develop a *general* athletic excellence. Interestingly, athletes at the pinnacle of their sport have traversed in both directions between multisports events and their individual discipline. Thus, an impressive list of stars in individual sports has tried multisport events with varying success. John Howard, Davis Phinney, George Sheehan, and Frank Shorter are among the more recognizable names who have tried multisport events. Few stars from single disciplines have dominated multisport events. Instead, they've learned the dictum of ITU President Les McDonald that competing in multisport events means more than just performing well at the individual sports. A multisporter who went the other way is triathlete-turned-professional-cyclist Lance Armstrong. One way that role specialization may have entered occasionally into these events has been via the use of a single discipline "rabbit" to increase the pace in a specific discipline (e.g., swimming), thereby enhancing the performance of elites in the field. For example, Olympic swimmer Lars Jorgensen set the swim record for the Hawaii Ironman Triathlon in 1995. Another paradoxical type of specialization is the triathlon or duathlon specialist (e.g., Ken Souza).

David N. Maynard (1994), in his illuminating analysis of cycling, points to the importance of establishing links between sport, material factors, and psychological processes. Thus, the elaboration of *equipment* dimension proposed by Blanchard and Cheska (1985) is consequential. The triathlon article in this encyclopedia has addressed several aspects of this elaboration. Duathletes (and triathletes) have an abundance of pricey gear. At major events it is not uncommon to see thousands of bicycles worth thousands of dollars each. Many have "tricked out" bikes. An athlete with a tricked-out bike and an out-of-shape (slow, undertrained) engine is likely to earn the appellation "techno-geek."

Many technical advances described in the triathlon piece are relevant here. Others include lace locks or elastic laces designed to speed transitions to and from the run. (The clock runs during the periods of equipment change, which are known as "transitions." Therefore the athletes value items that permit more rapid transitions.) One advance unique to duathlon is different varieties of platform pedal for bicycles. Platform pedals look like overgrown toe clips. They have a solid platform base that allows one to have the firmness of a bike shoe while pedaling in one's running shoes. In a duathlon this eliminates the user's need to change shoes.

Ingham and Loy (1993) have edited a work that examines the dominant (hegemonic) sport culture, residual components that tie it to the past, and emergent elements that offer the possibility of future culture change. Donnelly in that volume characterizes the dominant sport culture of today as professional, bureaucratic, and commercial.

The commercial value of duathlon and triathlon in the United States becomes apparent when one examines the statistics: between the early 1970s and the early 1990s, there were large increases in the United States in the number of runners and the number of bikers. By 1991 there were nearly 1.5 million people who were erstwhile participants in one of triathlon's disciplines.

An examination of multisport indicates that one emergent function that may already have become part of the dominant sport culture is *technologization*. In diverse sports, athletes are optimizing their performance via technological advancement: in nutrition, in training, and in equipment. Although technology is not independent of commercialization, it is a separate factor in that athletes would pursue the advances irrespective of their commercial value. Clearly, the development of several advances occurred purely with regard to performance considerations. Thus, for example, several duathletes have developed versions of pedal platforms that provide a stiff surface allowing the athlete to bike effectively (i.e., speedily) in biking shoes. Velcro closures (as opposed to laces) provide an alternative to those who choose to change shoes as quickly as they can.

Blanchard and Cheska (1985) cite Daniel Berlyne's distinction between *specific* and *diversive exploration*. The distinction between gaining functional information (specific) and gaining stimulation (diversive) appears useful for examining multisport technology. Although team sport athletes can express themselves through the *artistry* of their performance (e.g., a dunk in basketball or a catch in football), this is not a path open to duathletes. The only thing that can be artful in multisport races is speed. Speed is typically enhanced by efficiency rather than the type of styling to which other sports lend themselves so

well. Multisporters use specific exploration to create new technology (e.g., lace locks, aerobars). They use diversive exploration to decorate the equipment in eye-popping ways (e.g., blended neon colors, sleek glasses, and bike helmets).

The final Blanchard and Cheska dimension, *quantification*, is somewhat problematic in multisports. Thus, although most of the athletes are meticulous about timing their performance, race directors may not be. Often athletes can be heard discussing mismeasured courses and poorly reported "official" results. Because the courses are usually on public roads and open water (lakes, rivers, bays, oceans), the measured distances may not even be comparable from year to year. Some race directors take the quantification issue seriously. They may have components of their course certified by the appropriate governing body (e.g., the run course by a governing body in running) or use other accuracy-ensuring devices (e.g., laser-measured swim courses). They may report the time and rank of each athlete in each venue (including the transitions!). Other race directors may report only the overall finish time.

Maynard (1994) has urged that psychological processes be considered part of the mix. Space limitations permit only allusion to major themes pertinent to multisport. Thus, the extreme nature of some competitions clearly calls to mind Adler's notion of the compensatory striving for superiority. Many multisporters have had items in their experiential background that provided real or imagined physical challenges.

In a Freudian scheme, one might focus on the anxiety associated with increasing perception of lack of control over our lives. Following Blanchard and Cheska (1985), the clarity of the outcome of sporting events is unrivaled clarity in real life. The contest returns the perception of a modicum of control to the actor and thus reduces the *angst*. Sport also provides an ability to restructure opportunities through what Eifermann (1973) has called *metarules*. Metarules level the playing field (e.g., handicapping in golf). The multisport version of restructuring presents awards to age-group winners of both genders and the top finishers. Another manifestation of a metarule that leads to only idealized success is the sometime reporting in major multisport publications of age- and gender-adjusted finish times for major races.

Finally, the classic cross-cultural findings of Roberts and Sutton-Smith (1962) suggest testable cross-national hypotheses. According to those authors, games of physical skill are abundant in environments that reward achievement and where there is anxiety when one does not achieve. Although that dimension is confounded with economics, the major players in the multi-sport arena include Germany, the United States, Japan, and Australia.

—B. James Starr

Bibliography: Blanchard, Kendall, and Alyce Cheska. (1985) *The Anthropology of Sport: An Introduction.* South Hadley, MA: Bergin & Garvey.

Donnelly, Peter. (1993) "Subcultures in Sport: Resilience and Transformation." In *Sport in Social Development: Traditions, Transitions, and Transformations,* edited by Alan G. Ingham and John W. Loy. Champaign, IL: Human Kinetics Publishers, 119–145.

Eifermann, Rivka R. (1973) "Rules in Games." In *Artificial and Human Thinking,* edited by Alice Elithorn and David Jones. San Francisco: Jossey-Bass, 147–161.

Ingham, Alan G., and John W. Loy, eds. (1993) *Sport in Social Development: Traditions, Transitions, and Transformations.* Champaign, IL: Human Kinetics Publishers.

Maynard, David N. (1994) "The Divergent Evolution of Competitive Cycling in the United States and Europe." In *The Masks of Play,* edited by Brian Sutton-Smith and Diana Kelly-Byrne. New York: Leisure Press, 78–87.

Roberts, John, and Brian Sutton-Smith. (1962) "Child Training and Game Involvement." *Ethnology* 1, 2: 166–185.

Sisson, Mark. (1989) *Training and Racing Biathlons.* Los Angeles: Primal Urge Press.

Souza, Ken, with Bob Babbitt. (1989) *Biathlon: Training and Racing Techniques.* Chicago: Contemporary Books.

Tinley, Scott, with Mike Plant. (1986) *Winning Triathlon.* Chicago: Contemporary Books.

Environment

Like sport, environment is not easy to define. There is very little—if any—of the "natural" environment left since virtually every place as been affected, directly or indirectly, by human action. For convenience "environment" will be defined here as the phenomenon of the physical world in general.

The relationships between sport and the environment are varied and complex. The environment undoubtedly influences sports in numerous ways. Those responsible for the organization of sports have, in many cases, attempted to neutralize the impact of the physical environment—that is weather, climate, slope, soil, and water—by creating artificial environments in which sports are played. It is increasingly being recognized, however, that sports affect the environment also. It is often the artificial environments that have been designed to neutralize nature that have a negative effect on nature.

Effect of the Natural Environment

Sports can be categorized on the basis of environmental interference. Specialized environment sports *require* certain environmental conditions for them to take place at all. An obvious example is sailing; without wind the sport would not exist. Skiing would not have developed were it not for the existence of snow and hills; surfing owes its origins to the presence of waves and beaches.

More commonly, however, environmental influence on sport is thought of less in terms of being the basis for particular sports than of the effects it has on particular events. Environmental interference sports (i.e., sports in which the physical environment interferes in some way with the outcome and performance) are best suited to "environment-less" days. This means that ideally the ground should be flat and dry; the weather warm, dry, and bright but overcast; little or no wind; and with excellent visibility. Unfortunately, these are the conditions in which most specialized environment sports could not take place. Physical effects such as the weather may affect the playing surface and the comfort of players and spectators. These may, in turn, affect the athletes' performances, the attendance, and the economics of the sports event. Each of these effects may be examined in turn.

Environmental Advantage Sports

In some sports, changeable environmental conditions may influence some competitors and not others. In golf, for example, players starting on a clear morning would have an obvious advantage over those struggling over a wind-swept course later in the day. In a long-jump competition, the wind may assist one jumper to a leading position and blow against a fellow competitor and hinder performance. Any sport taking place in an arena too small to allow all participants to take part at the same time is open to the possibility of a change in the weather affecting the participants unequally. Indeed, the microclimate differs from place to place *within* most stadiums at any single time. The effect of an apparently constant environmental condition during the course of an event can be highly misleading. Take, for example, a 100-meter sprint race. An anemometer may record that the wind speed was above the permitted level for a record to be recognized. But it has been shown that even within a 100-meter stretch, the wind swirls in several directions, affecting to various degrees athletes in different lanes. In a soccer game, a strong wind may exist in the first half, hence affecting one of the teams either positively or negatively, but die away in the second half and affect neither side.

The unpredictability of the environment may bring unexpected outcomes to a game. In baseball the ball may strike a pebble and glance off in an unexpected direction. The type of soil making up baseball fields and cricket pitches varies from place to place. To some extent this may constitute a home field advantage, the opposing team being less familiar with the texture of the field. It has been shown that the degree of bounce, registered by using a standard test of dropping a cricket ball on to the field from a height of 5 meters (16 feet, 4¾ inches), varies directly with the clay content of the soil. Likewise, place-to-place differences in altitude are said to affect performance.

Recently the interaction between sport and the environment has been gaining attention. Even in an enclosed stadium, the wind can affect runners in different lanes to varying degrees.

Playing Surface

Traditionally, most playing surfaces have been made of natural or seminatural materials such as grass, clay, water, or snow. Changes during the course of an event, or differences from place to place, in such surfaces can affect the outcome of a sports event. Soil can become saturated during heavy rain, hence leading to the postponement or cancellation of an event. Snow-covered fields lead to soccer (association football) postponement; rain-outs are common in cricket and baseball; unseasonably mild weather has often led to the cancellation of ski events.

Player Comfort

A number of environmental considerations contribute to player comfort during a sports event. Player discomfort may impact performance. During the 1968 Olympic Games in Mexico City, many long distance runners felt physically distressed as a result of relative lack of oxygen at high altitudes. Times in events over 1,500 meters were slower than expected. In the case of the sprints and jumps, however, performances were thought to be greatly enhanced. The world long-jump record set by Bob Beamon (1945–) typified such altitude assistance.

As far as participant comfort is concerned, the temperature is important because different sports have different activity levels. For example, in swimming, evaporation heat loss is curtailed and most body cooling takes place via convection and conduction. As far as performance is concerned the optimum water temperature is regarded as being between 20 and 34.5 degrees Celsius (68 and 94 degrees Fahrenheit) for short races and between 23 and 26 degrees Celsius (73 and 79 degrees Fahrenheit) for 1,500 meters.

High temperatures can be extremely hazardous in long-distance cycling and running events. The 1908 Olympic marathon in London and the 1954 Empire Games marathon in Vancouver provide examples of races in which several runners collapsed due to excessively high temperatures. Low temperatures can be a hazard in sports where the hands play an important role, such as rugby, football, or field hockey. In cold conditions, the flow of blood to the hands and toes is reduced in greater proportion than to the rest of the body. Also, speed and power events tend to be performed poorly in cold conditions because human muscle functions best at 40 to 41 degrees Celsius (104 to 106 degrees Fahrenheit).

Spectator Comfort

Many of the effects of the environment on players also apply to the spectators. The anticipation of spectator discomfort at sports events may affect attendance and hence economics. In general, adverse environmental conditions tend to lure spectators away from sports events to the perceived comfort of the indoors and television sets. Attendance at sports events can be related to climatic factors because frequently the spectator has to put up with exactly the same weather conditions as the players, yet the activity level of the former is much lower.

Another aspect of environmental economics on sports is that sports-related marketing often has to take potential attendance into account in planning the amount of food, programs, and other concessions to be sold at a particular event. It has been recorded, for example, that in a rugby match in New Zealand, the weather was so bad that 10,000 meat pies went unsold because only half the expected 60,000 spectators turned up to watch.

One of the problems inherent in this discussion is that of isolating the effect of the weather or other environmental factors from other factors that may contribute to any of the possible outcomes. Take, for example, the effect of an assisting wind in the case of sprinters. Not all sprinters achieve their best times in wind-assisted races. Hence, wind is not the only factor influencing performance, and it is dangerous to assume cause and effect in such situations.

In recent years, scientists have recognized that there may be an environmental impact on sport taking place as a result of global warming. Such an occurrence threatens to limit the geographic area over which certain sports can take place. Skiing is the best-researched example. It has been shown that the effect of oxygen-induced warming may raise winter temperatures, leading to a reduction in snowfall and hence a shortening of the skiing seasons in particular parts of Quebec, Ontario, and Michigan.

Neutralizing the Environment

The interference caused by the physical environment, its unpredictability, and the risk to comfort, performance, and economics have led the sports business to neutralize environmental interference. This has assumed two basic forms: the decision not to recognize environment-assisted performances, and the attempt to eliminate the natural environment by making it artificial.

In track and field, performances in certain events are not recognized for record purposes if the wind is over a certain strength. Wind readings are taken by an anemometer and despite the inadequacies of such measurements (as noted earlier), critical readings of wind speeds are used to determine whether sprint times or long- and triple-jump distances are legal. Wind speeds of over 2.00 meters per second (6 feet, 6¾ inches per second) are deemed sufficient to nullify a performance for record purposes. On the other hand, this rule applies only to the sprints and the horizontal jumps; wind-aided javelin performances are not rejected; neither are performances achieved at high altitudes.

Environmental interference is also overcome by providing artificial environments where the activity takes place. The history of sport has been one of attempts to make its environment artificial. Early baseball, cricket, and soccer (association football) took place in natural environments; as the desire grew for improved performances and less unpredictable environments, grass playing surfaces were rolled and cut. Nature was tamed and manicured. Later, grass was replaced by plastic so that games could continue to be played in adverse weather conditions. The situation in track and field has been similar—from grass to cinder to synthetic tracks. The first synthetic running track made its appearance in the early 1960s; Astroturf was introduced in the United States in 1966. Other artificial environments include those produced by human-induced weather. Artificial snow is commonly found on ski slopes where natural snowfall cannot be guaranteed.

Moving sports indoors serves to nullify many environmental effects. Indoor sports arenas are now large enough to satisfy the needs of football, soccer, track and field, swimming, skating, and, in modified form golf, sailing, wind surfing, climbing, show jumping, and rodeo. Even in the case of indoor sports, however, microclimatic effects can be significant. Indoor environments for sports range from the high school gymnasium to the fully domed super stadium. Such latter facilities have grown dramatically in recent decades. In Toronto the distinction between an indoor and outdoor sports facility is blurred by the presence of the SkyDome with its retractable roof.

In outdoor sports the effects of environment could be reduced by establishing the climatically optimal season. In baseball, for example, it has been shown in a paper by Brent Skeeter that from a purely climatic viewpoint it would be appropriate to shift the season to a later date, although climate is not the only variable to be taken into account in such scheduling.

The Effect of Sports on the Natural Environment

It is only in recent decades that attention has turned to the influence of sport on the environment. The growing application of technology to sport has been a major contributor to this view although some observers believe that sport is intrinsically anti-nature. It is possible to argue that sports have a number of positive effects on the environment. A golf course in the Arizona desert brings a splash of greenery to an otherwise arid area. In Britain, the construction of golf courses has been said to increase the number of botanical and zoologic species in the course area. On the other hand, the very same sport, and a large number of others, had been shown to have a negative impact on the environment. It is now possible to conceive of sports pollution so widespread are the negative impacts of sports.

Such pollution has been well researched in the case of golf. Among the nations experiencing the most rapid rate of increase in golf courses is Japan. In 1956 the country had 72 golf courses; by the year 2000 it is estimated the figure will be about 3,000. With limited open space available for the construction of such courses, forests, usually near the foot of mountains, have been felled to

Sport as a Carrier of Deep Culture

Nature is there to be controlled, to be used—with "abused'" being just around the corner. The consequence of this is highly visible in the ecological crises of the world today: the decrease of maturity of ecosystems; depletion and pollution. In this field sport plays a minor role, but the inclination is in the same direction. Sporting events decreasingly take place in natural surroundings, and increasingly in special places made for the purpose, with an overwhelming amount of concrete rather than just pure, uncontaminated, unmanipulated. The sports palace and the stadium, Olympic or not, are anti-nature and have to be so because they are near-laboratory settings in which the unidimensionality of competitive sport can unfold itself under controlled conditions. Pure nature has too much variation in it, too much "noise.". . . Although the human body is nature and nature is also the human body, the distance between sport and nature in itself seems to be ever increasing.

—Johan Galtung, 1984

satisfy the demand. Herbicide, germicide, pesticide, coloring agents, organic chlorine, and other chemical fertilizers that are carcinogenic or may cause health problems are among the massive number of inputs associated with golf course construction. Widespread damage to bird, insect, animal, and human life has been reported. It has been noted that in Korea, pesticides spread on golf courses can be absorbed into the human body through inhalation or skin contact. Pesticide abuse is now seen as a problem requiring serious regulation. Golf is one sport that has witnessed the emergence of anti-golf ecological movements. The Global Anti-Golf Movement is a network of ecological organizations that is fighting against golf as a sport that destroys the natural environment.

Detailed studies also exist of the effect of ski facilities in mountain areas. During ski piste construction the natural terrain is modified to such an extent that soil erosion occurs, which in turn inhibits the regeneration of vegetation. The artificial modification of mountain slopes for improved skiing covers substantial areas of many alpine zones.

Spectator sports in urban areas also create pollution of various kinds. The development of urban stadium complexes has spillover effects in the form of increased traffic generation and its resultant pollution. Traffic congestion around older, inner-city stadiums is often perceived by local residents as being of greater nuisance than crowds, noise, or fan hooliganism. Few sports are completely free of environmental impact. Stadium and arena-based sports involve the removal of the entire natural ecosystem and the creation of an artificial environment. Motor sports create lead and noise pollution. Even wind surfing can produce some damage to water courses; nesting birds can be driven away from sites where the sport takes place. Orienteering lies at the other end of the spectrum and its effects are (almost) undetectable.

Sport is not independent of broader global concerns. As environmental concern grows in the decades ahead, its impact on sport, and the effects of sport itself, will need to be carefully monitored. Moves to ban environmentally unfriendly sports may grow in significance; at the same time, sport may, through its "need" to eliminate many environmental effects, unwittingly contribute to the very degradation that threatens it.

—John Bale

Bibliography: Bale, John. (1994) *Landscapes of Modern Sport.* Leicester, UK: Leicester University Press.

Digel, H. (1992) "Sports in a Risk Society." *International Review for the Sociology of Sport* 26, 2: 257–273.

Eichberg, Henning. (1988) *Leistungsraume.* Munster, Germany: Lit Forlag.

Galtung, Johan (1984) "Sport and International Understanding: Sport as a Carrier of Deep Culture and Structure." In *Sport and International Understanding,* edited by M. Illmarinen. Berlin: Springer-Verlag, 12–19.

Lipski, S., and G. McBoyle (1991) "The Impact of Global Warming on Downhill Skiing in Michigan." *East Lakes Geographer* 26: 37–51.

McCormack, G. (1991) "The Price of Affluence: The Political Economy of Japanese Leisure." *New Left Review* 188: 121–134.

Moon, Y., and D. Shin (1990) "Health Risks to Golfers from Pesticide Use on Golf Courses in Korea." In *Science and Golf,* edited by A. Cochran. London: Spon, 358–363.

Mossiman, T. (1985) "Geo-Ecological Impacts of Ski-Piste Construction in the Swiss Alps." *Applied Geography* 5: 29–38.

Skeeter, Brent. (1988) "The Climatically Optimal Major League Baseball Season in North America." *Geographical Bulletin* 30, 2: 97–102.

Thornes, John. (1977) "The Effect of Weather on Sport." *Weather* 32: 258–269.

Ethics

Suppose you are a coach, and you have always tried to do what is right. You have led an exemplary life; you keep your promises; you treat others as you would like to be treated; you follow the rules of society and the rules of your sport. Suppose, also, that the administrators that you work for do not share your sense of right and wrong. Suppose also that as luck and your hard work would have it, four members of your tennis team were the regional tournament champions and qualified for the state competition. Suppose, further, that it has always been your policy to take the whole team to the competition, even though only four will be competing. You have told your athletes that as a reward, everyone goes to the tournament. Four days before the scheduled trip, the administration informs you that only the four competing players will travel to the tournament, and that instead of the rest of the players riding in the van, prominent fans and parents will accompany you. Their reasoning is lodged in the fact that the fans and parents are generous boosters of the school and especially the tennis team. Also, the administration argues that only the actual qualifiers should be permitted to go to the state tournament. They say that your policy of letting everyone go detracts from the honor of the players who actually won the tournament. You are caught in a moral dilemma. You gave your word to your team, but now a higher authority is making the decision for you—or are they? What should you do?

At this point, you will probably get into a debate with the administration about your policy and about their politics. At some point, you and they will almost inevitably raise the issue of ethics. This will also probably lead to further argument about what is right, or good. When this happens, the discussion becomes a full-fledged philosophical one and will probably deteriorate and become quite emotional. One hopes the conflict will be resolved for the best, though often it is not.

The reason problems exist concerning what is considered right, is that few of us spend the time discovering what we value, why we value it, and how we apply what we value. As a society, we tend to make decisions about right and wrong from what we sense is right . . . or what feels good to us at the moment. Unfortunately, such a philosophy about decision making will lead us on a merry path of confusion and often will end in turmoil. Such confusion and turmoil does not have to be the case if we learn to use our own thought-out sense of right and wrong. We call the formal examination of what we value as right and wrong the study of ethics.

Ethics is one of the four branches of philosophy. To study philosophy is literally to study wisdom, or put another way, philosophy is the deliberate and rational quest to understand all and the parts of one's existence with the goal of improving one's life. To study any aspect of philosophy is to desire to understand more about Self in relation to the greater society. Traditionally, the four branches of philosophy are: metaphysics, epistemology, logic, and axiology. Metaphysics is the study of reality, epistemology is the study of knowledge, and logic the study of reasoning. The fourth branch, axiology, is the study of value. Historically, axiology has been divided into two subparts, aesthetics and ethics. Aesthetics is the study of the beautiful and the ugly, while ethics is the study of right and wrong, good and bad. All philosophic writing rests somewhat within each of these branches. Sport philosophers, in contrast, have divided their writing into three of the four branches of philosophy—metaphysics, epistemology, and axiology; outside departments of philosophy, few disciplines delve into the formal study of logic. Sport philosophers have focused on such metaphysical questions as the mind-body problem, the meaning of play, and the reality of the human being as he or she plays. [See Harper (1972, 1973–76, 1985); Hellison (1973); Hyland (1990); Kleinman (1986); Lenk (1979); Meier (1975, 1980, 1988); Metheny (1965, 1968, 1972); Morgan (1982); Morgan and Meier (1988); Nash (1931); Novak (1976); Slusher (1967); Suits (1972, 1978); Wood and Cassidy (1927).] Philosophers have also examined what we know when we play or participate in sport, i.e., epistemology. [See Fahlberg (1994): Steele (1985); Osterhoudt (1991); Metheny (1972); or Parry (1988).] And they have discussed the aesthetic experience. [See Best (1974); Wertz (1991); or Kleinman (1986).]

Our present focus is ethics, the subpart of axiology that is the study of right and wrong, good and bad. Specifically, ethics is moral philosophy or philosophically thinking about the moral questions, problems, and judgments that occur in our everyday lives. Moral philosophy is a special sort of thinking. It arises when we pass beyond the stage of only following rules to the stage of thinking for ourselves in a critical sense. The goal is to attain moral autonomy: self-governance in making decisions about right and wrong. This is not an easy journey, nor one that is accomplished through a quick and easy method. Critical self-examination about issues of right and wrong demands hard work and intense scrutiny of our own value system.

In formal ethical study, critical thinking can be separated into three kinds: (1) descriptive (i.e., empirical, historical, or scientific inquiry), (2) normative, and (3) meta-ethical. The goal of descriptive critical thinking is to describe morality; normative judgments deal with *how* should one decide what is right and wrong; and meta-ethics entails the sort of thinking one does when one goes "beyond" the normative to attempt a critical understanding of why and how one makes a normative decision. If we were to study formal ethical theory at a university or college, we would enroll in courses about classical ethics. In these courses, one usually studies the how and the who of different historical theories. It is believed that by reading and studying the great works, we will develop our ability to think critically about ethical and moral dilemmas. Typical writings to study in classical ethics are from the canons of Plato to Kant, Bentham to Mill, Augustine to Niebuhr. Sport ethics also has a very formal side and can be found in the writings of individuals known as sport ethicists. These individuals study in a classic sense the descriptive, the normative, and the meta-ethical.

For example, Earle Zeigler, author of *Ethics in Physical Education* (1976) and *Ethics and Morality in Sport and Physical Education* (1984), is a descriptive, normative ethicist who gives many good examples of how to attack ethical decisions. Warren Fraleigh, author of *Right Actions in Sport* (1984), is both an analytical and normative ethicist who argues that one cannot play a game and cheat at the same time—that it is illogical and impossible to do both, for when one cheats, one ceases to play.

Robert L. Simon, in *Fair Play: Sport, Values, and Society* (1991), analyzes the phenomenon of fair play and argues that sport is essentially a good and moral activity. John H. Gibson, in an interesting meta-ethical piece in *Performance versus Results* (1993), argues that American society has evolved to the point that it has lost sight of the meaning of sport, play, and performance and can logically only appreciate sport as a commodified product.

In contrast to the above formal study of ethics is common practice or applied usage of sport ethics. Today, current writings focus on the why and how of sport ethics. Rather than being theoretical and philosophical in the formal sense, these writings address the applied and focus on current social issues. These particular writers give presumably common-sense solutions to current problems. The writings can be separated into one of three areas: (1) personal morality, moral development, and the effect of moral reasoning; (2) ethics and the social community; and (3) formal written codes for a professional.

Personal Morality

Personal morality is our motive, intention, and action as that action impinges on and affects others. Morality in this sense is a social enterprise, it is not just a discovery of Self for our own benefits. Like most other social inventions, morality exists before we exist. We are inducted into the social morality of a community; however, we must also understand that personal morality also lies beyond the community. A truly morally educated individual is able to think critically beyond the social constructs of the community. That is, the individual is able to question the social mores and come to a decision about right and wrong based on either a higher authority or a deepened, reasoned sense of knowing.

Morality in its most general sense is concerned with our interpersonal relations. It involves a consideration of and concern for others (what is often called "common decency") as well as for ourselves and it attempts to distinguish right from wrong and good from bad. Morality in the theoretical sense is associated with values and principles that need to be evaluated, understood, and fleshed out before one chooses or engages in

a particular course of action (Arnold 1994, 76).

How we develop personal morality is based on our moral education. Moral education refers to the deliberate and intentional activity of cultivating both moral growth and moral judgment as well as the willing disposition to act upon that judgment. According to Kohlberg (1971, 25), moral education is the encouragement of a capacity for moral judgment. Moral education then is first about helping others form moral judgments and second to encourage others to act upon what they have learned. When moral judgment is translated into an appropriate moral action, moral education is most clearly expressed (Arnold 1994).

Moral education is much beyond the scope of moral training. The latter implies drilling to encourage individuals to conform to moral rules without much understanding of the principles involved. In contrast, moral education encourages students to reflect upon moral issues in light of fundamental moral principles and make their own rational judgments, which they can translate into appropriate moral action (Arnold 1994). Moral education as defined is imperative if morality is to be developed.

Moral Education and Character

Moral education is a lifelong endeavor. We are not necessarily born moral or immoral and morality does not mysteriously occur in childhood and stay rooted in our psyches for life. Rather, all of us grow, mature, and develop or do not develop morally through our education and environment and we are highly affected by moral role models.

Moral education (see Schematic) is a combined

lifelong informal and formal process of learning in which our own moral sense, personal values, and system of knowing about morality and moral issues influence our actual doing. All of these are inculcated by our life's experiences. This process culminates in what is otherwise known as our moral character. Specifically, the informal process of our moral education is highly influenced by our (a) environment, i.e., all our past and present experiences, and (b) modeling from significant others, i.e., family, friends, peers, respected others.

The formal process of moral education, however, may be different for each individual. Some of us may have more advanced and more consistent instruction, whereas others may have no or little instruction. Good moral education is about promoting the unsettling process of examining one's own personal values as well as the individual moral reasoning process. Moral reasoning occurs through systematic, reflective, and consistent reasoning with the goal of developing principled thinking, which is then applied to our relationships with others.

When we discuss the character or the moral development of the individual, we are referring to his or her ability to make moral or ethical judgments based on the reasoning process, past experiences, and from what has been learned from significant others.

Little has been written about how we improve moral development and thus the character of individuals involved in sport. Outside of the

sport process, much has been written about character development. It is usually believed that character is either innate, a product of the social construct, or a cognitive process. A few writers have examined character as it relates to sport. The best present sources in moral reasoning from a philosophic perspective is Lumpkin, Stoll, and Beller (1995), and from a psychological stance examining moral development, Bredemeier and Shields (1994) and Weiss and Bredemeier (1991). A good source on philosophical moral education is Arnold (1991).

Ethics and the Social Community

Our personal morality manifests itself in how we address issues in the greater social community; it directly affects how and if we believe we have an obligation to follow the basic moral tenets of our greater community. Most writing today on sport ethics issues is being done by either sport sociologists, journalists, or educators. Their writing is directed toward the perceived immoral or unethical nature of the sport community, focusing on the immoral or unethical conduct of players, coaches, fans, administrators, or parents. Some of the current social issues in sport today are:

1. The nature of competition. Is it good or bad? Should we compete, and if so, how should we compete? Alfie Kohn, in *No Contest: The Case against Competition* (1986), argues that competition negatively affects the moral growth of the competitor. He argues for a cooperative system. In contrast, Ronald M. Jeziorski, in *The Importance of School Sports in American Education and Socialization* (1994), argues that school sports are the key to developing effective U.S. citizens. In contrast to both is a 1994 work by A. W. Miracle and C. R. Rees, *Lessons of the Locker Room: The Myth of School Sports,* which focuses on the negative learned social experiences of youth and high school sport.
2. The importance of rules. What is the role of rules within the contest? Why do rules fail? What social problems occur because of unethical conduct in relation to the

Learning Personal Morality

Environment · Modeling · Cognitive Dissonance

Informal Learning · Formal Instruction

Moral Education

The Triad of Character Development

Valuing · Knowing

Doing

rules? See Richard Lapchick and John Slaughter, *The Rules of the Game: Ethics in College Sports* (1989), and Rick Telander, *The Hundred Yard Lie: The Corruption of College Football and What We Can Do To Stop It* (1989).

3. Sportsmanship and fair play. What are the social problems of poor sportsmanship? What has sport become? Does anyone play fairly? Typical writers and texts that cover this subject are: R. E. Lapchick, *Fractured Focus* (1986); Lumpkin, Stoll, and Beller (1995); James A. Michener (1976); A. W. Miracle and C. R. Rees (1994); and Stoll (1993).

4. Commercialization. Does commercialization negatively affect the ethical character of the player, the fan, the administrator? Should we commercialize or not? How does commercialization affect the nature of the game and the integrity of the organization? Numerous works appear on this topic, typical are Murray Sperber, *College Sports, Inc.: The Athletics Department vs. the University* (1991), who argues that commercialization of collegiate sport has completely violated the ethical nature of the university structure. H. G. Bissinger's *Friday Night Lights: A Town, a Team, a Dream* (1990) examines the social and commercialized structure of high school football. Another source on commercialization of professional athletics is *The Name of the Game: The Business of Sport* (1994), by J. Gorman, K. Calhoun, and S. Rozin.

5. Performance enhancement and drug abuse. What are the ethical concerns of performance-enhancing drug use? Should rules outlaw drug usage? What do drugs do to the validity of the performance? One of the best sources that philosophically argues both sides of performance enhancement is volume 11 (1984) of the *Journal of Sport Philosophy*. For a more social perspective on the dilemma of anabolic steroid abuse see *Death in the Locker Room: Steroids and Sports* (1984) by B. Goldman with P. Bush and R. Klatz; *Death in the Locker Room* (1992) by Goldman and Klatz.

6. Gender equity. An important topic to be discussed from the ethical perspective is gender equity. Should opportunities for men and women be equal or equitable? What effect does the status quo have on the participating female? Good beginning sources to examine this issue are M. Messner, *Power at Play: Sports and the Problem of Masculinity* (1992), and *Women and Sport: Interdisciplinary Perspectives* (1994), by M. Costa and S. A. Guthrie.

7. Racism. What are the ethical concerns and ramifications of racism in the sporting experience? What effect does racism have on the athlete? What should the experience be for the minority athlete? What ethical and legal issues are preeminent in discussing racism in sport? See H. Edwards (1973 and 1986). Numerous journals address issues in these areas, as well as various college sociology of sport texts: See Eitzen (1993), Eitzen and Sage (1993), and Leonard (1993).

8. Youth sport. Should children be in competitive experiences? What role should youth sport play in the lives of children? What do children learn from youth sport? What medical problems occur because of overuse and too much competition in children? See various issues of *Journal of Pediatric Exercise*, or selected issues of *Research Quarterly for Exercise and Sport*, as well as the *Journal of Sociology of Sport*.

9. Intercollegiate sport. Should intercollegiate sport exist? What are the ethical problems with intercollegiate sport? What solutions are available? See Bailey and Littleton (1991), Andre and James (1991), as well as current collegiate sport sociological texts.

Professional Ethics

The third area of common usage is professional ethics (see Figure 1). Professional ethics is the stated or implied professional conduct that each organization deems important. The acceptable professional conduct can be somewhat general or very specific. For example, 40 years ago in physical education, it was considered unprofessional if a female coach or physical education teacher married. It was standard professional conduct for women to "marry the profession." It was believed that a woman's being married jeopardized or compromised her ability to serve the profession, to be a good teacher, or to coach. Obviously, this particular standard of conduct is extinct today, though we have many social mores that are unacceptable, for example, personal relationships between coaches and players, plagiarism of research materials, cheating, violating rules, and so on. Many of these common social mores are not written down and interpretation can be very foggy. In today's litigious society, many if not most professional organizations are realizing that written codes of ethics are important for two reasons: to give some objective form to the common professional or social mores of the group and to serve as a legal guide to what is ethical and what is not. Most organizations realize that with a changing social climate, and little moral education, professionals really are in a quandary as to what is considered ethical behavior. What one individual believes is unfair practice, another might believe is a part of the competitive process. Also, in our litigious society, professional groups have discovered that expunging offending unethical behavior is legally impossible without a stated, concise code of acceptable ethical conduct. These professional ethics or rules of conduct can become as highly specific and technical as legal, medical, or military codes of conduct. The codes of ethics are developed based on some perceived moral conduct that the organization deems imperative to the professional process. They usually begin with an oratory about what the organization believes is its philosophic basis, then canons are written to state exactly what is considered to be ethical behavior. They are usually written in the negative so that the profession knows explicitly what is offensive behavior. Most governing bodies of sport organizations have stated codes of ethical conduct or codes of sportsmanlike behavior. For example, the National Federation of High School Activities Association as well as most of its state governing bodies have stated codes of fair play conduct. The National Youth Sport Coaches Association, under the umbrella of the National Alliance for Youth Sport, has explicit statements of acceptable ethical behavior. Other governing bodies such as the National Collegiate Athletic Association have very specific rules on conduct and behavior of coaches, players, and booster organizations.

Moral Reasoning or Applied Ethics

In our essay thus far we have examined the word *ethics* from two perspectives: formal study and informal common usage. We began with a scenario about a tennis coach. In both the applied and theoretical, we should attempt a resolution of the dilemma. To resolve an ethical dilemma demands a skill known as moral reasoning. Several different approaches exist on how exactly to perform philosophical moral reasoning in sport. Fraleigh (1984) uses what is known as the "good reasoned approach"; Zeigler (1984), the experiential approach; and Lumpkin, Stoll, and Beller (1995) a maieutic (i.e., a classical Socratic) approach. Any and all approaches attempt to ferret out the issue and decide first if it is an ethical dilemma and if so what possible alternatives are available. The alternatives are then weighed in relation to one or any combination of the following: one's personal values, the social climate, the rule, the principle, the ramifications of the action, or the amount of good achieved by the action. The stated purpose is to find the course of action that is the most fair, honest, and respectful of others.

For example, let us return to the dilemma posed at the beginning of this article: What should the tennis coach do? Should the coach follow the administrators' mandate or should the coach "buck the system" and fight to take all the athletes to the state competition?

The tennis coach has a moral dilemma because three stipulations are present: the coach must choose and act on which action to take; the coach does have a choice, with two or perhaps more alternatives available; and a moral value and condition exists. The administration has forced the coach to make a choice between what the coach told the team was policy and what the administration has decided (though it could be argued no choice exists because the administration is coercing the coach to follow its decision); the coach must choose between (a) following his own conscience and carrying out what he promised and (b) condescending to what the administration has mandated, either telling the players the circumstances or not. Either choice will have ramifications: if he chooses (a), his administration will surely respond with some sort of reprimand; if he chooses (b), he will suffer the consequences of his players knowing that he does not keep his word. Other possible alternatives are (c) quit his position and not have to deal with the problem and (d) solicit public support to back his position.

One possible way to access this dilemma is to look for the stated purpose of the activity and what rules and condition exist for the activity. In other words, what foresight was originally used to set up guidelines for the program? In our tennis scenario, the coach probably caused the original dilemma. Policies and procedures need to be developed not in a vacuum but in the light of day. When developing a policy, the coach should have taken into consideration any system procedures that might affect the policy. The policy then should have been approved or supported in writing by the administration. If done accordingly, the coach would have a history and stated philosophy about what is common practice and procedure, as well as a written document to support his practices. Unfortunately, the coach apparently did none of the above, and developed a vacuous policy that no one else knew about, giving rise to a moral dilemma.

Most of the coach's choices will cause hardship to either the coach, the players, the administration, or the parents and fans involved. One alternative possibility to solve the dilemma at hand is to contact individually the parents and fans who want to ride in the van to the state tournament and attempt to marshal them to coach's cause. Perhaps, by doing so, coach might find that the parents and fans would want all the team to travel to the tournament. Or, perhaps not. What would you do? And why?

—Sharon Kay Stoll

Bibliography: Andre, J., and D. N. James. (1991) *Rethinking College Athletics*. Philadelphia: Temple University Press.

Arnold, P. J. (1994) "Sport and Moral Education." *Journal of Moral Education* 23, 1: 75–89.

———. (1991) "The Preeminence of Skill as an Educational Value in the Movement Curriculum." *Quest* 43 (April): 66–67.

Bailey, W. S., and T. D. Littleton. (1991) *Athletics and Academe*. New York: Macmillan.

Best, D. (1974) *Expression in Movement of the Art: A Philosophical Inquiry*. London: Leups.

Bissinger, H. G. (1990) *Friday Night Lights: A Town, a Team, a Dream*. Reading, MA: Addison-Wesley.

Bredemeier, B. J. L., and D. L. Shields. (1994) *Character Development and Physical Activity*. Champaign, IL: Human Kinetics.

Costa, M., and S. A. Guthrie. (1994) *Women and Sport: Interdisciplinary Perspectives*. Champaign, IL: Human Kinetics.

Edwards, H. (1986) "The Collegiate Athletic Arms Race: Origins and Implications of the 'Rule 48' Controversy." In *Fractured Focus*, edited by R. E. Lapchick. Lexington, KY: Lexington Books.

———. (1973) *Sociology of Sport*. Homewood, IL: Dorsey Press.

Eitzen, D. S. (1993) *Sport in Contemporary Society*. New York: St. Martin's Press.

Eitzen, D. S., and G. Sage. (1993) *Sociology of North American Sport*, 5th ed. Dubuque, IA: Wm. Brown.

Fahlberg, L., and L. Fahlberg. (1994) "A Human Science for the Study of Movement: An Integration of Multiple Ways of Knowing." *Research Quarterly for Exercise and Sport* 65, 2: 100–103.

Fraleigh, W. (1984) *Right Actions in Sport: Ethics for Contestants*. Champaign, IL: Human Kinetics.

Gibson, J. H. (1993) *Performance versus Results*. Albany: State University of New York Press.

Goldman, R., with P. Bush and R. Klatz. (1984) *Death in the Locker Room: Steroids, and Sports*. South Bend, IL: Icarus Books.

Goldman, R., and R. Klatz. (1992) *Death in the Locker Room*. Chicago: Elite Sports Medicine.

Gorman, J., K. Calhoun, and S. Rozin. (1994) *The Name of the Game: The Business of Sport*. New York: John Wiley and Sons.

Harper, W. (1985) "The Philosopher in Us." In *Sport Inside Out: Readings in Literature and Philosophy*, edited by D. Vanderwerken and S. Wertz. Fort Worth, TX: Texas Christian University Press, 449–545.

———. (1973–1976) *The Play Factory Advocate*, vols. 1–4. Emporia, KS: William A. Harper.

———. (1972) "Giving and Taking." Paper presented at the meeting of the Philosophic Society for the Study of Sport, February, Brockport, NY.

Hellison, D. (1973) *Humanistic Physical Education*. Englewood Cliffs, NJ: Prentice-Hall.

Hyland, D. (1990) *Philosophy of Sport*. New York: Paragon House.

Jeziorski, R. J. (1994) *The Importance of School Sports in American Education and Socialization*. New York: University Press of America.

Kleinman, S., ed. (1986) *Mind and Body: East Meets West*. Champaign, IL: Human Kinetics.

Kohlberg, L. (1981) *The Philosophy of Cognitive Moral Development*. New York: Harper and Row.

Kohn, A. (1986) *No Contest: The Case against Competition*. Boston: Houghton Mifflin.

Kretchmar, S. (1985) "'Distancing': An Essay on Abstract Thinking in Sport Performances." In *Sport Inside Out: Readings in Literature and Philosophy*, edited by D. Vanderwerken and S. Wertz. Fort Worth: Texas Christian University Press, 87–102.

———. (1975) "From Test to Contest: An Analysis of Two Kinds of Counterpoint in Sport." *Journal of the Philosophy of Sport* 2: 23–30.

Lapchick, R. E. (1986) *Fractured Focus*. Lexington, MA: Lexington Books.

Lapchick, R. E., and J. B. Slaughter. (1989) *The Rules of the Game: Ethics in College Sports.* New York: Macmillan.

Lenk, H. (1979) *Social Philosophy of Athletics.* Champaign, IL: Stipes.

Leonard, W. M. (1993) *A Sociological Perspective of Sport.* New York: Macmillan.

Lumpkin, A., S. Stoll, and J. Beller. (1995) *Sport Ethics: Applications for Fair Play.* St. Louis: Mosby.

McIntosh, P. (1979) *Fair Play: Ethics in Sport and Education.* London: Heinemann.

Meier, K. (1988) "Embodiment, Sport, and Meaning." In *Philosophic Inquiry in Sport,* edited by W. Morgan and K. Meier. Champaign, IL: Human Kinetics, 93–101.

———. (1980) "An Affair of Flutes: An Appreciation of Play." *Journal of the Philosophy of Sport* 7: 24–45.

———. (1975) "Cartesian and Phenomenological Anthropology: The Radial Shift and Its Meaning for Sport." *Journal of the Philosophy of Sport* 2: 51–73.

Messner, M. A. (1992) *Power at Play: Sports and the Problem of Masculinity.* Boston: Beacon Press.

Metheny, E. (1972) "The Symbolic Power of Sport." In E. Gerber, ed., *Sport and the Body: A Philosophical Symposium,* edited by E. Gerber. Philadelphia: Lea and Febiger, 221–226.

———. (1968) *Movement and Meaning.* New York: McGraw-Hill.

———. (1965) *Connotations of Movement in Sport and Dance.* Dubuque, IA: Brown.

Michener, J. A. (1976) *Sports in America.* New York: Random House.

Miracle, A. W., and C. R. Rees (1994) *Lessons of the Locker Room: The Myth of School Sports.* Amherst, NY: Prometheus Books.

Morgan, W. (1982) "Play, Utopia, and Dystopia: Prologue to a Ludic Theory of the State." *Journal of the Philosophy of Sport* 9: 30–42.

Morgan, W., and K. Meier, eds. (1988) *Philosophic Inquiry in Sport.* Champaign, IL: Human Kinetics.

Nash, J., ed. (1931) *Interpretations of Physical Education: Mind-Body Relationships.* New York: Barnes.

Novak, M. (1976) *The Joy of Sports: End Zones, Bases, Baskets, Balls, and the Consecration of the American Spirit.* New York: Basic Books.

Osterhoudt, R. (1991) *The Philosophy of Sport: An Overview.* Champaign, IL: Stipes.

Parry, J. (1988) "Physical Education, Justification, and the National Curriculum." *Physical Education Review* 11: 106–118.

Sage, G. (1990) *Power and Ideology in American Sport: A Critical Perspective.* Champaign, IL: Human Kinetics.

Simon, R. (1991) *Fair Play: Sports, Values, and Society.* Boulder, CO: Westview Press.

Slusher, H. (1967) *Man, Sport and Existence: A Critical Analysis.* Philadelphia: Lea and Febiger.

Sperber, M. (1991) *College Sports, Inc.: The Athletic Department vs. the University.* New York: Henry Holt.

Steele, M. (1985) "What We Know When We Know a Game." In *Sport Inside Out: Readings in Literature and Philosophy,* edited by D. Vanderwerken and S. Wertz. Fort Worth, TX: Texas Christian University Press, 78–86.

Stoll, S. K. (1993) *Who Says It's Cheating?* Dubuque, IA: Kendall Hunt.

Suits, B. (1978) *The Grasshopper: Games, Life and Utopia.* Toronto: University of Toronto Press.

———. (1972) "What Is a Game?" In *Sport and the Body: A Philosophical Symposium,* edited by E. Gerber. Philadelphia: Lea and Febiger, 16–22.

Telander, R. (1989) *The Hundred Yard Lie: The Corruption of College Football and What We Can Do To Stop It.* New York: Simon and Schuster.

Thomas, C. (1983) *Sport in a Philosophic Context.* Philadelphia: Lea and Febiger.

Weiss, M. R., and B. J. L. Bredemeier. (1986) "Moral Development." In *Physical Activity and Well Being,* edited by V. Seefeldt. Reston, VA: American Alliance for Health, Physical Education, Recreation, and Dance, 373–390.

———. (1990) "Moral Development in Sport." In *Exercise and Sport Sciences Review* 18: 331–378.

Wertz, S. (1991) *Talking a Good Game: Inquiries into the Principles of Sport.* Dallas, TX: Southern Methodist University Press.

Wood, T., and R. Cassidy. (1927) *The New Physical Education: A Program of Naturalized Activities for Education toward Citizenship.* New York: Macmillan.

Zeigler, E. F. (1977) *Physical Education and Sport Philosophy.* Englewood Cliffs, NJ: Prentice-Hall.

———. (1984) *Ethics and Morality in Sport and Physical Education: An Experiential Approach.* Champaign, IL: Stipes.

Ethnicity

Whether we like it or not, we cannot discuss ethnicity without linking it to race. In the process, we will find that many social scientists and historians have reminded us that ethnicity and race are products of complex, contradictory, and historical human interactions. Ethnicity and race are, in other words, social constructions entangled with issues related to political power, class, gender, and nationality. If so, then we ought to look seriously at sport as one site among many for people forging complicated ethnic and racial identities combined with power relationships based on ethnic and racial ideologies.

Sport has long been identified as an assimilating tool in multiethnic and multiracial societies such as the United States. However, the concept of assimilation often varies from analyst to analyst. Sociologist Milton Gordon articulates one way of thinking about assimilation in the United States as a "merger of the Anglo-Saxon peoples with other immigrant groups and a blending of their respective cultures into a new indigenous American type." Accordingly, we could view sport as some kind of common or "middle ground" on which ethnic groups interact on relatively equal terms. The concept of the "middle ground" was used creatively in historian Peter Levine's *Ellis Island to Ebbets Field* to describe the Jewish-American sporting experiences. Another way to understand the concept of assimilation is to recognize that assimilation occurs with, as Milton Gordon writes, "the complete renunciation of the immigrant's ancestral culture in favor of the behavior and values of the [native-born] core group." Under such circumstances, there is no middle ground. The dominant racial and ethnic group generally assumes that nondominant racial and ethnic group members will assimilate or face the consequences.

From one perspective, sport becomes the tool of the dominant culture to encourage or compel assimilation. A century ago government run boarding schools for American Indians promoted athletic programs in order to make students over into "the white man's image." Similar kinds of programs were developed to "Americanize" white, Latin, and Asian immigrants. From another perspective, sport appears as an opportunity for individuals to make themselves over. By taking up a sport supported by the dominant culture, an ethnic minority group member is extended the freedom to fit in.

Among those countering assimilation are a number of thoughtful intellectuals who have articulated intriguing views on ethnicity, race, and culture. They have clearly jettisoned assimilation as a useful analytical tool while redefining a simplistic multiculturalism in such a way that it allows us to better see cultural convergence and separation among distinct social groups as well as the dynamic relationship between power and culture. Stuart Hall, Paul Gilroy, Renato Rosaldo, Gloria Anzaldua, George Lipsitz, and bell hooks stand out among these intellectuals. Gloria Anzaldua, for example, writes that in North America different racial and ethnic groups have constructed a "borderland." For Anzaldua, a borderland is terrain on which "two or more cultures edge each other, where people of different races occupy the same territory." The consequences for individual social identity seems potentially profound. Thus we traverse a myriad of socially constructed boundaries. We are not simply the legacies of homogenous, closed-off, and unchanging racial or ethnic identities, but carriers of interacting, often conflicting, gender, sexual orientation, class, and national cultures as well. In the borderland, we can find communal ground despite our differences. We can also find the powerful separating forces of racism, nativism, sexism, homophobia, imperialism, and class exploitation.

To situate sporting institutions and practices as constituting a borderland through which people of various racial and ethnic groups travel is to consider seriously the contradictory character of sport's relationship to society and power. On the one hand, sport has offered individuals from marginalized and exploited groups opportunities to develop and reinforce meaningful ethnic communities, to forge a bridge across cultural boundaries, to acquire a sense of liberation and even mastery. This is not to mention that commercialized sport has expanded, sometimes astonishingly so, the income and social status of a handful of athletes from historically oppressed and exploited racial and ethnic groups. On the other hand, sport has encouraged and buttressed racial and ethnic boundaries while supporting interrelated gender, class, and other socially constructed hierarchies. Indeed, even the presence of highly paid and seemingly well respected athletes of color or from white ethnic groups raises some troubling implications.

Border Crossings

It is possible to argue that sport can help develop an ethnic identity among people. For example, the largely agricultural people migrating to the United States from Japan during the late 1800s and early 1900s were like others possessing agrarian backgrounds in that they defined themselves politically in localistic terms. They identified themselves by way of their connections with family, kin, village, and region, and their identity with a place called Japan was not so close. In the United States, Japanese immigrants tried as well as they could to transplant their localistic social networks, while many seemingly displayed relatively little interest in seeming either Japanese or American.

However, in 1905 an early sign of a Japanese-American ethnic identity in the United States surfaced when Tokyo's Waseda University baseball team toured cities like Los Angeles, San Francisco, and Seattle. The Japanese immigrants in these cities reportedly attended Waseda's games with various college, high school, and other amateur teams in significant numbers and rooted for the Japanese team enthusiastically. In the process, they seemingly crossed boundaries between family and locality to link with other Japanese emigrants. In other words, they signaled the emergence of Japanese-American communities in West Coast cities.

One could see similar processes taking place later in the twentieth century among Mexican and Filipino immigrants living and working on the U.S. West Coast. In the 1920s and into the 1930s, the people performing migrant labor or domestic labor services in California were frequently either Mexican or Filipino. Very commonly these people were told that they were, at best, fit to serve Euroamericans. However, many prize-fighting promoters discovered as well that Mexican and Filipino immigrants were boxing fans and were, in particular, followers of Mexican and Filipino boxers brought into the United States to take on various U.S. opponents. Many of these boxers beat Euroamericans with regularity and provided a source of communal pride among marginalized and exploited Mexican and Filipino workers, who came from different regions of Mexico and the Philippines and possessed relatively little sense of Mexican or Filipino nationality.

Communities, for many us, seem to cross regional and national borders. If political scientist Benedict Anderson is correct, then nations are "imagined communities" and nationalism is the effort to build and maintain a sense of community among people who have little chance of seeing each other face to face. Sport has played an often underestimated role in engendering "imagined communities" among colonized people of color. Historian and political activist C. L. R. James has chronicled the relationship between colonialism, race, and sport in his classic *Beyond a Boundary*; it is a book about cricket, but as James reminds us: "What do they know of cricket who only cricket know?"

A Marxist, pan-Africanist, and remarkably versatile scholar, James played and followed cricket from his boyhood in the black colony of Trinidad. His *Beyond a Boundary* forcefully breaks down the stereotype of cricket as strictly an elitist, white Englishman's sport. Indeed, the English colonizers brought their love of cricket to the West Indies. They sought to use cricket as a way to Anglicize as much as they thought possible the less plebeian black West Indians. However, even if cricket was intended as a helpmate for British hegemony, black West Indians found in cricket multiple possibilities, some of which could well have troubled the colonizers.

James and many of his fellow black cricketers honored the ethos of fair play underlying cricket even if the source of this ethos was created by the English colonizers. However, by playing well against whites and doing so within the framework developed by English Victorians, black West Indian cricketers nurtured a sense of pride in themselves and in their own way helped construct a bridge among people of color throughout the British empire.

It seems that ethnicity and nationhood, according to Richard Holt, operate in an interesting way when it comes to sport. He writes:

> The rise of new kind of popular "Welshness" and "Scottishness" and its expression through rugby and football make British sport unique—in certain events Britain and Northern Ireland compete as a united nation, in others the UK is a federation of four nations each with its own teams; it is as if the French sent representatives from the Languedoc, Britanny and Provence alongside a team from "France" on the basis that these "countries" had once been self-governing states.

From the playground and sandlot to the professional arena, sport can aid the formation of racial and ethnic identities and communities across other social distinctions. The famous stars and teams often reflected and reinforced racial and ethnic pride, but so might the local athlete and the neighborhood team. Ethnic community leaders, moreover, often considered sport important in resolving social problems and conflicts disrupting their communities. Leading Chinese Americans and Japanese Americans often encouraged the creation of athletic teams for both sexes. In the 1930s and 1940s, San Francisco's Chinatown avidly supported Chinese-American basketball tournaments, while West Coast Japanese Americans just as avidly backed community baseball teams. The origins of such enthusiasm do not seem to have been an overwhelming need to achieve Euroamerican acceptance. Rather, Asian-American communities, like working class ethnic communities elsewhere, were sites of highly visible poverty, social cleavages, and criminal activities. To divert young people, especially working-class young people, from gambling, street gangs, and substance abuse, organizations such as the Young Men's Buddhist Association and the Young Women's Buddhist Association sponsored the formation of baseball, basketball, softball, and football teams among Americans of Japanese ancestry.

For Japanese Americans, this belief that sport could serve as a social bond was carried over into World War II; a time when the U.S. government interned over 100,000 West Coast Japanese Americans in concentration camps. Sports such as baseball, softball, and basketball helped maintain a sense of community among Japanese Americans during an immensely stressful period in their lives.

Sport could also bring solace and joy to people such as the Filipino migrant workers, overworked and underpaid while laboring in Alaska during the early 1930s. Filipino American writer Carlos Bulosan writes:

It was only at night we felt free, although the sun seemed never to disappear from the sky. It stayed on in the western horizon and its magnificence inflamed the snows . . . giving us a world of soft, continuous light, until the moon rose at about ten o'clock to take its place. Then trembling shadows began to form on the rise of the brilliant snow in our yard, and we would come out with baseball bats, gloves and balls, and the Indian girls who worked in the cannery would join us, shouting huskily like men.

In multiethnic, multiracial modern England, sociologist John Hargreaves has written, "Ethnic sport is growing in importance as ethnic minorities attempt to assert their independence and to establish their own cultural identities in a largely hostile society." Hargreaves informs us that during the 1980s, West Indians in Manchester organized "a thriving centre catering for a wide range of social, cultural, and recreational interests, among which sports are prominent." Manchester residents of African ancestry established their own football league, while blacks in London operated the Muhammad Ali Sports Development Association "to develop the talents and aspirations and confidence of young blacks."

While they could have done more, community sporting practices have often been relatively accessible to female participation. Women of Asian ancestry have had to struggle against the stereotype of them as physically, intellectually, and emotionally passive. However, in numerous Chinese-American and Japanese-American communities women eagerly played basketball and softball, as well as other sports.

Historically and today, the international movement of people of African, Asian, Latin American, Middle Eastern, Pacific Islander, and European ancestry has often meant the transplantation of sporting traditions along with the transplantation of communal ties. In nineteenth-century United States, European immigrants and their children played "old world" sports, as well as baseball, basketball, and American football. Irish games were played in cities such as Worcester, Massachusetts, where a large Irish working-class population resided. The Scottish Caledonia games attracted enthusiastic participation. German immigrants and their children organized and joined turnverein societies in American communities from St. Louis to El Paso to San Francisco. Asian immigrants to the United States also transplanted sporting traditions. For example, sumo wrestling tournaments were held by Japanese plantation workers in Hawaii before the turn of the century.

Migrants from India and Pakistan have brought their love of a Punjab-based game called Kabbadi to countries like the United Kingdom. However, social scientist Jennifer Hargreaves notes that while Kabbadi "is played by girls and young women in schools and colleges in India and Pakistan and has been played in the United Kingdom by men of Asian descent for the last thirty years, it was played by Asian women in the UK for the first time only in 1990, and in a spontaneous fashion as part of an Asian festival."

"Star" athletes seemingly reinforced community ties among members of racial and ethnic groups. Jackie Robinson's impact on African Americans is difficult to gauge. However, historian Jules Tygiel argues that the racial integration of mid-twentieth-century Euroamerican-organized professional baseball by Robinson encouraged the subsequent development of the American civil rights movement.

Robinson and black heavyweight champion Joe Louis became visible symbols of many African American aspirations during the first half of the twentieth century. They demonstrated the kind of courage and dignity Euroamericans so blindly ignored in the African American experience. While doing so, they time and time again outperformed whites. In her *Making a New Deal*, historian Liz Cohen claims that Joe Louis's popularity bridged the racial and cultural distinctions within Chicago's working class in the 1930s. In rooting for the great heavyweight, a Polish and African American worker could create a common ground between them that might otherwise have been lacking; a common ground from which a relatively effective labor movement was launched in the 1930s.

In the United States, renowned athletes like boxer John L. Sullivan, baseball players Joe DiMaggio and Hank Greenberg, and football player Jim Thorpe became ethnic symbols for Irish Americans, Italian Americans, Jewish Americans, and Native Americans, respectively. Similarly, the leading West Indian cricket players connected in a meaningful way to the experiences of black Caribbeans. C. L. R. James maintains: "All of us knew our West Indian cricketers, so to speak, from birth, when they made their first century, when they became engaged, if they drank whiskey or rum." No matter how good they might become, the West Indian cricketers were not just "read about in the papers and worshipped from afar. They were all over the place, ready to play in any match, ready to talk." The accessibility of these cricket stars was "one of our greatest strengths, why we have been able to do so much with so little." Likewise, professional baseball players associated with the U.S. Negro leagues and Caribbean leagues were often considered community heroes. This was so not just because they were highly accomplished ballplayers, but because they remained tied personally to the communities they were perceived as representing.

Of course, nowadays we are used to the notion that the "superstars" of sport transcend social boundaries. We are also becoming used to the notion that many of our sport idols might possess a different racial and ethnic identity than our own, while they get paid an obscene amount of money for playing games and advertising athletic shoes or breakfast cereals. Few can argue that sport has allowed some black athletes such as basketball star Michael Jordan and soccer star Pele to seemingly traverse racial barriers and become enormously admired and enormously wealthy. In the past and in the present, other athletes associated with marginalized and exploited racial and ethnic groups have crossed cultural boundaries to become universally respected and frequently well paid.

However rich and famous many of these athletes became, it is important to remember that some of the more moving stories in sport history revolve around the efforts of highly gifted amateur and professional athletes to endure and even contest racial and ethnic discrimination. The German Jewish athletes who were denied places on Hitler's Olympic team come to mind. Of course, Jackie Robinson's experience is well known. Lesser known is the courage of another baseball standout, Henry Aaron, who faced down unspeakable racism as he chased and moved ahead of Babe Ruth's home-run record.

That all sorts of people also cheered Aaron on is a reminder that star athletes can provide something of a common ground for people of different racial and ethnic groups. But even for lesser-known athletes, sport can cross otherwise powerful racial and ethnic barriers. Athletic teams organized in the Hawaiian Islands have historically been more multiethnic and multiracial than in other regions in the American empire. One can look at the all too unique rosters of Hawaiian football, basketball, and baseball teams in the 1920s, 1930s, and 1940s and note the existence of Asian, Hawaiian Islander, Hispanic, and Anglo last names. Hawaii, indeed, was arguably well ahead of the U.S. mainland in using sport to enhance democratic and egalitarian experiences and nurturing highly skilled athletes of Hawaiian Islander and Asian ancestry.

Sport, therefore, has allowed significant numbers of people of diverse racial and ethnic groups to move beyond ethnocentric assumptions developed about them. In many cases, it has even helped connect them as an "imagined community," prepared to battle racism, nativism, and colonialism. It has given opportunities for some of them to make money and achieve honors. It has given everyone wonderful stories of courageous struggles against bigotry and discrimination. However, if through sport, people can achieve movement across socially constructed boundaries, then it is important to note that there have been people who seem freer to travel about than others. In other words, sport has its border guards, discouraging movement for some, while allowing movement for others. It has made some borders more porous, while strengthening other racial and ethnic boundaries.

Sport and the Border Guard

If we just go back 400 or 500 years, we can see how sport can reinforce cultural barriers between people. By the 1700s, the Europeans characterized many of America's indigenous people as lazy. These Europeans defined hunting and fishing as sport and performing agricultural labor as work. Since many Native American groups depended at least in part upon hunting and fishing, they did quite a lot of it, much to the dismay of Europeans and then Euroamericans. The perception that Native Americans spent so much of their time engaging in "sport" and not in useful labor strengthened Europeans and Euroamericans in their beliefs that Native Americans were culturally and, perhaps, innately inferior.

A somewhat similar kind of cultural barrier was erected in California during the mid-nineteenth century. Before the United States obtained California as a consequence of the Mexican War, horse racing and other displays of equestrian skills ranked among the Californians' favorite pastimes. These equestrian events possessed a utilitarian value since so much of the region's economy was based upon cattle ranching and the horse-riding skills of the people who worked on these ranches. Nevertheless, those from the United States who came to California during and after the Gold Rush generally frowned upon these Mexican pastimes. This was especially true among those Americans known as Sabbatarians. These pious Protestants professed a belief in hard work from Monday through Saturday but allowed that Sunday was, according to their interpretation of God's will, a day of rest; a day of rest from work but also from play.

Sunday, however, was a favored day for Mexican Catholics to engage in horse racing, as well as put on bullfights and other activities that repulsed good Protestant Americans. In the early 1850s, the Anglo-controlled town government of San Jose banned horse racing. At about the same time, the California state legislature distressed the state's Mexican population by passing a Sunday law that declared as illegal on Sunday many of Mexican Californians' favorite sporting activities.

In California and throughout the nineteenth-century United States, the sporting practices of immigrants and children of immigrants often provoked nativistic responses. Immigrants were often seen as too inclined to patronize such "disreputable" activities as prize fights and too little inclined toward hard work and sobriety. Of course, class issues intertwined with the development of industrial capitalism weighed heavily here; especially when it came to Sunday sporting and recreational practices. The country's native-born Protestant elite clung tenaciously to the notion that Sunday laws would keep ethnic workers controllable. Its industrial capitalists often viewed Sunday laws favorably, because they would encourage a rested and sober workforce ready for 50 to 60 hours of labor from Monday through Saturday.

Into the twentieth century, people identified with other racial and ethnic groups have been stereotyped as more interested in play than in work. Often such stereotyping becomes clearly racist, because it connects a person's interest with some kind of innate predisposition. In the United Kingdom, Jennifer Hargreaves writes: "Whereas the successes of white women in sports are assumed to be the result of dedicated training and self-sacrifice (or drug-taking, particularly in the case of Eastern Europeans), the visibility of elite black sportswomen is assumed to be because they are genetically predisposed to be superior athletes."

Of course, the view that people of African ancestry harbored innate talents for at least certain sports, especially sports requiring considerable running and jumping, has scarcely been unique to the United Kingdom. The issue of whether blacks are naturally gifted athletically has long provoked controversy and has long helped construct a racial ideology in the United States, the UK, and elsewhere. Ironically, among the early supporters of athletic competition in Europe and North America there was little doubt that whites were more naturally gifted athletes than nonwhites. Indeed, for many, athletic competition buttressed Social Darwinism; races did exist and some races were more fit than others. Athletic competition, according to these racial ideologues, demanded brains, discipline, and "pluck," as well as coordination and strength. Nonwhites might claim the latter two characteristics, but when it came to intelligence, discipline, and courage, they were lacking. The rugby and American football stadium seemed to prove that time and again to white supremacists; despite the accomplishments of athletes such as the Native American Jim Thorpe during the first decades of the twentieth century.

Therefore, sport helped draw the color line in the United States and it helped justify European imperialism. To the extent that people of color might display some ability to compete athletically, they were simply showing that they were "white inside." The dominant racial ideology was scarcely disturbed at all. At the same time, some Europeans and Euroamericans who regarded people of color as not so closely bound by their natures also considered sport as a civilizing tool. If East or West Indians learned cricket, then those "natives" would take one step closer to Western Civilization, while, hopefully, gaining new respect for their colonizers. In the Philippines, during the early twentieth century, baseball was used to "Americanize" a population, a significant portion of whom had fought a protracted guerrilla war against U.S. rule.

Within the United States, sport took on a highly visible role in supporting a racial hierarchy. Major League Baseball and other professional baseball organizations affiliated with it barred African Americans from team rosters in the 1880s and backed "Jim Crow" segregation until after World War II. While prominent as jockeys for many years, African Americans found that by the twentieth century commercial horse racing had drawn the color line as well. Occasionally during the late nineteenth century and early twentieth century, blacks such as Paul Robeson might play for college football teams and some African American boxers were prominent. However, as Jeffrey Samuels points out, African American prizefighters faced substantial challenges in crossing the color line:

Since prizefighting has been characterized by some as a true test of skill, courage,

intelligence, and manhood, boxing champions have traditionally stood as symbols of national and racial superiority. Consequently, black challengers to white American champions have been perceived as threats to white and national superiority. If football was "the expression of the strength of the Anglo-Saxon . . . the dominant spirit of the dominant race," then boxing reduced this expression to individual terms.

Black heavyweight champions such as Jack Johnson and Muhammad Ali expressed an unapologetic awareness that they challenged white supremacy. Johnson, in particular, aroused white resentment and quests for "white hopes" to unseat him from his heavyweight throne during the 1900s and 1910s.

Non–African American athletes of color have also faced discriminatory treatment in the world of sport. A few athletes of indigenous, Asian, and Latin American ancestry have reached the higher echelons of competitive sports. However, for decades a racial ideology has proclaimed all people of color as lacking the characteristics of true sporting champions. At the dawn of the twentieth century, U.S. sportswriters expressed astonishment that prizefighters of Mexican ancestry and Asian ancestry could manage adeptly in the boxing ring. Such athletes were perceived as generally lacking the white man's fortitude. When it seemed clear that some Asian boxers, in particular those hailing from the Philippines, were challenging white supremacy time and again in the boxing ring, the state of California tried to ban Filipino boxers in 1930.

Recreational sport has offered too many instances of racial and ethnic hierarchies as well. Swimming pools and other recreational facilities were declared off limits to Americans of color for decades. Private golf clubs and athletic clubs not only have restricted membership to white Americans, but they have banned Jews and others normally identified as white.

Even if unintentional, such discrimination persists, as Jennifer Hargreaves asserts is the case in the United Kingdom. Race, gender, and class factors combine, Hargreaves maintains, to limit the participation of British women of Asian ancestry in recreational sports. Asian women are stereotyped as not interested in participating in sports.

Thus, their need for physical health and fun is ignored by recreational policy-makers. At the same time, many recreational activities remain too costly to be accessible to working-class Asian women. Indeed, Hargreaves work suggests that we can easily exaggerate the bonding power of sport in racial and ethnic communities. Class and gender, for example, can divide such communities and sport can reinforce such divisions.

In recent decades, the relationship between racial ideology and sport has been altered. The success of athletes of color in many competitive sports has, of course, weakened the argument that people of European ancestry are athletically superior. Instead, too many of those involved in sports in one form or another now argue that people of African ancestry possess some natural abilities that make them particularly adept in sports that require a great deal of running and jumping, such as basketball. On the other hand, it has also been claimed that people of African ancestry have a natural tendency to fail at competitive water sports.

Whether supposedly complimentary or not and whether people of African ancestry internalize these assumptions about their athletic capabilities or not, it ought to be clear that sport remains a powerful racializing tool. In other words, historically and today it can ascribe to a group of people certain characteristics that they cannot alter. Despite the evidence provided by substantial numbers of physical anthropologists, sport continues to insist that race has a scientific validity.

The fact that numerous athletes of color have achieved fame and fortune should not divert us from looking at the downside of all this. As sociologist Harry Edwards points out, the stereotype of blacks as naturally inclined toward athletics has more than likely dissuaded African Americans from seeking careers more realistic than those of professional athletes and more beneficial, in the long run, to themselves, their families, and communities. Even those very few athletes of color who do become well known remain subject to discrimination. Disproportionately their employers and coaches are white. If team players, they disproportionately play positions that supposedly require more athleticism and less intelligence. And very often they will hear how naturally gifted they are from pundits and fans and how intelligent and hard working their white teammates are.

Admittedly, the last decade or so has seen less in the way of overt racial and ethnic hostility in the sporting world. Yet such hostility or indifference to such hostility persists. "Football hooliganism" emerging in the United Kingdom during the 1970s has expressed a white racial chauvinism frightening in its openness. But even more frightening is the silence expressed by many clubs and players in response to crowd abuse of players of color. Moreover, the anti-apartheid movement called upon the sporting elite to condemn racial policy in South Africa and refuse competition with South African athletes until apartheid was ended. Instead, this elite frequently turned away in silence and complained about those who fail to understand that sport and politics do not mix.

Racial and ethnic conventions seem rooted in the historical development of sport; especially commercialized sport. Indeed, commercialized sports have long marketed race and ethnicity as a sound business practice. For years, professional baseball's New York Giants sought a Jewish player who would attract Jewish fans to New York's Polo Grounds. Moreover, racial integration of post–World War II professional baseball would not have been undertaken if baseball entrepreneurs such as Branch Rickey were not convinced that terminating "Jim Crow" baseball made good business sense. In San Francisco, a prize-fight promoter in the 1930s was so anxious to attract Jewish customers that he used the services of a non-Jewish boxer because he possessed a Jewish-sounding last name. Meanwhile, in Los Angeles, prize fight promoters employed boxers of Mexican and Filipino ancestry to lure fans of Mexican and Filipino ancestry.

Entrepreneurs may not now exploit race and ethnicity so overtly as a marketing strategy for commercialized sport. But the close ties between commercialized sport and manufacturers of athletic shoes combined with the knowledge that such highly expensive shoes have found a market among African American ghetto youth has been and remains troubling. Consequently, there are two sure places to see an African American male on television; during a telecast of a sporting event or in an advertisement showing him jumping, running, or being physically intimidating.

Exercise

Conclusion

Through sport, people have crossed racial and ethnic borders and shown time and again that bigotry can lose. However, borders, particularly racial borders, endure and racism's border guards seem ever vigilant. Those of us who look at the Michael Jordans and Peles and optimistically argue that things have gotten better in recent years and will get even better in the future haven't been paying that much attention to human history. Far too many of us have not noticed or chosen not to notice what literary critic Elaine Kim has referred to "racism's traveling eye," which shadows our movements across the borderlands.

—Joel S. Franks

Bibliography: Coakley, Jay J. (1990) *Sport in Society*. St. Louis: Missouri Times Mirror.

Edwards, Harry. (1973) *The Sociology of Sport*. Homewood, IL: Dorsey Press.

Eisen, George, and Wiggins, David K., eds. (1994) *Ethnicity and Sport in North American History and Culture*. Westport, CT: Greenwood Press.

Gorn, Elliot. (1986) *The Manly Art: Bare Knuckle Prize Fighting in America*. Ithaca, NY: Cornell University Press.

Guttmann, Allen. (1978) *From Ritual to Record*. New York: Columbia University.

———. (1991) *Women's Sports: A History*. New York: Columbia University Press.

Hargreaves, Jennifer. (1994) *Sporting Females: Critical Issues in the History and Sociology of Women's Sports*. London and New York: Routledge.

Hargreaves, John. (1986) *Sport, Power and Culture: A Social and Historical Analysis of Popular Sports in Britain*. New York: St. Martin's Press.

Holt, Richard. (1990) *Sport and the British*. Oxford and New York: Oxford University Press.

James, C. L. R. (1983) *Beyond a Boundary*. New York: Pantheon Books.

Roberts, Randy. (1983) *Papa Jack: Jack Johnson and the Era of White Hopes*. New York: Free Press.

Lapchick, Richard. (1986) *Fractured Focus: Sport as a Reflection of Society*. Lexington, MA: D. C. Heath and Co.

Levine, Peter. (1992) *Ellis Island to Ebbets Field: Sport and the American Jewish Experience*. New York and Oxford: Oxford University Press.

Nasaw, David. (1985) *Children of the City: At Work and at Play*. Garden, City, NY: Doubleday.

Riess, Steven A. (1989) *City Games: The Evolution of American Urban Society and the Rise of Sports*. Urbana and Chicago: University of Illinois Press.

Rosenzweig, Roy. (1983) *Eight Hours for What We Will: Workers and Leisure in an Industrial City, 1870–1920*. Cambridge: Cambridge University Press.

Ruck, Rob. (1987) *Sandlot Seasons: Sport in Black Pittsburgh*. Urbana and Chicago: University of Illinois Press.

———. (1990) *The Tropic of Baseball: Baseball in the Dominican Republic*. New York: Carroll & Graf Publishers.

Sammons, Jeffrey T. (1988) *Beyond the Ring: The Role of Boxing in American Society*. Urbana and Chicago: University of Illinois Press.

Tygiel, Jules. (1983) *Baseball's Great Experiment: Jackie Robinson and His Legacy*. New York and Oxford: Oxford University Press.

Exercise

Exercise is a component of physical activity or physical fitness and is a structured activity specifically planned to develop and maintain physical fitness. Physical fitness has been defined by the U.S. President's Council on Physical Fitness and Sports as "the ability to carry out daily tasks efficiently with enough energy left over to enjoy leisure time pursuits and to meet unforeseen emergencies." The position of the American Alliance for Health, Physical Education, Recreation, and Dance (AAHPERD) is that "physical fitness is a multifaceted continuum extending from birth to death. Affected by physical activity, it ranges from optimal abilities in all aspects of life through high and low levels of different physical fitness, to severely limiting disease and dysfunction."

Since early in human development, people have realized the benefits of being physically fit. Only recently have contemporary societies actively engaged in exercise to obtain varying levels of physical fitness. Exercise keeps the body healthy and fit; it is beneficial to physical health as well as mental health. Exercise includes such activities as running, walking, biking, dancing, rowing, skating, and weight training. Exercise or fitness activities must be engaged in on a regular basis to maintain or increase fitness levels.

History

From the beginning of humankind's existence on earth, movement of the human body has been an integral and necessary part of human life. Exercise as physical labor was an essential and mandatory part of life. In the early hunting and gathering days there was no use for exercise as we define and use it now. People moved all day in order to survive.

Their exercise, however, was not for labor alone. They engaged in activities of a warlike nature, and in times of peace they practiced these skills as recreational pastimes. Dance was an important aspect of early physical activity. It was interwoven into many areas of the lives of the early hunters and gatherers. Dance was used to placate the gods for wrongdoings and to thank the gods for assistance and blessings. The dancers imitated not only their own activities of hunting and war, but also animals and forces of nature, such as bears, snakes, rain, and fire. The earliest evidence of organized exercise, running, occurred in 3800 B.C.E. at Memphis in Egypt. However, ritual races around the walls of Memphis may have actually predated 4100 B.C.E. Drawings dating from 3300 B.C.E. show a form of high jumping, with children jumping over the linked arms of other children.

The ancient Greeks are credited with instituting and promoting the idea of exercise and athletics. The Greeks placed more emphasis on exercise than any previous society. The Athenians exercised and played for the sheer enjoyment of it. They admired a beautiful body and actively strove to attain it. They believed in both a healthy body and a healthy mind and felt that these two concepts worked together to create the whole person. The Spartans, by contrast, were motivated by militarism. Physical exercise was undertaken to develop strong bodies to withstand the rigors of war. This idea of fitness for military strength has continued to have an overwhelming impact on many societies since that of early Sparta.

The Greeks held the first Olympic Games in 776 B.C.E. The Games convened every four years until they were discontinued in C.E. 394. The modern Olympic Games reconvened in 1896, in Athens, Greece, a fitting tribute to the ancient Greeks who had placed such emphasis on these games in their culture. The Romans never embraced the games as the Greeks did. The Romans, like the Spartans, were a military nation, so military exercises took precedence over games. However, the Romans were known to bring Greek athletes to their cities to watch the gladiatorial games and professional exhibitions, as they did appreciate the physical pursuits of these athletes.

On the other side of the world there were also some strong early influences of Eastern exercise and physical activity in the form of the martial arts. Historians believe that the martial arts began in India with the practice of Veda. Later Taoism and Zen were documented in Asian cultures. The martial arts practice a highly disciplined type of exercise that combines the workings of the mind and the body.

With the decline of the Roman Empire, the Christian concept of life began its dominance, which continued for many centuries. Most recreational or physical activities had to be approved by the church and mandated a strong religious theme. Germany is credited with developing in the early nineteenth century a system of physical exercises that became a model for many other European nations in modern times. Denmark, Sweden, and Finland followed the German lead of implementing gymnastic-type programs to increase the fitness levels and health of their citizens. England also adopted and developed a strong sport and exercise culture. The Church of England promoted the idea of muscular Christianity, which espoused the attainment of spiritual well-being through physical exercise. The athletic and sport traditions of England were transplanted to America by the early colonists; from both North America and Britain these traditions spread throughout the world. England and the United States are credited with the evolution of modern sport and exercise.

The industrial period began during the mid-eighteenth century and lasted to the end of World War II in 1945. This period was marked by the development of the steam engine and electrical power. The population showed a shift from rural life to urban life, from farms to cities. This was the beginning of a less physically challenging way of life. A small but vocal group of educators and reformers in both England and the United States in the mid-1800s advocated exercise for both men and women for increased health. Writers, ministers, educators, and statesmen launched a crusade in favor of exercise, criticizing the sedentary nature of city dwellers. For the first time exercise and recreation were promoted as a respite from the pressures of work. However, people in this industrial age still faced significant energy demands in their daily functioning compared to the future technological period.

The physical and mental benefits of fitness have been recognized by almost every culture throughout history. Here women training to become U.S. Navy machinist mates during World War II do their daily stint.

Health Benefits

The technological period after World War II marked a significant change in the energy expenditure of the human being. Technology developed to make life easier and less physical, both at home and in the workplace. Automobiles became the major mode of transportation. Elevators and escalators took the place of stairs, and with remote control one can do just about anything from the comfort of the living room couch. Today we walk for fitness, whereas our ancestors walked to get from one place to another. Exercise and physical fitness became necessary in order to counteract the negative effects of a sedentary lifestyle. During this time, significant increases in illness and disease attributed to lack of activity grew at alarming rates. Exercise became medicine; however, the concept was not really a new one. It was Hippocrates, the fifth-century B.C.E. Greek physician, who said: "All parts of the body which have a function, if used in moderation and exercised in labours in which each is accustomed, become thereby healthy, well-developed and age more slowly; but if unused and left idle they become liable to disease, defective in growth, and age quickly." Greek physicians emphasized the value of exercise in health maintenance and longevity.

In the early 1950s, British physician Jeremy N. Morris developed what has become known as the "exercise hypothesis." He found that workers who were more active were at less risk for coronary artery disease. Morris started the trend to research the relationships between a sedentary lifestyle and disease. In the 1960s, with increases in both mechanization and cardiovascular disease, the idea of using exercise to prevent and rehabilitate illness began to become accepted in medicine. This idea helped to jump start the exercise revolution of the 1970s.

In the 1970s, exercise was seen as a way to combat the rising incidence of cardiovascular disease and to counteract the effects of stress, excess weight, smoking, drugs, and alcohol. Running, aerobic dance, high-impact aerobics, and the "no pain, no gain" mentality flourished. However, people began to get confused and burned out with all of this exercise and began looking for a gentler, more-well-rounded approach to wellness and physical fitness. The 1980s marked the beginning of the wellness revolution. This revolution looked at many aspects of lifestyle, including diet, stress reduction, and elimination of tobacco, drugs, and alcohol as a means to a healthier life, rather than focusing exclusively on exercise. During the 1990s, there has been an even gentler and more diverse approach to exercise. The "no pain, no gain" mentality is gone, and walking has taken the place of running and high-impact aerobics as the exercise of choice.

The benefits of exercise are numerous, and there is an overwhelming amount of research to support these benefits. Weight management is one of the most widely recognized effects of regular exercise. Exercise is considered a critical element in most weight-loss programs. The American College of Sports Medicine generally recommends a combination of a medically supervised program of dieting along with exercise as the best way to lose weight. Exercise can increase longevity and improve quality of life.

Other benefits of exercise include reductions in coronary heart disease, cholesterol levels, and atherosclerosis. These are significant benefits, as coronary heart disease is the leading cause of death in the United States. With regular exercise, blood pressure is lowered and the effects of pulmonary disease are decreased or diminished. Osteoarthritis, osteoporosis, back pain, and recovery from surgery have all been found to benefit from a regular exercise program, and such a program can reduce the chances of getting cancer. There are also psychological benefits to exercise. Research shows that people who are physically fit are also more likely to be psychologically fit. The symptoms of stress, depression, and anxiety are all reduced by a regular exercise program, while self-esteem is raised.

Components of Exercise

There are many different types of exercise. Exercise could mean running a marathon to one person and walking the dog or taking the stairs instead of an elevator to another person. The key is physical movement. Exercise is a means to physical fitness. There are four major components to physical fitness that should be addressed when exercising. Cardiorespiratory fitness is the heart's ability to pump blood and deliver oxygen throughout the body. Walking, running, cycling, aerobic dance, and swimming are examples of exercises that increase cardiorespiratory fitness.

Exercise

Muscular fitness is the second component of physical fitness and is usually obtained by some sort of weightlifting exercise program. There are two components to muscular fitness: muscular strength—how much weight one can lift—and muscular endurance—how many times one can lift a weight. Flexibility or range of motion is the third component of physical fitness. Flexibility is important for the performance in sport activities as well as for functioning in daily life. Stretching exercises will help improve the flexibility of the body's muscles and joints. The last component of fitness concerns body composition, the portion of body weight that is made up of fat. The level of body fat can affect the risk of developing health problems, including heart disease, high blood pressure, and diabetes. Some of the same exercises recommended for cardiorespiratory fitness and muscular fitness are also recommended for controlling body composition. A minimum of three 20- to 30-minute exercise periods per week, or 30 minutes every other day, is recommended.

Along with the four components of exercise are the principles of exercise training. The first, specificity, is the idea that the adaptation of the body or change in physical fitness is specific to the type of training undertaken. To increase cardiovascular fitness, one must specifically train the cardiovascular system. The second principle is overload: to improve any aspect of physical fitness one must continually increase the demands placed on the appropriate body systems. Progression, or increasing the level of the activity, is important to increased fitness levels. Everyone has different capabilities of progression, so this progression should be slow to avoid injury or fatigue.

There has been much research on the frequency, duration, and intensity of exercise, three additional components of exercise training. To develop and maintain fitness, exercise must be performed regularly. A frequency of about three to five times a week is thought to be sufficient. The intensity of exercise has been the subject of much debate and research. In the past, it was thought that in order to reap the health benefits of exercise one needed to exercise at 80 percent of maximum heart rate. However, in more recent years, researchers have found fitness benefits at only 50 percent of maximum heart rate. Exercise heart rate has been found to be a reliable way to gauge exercise intensity. Duration of exercise is related to the intensity of the exercise. If the exercise is of a high intensity then the duration does not need to be as long; if the exercise is of low intensity then the duration must be longer to derive similar effects. All of these components and principles of exercise need to be considered when considering an exercise program.

Exercise is a relatively new phenomenon. In early times exercise was not necessary because people lived a much more active lifestyle. In today's technological age, lifestyles have become less active, and there has been an increase in sedentary-related illness and disease. The exercise boom is alive and well. According to American Sports Data (ASD), the number of people who participated 100 times or more in at least one fitness activity in the previous 12 months numbered 42.2 million. The U.S. running population was 30.4 million and the number of people using home exercise machines has increased tremendously. Since 1991, in-line skating has increased 51 percent and mountain biking 16 percent. Exercise and wellness constitute a long-term trend that is here to stay.

—Sally Crawford

See also Aerobics; Conditioning; Medicine.

Bibliography: American College of Sports Medicine. (1992) *ACSM Fitness Book.* Champaign, IL: Leisure Press.

Cooper, Kenneth. (1969) *Aerobics.* New York: M. Evans and Co.

Durant, Will. (1939) *The Life of Greece.* New York: Simon and Schuster.

Floyd, P. et al. *Wellness: A Lifetime Commitment.* Winston-Salem, NC: Hunter Textbooks.

Gavin, James. (1992) *The Exercise Habit.* Champaign, IL: Leisure Press.

Gordon, Neil F., and Larry W. Gibbons. (1990) *The Cooper Clinic Cardiac Rehabilitation Program.* New York: Simon and Schuster.

Harris, Harold A. (1964) *Greek Athletes and Athletics.* London: Hutchinson and Company.

Henderson, Joe. (1988) *Total Fitness: Training for Life.* Dubuque, IA: W. C. Brown.

Hoeger, W., and S. Hoeger. (1992) *Lifetime Physical Fitness and Wellness.* Englewood, CO: Morton Publishing.

Ramsey, F., T. Paul, and F. Murray. (1982) *Fundamentals: Concepts in Exercise and Fitness.* Dubuque, IA: Kendall/Hunt Publishing.

Sharkey, B. J. (1990) *Physiology of Fitness.* Champaign, IL: Human Kinetics.

Stone, William J. (1987) *Adult Fitness Programs: Planning, Designing, Managing, and Improving Fitness Programs.* Glenview, IL: Scott, Foresman and Company.

Extreme Sports

Extreme sports is the generic label used for sports that in some way go beyond—in endurance, testing the limits, or danger—traditional sports. The label was promoted in the 1990s by athletes, promoters, the sports equipment industry, and advertisers to bring mainstream attention to these sports and, at the same time, to differentiate them from related sports. While most sports now classified as extreme have all existed for some time and most have governing bodies and regional and world competitions, extreme sports as a category of sports achieved their highest level of public exposure in 1995 with the First Extreme Games held in June in Newport, Rhode Island. These games were given 45 hours of week-long coverage on the ESPN (Entertainment and Sports Programming Network) cable network. The extreme games included street luge, eco-challenge, skysurfing, sport climbing, barefoot water ski jumping, in-line skating, BMX dirt biking, mountain biking, and bungy jumping. To some extent, all of these sports are extensions of already existing sports or recreational activities:

street luge—skateboarding, roller skating, luge, tobogganing
eco-challenge—orienteering, canoeing, rafting, kayaking, swimming
skysurfing—sky diving, surfing
sport climbing—rock climbing
barefoot water ski jumping—water ski jumping, trick water skiing
in-line skating—roller skating, skate boarding
BMX dirt biking—bicycle racing, motorcross
mountain biking—bicycle racing, cross-country racing
bungy jumping—diving

What differentiates these sports from the related sports varies from sport to sport and might involve changes in the rules, the combining of different events, use of different equipment and venues, and a greater degree of risk to the athletes. Additionally, some extreme sports have been called "outlaw" sports because they have been banned in some jurisdictions as too dangerous. In street luge, for example, the participants lie flat on their backs on wheeled luges or "rails" and race downhill on roads. When these roads are used also by pedestrians, bikers, and vehicles, the sport is dangerous for both the competitors and others. Perhaps the common feature of extreme sports and what makes them extreme are requirements of the activities that make the sport especially dangerous and/or that test the limits of human physical ability or endurance.

The following are brief descriptions of each of nine major extreme sports, although it should be noted that the rules and events for each sport may vary from competition to competition, and, as relatively new sports, the rules, activities, events, and equipment that comprise the sports are still developing.

Street Luge

Events are conducted on a winding, downhill course on city streets or country roads. In sanctioned competitions, the course is bordered by a barrier of a protective material such as hay bales to protect lugers who crash as well as spectators. Racers wear helmets and other protective gear and lie flat on their backs on either a luge or rail, both of which are metal or plastic with wheels, but a rail is flatter than a luge. As a new sport, with a small following, equipment is still rather crude with competitors often making their own luges and rails with wheels taken from skateboards. Participants either race against the clock or each other, steering with body movement and by dragging their feet.

Eco-Challenge

Eco-challenge is a form of adventure racing in which teams race from a starting point to a finish line over a course several hundred miles in length. The course is unfamiliar to the participants who are given a map of it the day before the start of the race. Participants use canoes, rafts, kayaks, mountain bikes, and also must swim, hike, and portage over rough terrain while carrying about 136 kilograms (300 pounds) of supplies per team. The teams can set their own course for part of the competition using survey maps and compass, but they must pass specific checkpoints along the route. Participants see the event as about "challenging oneself" and developing

Skysurfing is just one of the developing forms of exciting "extreme sports" that extend existing sports in dangerous or physically challenging ways.

teamwork. A long course might take five days to complete with a team getting as little as five hours of sleep during the competition.

Skysurfing

This sport is a combination of sky diving, surfing, and aerial photography. Two-person teams jump from a plane at about 4,000 meters (13,000 feet). One team member is the surfer and wears a surf board on his or her feet, the other member is the photographer who photographs the surfer with a videocamera attached to her or her head. The surfer performs a 50-second routine of glides, twists, turns, spins, and jumps which the camera operator films for judging by a panel of judges. Both perform while free-falling toward earth at speeds ranging from 175 to 240 kilometers (110 to 150 miles) per hour. The judges award points for technical and artistic merit. While it is the surfer whose performance is judged, the photographer is equally important as he or she must stay close to and in alignment with the surfer to produce a clear and focused record of the performance. The surfer champion of the 1995 Extreme Games died in an accident in late 1995 while shooting a commercial.

Sport Climbing

Closely related to rock climbing, this sport requires participants to scale artificial "rock walls." Separate events for men and women require the participants to scale a series of different types of walls with strategically placed hand and foot holds in six-minute trials. The three different events that comprise the sport emphasize speed, difficulty, and strategy, with speed in completing the different courses determining the winners.

Barefoot Water Ski Jumping

This sport is water ski jumping without the skis. Competitors are towed across the water at 65 kilometers (40 miles) per hour, using only their bare feet as skis and then launch off an angled ramp into the air, landing some 21 to 27 meters (70 to 90 feet) ahead. A successful landing requires that the jumper hold on to the tow rope handle and maintain his balance upon landing. Victory is determined by the distance jumped. In a recent innovation, competitors are allowed to perform tricks while being towed toward the launch ramp. Tricks include jumping from a 3.7-meter (12-foot)

platform at the start of the run, spinning on one's back while being towed, and skiing backwards. Distance points are awarded for successful tricks and added to the actual distance jumped.

In-Line Skating

In this sport, sometimes called "aggressive skating," competitors use in-line roller skates and compete in three types of events. In the in-line vertical ("vert") event competitors skate on a half-pike ramp (two curved, ten foot walls facing each other) and jump, twist, spin, and flip in order to earn points for their performance. On the street course, competitors navigate walls, ramps, stairs, and railings in 75 seconds, earning points for style, creativity, and the difficulty of the stunts they perform. In the downhill course, on streets or roads, the competitors race against each other in groups.

BMX Dirt Biking

BMX dirt bikes have been used by children and teenagers for several decades, for recreation, transportation, and in competitions on dirt courses. Dirt biking as an extreme sport involves racing, jumping over and off dirt mounds, and riding on vertical ramps. Competitors are judged for style, difficulty of maneuvers, execution, and the height reached in jumps.

Mountain Biking

This sport combines a number of different racing events on mountain bikes. In one event, competitors race through woods on rough trails against the clock. In a second event, the dual slalom, they race head-to-head on 274-meter (300-yard) dirt courses, through gates and over jumps in a combination of slalom and freestyle snow skiing on bikes.

Bungy Jumping

This is a new extreme sport that evolved from the recreational activity of bungee jumping—jumping from a high place (usually a bridge) with an elastic cord attached to one's feet that stops the fall before the jumper reaches the ground or water. In competitive bungy jumping, competitors leap from a 49-meter (160-foot) tower and compete in a number of events including backward and forward jumping and freestyle jumping, which requires the performance of various turns, flips, and twists.

Extreme Sports

Extreme sports are international: the Extreme Games in 1995 attracted competitors from 25 nations. Different sports have developed in different nations—skysurfing in France, barefoot ski jumping in Australia, and some sports such as street luge, sport climbing, eco-challenge, and mountain biking draw participants from a variety of nations. For the most part, however, competitors are from Western nations, with most coming from the United States, Australia, Canada, Germany, New Zealand, France, and England. Some sports, such as sport climbing and eco-challenge, draw competitors who are in their thirties and forties, but most competitors in the other sports are usually in their twenties or even teens. Most extreme sports draw only male competitors, with only eco-challenge and sport climbing having significant numbers of women competitors. Sport climbing is the only extreme sport with separate divisions for men and women. All extreme sports, except for eco-challenge and skysurfing, are individual sports.

The 1995 Extreme Games marked a major effort to broaden interest in these sports among the general public. As all competitors at the games were invited and were the best in their respective sports, the games were as much an exhibition as a competition for world supremacy. Coverage of the sports emphasized the "exciting" nature of the events, although it is not clear that any of these sports currently generate such excitement among large segments of the public.

—David Levinson

Bibliography: Bane, Michael. (1996) *Over the Edge: An Odyssey of Extreme Sports*. New York: Macmillan.

Falconry

Falconry is a form of hunting in which birds of prey are trained to find and kill game for their human owners. It is an ancient sport that was once extremely popular, and although it is far less prevalent today, it still has numerous enthusiasts in many parts of the world. An important element of falconry is the training of the birds—a slow, complex process that requires patience, skill, and careful attention to detail. For many falconers this aspect of the sport, together with the appreciation of watching the magnificent birds in flight and the opportunity to preserve and display the birds for others, is just as important as the actual hunt.

Falcons are members of the Falconidae family, a category of hawks. They are powerful, fast birds of prey that swoop down and catch their quarry in their claws and talons. Eagles and other birds of prey are also used in the sport on a more limited basis; however, technically, falconry refers specifically to the use of falcons. When other species of hawks are used, the sport is called hawking. Nevertheless, people often refer to the general use of any of these birds as falconry.

Origins

Falcons and other hawks are found throughout the world, and they have had symbolic importance in many cultures. While the exact origins of the sport of falconry are not known, it is believed to have started in Asia and the Middle East, possibly as early as 2000 B.C.E. Falconry spread to Europe in the centuries following the death of Christ, with the increased contact between Eastern and Western civilizations. It became especially popular in the British Isles during the Middle Ages. The wealthy often had prized collections of birds, and they employed staffs of skilled trainers to manage them. In Europe, falconry was among the sports governed by feudal laws in the Middle Ages that restricted hunting and the ownership and use of sporting animals based on social class. These were imposed on the inhabitants of Britain around 1000 B.C.E., especially after William the Conqueror took over the throne of Britain in 1066. These became known as the Forest Laws. Although these laws were altered and relaxed in the following centuries, vestiges of them remained into the nineteenth century. While all people could participate in falconry, specific types of hawks and falcons were designated for each class. Only members of the royalty could own gyrfalcons, the largest falcons. Lesser royalty and nobles used peregrine falcons. This system extended down to the servants and serfs, who were only allowed to use smaller birds such as sparrow hawks.

Interest in falconry diminished around the seventeenth century, as the emphasis in hunting shifted more to the use of guns and to other hunting animals such as dogs. Since then, falconry has not been nearly as widely practiced as other forms of hunting or animal sports. The sport, however, has been carried on by individual falconers and by regional and national organizations, such as the North American Falconers Association.

In the mid-twentieth century, falconry faced new challenges. In many regions, modern community development significantly reduced the amount of open and accessible countryside necessary for falconry. Also, many species of birds were in danger of extinction from chemical pesticides and other environmental threats, and they were placed on protected endangered species lists. Their use became carefully regulated, and breeding programs were initiated to rebuild the population. In the 1990s, these programs have shown signs of success, and once-rare species are becoming reestablished.

Practice

The hunting characteristics and other traits of hawk species vary greatly. Some hawks prey mainly on other birds, flying high above them before suddenly diving down and catching them in mid-air. Other hawks hunt and eat insects and small animals that dwell on the ground.

There are approximately 40 individual species of falcons, ranging in length from about 15 centimeters (6 inches) up to 60 centimeters (2 feet) or more. They differ from other hawks in several respects. Most falcons, for example, are characterized by dark-colored eyes, while the eyes of other hawks are lighter. Falcons also have two grooves

Often associated with Europe in the Middle Ages, as seen in this illustration, falconry was practiced in Asia and the Middle East before the time of Christ. The training of the birds requires enormous patience and skill.

on either side of their beak, and they usually have longer, more pointed wings than other hawks. They also rely on their beaks to kill their prey to a greater extent than other hawks.

Several different falcons can be trained for the sport of falconry. The gyrfalcon is among the largest species of falcon used; it can grow up to 60 centimeters (2 feet). The peregrine, another large falcon, is considered one of the world's fastest animals, with a flying speed as high as 320 kilometers per hour (200 miles per hour). Merlins are smaller peregrines that are typically used in falconry. Kestrels are small, long-winged falcons that live primarily in woods and grassy areas. They are among the most common species of falcon and are considered easy to train, so they are very adaptable to the sport. Sparrow hawks and, less frequently, other hawk species, eagles, and other birds are used.

During a hunt, the falcon is brought to a site attached by leather leg straps to a special perch or to the hand of the falconer, which is protected by a large leather glove. The bird is released to fly after its quarry, which may be other airborne birds or ground-dwelling animals. Many kinds of game animals are hunted in the sport of falconry, including rabbits, ducks, pheasants, grouse, and squirrels. After the kill, the bird is trained either to fly back to the master's glove, return to the perch, or stay with the dead prey until it is retrieved by its master. Small bells or radio transmitters are attached to the bird so it can be easily located in the field by sound or radio signal.

Different hunting techniques are used. The bird might be restrained and only allowed to fly when the falconer is very close to a specific quarry. In training, or on some hunts, a rabbit or other animal might be brought along in a cage and released for the bird to follow. In other instances, the falcon may be released to find its own prey. Some falconers also use hunting dogs to flush out prey for the birds.

Tradition has an important role in falconry. It is a sport with very specific equipment, procedures, and vocabulary. The sport's heritage is a basic element of its appeal for many falconers. Etiquette, methods of training, and care date back to the earliest days of the sport. These grew out of the very specific demands that are required to care for the birds, as well as a respect for the traditions and values embodied by the sport. Falconry's ex-

tensive vocabulary of specific terms for equipment, training, hunting procedures, and other facets of the sport date back to its early years. For example, when a bird drinks, it is called bowsing. Features of birds also have unique names in falconry. Wings, for example, are frequently called sails. Procedures also have defined names, such as weathering, which is the process of gradually readjusting the bird to the outdoors after it has been kept indoors for a period after its initial captivity. Nevertheless, definitions in the sport of falconry are not always universal and can seem confusing to the novice. Words and spellings vary among languages and contexts. Even the names used to identify birds are somewhat variable. For example, the word *falcon* generally refers to a broad category of species; however, *falcon* also specifically refers to the females of certain species, while the males are called tiercels. There are also distinctions between the long-winged "true" falcons and the shorter-winged species of falcon. In some instances, the basic name and classification of a bird differ among geographic regions. For example, in North America, kestrels are sometimes called sparrow hawks, but in Europe sparrow hawks are considered a distinct species.

Falcons and other predatory birds are difficult to breed in captivity. Traditionally, very young birds, or eyesses, are taken from their nests (eyries) in the wild soon after their birth, before they can fly or leave the nest on their own. They are also captured in their very early stages of flight or when they are migrating during their first year. In the late twentieth century, the ability to collect wild bird species has become increasingly regulated. Many localities require falconers to obtain special permits prior to capturing the young birds. Falconry is also subject to laws covering the game that is hunted by the trained birds. Many areas have specific hunting seasons for falconers, similar to those for other types of hunters.

Hawks of all types have an instinctive fear and mistrust of humans, so their training is undertaken very carefully. The exact procedures vary for different species, to reflect differences in their habits and temperaments. The more docile birds may be basically trained within a month, while others may take much longer. During these early stages, young birds are also growing and their feathers are maturing, so they require careful handling.

The first basic step in training is adapting the wild bird to captivity and the presence of people. This process, called manning, takes place indoors in special houses called mews. The trainer gradually makes the bird accept him by visiting it regularly and feeding it by hand. Once a degree of trust has been established, the bird is trained to perch on the falconer's hand, which is protected by a large leather glove. During training and at other times, the bird's legs are attached to leather straps, called jessups, to restrain it from flying away. In its early captivity, or later when a bird in training is being moved from its usual perch to another location for training or hunting, the head is often covered with a hood to keep it calm. In the past, the eyes of young birds were temporarily sewn shut.

Eventually the bird is taken outside to become readjusted to the open air, a process known as weathering. During this phase, the birds are attached to outdoor perches for regular periods during the day. Then they are allowed to fly while attached to leather straps. The birds are trained to hunt with the use of meat attached to lures and string, which are swung out for the bird to catch. Gradually they are trained to fly loose and hunt without flying away permanently from their demarcated territory, or from the master's control when taken to another location for a hunt. However, unfettered birds sometimes do fly off, no matter how well they have been trained. Falconers accept this tragedy as an inevitable aspect of the sport.

—John Townes

See also Hunting.

Bibliography: Ford, Emma. (1992, 1995) *Falconry: Art and Practice.* London: Cassell.

Hare, C. E. (1939, 1949) *The Language of Field Sport.* London: Country Life Ltd.; New York: Charles Scribner's Sons.

Longrigg, Roger. (1977) *The English Squire and His Sport.* New York: St. Martin's Press.

Woodford, M. H. (1960, 1972) *A Manual of Falconry.* London: Adam & Charles Black Ltd.

Fencing

Fencing is the art and sport of swordsmanship using blunted weapons. It features several aspects that render it distinctive, if not unique, in the athletic community. For more than 100 years and until quite recently, it was the only combative sport open to both men and women, although men and women compete apart from each other. It is the only combative sport with neither weight classes nor height restrictions. Fencing champions come in all shapes and sizes and all competitors meet each other as equals, separated by ability alone. It is an activity that one can initiate at any age and, having commenced, can be continued for the remainder of one's life. It requires few players (any number greater than two may meet to fence, and a growing or declining group is readily accommodated) and requires no specially built venue or expensive equipment. The nature of fencing is such that an athlete whose visual or physical impairments might prevent him or her from taking an active role in some other vigorous sports is not only welcome, but encounters no limit but that of talent to achieve any level of success. There have been highly successful fencers who were deaf, blind in one eye, or missing a limb.

Origins

Fencing is an activity of the most pronounced antiquity, with several millennia of tradition behind it. Perhaps the earliest reference to a fencing match appears in a relief carving in the temple at Madinet-Habu near Luxor in upper Egypt built by Ramses III about 1190 B.C.E. The fencers depicted there are using weapons with well-covered points and masks not dissimilar to those currently in use. A panel of officials and administrators is depicted and distinguished by the feathered wands they hold.

Every succeeding ancient civilization—Chinese, Japanese, Egyptian, Persian, Babylonian, Greek, and Roman—practiced swordsmanship as a sport as well as training for combat. It is a curious anomaly that European swordsmanship—the most immediate antecedent of modern fencing—did not commence its development until after the advent of gunpowder and firearms (black weapons) in the fourteenth century. Until that time, men wielded ever-heavier swords to cleave through ever-more-ponderous armor. Strength was more critical than skill. However, the advent of ballistic weapons rendered armor obsolete, enabling speed, mobility, and skill to prove a greater influence than mere force. This led to the development of lighter swords (white weapons) used with faster, more subtle handwork for better use in close quarters. Thus the art of fencing arose.

German fencing masters were the first to organize themselves into guilds, such as the famous Marxbruder of Frankfort, which was granted letters patent by Emperor Frederick at Nuremberg in 1480. Other such associations flourished throughout Europe. The masters of these schools of fencing advocated techniques and styles of play that included wrestling and boxing tricks, in addition to swordsmanship. For a price, they would sell "secret strokes" to their members. In Great Britain, such a fraternity was the Corporation of the Masters of Defence, founded under letters patent issued by King Henry VIII sometime before 1540. Until Henry's act swordsmen were regarded with disfavor and suspicion in Britain. A statute of Edward I enacted in 1285 forbade the teaching of fencing or the holding of tournaments within the precincts of the city of London. The London city fathers regarded fencing schools as dens of iniquity that encouraged dueling, brawling, and all manner of ruffianism. Fencing masters were held in the same low esteem as members of the acting profession, and both groups were encouraged to stay south of the Thames River. Fencing was also unpopular with the army, as it was so much fun that officers felt fencing distracted soldiers from practicing their archery.

The Italian masters were the earliest to advocate the use of the point in preference to the cutting edge for subtlety and effectiveness, which led to the development of the rapier. From then on, swordsmanship grew detached from tricks of wrestling and boxing.

From the sixteenth to the eighteenth centuries, prize fights consisted of displays and tests of swordsmanship. These were frequented by all ranks and segments of the population and patronized by members of the royal family. Champions met challengers in bouts at a variety of weapons, such as singlesticks, quarterstaffs, and

Fencing has been present in almost every culture for millennia. After severe fluctuations in popularity in recent times, fencing gained stability with its inclusion in the modern Olympic Games.

backswords, and the blood flowed freely. At the end of the eighteenth century, James Figg (ca. 1695–1734), the champion of the Corporation of Fencing Masters (as well as the first British boxing champion), introduced pugilism into these prize fights. Since fisticuffs was easier to learn than swordplay, and less likely to be fatal, these encounters soon eclipsed fencing in popularity. Fencing found itself relegated to provincial contests and fairs, where the old ways were held fast.

Learning to use a sword was difficult. The wounds resulting from it often became infected. Threats to one's vision were a particular risk: It was said no competent fencing master could expect to close his career with two good eyes. But three innovations made fencing more appealing to prospective students concerned with their safety. The first of these came in the seventeenth century, when a light practice weapon was developed. It was called a foil because its point had been flattened—or "foiled"—and then padded to reduce the chance of injury. The second safety innovation was the development of rules of engagement known as "conventions"—in which the valid target was limited to the breast and the fencer who initiated the attack had precedence unless completely parried by the defender. Fencing with foils thus became a "conversation" of blades. But even with the advent of the foil and its conventions of play, fencing was a slow, stylized activity because of the chance of injury to the face and the eyes. The third innovation—the invention of the quadrille wire-mesh fencing mask by the French master La Boiëssière père and the English master Joseph Boulogne, Chevalier de St. George (ca. 1739–1799), at the close of the eighteenth century—was the final step necessary to make fencing a completely safe activity. (They actually reinvented the mask, which had been lost to history since the time of the ancient Egyptians.)

Once the mask was in widespread use, more complex "phrases" (exchanges of blows) could become possible and foil fencing as it is now known was developed. The rules and conventions already mentioned prevented the play from degenerating into a brawl. These conventions are the basis of modern foil and sabre fencing.

While foil fencing was developing, dueling continued concurrently, and a more realistic fencing experience was considered desirable. The *épée de combat* was transformed from a combat weapon of affairs of honor to a weapon of sport. Its target was expanded from that of foil to simulate a real duel and conventions were discarded. Verisimilitude was enhanced when épée competitions were conducted outdoors, on terrain of grass or gravel; with street shoes and regular trousers de rigeur; finally, bouts were fenced to the best touch (that is, for one hit).

The traditions of the cutting weapons of medieval times were continued by the backsword or broadsword, which was an Englishman's traditional weapon until well into the eighteenth century. The modern sabre owes its appearance to the scimitar, the curved weapon of the Middle East, introduced to Europe by the Hungarians for use in their cavalry. Other western European armies soon adopted the sabre as well and copied the hussar mode of dress for their mounted troops.

A light sabre was developed by the Italians during the last quarter of the nineteenth century and was soon universally adopted for fencing, although many still preferred the heavy sabre, and these coexisted for a time. Light sabre play became a sport in its own right, with conventions similar to those of foil. Heavy sabers continued to be used by the cavalry and in duels.

Practice

A modern fencer uses one of three types of weapons—the foil, the épée, or the sabre. Competitions for men or women are conducted at all three weapons; although until quite recently, women competed exclusively at foil. Fencing meets may be conducted as individual events or as team events. Even in team events only two fencers compete against each other at any one time. Teams are usually made up of three or four on a side, with each competitor meeting each competitor on the opposing squad.

In the earlier years of the twentieth century, fencers were frequently three-weapon men and practiced all three arms. As time passed, the size of the starting fields and the duration of competitions, as well as their concomitant expenses, kept increasing. The desire for success led increasingly to specialization in one weapon, at most two. Each weapon has its own aficionados.

The modern foil has a slender, flexible blade, quadrilateral in cross-section, and a small, circular guard centrally mounted. The blade is a maximum of 90 centimeters long. Foil fencers try to score, using the point of their weapon only, by hitting their opponent on the torso. If the fencer touches his or her opponent on the head, legs, or arms, no point is scored and the action resumes. If a fencer touches his or her opponent on the torso, then a point or a touch is scored. If both fencers hit each other, then the official applies the conventions of right of way to assess the situation and awards a touch, if any. Usually, bouts are for five touches in elimination pools leading to a final round-robin pool; or 10 or 15 touches in direct elimination ladders leading to the title bout; or a combination of both methods.

The modern épée has a wide blade, more rigid than that of a foil, Y-shaped in cross-section, and a large circular guard that may be centrally or eccentrically mounted. The blade is a maximum of

90 centimeters (35 inches) long. Epée fencing observes no conventions, and touches are made with the point only anywhere on an opponent. If both fencers hit together, then a double-touch is scored against each and both fencers are counted as hit. Epée bouts may be fenced to one touch or multiple touch bouts, in pools or direct elimination, or a combination of both. Epée fencing for one touch is an element of the five-event competition called the modern pentathlon.

The modern sabre has a flexible blade, usually T-, Y-, or I-shaped in cross-section, and a large guard that curves around the knuckles and may be centrally or eccentrically mounted. The blade is a maximum of 88 centimeters (34 inches) long. In sabre fencing, touches made with either the point or one of the two cutting edges count if they land above the opponent's hips (a tribute to saber's cavalry origins). Sabre fencing observes the same conventions as foil fencing, although before World War II it observed some rules more characteristic of a combative weapon.

With all three weapons, bouts in a round-robin pool are of four minutes' duration. Direct-elimination contests are encounters of 10 or 15 minute's duration, depending on the maximum number of touches.

To avoid injuries, fencers wear a heavy wire-mesh mask with a thick canvas bib to protect the head and neck. They also wear thick canvas or nylon jackets and knickers and a padded glove on the hand holding the weapon. When competing, in addition to the above equipment, fencers wear additional equipment that permits electric scoring apparatus to function.

Fencing is conducted on a field of play called a strip, or piste, that is 14 meters (46 feet) long and 2 meters (6½ feet) wide. A fencer exiting from the side of the piste is penalized in distance. A fencer exiting from the rear of the piste is penalized a touch for loss of ground.

Until the advent of electric scoring devices, fencing matches were adjudicated by a jury composed of a "president" and four "assistants." The president has also been referred to as a director, or more recently, a referee and the assistants as "judges." At the end of the nineteenth century, foil fencers wore black uniforms and chalk tips were used on foils to aid in the scoring; but this system was not very popular, particularly in Europe and in American colleges, where "form"

was also taken into account in scoring. Around the time of World War I, and for the next 30 years, white uniforms were worn and red ink was used on the tips of épées to indicate a touch.

Since the invention of the mask, no innovation in fencing has had so great an impact on the sport as the advent of electrified scoring. It has completely eliminated the need for assistants, leaving only the president to officiate. Epée was electrified in time for the 1935 world championships at Lausanne, Switzerland; foil was electrified for the 1955 world championships in Rome, Italy; and sabre was electrified for the 1989 world championships in Denver, Colorado. However, these advances have not been without complications. Electrification of the sport has increased the startup and maintenance costs considerably and has had a debilitating effect on the technique of competitors since its introduction. Also, in spite of the objectivity of the equipment, biased officials remain entrenched and are among the biggest hazards of the sport.

Much of the history of modern fencing is connected with the Olympic Games. Fencing was one of the eight sports comprising the program of the first modern Olympic Games when it was revived in 1896 by Baron Pierre de Coubertin, who was himself a fencer. It shares with only three other sports (athletics, swimming, and gymnastics) the distinction of being on the program of every Olympic Games observance.

The first modern Olympic Games at Athens in 1896 included three fencing events: a foil individual won by Eugène-Henri Gravelotte of France; a sabre individual won by George Georgiadis of Greece; and a foil individual for fencing masters won by Leon Pyrgos of Greece. In the case of the last named event, fencing was the first sport in the Olympics to conduct events for professionals. At the Olympic Games of 1900 at Paris an épée individual event was added and was won by Ramon Fonst of Cuba. Other events for fencing masters that attracted very limited fields were added on a short-term basis. At the Olympic Games in St. Louis in 1904 a foil team event was added, which was won by Cuba. Most of the best European fencers did not attend this Olympics because of the great distance between Europe and St. Louis. At the intercalated Olympic Games of 1906 at Athens an épée team event was added, won by France; and a sabre team event was

Fencing

added, won by Germany. At the Olympic Games in Paris in 1924, a women's foil individual event was added. It was won by Ellen Osiier of Denmark. At the 1960 Olympic Games in Rome a women's foil team event was added and was won by the Russians. At the Olympic Games of 1996 at Atlanta, women's épée individual and women's épée team events were contested for the first time.

The record for the most championships won by any fencer is seven. Aladar Gerevich (1910–) of Hungary won in sabre individual and team between 1932 and 1960. He is also the only athlete in any sport to win an Olympic championship in six different Olympic observances. The record for the most medals of any types is 13 held by Edoardo Mangiarotti (1920–) of Italy in foil and épée, individual and team, between 1936 and 1960; he won five gold, five silver, and three bronze.

At the end of the nineteenth century, the international competitions at foil and épée were dominated by the French and the Italians and those at sabre by Hungary. This situation lasted until about 1960, when Russia became the dominant nation in all three weapons, with occasional successes by Poland and Romania. After 1972, there was another reordering, which included a resurgence of fencing in Italy and later in France, as well as a new flourishing in Cuba and China.

A renaissance of interest in fencing occurred simultaneously in the United States and Great Britain during the last decade of the nineteenth century, nearly concurrent with the revived interest in the Olympic Games and the expansion of collegiate sports. In the United States, several New York fencers were dissatisfied with the conduct of fencing competitions by the Amateur Athletic Union from 1888 through 1891. Led by Graeme M. Hammond (1858–1944), these insurgents broke away and formed their own organization, the Amateur Fencers League of America (AFLA) in 1891. In Great Britain, Captain Alfred E. Hutton (1839–1910) joined with his fellow enthusiasts to stage displays and lectures throughout the country. As a result, the Amateur Fencing Association (AFA) of Great Britain was founded in 1902.

The U.S. Fencing Association (USFA), as the AFLA has called itself since 1981, administers the sport in the United States, conducting its national championships and other important events. It is the American member of the International Fencing Federation (FIE) which was founded in 1913 because of disputes over the rules governing foil at the 1908 Olympics and the rules governing épée at the 1912 Olympics. The FIE conducts the world fencing championships, the junior world championships (for competitors under 20 years of age), and the cadet world championships (for competitors under 17 years of age), as well as the fencing events of the Olympic Games. The FIE also establishes the official rules of the sport.

The U.S. Fencing Coaches Association (USFCA), founded in 1941, administers the teaching of fencing in the United States and is the American member of the International Academy of Arms (AAI), the international governing body of fencing masters.

Collegiate fencing in the United States is administered by the National Collegiate Athletic Association (NCAA), which conducted its first fencing championship in 1941; the Intercollegiate Fencing Association (IFA), which was founded in 1894 by Columbia, Harvard, and Yale; and the National Intercollegiate Women's Fencing Association (NIWFA), which was founded in 1929 by Bryn Mawr, Cornell, New York University, and the University of Pennsylvania. Other, smaller organizations play a role in the conduct of collegiate fencing in their geographic areas. Collegiate fencing flourished for decades in the United States, but over the past twenty years, owing to the pernicious policies of the NCAA and USFA, sponsorship of collegiate fencing teams has declined precipitously. Interscholastic fencing still exists in some parts of the United States, such as New York City and New Jersey, but it clearly owes its considerable decline in recent years to the shoddy operation of collegiate fencing, which serves as its role model.

—Jeffrey R. Tishman

Bibliography: Castle, Egerton. (1969) *Schools and Masters of Fence: From the Middle Ages to the Eighteenth Century.* York, PA: George Shumway.

De Beaumont, Charles L. (1970) *Fencing: Ancient Art and Modern Sport.* South Brunswick, NJ: A. S. Barnes.

De Capriles, Jose R., ed. (1965) *AFLA Rulebook.* Worcester, MA: Heffernan Press.

Thimm, Captain Carl A. (1896) *A Bibliography of Fencing and Dueling.* Bronx, NY: Benjamin Blom.

Tishman, Jeffrey R. (1990) "College Fencing Damaged by NCAA and USFA Policies." *Swordmaster* (Spring).

———. (1990) "Collegiate Fencing at Risk." *American Fencing* 42, 1 (Spring).

Films

See Movies

Fishing, Freshwater

Freshwater sport fishing evolved from mere subsistence fishing. Waterman (1981) suggests that it is the self-imposed handicaps that make sport fishing different from its commercial and subsistence kin. Freshwater fishing takes place in waters that are in-land, as opposed to ocean waters. This includes a tremendous variety of in-land lakes (man-made and natural), ponds, marshes, creeks, streams, and large rivers.

Some have raised the issue of whether or not fishing is sport at all. At first glance, the activity is strikingly different from many of the more conventional sports. However, there are important similarities. McPherson, Curtis, and Loy (1989) posited five essential elements of sport. When freshwater fishing is compared to these elements, it is clear that it is indeed sport. Fishing is goal oriented. The specificity of the goals varies from situation to situation but for nearly all anglers, goals do exist. Fishing contains an element of competition. Fishing may include competition between anglers, competition with oneself, or competition with a standard. In most cases, there is a demonstration of physical prowess, although some freshwater fishing (particularly bait fishing) may require less physical ability. However, fishing with artificial baits requires tremendous physical skill. Sports require a high degree of concentration, and this is also true of freshwater fishing. Finally, sport has a ludic quality. This consists of an uncertain outcome and sanctioned display. Freshwater fishing always has an uncertain outcome. Factors such as weather, water conditions, and the angler's skill and knowledge make catching fish an uncertain endeavor. Indeed, that is one of the qualities that many an-

glers mention as a motivation for their participation. The element of display in fishing is sanctioned, although it is not always highly structured.

Origins and Development

Subsistence fishing, practiced by most past and contemporary cultures, is the mother of sport fishing. It is difficult to determine when fishing "for the fun of it" branched off on its own. The earliest writing about sport fishing comes from eighth century Japan. Even in that very early culture, the sport was apparently quite socially prestigious. This thread of class distinction was to follow the sport until the modern day.

One of the earliest English writings on the topic came from Dame Juliana Barnes, who wrote *Treatyse of Fyshinge wyth an Angle* in 1496. She indicated that fishing in English-speaking cultures was also a sport of aristocrats. British iron-monger Izaak Walton read Dame Juliana's book and went on to author the most influential book on the subject ever written. Not only did his book, *The Compleat Angler*, address fishing technique, it addressed the philosophical side of the sport. The book is now in its 121st edition. For several centuries the sport was reserved for the aristocracy, and most fished for trout and salmon. Many English people, even today, consider all fish except trout and salmon "coarse fish." Freshwater sport fishing continues to be an extremely popular activity in the British Isles and most parts of Europe.

The sport traveled across the Atlantic Ocean and arrived in the United States with the colonists. Little information is available on the sport fishing of the early United States. Waterman (1981) noted, "No matter how carefully historians try to avoid the subject, there is a great void in American sport fishing history, some 200 hundred years during which little was reported about it" (p. 69). We do know that the Puritans looked down on fishing as a waste of precious time. This probably contributed to the paucity of historical information during this period.

Americans began fishing in earnest in the early 1800s. For the most part, the chosen fish species were not the high-class trout and salmon of the English but the rough-and-tumble bass, walleye, and muskellunge found in the new frontier. From the mid-1850s, the growth of freshwater fishing

One of the most popular outdoor sports, freshwater fishing requires great knowledge, skill, and practice.

in America is closely linked to the development of fishing equipment—some of the most important of which came from the United States. Perhaps the most significant development for freshwater fishing in the United States was the invention of the Kentucky reel. When this reel was combined with another U.S. fishing contribution, the split bamboo rod, anglers were able to cast a bait considerably farther than previously had been thought possible. This fit in very well with the type of fishing available to Americans. By the late 1800s freshwater fishing was a permanent fixture on the American sporting scene (Waterman 1981).

Freshwater Fishing Today

Freshwater fishing is enjoyed in all but the most impoverished countries. While there is great variation in the sport, there is also considerable similarity. The differences are due to several factors: geography, types of fish available, technology,

and culture. Some of these variations have been reduced with increasing interaction between fishers of different cultures. It is not uncommon for anglers to travel to other countries with vastly different cultures to try their hand at fishing "over there." This has served to standardize the sport around the world. One can now travel to the most remote parts of each continent and catch fish in relative comfort using fairly standard fishing equipment and techniques.

Rates of participation for freshwater fishing on a worldwide basis are impossible to ascertain. However, it is possible to get an idea of the sport's popularity by considering participation in the United States. There are about 40 million freshwater anglers in the United States (Krause 1994). It is one of the most popular outdoor sports activities in the country with approximately 19 percent of the population participating at least once each year. Freshwater fishing surpasses hunting almost three to one. In the United

Bass Fishing

The bass family is a small group of freshwater sunfishes known as Centrarchidae that includes, among other species, the largemouth bass, the smallmouth bass, and the spotted bass. These fish are common to North America, although in recent years they have been successfully transplanted to several other countries (Bennett 1970). American anglers had pursued bass for at least a century before the construction of large dams in the 1940s. However, with the emergence of large impoundments of fresh water in the southern part of the country, fishing for bass became accessible and increasingly popular.

Bass are a predatory species and can be taken with a variety of techniques and equipment. This includes the use of natural baits, lures, and artificial flies. The largemouth bass is the most common of the basses. The world-record largemouth, a 10.1 kilogram (22.25 pound) lunker, was taken in 1932 in Georgia. Most bass weigh between one and three pounds (one-half to one and a half kilograms), although several fish over 18 pounds (8 kilograms) are caught each year (Harbour 1979).

Waterman (1982) noted that bass fishing boomed into the consciousness of the American angler in the 1960s. Part of this was undoubtedly the result of bass fishing tournaments and the Bass Anglers Sportsman's Society (B.A.S.S.). B.A.S.S. signed up its first member in 1968, about six months after the first bass tournament, which took place in 1967 when an enterprising young insurance salesman envisioned that money could be made from tightly structured fishing contests. Within a decade, B.A.S.S. had 250,000 members. The concept started out slowly but today bass tournaments are held on virtually every large lake and river in the United States. The Bass Anglers Sportsman's Society today has over 500,000 members in 52 countries, sponsors a weekly fishing series on television, and publishes four different periodicals on the sport of tournament bass fishing (Burek 1992).

Tournaments for freshwater bass range from small-club tournaments with 10 or 15 anglers and no monetary reward to national tournaments with hundreds of professional anglers and first place prizes of $100,000 and more. Anglers compete in head-to-head competition in an effort to catch the largest and greatest number of bass (within the limits set by the particular state fish and game regulatory agencies). An elaborate set of rules has evolved to deter cheating by participants.

A small but visible group of professional bass fishermen composed almost entirely of white, middle-aged males competes in elite bass tournaments. Just like professionals in other sports, these men have loyal fans who follow their activities. They are sponsored by the manufacturers of fishing equipment. In return, they are walking billboards for a dazzling array of boats, recreational vehicles, tackle, fishing clothing, and electronic fishing equipment (Taylor 1988).

—Daniel G. Yoder

States the sport also has a significant economic impact. Freshwater anglers spend about $15 billion annually on a surprisingly diverse variety of fishing goods and services (U.S. Fish and Wildlife Service 1993; Edginton, Jordan, DeGraaf, and Edginton 1995).

The fishes pursued by freshwater fishers run the gamut from big to small, reclusive to bold, flashy to down-home. Only a few of the more popular species will be mentioned here, but each species requires different techniques or equipment (Tryckar, Cagner, and Dybern 1976). One of the most visible and popular fish groups, the salmon group, includes different varieties of trout, whitefish, and salmon. The fishes in this group are a diverse collection that are scattered over the cold waters of a large part of the world including Europe, North and South America, Australia, and New Zealand. Consequently, they are pursued by more people than any other group of fishes. Trout and salmon anglers tend to be a particular breed.

Perhaps more than any other angler they are defined by technique and a special ethos, and they are likely the most exclusive of all anglers. While fish in this family may be caught by various methods, fly fishing for trout is the most well known. Not only are members of the trout family great sport fish, they are also prized for their taste.

Members of the pike family of fishes are very popular game fish. They too range over a large part of the world. Pike are largely predatory fish. The fishing methods and equipment reflect this characteristic. For the most part, these freshwater fish are caught with either small, live bait fish or with artificial baits that resemble this type of forage. Pike are noted for their fighting ability. They are not generally considered great table fare (Carhart 1949).

The catfish family is also a diverse group of fishes. These are warm-water fish that range from the one-quarter kilogram (one-half pound) bullhead catfish to the flathead catfish that may weigh well over 45 kilograms (100 pounds). Catfish eat other fish, frogs, small birds, and carrion. Those who fish for this type of fish are generally not considered to be as refined as their pike, trout, and bass fishing cousins.

Rivaling the trout family as the most popular type of fish in North America is the bass family. This class of fish includes a variety of sunfish and bass. Bass fishing, while currently practiced in many parts of the world, originated in the southern United States. Since the early 1800s it has been exported to many other countries with varying degrees of success. Bass fishers have been unflatteringly compared to trout fishers. Whereas trout fishers are interested in technique, style, and simplicity, bass fishers surround themselves with the latest fishing technology and seem less concerned with how they catch their prey.

Fly Fishing

Fly fishing, whether for trout or for bass, is the most formal—and many feel the most prestigious—type of fishing. Nearly all freshwater fish can be taken with flies. Flies are artificial fish attractants that often resemble the insects on which fish feed. Anglers cast a relatively heavy line with a fly attached to its end with a relatively light fishing rod. Although the art of fly fishing may intimidate many novice anglers, the basic skills of presenting the fly to the fish are not difficult. Most can learn the techniques after only a couple of lessons. Of course, as with all sports, the advanced skills and techniques come only after years of study and practice. In fly fishing, it is the weight of the line that provides the momentum to carry the fly to the fish. Wulff (1982) noted that changes in fly-fishing equipment over the past 60 years have modified the sport considerably and made the sport more accessible to more people. Important changes have taken place in fly rods, reels, and most importantly fly-fishing lines.

Fishing with Lures

Fishing with lures is similar to fly fishing except that the lure is usually much larger and heavier. The lure is cast out and then retrieved in such a way as to make a fish strike or bite the hook. Lures come in an incredible variety of styles, materials, colors, and shapes. Most lures are made from wood, plastic, and metal and contain from one to five hooks. Bennett (1970) suggested five

types of lures: spinners, spoons, plugs, jigs, and plastic baits. Some lures appeal more to specific types of fish; however, other lures are appealing to a great variety of fish species. It has been humorously noted that a few lures are designed to catch fish and a great many lures are designed to catch the fishers of fish.

Angling Song

I would seek a blest retreat
To my mind.
Oh: remove me from the great,
And a rural pleasant seat
Let me find.

In a vale pray let it be
That I love:
Where the blackbird on the tree,
piping forth its melody,
Fills the grove.
Let a limpid stream I pray
Murmur near,
That at eve sweet Echo may
Sound of village bells convey
To mine ear.
There I'd watch the speckled trout,
Ever shy,
In the water play about,
Or perhaps leap fairly out
At a fly.
Let a steeple stand in view,
That should be:
And the poor man's cottage too,
'Twill remind me what to do
In charity.
As my poultry, let the poor,
Without dread,
From the village cot or moor,
Crowd around my wicker door,
To be fed.
Thus my time I'd pass away
With delight:
Blithe as lambkins at their play,
Social, innocent and gay,
Morn and night.
Think not this is a fancied view—
You'll be wrong:
From a well-known spot I drew,
And of me you've nothing new,
But a song.

—*The Angler's Progress, 1820*, Newcastle, England, by Mr. Charnley.

Fishing, Freshwater

Fishing with Natural Bait

On the other end of the style and prestige spectrum is fishing with natural bait. The equipment for this type of fishing has considerable diversity but is considerably less diverse than the variety of baits used. Among other baits, natural bait anglers use minnows of different species, a variety of worms, crayfish, shrimp, insects, salamanders, frogs, caterpillars, and mollusks. It is likely that this is the oldest and most common method of fishing. Ancient anglers had few other ways of catching fish. They were forced to use the baits they found in the areas they were fishing. The secret of using natural baits is to match the bait with the preference of the fish at the particular time and location. Each bait requires a particular method of attachment to the hook. In some cases, it is important to attach the bait in such a way as to keep it alive. At other times, it is acceptable to kill the bait in the process. Most countries and all states in the United States have restrictions regarding the types of natural baits allowed and the methods for using them.

Freshwater Fishing Equipment

Rods and reels for freshwater fishing vary considerably. For optimum results they should be matched to the fishing conditions. There are five basic types of rod and reel combinations. Spinning rods and reels are designed to cast a weighted artificial bait a considerable distance. The reel used in this combination is "open faced." This means that the angler can see the line as it comes off an exposed spool. Spin casting combinations are similar except that the reel is "closed faced." The enclosed spool reduces the chances of tangled line but the distance of the cast is reduced as well. Fly-casting combinations consist of a relatively long rod and a very simple reel. In fly fishing the reel merely acts as a place on which to store line. Bait-casting outfits are the most accurate. The rod is stiff and the reel can be manipulated to allow for accurate casts. Trolling rods and reels are much heavier than their bait-casting cousins. They are used out of moving boats and are cast only very short distances (Sternberg 1982).

Challenges

While it may seem out of character with freshwater fishing, the sport has its share of controversy and challenge. At the center of many issues is the notion of the self imposition of handicaps. The sporting quality of the activity is based on the principle of a "fighting chance." Writers have bemoaned the fact that as technology has provided new means of catching fish, it has also reduced the opportunity of an equal contest between fish and fisher. Freshwater anglers must maintain the balance between their equipment and techniques and the skills and abilities of the fish. This is a dynamic balance, and anglers must be aware of changes in the relationship between freshwater fish and man. For example, electronic fishing aids have become common over the past twenty years. Highly technical sonar equipment can detect the presence of fish. They are so sensitive they are able to tell the type and size of the fish. Electronic temperature gauges also help the angler pinpoint the prey. Obviously, fish have not made the advances that man has made. Many argue that the game of catching fish is now grossly unfair. They call for formal and informal methods to level the playing field once more (Sternberg 1982).

One of the most positive developments in the last two decades is the catch-and-release concept. Although it started out as a practice of a few fringe sports participants, it has now become accepted in most fishing circles. With increased fishing pressure and dwindling resources, the practice of killing large numbers of fish after catching them may have to come to an end. Experts suggest that if fish are released after they are caught, they can return to their natural state and be caught at some future time by other anglers. They contend that game fish are too valuable to be caught just once. This is especially true of some of the more delicate and less prolific fishes such as trout and bass. To provide freshwater fish with the best chance of recovery, McNally (1993) suggests that fish should not be played to exhaustion and should be handled as little as possible; the fishes' gills should never be touched and hooks removed as gently as possible. In some cases, it is better to cut the line than harm the fish by trying to remove a hook deeply imbedded in it. The fish should always be released carefully. It should never be thrown onto the water's surface as this may harm the fish's delicate inner organs.

In most countries wide-scale pollution of fresh water has become a major threat to the sport.

Many lakes and streams in several countries no longer contain fish because of an increase of insecticide residues, industrial wastes, and acid rain. The situation may have reached its zenith in the late 1970s when there were alarming deaths of freshwater fish in many countries. Thanks to the efforts of individual anglers, angling clubs, and resource managers, the trend seems to have been reversed. Many lakes and streams are being returned to their prepollution condition, and the fish that inhabited them have been reintroduced. Serious threats to the resources, however, still remain (Netherby 1974).

—Daniel G. Yoder

See also Animal Rights.

Bibliography: Bennett, Tiny. (1970) *The Art of Angling.* Ontario: Prentice-Hall.

Burek, Deborah M. (1992) *Encyclopedia of Associations.* Vol. 1. Detroit: Gale Research.

Carhart, Arthur Hawthorne. (1949) *Fresh Water Fishing.* New York: A. S. Barnes.

Edginton, Christopher R., D. Jordan, D. DeGraaf, and S. Edginton. (1995) *Leisure and Life Satisfaction: Foundational Perspectives.* Dubuque, IA: Brown & Benchmark.

Harbour, Dave. (1979) "Trophy Bass: The Challenge and the Prize." In *L. Underwood's Bass Almana,* edited by L. Underwood. Garden City, NY: Doubleday, 200–212.

Krause, Richard. (1994) *Leisure in a Changing America: Multicultural Perspectives.* New York: Macmillan.

McNally, Tom. (1993) *The Complete Book of Fly Fishing.* 2d ed. Camden, ME: Ragged Mountain Press.

McPherson, Barry D., James E. Curtis, and John W. Loy. (1989) *The Social Significance of Sport: An Introduction to the Sociology of Sport.* Champaign, IL: Human Kinetics.

Netherby, Steve. (1974) *The Experts' Book of Fresh Water Fishing.* New York: Simon and Schuster.

Sternberg, Dick. (1982) *The Art of Fresh Water Fishing.* Minnetonka, MN: Cy DeCosse Inc.

Taylor, Nick. (1987) *Bass Wars: A Story of Fishing Fame and Fortune.* New York: McGraw-Hill.

Trench, Charles Chenvix. (1974). *A History of Angling.* Chicago: Follett.

Tryckare, Tre, Ewart Cagner, and Bernt Dybern. (1976) *The Lore of Sportfishing.* New York: Crown.

U.S. Fish and Wildlife Service. (1993) *1991 National Survey of Fishing, Hunting, and Wildlife Associated Recreation.* Washington, DC: Government Printing Office.

Waterman, Charles F. (1981). *A History of Angling.* Tulsa, OK: Winchester Press.

Wulff, Lee. (1982). "Fly Fishing: An Angler's Perspective." In *Water Swift and Small,* edited by G. LaFontaine and D. Seybold. Tulsa, OK: Winchester Press, 121–137.

Fishing, Saltwater

Although some people may ask the question, "Is saltwater fishing truly a sport?" it does in fact satisfy the qualifying criteria for sport put forth by B. D. McPherson, J. E. Curtis, and J. W. Loy (1989, 1–7) It is goal-oriented, has competition, involves physical prowess (most types of saltwater fishing require considerable physical skill and stamina), requires concentration, and has the ludic quality—uncertain outcome and sanctioned display—of sports. The majority of saltwater fishing actually takes place in the world's estuaries, which are the diverse and very fertile areas where freshwater rivers and streams enter the ocean. While these brackish waters have very low salinity, they are considered saltwater, and thus the fishing there is considered saltwater as well.

E. Cagner suggests that there are two main reasons that saltwater fishing is different from freshwater fishing (1976, 276). First, "ocean fish are governed by the ebb and flow of the tides as well as the daily and seasonal fluctuations of sunlight, temperature and weather." The second and more important distinction is the tremendous diversity of saltwater fish species available to the angler. Such diversity can present problems; some of which are quite serious. For example, unexpectedly hooking a 68-kilogram (150-pound) shark instead of a 4.5-kilogram (10-pound) permit can be particularly unnerving.

Origins and Development

Saltwater sport fishing is not as old as freshwater sport fishing. It took longer for people to recognize that fishing in the sea could be recreational. Part of this lag can be attributed to the difficulty and danger encountered by subsistence and commercial ocean fishermen. Given the fact that boats and men failed to return on a regular basis from ocean fishing expeditions, it is not surprising that people were hesitant to go out and fish for fun. In addition, fishing equipment and boats simply were not available to most saltwater anglers. Whereas one could get by with less than ideal equipment for freshwater fishing, it was much less possible for the saltwater angler.

Waterman (1981), one of the foremost authorities on the history of salt-water fishing, illustrates some of the confusion about the history of the sport. At one point he notes, "Striped bass clubs of the New England coast probably started serious coastal sport fishing in America" (p. 122). However, at another point he writes, "So although it was in the Pacific that offshore angling really began, it was the Atlantic tarpon that stirred enthusiasm for giant fish on light gear" (p. 125). The problem is that east coast fishers initiated saltwater fishing from shore and west coast fishers were more instrumental in starting saltwater fishing in deep water far from shore. They actually developed at approximately the same time, the late 1800s.

For unexplained reasons, striped bass disappeared from the U.S. Atlantic coast from 1900 to 1930. By this time, the nucleus of saltwater fishing had shifted to Florida. Tarpon had long been considered uncatchable with light fishing gear, but this did not stop some from forcing the issue. Slowly, techniques and equipment that allowed anglers to catch large specimens of the powerful fish were developed. Tarpon fishing stimulated saltwater fishing, and it was not long before another fish of the Florida Flats, the bonefish, was sharing center stage with the tarpon (Waterman 1981, 141). These two fish spurred a sudden interest for in-shore fishing.

The Pacific tuna served as the impetus for saltwater fishing farther off shore. At the turn of the last century, a few California anglers brought in large Pacific tuna weighing over 45 kilograms (100 pounds). The Catalina Tuna Club was a prestigious fishing club that catered to the rich and occasionally eccentric. American author and Catalina Tuna Club member Zane Grey (1872–1939) "did more to promote deep water fishing than any other man" (Waterman 1981, 130). His particular passion was catching billfish—sailfish, swordfish, and marlin. Grey wrote of the adventure of deep-sea fishing and spread the word to the rest of the Western world. By the 1940s, saltwater fishing was firmly established, although its growth was slowed temporarily by World War II.

Practice

Saltwater fishing may best be divided into in-shore fishing and off-shore fishing. One of the

Writer Ernest Hemingway shows off his marlin, certain kinds of which can weigh up to 1,600 pounds. The challenges of the sport and the great variety of fish attract many people to saltwater fishing.

most popular types of in-shore fishing is surf fishing. The angler wades as far out into the water as possible, keeping in mind the incoming waves that may be four feet high and very powerful. On other occasions the fisher stands on a rock jetty that protrudes out into the water, and casts as far as possible (Cagner 1976, 271). Some purists, however, do not consider fishing from a jetty true surf fishing.

As early as the mid-1970s there were approximately 1 million surf anglers (p. 269). R. Scharff called surf fishing "the most rapidly growing branch of salt water fishing" (1966, 116). Surf fishing is most popular on the Atlantic and Pacific coasts of the United States. Some of the advantages of this type of saltwater fishing include its relative low cost and its close relation to freshwater trout fishing and its status as the sport of the upper class. In addition, it can be more interesting than most other saltwater fishing. Surf anglers are on their own; they have no mate or guide to help them find and catch fish. Consequently, surf fishing appeals to anglers with an individualistic bent.

The equipment for surf fishing, although less expensive than that used for some other types of saltwater fishing, is critical. The spinning reel is the most common type of reel used for fishing the surf. This reel allows the angler to continually cast long distances and to retrieve artificial lures or baits at a high rate of speed. Surf casting rods must be strong and flexible enough to cast large bait, but sensitive enough to detect small taps by cautious fish. Most surf rods are fairly long and have a long rod butt, which provides the two-handed leverage essential for surf casting.

Most surf fishers prefer to use artificial lures. Surf fishers tend to be action-oriented men and women who would not be interested in casting out a bait and waiting for a fish to take it. Artificial lures allow surf fishers to be proactive rather than reactive. One of the oldest lures is the metal squids, which come in a variety of sizes, shapes, and colors and are designed to look like the fish's natural food. Plugs are also used extensively by surf fishers. They are usually made from wood and plastic and tend to be lighter than squids. For this reason, they are less popular when the surf fisher has to cast a long distance (Scharff 1966). Occasionally surf anglers do use natural bait. Sometimes these baits are cast and retrieved as one might cast an artificial lure. At other times, the natural bait is still fished, where the bait is allowed to lie motionless on the bottom. This is usually accomplished with the use of a large lead weight or "sinker."

Fishing from rocky shores and piers is very close to surf fishing. It is very popular in the United States, which has accessible shoreline and very long piers that jut out into the ocean. When the fishing is good, anglers are lined up on the piers shoulder to shoulder. Man-made jetties are especially productive areas for saltwater fishing, because smaller bait fish tend to congregate around areas with underwater structures such as piers and jetties, larger game fish move in to feed. Fishing around jetties is done both with artificial baits and with natural baits, which are retrieved and still fished.

The previously mentioned saltwater fishing techniques involve special hazards. For the beach surf fishers, ocean tides and waves can be deadly. Anglers have been washed off their feet with un-

expected waves, and some have been stranded on points when tides have risen. Jetties have the reputation of being the most dangerous of all fishing areas. The jetties' rocks are usually covered with moss. The combination of poor footing and rushing waters from waves and swells can be a recipe for disaster (Scharff 1966). Night fishing, which is popular in these areas, adds yet another level of risk. Specialized equipment and techniques for surf and rock fishers, such as cleated footwear and flotation devices, have been developed to reduce some of the danger.

Trolling for fish, either on the surface or at considerable depth, is the most effective method of catching world-record saltwater species. By pulling a lure or a natural bait from a slow moving boat, one is able to cover a great amount of water. Anglers do not have to concern themselves with the fatigue they might experience in surf fishing. They can have their equipment in the water at all times. Much trolling is provided by charter boats because the cost of equipment is too great for many anglers, but many smaller vessels also troll for in-shore and off-shore species. Trolling reels are not designed for casting. They are often heavy, dependable, and built for extended use. The rods are usually somewhat shorter and heavier than those used for surf fishing. Outriggers are long poles that extend 3 to 6 meters (10–18 feet) from the sides of boats. These allow the lures and baits to be trolled away from the boat's wakes at different depths and with different actions. With outriggers several anglers, as many as eight, are able to simultaneously fish from a single boat. On the heavier lines, anglers can fish for marlins and sailfish, and on the lighter or "flat" lines anglers can fish for species such as wahoo, albacore, and dolphin.

Party boat fishing is designed for the saltwater angler who wants to fish but lacks the necessary skill and/or equipment for participating on his or her own. This method of fishing is not new; in the last half of the nineteenth-century, skippers took groups of paying individuals to locations in the sea known to have fish. Party boats were especially popular on the West Coast and, initially, in the East (Waterman 1981, 136). Recently, they have become popular in Florida. The early boats were not specifically designed to allow a large number of people to fish simultaneously; they were merely large boats that were modified to more or less serve the purpose. As the sport became more popular and profitable, boats were designed with large decks that allowed up to 100 anglers to get bait from a central location and conveniently fish over the sides of the boat. Today, most often a flat rate is charged either on a day or a half-day basis. Fishing gear is provided if anglers do not own their own equipment. In fact, some party boats prefer to provide fishing equipment to ensure that anglers have a reasonable chance of success. In addition, the equipment they provide is specifically designed to account for the limited space aboard vessels that have a full load of anglers. Party boat fishing consists of fishing straight down off the sides of the boat. The boat stations itself over the fishing area (sometimes a shipwreck or a reef) and anglers simply release line on the reel until the bait is at the proper depth (Cagner 1976, 282). A variety of species can be taken from these boats using these techniques, including grouper, snappers, shark, flounder, salmon, and others.

Party boats are often equipped with the latest in sonar equipment to detect underwater structures, such as wrecked ships, that attract game fish. Some of this equipment is sensitive enough to detect the fish themselves. Many captains of party boats guard their fishing waters seriously. They understand that too much fishing pressure can reduce fishers' success and consequently their profits (Cagner 1976, 282).

Charter boats are similar to party boats except that there is more privacy on a chartered vessel. Instead of fishing with 60 strangers as on a party boat, a charter angler usually fishes with a small group of friends or relatives. This fishing is usually more exciting, with greater chances of catching trophy fish of various species. The trade-off is the expense; charter boat fishing is considerably more expensive than party boat fishing (Scharff 1966).

The fastest-growing and most prestigious form of saltwater fishing is fly-fishing. Freshwater fly fishers are able to convert without too much difficulty, and other saltwater anglers are realizing the thrill of the challenge of taking large, strong fish with relatively light tackle. Saltwater fly-fishing includes in-shore fishing and off-shore fishing. In-shore fly-fishing is by far the most popular. More species and a greater number of fishing areas are available to the in-shore angler.

Fishing Spiritualized

Chap. 1. Of the Fisherman's Ship or Boat
Chap. 2. Of the waters that are for this fishing
Chap. 3. Of the nets and angle-rod that are for this fishing
Chap. 4. Of the fishermen that principally are appointed for this office
Chap. 5. The especiall duties of the spirituall fisherman
Chap. 6. Of the Fisherman's baytes
Chap. 7. Of the fishes that the spirituall Angler or Fisherman onely fisheth for
Chap. 8. The Sympathie of natures, of the fishes of both natures
Chap. 9. Of the Antipathie and differences of fishes of both sortes, and of the angling of both kindes

Every Fisher-man hath his proper baytes, agreeable to the nature of those fishes that hee trowleth or angleth for. For at a bare hooke no Fish will bite. The case-worme, the dewe-worme, the gentile, the flye, the small Roache, and suche-like, are for their turnes according to the nature of the waters, and the times, and the kindes of fishes. Whoso fisheth not with a right bayte, shall neuer do good. Wee that are spirituall fishermen, haue our seurall baites suitable to the stomackes we angle for. If we obserue not the natures of our auditors, and fit ourselves to them, we shall not do wisely. Let such as will not bee led by love bee drawne by feare. But with some the spirit of meeknes will doe most, and loue rather than a rodde doth more good and we shall do indiscreetly, to deale roughly with such. For as the water of a spacious and deepe lake, being still and quiet by nature, by ruffling windes is moued and disquieted; so a people tractable by nature, by the rough behauiour of the Minister may be as much turmoyled and altered from his nature.

The fisherman baiteth not his hook that the fish might only take it, but be taken of it. The red-worme, the case-worme, maggot-flies, small flie, small roche, or such like, are glorious in outward appearance to the fish. So the riches, prioritie, authoritie, of the world, are but pleasant bayts laid out for our destruction. The fisherman's bayte is a deadly deceite: so are all the pleasures of the world. As all the waters of the riuers runne into the salt sea, so all worldly delights, in the saltish sea of sorrows finish their course. Wherefore mistrust worldly benefits as baites, and feed not upon them in hungry wise.

—A Booke of Angling or Fishing. Wherein is shewed, by conference with Scriptures, the agreement between the Fisherman, Fishes, Fishing of both natures, Temporall and Spirituall. By Samuel Gardiner, *Doctor of Divinitie.* Mathew iv. 19. *"I will make you fishers of men."* London: Printed for Thomas Purfoot, 1606.

It is also less expensive than its off-shore counterpart (McNally 1993, 306). Hot spots for fly-fishing for saltwater species, both in-shore and off-shore, include the waters of Florida, Australia, the Caribbean, and the Gulf of Mexico. Popular species pursued by fly fishers include bonefish, tarpon, snook, sea trout, barracuda, channel bass, cravelle, and mackerel.

No discussion of saltwater fishing would be complete without mention of the big game fish of the open seas. These are the fish in the novels of Zane Grey and Ernest Hemingway. Before the advent of charter boats, the pursuit of the "big boys of the sea" was limited to the rich and influential. The modern charter boat, however, has made the sport much more accessible to greater numbers of people. With equipment and boat rental, one can pursue big game fish with relatively little expenditure.

Various species of tuna roam the cool waters of the Atlantic and Pacific oceans. The bluefin tuna has a special place in the sport of big game fishing. The bluefin was one of the first widely recognized big game fish. C. F. Waterman noted, "The Pacific tuna moved sportsmen into deep water" (1981, 130). The largest specimens of this migratory fish weigh over 450 kilograms (1,000 pounds). They are noted for their tremendous strength, endurance, and speed (Cagner 1976, 216). The preferred method of catching tuna is by trolling in the open seas.

Most anglers consider the swordfish the greatest big game fish of all. They are found on the deep water edges of off-shore banks throughout the warm waters of the world. Although the average weight is in the 180–250 kilogram (400–600 pounds) range, specimens over 450 kilograms are occasionally taken. The broad sword on these fish distinguishes them from the marlins and sailfish that have shorter and rounder spikes. The most common way of catching swordfish is to skip an artificial or a natural bait past them while trolling. First, however, it is necessary to locate them. The sea is too big and the fish too few to catch them by blindly trolling. Tall platforms mounted on fishing boats allow anglers to see swordfish from long distances because "swords" often bask very near the water's surface.

The five different species of marlin are noted for their spectacular surface fighting. They sometimes make several leaps that clear the water by 3

meters (10 feet). White marlin average around 27 kilograms (60 pounds). At the other end of the size spectrum is the black marlin of the Pacific Ocean. Excluding sharks, the black marlin is the largest game fish, with individuals weighing well over 727 kilograms (1,600 pounds) (Cagner 1976, 221).

The different types of sailfish are especially popular big game fish. While they do not have the size of either the marlins or the swordfishes, they are exceptional fighters. The large "sail" is actually a dorsal fin that can be folded into a groove in the fish's back or extended when the fish jumps after being hooked.

Sharks are the final category of big game fish. They inhabit the cold and warm waters of the world. Anglers are slow to recognize them as worthy game until they experience the strength and endurance of them on a line. Although there are many species of sharks in the world's ocean waters, only mako, white, tiger, porbeagle, and thresher sharks are recognized as game fish by the International Game Fishing Association (IGFA). The white shark is the largest game fish in the world, with record-holding specimens weighing over 1,180 kilograms (2,600 pounds). Special care must be taken when fishing for sharks, for even those species that are not man-eaters are equipped with several rows of teeth and powerful tails that can injure or kill careless anglers. In addition, sharks have razor-sharp skin consisting of thousands of denticles that make the skin feel like sandpaper (Cagner 1976, 304).

Although some lay persons and anglers persist in the belief that the fish in the seas are unlimited, recent evidence disputes such a position. The numbers of many in-shore and off-shore species are in fact dangerously low. Restrictions on the length of seasons, types of equipment, and fishing techniques have been imposed in an effort to reverse the trends. In addition, at least for many of the big game fish, the catch-and-release concept has firmly established itself. Amazing results have been realized for some species of saltwater game fish, but for others the outlook is less than bright (Boyle 1995, 5–10).

Saltwater fishing has competitive formats similar to its freshwater counterpart. These competitions include record-keeping and organized fishing tournaments. The IGFA, organized in 1940, initially kept records of saltwater species only. The organization is now responsible for both saltwater and freshwater records. Although tournaments are organized to fish for a variety of saltwater species, probably the most popular and visible tournaments are for billfish such as marlins and sailfish. Winners are judged on the number of fish caught within a specified time and the weight of the fish (Waterman 1981, 19–95).

—Daniel G. Yoder

Bibliography: Boyle, R. (1995) "Management School." *Outdoor Life* 195 (April): 53–60.

Cagner, E. (1976) *The Lore of Sportfishing*. New York: Crown.

McNally, T. (1993) *The Complete Book of Fly Fishing*. 2d ed. Camden, ME: Ragged Mountain Press.

McPherson, B. D., J. E. Curtis, and J. W. Loy. (1989) *The Social Significance of Sport: An Introduction to the Sociology of Sport*. Champaign, IL: Human Kinetics.

Scharff, R. (1966) *Standard Handbook of Salt-Water Fishing*. New York: Thomas Y. Crowell.

Waterman, C. F. (1981) *A History of Angling*. Tulsa, OK: Winchester Press.

———. (1982) "The Bonefish Flats." In *Waters Swift and Small*, edited by C. Woods and D. Seybold. Tulsa, OK: Winchester Press.

Flying Disc

Flying discs are lightweight objects shaped like saucers that players throw and catch. "Flying disc" is a generic term, and discs are often referred to as a "Frisbee," which actually is the trademarked name of the most famous brand of them. Since the 1950s flying discs have become extremely popular recreational products. According to its manufacturer, Mattel Corp., over 100 million Frisbees have been made since the product was introduced in 1957, and they annually outsell baseballs, basketballs, and footballs.

The flying disc has become a prominent feature of popular culture. Initially, the design and performance of these plastic discs (which have also been called "flying saucers") reflected the nation's fascination with space flight and science fiction. In the 1960s and 1970s, the gentle flight characteristics of the discs became associated with the relaxed attitudes of the counterculture. Casual players simply enjoy the act of tossing and catching the disc as a relaxing way to spend time. The flying disc also reflects the increased emphasis on sports and exercise that emerged after 1970. Flying discs are also used in a wide range of challenging competitive sports and in exercise programs in schools.

Origins

There have been many different versions told about the origins of the modern flying disc. Throwing discs as sport can be traced back to ancient cultures, such as the historic track-and-field event of discus throwing.

The contemporary lightweight flying disc is believed to have originated in a game college students invented by tossing metal pie plates or cookie-tin tops among themselves for amusement. This fad was generally thought to have started in the 1930s and 1940s, but some accounts trace it back as far as the nineteenth century. It is not known where this game started either. It has been attributed to several schools. At Middlebury College in Vermont, for example, a statue of a dog catching a flying disc commemorates a day in 1939 when, according to college lore, several Middlebury students invented the game by tossing a pie tin while they were on a trip.

The plastic flying disc as a recreational product was developed in the late 1940s and the 1950s. The idea apparently occurred to more than one person simultaneously, and several versions were sold in that era. Ernest Robes, a New Hampshire inventor, made and sold a disc called the Space Saucer for several years in the 1950s.

The genesis of the specific product known as the Frisbee—the version that made flying discs popular—is clearer. Fred Morrison was a building inspector and pilot in California. In 1948, Morrison developed a small flying disc made of plastic. He first named his invention the "Flyin' Saucer" and later the "Pluto Platter." For several years he made personal appearances at public gatherings to sell his new toy to bystanders.

In 1956, Morrison sold the rights to the product to Wham-O, a San Gabriel, California, company owned by entrepreneurs Rich Knerr and A. K. Melin. They had already marketed a popular slingshot, and later developed many other famous

Since their invention in the 1950s flying discs (Frisbees) have become a familiar sight to people everywhere.

Wham-O inscribed on the original Frisbees the motto "Play Catch! Invent Games." Many people did invent new games and variations of old sports using the versatile flying disc. Competitive flying-disc sports emerged, and many tournaments, leagues, and other associations have been formed over the years. In 1958, the first International Frisbee Tournament was held in Escanaba, Michigan. Wham-O executive Ed Headrick founded the International Frisbee Association to promote disc sports in 1967.

In 1985, the first World Flying Disc Conference was held in Helsinborg, Sweden, with 19 nations represented, which led to the formation of the World Flying Disc Federation. This organization was accepted as a member of the General Association of International Sports Federations in 1987. In the United States, the flying disc was also accepted as a new category for the Presidential Sports Award in 1993.

Practice

Flying discs are designed to move forward through the air with a spinning motion. The specific characteristics of this movement depend on a combination of factors, including the force of the throw, the speed of the spin, and the angle of flight. A disc can be thrown so that it slowly floats to its destination or it can be made to fly in a fast, direct path. The skill of throwing a disc is based on the ability of a player to control these variables. These include the way the disk is held in the fingers and the angle and speed of the arm and wrist movements as it is thrown.

There are several basic tosses, and players devise their own variations to achieve specific results. One common throwing style is an even, level movement of the arm, extending forward from the chest, while the disk is released by a steady flick of the wrist, which propels the disc with a straight, even movement. This is one of the gentler tosses, although it can also be thrown hard and fast with that method. Another variation is an overhand toss, with the arm held at shoulder height, and the disc thrown from behind the player's head forward (similar to the way a baseball is thrown). The disc is held by the thumb and is often thrown with a more distinct snap of the fingers and wrist, which causes a fast, direct flight. A disc can also be thrown with an

recreational products, including the hula hoop. Wham-O changed the name of the Pluto Platter to Frisbee in 1958. Backed by Wham-O's marketing skill, the Frisbee soon achieved great popularity.

The origin of the name "Frisbee" is also open to question. The most frequent explanation is that it refers to the Frisbie Baking Co., whose containers were originally thrown by students. However, one of the cofounders of Wham-O once said he took the name for the product from an old comic strip.

For serious players, Wham-O introduced the heavier "Professional Model" Frisbee in 1964. Wham-O eventually was sold and absorbed into other companies, and the Frisbee rights are now owned by Mattel Corp. Other companies have marketed their own brands and designs of flying discs.

underhand movement beginning low from the player's side and then swinging upward as the disk is released. This often creates a high, long throw.

Flying discs are also used in a wide variety of competitive games and sports and for physical conditioning. In "Guts," individual players or teams, generally with five players on each side, face each other, and toss the disc back and forth. Their goal is to throw it as hard and fast as possible to prevent opponents from catching it. (The origin of Guts is not known, but it is believed to be a safer version of a game that college students once played with a circular saw blade!) The modern rules of Guts were formalized in 1975 by the Guts Players Association. Ultimate is a field sport played with a flying disc (see sidebar). Freestyle flying-disc events are displays of especially dramatic and creative movements. Canine Frisbee, games in which dogs catch and retrieve discs, are also popular.

Numerous variations of bowling and other traditional games have also been tailored for the flying disc. Disc Golf is a variation of its namesake, played with specially designed discs rather than golf balls and with poles as the targets instead of holes. There are at least 500 Disc Golf courses in the United States, often in public parks.

In addition to direct competition among themselves, serious flying-disc players also attempt to break records, such as those listed in the *Guinness Book of Records*. In 1993, Niclas Bergehamm of Sweden set a long-distance flying-disc record by throwing a disc 197.38 meters (215 yards, 2 feet, 9½ inches).

A newer flying disc, known as the Aerobie, became popular in the 1990s. Unlike the traditional flying disc, the Aerobie is hollow at the center, and is designed to fly especially far, commonly 200 yards or more. The Aerobie was recorded in one edition of the *Guinness Book of Records* as the object thrown farthest in the world, a record set with a 383.13-meter (419-yard) toss by Scott Zimmerman of San Francisco.

—John Townes

Ultimate

The sport of Ultimate is a fast-paced game played according to a simple set of rules, with no referee. Played with a Frisbee, the game combines elements of soccer, football, and basketball. Every player is a quarterback and every player is a receiver.

Ultimate was first played by a group of high school students in 1968 in the parking lot of the Columbia High School in Maplewood, New Jersey. Within a few years the sport had spread to colleges throughout the United States; the first intercollegiate Ultimate game took place on 6 November 1972 in New Brunswick, New Jersey, between players from Rutgers and Princeton. The game is particularly popular among high school and college students, but many others participate as members of club teams or in informal settings. There are now over 15,000 players in 20 countries around the world.

A regulation game of Ultimate is played by two teams of seven players on a field measuring 70 yards by 40 yards (64 meters by 36 meters) with 25 yard (23 meter) deep endzones. At the start of each point, the teams line up in front of their respective end zones; a point is scored when the offensive team completes a pass within the defensive team's end zone. The disc (Frisbee) may be advanced in any direction by completing a pass to a teammate. Possession changes sides when a pass is not completed; the defense immediately takes possession and becomes the offense. Players may not run with the disc; the person with the disc ("thrower") has ten seconds to throw the disc to a teammate. No physical contact is allowed between players; a foul occurs when contact is made. When a foul disrupts possession, the play resumes as if the possession was retained. If the player committing the foul disagrees with the foul call, the play is redone.

According to participants, Ultimate depends on a spirit of sportsmanship and fair play. Players are responsible for their own foul and line calls and resolve their own disputes. Competitive play is encouraged but never at the expense of respect between players, adherence to the rules, or the basic joy of play. Under the rules of the game, behavior such as taunting opponents, dangerous aggression, intentional fouls, or a "win-at-all-costs" attitude is contrary to the spirit of the game and must be discouraged by all players.

Bonnie Dyer-Bennet

Footbag

Footbag is a popular contemporary sport based on the activity of kicking a stuffed, pliable ball that is usually about two inches in diameter. Players keep the footbag moving in the air using only their feet, legs, or thighs. "Footbag" is a generic name for the sport; it is also known as Hacky Sack, which is the trademarked name of one of the most popular brands of footbag.

Footbag was developed in the 1970s. By the mid-1990s footbag was played in at least 15 countries, and an estimated 20 million footbags had been sold. Many people simply enjoy kicking footbags alone, in pairs, or in groups as a casual pastime. The sport has also attracted serious amateur enthusiasts and professional players, and a network of organized footbag competitions has developed.

Origins

Footbag is similar to older kick-based sports, such as soccer and the Malaysian national sport of *sepak takraw*. One of its oldest ancestors is believed to be a game that originated in China around 2600 B.C.E. in which an object filled with hair was kicked as a sport and a conditioning exercise for soldiers. Another forerunner, the game of shuttlecock, was developed approximately 2,000 years ago in Asia, using a feathered disc that was kicked and passed by players.

The contemporary sport of footbag was developed in the western United States in the early 1970s by John Stalberger and Mike Marshall, two friends who enjoyed kicking around a small stuffed sock for enjoyment and physical conditioning. They called this pastime "hacking the sack," and they began to develop and promote their hobby as a sport.

Although Marshall died in 1975, Stalberger continued to be an active promoter of the footbag. He invented a footbag game called Net. After experimenting with footbags of different sizes made of various materials, he obtained a patent for the Hacky Sack footbag in 1979. In 1983, he sold the rights for the Hacky Sack to Wham-O, a company that had already marketed many other popular recreational products, including the Frisbee and the Hula Hoop. (Many of Wham-O's products are now owned by the Mattel Corp.) Supported by the promotional resources of Wham-O, the footbag gained many enthusiasts and became a fad in the early 1980s. It was not a briefly popular flash in the pan, however. Instead, it has evolved into an established form of recreation and exercise, and many other makers of footbags and accessories have emerged.

In 1983 the World Footbag Association (WFA), based in Golden, Colorado, was formed as an official promotional and players' organization. By late 1995, the WFA's membership had surpassed 34,000 and was increasing at a rate of 600 new members per month. To promote the footbag as a form of physical education, the WFA sponsors many demonstrations and classes in schools.

The first National Footbag Championship tournament was held in Oregon City, Oregon, in 1980. It has since become an annual event and was renamed the World Footbag Championships in 1986. Approximately 150 players from various nations were registered to play in the 1995 World Footbag Championships held in San Francisco. Many other local and regional events are held throughout the world, either as general competitions or for specific games played with the footbag.

Practice

Many different games have been developed for the footbag. These include completely new games as well as older sports that have been adapted to use the footbag instead of balls.

According to its proponents, footbag is a valuable form of exercise that develops endurance, coordination, balance, and mental concentration in unique ways because of its emphasis on muscles and movements that are not often used in daily life or in other sports.

Most footbag games do not allow any movements in which the player uses their hands, arms, or upper torso to control the bag. With some exceptions, only the feet and lower body are supposed to touch the footbag while it is in play. One of the principles of the sport is the use of kicks on alternate sides of the lower body to keep the footbag in motion. Many standard movements are

Footbag net, just one variant of footbag, allows players the individual creative freedom that attracts many people to the sport.

learned and used by footbag players as they become proficient in the sport. Controlling the footbag requires the ability to move quickly while maintaining balance, to see where the footbag is and then instinctually direct the movement of feet, legs, and torso to control it. It also requires endurance to sustain the continuous exertion required to keep the footbag in play. Individual games also involve more specific skills.

The sport's most basic format is known as Footbag Consecutive, which is played either informally or in competition. Consecutive play can be an individual activity or played by pairs or teams who pass the footbag among themselves. In basic Consecutive, players keep the footbag in the air for as long as possible and perform as many kicks as they can before they either miss the footbag, lose control of it, or become too tired to continue. In organized events, players or teams compete against each other. In Singles Timed Footbag Consecutive individual players try to make as many kicks as possible in five minutes, without losing points for upper-body fouls, for dropping the bag or for not alternating their feet or knees. In Doubles Distance One Pass Foot Consecutive, two players try to successively pass a footbag in a rally over a 3-meter (10-foot) distance. Serious footbag players also try to break records in such categories as men's and women's Single Consecutive, Doubles Consecutive, One-Pass Consecutive, and Timed Consecutive. The best players have shown high levels of endurance and mental discipline, and the records are continually being expanded. In 1978, for example, Stalberger set the record for Men's Single Footbag Consecutive by kicking a footbag 1,518 times in a period of 23 minutes, 42 seconds. By 1993, Ted Martin had set a new record with 51,155 kicks over a period of 7 hours, 1 minute, 37 seconds. In 1980, Jack Schoolcraft and Will Wingert established a Men's Doubles record of 2,069 kicks in 25 minutes. In 1995, Tricia George and Gary Lautt made 123,456 kicks over 19 hours, 19 minutes, 20 seconds.

Footbag Freestyle is somewhat similar to Consecutive. However, in Freestyle the emphasis is on the individual display of especially creative and dramatic kicks and routines, which are scored by a panel of judges. The rules of Freestyle are more lenient regarding the use of the upper body to allow players greater freedom and variety in their actions. Players choreograph their routines to music and incorporate many elements to add to the impact of their displays. Because of their free-form and creative nature, Freestyle competitions are inherently difficult to judge objectively. To resolve controversies that have occasionally arisen, systematic guidelines have been devised. Judging is based on a point system, with difficulty ratings from one to four points awarded for individual movements and the overall routine. Judges also rate other factors, such as leg dexterity, delays, cross-body movement, originality, and the player's coordination with selected music.

Footbag Net is played by pairs of individuals, doubles, or larger teams. Its rules, strategy, and scoring combine elements of volleyball and tennis. The official court size is 13 meters by 6 meters (44 feet by 20 feet), divided by a net 1.5 meters (five feet) high in the center. Players stand on either side of the net and kick the footbag back and forth, attempting to score points by making spikes and other shots their opponents cannot return. Two kicks can be made per side in singles play, while three kicks are allowed in doubles (but a doubles player cannot make two consecutive kicks). A game is played to 11 or 15 points, and a match is won by the victor in two out of three games. Players are ranked in regional and national tournaments to qualify for the World Championships. The best Net players are able to make spectacular shots, kicking their feet high in the air as they hit the fast-moving footbag.

In Footbag Golf, players move the footbag around a specially designed course with the goal of kicking it into a series of holes. The basic format and scoring are similar to the traditional game of golf. Players tee off with a hand toss and kick. The course can include a variety of obstacles. The hole is a raised cone-like object.

The common footbag is generally two inches in diameter, covered with suede or leather and stuffed with plastic pellets. The surface is often a series of smaller panels stitched together. However, many other types of footbags have been introduced, including those made with other materials and of different sizes and weights. Some footbags have knitted or crocheted textile surfaces. Footbags also include both commercial models and homemade versions. Certain footbags are designed to give specific performance characteristics, such as those designed for freestyle events. Footbags often feature colorful designs on their surface, including a player's name and other personalized graphics or messages. Some enthusiasts enjoy collecting different footbags.

—John Townes

See also Takraw.

Bibliography: *Footbag World Magazine* (Golden, CO).

Football, American

American football was adapted from English rugby in the period from the 1870s to the early 1900s. The game first became popular in the elite colleges of the East after Harvard refused to play soccer (association football). Led by Yale's Walter Camp (1859–1925), rugby football rules were changed to reflect America's desire for a more scientific, rational game. Only after football became the most prominent college sport, based on a felt need for a manly game, did football become professionalized, and the professional game did not challenge the dominance of college football until the 1960s, when television coverage of the National Football League became popular. By that time African Americans had become prominent in both college and professional football. With increased revenues, professional players formed a labor union and demanded a higher portion of the profits being made by team owners. By the close of the twentieth century, the colleges continued to be "feeders" for the professional leagues, and college and professional teams prospered.

Origins

American football is a nineteenth-century adaptation of the game of rugby football that evolved at the Rugby School, one of England's elite private secondary schools known as "public schools." Two distinct forms of football had developed in Britain, association football (soccer) and rugby, a contest emphasizing running more than kicking. The English Football Association codified the rules of soccer in 1863, when it was founded by elite ex–public school and Oxford and Cambridge players working in London. The Football Association had hoped to create one game of the various school and college games but was unable to convince the rugby players of the need for one unified game of football. The Rugby Football Union was formed in 1871 to promote the running game with one set of codified rules. In the 1860s and early 1870s, many American collegians were playing forms of soccer, while Harvard students had created a game more akin to English rugby than soccer.

On most U.S. campuses football, of the soccer type, had evolved as part of class battles. The sophomores would challenge the freshmen to a kicking game in which the kicking of opponents appeared to be as common as booting the ball. These games were part of the traditional indoctrination process found on all college campuses where cocky sophomores initiated freshmen through various forms of hazing. At Harvard, the first day of school in the fall was concluded annually with what was known as "Bloody Monday," when the sophomores generally beat the freshman into submission on the campus delta. Other matches throughout the year might include the freshmen combining with the juniors to battle the sophomores and seniors. These contests became so brutal, especially the Bloody Monday encounters, that Harvard authorities banned football in 1860.

Most other colleges, however, continued to play football, including two New Jersey institutions, Princeton and Rutgers, which were located only about 32 kilometers (20 miles) apart. A year after the Civil War, when baseball was expanding greatly throughout the United States, Princeton had beaten Rutgers in their first intercollegiate baseball contest 40–2. Three years later Rutgers challenged Princeton to a two-out-of-three football contest. On 6 November 1869, the first intercollegiate football game was played on the Rutgers campus with teams of 25 on a side. The agreed-upon rules resembled soccer, but the players could bat the inflated rubber ball with hands or fists as well as with feet. The goal posts were eight paces wide and were located at the ends of a 69-meter (225-foot) field. Rutgers accumulated six goals first and won 6–4 before a crowd that included a small number of Princeton partisans, who took the train to New Brunswick. They and the Rutgers fans saw a contest featuring "headlong running, wild shouting, and frantic kicking," and a Princeton player who forgot which end was his and sent the ball to his own goal. The game was followed by a gastronomic and convivial evening including a roast game dinner, impromptu speeches, and the singing of college songs. A week later Rutgers visited Princeton, playing under Princeton's usual rules that allowed the free kick, whereby a player could catch the ball in the air or on first bounce and kick it without hindrance. Princeton's 8–0

victory called for a third and decisive game, but it was not played, possibly due to institutional administrative interference but more likely because the two institutions were not able to agree on common rules.

While most colleges were playing a variation of association football, the soccer-like game was short-lived despite the rules being codified on several campuses. Harvard was the only major school not playing a form of soccer. The Harvard men called their pastime the Boston game, in which a player could catch or pick up the ball and then kick it or even run with it. The opportunity to run with the ball was a key development of a nonsoccer game in America. It resembled the rugby game, not followed by any other college. Yale, Harvard's chief rival in crew and baseball in the early 1870s, played its first intercollegiate soccer contest when it beat Columbia in 1872. The Yale victory began what would become the most successful college program in the first century of intercollegiate football. The next year, a "Western" school, Michigan, challenged Cornell to a football game, but Cornell's president, Andrew D. White (1882–1918), banned it when he made his classic comment: "I will not permit 30 men to travel 400 miles merely to agitate a bag of wind." With interest expanding, Yale called a convention to write common rules for league play in 1873.

Harvard absented itself from the convention, protesting the soccer game as inferior to its own, and its action drastically changed the history of American football. While Yale, Princeton, Columbia, and Rutgers agreed to common rules, Harvard kept its own. This led Harvard to two matches in May 1874 with McGill University from Montreal, Canada. The first game between the most elite institutions in each country was played under Harvard rules and the second under McGill's rugby rules. Harvard men enjoyed the rugby game, and in the spring of 1875 played nearby Tufts College in the first intercollegiate rugby game between colleges in the United States. Soon Yale asked Harvard to play a football game, but Harvard would only agree if rugby rules were the basis. Yale, to save face, agreed to "concessionary" rules, but they were really those of rugby. Some Princeton men traveled to New England to see the contest. Wanting to play the more prestigious Yale and Harvard in the future, Princeton had to change to the rugby game.

Number 60 (Bednarik) hopes to make the tackle for the University of Pennsylvania in this 1947 game. Football owes much of its popularity in the United States to the intercollegiate arena.

Once Princeton accepted rugby, a convention was called in which the future "Big Three" and Columbia met to adopt standard rugby rules and form an Intercollegiate Football Association (IFA) in the fall of 1876. Yale was reluctant to accept 15 men on a team rather than its favored 11. Nevertheless, the IFA decided to initiate a Thanksgiving Day championship contest between the two leading teams of the previous year. Yale and Princeton were chosen for the first of the traditional Thanksgiving Day games, and the two schools continued to dominate the game for the next two decades. By the 1890s, the contest kicked-off New York City elite's social season, giving added social significance to the event. As

many as 40,000 viewed the contest in the Polo Grounds or at Manhattan Field, and the Thanksgiving Day tradition spread across America as "a holiday granted by the State and the nation to see a game of football" (*New York Herald*, 1 December 1893, 3).

Development

The Eastern elites Americanized the rugby rules that the rest of the colleges and schools accepted as their own. Walter Camp, the "father" of American football, had played for Yale in the first Thanksgiving Day championship game. He remained involved in football and rule changes for the next half-century. Camp, more than any other individual, created the American version of football. Camp began attending football rules meetings in 1877 as a sophomore and continued for the next 48 years. In 1880, he suggested possibly the most radical rule in football history, one giving continuous possession of the ball to one team after a player was tackled. In rugby, when a player was downed, the ball would be placed in a "scrummage." The ball might go forward or backward, with possession in doubt. To Camp, this was not rational. Camp proposed a "scrimmage" in which the team in original possession would snap (center) the ball back to a quarterback who would hand it to another back in a logical play. One team could control the ball for as much as an entire half unless it was fumbled away or was kicked to the opponents. Camp, by the early 1880s, suggested incorporating the notion of "downs," in which one team was given three attempts (downs) to make 5 yards (4.5 meters) or lose possession of the ball. The 5-yard chalk lines created a "gridiron" effect and a new name for the game. The consequence of the short distance to be gained in three attempts created the need for exacting plays, the development of signals for calling the plays, and the introduction of players running interference for the ball carrier, another modification of rugby.

Mass plays led to the charge of brutality in the late nineteenth century. The change from the more open running of the original rugby game to tight line smashes resulted from a rule to allow tackling below the waist in 1887. The low tackle did much to reduce the effectiveness of open field running, and contributed to the unfolding of various wedge formations including the famous "flying wedge." Wedges were V-shaped formations that "snowplowed" a particular position in the defense. In the flying wedge, players began about 25 yards (23 meters) behind the scrimmage line, progressed at full speed from two angles to form a "V" formation just before the ball was passed to the runner behind the "V." The play was so brutal to the defensive player at whom it was aimed that it existed for only one season before it was outlawed. Plays such as the flying wedge and other mass plays eventually led to the forward pass, a radical change legislated in 1906 to open up the game.

The game's brutality was evidenced at a time when American society was urbanizing and thought to be losing manly qualities found on the frontier. College students had often been the symbol of the effete, pale, and dyspeptic scholars, individuals lacking the virile element considered to be an important aspect of American society. Football could counteract this negative, demasculinized image and give college life the picture of vitality and manliness. As the century waned, Theodore Roosevelt (1858–1919), more than any other individual stood for the strenuous life needed for America's leadership in the world. Football, if played fairly, Roosevelt believed, could add to the vigor of the nation. "Hit the line hard: don't foul and don't shirk, but hit the line hard" was to Roosevelt and many other people a metaphor worth pursuing in life as in football.

College and Professional Football

College football was an American symbol of virility before the first identified contest in which players were known to be paid. The professional game has been traced to the payment of Walter "Pudge" Heffelfinger (1867–1954), the acknowledged greatest college player of the nineteenth century. Heffelfinger was on Walter Camp's first all-American team in 1889 as well as the following two years. In the fall following his graduation from Yale, he was playing for the Chicago Athletic Club, as did Ben "Sport" Donnelly, formerly of Princeton. When the club concluded a tour of the Eastern United States, Heffelfinger and Donnelly did not return to Chicago. The Allegheny Athletic Association, located near Pittsburgh, saw an opportunity to defeat the rival Pittsburgh Athletic Club with the help of outsiders and recruited Heffelfinger and Donnelly to play for them. Heffelfinger received the enormous sum of $500, approximately a worker's yearly wage, plus travel expenses, and Donnelly received $250 plus expenses. In a contest with high betting stakes, Heffelfinger picked up a fumble and ran for the game's only touchdown.

Other "amateur" teams began paying their players in western Pennsylvania, upper New York, and especially Ohio. Most of the better players were collegians, who at times played on Saturdays for college teams and competed under assumed names for pro teams on Sundays. Some of the players were professional baseball players

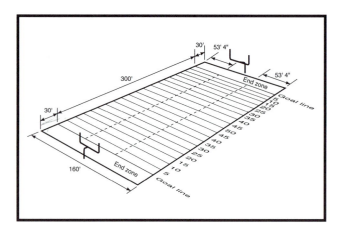

Two of the most important pro franchises were a result of industry-sponsored teams—the Green Bay Packers and the Chicago Bears. In Wisconsin in 1919, Curly Lambeau (1898–1965), a Notre Dame dropout, received $500 from the Indian Packing Company of Green Bay to organize a team, the Green Bay Packers. After a 10–1 season playing regional teams, each player was paid $16.75. The following year George Halas (1895–1983), a former University of Illinois player, organized a team with money from the Staley Starch Company of Decatur, Illinois. Players on Halas's Decatur Staleys were hired by the company and paid $50 a week, with two hours off each day to practice football. After a 10 win, 1 loss, and 2 tie season, the average payment for playing was $125 a game. Halas, with the blessing of the Staley Company, moved his team to Chicago, where he renamed them the Bears because they shared Wrigley Field with the Chicago Cubs baseball team. He soon joined a group in 1920 that was the forerunner of the National Football League (NFL). Green Bay and Chicago, along with the New York Giants and the Washington Redskins, came to dominate the NFL until the end of World War II.

The relationship between the professional and intercollegiate game has been a long one and close in many ways. The star players of the professional teams were mostly collegians from the time of Heffelfinger in the 1890s. Nearly as important, many college coaches had played professional football, including such renowned coaches as Knute Rockne of Notre Dame, Hugo Bezdek (1884–1952) of Penn State, Bert Ingwerson (1898–1969) of Illinois, and Jimmy Conzelman (1898–1970) of St. Louis. Coaches, too, shifted between college and pro teams. Examples included Arnold Horween (1898–1985), who moved from the Chicago Cardinals pro team in the 1920s to head Harvard University's squad, and Jock Sutherland (1889–1948), who took over the Brooklyn professional team after a successful career at the University of Pittsburgh. The midwestern Big 10 Conference and the Ivy League in the East were so concerned about pro football in the mid-1920s that they legislated that all employees of athletic departments who took part in professional football games as players or officials were disqualified from employment in athletics at conference institutions. The case of Harold

as well as collegians. Christy Mathewson (1880–1925), a Bucknell University player and later a star pitcher for the New York Giants, played for Pittsburgh Pirate owner, Barney Dreyfuss (1865–1932), who fielded a football team in 1898. The strongest teams early in the twentieth century were formed in Ohio, where Akron, Canton, Columbus, Dayton, and Massillon created unparalleled rivalries, particularly the Canton Bulldogs and Massillon Tigers, towns a buggy ride apart. A scandal emanating from a bribe offer disrupted continuous play, but pro football in the area was renewed in 1912. By then, the game resembled the modern one with the legalization of the forward pass, touchdowns counting six points and field goals three, and four downs to gain 10 yards (9.1 meters).

Ohio again led the way in the professional game. Collegians such as Knute Rockne (1888–1931) of Notre Dame and the great African American stars, Paul Robeson (1898–1976) of Rutgers and Fritz Pollard (1894–1986) of Brown, played in Ohio. Rockne once played for six different teams in a two-month period. Massillon hired 45 top players for one game to ensure that the opponent would not hire any of them. Jim Thorpe (1888–1953), the star of the Carlisle Indian School around 1910, was paid $250 a game in 1915 to play for the Canton Bulldogs. When the "greatest athlete" of the first half of the twentieth century made his debut at Canton, 8,000 spectators saw him lead the Bulldogs to a victory over the hated Massillon Tigers. While the crowds at professional games did not compare to the best of the colleges, interest in football was increasing when World War I, momentarily, halted the game.

"Red" Grange (1903–1991), a star halfback from the University of Illinois, led to an outcry by colleges against the pros for signing a player before he graduated from college. In his senior year, Grange signed a football contract with the Chicago Bears within a week of playing his last college game against Ohio State in 1925. The reaction was so negative that the NFL decided to make an agreement with the colleges not to sign any football player before his eligibility was completed or the athlete's class had graduated. The so-called "Red Grange Rule" lasted for more than a half-century, when the agreement could no longer stand up under federal antitrust law as it violated the freedom of individuals to sign contracts, a conspiracy in restraint of trade.

Pro football was given a degree of national attention when Red Grange joined the Chicago Bears and went on an Eastern and then Southern and Western tour, at one point playing seven games in 11 days. It was clearly more important for the pros to feed off the colleges than for the colleges to benefit from the pros. Pro football gained stature because it increasingly used the colleges as "farm teams" of the professional clubs. In an attempt to ensure an equitable distribution of college players within the professional ranks, the annual draft of college players was devised in 1936. When Jay Berwanger (1914–) of the University of Chicago and first Heisman Trophy winner was chosen by the worst team in the NFL, the Philadelphia Eagles, it was an attempt to give weaker teams an opportunity to improve their teams immediately. That Berwanger chose to enter business and not the NFL was a reflection of the lack of esteem accorded professional football in the 1930s. Some other star college players, however, were drafted and joined pro teams, including Byron "Whizzer" White (1917–) of the University of Colorado and later a U.S. Supreme Court Justice, who was paid the NFL's highest salary of $15,800 to join the Pittsburgh Steelers in 1938.

College coaches and other college athletic officials feared the growth of professional football. At about the same time the NFL came into existence, college coaches formed the Football Coaches Association (FCA). One of the association's first actions in 1921 was to unanimously resolve that "professional football was detrimental to the best interests of American football and American youth and that football coaches [should] lend their influence to discourage the professional game." The fear of pro football hurting the college game continued through the century. It was seen early in creation of the "Red Grange Rule," and it continued with such 1960s actions as forbidding the mention of pro football in college football telecasts and the successful lobbying to pass federal legislation to prohibit pro football from televising games on Saturdays, when college football is traditionally played. The fear of the pros was a major stimulus in the 1960s decision to allow unlimited substitutions (two platoon football) to increase fan interest, which was being lost to the more exciting pro game. The fear of professional competition almost led to the creation of a playoff system for college football in the 1960s, but the previous development of "bowl" games at the end of each season made the playoff problematical and less attractive. In a similar way, the success of the Pro Football Hall of Fame in Canton, Ohio, put pressure on colleges to create their own hall of fame. As with the playoff, the colleges did not financially support the hall of fame idea and the development of a College Football Hall of Fame has languished for decades.

College football far outstripped professional football until the 1960s. The college game took advantage of claiming to be amateur, with athletes playing for the honor of their alma mater. British amateurism's upper-class notions of participating in sport purely for enjoyment, not financial benefits, applied to college football in America as well. Even though the college game had been developed on a commercial model with huge stadiums, highly paid coaches, and subsidized athletes (either overtly or covertly), there was a general belief that the athletes were amateurs. The positive virtue of "amateurism" added to the luster of football traditions of "homecoming," pep rallies, "tailgating," cheerleaders, and marching bands. Season-ending bowl games added to the interest. The Rose Bowl in Pasadena, California, began in 1902 and has been continually contested since 1916. During the Depression of the 1930s, several communities, principally in the South, decided that they could help the local economy by hosting bowl games. The Orange Bowl in Miami and the Sugar Bowl in New Orleans started the rush to season-ending contests and were followed by the Cotton Bowl in Dallas and a host of new bowls after World War II.

Both college and professional teams lacked a large number of African-American players during the first half of the twentieth century. Southern institutions of higher learning refused to admit blacks until forced to do so by desegregation during the 1960s, and there were only a few institutions in the North with black students until after World War II. Outstanding players such as Fritz Pollard of Brown and Paul Robeson of Rutgers in the 1910s, Duke Slater (1898–1966) of Iowa and Joe Lillard (1918–) of Oregon in the 1920s, Wilmeth Sidat-Singh (1917–1943) of Syracuse and Kenny Washington (1918–1971) of UCLA in the 1930s, and Buddy Young (1926–1983) of Illinois and Marion Motley (1920–) of Nevada in the 1940s were exceptions to the rule. Professional football's first black player was Charles Follis (1879–1919) who in 1904 played for the Shelby Athletic Club in Ohio. Fritz Pollard played pro football after his Brown experience, becoming the first African American head football coach in 1919 when he coached the Akron Pros. There were blacks in the NFL until the "color line" was drawn in 1933. Football remained segregated until the end of World War II, when the Los Angeles Rams of the National Football League and the Cleveland Browns of the All-American Football Conference added black players shortly before Jackie Robinson (1917–1972) desegregated professional baseball.

Television and Football

Another dramatic change affected college and pro football following World War II with the introduction of television. Football contests were first telecast in the fall of 1939, but it took another decade for the cable required to carry signals to spread from the East coast to as far west as Chicago. By about 1950, the growth of television made commercial telecasts of sport contests profitable. Colleges were concerned that telecasts would have a negative impact on attendance at stadiums, and in 1951 members of the National Collegiate Athletic Association decided to control the number of telecasts of their football games. From 1951 to 1984, the NCAA plan provided for national and regional telecasts each Saturday during the season. This monopoly existed first to

Football Shapes Up

The year 1905–1906 was probably the most critical to the development of American football. In that year, intercollegiate football, the leader in the evolution of the American game, went through a crisis of ethics and brutality. During the middle of the season, President Theodore Roosevelt, feeling the pressure of the "muckrakers" attacking football, called a White House conference of football authorities from the Big Three, Harvard, Yale, and Princeton. Led by Walter Camp, the Big Three agreed in the future to "carry out the letter and in spirit the rules of the game of football, relating to roughness, holding and foul play." It was not enough. A number of institutions banned football at the end of the season including Columbia, Northwestern, California, and Stanford. Harvard, the leading educational institution in America, banned it for several months. Following the death of a Union College halfback in its final game with New York University, 13 institutions met to choose between banning or reforming football. Out of this meeting a second reform meeting was called at the end of December 1905, at which 68 institutions from across the nation took part. This meeting of faculty and college administrators was the beginning of the National Collegiate Athletic Association, the eventual governing body of intercollegiate athletics in many American colleges. A new football rules committee was appointed and joined with the old and rather inflexible rules group. Rule changes resulted to counter brutal play, including lengthening the yardage needed to retain the ball to 10 yards, prohibiting runners from hurdling the line, placing a neutral zone between the two teams, and introducing the forward pass. While the forward pass was unsuccessfully fought by Walter Camp, it was greatly limited by restrictions placed on its use. The forward pass had to be made from behind the line of scrimmage and thrown at least 5 yards to either side of the center. It could only be caught by one of the backs or the two players at the end of the offensive line. If the ball was not touched by a player on either side, the ball was turned over to the opponent at the spot where the ball was thrown. The pass at first was used sparingly, and generally only as a desperation device. However, restrictive rules were eventually eased, and with the appearance of the forward pass, the modern twentieth-century game was created.

—Ronald A. Smith

limit games on TV and preserve gate receipts. Later, when the NCAA contract with television networks was worth over $65 million per year, television revenues going to big-time colleges became more important than preserving stadium attendance. A power struggle erupted between the smaller NCAA institutions and those that had regular game telecasts. The smaller institutions, demanding a greater percentage of television funds, helped spur the creation of the College Football Association (CFA). The CFA was created in 1976 to promote big-time football. Within five years, the CFA helped sponsor a legal suit against the NCAA by the Universities of Oklahoma and Georgia to break up the NCAA football TV monopoly. A 1984 U.S. Supreme Court decision went against the NCAA, and colleges were thereafter free to create their own television plans. The result was an oversupply of games and lower fees being paid to most institutions.

The professional National Football League had different results from television. The league's popularity rose greatly after its championship game in 1958, when the Baltimore Colts defeated the New York Giants in a dramatic overtime contest seen by millions on television. In that decade, the NFL solution to protect stadium attendance was to prevent televising within a radius of 75 miles without permission of the home team. Second, the NFL decided to pool television money, dividing the TV revenues equally among all the teams. This brilliant decision allowed smaller market teams, such as the Green Bay Packers and the Pittsburgh Steelers, to remain financially competitive.

Competition from a new league also had an impact on professional football. Lamar Hunt (1932–), disgruntled at being unable to purchase an NFL franchise, decided to form the American Football League (AFL) in 1960, which soon received a multimillion dollar television contract from the National Broadcasting Corporation (NBC). With the signing of star college players such as Joe Namath (1943–) of Alabama, the AFL received recognition, and in 1966 the NFL, which fought the AFL, accepted a merger of the two leagues. The merger, under the NFL name, became official as a 26-team league in 1970. A playoff between the NFL and AFL beginning in 1967 added excitement and created greater wealth. The championship was called the Super Bowl, and Green Bay won the first two contests. The Super Bowl, a kind of American holiday, has had some of the highest ratings in television history, easily surpassing baseball's World Series in popularity. The NFL introduced Monday Night Football to supplement the traditional Sunday games beginning in 1970. The first "prime time" evening football was the creation of the NFL's commissioner, Pete Rozelle (1926–), and the innovative Roone Arledge (1931–) of the American Broadcasting Company (ABC). For two decades, Monday Night Football surpassed all regular televised sporting events in popularity.

Professional football's increase in wealth from television has spurred both new labor disputes and competing leagues. Players formed the National Football League Players Association in 1956, but the union was not recognized by NFL owners until 1968. A desire for a larger share of the profits eventually led to several players' strikes between 1968 and the mid-1980s. New football leagues, also looking at the growing wealth in the professional game, were formed. The World Football League lasted only one season in the mid-1970s. Eight years later, the United States Football League (USFL) began as a spring sport in 1983. The March to July schedule did not conflict with the stronger NFL for a television audience, but the USFL survived for only three years due to low television ratings. Three years later the NFL established the World League of American Football (WLAF) with teams in Europe and North America. The WLAF acts like a farm system for the NFL and expanded the college football feeder system that has existed for much of the century.

Since the nineteenth century, football in America has developed differently than in the rest of the world where soccer football is the dominant sport. The game was thriving in colleges well before the professional game took hold. It has remained a game played almost exclusively by boys and men, unlike other popular team sports such as baseball, for which women formed a professional league in the 1940s and 1950s, and basketball, which girls and women made the most popular sport in schools and colleges for most of the twentieth century.

—Ronald A. Smith

Bibliography: Baker, L. H. (1945) *Football: Facts and Figures.* New York: Farrar & Rinehart.

Braunwart, Bob, and Bob Carroll. (1981) *The Alphabet Wars: The Birth of Professional Football, 1890–1892.* Canton, OH: Professional Football Researchers Association.

Cope, Myron. (1974) *The Game That Was.* New York: Thomas Y. Crowell.

Richard O. Davies. (1994) *America's Obsession: Sports and Society since 1945.* Fort Worth, TX: Harcourt Brace.

Davis, Parke H. (1911) *Football, the American Intercollegiate Game.* New York: Scribner's Sons.

Falla, Jack. (1981) *NCAA: The Voice of College Sports.* Mission, KS: National Collegiate Athletic Association.

Hickok, Ralph. (1992) *The Encyclopedia of North American Sports History.* New York: Facts on File.

Jable, J. Thomas. (1978) "The Birth of Professional Football: Pittsburgh Athletic Clubs Ring in Professionals in 1892," *Western Pennsylvania Historical Magazine* 62 (April): 131–147.

March, Harry A. (1934) *Pro Football: Its "Ups" and "Downs."* Albany, NY: J. B. Lyon.

Neft, David S., Richard M. Cohen, and Rick Korch. (1992) *The Sports Encyclopedia: Pro Football.* New York: St. Martin's Press.

Neft, David S., Roland T. Johnson, and Richard M. Cohen. (1974) *The Sports Encyclopedia: Pro Football.* New York: Grosset & Dunlap.

Ours, Robert. (1984) *College Football Almanac.* New York: Harper & Row.

Porter, David L., ed. (1987) *Biographical Dictionary of American Sports: Football.* Westport, CT: Greenwood Press.

Roberts, Randy, and James Olson. (1989) *Winning Is the Only Thing: Sports in America since 1945.* Baltimore: Johns Hopkins University Press.

Rowe, Peter. (1988) *American Football: The Records.* Enfield, UK: Guinness Publishing.

Smith, Robert. (1972) *Illustrated History of Pro Football.* New York: Grosset & Dunlap.

Smith, Ronald A. (1994) *Big-Time Football at Harvard, 1905: The Diary of Coach Bill Reid.* Urbana: University of Illinois Press.

———. (1988) *Sports and Freedom: The Rise of Big-Time College Athletics.* New York: Oxford University Press.

Weyand, A. M. (1926) *Football, Its History and Development.* New York: D. Appleton.

Whittingham, Richard. (1984) *What a Game They Played.* New York: Harper & Row.

Football, Australian

Australian Rules Football is a unique Australian sport that evolved in Melbourne in the nineteenth century. Earlier forms of football had previously been played in the Port Phillip District of New South Wales (later Victoria), but these would have been soccer, rugby, or Gaelic football.

In 1844 a hurling match was held at Batman's Hill between representatives of Clare and Tipperary, and on Christmas Day 1845 the *Port Phillip Herald* advertised various old country sports, including a "grand match of the old English game of football," which could have been the folk variant of the game.

The game is played on an oval field by two teams of 18 players. There are four goalposts at each end of the field. If the ball is kicked through the center posts, the team is awarded 6 points; if the kick goes between the outside posts, the team is awarded 1 point. There is no offside, and no goalie, and it is essentially a kicking and catching game, with points scored only by kicking. The ball is kicked or hand-passed between teammates and features high leaps, or "marks" for the ball. Although the sport is now national in scope, its greatest following is in the state of Victoria.

Origins

In 1857 there were only 100,000 people in Melbourne, and the town was just 20 years old. The gold rush changed the nature of the area, and within 10 years the population had doubled. The majority were from the British Isles, then came immigrants and transients from North America, Europe, and China. Their cultural baggage accompanied them, and this included their sports and games. The climate was particularly conducive to outdoor games.

Australia was a pioneer in the rights of the working man, and by 1865 stonemasons and other artisans had secured an eight-hour working day, with Sunday a rest day. Bank and office workers enjoyed a Saturday half-holiday. These developments enhanced leisure opportunities. Though certainly not a classless society, there was little poverty in comparison with most of the countries from whence the inhabitants came, and sporting activities were available for most males. The middle and upper classes organized sporting endeavors, particularly the former, and argued that they should be available for every man regardless of status. The main sports were cricket and horse racing.

It was within this cultural milieu that this new game evolved. There were games of football in 1858 between Melbourne Grammar and St. Kilda, and also at Scotch College and Melbourne

An influx of immigrants to Australia in the late nineteenth century gave rise to this less-violent derivative of rugby. Here Melbourne and Essendon compete for the 1989 Fosters Cup.

Grammar, the Australian equivalents of the English public schools, but these undoubtedly were influenced by the rules played at such schools, particularly Rugby.

The genesis of the new game can be attributed to one individual, Thomas Wentworth Wills (1835–1880). Wills was born in Australia and was sent to Rugby School in England for his education. He was the scholastic head of his class, captain of the school eleven, and outstanding at football. After he returned to Victoria, he was chosen for the international cricket team in 1857 and was captain in the following seasons.

On July 10, 1858, he wrote to *Bell's Life*, a newspaper, suggesting that as the cricket season was over a football club should be formed, with a committee of three or more to draw up rules. It is obvious he mainly wanted to keep cricketers fit, though he felt that trampling on the cricket fields in the off-season would be good for them. He followed this letter up with an approach to the Melbourne Cricket Club Committee and after

consideration they asked him to create such a game. The novel *Tom Brown's Schooldays*, which was published in 1857 and was being read in Melbourne at this precise time, espoused the creed of "muscular Christianity." The time was opportune for the delineation of a football code in Melbourne.

Development

An impromptu game was subsequently played between members of the Melbourne Cricket Club and "others who happened to be present in August of 1858," next "about fifty gentlemen" played the game, and then 26 players from Melbourne played against a like number from South Yarra. Football interest grew rapidly, and formal rules were developed in May 1859 by seven men from the Melbourne Cricket Club.

There is little doubt that the rules that were generated were a compromise from those in force in the public schools in England. Harrow and

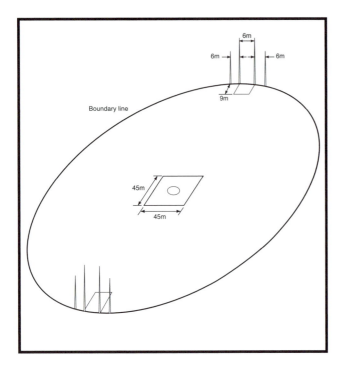

Winchester rules were merged with those of Rugby. Handling was allowed, but a player could run no farther than was necessary to kick the ball. Eventually, the rules stipulated that an individual could run, but the ball had to be bounced every 5 or 6 yards (4.5 or 5.5 meters). If there was a "mark," that is, if the ball was caught cleanly, the player with the ball would have an unobstructed kick. This rule perseveres in the modern sport of rugby as well as Australian Rules. A unique innovation was to allow for a no-offsides rule, which clearly distinguished the game from rugby.

The original rules agreed upon were those of 1859, but most historians incorrectly place the origin of the codification of the game to 1866, when Henry Colden Antill Harrison (1836–1929), a cousin of Wills, was asked to rewrite the rules. By 1874 points were gained by kicking through the posts rather than carrying the ball between them.

This new game would appear therefore to have been based on English public school games, particularly rugby, but it was soon modified for Victorian conditions and needs with less body contact than is associated with other variants of football. As the writer J. B. Thompson noted: "Black eyes don't look so well on Collins Street (Melbourne)." A unique Australian game had

emerged and it diffused rapidly. Until about 1870 this new game was known as "Victorian Rules," but this term was not a sensible one for broader adoption of the code. It became known as "Australian Rules," though Wills himself preferred "Ausball."

The game spread to the other states of Australia and to New Zealand. Though cricket was never questioned as the summer sport, rugby struggled as the universal winter sport, there being a tendency for adoption of the indigenous game. This was even apparent in the English-influenced grammar schools of Queensland. It was only in Sydney that the game of rugby was pre-eminent. For some reason Sydneyites preferred the more rugged body-contact game. New Zealand had 44 clubs by 1893, and the game was more established there than rugby. By 1890 the tide had turned in both New Zealand and Queensland, and rugby became the principal game.

In 1877 the Victorian Football Association (VFA) was formed, with the principal aims of regulating the sport and promoting intercolonial contests, the original clubs being Hotham (North Melbourne), Melbourne, Geelong, Carlton, Albert Park (South Melbourne), St. Kilda, Essendon, and East Melbourne. These were the major clubs, but there was an additional base of 125 clubs in Melbourne alone. The South Australian Football Association formed in the same year, adopting Victorian rules.

There were societal shifts in the 1870s and 1880s as Australian football was increasingly adopted by the lower classes, instead of remaining a haven for middle-class cricketers. Some of the factors that occasioned these changes in public participation and acceptance were the increase in professionalism in various sports in this time period such as boxing, snooker, cycling, and pedestrianism, the extension of the half-day holiday to tradesmen and shop workers, and the playing of matches at parks without admission charges, which attracted legions of local spectators. In 1880, 15,000 spectators attended a football game in Melbourne, and some 34,000 attended a match in 1886. The game became *the* winter sport of Melbourne. Its popularity was due to a need for a body-contact sport and partly as a reaction against the rampant professionalism in other sports.

The depression of 1893–1895 affected some clubs, and the increasing acceptance of professionalism in sport caused the gradual demise of the VFA and heralded the emergence of the Victorian Football League (VFL) in 1897, which was initially amateur in scope. The eight most successful clubs—Melbourne, Essendon, Geelong, Collingwood, South Melbourne, Fitzroy, Carlton, and St. Kilda—made up the VFL, and it became the dominant organizational body in the sport. In order to speed up and commercialize the game, various rule innovations were introduced, the principal one being a reduction of team members from 20 to 18.

A national body was formed in 1906, the Australian National Football Council (ANFC), which controlled interstate player exchanges and developed a national championship contest. The ANFC gave way to the National Football League, but both were under the control of the VFL. The game became truly national when first Sydney (1983), then Brisbane and Western Australia (1987), joined a national league comprising 14 teams. The VFL then altered its name in 1990 to the Australian Football League (AFL), and in 1991 Adelaide entered a team into the national competition.

Though there have been attempts to spread the adoption of the game to other countries, even Ireland because of its predilection for hurling and Gaelic football, it has not made significant inroads elsewhere. Crowds of over 100,000 have been common in Melbourne, and though it remains the principal winter sport in Tasmania, South Australia, Western Australia, Victoria, and the Northern Territory, it has never dented the popularity of rugby in Queensland and New South Wales.

The heroes of the sport, because of its regional nature, have not been truly national heroes, particularly in comparison with those of the summer sport of cricket. Among the more illustrious figures are Ivor Warne-Smith, Haydn Bunton, Dick Reynolds, Bob Skilton, Ian Stewart, Jack Dyer, Roy Cazaly, Tom Hafey, Alex Jesaulenko, Leigh Mathews, Bob Pratt, Lou Richards, and Ted Whitten.

The most prestigious award in the sport is the Brownlow Medal, given to commemorate the contributions of Charles Brownlow (1861–1924), former Australian National Council President. It is given to the best and fairest player each year.

Letter from Thomas Wentworth Wills

Sir,— Now that cricket has been put aside for some months to come, and cricketers have assumed somewhat of the chrysalis nature (for a time only 'tis true), but at length will again burst forth in all their varied hues, rather than allow this state of torpor to creep over them, and stifle their now supple limbs, why can they not, I say, form a foot-ball club, and form a committee of three or more to draw up a code of laws? If a club of this sort were got up it would be of vast benefit to any cricket-ground to be trampled upon, and would make the turf quite firm and durable; besides which, it would keep those who are inclined to be stout from having their joints encased in useless superabundant flesh. If it is not possible to form a foot-ball club, why should not these young men who have adopted this new-born country for their mother land, why I say, do they not form themselves into a rifle club, so as at any rate they may some day be called upon to aid their adopted land against a tyrant's band, that may some day 'pop' upon us when we least expect a foe at our very doors. Surely our young cricketers are not afraid of the crack of the rifle, when they face so courageously the leather sphere, and it would disgrace no one to learn in time how to defend his country and his hearth. A firm heart, a steady hand, a quick eye, are all that are requisite, and with practice, all these may be attained. Trusting that some one will take up the matter, and form either of the above clubs, or at any rate, some athletic games.

I remain, yours truly, T. W. Wills.

—*Bell's Life*, 10 July 1858.

"Up there Cazaly" was reputedly the battle-cry of Australian soldiers in World War II as they stormed out of the trenches. It was associated with the high marks of legendary player Roy Cazaly (1893–1963), who played 422 senior games between 1910 and 1927. A song "Up there Cazaly" became the anthem of the AFL. There have been numerous poems, paintings, short stories, and even a stage play, *The Club*, all of which have endeavored to capture the exhilaration of the sport.

Commercialism is increasingly eroding the fundamental reasons for the emergence of this unique game, and it is in danger of losing its traditional roots. It is becoming more and more a spectacle engineered by public relations and

Football, Canadian

Tradition

The new president of the club says: "We might have the proudest tradition in the League but we haven't won a premiership in nineteen years. Tradition, tradition, tradition. We're been strangled by it. The days when recruits would flock to the club from all over the country simply because of its name are long since game. It's no good waiting for players to come to you; you've got to go out there into the market-place and fight for them."

—From David Williams's play *The Club*

mass consumption experts who mainly wish to market a game for a consumer-oriented society. This rampant commercialization is in danger of creating larger-than-life figures who become more distant from (and unlike) the ordinary fan, who is the basis for the game's popularity. Local clubs are gradually losing meaning as spectators are asked to change their affiliations from their local community team to a city or even a state conglomeration.

—Maxwell Howell

See also Cricket; Rugby League; Rugby Union.

Bibliography: Atkinson, Graeme. (1982) *Everything You Ever Wanted To Know about Australian Rules Football But Couldn't Be Bothered Asking.* Melbourne: Five Mile Press.

Craven, John, ed. (1969) *Football the Australian Way.* Melbourne: Lansdowne Press

Dyer, Jack, and Brian Hansen. (1968) *The Wild Men of Football.* Melbourne: Southdown Press.

Fiddian, Marc. (1977) *The Pioneers.* Melbourne: Victorian Football Association.

Main, Jim. (1974) *Australian Rules Football.* Melbourne: Lansdowne Press.

Sandercock, Leonie, and Ian Turner. (1982) *Up Where, Cazaly?* Sydney: Grenada.

Stewart, Bob. (1983) *The Australian Football Business.* Kenthurst: Kangaroo Press.

Stremski, Richard. (1986) *Kill for Collingwood.* Sydney: Allen and Unwin.

Vamplew, Wray, Katharine Moore, John O'Hara, Richard Cashman, and Ian Jobling. (1992) *The Oxford Companion to Australian Sport.* Melbourne: Oxford University Press.

Williams, David. (1978) *The Club.* Sydney: Currency Press.

Football, Canadian

Because Canada was a British colony, it is only natural that sports and games in its formative years mirrored those of the motherland. Of the two types of football, association (soccer) and rugby, it was the latter that became the game of choice among the new settlers. After all, soccer had the reputation of being a gentleman's game that was played by hooligans, while rugby might have been considered a hooligan's game that was played by gentlemen.

Rugby football simply meant that it was the code of play developed and in use at the British school of the same name. It was distinct from the versions played at Harrow or Eton and other elite private secondary schools known in Britain as "public schools." Graduates of these schools who moved to the colonies as immigrants, civil servants, or members of the professions or the military took their culture with them. The game at Rugby had been distinctive since 1823 when, legend has it, a day student, William Webb Ellis (the trophy for the World Cup of Rugby is named in his honor), picked up the ball contrary to the rules and began to run with it. The subsequent chase and passing the ball back and forth among the team members was so exhilarating that the students decided to frame a set of rules for their new game. Thirty-seven "Laws of Football played at Rugby School" were declared and codified on 28 August 1845.

By the 1860s, it was being played in Canada, particularly Montreal. There, members of the town and garrison had formed a team, the Montreal Football Club, in 1868, from which it was introduced into McGill University. In England, the game had been adopted by a number of clubs, and by 1871 the rules were standardized with the formation of the Rugby Football Union. By 1874, McGill had its own hybrid version of the rules codified for its own use. In that year, Captain David Rodgers challenged Harvard University to two games, one in Cambridge in May, the other to be played in Montreal in the autumn. The one game at Cambridge turned out to be two. When the Montreal team arrived after its train trip and took to the practice field, it drew a curious crowd

British immigrants to Canada brought rugby, but the exposure to football in the neighboring United States ultimately produced a distinctive Canadian game.

of onlookers. The bewildered Harvard players asked them what game McGill was playing, for Harvard's game was an amalgam of the rugby and soccer varieties of football. The teams agreed to play two games, one under each other's set of rules. Harvard won the first game on May 14 under its rules by a 3–0 score. The second game was played the next day under McGill rules but with Harvard's round ball; McGill's was lost. It was a scoreless tie but Harvard was so impressed—the *Magenta* described it as much better "than the somewhat sleepy game now played by our men"—that it asked McGill for its rules and subsequently wrote to Rugby for the "official" version of the game. Harvard began playing rugby the next year and persuaded some of its northeastern school neighbors to adopt the new game. American and Canadian versions of football continued to influence each other as the years went by.

Canadian football was much like the country that created it in that it was bound to British tra-

dition and yet increasingly subject to influences from the United States. By 1882, the traditional English scrummage, the unpredictable way of putting the ball into play, was removed. Unlike the Americans, who had replaced it with the snapback system of putting the ball into play, the Canadians "heeled" it, that is, the center put the ball into play by tapping it with his heel to the quarterback. On either side of the center was a "scrim support" to protect the center and delay any rush from the opposition. The rule change also meant that possession took precedence over spontaneity.

By 1892, a reorganized Canadian Rugby Union was formed (an earlier union had been founded in 1882 but soon dissolved because it was unable to arrange an accepted set of rules for championship games between Ontario and Quebec). The new organization governed the sport and was responsible for a national championship contest. The field was set at a length of 110 yards (100 meters) with a 25-yard (22.9-meter) goal area and a width of 65 yards (59.5 meters). There were 15 players on a side, and a game consisted of two 45-minute halves. A majority of points determined the winner of the game. A team was awarded six points for a goal from a try, five from a drop kick, four from a flying or free kick and a try, two from a safety touch, and one from a rouge. The only two values remaining in Canadian football today are the safety touch and the rouge or single point given when a kick is not returned from the end zone. The field dimensions are the same with one exception. Since 1986 the Canadian Football League changed its end zone to 20 yards (18 meters).

In 1897, a team had to advance the ball at least 5 yards or lose 20 in three downs or it would lose possession. Today, teams must gain 10 yards in three downs or lose possession. Prior to World War I, in 1909, there were a number of "Unions" or leagues in operation. The Quebec Rugby Football Union (1882), the Ontario Rugby Football Union (1883), the Intercollegiate Rugby Football Union (1898), the Interprovincial Rugby Football Union (1907). The Western Canada Rugby Football Union was formed in 1911 and was a governing body for unions in Manitoba, Saskatchewan, and Alberta. The Canadian Rugby Football Union was responsible for coordinating a "Dominion Championship." It had been doing so since 1892, but in 1909 the title was symbolized by a trophy donated by the Governor General of Canada, Lord Earl Grey (1851–1917). The Grey Cup continues to be the sought-after trophy of teams playing in the Canadian Football League (CFL).

By 1909, the game was neither rugby in the traditional sense nor football in the modern. There were 14 players; the ball was still being heeled out, and there was no interference and no forward passing. It was a sport developing its own approach, somewhat removed from its British roots, but always with them in mind, and consistently emulating the American refinements—the typical Canadian compromise. By 1921, more changes had been made. Teams were reduced to 12 to a side as they are today, and the ball could be snapped back, although the quarterback had to stay 5 yards behind the snapper. That year was also the first that the Dominion Championship, or the Grey Cup Game as it was increasingly called, became an East-West affair. The Toronto Argonauts, representing the East, defeated the Edmonton Eskimos of the West by a 23–0 score.

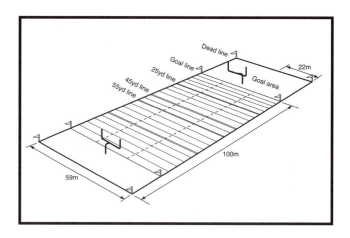

The forward pass was approved for all leagues in 1931, although it had been used in the Grey Cup game of 1929 between the Hamilton Tigers and the Regina Roughriders. Recruitment of American players and coaches began in earnest after Warren Stevens of Syracuse University led the Montreal Amateur Athletic Association's "Winged Wheelers" to an undefeated season and the Grey Cup in 1931. In 1935, the Winnipeg Football Club, who had nine Americans in the lineup, won the Grey Cup. In a bid to halt the flow of American talent and develop the Canadian talent pool, the Canadian Rugby Football Union imposed a residence rule requirement for 1936. Players had to live in the community they represented for one year prior to the season. It was as much an attempt to adhere to the "amateur code" that teams were supposed to profess as it was to ensure that Canadians would continue to be able to develop and play the game in their own land.

After the end of World War II, amateur status was often overlooked. In 1946, the Canadian Rugby Football Union allowed teams to carry five American "imports," and the residence rule of 1936 was abolished. Not all teams rushed to embrace the new reality: The Toronto Argonauts preferred to play with an all-Canadian roster and won the Grey Cup in 1945, 1946, and 1947. The 1947 game was a watershed of sorts. The following year, 1948, saw the Calgary Stampeders defeat the Montreal Alouettes to win the Grey Cup and turn the game into a national festival with its array of cowboys, chuck wagons, pancake breakfasts, horses, and boisterous fans who arrived by the train load in Toronto, the site of the game, for a week-long celebration.

The popularity of the game increased as did the dependence on American talent. The term

The Grey Cup

Although "national championships" have been held in Canada since 1892, it was in 1909 that a trophy was given for that purpose. The Governor General of Canada, Lord Earl Grey, donated a silver cup for the "Amateur Rugby Football Championship of Canada." Three trustees were named to draw up rules for the competition. They were: H.P. McGiverin (1870–1931), MP for Ottawa, Percival Molson (1880–1917) of the National Trust Company of Montreal, and the Rev. D. M. Macdonald (1872–1962), Rector of St. Andrew's College in Toronto. While the term *rugby* was used, there was no question that the Canadian version of football was meant. The other condition to guide the trustees was that the competition must *remain always* (emphasis in guidelines) under purely amateur conditions.

The first championship was won by the University of Toronto, which defeated the Parkdale Canoe Club of the Ontario Rugby Football Union, 26–6. University teams dominated the early years of the Grey Cup game, with the University of Toronto winning three consecutive years (1909, 1910, and 1911) and Queen's University in 1922, 1923, and 1924. McGill, too, won its share of university titles but declined to move into the national competition citing students' loss of study time. The Intercollegiate Union was so strong that its representative, Queen's, defeated the West's Regina Roughriders by a 54–0 score in 1923.

In 1921, the trusteeship was turned over to the Canadian Rugby Football Union. That same year, the Western Canada Rugby Union sent its first representative to the game, the Edmonton Eskimos. The Toronto Argonauts defeated them by a score of 23–0. After 1925, city-based teams became stronger because of their ability to attract good players through employment opportunities. Football was officially "amateur," but a blind eye was being turned toward the situation. The 1924 Queen's victory represented the last time that the universities were able to compete successfully for the Cup. As long as smaller centers, such as Sarnia, Ontario, with its oil industry, could attract players through jobs, the Ontario Rugby Football Union continued to challenge (Sarnia won the Grey Cup in 1934 and 1936). But by 1955, the union withdrew from Grey Cup competition.

The first Grey Cup game won by the West was in 1935. The Winnipeg Blue Bombers defeated the Hamilton Tigers by an 18–12 score. It was in 1948 that the game, an East-West focus since 1921, took on the aspects of a national celebration. The Calgary Stampeders, with a huge contingent of horses, chuckwagons, flap jacks, and boisterous enthusiasm, captured the nation's imagination and fueled the rich lore that was becoming the Grey Cup Festival.

The game was becoming as important as the railway was in forging links between the East and West. The government perceived it to be a force for national unity, so much so that in the 1960s private and public television had to combine resources, by law, so that all parts of the country could watch the game. The first televised game was in 1952, but it was the three games between the Edmonton Eskimos and the Montreal Alouettes in 1954, 1955, and 1956 that were etched in people's minds, especially the 1954 game, where Jackie Parker of Edmonton scooped up a loose ball and ran 95 yards (87 meters) for the tying touchdown. The convert by Bob Dean won it. There were other memorable confrontations. The Winnipeg Blue Bombers and the Hamilton Tiger-Cats engaged in memorable contests during the 1960s: the first overtime game in 1961, won by Winnipeg 21–14; the "fog bowl" of 1962, where the game was called in the fourth quarter and continued the next day, Sunday, the score remaining 28–27 for Winnipeg; the "wind game" of 1965 played in a gale force wind, forcing Winnipeg to concede three safety touches, the margin of victory for Hamilton's 22–16 win.

There was the 1969 game, the last of Quarterback Russ Jackson's career, capping off an award-winning season and leading the Ottawa Rough Riders to a 29–11 win over the Saskatchewan Roughriders. The game was played at the Autostade in Montreal, death threats having been made on Jackson's life. The Front de Liberation de Quebec was active, and the threats were taken seriously, with armed personnel discreetly placed around the benches and the roof tops.

In the 1970s and 1980s, Montreal and Edmonton were the dominant teams, the Eskimos winning five consecutive titles from 1978 through 1982. The first international Grey Cup game was played in 1994 when the British Columbia Lions defeated the Baltimore CFLers 26–23. For the 1995 season, the CFL realigned its teams in a North-South divisional alignment in order to achieve an American versus Canadian based game, thus moving away from the traditional East-West match-up.

In 1995, the Baltimore Stallions defeated the Calgary Stampeders 37–20 before 52,564 fans at Regina and a national television audience. They became the first U.S. team to win the trophy. It might be the last time. The American experiment seemed doomed when the NFL returned to Baltimore for the 1996, the Stallions moved to Montreal and became the Alouettes, and the other four U.S. teams disbanded. The Grey Cup for 1996 was scheduled for Hamilton.

—Frank Cosentino

"rugby" disappeared as a descriptor, replaced by "football" since it was more easily understood by American prospects. In 1956, the touchdown was increased in value from five to six points, and the following year the American names for the positions of center, guard, tackle and end replaced the Canadian snap, inside wing, middle wing, and outside wing. The twelfth position was retained, but its name was changed from flying wing to wingback, and later to slot back, flanker, or wide out.

Meanwhile, the two dominant leagues in the country from the West and the East formed the Canadian Football Council in 1956, which was renamed the Canadian Football League (CFL) in 1958. It was organized into Eastern (Hamilton, Toronto, Ottawa, and Montreal) and Western (Winnipeg, Saskatchewan, Edmonton, Calgary, and British Columbia) Conferences in 1960. The British Columbia Lions had joined the Western Conference in 1954. The first Commissioner was G. Sydney Halter (1905–1990) of Winnipeg. The Canadian Rugby Football Union turned over the trusteeship of the Grey Cup to the CFL in 1966 and became the Canadian Amateur Football Association (CAFA). In 1986, it changed its name to Football Canada and oversees playoffs of developmental football outside the university system and manages coaching certifications. The universities had already formed their own national playoffs beginning in 1965. The Vanier Cup, named for Governor General Georges Vanier (1888–1967), is presented annually to the university team winning the national championship.

Since 1965, the CFL has described its players as "imports" (those who played football outside Canada prior to their seventeenth birthday) and "nonimports" (those who had not played football outside Canada prior to their seventeenth birthday). For all intents and purposes, imports were Americans and nonimports Canadians. This legislation meant that naturalized Canadians would continue to be classified as "imports" and therefore not increase the cost of the Canadian side of the budget. The legislation was responsible for the formation of the Canadian Football League Players' Association (CFLPA).

In the 1960s and 1970s, CFL football grew in popularity until a series of influences minimized its acceptance. A contentious "Designated Import Rule" passed in 1970 allowed two American quarterbacks to substitute freely and virtually guaranteed that a Canadian would not play at that position. Some referred to the Canadians' status as "nonimportant." In the 1980s, a lucrative television contract was canceled, leaving teams in the CFL to scramble to make up the shortfall in revenue. The Montreal Alouettes folded in 1987 immediately prior to the season. The league found itself competing with Major League Baseball and other entertainment options for the public's favor and money. By 1993, the league expanded into the United States when it added the Sacramento Gold Miners. The following year, teams from Las Vegas, Shreveport, and Baltimore joined, and in 1995, Memphis, Tennessee, and Birmingham, Alabama, became members of the CFL. Also in 1985, the Sacramento franchise moved to San Antonio and the Las Vegas Posse disbanded.

The CFL game today differs from the American chiefly in its size of field, no fair catch, unlimited motion by the backs, three downs to make 10 yards, 20 seconds to put the ball into play, and a single point awarded for a punt or missed field goal when the returning player is tackled in or the ball is kicked out of the goal area. In 1995, the CFL moved to two divisions that would play for the Grey Cup. In the North were Toronto, Hamilton, Ottawa, Winnipeg, Saskatchewan, Edmonton, Calgary, and British Columbia. In the South were Baltimore, Shreveport, Memphis, Birmingham, and San Antonio. Rosters per game were set at 37: The North could carry 14 imports, 3 quarterbacks and 20 nonimports; the South was allowed to carry whomever it wished. A $2.5 million (Canadian) salary cap was in place.

Baltimore, now known as the Stallions, won the Grey Cup in 1995. It was the first American team to do so. The return of the NFL to the Maryland city resulted in the shifting of the CFL franchise to Montreal, to be known as the Alouettes, for the 1996 season. The four other American teams withdrew from the league and the CFL reverted to an all-Canadian city format in 1996. Rosters were set at 36 players, including 17 nonimports, 2 quarterbacks, and 17 imports, one identified as a "designated import." The player he is substituted for cannot return to the game. In the Western Division were British Columbia, Calgary, Edmonton, Saskatchewan, and Winnipeg.

In the Eastern Division were Montreal, Ottawa, Toronto, and Hamilton.

—Frank Cosentino

Bibliography: Cosentino, Frank. (1969) *Canadian Football: The Grey Cup Years.* Toronto: Musson Book Co.
————. (1995) *The Passing Game: A History of the CFL.* Winnipeg: Bain & Cox.

Football, Gaelic

Gaelic football is the most popular participation and spectator sport in Ireland. It is one of the main sports affiliated with the Gaelic Athletic Association (GAA), which oversees traditional Irish sports in Ireland. Closely tied to Irish nationalism and national culture, Gaelic football is a central cultural activity in Ireland and an important sporting activity among emigrant Irish communities in Britain, North America, and Australasia.

Origins

One of the many football games in the world, Gaelic football has its origins and primary roots in various forms of football played in Ireland since at least the seventh century. Although it is played in several other countries, Gaelic football is a significant part of popular culture only in Ireland. Gaelic football and hurling are the two main sports administered by the Gaelic Athletic Association, which was formed in 1884 to organize Irish sports, codify their rules, and fight against competition from British sports such as soccer and rugby. The Irish Football Association formed in 1880 and the Combined Irish Rugby Union formed in 1881. As a result, English codes of football began to dominate in Ireland as other forms of English culture also expanded. The GAA was closely tied to the nationalist movement in Ireland, particularly the Irish Republican Brotherhood (IRB), and received support from many leading Irish nationalists. The GAA was founded by Michael Cusack (1847–1906), from

Bloody Sunday

Gaelic football moved to the center of Irish nationalist consciousness during the events surrounding an exhibition match, perhaps arranged in conjunction with Irish republican activities, although the evidence is not clear. The match was held at Croke Park on Sunday, 21 November 1920. The match was played between Dublin and Tipperary and proceeds were designated to buy arms for the Irish Volunteers, who were fighting against British rule. On the same day, a group led by Michael Collins shot dead 12 British officers and wounded several others in Dublin because British soldiers had infiltrated Irish nationalist organizations. A quarter-hour into the football match, British troops (Black and Tans) and Dublin police entered the stadium and began firing at the field and on the crowd of 10,000 spectators. Numbers killed have varied between 12 and 14, but one of the dead was Michael Hogan, a back from Tipperary, who later had a stand at Croke Park named after him. "Bloody Sunday" was thus indelibly etched on the memory of Irish nationalists and Gaelic footballers.

—John Nauright and Michael Letters

County Clare, with the support of Maurice Davin. Ireland's most famous athlete of the 1870s, Davin at one time held the world record for the hammer throw and opposed the domination of English sports and their accompanying values of amateurism, which excluded the majority of Irishmen from participation. Cusack and Davin secured the support of major nationalist leaders such as Charles Stuart Parnell (1846–1891), the leader of Ireland's Home Rule movement; Michael Davitt (1846–1906), the leader of the Irish Land League; and Thomas William Croke (1824–1902), the Archbishop of Cashel and a supporter of Irish reform movements. The GAA was quickly dominated by the IRB. The involvement of a political organization in sport like the IRB has perhaps only been equaled by the Afrikaner Broederbond's domination of rugby union in South Africa during the apartheid period. After some internal difficulties, the GAA slowly got off the ground. The first Gaelic football championship was held in 1887 between Young from Louth and Commercials from Limerick, who were victorious. From 1889, teams representing counties competed for the football championship.

Development

Gaelic football and other GAA sports were some of the first modern sports to be openly political in context. In 1887 the GAA prohibited participation by anyone who had played, watched, or supported "foreign" (meaning British) games, by any member of the British occupying forces, particularly the Royal Irish Constabulary and the Dublin Police, or by anyone who was suspected of working or spying for the British. The support of Archbishop Croke and the Catholic Church helped GAA sports become immensely popular in rural Ireland. Gaelic football and hurling contests thus soon appeared at the forefront of nationalist struggle. Battles for control of the GAA took place between militant and moderate nationalists, but with the formation of the Irish Free State in 1922, Gaelic football and other Irish games came to symbolize the expression of Irish culture, losing some of the overtly political associations. In Northern Ireland, however, Irish sports remained tied to the nationalist struggle of Irish Catholics who sought a united and independent Ireland.

The GAA is the largest sporting organization in Ireland today. It has over 2,800 affiliated clubs that have as members 182,000 football players and 97,000 hurlers. The membership of the GAA, at home and abroad, is over 800,000. Gaelic football is Ireland's most popular participation sport with approximately 250,000 men and women playing, or about 20 percent of the adult population. The difference in numbers between total footballers and those registered with the GAA is largely accounted for by participants in church leagues. Links between Irish nationalism and the Catholic Church explain the cultural centrality of the GAA and Gaelic football in Irish society.

Practice

Gaelic football is played on a field that is 140–160 yards (129–147 meters) long and 84–100 yards (77.5–92 meters) wide. At each end of the field there is a goal that looks like a combination of a soccer goal and rugby union or American football goalposts. Many rule changes took place in the 1890s and early 1900s as the number of players decreased from 21 to 15 and a point for kicking the ball between the uprights was added, all to

Like hurling, Gaelic football, a strictly amateur sport, came to be associated with Irish nationalism and anti-British sentiments.

speed up the game. Three points are scored for a goal when a player kicks the ball into the lower goal, as in soccer, and one point is scored when the ball is kicked between the posts above the crossbar. Scoring is rendered in the form of team A 2–7 and team B 1–9, which means that team A won the game 13–12 after adding three points for each goal recorded in the first column plus one point for each in the second. Teams consist of 15 players, including one goalkeeper. Players can carry the ball but must bounce the ball off the turf or their feet after every four steps. Passing occurs through long and short kicks or by slapping or punching the ball with the hand to a nearby teammate; throwing is not allowed. Players may not pick up the ball from the ground unless they first get their toe under the ball. The ball may also

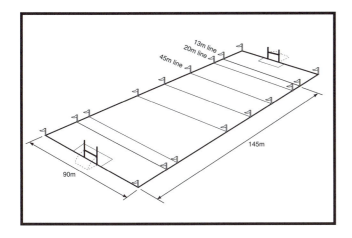

be played on the ground or in the air as in soccer. Games consist of two 35-minute halves.

Competitions are divided according to age: Juniors up to age 16, minor football up to age 18, and senior football 18 and over. The All-Ireland championships are conducted in the summer, while the National League is played during the winter. The All-Ireland semi-finalists are the provincial champions of the four historical Irish provinces of Ulster, Munster, Leinster, and Connacht. The champion of each province is determined by competition between representative teams from the counties within that province. The county teams are selected from the best players on the parish teams within the county. The All-Ireland final is held on the third Sunday of September. The Dubs (Dublin) are the 1995 holders of the Sam Maguire Trophy given to the All-Ireland champions after their one-point defeat of Tyrone 1–10 to 0–12.

The National League takes place during the winter and is considered less prestigious than the All-Ireland championships and generally viewed as a preparation for the All-Irelands, particularly with respect to developing new players. The National League is a county competition divided into four divisions with a two up, two down relegation/promotion system. At the end of the season, the top two teams in divisions two through four are promoted to the next higher division, while the bottom two teams from divisions one through three are relegated to the next lower division. Given that playing at the county level is a huge time and personal commitment and that all players are amateurs, good players normally stay at the county level for about three seasons and often retire from county football in their mid-twenties. Having said this, there are also players who stay at the top level for more than ten years. Because soccer (association football) is Ireland's second most popular sport, and many of the Gaelic footballers also possess the athletic capacities and skills to play soccer (and are allowed to do so with the passing of the "ban"), several top players are signed to play with teams in the Football Association of Ireland. Players from the parish to the county level often have commitments with soccer teams, particularly university students who might play Gaelic football for their county and soccer for their university.

Gaelic football competitions also occur in Australia, New Zealand, Canada, the United States, England, and Scotland. The competitions in Britain are dominated by Irish citizens living and working there. In Australia there are state-based competitions, with representative teams from Australia and New Zealand competing in the Australasian Championships held each year for seniors and under-19s. There are also competitions held on the North and South islands of New Zealand. A national Australian team is selected about every five years to play an Irish 15, often in conjunction with the touring of the Irish rugby team or Australian rugby tours of Ireland. In Canada there are two separate competitions, one based in Ontario and the other in British Columbia. The Ontario competition has seven teams from Toronto, one from Ottawa, and one from Montreal in Quebec. There are also seven women's teams. The champions of the Ontario and British Columbia competitions do not meet in an all-Canadian final, though teams have traveled to play informal championships off and on over the last couple of years. In the United States, competition is centered around New York City, Boston, and Chicago, all cities with large Irish populations. There are also Irish teams who travel to the United States on tour.

Gaelic football competitions are important to members of emigrant Irish communities as they serve to maintain cultural ties to Ireland. While many Irish and Irish-descended people move into local sports such as American football or Australian football, the existence of Irish sporting competitions continues a link to Irish sporting culture and life. As with other elements of Irish culture, Gaelic football has spread to other communities within North America and Australasia as a subcultural activity. The similarities between Gaelic and Australian football, for example, allow talented players to participate in both games quite easily.

Within Ireland, spectating is also an important component of Gaelic football. The All-Ireland finals regularly attract capacity crowds of nearly 80,000 at Croke Park in Dublin, Ireland's largest sporting stadium. The highest recorded attendance at a Gaelic football match was 90,556 at Croke Park for the All-Ireland final in 1961, but renovations to the stadium have limited its capacity to 79,500. The headquarters of the GAA is thus the premier stadium in Ireland, with Lansdowne Road (home of the Irish Rugby Union) the next largest stadium with a capacity of 51,000.

—John Nauright and Michael Letters

Bibliography: Mandle, W. F. (1977) "The IRB and the Beginnings of the GAA." *Irish Historical Studies* 20 (September): 418–438.

Mandle, W. F. (1987) *The Gaelic Athletic Association and Irish Nationalist Politics 1884–1924.* London: Croom Helm.

Mullan, Michael. (1995) "Opposition, Social Closure and Sport: The Gaelic Athletic Association in the 19th Century." *Sociology of Sport Journal* 12: 268–289.

Rouse, Paul. (1993) "The Politics and Culture of Sport in Ireland: A History of the GAA Ban on Foreign Games 1884–1971, Part 1 1884–1921." *International Journal of the History of Sport* 10, 3 (December): 333–366.

Sugden, John, and Alan Bairner. (1993) "National Identity, Community Relations, and the Sporting Life in Northern Ireland." In *The Changing Politics of Sport,* edited by Lincoln Allison. Manchester: Manchester University Press.

Formula 1 Auto Racing

Formula 1 (F1) cars are single-seat vehicles that are built according to specifications developed by the Fédération Internationale de l'Automobile (FIA) and used for no purpose other than racing. Most F1 races are now held on specially constructed racecourses, although some, such as the Grand Prix of Monaco, are still contested on city streets or country roads that have been closed and prepared for the race but are at other times used for normal vehicular traffic. Racing-only courses for F1 events are closed, but they are designed to simulate features that are encountered in ordinary everyday driving, including acceleration, straight-line speed, cornering, braking, and endurance. Drivers comprise the elite corps of auto racers and reach F1 only after demonstrating exceptional skills in lower levels of racing, such as Formula 3 or sports cars. Like professional athletes in a few other sports today, the top F1 drivers earn enormous amounts of money. Though now much safer than in its earlier years, F1 is still probably the most dangerous of all internationally contested sports.

Origins

In auto racing circles it is often said that the first auto race was predestined as soon as the second car was built. The first automobile races were created to determine which manufacturers produced the fastest and most durable vehicles (Hodges, Nye, and Roebuck 1981). The first international race, from Paris to Bordeaux and back, took place in 1895 and was won by a French Panhard that averaged 24 kilometers per mile (kph) (15 miles per hour [mph]). The first Grand Prix race was held at Le Mans, France, in June 1906 and required 12 laps of a 100-kilometer (62.14-mile) circuit, six to be completed on each of two consecutive days. Of the 32 entrants, 11 finished, with Ferenc Szisz winning in a Renault at an average speed of 101.17 kph (62.88 mph) (Hodges, Nye, and Roebuck 1981). Grand Prix style road racing enjoyed a brief flowering in the United States, beginning with the American Grand Prize race held at Savannah, Georgia, in 1908. Though it continued through 1916, Grand Prize racing was soon superseded in popularity by the Indianapolis 500, first held in 1911 (Hodges, Nye, and Roebuck 1981).

World War I put a halt to auto racing in Europe, but in 1921 Grand Prix races were held in both France and Italy. The early 1920s saw numerous technical developments in race cars, including supercharging, exotic fuels, brakes on all four wheels, and aerodynamic body styles. In 1926, the first world championship was instituted, though it was for manufacturers, rather than drivers. Qualifying races included the Indianapolis 500 and the Belgian, French, and Italian Grands Prix (Hodges, Nye, and Roebuck 1981).

Grand Prix racing always had nationalistic overtones and this trend reached its zenith in the

Formula 1 Auto Racing

The most challenging and dangerous form of auto racing, Formula 1 racing tracks mimic conditions encountered on dangerous roads. Improved technologies have led to safer conditions since this Grand Prix de Monaco.

1930s. Regulations for 1934 limited the dry weight of cars to 750 kilograms (1,654 pounds) and minimum race distance to 500 kilometers (310.7 miles) (Hodges, Nye, and Roebuck 1981). The intent was to stabilize Grand Prix racing at speeds roughly equivalent to those achieved during 1932. While the French and Italian teams continued with minor modifications to their existing cars, under Hitler's intense nationalism the Germans designed entirely new cars. The new German cars had powerful engines, but their superiority was due more to revolutionary chassis and running gear designs that gave them better road-holding and handling than the competition (Hodges, Nye, and Roebuck 1981). By 1937, German domination was such that, of the 12 Grands Prix in which their cars raced, 7 were won by Mercedes while Auto Union took the other 5. The best finish by a non-German car was a third place by an Alfa Romeo in the Vanderbilt Cup race (Hodges, Nye, and Roebuck 1981).

In the early post–World War II era, Grand Prix racing was revived using cars that had survived the war. A new set of technical specifications, or formulas, for international Grand Prix auto racing was institutionalized in 1948 with Formulas 1 and 2. A World Driver's Championship was created in 1950 and a manufacturer's championship in 1958. Points for the championships were awarded to the first six finishers. The first-place car received 9 points while second through sixth places received 6, 5, 4, 3, 2, and 1 points each. One point for the fastest lap during each race was awarded until 1959. In recent years, 10 points have been awarded for first place while points for the remaining cars finishing in the top six remain the same.

Formula 1 Cars

The first Grand Prix cars were derived for the most part from passenger cars. They were typically

Formula 1 Auto Racing

chain driven, had brakes only on the rear wheels, sat high with minimal bodywork around the driver, and had large, slow-turning engines that often differed widely in design. A second phase of Grand Prix cars, those of the 1920s through the end of the 1950s, typically were streamlined, front-engine, rear-drive roadsters, though the Auto Unions of the 1930s were mid-engine models. Finally, since 1960 all F1 cars have been mid-engined with the engine behind the driver's cockpit and in front of the rear wheels. In the 1970s, F1 car bodies were wedge-shaped with inverted airfoils both front and rear in order to create aerodynamic downforce that permitted cars to corner at far greater speeds than previously possible. Wind tunnel and track testing, in addition to rule changes, have led to some modification in car shapes since the 1970s, although these have not been as radical as the changes from front to rear engines or from cigar-shape streamlining to ground-effect aerodynamics.

In the early years of Grand Prix racing, specifications for cars commonly changed on an annual basis. Currently, formulas are established by the FIA to run for several years at a time. The primary stipulations limit engine displacement and minimum car weight, although virtually all aspects of car design are regulated to some extent. Naturally, with each new formula, engineers try to exact the maximum amount of performance from cars, often through novel designs that are not covered by the rules. For this reason, racing rules and car specifications are under constant modification over the life of each formula in order to keep competition as level as possible, to keep costs down (though F1 cars are wildly expensive), and to make racing as safe as possible for drivers, crews, and spectators.

Formula 1 regulations for 1948–1953 specified maximum engine capacity at 4.5 liters unsupercharged or 1.5 liters supercharged. For 1954 through 1960 engine capacity was limited to 2.5 liters unsupercharged and 750 cc supercharged. Though earlier cars had been open-wheeled, new regulations for the 1959 season stipulated that they be so constructed. Engine capacity was limited to 1.5 liters unsupercharged while supercharged engines were prohibited from 1961 through 1966. Minimum car weight, with oil and water but without fuel was 450 kilograms (992.25 pounds). For 1966 through 1988, unsupercharged

engines were limited to 3.0 liters while supercharged engines could be no more than 1.5 liters. This was an extremely popular formula and numerous technological advances in racing car design occurred while it was in effect. These included the use of exotic materials in the construction of cars, such as Kevlar and carbon fiber, and the incorporation of design principles derived from the aircraft industry.

Renault changed F1 racing in 1977 with the introduction of a new 1.5 liter turbocharged engine. Though 1.5 liter turbocharged engines could produce far more horsepower than normally aspirated 3.0 liter engines, abrupt changes in the power curves of early turbocharged engines made cars using them difficult to drive. These problems were eventually overcome and the world champion drivers from 1983 through 1988 all drove cars with 1.5 liter turbocharged engines (Nye 1992). For one year, 1986, normally aspirated engines were prohibited in F1. Turbocharged engines were banned after the 1988 season and replaced by normally aspirated 3.5 liter engines. In 1995, engine size was reduced to 3.0 liters.

FIA regulations for F1 for 1996 stipulate that engines must be 4-stroke, reciprocating, unsupercharged, with no more than 12 cylinders, and have a maximum displacement of no more than 3.0 liters. Unlike the early years of Grand Prix racing, where maximum car weight was set, current F1 cars must weigh a minimum of 600 kilograms (1,323 pounds). Cars are not permitted to utilize 4-wheel drive, traction control, antilock brakes, active suspension, or 4-wheel steering (FIA 1995b). At one time or another, each of these technologies was used in F1. They are now prohibited for reasons of cost, safety, and competition.

Cars are designated by the names of the manufacturers of their chassis and engines. In a few cases, including BRM, Honda, Ferrari, Mercedes, Maserati, Alfa Romeo, Porsche, Vanwall, and Matra, companies made both chassis and engine, but today most F1 cars are hybrids with a chassis constructed by one manufacturer fitted with an engine produced by another. Most successful engines have been built by major auto manufacturers, including Honda, Ford, BMW, and Renault, although, among smaller companies, Ferrari has been singularly successful. A few specialized racing-only engine producers, such as Hart, Judd, and Weslake, have enjoyed limited success. In recent years, the most successful chassis have been built by specialized race car manufacturers, including Williams, McLaren, and Benetton.

Formula 1 Drivers

Formula 1 is the pinnacle of auto racing and few drivers ever manage to compete at that level. Of those who do, not many are successful. From 1950 through 1993, 543 different drivers competed in F1 and 124 captured World Championship points. However, only 70 won races and, of those, 17 only won once (Chimits and Granet 1994). In 1995, 34 different drivers contested F1 races but only 18 scored championship points. Five drivers won races with Michael Schumacher of Germany the victor in 9. At the end of the 1995 season, drivers from Great Britain have produced the most wins in F1 (164) and the most world champions (7). Brazil, on the shoulders of World Champions Ayrton Senna (41 wins), Nelson Piquet (23 wins), and Emerson Fittipaldi (14 wins), ranks second. Italy, which has supplied the second most drivers to F1 behind Great Britain, has produced but two world champions (Giuseppe Farina in 1950 and Alberto Ascari in 1952 and 1953) and the fifth most victories (39), after Great Britain, Brazil, France, and Austria. Four-time World Champion Alain Prost, with 51 wins, holds nearly two-thirds of the 78 Grand Prix victories scored by French drivers. Five American drivers have won Grands Prix (a total of 22), although only two have captured the World Driver's Championship (Phil Hill in 1961 and Mario Andretti in 1978).

Formula 1 racing is a very dangerous sport, and drivers, track personnel, race team crew members, and spectators have been killed or injured during events. Since 1950, 24 drivers have lost their lives from injuries received during races or during practice or qualifying for races. Others have been killed while testing F1 cars or racing other types of cars. Fortunately, advances in the design and construction of tracks, cars, and driver equipment (fireproof suits, helmets, etc.) have made modern F1 racing much safer than it was during its first three decades. No drivers died in sanctioned F1 events after 1982 until the tragic losses of rookie driver Roland Ratzenberger in qualifying and three-time world champion Ayr-

What Makes a Driver Great?

It is as difficult to compare Formula 1 drivers from different eras as it is to compare individuals who competed at different times in other sports, such as Babe Ruth and Hank Aaron in baseball. Alain Prost of France holds the record for most victories in F1 (51), but he is also among the leaders in number of starts in races. Ayrton Senna is second, with 41 victories, but his career was cut short at the age of 32 when he lost his life in a crash at the 1994 San Marino Grand Prix. Similarly, Jim Clark is regarded by many as the greatest driver ever and would surely have added to his victory total of 25 had he not died in a Formula 2 race at Hockenheim, Germany, in 1968. Juan Manuel Fangio, of Argentina, holds more world championships (5) than any other driver. Prost has four, while Scotland's Jackie Stewart, Brazilians Nelson Piquet and Ayrton Senna, and Niki Lauda of Austria have three. Several other drivers hold two championships.

Another way of comparing drivers is to look at their ratio of wins versus starts. By this measure, Fangio is in a class by himself, having won 24 of his 51 F1 races (47 percent), starting from the pole in 27. Moreover, he won the world championship five of the eight years that he competed. By contrast, Prost started 199 races in order to accumulate his 51 wins (25.6 percent) while Senna won 41 times in 161 starts (25.5 percent).

Finally, a more subjective way of comparing drivers is in terms of wins or high placements when they were driving cars generally judged to be inferior to those of their competitors. An example is Tazio Nuvolari's legendary victory at the 1935 German Grand Prix, where he defeated the superior Mercedes and Auto Union cars in an obsolescent Alfa Romeo. Though never a world champion, Sterling Moss of Great Britain achieved several of his 16 F1 victories in cars that were probably inferior to those of his competitors. With few exceptions, however, victories in F1 are achieved by a combination of the best car driven by a first-rate driver.

—Garry Chick

ton Senna during the race at the 1994 San Marino Grand Prix. The recent safety record is all the more remarkable because retirements during races due to collisions between cars and crashes resulting from cars leaving the track have become more common in recent years while retirements due to mechanical failures have decreased. In 1992, for example, 211 cars out of 416 starts failed to complete races. Of those failures, 76 (36 percent) were due to accidents and collisions. In contrast, only 15 percent of retirements in 1960 were due to accidents and collisions (Chimits and Granet 1994). The reason for the increase in accidents and collisions is not due to a decrease in driver skill but to the magnitude and equality of car performance, forcing drivers to take additional risks if they wish to improve their placing during practice or a race (Chimits and Granet 1994).

In order to be successful, F1 drivers must combine excellent athletic skills, such as strength, stamina, and quick reactions, with keen vision (though some wear glasses) and the ability to sustain concentration. Because of the enormous acceleration, braking, and cornering forces generated by F1 cars, drivers are put under tremendous physical stress. Drivers also must withstand the effects of vibration, heat, and physical wear-and-tear on hands, feet, and other parts of the body through contact with car controls or bodywork in the cockpit (Chimits and Granet 1994).

Formula 1 Races

FIA regulations (1995a) require that there be at least 8 and no more than 16 F1 Grands Prix per year, each contested by no more than 26 cars. Starting grid alignment is determined by qualifying, with the fastest driver in the pole position. When the cars are properly aligned on the grid after a formation lap around the track, a red light is displayed by the starter. Anytime between four and seven seconds after the red light is illuminated, the starter switches on a green light to start the race. Under current regulations, race distance is the fewest number of complete laps that exceed a total distance of 305 kilometers (189.5 miles). In addition, races are limited to two hours. If the race is slowed due to weather or some other reason, the driver in the lead is shown the checkered flag at the end of the lap during which the two-hour limit is reached.

Due to restricted fuel capacity, it is necessary for F1 cars to make at least one, and more often two, pit stops during races in order to refuel and take on new tires. Quick pit stops figure prominently in winning or losing races and teams practice pit stops intensely. Tires can usually be changed in 5 to 10 seconds so the duration of pit stops is more dependent on the amount of fuel re-

plenished. Good pit stops usually take less than 15 seconds.

During races, electronic telemetry constantly provides information about the engine and chassis to pit crews. In the cars, liquid crystal display instruments inform the driver of engine speed, fuel remaining, water temperature, lap times, and other variables. At the same time, miniaturized TV cameras mounted on the cars transmit the experience of F1 speed to viewers around the world. It is estimated that some 30 billion viewers followed the 1993 season on TV (Chimits and Granet 1994), making F1 among the world's most popular spectator sports.

—Garry Chick

Bibliography: Chimits, Xavier, and François Granet. (1994) *The Williams Renault Formula 1 Motor Racing Book.* New York: Dorling Kindersley.

Fédération Internationale de l'Automobile (FIA). (1995a) *1996 Formula One World Championship Sporting Regulations.* Paris: FIA.

———. (1995b) *1996 Formula One Technical Regulations.* Paris: FIA.

Griffiths, Trevor R. (1993) *Grand Prix.* London: Bloomsburg Publishing.

Hodges, David, Doug Nye, and Nigel Roebuck. (1981) *Grand Prix.* New York: St. Martin's Press.

Nye, Doug. (1992) *The Autocourse History of the Grand Prix Car 1966–91.* Richmond, UK: Hazleton Publishing.

Rosiniski, José. (1974) *Formula 1 Racing: The Modern Era.* New York: Madison Square Press.

Foxhunting

Foxhunting is an adaptation of the prehistoric and medieval chase that justifies its existence as an exterminator of vermin. English in its origins, it has an international following that finds "Britishness" attractive. Since its "scientific" reorganization in the eighteenth century the sport has grown because it provided a means by which affluent city-dwellers could adopt the lifestyle of the landed elite and boost their own social prestige. Modern economics have changed its financing and strengthened it in the process, and changes in the transportation systems, once feared, have actually boosted participation. With artistic and literary underpinnings, it represents the essence of rural life for far more people than those who actually hunt. Its security is, however, threatened by changes in attitudes toward animal rights and toward social hierarchies, and the hunting field is now often literally a battleground between the sport's supporters and saboteurs. Yet its cultural impact remains far wider than many people realize.

Origins

Foxhunting is essentially an English sport, although it and similar sports are practiced elsewhere. The prehistoric pursuit of wild animals with hounds, initially for food and then for thrills, had many regional variations, and by the Middle Ages the prized English quarry had become deer, hunted in strictly defined and enclosed parks from which farming was largely banned. Subsequent changes in agriculture opened up a wider countryside for hunting when whole swaths of grass, divided by hedges and small woods or "coverts" and suitable for fast riding and jumping, were created, providing new habitats for foxes and their natural prey. This was reinforced when aristocrats such as the second Duke of Buckingham (1797–1861) and the landed gentry changed from chasing stags to hunting foxes and made what had once been regarded as vermin a socially acceptable quarry. By the mid-eighteenth century the sport was widely established but comparatively disorganized and informal. To this circumstance, Hugo Meynell (1735–?), a wealthy country gentleman, brought a sporting revolution. He took over a pack of hounds in Leicestershire, in the English Midlands, in 1753 and introduced scientific breeding and a new fast mode of riding. His hunt, the Quorn, became the model for a boom in foxhunting that has barely slowed since.

Practice

Modern foxhunting is a sport of custom, ritual, and etiquette rather than rules and bureaucracy; it is essentially noncompetitive and defines itself in terms of older usage wherein "sport" is a contest with nature. Although there are formal associations of Masters of Fox Hounds and Hunt Secretaries, national organization is minimal. Each hunt has its own agreed "country," and these vary in size according to the subtle complexities of the local terrain. It has a Master (sometimes several), nowadays often elected, who presides over an establishment that usually has some paid servants, "huntsmen" and "whippers-in," who manage the kennels and hounds. It is essentially a winter sport, inherited from the days when agriculture was largely a spring and summer activity and there were long months of gentry leisure. Nowadays men and women hunt in roughly equal numbers, a Victorian innovation, and about a third of Masters are female.

On the two or three days a week when most hunts take place, a "field" of mounted riders follows their pack of carefully bred and trained hounds (always numbered in twos or "couples") to a different meeting place, where the hunt begins. If a fox is located, it is chased until it either escapes or is killed. Although the justification for foxhunting is the killing of vermin, its appeal for most participants lies in the thrill and risks of fast cross-country riding, the attraction of the winter landscape, and in the social relationships the sport engenders. In addition to the riders, large numbers of people follow most hunts by foot, bicycle, or motor vehicle. The sport is traditionally "pan-class," pursued by the relatively wealthy or socially ambitious but offering a rural spectacle for humbler watchers and giving an impression of social cohesion at odds with many of the other divisions of modern society. Although most hunts are mounted, there are a few places, such as the English Lake District, where hunting takes place on foot because the terrain is too difficult for riding.

Full participation in hunting is comparatively expensive, demanding the maintenance and transport of individual horses and the purchase of the correct accessories. Most established hunts have a uniform in which the buttons are the key distinctive feature. Established full members and hunt servants usually wear scarlet coats (often known as "pink" after a London tailor), others black. The actual apparatus of the hunt, particularly the pack of hounds, is maintained largely by members' subscriptions, topped up by "cap" fees charged to visitors and hunt followers. This has become almost universal since the late-Victorian agricultural depressions made it almost impossible for individual

Foxhunting was popular among the upper classes in Victorian England. It offers more than just the thrill of the hunt; its aristocratic associations lend an air of prestige and nobility to the participant.

landlords to follow the customary practice of keeping hounds at their own expense. It has long been argued that this cooperative financing made the sport more "democratic." It would be more accurate to say that it widened the boundaries of those who could choose to mark their social mobility, wealth, and control of time by taking up the activities of a traditional and venerated elite. The involvement of several members of the British royal family, especially Prince Charles (1948–), still reinforces the social cachet that has made the sport so attractive to newcomers.

Social ambition has always fueled the sport's growth. When new roads were built across eighteenth century England, they allowed an increasing number of prosperous Londoners to visit the "Shires," the Midland counties where the sport was strongest. The construction of the railways a century later was initially seen as a threat, divid-

ing up the hunting countryside. Instead, they offered a major boost, speeding up the transport of horses and making it possible for city-dwellers to commute for a day's sport. During the reign (1837–1901) of Queen Victoria (1819–1901), the number of British hunts more than doubled, coming close to the present 200 or so. At least 50,000 "rode to hounds" by the beginning of the twentieth century and many more were followers and spectators. It was this influx that prompted a tightening of hunting etiquette, with a subtle refining of the codes of acceptability. Within the "democracy," there were many social circles to which entrance was far more restricted.

This pattern of social stratification still survives despite agricultural vicissitudes and a continued shift in the economic power of the traditional landed leadership. Despite the motor car and its road networks, the popularity of the horse as an object for recreation continues unabated. The automobile has replaced the train in increasing the mobility of hunting's participants and the horse trailer, towed behind a four-wheel drive vehicle, is now a major hunting accessory. The car has also boosted the number of spectators considerably; road traffic management is now a constant headache for most hunts, particularly those that meet on a Saturday, when spectatorship is at its highest.

Foxhunting also fostered two satellite sports. In order to compensate farmers whose land was damaged and to test boasts about horses' abilities, most hunts arranged "point-to-point" races at the end of the season, run across the countryside. Although they still continue, they have been formalized into the steeplechase, or National Hunt fence-jumping winter calendar of horseracing, using normal racetracks. The Grand National is the peak of these. The other sport, show jumping, ritualizes the testing of a natural course in the context of an arena while its riders wear hunting clothing.

Against social acceptability, however, other problems have emerged. One has been a significant shift in farming activity due to membership in the European Union. Considerable areas of grass and woodland, with their attendant hedgerows, have been replaced by vast plowed areas that offer poor wildlife habitat and inhibit fast riding; they also do not hold a fox's scent as well as grass. This may change as the over-production of cereals gives way at the end of the twentieth century to the reintroduction of grassland.

The other problem arises out of a fundamental shift in attitudes to animals and social deference. Late Victorian England produced middle-class groups opposed to what they perceived as the vicious cruelty of hunting and saw the formation in 1891 of the relatively short-lived Humanitarian League, which sought change by reasoned persuasion; in the case of foxhunting it failed. An undercurrent of protest that has existed throughout the twentieth century became more sharp since the early 1980s with the emergence of groups committed either to the legal banning of the sport or to disruption of events and intimidation of participants. The League Against Cruel Sports stands first among these and still limits its activities to orderly protest and parliamentary lobbying. Around it, however, have emerged bodies

The Idealized Huntsman: John Peel (1776–1854)

John Peel was a "yeoman" (small farmer) in Caldbeck, Cumberland, on the edge of the English Lake District. Although far from wealthy, he was so addicted to foxhunting that he kept two horses and his own pack of hounds for 55 years. His knowledge of the landscape and the sport was legendary. A jovial character, he was seen as the epitome of the English sporting character of honest values. For many people he has long been more famous than many sporting aristocrats and is far better known than Hugo Meynell. The reason for this lies in a song that was composed around 1820 by his friend, John Woodock Graves, who also set it to an old folk tune, "Bonnie Annie"; it names his horse and some of the hounds. The song has passed into English culture as an expression of rural virtue, nationalism, and manly spirit. It has been adapted as a regimental march and been taught to generations of English schoolchildren. Here are three of the verses and the chorus, sung between them:

D'ye ken John Peel with his coat so gay?
D'ye ken John Peel at the break of day,
D'ye ken John Peel when he's far, far away,
With his hounds and his horn in the morning?

Yes, I ken John Peel, with Ruby too,
Ranter and Ringwood, Bellman and True,
From a find to a check, from a check to a view,
From a view to a death in the morning.

D'ye ken John Peel with his coat so gay?
He lived in Troutbeck once on a day,
Now he has gone far, far away,
We shall ne'er hear his voice in the morning.

Chorus
'Twas the sound of his horn brought me from
   my bed,
And the cry of his hounds which he oft-times
   led,
For Peel's "View hallo" would awaken the
   dead,
Or the fox from his lair in the morning.

—John Lowerson

committed to the active sabotage of hunts and, if necessary, to arson, personal violence, and bomb threats.

Opposed to these groups is an umbrella defense organization, the British Field Sports Society. The

Foxhunting in North America

Foxhunting has existed in North America since colonial days. However, foxhunting here was not highly organized until much later. Night hunters, farmers, and landed gentry were the early foxhunters. The earliest surviving records of American foxhunting in the modern manner, by what is now known as an organized hunt—maintained for the benefit of a group of foxhunters rather than for a single owner—are of the pack instituted by Thomas, Sixth Lord Fairfax, in 1747, who claimed an inheritance of 5 million acres in the northern neck of Virginia. The Blue Ridge hounds now hunt over much of his former lands. Much of what little is recorded on early foxhunting comes from letters written by Lord Fairfax and from the diaries of George Washington. Washington, the first president of the United States, was an ardent foxhunter who owned his own pack of hounds. Washington's diaries are laced with frequent references to foxhunts near the nation's capitol. On one occasion Congress was in session as hounds ran near the capitol; the congressmen ran outside to watch the hounds, and some jumped on horses and joined the chase. The earliest established North American foxhound club was the Montreal Hunt in Canada (1826). In the United States, the Piedmont Foxhounds were established in Virginia in 1840, and the Rose Tree Foxhunting Club in 1859.

Through the years, American (Canada and the United States) foxhunting has evolved with its own distinct flavor, noticeably different from the British. The most obvious is that in the Americas the emphasis is the chase rather than the kill. In Britain the goal is to kill the fox. This is because fox are considered vermin in Britain. Farmers with large sheep farms want the animals killed. In America such is not normally the case. They want the fox to get away so it can be chased another day. A successful hunt ends when the fox is accounted for by entering its hold in the ground, called an earth. Once there, the hounds are rewarded with praise from their huntsman and that is the end of the chase.

The generic term *foxhunting* applied to red fox, gray fox, coyote chasing, and bobcat chasing. In colonial days, the primary quarry was the gray fox. Red fox were found only in Canada and the northern states, the dividing line being about the middle of New Jersey and Pennsylvania, with the gray fox native to the country south of this. Some red fox may have migrated to the southern states; others were imported from England or trapped and moved by hunters. What animal is hunted depends on the geographic location of the hunt. Today in America the coyote has become a significant quarry as well as the fox. Coyotes are very adaptable and have migrated across America, reaching all but the most eastern portions of Virginia, Maryland, and Pennsylvania.

There is tremendous variety of both terrain and quarry in the United States and Canada. Hounds hunt red fox along the sand dunes of Long Island Sound. They hunt red and gray foxes, coyotes, and bobcats in the pine woods of Alabama, Georgia, and the Carolinas. The stony fields and thick deciduous growth of New England make perfect cover for the red fox. Virginia, Maryland, Pennsylvania, and Delaware offer a countryside closer to the traditional English landscape. Here, the fox is plentiful. Moving westward, there is hunting on the Great Plains of the Midwest, in the high altitudes of the Rocky Mountains, and along the shores of the Pacific Ocean. Coyotes predominate as one moves westward. Canada has the same variety of terrain and quarry as one moves from east to west. Foxhunting exists in 34 states and 5 Canadian provinces.

—Dennis J. Foster

battle is now fought in the media, in politics, and in the hunting field; some farmers and local authorities have now banned the hunts from their land. Recent legislation has attempted to curb sabotage, but the battles rage and many hunts now use police protection or employ private security firms, which raise costs considerably. The protesters argue that foxhunting is a vicious and inefficient form of vermin control that has more to do with social prestige than rural necessity. Hunt supporters claim they are victims of an urban-rural rivalry at the heart of British society and that banning foxhunting, with its wide social dependencies, would both reduce the spectacle of country life and do serious damage to local economies.

Although the sport is very much associated with carefully constructed images of "Englishness" it is not restricted to that country. There is a small number of Scottish and Welsh hunts, limited by local mountainous terrain. Ireland has nearly 30. The sport is less costly there than in England and this has attracted both English and transatlantic participants. Anglophiles elsewhere have also adapted the sport to suit local conditions, sometimes breeding from imported foxes to provide a quarry. This was the case in Australia, where some 8 hunts were established in southern states fairly close in pattern to the English landscape. In Portugal, Spain, and Italy there are also hunts run on very English lines. But by far the most important growth has been in North America, where the legacy of colonialism merged with the leisure wishes of a nineteenth-century plutocracy to encourage this "gentry" activity. The United States has had some 130 hunts; while the majority of these are associated with the East Coast former colonies, the midwest and desert states have also seen small numbers of hunts emerge. Their quarry is usually the native gray fox, and much of the sport's justification comes less from the need to control vermin than the marking of social exclusiveness which membership provides.

This was nowhere clearer than in the boom of the 1880s and 1890s when country clubs formed on the Eastern seaboard developed hunts as part of their overall provision for the very wealthy; perhaps the best example of this is the Orange County, Virginia, club, which moved there from New York in the 1920s to escape creeping suburbia. This obsession with "Britishness" is also matched on a much smaller scale in Canada, which has some 12 hunts scattered widely from Montreal to British Columbia, of which the Eglinton and Caledon near Toronto is probably supreme.

Foxhunting has had an even greater impact than this distribution would suggest. It has provided a singular iconography for the English countryside and elegant input to English literature. Many landed aristocrats sought to have themselves and their horses and hounds immortalized by specially commissioned painters. Of these, perhaps the most important have been George Stubbs (1724–1806), the first great painter of horses, John Fernley Senior (1782–1860), who portrayed the new "scientific" hunts, and Sir Alfred Munnings (1878–1959), who provided many twentieth century stereotypes. These and their many imitators had a much wider importance than their immediate patronage suggests; cheap prints brought an idealized rural world centered on the hunts to a huge public. Perhaps the most important and bizarre manifestation of this was the role that winter hunting scenes played in British Christmas card production, sanctifying a neo-pagan love of the land for an increasingly secular culture.

In literature, novelists have performed a similar task, combining fun with sporting idealism.

Probably the most significant of these was Robert Smith Surtees (1805–1864), whose principal character, Jorrocks, became the epitome of the honest and jolly hunting squire. Anthony Trollope (1815–1882) built hunting scenes into many of his 47 novels, which he wrote largely to finance his own love of the sport. In this century Siegfried Sassoon (1886–1967) offered an account of a youth spent foxhunting that did much to reinforce a widespread nostalgia for pre–World War I England as a genteel Golden Age.

Perhaps the sport's most surprising impact has been in providing colloquial phrases that have become commonplace in British and American life without their users' realizing their origins. Just two examples must suffice: when a scholar is described as "prominent in his field," he little realizes that it once referred to a fast-riding risk taker, and when we are told to "Have a nice day," how many know that it is a modification of hunting's traditional greeting, "Have a good day," with its promise of a fast ride and a good kill?

—John Lowerson

See also Animal Rights.

Bibliography: Blackwood, Caroline. (1987) *In the Pink*. London: Bloomsbury

Carr, Raymond. (1976) *English Foxhunting: A History*. London: Weidenfeld and Nicolson.

Dencher, Stepehen. (1988) *Sporting Art in Eighteenth Century England*. New Haven, CT: Yale University Press.

Itzkowitz, David C. (1977) *Peculiar Privilege: a Social History of English Foxhunting*. Hassocks, UK: Harvester.

Jackson, Alastair. (1989) *The Great Hunts: Foxhunting Centres of the World*. Newton Abbot, UK: David and Charles.

Lowerson, John. (1993) *Sport and the English Middle Classes, 1870–1914*. Manchester: Manchester University Press.

Sassoon, Siegfried. (1928) *Memoirs of a Foxhunting Man*. London: Faber.

Surtees, Robert Smith. (1901 [1838]) *Jorrocks Jaunts and Jollities*. London: Downey.

Thomas, Sir William Beach. (1936) *Hunting England*. London: Batsford.

Trollope, Anthony. (1952 [1865]) *Hunting Sketches*. London: Benn.

Walker, Stella A. (1972) *Sporting Art; England 1700–1900*. London: Studio Vista.

Watson, John N. P. (1977) *The Book of Foxhunting*. London: Batsford.

Gambling

The need, desire, and drive to compete are deeply ingrained in many cultures. The basis for this characteristic is unimportant; but, be it innate or learned, it is unquestionably pervasive in Western society. This tendency toward competitiveness is reflected in government, politics, business, education, and every other societal institution. Mutually beneficial events and outcomes rarely have a place in the Western credo. The following is a discussion of how this spirit as manifested in sport can surface in a very innocent fashion and become an integral part of the relationship between spectators and sport (Schuetz 1976).

In all preindustrial societies almost every aristocratic male was involved in some form of physical activity such as hunting, hawking, court tennis, and ball games, which were the precursors to baseball, football, soccer, golf, and bowling—pastimes that were more popular among "commoners." Sports, played on a localized basis among friends and kin, were chiefly a recreational outlet that furthered social cohesion.

As technological advancements expanded at an ever-increasing rate during the mid-nineteenth century in communication, transportation, and the mass production of consumer products, national populations began an exponential growth pattern of unknown proportions (Kaplan 1986; Schuetz 1976). The nature of the labor market also changed dramatically as jobs in the service and professional sectors boomed, leading to both the growth of population centers and the widespread loss of muscle tone among males, as fewer jobs now required hard physical labor.

As people began to mass in urban centers, sports now had a large population to draw from, and the demand for talent to produce winning teams began to eclipse the mere desire for recreation. The physical requirements of the competitive sports arena were transforming sport into a commercial venture restricting many from participation. Eventually those who could not participate were conceded the right to watch those who could. Thus, a new relationship began to form between the spectator and the team as a whole. People began to align themselves with a team because

of some identifying characteristic, and during the play of the contest they attached themselves emotionally to the outcome (Kaplan 1986; Schuetz 1976). The spectator was now developing.

By watching a contest, individuals could continue to experience vicariously that competitive spirit which they had at one time received from the actual competition. This meant that for spectators their competitive counterparts were now in the opposing stands and could only gain at their loss or lose at their gain.

As the population of the United States continued to explode during the 1940s a new sound joined the pounding of machinery—the whir of the computer (Schuetz 1976). The nature of human inputs within U.S. society was forced to change because of technological leadership, and with this change, the role of sports again adopted a new relationship with the people—the nuclear relationship.

No longer could the individual assimilate the competitive spirit of the contest by being a spectator. The spectator was prohibited from fulfilling his role by stadium capacity, distances, and time. Essentially, technological advances such as computers and television transformed the relationship between sport and the spectator in that it was no longer necessary to be present at a contest to satisfy one's competitive desires.

Sports betting developed as an alternative to the American male's exclusion from competition by the surrounding environment over which he had no control. The betting arena emulated the bipolar nature inherent in the spirit of competition, allowing for a winner and a loser and the opportunity to be one or the other (Schuetz 1976; Shecter 1970). This alternative has often suffered from the taint of illegality and has been usually perceived by most governmental agencies as harmless. Unfortunately, this attitude toward sports gambling renders it difficult to precisely identify those who gamble regularly (most are reluctant to admit they gamble illegally), although it appears that most of the action involves males, many of whom have substantial money to allow regular wagering on sporting contests. In recent years, an increasing number of women seem to be gambling on sport events (McPherson, Curtis, and Loy 1989).

The effects of gambling on sport have resulted in a marked increase in the interest and degree of interest bestowed upon sport, especially by males. Even though separated at times by hundreds of miles from the event itself, the viewer now assumed partial responsibility for the contest outcome as personal participation was as essential as that of the actual participants in terms of outcome. This participation would become mandatory for some when the competitive spirit was awakened by the ability to bet because economic gain was now the motivation for a renewed interest in sport.

U.S. Origins

Two inventions shaped modern sports betting and bookmaking in the United States. The first and more obtrusive was television. From the early 1950s, live telecasts of sports steadily gained popularity and generated huge profits for owners. Professional sport franchise owners, especially in football and baseball, and players with new collective bargaining agreements and favorable court decisions were able to accumulate huge amounts of wealth. Sports betting was the unrecorded part of the flood of money that television generated (Rader 1990; Roberts and Olson 1989).

Television in its own innocent way provided a background of mocking laughter for the old and tired refrain of previous congressional committee hearings: "Cut off the wire service and you stop bookmaking" (Figone 1989). Nowadays on virtually any given day, every saloon in the country has its own "wire service" on the wall courtesy of advertisers with instant replay. In many homes, the television set has taken over the function of the horse parlor of the past. The serious bettor after seeing the outcome of a bet develops a new set of opinions and backs these opinions with further wagers (Sasuly 1982).

The second invention involved not technology but an idea—the bookmaker's point spread. For 200 years individuals who sponsored sports betting (that is, bookmakers) had wrestled with the problem of setting the stakes in an event in which one party (that is, a horse, fighter, or team) appeared clearly superior. In mid-nineteenth-century England, different weights or handicaps were assigned to faster horses in a race (Sasuly 1982); but rarely did the weights equalize or bring the field together. A really fast horse running

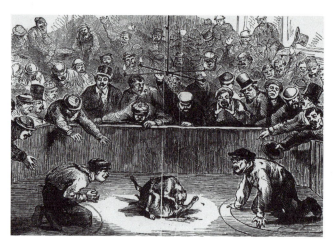

Betting can provide spectators a feeling of vicarious participation in sports, as seen here among gamblers at a New York dog fight.

against a slower one could most often pick up the extra 9 kilograms (20 pounds) of handicapped weight, take the track, and win easily. To entice more bettors, bookmakers began to offer different odds so that an unlikely horse assigned long odds would reward his backers with a rare but handsome return. The bookmaker's goal was to attract different amounts of betting at different odds so that no matter which horse won, the payout would be the same, guaranteeing the bookie a profit (Sasuly 1982).

In a prize fight or a contest between two teams, one fighter or team was likely to be favored, sometimes heavily. If a bettor wished to wager on a heavily favored fighter or team, $6 might have to be wagered to win $1, while if the bettor chose the underdog, $5 would be returned for a $1 bet. The bookmaker was adjusting the odds to the strength of the bettors' opinions—in this case producing about five times as much betting on the favorite as on the underdog to protect his commission no matter who won. The bookmaking trade used the odds to split the payoffs profitably, until the early 1920s or 1930s when the point spread was introduced. Before World War II, giving or taking points was rare. After the war it became standard practice, especially in football and basketball.

With the point spread no odds are offered. Even money is bet by everyone and the bettor stakes $11 to win $10—the difference is the bookie's commission. No odds are posted with the point spread; the favored team must win by a set number of points. The underdog bettor's team may lose the contest but its backer wins the bet if the margin of defeat is less than the number of points offered. For example, if one bettor wagers on an underdog football team and is given three points, the bet is won if the underdog team loses by two points. In effect, the underdog team, for purposes of wagering, won the game by one point (Figone 1989; Sasuly 1982). The advantage of the point spread was that it stimulated a sports bettor to act on opinion in any contest in which points are offered. A bettor can persuade himself that there is reason to favor one side or the other—and the bookmaker's commission proportionally increases.

Since the inception of the point spread a substantial number of collegiate basketball players in the United States have been involved in "fixing" scandals. These scandals have involved either a favored team playing to stay under the point spread (that is, "shaving points") or one of the teams outright losing or "dumping" the game. "Shaving" has been more commonplace since the game still can be won and players are less likely to draw attention to their manipulation of the final score. For the most part, professional and college football have evaded these scandals.

The Attraction of Betting

In sports gambling the primary satisfaction is derived from the feeling that one "knows" something, that one has outsmarted the cosmos by guessing correctly. When a bettor wins, the ascription is to superior power of analysis. When a bettor loses, it's bad luck.

Financial gain may be the underlying desire. But there are many avenues to financial gain: hard work, theft, investment, invention. The habitual gambler who hopes to strike it rich, and for whom the money to be won is the primary motivation, has at his or her disposal cards, dice, roulette wheels, and even elections. Bingo, lotteries, and other forms of gambling are now common in most states. However, the sports bettor is a hybrid (Koppett 1981). He or she loves to bet, but also enjoys the game. Because the sports bettor believes the game can be figured out, sports betting is the ideal outlet for satisfying gambling desire.

The "real" sports bettor is a minority of the sports audience but an appreciable fraction of it,

and a disproportionate number of those who constitute the passionate following. More numerous are those who desire a little stimulant to their involvement. If one makes a small side bet with a friend, the game becomes more interesting. The first type is labeled the "habitual bettor" and the second type the "casual bettor" (Koppett 1981). Between them, they form the backbone of the adult sports betting audience.

Thoroughbred and harness horse racing are devices for legal betting, and the $2 bettor is no more interested in the horse as an animal than in a playing card as an artistic illustration. There are certainly people interested in horses who breed, train, and race them to "improve the breed." If only those individuals were involved, horse races would be as frequent—and as expensive and exclusive—as yacht races of the America's Cup class. The democracy of horse racing, which attracts more customers through its turnstiles each year than any other sport in the United States, is totally based on the equal opportunity to cash a bet (Koppett 1981).

Without the opportunity to bet, openly, under supervision that guarantees the winners will be paid off and ensures a fair contest, horse racing and other events such as dog racing and jai alai would not draw crowds. A few historic events, such as the Kentucky Derby, transcend betting interest and become entertaining, competitive sports events steeped in tradition for millions who do not bet. But these events are exceptions to the rule and survive only in a context that day-to-day betting provides (Figone 1989).

In other sports, betting is less fundamental but not necessarily less present. Horse racing, dog racing, and jai alai are legalized and licensed for betting by some states, and they do not exist where they are not. Other sports such as professional baseball and basketball are automatically legal and need no licensing (except for business purposes), while betting on them is illegal (except in Nevada, and professional football in Oregon). Boxing requires licensing for a different reason—in theory to protect the health and safety of the contestants—but does not involve legalized betting (Brenner and Brenner 1990; Koppett 1981). And a few other sports, such as cock fighting, may be outlawed with betting on them also illegal.

The reasons for this distinction between licensed and unlicensed professional sports become apparent when the requirements for attracting bettors are presented. First, the event wagered on must be sufficiently complex to provide suspense and mental stimulation, but simple enough to be easily followed. And entertainment sports or sports whose rules are designed to meet the above function (that is, professional football and basketball) are constructed to attract spectators by promoting a lot of scoring or thrilling plays.

Second, there must be the conviction that the contest is truly unpredictable—that is, the outcome is not prearranged. A high-wire act in the circus may arouse suspense and a sense of hazard, but it is most assuredly rehearsed. An improvisation by an actor or musician may be unrehearsed; however, it is not a contest. Neither is suitable material for betting. Similarly, a lopsided pair of dice would also be unsuitable, as would a tennis match between a world-class player and an 11-year-old boy. The concepts of "doubt" and "fair shake" must be present; entertainment sports have been designed for that as well (Brenner and Brenner 1990; Sasuly 1982).

Third, the contest being bet on must occur frequently with its result easily accessible to all interested parties. Casinos, legal and otherwise, are often difficult or expensive to reach, and the result of the bet is not broadcast beyond the immediate area within the casino. Theoretically, one could bet on the number of sunspots recorded by major telescopes every day; obtaining the results would probably be impossible. Entertainment sports for their own purposes are frequent and accessible, with every result promptly publicized (Figone 1989; Sasuly 1982).

Further, the bettor needs continuity—repeated instances of the same basic circumstances. The comparable event must continue occurring, time after time, to allow one to get even after losing. And it has to be recognizably similar each time, so one feels that accumulated knowledge will provide an "edge"—increasing one's chances of winning.

Finally, there must be someone to bet with. A large body of other bettors, with similar interests, must exist to create a "market"—in the sense of the floor of a stock market—where pools of winnings can be formed by collecting from losers. Gambling is not practicable without someone to function as a broker, whether it's an illegal bookmaker, a legal one, the operator of a pool, or the

state. Entertainment sports, by generating a large audience for their activities, create just such a market for betting (Koppett 1981).

Different sports with variable characteristics create interesting contexts for betting. Most sports, like horse racing, are competitions with elemental simplicity; the only factor one must follow or know is the "score," "the winner," or "order of finish." As soon as one wants to bet, marvelous complications appear. Past performances, horse lineage, records of jockeys, trainers, owners and coaches, weather conditions, injuries to key players, and just plain hunches can all be considered by the bettor. Since the complications lie almost entirely in the area of predicting, rather than in complex rules or tactics during the event itself, only betting sustains interest (Koppett 1981). The role of state governments in sports betting is to ensure that an honest event is being offered to the public. The power of the state is implemented because so much tax revenue is generated from legal sports betting and state governments must ensure that the taint of corruption does not permeate legal sports betting since this would decrease needed tax revenues.

U.S. Betting Corruption

The problem of "manipulation" or fixing of sporting events has plagued sports betting since its beginnings. Manipulation in state-run betting is certainly possible, but less likely since the state's elaborate security machinery is designed to prevent such occurrences. However, anyone who bets has, or quickly acquires, sensitivity to the possibility of "fixing" results. No one doubts that humans could manipulate without detection, if they were so inclined. Boxing offers such an opportunity (Shecter 1970).

Boxers can easily manipulate an event. There are only two people in the ring, and if one does not hit quite as hard as he could, or falls down when hit, it is relatively difficult to prove it occurred on purpose. Yet boxing remains one of the biggest betting sports, because it meets the four necessary conditions so well. It is elemental yet technically complex, accessible, frequent, with some individuals enjoying long careers followed by plenty of fans. More importantly, there is a public feeling that most major fights are honest, because the stakes are high (not only in terms of the winning purse, but also in terms of status for future earnings) and because each boxer faces real physical danger in terms of injury in the ring and, if suspected of manipulating the outcome, physical attack from "losers of big money."

"Point betting" has also led to serious problems with "fixing" in sports gambling, primarily in collegiate basketball. With "point betting" or the bookmakers' point spread, the suspense in an event can become even greater, and more prolonged, in a one-sided game. Suppose Michigan is a 15-point favorite over Indiana, a fact that has already established the belief that Michigan is most likely to win and is considered the superior team. Sure enough, Michigan dominates the football game and is leading 21–0 in the fourth quarter, content to end the game that way, not going out of its way to embarrass the loser unnecessarily. But right down to the last play, an Indiana touchdown and an extra point can decide the bet, one way or the other. A 21–7 Michigan victory, every bit as good in the league standings as a 21–0 victory, would be a 15-point bettor's defeat (or an underdog's bettor's triumph). The element of hazard and suspense has been prolonged and intensified (Koppett 1981; Shecter 1970). Before the point spread was implemented by bookies, if Michigan was a 4-to-1 favorite, the late touchdown would have made no difference. The betting would have been decided long before the game ended. Also, many practical betting benefits arise from point betting. The illusion of figuring things out, so fundamental to sports betting, is enhanced when one tries to calculate the margin of victory, not merely the identity of the winner. Point-spread betting is even better for basketball than for football, since so many points are scored quickly, and late-game margins can fluctuate so rapidly (Figone 1989).

But every benefit contains its drawbacks—crookedness, to be blunt, is much easier. To play badly enough to lose deliberately to an inferior team requires not only a callous moral sense but also involves substantial risk of arousing suspicion (Figone 1989). However, if a favorite can guarantee that a bet on the underdog will pay off, without giving up his own victory, the moral question is blunted and the risks are fewer. All a team has to do is win by a margin smaller than the point spread—which was set illegally in the first place. Why not? Who will be hurt except those illegal bettors who are in no position to complain?

Such a rationale has been behind the fixing scandals that have plagued college basketball since the early 1930s. Involved teams that were favored attempted to play well enough to win "under the points" without actually losing. If the game got out of hand and the favored team lost, that was a shame—but the bet's success was not altered (Figone 1989).

The bookies were hurt, since illegal or not, a bookie is simply a banker whose primary function is bookmaking and needs approximately equal amounts bet each way to have enough money to pay off the winners. Ten dollars is paid for every $11 bet; the $1 profit is his commission. If the "fix is in" and the bookie does not know it, he or she will get burned because those arranging the fix will bet large amounts in the right direction. Thus, bookies have become the first line of defense against indiscriminate fixing. The fans, the club managers, the press, and the excluded players may not know that "business" is being generated, but the bookmaking community is instantly alerted to money flowing in an unexpected direction. It is usually very difficult to carry out a fix for a substantial payoff without creating a strong degree of suspicion within the bookmaking community (Figone 1989; Kaplan 1986; Sasuly 1982). And if substantial money was not involved, the event would not be worth fixing.

Of course, a bookmaker may attempt to profit from a fix by betting along with it and this has occurred in rare cases. But to the degree that a bookie functions as a broker alone, he or she needs an honest game as much as the sports promoter to avoid being "sandbagged" or "tricked" by a specific event. More importantly, a clientele of customers must be maintained and any hint of a dishonest business would cast doubt about the fairness of an event bet on which in all probability would reduce amounts of money wagered (Sasuly 1982).

Recently, there have been numerous debates regarding the legalization of sports betting. All of the established sports have pronounced their opposition to legalized betting, based on the fear that athletes might perceive that society through governmental action is putting a stamp of approval on sports betting. With this view, athletes might still bet on themselves to win and play as

Gambling

hard as possible. However, sooner or later, there is a loss and to get even the only result that athletes can guarantee is to lose the next time out (Frey 1987).

While the above concern appears realistic, sports promoters probably have a stronger interest in ensuring that sport remains for fans (especially children) an event based on the illusion that winning is "all that counts." Under legalized betting, this would subtly change to "winning the bet," and the media will invariably reflect this view, as they now do in horse racing coverage. Children will just as inevitably quickly learn to become bettors rather than sports fans. Whether this is harmful or desirable from the standpoint of society, morality, mental health, economics, and ideation may be endlessly debated. Most assuredly, legalized betting will certainly stop the growth of those particular subliminal associations that allow sports to be marketable as a reenactment of one's early life's pleasures and experiences (Koppett 1981).

Scandals Outside the United States

Over the past decade soccer (association football) has become big business in France. Many clubs have annual budgets of over 200 million francs ($37 million). However, rumors have abounded of bribes, tax evasion, fraud, and doping. In 1993, France's Olympique de Marseilles soccer team were national heroes. Not only had Marseilles won the French league championships for the fifth consecutive year, but it had also become the first French club to win the European Cup ("Corrupt" 1993).

Shortly after completing its season, one of Marseilles' players, Jean-Jacques Eydelie, was arrested and charged with attempting to bribe members of a rival team. A Valenciennes player claimed that on the eve of their French league championship game with Marseilles, he and two teammates were contacted by men whom they identified as Eydelie and Jean-Pierre Barnes, Marseilles' managing director ("Corrupt" 1993). The three players reported they were offered 200,000 francs ($34,800) to lose the game. One of the Valenciennes players, Christophe Robert, corroborated the allegation when he admitted accepting 250,000 francs ($45,750) for all three

teammates. Another Valenciennes player, Jorge Burruchaga, later acknowledged that he was approached to throw the game but said he denied accepting any money ("Corrupt" 1993). Although Marseilles and eight other French league clubs had already been investigated on various charges (including "fixing" of games), this was the first time hard evidence had surfaced in connection with French soccer.

Outside Europe, soccer's immense popularity has also been accompanied at times by scandal. In 1981, journalist Fauzy Omar detailed the rigging of a football match between Singapore and Malaysia's Selangor State. Omar quoted Singapore's coach, Jeta Singh, as admitting five of his players had accepted bribes to lose the game (Jayasankaran 1995). Omar, now senior editor of the *New Straits Times* Group and president of the Sports Writers Association of Malaysia, has disclosed that soccer corruption has been in existence since the 1970s. Government sources have reported that 85 percent of Malaysia's Premier League matches were fixed in 1994. Police investigations portray an even more dismal picture as they estimated that 95 percent of Malaysian match outcomes were rigged, with betting on certain games running as high as $2 to $4 million (Jayasankaran 1995).

Former players in the Malaysia league have detailed the manner in which betting syndicates would usually offer large sums of money to star players in return for getting these players to persuade other players to join in the fixing. Despite these alarming allegations of massive fixing in a sport that enjoys immense popularity in this country, such bribery has been hard to prosecute, according to police, due to a scarcity of evidence (Jayasankaran 1995). Interestingly, Malaysian soccer fans have not lost faith in their players even as they continue to be charged with fixing games. In the Malaysian Cup Final between Singapore and Pahang in early December 1994, 120,000 fans jammed the Shah Alam Stadium to cheer on their heroes.

Conclusion

Gambling is a multibillion-dollar industry composed of illegal and legal gambling. In some countries where sports are highly commercialized it has been estimated that both legal and illegal gambling generate profits larger than the combined profits of several of the largest manufacturers in these countries. In many societies, the difference between buying a football card from a local bookie and buying stocks lies in cultural definitions of worthiness. Some cultures define one act as disreputable and illegal, the other as an investment and praiseworthy. Both are gambles, and at some point for many people gambling becomes truly indistinguishable from the normal involvement with elements of chance that is part of living itself. As long as societies condone (or do not strongly resist gambling), and as billions of dollars continue to be wagered on sports events by millions of people, fixes will occasionally take place. The sheer volume of dollars, gamblers, and opportunities guarantees it.

—Albert J. Figone

Bibliography: Abt, Vicki, James F. Smith, and Eugene Martin Christiansen. (1985) *The Business of Risk*. Lawrence: University Press of Kansas.

Brenner, Reuven, and Gabrielle A. Brenner. (1990) *Gambling and Speculation: A Theory, a History, and a Future of Some Human Decisions*. New York: Cambridge University Press.

Coakley, Jay J. (1994) *Sport in Society: Issues and Controversies*. St. Louis: Mosby-Year Book.

Cohen, Stanley. (1977) *The Game They Played*. New York: Farrar, Straus & Giroux.

"Corrupt as a Parrot." (1993) *Economist* 328 (7818): 46.

Figone, Albert J. (1989) "Gambling and College Basketball: The Scandal of 1951." *Journal of Sport History* 16, 1: 44–61.

Frey, James H., ed. (1987) "Gambling on Sports." *Arena Review* 11, 1: 8–14.

Isaacs, N. D. (1975) *All the Moves: A History of College Basketball*. New York: J. B. Lippincott Co.

Jayasankaran, J. (1995) "Offside: Red Faces Follow Match Fixing Revelations." *Far Eastern Economic Review* 158, 2: 20.

Kaplan, H. Roy (1986) "Sports, Gambling, and Television: The Emerging Alliance." In *Fractured Focus: Sport as a Reflection of Society*, edited by Richard E. Lapchick. Lexington, MA: D. C. Heath & Co.

Koppett, Leonard. (1981) *Sports Illusion, Sports Reality: A Reporter's View of Sports, Journalism and Society*. Boston: Houghton Mifflin.

McPherson, B. D., J. E. Curtis, and J. W. Loy. (1989) *The Social Significance of Sport: An Introduction to the Sociology of Sport*. Champaign, IL: Human Kinetics.

Merchant, Larry. (1973) *The National Football League Lottery*. New York: Holt, Rinehart, and Winston.

Rader, Benjamin G. (1990) *American Sports: From the Age of Folk Games to the Age of Televised Sports*. Englewood Cliffs, NJ: Prentice-Hall.

Roberts, Randy, and James S. Olson. (1989) *Winning Is the Only Thing: Sports in America since 1945*. Baltimore: Johns Hopkins University Press.

Rosen, Charles. (1978) *Scandals of 51: How the Gamblers Almost Killed College Basketball*. New York: Holt, Rinehart & Winston.

Sasuly, Richard. (1982) *Bookies and Bettors: Two Hundred Years of Gambling*. New York: Holt, Rinehart, and Winston.

Schuetz, Richard J., Jr. (1976) "Sports, Technology, and Gambling." In *Gambling and Society: Interdisciplinary Studies on the Subject of Gambling*, edited by William R. Eadington. Springfield, IL: Charles C. Thomas.

Shecter, Leonard. (1970) *The Jocks*. New York: Bobbs-Merrill.

Gay Games

The Gay Games are a group of international athletic contests for homosexual men and women. Held once every four years in a designated city, they feature a week of competitions in swimming, track and field, tennis, and many other sports. The name derives from the word "gay," which is a term that refers to homosexuals, who are people sexually attracted to others of the same gender. The word also refers to the community and culture of homosexuals.

In terms of participation and attendance, the Gay Games are among the largest athletic events in the world. They are organized largely on a volunteer basis by members and supporters of the Federation of Gay Games and by local residents in the city where they are to be held. The Gay Games are a nonprofit venture, financed by corporate sponsorships, private contributions, registration and admission fees, and other revenue sources.

Origins

The Gay Games originated in the early 1980s in San Francisco, California. They were founded by Dr. Tom Waddell, a gay physician who was active in athletics all his life. In 1968 he competed in the decathlon in the Olympic Games. He had also been an army paratrooper and traveled extensively. Waddell decided to organize an international athletic event that would showcase gay athletes and emphasize fellowship and widespread participation. While the event is primarily oriented to the gay community, Waddell also wanted the Gay Games to help reduce stereotypes of homosexuals and to foster a larger sense of unity among all people. Reflecting these goals, participation in the Gay Games is open to men and women of all levels of athletic ability, ages, backgrounds, political beliefs, and sexual orientations. Heterosexuals are invited to participate as both athletes and spectators.

The first Gay Games were held in San Francisco in 1982. San Francisco was also the site of the second Gay Games in 1986. Gay Games III took place in Vancouver, British Columbia, in 1990. Gay Games IV were held in New York City in June 1994, and Gay Games V is scheduled to take place in Amsterdam, Holland, in August 1998.

The basic format of the Gay Games is similar to that of the Olympics, and Waddell originally intended to call the event the Gay Olympics. However, the U.S. Olympic Organizing Committee filed a suit that legally prevented Waddell from using that name, and the event became the Gay Games instead. In addition, each quadrennial event often has a separate name based on a theme. The 1982 Gay Games were also known as Challenge '82, the 1986 games as Triumph '86, the 1990 Gay Games as Celebration '90, and the 1994 Gay Games were Unity '94.

Development

The scope of the Gay Games expanded markedly in their early years. The first Gay Games in 1982 had a field of approximately 1,300 athletes competing in 16 events. The 1986 Gay Games drew approximately 3,500 participants. Over 7,000 athletes competed in the 1990 Gay Games in Vancouver. By 1994, Gay Games IV featured approximately 11,000 athletes from 44 countries, with events representing over 30 sports held at 42 different locations in the New York area. The initial field in the 1994 tennis tournament alone included approximately 900 players. It was estimated that 500,000 people went to New York as participants and spectators during the eight-day 1994 event. The Gay Games also feature large opening and closing ceremonies. A crowd of 40,000 people attended the closing ceremony in 1994.

The event has grown in other ways. The first Gay Games had an operating budget of approximately $100,000. The 1994 Gay Games budget was over $6 million, and the event was estimated to have brought $100 million in added tourism and other revenue into the New York City economy. The projected budget for the 1998 games in Amsterdam is $9.3 million. As the Gay Games have become more visible and prominent, they have attracted sponsorship funding from large corporations and other businesses, who see the games as a way to promote themselves to a large market. Some people, however, have contended that the Gay Games should not become too large and commercialized.

The multifaceted event reflects the diversity that exists within the international gay community. In many respects, its events, athletes, and spectators are indistinguishable from those in other athletic tournaments. The Gay Games have been largely accepted by people who are not gay, and many cities compete to be selected as the site. In other ways, however, the Gay Games have reflected issues, lifestyles, and social and cultural interests that are more specific to the gay community.

Events

The roster of sports in the Gay Games includes a wide range of Olympic events and other popular traditional sports, as well as newer or more specialized ones. In addition to a basic core of perennial sports, other events have been added or replaced in different years. Sports represented in the Gay Games have included track and field events and endurance marathons, ice hockey, swimming, tennis, wrestling, figure skating, volleyball, flag football, in-line skating, rock climbing, martial arts, bodybuilding, softball, competitive aerobics, golf, billiards, bowling, croquet, squash, cycling, and many others. The Gay Games also feature events that are not based on athletic ability to augment the other contests. The scheduled roster for the 1998 games included bridge, chess, ballroom dancing, and other recreational activities. In addition to mainstream sports and recreational activities, the less conventional aspects of gay culture are also represented in the Games. One of the more unusual Gay Games events has been the Pink Flamingo, a swimming relay in which participants are

The Gay Games, seen here at New York University in 1994, serve to shatter stereotypes about homosexuals.

dressed in drag and other flamboyant costumes and hand off a plastic flamingo during the relay switch-offs. In 1994, the first international same-sex ice-dancing skating competition was held at the Gay Games.

Reflecting its basic purpose as an international celebration, the Gay Games also feature activities other than athletics, including an extensive arts and cultural festival. Events sponsored by other organizations or individuals take place in the cities where the games are held. The Gay Games gained particular visibility in 1994, because they were scheduled to coincide with rallies and other events to commemorate the anniversary of the 1969 Stonewall riot in New York. (The Stonewall riot is considered a landmark in the history of gay activism.)

Participation in the Gay Games is open to athletes of all levels of ability, and participants are encouraged to focus on camaraderie and accomplishing "personal bests" rather than victory. There are no eligibility requirements based on current or past performance in a sport. As a result, the field for competitions has included participants of many different skill levels. In addition to those of limited ability who participate simply for enjoyment, the Gay Games attract many serious and accomplished athletes. In 1994, former Olympic gold medalist Bruce Hayes broke three world freestyle swimming records for men ages 30 to 34 at the Gay Games. Another swimmer, James Ballard, set a 100-meter backstroke record in the same age category.

However, some debates have arisen over how to balance the competitive and noncompetitive aspects of the Gay Games. As in other tournaments, winners receive awards based on how they place in the events. Some people believe that too much emphasis on serious competition detracts from the open philosophy the games are based on. Others, however, contend that the most accomplished athletes at the games should be awarded.

The Gay Games have also reflected larger issues, such as the differences and conflicts that sometimes exist among different segments of gay people and between the gay community and heterosexual society. In 1994, for example, critics of homosexuality tried to stop the New York City administration from supporting the presence of the Gay Games there. While most participants in the games are open about their sexual orientation, some athletes have competed anonymously to avoid facing discrimination in their personal lives by revealing their sexual orientation. On occasion, open displays of the more unconventional aspects of gay life have also caused discomfort and criticism. The conservative journal *National Review,* for example, expressed strong disapproval in an editorial (1 August 1994) about a contingent of naked marchers in a Gay Games parade in New York.

The Gay Games have also been affected by the disease AIDS (acquired immune deficiency syndrome), which has been a major crisis in the gay community in the 1980s and 1990s. Gay Games founder Tom Waddell died at age 49 of AIDS in 1987. Participants and spectators in the games have included people infected with the HIV virus (which causes AIDS). In 1994, the administration of President Bill Clinton temporarily relaxed government immigration restrictions by granting a ten-day waiver to allow HIV-infected athletes from other nations to enter the United States to participate in the Gay Games. In addition to other personal reasons for participating in the Gay Games, HIV-infected athletes have often taken part in them to offer inspiration and to demonstrate that people with the virus can continue to live vigorous lives.

—John Townes

Bibliography: Clark, Joe. (1994) "Let the Games Begin." *Village Voice* (New York), 21 June.

Clines, Francis X. (1994) "Let the Games and the Lobbying Begin." *New York Times,* 17 June.

McKinley, James, Jr. (1994) "Marathon and Ceremony Bring Gay Games to a Close." *New York Times,* 26 June.

Schaap, Dick. (1987) "The Death of an Athlete." *Sports Illustrated,* 27 July.

Smith, Chris. (1994) "A Guide to the Games." *New York Magazine,* 20 June.

Geography

It is only in the last two decades that geographers have begun to apply their skills and concepts to the serious study of sports. Geographers explore the regional variations in sporting participation, the spatial and environmental impact of sports, the geographic diffusion of sport, and the character of the sports landscape. In addition to the interest in sports shown by a number of professional geographers, it is also evident that much implicitly geographical work on sports has been undertaken by scholars in other disciplines. The journal *Sports Place* carries articles reflecting current geographical approaches to the study of sports.

It is always possible to find antecedents to geographers' current interest in sports. In 1919, for example, *National Geographic* magazine published an article entitled "Geography of Games." The article reflected the prevailing approach to geography, emphasizing environmental influences on athletic participation and performance. Such environmentally deterministic studies of sports

continued into the 1950s, but they were extremely few in number. Since then sports geographic studies have tended to reflect the broad approaches that have characterized geography per se. As geography itself has tended to branch toward anarchy, a wide variety of approaches have also been applied to the geography of sports.

Geographic Variations

Professor John Rooney of Oklahoma State University published the first academic paper of any note on the geography of sport. His paper "Up from the Mines and Out from the Prairies" was published in the *Geographical Review* in 1969. Rooney highlighted the marked spatial variations in the high school origins of college footballers. This led him to identify a number of football regions in the United States. These regions often varied according to whether state footballer output was measured in absolute or per capita terms. For example, Rooney was able to show that Texas had a number of "hotbeds" of footballer production when using a per capita approach, whereas in absolute terms the largest cities were the major producers.

Because some states in the United States produce more college-level footballers than their instate colleges can "consume," a considerable amount of interstate talent migration takes place. A number of maps accompanying Rooney's text dramatically illustrate not only the interstate patterns of footballer production but also the interstate flows of the sport's migrant athletes. Rooney's pioneering paper was followed by many others on interstate variations in sports talent production (in a number of sports) and the associated migration patterns. Some of the migration studies tried to model or predict the number of footballers who would migrate to particular destinations from a given state. Such studies adopted the use of the "gravity model" (a model that has been used to account for a wide variety of flow patterns in human geography) and hence reflected the quantitative approach many geographers had adopted during the 1960s and 1970s.

Rooney wrote the first book on the geography of sport in 1972. The book focused on the per capita approach and included a large number of

Geography

Sunshine

The relationship between sunshine and sport has in the main been largely ignored by sport analysts. The only direct considerations are those made by sports scientists in terms of human performance and by those concerned with the dangers of excessive exposure to the sun's harmful rays. This is strange when one reflects upon the centrality of the sun in our myths, religions, history, in all aspects of our daily lives.

Indigenous peoples from places as disparate as Mexico and Australia enlisted sporting activities or at least games in their ritualistic attempts to appease the elements or to call for their gods to grant them bountiful harvests. The athletes of ancient Greece are said to have trained in the full heat of the day to strengthen their bodies yet they also covered themselves in exotic oils to offset the harmful effects of the same rays. There is even a theory that some of the events of the ancient games were held in the light of the full moon, now would not that debunk many a myth relating to origins of modern sport? It is said that nations and cultures are products of their climate and geography. Sports are similarly products of their environments, winter sports and aquatics most obviously spring to mind. The greatest exportation of sport as a cultural form came with the cultural imperialism that followed the rise of the British Empire. This saw the proselytization of what were essentially cold climate sports to hot climates. When considered logically, cricket is hardly a suitable game to be played under the ravages of the Australian or the South African sun, let alone the oppressive heat and humidity of the Indian subcontinent. Similarly, rugby played on the concrete-like grounds of outback Queensland or the Veldt is not a pleasant experience. However, such sports were avidly adopted by the young colonies of the empire and soon they challenged the motherland for supremacy in the games that formed her very cultural core. Australians proved to be more than a match at cricket whilst the New Zealand All Blacks of the Edwardian era were virtually unbeatable. And, in the greatest game of all, warfare, these colonial upstarts also proved themselves superior to the pale, wan, and apparently unathletic British conscripts. Clearly, it was the far healthier environment, the sun, clean air, and the vigorous outdoor lives these young colonials experienced that had produced this eugenic miracle, or so the story went. Undoubtedly, their lifestyles were in the main more physical and their diets and living environments more wholesome, yet it was also the very finest and the fittest from these young nations that volunteered to fight.

As tennis, golf, swimming, and athletics began to establish themselves as world sports, the countries that were best endowed in terms of the climate initially gained the ascendancy. Australians and Americans dominated the rankings, as their players could always be assured of at least a good (sunny) summer and in such places as California, Queensland, and Hawaii the sun apparently always shone. Talent abounded and opportunity and access existed for all aspiring hopefuls in these sunshine states. The need for scientific coaching and training was minimal, as just doing it was enough. This soon changed as sport became more and more commercialized and as it was enlisted in the race for ideological supremacy. It was no longer sufficient just to be able to swim or play in the sun. Much sport came to require a systematized regime of professionals, ranging from physiologists to business managers. The sun alone was no longer enough.

—Peter A. Horton

maps and tables documenting the marked regional differences in the number of participants, clubs, and facilities for sports. His approach produced meticulously researched and drawn maps that are of intrinsic interest. They are also of significance to planners, development agencies, and sports goods industries concerned with exploring gaps in the market for sports or with the recruitment of sports talent. This latter theme, athletic recruitment, was the subject of Rooney's second book, *The Recruiting Game*. This was essentially an exercise in applied sports geography, taking the scramble for collegiate athletic talent as its focus. A mixture of cartography, sensitive writing, and ethnography, it sought geographic solutions to the abuses of recruiting by America's sport-oriented universities. It suggested, for example, that the draft should be organized on regional lines, hence producing teams with players primarily from their own locale. Teams would then be truly representative of their home areas and would retain their regional identity.

Geographic variations in sports were also explored by geographers outside the United States. In Britain Rooney's approach was followed, albeit 10 years later, with studies of a wide variety of sports in the United Kingdom with special emphasis placed on soccer (Bale 1982). Studies confirmed that northeast England was a hotbed of soccer player production, although the geographic extremes of productivity had become less polarized over time. Similar studies were authored in

Canada, Italy, France, and Sweden. The per capita approach was taken beyond the national level to explore geographic differences at the continental and even global scale (Bale 1996). The logical outcome of the regional variations approach to a geography of sports was the emergence of a number of national sports atlases. These have been published in various formats for France, Italy, Canada, Sweden, and the United States. The monumental *Atlas of American Sport* is arguably the most ambitious and successful publication of its kind. Athletic migration was also studied, but at the global scale. The international recruiting of sports talent by American colleges and universities was examined, mapping the origins and destinations of such migrant athletes and exploring, as Rooney had done earlier at the U.S. level, the nuts-and-bolts of collegiate recruiting (Bale 1991).

Geographical Diffusion

Studies of regional variations in aspects of sports have been paralleled by those exploring the geographical diffusion of sports. In a sense, this approach adopts the perspective of geographical history, adding a spatial dimension to the evolution of sports. Such studies are much fewer in number than those from the geographical variations school. Diffusion in sports can be studied locally and globally. The stages of spatial diffusion include the place of introduction of a sport, its point of adoption, and its geographic spread. A prime problem in sports diffusion studies involves the defusing terms like "adoption." In one study of the diffusion of sport at the international scale, date of formation of a national governing body was taken as the date of a sport's adoption (see Bale 1989). This poses a number of problems because de facto governing bodies may have predated the establishment of the formal national bureaucracy. The use of date of formation of the de jure organization may therefore imply that the sport was adopted in a particular country at a later period than it in fact was.

Studies of three sports in Europe revealed that each diffused both spatially and hierarchically (see Bale 1989). A twin diffusion process seemed to take place; sports scattered outward from their country of origin and also "down" the continent's economic hierarchy. The caveat about the problems of defining the national date of adoption of a sport remains a methodological hazard, however. Such diffusion studies, like those focusing on regional variations, have been criticized because they tend to reduce human beings to dots on maps or flow lines between places. The significance of human agency in such studies is neglected.

Spatial and Environmental Impact

The impact of a sports event, be it the Olympic Games or a high school basketball game, extends beyond the site of the event itself. It has, therefore, spatial (geographic) impacts of various kinds. These may be positive or negative. Positive impacts from sports events include community well-being, additional income, and pride in a place. Research on the economic impact and regional multiplier effects of sports conducted by economist Robert Baade suggests that the regional benefits of new stadium construction or the attraction of a new franchise are more apparent than real. A study exploring the positive impacts of sports geographically was undertaken by Swedish geographer, Hans Aldskogius of Uppsala University. He examined the geographic effects of the major league ice hockey club in the small Swedish town of Leksand. He discovered that the club's impact was felt all over Sweden; indeed, some of its players were recruited from North America and other parts of Europe.

The negative impacts of sports events have been examined primarily in Britain, especially in the context of professional soccer (association football). Such studies were related to the emergence of hooliganism in soccer and sought to place hooliganism within the broader negative impacts of the sport. One finding of these studies is that negative effects of soccer may be felt among residents living more than 1 mile (1.6 kilometers) from the site of the game. Generally, the intensity of perceived nuisance declines with distance from the stadium. The major nuisances perceived by residents living around British stadiums have been found to be traffic congestion, crowding, and parking. Hooliganism is rarely viewed as the main source of soccer "pollution." Such findings have been of considerable interest in Britain because of plans to relocate many of the soccer stadiums away from residential areas.

Geography

Landscapes

The kinds of geographical studies described so far reflect the regional, quantitative, and spatial traditions of geography. A more humanistic and interpretive approach is found in studies of the landscapes of sports. A pioneer of sports landscape studies is Professor Karl Raitz of the University of Kentucky. His book, *The Theater of Sports*, contains a large number of original essays on different sports and their landscapes. Many of these essays reveal two basic features characterizing the landscapes of modern sports: The first is their high level of *spatiality*; the other is their increasing *artificiality*. They are not natural but cultural landscapes.

A pioneering paper by cultural geographer Philip Wagner drew attention to the intrinsically *spatial* nature of sports. Sports are essentially attempts to conquer space. This is not only done by the participants themselves who seek to get from one place to another faster than their opponent or who try to tactically use the area on which the game is played to their advantage. It is also found in the way the rules of sport impose geometry on the landscape and change the area of play from what was originally multifunctional land into space specifically designated for sport. A lawn tennis court, for example, can be used for little else but lawn tennis. The impact of geometry on the landscape of sport is obvious from the plans of various fields of play. It is a world of accurately measured territories, segmented and delimited. In many sports the place where a game is played has to be the same, exactly the same, as any other. There is a tendency, therefore, for sports places to typify "placelessness," relatively homogenous and standardized landscapes.

The geometry of sport means that participants literally know their places. Each player has a position. The spectators are rigidly segregated from the players, a situation that did not exist in the early days of sports. This has led some observers (particularly those taking a neo-Marxist view) to describe sports places as "prisons," but other metaphors (e.g., theater or garden) remain equally appropriate (Bale 1994).

Although sports landscapes are not natural, many sports started by using natural landscapes to which the sport appeared well suited. Golf, for example, started in Scotland on the eastern linkslands—the sand dune coastal areas. As physical geographer Robert Pryce has shown in *Scotland's Golf Courses*, however, it did not take long for it to colonize a wide variety of Scottish land forms. Today golf is played everywhere from deserts in Arizona to coniferous forests in Finland. It can also be played indoors in simulated conditions. The artificiality of many landscapes of sport is reflected in the use of technology. Concrete, plastic, and steel often characterize many landscapes of sport. Among the reasons for making the sports landscape artificial is the neutralization of the physical environment, which all too often interferes with the "ideal" sporting milieu. As a result of the imposition of geometry and artifice, the locations where sports take place are often ambiguous places. The SkyDome in Toronto, for example, is more than a sports stadium. It is part stadium, part hotel, part restaurant, part exhibition center; it is sometimes indoors, sometimes outdoors. In some ways, the introduction of artificial surfaces returns sport to the multifunctional landscape of former times.

There is not yet a geographical *theory* of sport and this is an area to which geographers may attend in the future. Given the centrality of space, place, and environment in sports, it is also possible that geography will play a greater role in the conceptualizing of modern sports.

—John Bale

Bibliography: Baade, Robert. (1995) "Stadiums, Professional Sports and City Economies: An Analysis of the United States Experience." In *The Stadium and the City,* edited by John Bale and Olof Moen. Keele, UK: Keele University Press, 277–294.

Bale, John. (1982) *Sport and Place.* London: Hurst.

———. (1991) *The Brawn Drain: Foreign Student-Athletes in American Universities.* Urbana: University of Illinois Press.

———. (1994) *Landscapes of Modern Sport.* London: Leicester University Press.

———. (1993) *Sport, Space and the City.* New York: Routledge.

———. (1989) *Sports Geography.* New York: Spon.

Dudycha, Douglas, Stephen Smith, Terry Stewart, and Barry McPherson. (1983) *The Canadian Atlas of Recreation and Exercise.* Waterloo: University of Waterloo, Department of Geography.

Kidd, Bruce. (1995) "Toronto's Sky Dome: The World's Greatest Entertainment Centre." In *The Stadium and the City,* edited by John Bale and Olof Moen. Keele, UK: Keele University Press, 175–196.

McConnell, Harold. (1984) "Recruiting Patterns of Midwestern Major College Football." *Geographical Perspectives* 53: 27–43.

Pryce, Robert. (1989) *Scotland's Golf Courses.* Aberdeen: Aberdeen University Press.

Raitz, Karl, ed. (1995) *The Theater of Sports.* Baltimore: Johns Hopkins University Press,

Rooney, John. (1972) *A Geography of American Sport: From Cabin Creek to Anaheim.* Reading, MA: Addison-Wesley.

———. (1978) *The Recruiting Game: Toward a New System of Intercollegiate Sport,* 2d ed. Lincoln: University of Nebraska Press.

Rooney, John, and Richard Pillsbury. (1992) *Atlas of American Sport.* New York: Macmillan.

Springwood, Charles. (1996) *Cooperstown to Dyersville: A Geography of Baseball Nostalgia.* Boulder, CO: Westview.

Wagner, Philip. (1983) "Sport: Geography and Culture." In *Time and Space in Geography,* edited by Allen Pred. Lund, Sweden: Gleerup, 85–108.

Gliding
See Soaring

Golf

Origins

Golf is generally stereotyped as the national game of Scotland, and St. Andrews, Fife, is recognized as its birthplace. Notwithstanding its distinctive Scottish development, however, the game claims a rich multicultural heritage that leads back to the Scottish game of shinty, Cornish and Irish hurling, and even to ancient Egyptian fertility rituals (Henderson 1974).

Golf predates cricket (1788) and association football (1863) as an organized sport. The Royal and Ancient Golf Club was founded in 1754, only a few years after the beginning of the first national sports organization, the Jockey Club (circa 1750), and the first universal rules were drawn up at the Royal and Ancient Golf Club at St. Andrews in 1822. The world's first golf tournament took place in 1860 on the Prestwick course in western Scotland, but the game itself was played well before the eighteenth century—as early as 1457, King James II prohibited the game because it was interfering with archery practice.

A list of 13 rules, the *Articles and Code of Playing Golf, St. Andrews, 1754,* is the oldest surviving official document on the sport. The St. Andrews Golf Club assumed the title "Royal and Ancient" as a result of the patronage of King William IV in 1834.

Development

Golf profited indirectly from the Catholic-tinged Protestant culture of Scotland. James VI of Scotland, for example, encouraged the adoption of a continental sort of Sabbath observance: after church, people were to be allowed to engage in appropriate recreational activities such as golf.

During the eighteenth century the game spread to England, and Scottish emigrants played a vital role in spreading it around the world. For example, New Zealand's first golf club—the Dunedin Golf Club—advertised the game in the *Otago Daily Times* of 28 September 1871 as adding "many happy (because healthful) years to the lives of those who practice it." The association was founded by a golf lover and Scotsman, C. R. Howden, who carried his love of the game to New Zealand. Despite the lack of suitable land, the golfers set up a nine-hole course in the town green belt at Mornington and fenced it off from wandering stock. Without the grazing animals, however, the grass grew so long that play eventually became impossible.

Despite the elitist aura of golf (stately golf club houses set on spacious territories of open land), the first star players were unquestionably professional and working class. In the nineteenth century the dichotomy between the professional and the amateur athlete was a major political, social, and economic divide. It is true that the greatest cricketer of his generation, W. C. Grace, enjoyed the label amateur while amassing a considerable fortune, but he was, in every sense of the word, exceptional. The norm was more accurately expressed by the British Rowing Association in 1878; it stipulated that individual membership was open to the military, civil servants, lawyers, doctors, university students and graduates, and public (that is, private) school boys. Any application from a club that had "mechanics or professional," however, was rejected.

Since 1985 the increase in corporate sponsorship and television money for golf has been extraordinary. Ever more celebrity players emerge from countries all over the world. Ernie Els (South Africa, 1969–), Vijay Singh (Fiji, 1963–), and Constantino Rocca (Italy, 1956–) are three impressive newcomers. In 1995 the controversial 29-year-old John Daly (United States) blasted his way to a British Open victory at St. Andrews, and the Ryder Cup, a biannual regional golf challenge tournament between Europe and the United States, turned into one of the most exciting sports team competitions of all time.

Canada

The first mention of golf in Canada was a Christmas 1824 announcement of a golf outing at Priest's Farm, Montreal. The Scottish connection and influence was considerable: the founding president of Canada's (and North America's) first golf club—the Montreal Golf Club (1873)—was Scottish émigré Alexander Dennistoun.

By the 1890s, greatly aided by the transcontinental network of the Canadian Pacific Railway, most Canadian cities had one golf course. Women's golf clubs were also institutionalized at this same time, and in 1898 the Ottawa Golf Club had 48 women members. Nevertheless, golf existed against a background of gender segregation.

The first golf match between U.S. and Canadian golf clubs took place at Niagara in 1896. The inaugural Canada–United States team competition occurred two years later. The United States triumphed by a score of 27–7.

Despite Canada's vast land mass, the growth of golf has nonetheless been inhibited by insufficient courses for the numbers of people wanting to play the game. By the early 1970s there were nearly 900 golf clubs in Canada with over one million male members and a quarter of a million female players.

Australia

The development of golf in Australia was also markedly influenced by Scotland. The first players, the pioneer foundation clubs, and the majority of the game's professional players were Scottish. Moreover, in the nineteenth century, the game actually exacerbated class consciousness and social divisions, for golf professionals enjoyed only restricted use of clubhouses and other facilities, and although their opinions and skills were respected, they were definitely looked down upon by the purist (and socially better-connected) amateur player.

In the twentieth century Australia has contributed much to international golf. Precision Golf Forgings and Dunlop were two Australian firms that by the innovative, indeed, radical, design and manufacture of golf clubs improved the game for novice and elite player alike. The stature of the game has been enhanced by outstanding Australian women such as Joan Hammond (made a Dame because of her lifelong services to world opera as a soprano) and Jan Stephenson (1951–), who despite moving to the United States has retained her pronounced Australian drawl. Stephenson, as well as establishing herself as a successful Ladies Professional Golf Association tour player, has also been a pioneer in accumulating commercial endorsements, helping women's golf earn commercial credibility in a world where financial sponsorship is critical to the expansion of the women's game.

Today star amateur and professional players dream of success on the lucrative stage of world golf. The celebrity status of multimillionaire Greg Norman (1952–), "The Great White Shark," serves as a powerful role model for all young and aspiring Australian golfers.

Great Britain

In Great Britain the development of golf during the twentieth century has been extraordinary. Conservative estimates suggest that more than 2 million men, women, and children regularly play golf. Despite the modernity of the game—oversized driving clubs shaped out of space-age materials, vast television, cable and satellite coverage of golfing events, Ryder Cup teams crossing the Atlantic on the Concorde—golf's ruling body seems to draw strength and stability from its autocratic heritage. In 1919 the Royal and Ancient Club, St. Andrews, became the international organization for golf. The Royal and Ancient Club has a maximum of 1,750 members, 700 of whom must be resident overseas. These 700 members represent nearly 50 countries.

United States

Although Scotland remains the traditional home of golf, the United States has become the dominant golf nation in the twentieth century.

Although the sport's origins remain unclear, golf was popularized in Scotland and was spread around the world by Scottish emigrants. A recent explosion of media attention to the sport mirrors its popularity.

The sport grew from 1,000 clubs in 1900 to 6,000 by 1930. The Professional Golfers' Association (PGA) was founded in 1916 and in that year the first PGA championship took place on the Bronxville, New York, course. The versatile athlete Babe Didrikson Zaharias (1914–1956) transformed the women's game into a major sport. Meanwhile, golfers such as Ben Hogan (1912–) demonstrated the sheer depth and toughness of stellar U.S. male golfers.

The United States' two premier golfers in the 1920s were Walter Hagen (1892–1969) and Bobby Jones (1902–1971). Hagen, who won four British Opens, is recognized as much more than a great golfer, for he virtually single-handedly changed the exclusionary nature of golf clubhouses. Hagen was a flamboyantly dressed showman and an innovator in shot making and sports psychology. His favorite one liner was, "Who's going to be second?"

Bobby Jones, meanwhile, played such a complete game that in tournament after tournament he dominated his opponents by a wide margin. Jones won all 4 major tournaments—the British Open, U.S. Open, U.S. Masters, and USPGA—and in 14 years of golf he had 13 major title successes. Whereas Hagen was a full-time professional, Jones was a part-time amateur, which makes his feats all the more remarkable. For Jones, golf was a recreation. His paid job was working in a law office. He was proud of his golfing trophies, but in his office he prominently displayed his university degrees in engineering, English, and law. Jones continued to exert a tremendous influence over golf even after his retirement from tournament play. He built the Augusta (Georgia) National Course and supervised the first Masters Tournament in 1934.

In the 1930s and 1940s the leading U.S. golfer was Byron Nelson (1912–). In 1945 he won 18 tournaments. The standard of golf is so high in the 1990s that no current golfer could hope to challenge Nelson's record total. Following Nelson came Ben Hogan and Sam Snead (1912–). The major development of golf in the post–World War II United States can be summarized in two names, Arnold Palmer (1929–) and Jack Nicklaus (1940–). Palmer internationalized the game by going to Great Britain and succeeding in the British Open. His cheerful persona and genial disposition, as well as his golfing skills, endeared him to millions. "Arnie's Army" became the label for swarms of golf aficionados who came to watch—not golf, but Arnold Palmer. Jack Nicklaus further popularized the game because he had won in his twenties—and continued to enjoy success after the age of 50 on the senior tour.

Women in Golf

Women have long been involved in golf, but they have had to struggle to gain equal standing with men. In the late nineteenth century, one Canadian golf club ruled that "lady members could use the links every morning except Saturday, and on Monday, Tuesday, Thursday, and Friday afternoons" (Redmond 1982). The major figure in establishing women's golf was Babe Didrikson Zaharias, the track and field star of the 1932 Olympics. Zaharias was the top female earner in 1948 with $3,400.00. In 1976 Judy Rankin (1945–) became the first woman golfer to top $100,000, and in 1985 Nancy Lopez (1957–) earned over $400,000.

Practice

Golf is unique among ball games in matching a single human being's skill against the forces of nature; any connection with anyone else doing the same thing at the same time is fortuitous and inessential. It is the only ball game in which one can legitimately play against oneself.

Equipment

Golf clubs evolved from primitive sticks or strong branches cut from a tree (all of one piece) to carefully crafted hickory shafts that were joined to separate wooden heads. At the beginning of the twentieth century other materials were experimented with, such as bamboo and steel. In 1926 a tubular steel shaft was accepted and, despite strong objections from the Royal and Ancient Club, St. Andrews, within a decade it became the international standard for golf clubs.

Golf bags are traced back to an innovative English sail-maker of the 1870s who introduced them to the Royal North Devon Club. Prior to that golf clubs had been carried under the arm just as a sporting gentleman transported his hunting weapons.

A complex process governed manufacture of the featherie, as the golf ball was originally known. Three narrow strips of leather were sewn together to form a bag, which was then stuffed with boiled goose feathers and covered with white paint. The expansion of the feathers made the ball more lively (Brasch 1970). Clearly such a ball had several imperfections. In wet weather it absorbed too much moisture. Eventually, as a result of wear and tear, it burst, and its design precluded it from being driven long distances.

The invention of the gutta-percha ball in 1848 (a solid ball molded from rubber), and its eventual refinement by means of pitted markings on the outside, played a crucial role in modernizing the game of golf. "Gutties" as they were known, opened up golf and made the sport available for more people at a more reasonable cost. At the beginning of the twentieth century the rubber core ball, invented in the United States, came to replace the gutta-percha ball. The production of golf equipment was an important segment of the British sports requisites trade. For example, in 1935 British firms manufactured 588,000 golf clubs and almost 11 million golf balls. The Dunlop Rubber Company was a British multinational

Golf

1995 Ryder Cup

In 1995 yachting enthusiasts smacked their lips at the prospect of a series of titanic encounters between the United States and New Zealand as these nautical adversaries battled for the America's Cup. The actual competition was a letdown; the New Zealanders won by a landslide. Later in the year the World Series in U.S. baseball promised to be a nip-and-tuck affair between the Atlanta Braves and the Cleveland Indians, but the Braves won handsomely. In international golf that same year there was a reversal of expectation and outcome. Many pundits secretly wondered if the European team stood any chance to win the Ryder Cup against the might of the United States. In fact, the three-day event (22–24 September 1995) evolved into a magnificent sport spectacular in which see-sawing fortunes transformed a seemingly gentle and elegant sport into a dramatic theater of triumph, disaster, courage, luck, derring-do, and downright nail-biting, heart-pumping suspense.

Bookmakers in Las Vegas and London offered odds of 5 to 2 against Europe. Although Europe seemed to have strong players in the likes of Nick Faldo (England), Colin Montgomerie (Scotland), and Phil Woosnam (Wales), the balance of the team seemed fragile. The in-form Jose Maria Olazabal (Spain)had to withdraw because of a leg injury, and team members Seve Ballesteros (Spain) and Berhard Langer (Germany), despite magnificent histories, were wrapping up undistinguished 1995 seasons. Moreover, the Italian on the team, Constantino Rocca, had been nastily dubbed by certain Fleet Street dailies as being Rocca "the choka" because of his faltering play two years earlier. As a result, the Belfry course in the English Midlands had witnessed a European collapse and a last-gasp U.S. triumph in the 1993 Ryder Cup. The United States, because of its vast college-based golf

"nursery," and the lucrative Professional Golf Association Tour (as well as the many satellite tours), creates a playing depth in professional golf that is, without any exaggeration, awesome. However, the U.S. 1995 team selection process was flawed, for five relative rookies made the team, whereas several seasoned professionals did not.

Since the United States had won the biennial Ryder Cup in 1993, under the rules, a draw would mean that the cup remained a U.S. trophy. At the end of the first day of competition the United States led 5 to 3. By the end of the second day the United States had retained its advantage and was up by the score of 9 to 7.

The final day contest (a series of match-play singles events) seemed like an athletic version of the Battle of Waterloo. Victories—and defeats—to paraphrase the Duke of Wellington, were a "near run thing." The military analogy was reinforced by spectators wearing camouflage fatigues and cheering "European misfits with rebel yells" ("Caps off for Europe," 1995).

Officially, Europe regained the Ryder Cup (14 1/2 to 13 1/2) when Ireland's Philip Walton defeated Jay Haas on the final hole. "Maybe the Americans know me now," gloated a delirious Walton, draped in an Irish flag and about 50 rabid fans. "Tell 'em I'm related to all those Waltons on that TV show" (Garrity 1995). Team captain and tough Texan Lanny Wadkins appeared shell-shocked as Haas, and especially Curtis Strange (one of Wadkins's special "personal" selections), seemed to lose composure in the cauldron that was Oak Hill. Nevertheless, Wadkins maintained a feisty persona at the closing ceremonies, where he advised: "Enjoy your time with this pretty little thing [Ryder Cup] . . . 'Cause two years from now, we're comin' to get it."

—Scott A. G. M. Crawford

that developed and marketed golf balls for the national and international marketplace.

Many of golf's singular "architectural" characteristics happened by chance rather than by any preconceived plan. All "cups" (golf holes on the putting greens) measure 11 centimeters (4 1/2 inches) across simply because two St. Andrews golfers found that a hole was so badly worn that they could not finish the hole. The looked around, found an old drainpipe, and used it. The size of the pipe happened to be 4 1/2 inches across, which remains today the globally recognized size of a cup. Even the concept of playing 18 holes (the first such course was at St. Andrews in 1764) evolved haphazardly. Scoring took place with an out-and-back playing sequence. In other words, 9-hole courses (9 holes "out" and then the same 9 holes back

"in"), allowed for 18 actual holes of golf. St. Andrews eventually discarded this method and adopted a standard of separate fairways.

Bunkers, or hollow depressions filled with sand, were originally created as a result of the impact of weather on golfing land, especially on links golf courses, which are shaped out of the terrain adjoining sea and ocean.

In the United States, spectator facilities have become important in the Tournament Players clubs built by the PGA since 1980. These massive architectural creations, with grass amphitheaters and colossal spectator mounds, capitalize on a sport that is "part golf course, part theater." The exemplar is the Augusta National Golf Club, site of the Masters, which has taken on a legendary, heroic and mystical aura.

While golf is now a global sport, the contrasting protocols of British and U.S. golf are intriguing. Transatlantic radio commentator Alistair Cooke (1985) noticed at least one cultural quirk:

So the British, of all ages, still walk to the course. On trips to Florida or the American Desert, they still marvel, or shudder, at the fleets of electric carts going off in the morning like the first assault wave of the Battle of El Alamein. It is unlikely, for sometime, that a Briton will come across in his native land such a scorecard as Henry Longhurst rescued from a California club and cherished till the day he died. The last on its list of local rules printed the firm warning: "A player on foot has no standing on the course."

Caddies

Linguistically, the word caddie had a French root (cadet), and then in Scotland, the word came to be spelled "caddie." Originally caddies cleaned and carried clubs, marked the holes, and indicated the exact location of the cup and green (the sticks that were used eventually became a permanent addition to the game and were known as "flagsticks"). In the pre-tee-peg era, the caddies sprinkled a small mound of sand on the driving area so that the golfer could more easily strike and drive the ball.

Caddies occupied the lowest rung on the golf course occupational ladder; above them were the professionals and the green keepers. At the outbreak of World War I there were an estimated 11,000 caddies in England and Wales. It was possible for caddies to move up the job ladder (Lowerson 1993). Some made it a career. Scotland's most famous caddie, Tip Anderson of St. Andrews, caddied for the victorious Arnold Palmer at the 1995 British Open as he had 32 years before; the two announced it would be their last tandem performance.

Big Games and Big Purses

In 1995 the Professional Golf Association (European Tour division) decided to climax the season by crossing the Atlantic and playing on a Braselton, Georgia, course designed by Hall of Famers Gene Sarazen (1902–), Sam Snead (1912–), and Kathy Whitworth (1939–). The course, called "The Legends," is 6,368 meters (6,967 yards). The purse is $1.9 million dollars with a first prize of $350,000. The tournament (the final days) was covered live by U.S. cable television. In 1994 South African Ernie Els (1969–) won the inaugural tournament with a 3-stroke victory over American Fred Funk.

The winners of the four majors and 61 national opens in the two-year period ending with 1995 British Open were invited. The field included British Open victor John Daly (1966–), Sam Torrance (1953–) of Scotland (winner of the 1995 Italian and Irish Open), Mark Calcavecchia (1960–) of the United States (1993 Argentina Open), Brad Faxon (1961–) of the United States (1993 Australian Open), and Mark O'Meara (1957–) of the United States (1994 Argentina Open).

Gene Sarazen, as befits one of golf's legends, was allowed to select for the tournament his "Squire's Selections." Sarazen, who popularized the golf cap and knickerbockers, had an electrifying start to his career in 1922 when, at the age of 20, he won both the U.S. Open and the USA PGA Championship. In 1995 golf's eldest legend (93 years old) was living on Marco Island, Florida. In an interview he reminded his audience that he dropped out of school in the sixth grade and changed his name from Eugenio Saraceni to Gene Sarazen (in 1918) so he sounded like a golfer, not a violinist. Currently, his favorite golfer is Greg Norman, and his major hobby is watching televised senior golf. The "Squire's Selections" were three golfers from the United States (Lee Janzen (1964–), Craig Stadler (1953–), and Fuzzy Zoeller (1951–) and one from Zimbabwe (Mark McNulty (1953–).

The internationalism of golf is nicely reflected by the sponsor site and the countries of origin (of the top players) at the penultimate event of the PGA European Tour (late October 1995). The sponsor was the Swedish automobile manufacturer Volvo; the location was the Valderrama course in Sotogrande, Spain; the winner was a Czech-born German, Alexander Cejka (1970–); the runner up was Scotland's Colin Montgomerie (1963–). This second place took Montgomerie to the year's record-breaking purse—$1,319,381.

The season-ending PGA Tour Championship was won by Billy Mayfair (1946–) of the United States. He closed with a 3 over par 73 for a two-stroke victory over Corey Pavin of the United

States and Australia's Steve Elkington (1962–). Mayfair took home a check for $540,000. The first two rounds were televised by ESPN and the final rounds by ABC.

The 1995 PGA tour circuit ended with Greg Norman winning his third career money title. He won a record $1,654,959 in 16 starts. He also leads the PGA career tour list with $9,592,829. Tour championship winner Billy Mayfair was second with $1,543,192. Norman won the PGA of America's Player of the Year Award.

In 1954 the average purse on the PGA was $23,108. Nine years later the figure was $47,550. In 1962 Arnold Palmer became the first golfer to earn six figures in a single season. A decade later the "Golden Bear" Jack Nicklaus won more than $300,000. In 1980 Tom Watson (1949– , the captain of the successful 1993 U.S. Ryder Cup team) grossed over half a million dollars.

The game's rewards are such that players' preparations are extraordinary. *Sports Illustrated* very matter-of-factly described Mayfair's daily counseling sessions with his sport psychologist, Dr. Bob Rottela, a professor at the University of Virginia.

The Senior Tour (designed for male players aged 50 and over) was launched in 1981 and has become sensationally successful. In 1990 the tour totaled 42 tournaments worth $25 million in prize money. The final event of the 1995 Senior PGA Tour was the Emerald Coast Classic played in November on the 6,115 meters (6,691 yards), par 71 course at Milton, Florida. The prize winner receives $150,000 out of a total purse of $1 million and the event receives delayed cable television coverage. Dave Stockton (1941–) of the United States leads the money list with $1,303,280 earnings in 1995. Other Americans Jim Colbert (1941– ; $1,167,352) and Bob Murphy (1943– ; $1,146,591) are in second and third places. The "seniors" structure not only extends the playing life of professionals but it enhances their potential for achievement and recognition. Stockton, Colbert, and Murphy were good but not outstanding players as younger professionals; as senior citizens (over the age of 50) they are prospering. No other sport remotely approaches golf in offering athletic fame and fortune for older participants. Left-hander Bob Charles (1936–) of New Zealand, for example, won the 1963 Open as a young visitor to Great Britain. In

late 1995, Charles, who divides his time between the United States and New Zealand, won the Kaanapali Seniors Classic in Hawaii at the age of 59. His six-figure winner's check gives some indication of the incentive for golfers to continue the peripatetic existence of the touring pro.

The climax to the Ladies Professional Golf Association 1995 Tour was at the 5,870 meters (6,423 yards), par 72 course in Hashimotocho, Japan, in November. Of a total purse of $700,000, $105,000 will go to the winner. A significant factor for the women's tour in the last two years has been the impact of European golfers. The driving power of Britain's Laura Davies (1963–) has helped to legitimize the women's game. Scandinavian players (recruited to play golf for intercollegiate athletics programs at U.S. universities), such as Annika Sorenstam (1970–) and Helen Alfredsson (1965–), have also arrived on the women's golf scene. Sorenstam won the 1995 World Championship of Women's Golf and heads the money title list with $660,224. She also won the 1995 U.S. Women's Open Championship—the sixth foreign winner in the tournament's 50-year history. Alfredsson was voted the 1995 Most Valued Player on the LPGA tour.

The development of professional golf is graphically illustrated by the growth of the PGA tour. In 1950 it was hosted by 12 cities, largely in California, Arizona, and Texas. Twenty years later the tour embraced 30 cities, and by 1990 there were 41 states on the tour. In the same year the LPGA tour included 37 cities. The two tours are coordinated so that the events complement rather than compete with each other.

The growth of amateur golf in the United States has also been phenomenal. It has been estimated that 21.7 million Americans play at least one round of golf and spent $20 billion on golf and golf-related services per year (Stoddart 1994).

Elitism

Private courses restrict play to members. Annual dues range from several hundred dollars to six figure totals for the most expensive metropolitan areas. Golf in the United States has been accused of discriminating against minority groups. In a 1995 *Sports Illustrated* profile, golf celebrity Tom Watson observed that he gave up his membership in the Kansas City Country Club in 1990 "over its blackballing of a prospective Jewish member."

Golf historically has shown a grave insensitivity to race relations. During the worst years of South Africa's apartheid system one of the country's so-called homelands (satellite states set up to avoid granting political rights to blacks in South Africa itself), Bophuthatswana, organized an annual rich golf tournament at the Sun City resort. Despite the international sports boycott of South Africa and warnings from the U.S. State Department, Jack Nicklaus, Lee Trevino, and other big-name players continued to attend the tournament. Only Tom Watson stayed away.

There are very few successful African American professional golfers—a phenomenon that is not merely puzzling but disturbing. The history of black involvement in golf, the history of their primary sport involvement (as players), and the history of their secondary sport involvement (as spectators) reveal reprehensible levels of social segregation and racial discrimination. Indeed revisionist histories are urgently needed to address, for example, the role of the Augusta National Golf Club and the Masters tournament in excluding black members and players long after the civil rights movement of the 1960s. A case can be made that golfing icons such as Palmer and Nicklaus failed to be the catalysts for racial integration that they could have been had they considered it a priority. It is not sufficient to point to the talented African-American golfer "Tiger" Woods—now a student and an amateur athlete at Stanford University—and argue that his case offers an effective rebuttal of claims about institutional discrimination. The PGA does not seem to have explored strategies for raising the numbers of minority groups involved in professional golf. The mentoring of young black professionals, the employment of black caddies, and school programs designed to attract minorities to golf rather than to football, basketball, or baseball seem to have been ignored.

Golf in Popular Culture

Golf lends itself to wonderful story telling. Great comics frequently spike their repertoire with "tall tales" and amusing anecdotes about golf. P. G. Wodehouse, the artful creator of Jeeves and Wooster, delighted in parodying upper-crust English eccentricity. He adored golf and repeatedly used it as an artistic backdrop for gossip, romantic intrigue, and melodrama. In *Chester Forgets Himself* Wodehouse describes one luckless golfer: "He never spared himself in his efforts to do it [the ball] a violent injury. Frequently he had cut a blue dot almost in half with his niblick."

Alec Morrison, in an anthology of golf writing, gives a taste of golf literature, from the erotic (James Bond's golf match with Goldfinger), to the existential (John Updike's Rabbit Angstrom savoring the cerebral ecstasy of a glorious five-iron shot), to the farcical (Dan Jenkins and *The Dogged Victims of Inexorable Fate*).

H. M. Zucker and L. J. Babich profile 48 golf films in their *Sports Films*. The 1980 movie *Caddyshack* with Chevy Chase, Bill Murray, and Rodney Dangerfield offers hilarious clowning. *Follow the Sun* (1951) is a nicely told story of Ben Hogan's life, with Glen Ford in the starring role. Real-life golfers Sam Snead, James Demaret, and Cary Middlecoff have cameo roles. In the 1952 classic *Pat and Mike*, Pat Pemberton (played by Katherine Hepburn) becomes a professional touring athlete (golf and tennis), Mike Conovan (played by Spencer Tracy) is her manager, and Babe Zaharias displays her considerable athletic gifts as a golf champion.

—Scott A. G. M. Crawford

Bibliography: Abrahams, R. L. A. (1995) "Golf." In *The Theater of Sport*, edited by K. B. Kaitz. Baltimore: Johns Hopkins University Press.

Brasch, R. (1970) *How Did Sports Begin?* New York: David McKay.

Bomberger, M. (1995) "Par for the Course." *Sports Illustrated* 83, 20 (6 November).

"Caps off for Europe." (1995) *Economist* 336 (30 September): 7934.

Cayleff, S. E. (1995) *Babe, The Life and Legend of Babe Didrikson Zaharias*. Urbana: University of Illinois Press.

Cooke, A. (1985) "Golf—The Old Fashioned Way." *New York Times Sports Magazine*, 31 March.

Cousins, G. (1975) *Golf in Britain*. London: Routledge and Kegan Paul.

Crosset, T. W. (1995) *Outsiders in the Clubhouse—The World of Women's Professional Golf*. Albany: State University of New York Press.

Dobereiner, P. (1973) *The Glorious World of Golf*. London: Hamlyn.

Fields, B. (1995) "Man of the Century." *Golf World* 49, 21 (24 November).

Garrity, J. (1995) "Point of View." *Sports Illustrated*. 83, 3 (17 July).

Harris, H. A. (1975) *Sport in Britain*. London: Hutchinson.

Henderson, R. W. (1974) *Ball, Bat and Bishop—The Origin of Ball Games*. Detroit: Gale Research Company.

Hickok, R. (1992) *The Encyclopedia of North American Sports History*. New York: Facts on File.

Jones, S. G. (1988) *Sport, Politics and the Working Class—Organized Labor and Sport in Inter-war Britain*. Manchester: Manchester University Press.

Lowerson, J. (1993) *Sport and the English Middle Classes, 1870–1914*. Manchester: Manchester University Press.

Morrison, A. (1995) *The Impossible Art of Golf: An Anthology of Golf Writing*. New York: Oxford University Press.

One Hundred Years of Golf. (1971) Dunedin: Otago Golf Club.

Porter, D. L. ed. (1995). *African-American Sports Greats—A Biographical Dictionary*. Westport, CT: Greenwood Press.

Redmond, G. (1982) *The Sporting Scots of Nineteenth Century Canada*. East Brunswick, NJ: Fairleigh Dickinson University Press.

Reilly, R. (1995a) "Road Test." *Sports Illustrated* 83, 4 (24 July).

———. (1995b) "Wrong Man, Wrong Time." *Sports Illustrated* 83, 14 (2 October).

———. (1995c) "Another World." *Sports Illustrated* 83, 25 (11 December).

Rooney, J. F., and R. Pillsbury. (1992) *Atlas of American Sport*. New York: Macmillan.

Stoddart, B. (1994) "Golf International: Considerations of Sport in the Global Marketplace." In *Sport in the Global Village*, edited by R. C. Wilcox. Morgantown, WV: Fitness Information Technology.

Wind, H. W. (1975) *The Story of American Golf*. New York: Alfred A. Knopf.

Vamplew, W., K. Moore, J. O'Hara, R. Cashman, and I. Jobling. (1992) *Oxford Companion to Australian Sport*. Melbourne: Oxford University Press.

Zucker, H. M., and L. J. Babich. (1987) *Sports Films—A Complete Reference*. Jefferson, NC: McFarland.

Greyhound Racing

See Coursing

Gymkhana

See Horseback Riding, Gymkhana

Gymnastics

Some form of gymnastics has existed since the earliest known sport activity in human history. Modern apparatus and the modern form of the sport began to appear early in the nineteenth century and have continued evolving to the present time. As a competitive sport today, *artistic gymnastics* includes six events for men (floor exercise, high bar, parallel bars, pommel horse, rings, and vault) and four for women (floor exercise, uneven bars, balance beam, and vault). *Modern rhythmic gymnastics* is a women's sport in which light hand apparatus is used to accompany dance movements.

Once nearly exclusively a European sport, gymnastics has become universally practiced, although its development is still minor in Africa and much of Latin America and Asia. International competition in artistic gymnastics since 1952 has been dominated by men and women of the former Soviet Union, Japanese men, and Romanian women, with additional top performances from Germany, Czechoslovakia, and other European countries and more recently from China and the United States.

Origins

Tumbling and balancing activities were performed in China and Egypt before 2000 B.C.E. In the second millennium B.C.E. Minoan athletes on Crete not only tumbled and balanced, but grasped the horns of a charging bull and vaulted with a front handspring to a landing on the animal's back. As part of their practice of skills needed in war, the ancient Romans used wooden horses to practice mounting and dismounting. This apparatus evolved into the gymnastics vaulting and pommel horses, early models of which were built to look like horses with saddles or at least had one end curved upwards like a horse's neck. The three sections of the gymnastics horse still retain the names *neck*, *saddle*, and *croup*.

During the Middle Ages and early Renaissance, acrobats made a living as court entertainers, but it was not until the late eighteenth and early nineteenth centuries that a modern form of gymnastics began to take shape. Around that time many pieces of gymnastics apparatus were invented, mostly by Germans such as Johann Friedrich Guts Muths (1759–1839) and Friedrich Ludwig Jahn (1778–1852). Danish, Swiss, and Italian educators also promoted gymnastics activity. In the early nineteenth century, important contributions to gymnastics originated in Sweden, and gymnastics activity began in the United States.

In the United States, German and Swiss immigrants established Turnverein clubs (American Turners) and Czechoslovakians established Sokol clubs (American Sokols). The American Turners promoted the introduction of physical education classes in American schools, and most early school physical education activity involved gymnastics. In the late 1800s many schools favored Swedish gymnastics, a highly structured system of exercises that used specialized apparatus and was advocated as having healthful benefits for both men and women. The Young Men's Christian Association (YMCA) has also been an important force in promoting gymnastics and sponsoring competition for both men and women. The Amateur Athletic Union (AAU) held its first national gymnastics championships in 1888 and controlled the sport for the next half century until conflicts with the National Collegiate Athletic Association (NCAA) and other considerations eventually led to formation of the U.S. Gymnastics Federation in 1962.

Around the turn of the twentieth century there was a de-emphasis of gymnastics in the United States, responding to American educators' preference for team sports as fostering democratic and social skills and developing more physical symmetry and grace. Except for the anomalous 1904 Games in St. Louis, Americans did not participate in Olympic gymnastics until 1920. College gymnastics competition grew after that time, and the NCAA held its first national gymnastics championships in 1938. However, NCAA competition was for men only until 1980. A national gymnastics championship for women was first held in 1969, sponsored by the American Association for Health, Physical Education and Recreation's Division for Girls and Women's Sport, and the Association for Intercollegiate Athletics for Women sponsored championships for women from 1971 until 1982, when the NCAA gained control of this function.

After World War II, and especially since the early 1960s, gymnastics has grown phenomenally in the United States. Much of this growth has been due to the greatly increased coverage of gymnastics on television, and especially to the Olympic performances of Olga Korbut in 1972 and Nadia Comaneci in 1976. Growth of women's gymnastics in the United States has been especially great since 1972, with most of the activity taking place in private clubs, and the participation of these clubs in the Junior Olympic program. Rising support of gymnastics was closely related to America's poor showing in the sport in international competition (especially in comparison with the Soviet Union).

International gymnastics competition before World War II was dominated by Western European countries. In the Olympic Games of 1896 through 1948, Switzerland, Finland, and Italy won team medals four times each, the United States, France, and Hungary, twice each, and eight other countries (all European), once each. The team gold was won by Italy four times, and once each by Switzerland, Finland, the United States, Germany, and Sweden. Individual medals were won by the United States (22.1 percent), Switzerland (19.5 percent), Germany (11.1 percent), Finland (8.9 percent), Czechoslovakia (8.4 percent), Italy (6.8 percent), France (6.3 percent), and all others (nine European countries; 16.9 percent). The proportion of U.S. medals is strongly affected by the results of the 1904 St. Louis Olympics, where almost all of the participants (and medal winners) were Americans. Women's Olympic gymnastics competition was held in 1928, 1936, and 1948, with Czechoslovakia, Germany, and Holland winning the team gold medal once each, and Hungary (2), Czechoslovakia, Great Britain, Italy, and the United States winning other team medals.

With the entrance of the Soviet Union into Olympic competition in 1952 and the rise of Japan as a gymnastics power, the picture changed radically. In the eleven Olympic Games between 1952 and 1992 the men's team gold medal was won five times each by the Soviet Union and Japan and once by the United States. Over this period, men's team medals were won by the Soviet Union (10), Japan (9), East Germany (5), China (2), Finland (2), and one each by the United States, Germany, Hungary, Italy, and Switzerland. The Soviet men won a team medal in every Olympics they par-

Gymnastics offers a superb conditioning workout and demands perfect physical control, as this French gymnast demonstrates.

ticipated in, and Japan in all but one during this period (Japan boycotted the 1980 Games and the Soviet Union boycotted in 1984). Most individual medals were won by the Soviet Union (39.4 percent) and Japan (30.5 percent), with others going to China (6.1 percent), East Germany (4.5 percent), the United States (3.7 percent), and 13 other countries (all European except for three medals to the two Koreas, for a total of 15.8 percent). In the 1996 Olympics Russia won the overall team gold and 5 individual medals; Belarus took 4. Fewer countries participated in women's gymnastics during this period and the Soviet Union was even more dominant, winning the team gold medal in all ten Olympic Games in which they participated (Romania won in 1984). Women's team medals were also won by Romania (7; including gold in 1984), East Germany (5), Czechoslovakia (4), Hungary (3), the United States (2), Japan (1), and China (1). Most women's individual medals were won by the Soviet Union (36.9 percent) and Romania (26.1 percent), with others

for East Germany (13.5 percent), the United States (10.8 percent), and four other countries (12.7 percent). In 1996 the United States won the team competition but only 3 individual medals; Romania won 7, Ukraine 3, China 2, and Russia 1.

In most countries competitive gymnastics is organized and administered under the control of a national federation. In the United States gymnastics activities have been organized on different levels and under the auspices of various organizations. The American Turners and Sokols and the YMCA have long histories of holding competitions for their members, and the AAU sponsored most open gymnastics competition for many years. The NCAA controls collegiate competition, and many state athletic associations hold interschool competition at the high school level. Private gymnastics schools hold interclub meets, especially for young women. USA Gymnastics, formerly known as the U.S. Gymnastics Federation (USGF) is the parent organization for all American gymnastics competition and is responsible for

American participation in international events. National federations in turn belong to the International Gymnastics Federation (FIG), which was founded in 1881 and is the ultimate arbitrator of international gymnastics.

World Gymnastics Championships and World Cups offer opportunities for international competition at the highest level, as do the European and U.S. Championships and multisport festivals such as the Olympic, World University, Goodwill, Commonwealth, Pan American, and Central American and Caribbean Games. With the rise of international gymnastics competition after World War II, great need was felt for rules standards and improved judging. The first *Code of Points* was formulated by the International Gymnastics Federation in 1949 in order to have guidelines for use at the 1950 World Gymnastics Championships. Before that time there was little consistency in judging practices from country to country. In the 1948 Olympic Games significant differences among judges' scores had led to noticeably inaccurate judging. Subsequent editions of the code added more specific rules and defined difficulty levels of skills.

Practice

Once the word *gymnastics* connoted almost any form of exercise, including calisthenics and the use of light and heavy apparatus. Today the terms *developmental* or *educational gymnastics* still refer to a broad spectrum of basic movement and manipulative activities for children and young people. Educational gymnastics activities promote the development of strength, flexibility, balance, coordination, and agility, as well as courage and self-reliance.

Competitive gymnastics includes two distinctly different sports: (1) artistic gymnastics, consisting of six men's and four women's events, and (2) modern rhythmic gymnastics, an activity for women that makes use of light hand apparatus such as hoops, balls, ropes, clubs, and ribbons.

Artistic Gymnastics (Olympic Gymnastics)

In artistic gymnastics competition, individual skills are combined into routines that are evaluated by a panel of judges. At the higher levels, five judges are used. The marks of four acting judges are reported to the head judge, who discards the high and low marks and averages the two middle marks to determine the gymnast's score. The head judge also evaluates the exercise, but his/her score is not utilized unless it differs significantly from the average of the two middle scores or unless the two middle scores differ from each other by more than a set amount. In local competition and even state meets, commonly only two judges are used for each event, and the gymnast's score is the average of these two judges' marks. In international FIG competitions such as the Olympic Games, six judges evaluate the routines and the middle four marks are averaged to arrive at the gymnast's score. Each judging panel also includes a head judge and/or other officials with special duties.

Competitions may include compulsory and/or optional routines. Compulsories are prescribed routines that all gymnasts at a particular level are required to perform. Judging then becomes a task of evaluating each gymnast's execution and form in the prescribed exercise (since difficulty and composition are the same for all competitors). Each compulsory routine (or vault) is worth 10 points; and deductions are made for faults. (In men's compulsory competition the total value of the exercise is considered to be 9.8; the additional 0.2 points can be awarded for virtuosity, i.e., extremely well-performed skills.)

Optional routines are composed individually by each gymnast, making the judging of optionals a complicated process. For women the evaluation factors of difficulty, combination (or composition), and execution are used to arrive at a score of up to 9.4; an additional 0.6 points may be awarded for the inclusion of additional especially difficult skills. Men's optionals judging uses the factors of difficulty, presentation, and special requirements to account for 9 points, with up to 1 point awarded for additional highly difficult skills. Thus, the maximum score that can be made is 10. There are prescribed deductions or ranges of deductions for each type of error that may be made. Optional vaulting is handled differently; each vault has a predetermined point value based on its difficulty, so optional vaulting is judged similarly to compulsories.

Compulsory routines describe the body positions required during performance of each skill, whereas in optionals, the gymnast may elect the position he or she prefers. Standard positions for somersaults and twists include: (1) pike (straight legs with body bent at hips); tuck (bent legs with body bent at hips); and (3) straight or layout (body straight). Rotations become more difficult as the distance from the rotational axis to each part of the body increases. Thus, twists are easiest in layout position and somersaults are easiest in a tuck, and judging of difficulty takes this fact into consideration (e.g., a layout double back somersault is worth more than one done piked, which in turn is worth more than one in tuck position. Gymnastics judging has evolved from strictly defined traditional ideas of good form to greater emphasis on higher difficulty, with less concern about details of form. One example from gymnastics (also found in tumbling, trampoline, and diving) is the currently accepted tuck style for multiple somersaults. Most performers of double and triple somersaults "cowboy" the tuck, i.e., they use their arms to pull their legs closer, with the knees widely separated. Separation of the knees allows a tighter tuck, thus decreasing the radius of rotation maximally and allowing greater speed of rotation, but according to traditionalists it constitutes a distinct form break.

In international championships such as the World Gymnastics Championships and the Olympic Games there are three forms of competition: (1) team competition (compulsory and optional exercises; six-member teams with low score omitted), (2) individual all-around finals (optionals by 36 best gymnasts from the team competition), and (3) individual event finals (optionals by 6 best gymnasts on each apparatus in the team competition).

The International Gymnastics Federation publishes a *Code of Points* for both men's and women's competitions. The code contains general rules and specifies the difficulty rating of many gymnastics skills (omitted are the easier ones and new ones that are constantly being dreamed up). Skills are classified as A (easiest), B, C, D, and E (most difficult). To receive all of the possible points for difficulty (3 for women; 2.4 for men), a competitive routine must contain a certain number of skills of the higher-difficulty ratings. Lower-difficulty skills are used for purposes of fulfilling requirements for total length of the routine and for making connections between skills of greater difficulty.

Gymnastics judging attempts to put evaluation of routines on as objective a basis as possible, but some subjectivity is always present. Each judge views a performance from a somewhat different position, and personal criteria come into play when there are ranges of deductions allowed for specific classes of faults. Gymnastics scores can be affected by nationality, reputation, and appearance of a contestant, and order of competition (later scores better than earlier ones) is also a factor. There have been instances of judges' scores' reflecting their political allegiances, and in international competitions, judges have been removed for giving biased scores.

Men's Events

Men's artistic gymnastics consists of the following events: horizontal bar (high bar), parallel bars, floor exercise, rings, pommel horse, and vault. An additional category, all-around, is treated as an event, and awards are given to the top finishers in all-around. However, it is not actually a separate activity but is scored as the total points for the competitors who participate in all six events.

Horizontal Bar (High Bar). The horizontal bar is a flexible steel bar, about 2.8 centimeters (1-1/8 inches) in diameter and 2.4 meters (7 feet, 10 inches) long, mounted for competition purposes approximately 2.6 meters (8 feet, 6 inches) above floor level. Skills on the horizontal bar consist of swinging and vaulting types of movements. Swinging movements are done either with the trunk and legs close to the bar (in-bar moves) or with the body fully extended from the hands (giant swings). In competitive routines there should be no stops, body parts other than the hands or soles of the feet are rarely in more than momentary contact with the bar, releases of one and both hands from the bar are common, and dismounts often consist of multiple somersaults (triples have been done), sometimes with one or more twists. In high-level routines of recent years, one-arm giant swings and release moves from one-arm giants have become common. Special requirements for FIG competitions include at least (1) one giant swing with eagle grip (palms toward the gymnast, but with a 360-degree pronation of the forearms) or the arms behind the body (German giant), (2) one in-bar element, and (3) one element with released grip and flight.

Gymnastics

Extinct Events

International gymnastics competitions of the past included many activities no longer performed. The first modern Olympic Games in Greece in 1896 featured rope climbing, flying rings, and special team and combined events, and later Olympics included Indian club swinging (1904 and 1932), rope climb (1904, 1924, and 1932), Swedish System gymnastics (1920), flying rings (1920), side horse vault for men (1924), and tumbling (1932). Early World Gymnastics Championships included pole vault, broad jump, shot put, rope climb, and 100-meter sprint. An exclusively gymnastics program did not appear in the World Gymnastics Championships until 1954.

In the United States until the 1960s, men's AAU, club, school, and college gymnastics meets included flying rings (swinging rings), rope climb, tumbling, and trampoline, in addition to the international events. Women's competition included tumbling and trampoline and earlier, even flying rings and parallel bars. Because of the poor showing of the United States in international gymnastics competition, especially relative to its cold war adversary, the Soviet Union, these special events were dropped in order to encourage American gymnasts to concentrate on the international events. They had disappeared from most U.S. gymnastics meets by the mid-1970s.

In the flying rings event the gymnast was swung by a teammate to initiate his routine, and then had to maintain a large swing throughout his sequence of skills. Moves such as dislocates, inlocates, and uprises were used at the ends of each swing in order to build and maintain height. Handstands and iron crosses were held through entire swings. The event was exciting and dangerous because of the great heights involved. At Santa Monica, California, quadruple flyaways have been performed on flying rings set up on the beach.

Rope climb was an exciting event in which the gymnast, using hands only, was timed from a seated position on the floor to the top of a 6.1-meter (20-foot) rope (greater heights were used in some competitions). The world record time for this event is a nearly unbelievable 2.8 seconds.

Tumbling was conducted along a strip of mats, commonly 18 meters (60 feet) long, and four passes were required, with a time limit for the entire performance of forward and backward tumbling. Trampoline competition involved the judging of skills performed during a set number of contacts with the trampoline bed (usually eight or ten). Commonly two or three such sequences were performed by each contestant, with a time limit for the entire presentation. The skills consisted of somersaults, with or without twists, and with landings allowed on the feet, stomach, and back.

Sports closely related to gymnastics in which local and international competitions continue to be held include trampoline and sport acrobatics, the latter consisting of tumbling and group balancing with teams of two, three, and four athletes. The U.S. Sports Acrobatics Federation was formed in 1975, and annual national championships began the next year. Biennial world championships have been held since 1974.

—Richard V. McGehee

Parallel Bars. The parallel bars are flexible wooden rails 3.5 meters (11 feet, 6 inches) long. Their width and height is adjustable, but for competition the height is set at about 1.7 meters (5 feet, 8 inches) above the floor. Movements consist of swings, vaults, balance positions (held for 2 seconds), and slow movements emphasizing strength (e.g., presses to handstands). The bars are released and regrasped with one hand at a time or with both hands simultaneously (and with the gymnast above or below the bars). Most skills involve movement of the body in the plane of the central long dimension of the bars. However, the bars may be worked with the body moving perpendicularly to the bars or circling a position on the bars, and with both hands placed on the same bar. In competitive routines only the hands and, occasionally, the upper arms are ever in contact with the bars. Special requirements include at least one swinging move above the rails and one below, and one release move. A maximum of three held positions is allowed. A springboard may be used for mounting the bars.

Pommel Horse (Side Horse). The pommel horse is a leather- or fabric-covered cylinder 35.5 centimeters (14 inches) in diameter and 162.5 centimeters (64 inches) long. The pommels are set about 40 to 45 centimeters (16 to 18 inches) apart and the height of the horse for competition is 1.25 meters (4 feet, 2 inches) to the top of the pommels. All movements on the horse are swinging movements (no stops are permitted and neither are slow movements employing obvious strength). Only the hands should touch the horse. Support is with the hands on the horse itself or on the pommels, and swings may be circular or pendular. With the exception of a few advanced skills, at least one hand is always in contact with the horse or a pommel, and mounts and dismounts are not distinctly different in style from moves performed on the horse. Advanced pommel horse performers may take their dismounts, and occasionally even some swings within their routine, all the way through a handstand position. All three parts of the horse must be used and special requirements include at least two scissors, moves on both ends of the horse, and at least one element done on a single pommel.

Vault (Long Horse). The vaulting horse is the same apparatus as the pommel horse, with the pommels removed. For competition the height to the top of the horse is 1.35 meters (4 feet, 5 inches). The horse is vaulted along its length, with an approach run of up to 25 meters (27 yards). Evaluation of the vault begins with the takeoff from a springboard and focuses on the flight onto the horse, repulsion with one or both hands, and especially, the second flight phase to landing. One attempt at each vault is allowed during competition; however, in individual finals, two different vaults must be presented. Vaults are classified into five difficulty groups, from 8.6 to 9.8, and an additional 0.1 or 0.2 points may be awarded for second flights of greater than 3.5 meters (11 feet, 6 inches) and 4 meters (13 feet, 1 inch), respectively.

Rings (Still Rings). The rings are wooden and are spaced 50 centimeters (20 inches) apart and suspended from a height of about 5.6 meters (18 feet, 6 inches). For competition the lowest part of the rings is about 2.6 meters (8 feet, 6 inches) above the floor. Ring activities include swinging movements, held positions, and slow movements emphasizing strength. Advanced competitive optional routines require two handstands, one reached with strength (press) and one with swing. One additional static strength element is required; it and the two handstands must be held two seconds. Dismounts involve some form of somersault, with or without twists. Any swinging of the rings during held positions is penalized. Assistance is permitted while obtaining the initial grip.

Floor Exercise (Free Calisthenics). This event utilizes a square floor area, 12 meters (40 feet) on each side, and is performed on a mat 3.2 centimeters (1-1/4 inches) thick. Tumbling skills are combined with balance and positions and movements emphasizing flexibility and strength. In

competition all parts of the floor area and all directions should be used, and a time limit of 50 to 70 seconds is placed on the exercise. Special requirements include one acrobatic series forward and one backward and a balance on one leg or one arm held for two seconds.

Women's Events

Women's artistic gymnastics consists of the following events: uneven bars, balance beam, floor exercise, and vault. All-around scores are totaled from the four women's events.

Uneven Bars (Uneven Parallel Bars). The uneven bars were originally an adaptation of the men's parallel bars, and thus the bars were identical to the men's bars but with one bar set higher than the other. To stabilize the top rail, rigid supports were added to its pistons. Uneven bar work evolved toward greater swinging motions, which required modification of the apparatus to withstand the large forces produced. In the late 1960s guyed bars with the rails extending only over the distance between the uprights began to be used. Other changes involved the adoption of strong tubular fiberglass rails with a thin wood lamination and modification of their cross-section to a more circular shape.

The bars are worked in the direction perpendicular to their length, with many of the skills being very similar to those used in men's horizontal bar work. For competition there are requirements for height and separation of the two bars. However, they may be set very wide in order to facilitate giant swings on the top bar. Only swinging and vaulting movements are permitted, and no stops are allowed. Skills must involve in-bar and giant circles, kips, swings to handstands, twists, and somersaults and other flight moves. The optional routine must have at least ten parts, with three bar changes, two flight elements (complete release of a bar and regrasp of it or the other bar), and one rotation around the long axis of the body. A springboard may be used for mounting the bars.

Balance Beam. The balance beam was originally of wooden construction, 5 meters (16 feet, 4 inches) long and 10 centimeters (4 inches) wide. For competition the beam height is set at 1.2 meters (47 inches). In the 1970s beams began to be thinly padded and covered with a material giving the feel of suede leather. Competitive routines consist of tumbling, balance, and gymnastic movements. The entire length of the beam should be used and the exercise should be continuous and last between 1 minute, 10 seconds, and 1 minute, 30 seconds; only two held positions are permitted. One acrobatic series must have two or more flight elements. One skill must be performed close to the beam, and there are special requirements for gymnastic elements, such as a 360-degree turn on one foot and a high leap or jump. A springboard may be used for mounting the beam.

Floor Exercise. The same floor area and the same mat are used as in the men's event. Movements are continuous and involve tumbling, gymnastic, and dance movements, as well as momentary balance positions. The competitive routine must have two acrobatic series, one with at least two somersaults and another with at least one somersault (the three somersaults being of different types). All of the area and all directions should be used in a competitive routine and the exercise must last between 1 minute, 10 seconds, and 1 minute, 30 seconds. Music (taped orchestra or piano) is used and the movements should conform to the rhythm, tempo, and spirit of the music.

Vault (Side Horse Vault). The vaulting horse for women is the same apparatus as that used in men's vaulting. However, the vaults are performed across the short dimension of the horse, and its height for competition is set at 1.2 meters (47 inches). One vault is performed in compulsory competition. Two vaults are permitted in team optionals, the better score to count. In all-around finals two vaults are required and their scores averaged; in individual finals the scores of two different vaults are averaged. The takeoff is made from a springboard. Each vault has its own difficulty rating, and judging emphasizes flight, form, and landing. Both hands must touch the horse, but the duration of contact of the hands with the horse should be extremely brief.

Gymnasts and Their Training

Although there have been exceptions, such as 1950s U.S. Olympian Jack Beckner, who was 185.4 centimeters (6 feet, 1 inches) tall, the ideal body type for gymnastics is short and light. Gymnastics skills require great strength and flexibility, as well as balance and explosive power. Ages and

sizes of competitive gymnasts have been decreasing progressively as their selection and training has become more demanding. Averages of age, weight, and height for gymnasts at the 1964 Olympics were for men: 26 years, 63.3 kilograms (140 pounds), and 167.2 centimeters (5 feet, 6 inches); for women: 22.7 years, 52 kilograms (115 pounds), and 157 centimeters (5 feet, 2 inches). The same averages for the top six gymnasts at the 1972 Olympics were for men: 24.3 years, 59 kilograms (130 pounds), and 165.3 centimeters (5 feet, 5 inches); for women: 19.9 years, 48 kilograms (106 pounds), and 160 centimeters (5 feet, 3 inches). In 1976 U.S. women Olympians averaged 17.5 years, 48 kilograms (106 pounds), and 161 centimeters (5 feet, 3-1/2 inches), and by 1992 they averaged 16 years, 38 kilograms (83 pounds), and 145 centimeters (4 feet, 9 inches). The two top female gymnasts in the 1992 Olympics were 15 years old, 137 centimeters (4 feet, 6 inches), and one weighed 31.7 kilograms (70 pounds) and the other 31.3 kilograms (69 pounds).

To produce the strength, flexibility, and power essential for competitive gymnastics requires long hours of strenuous practice, and training procedures are designed to develop not only these physical qualities but also the great courage required to perform intrinsically dangerous movements. Modifications of apparatus and special training aids include placement of bars, beam, vaulting horse, and rings at lower heights for learning new skills, the use of special padding and spotting procedures, and extra cushioning for landings. An innovative training device that is used in connection with high bar and other events is a deep pit filled with pieces of foam rubber. A gymnast can plunge into the foam-filled pit even head-first without fear of injury. For advanced work on uneven bars, high bar, and rings, dowel hand grips are used to assure a more secure grip on the bar or rings. Modifications of apparatus that aid the safety of gymnasts and improve performance include the use of springy platforms under floor exercise pads (until the 1960s competitive exercises were done directly on the wooden floor, and the first pads were only 0.6 to 1.2 centimeters [¼ to ½ inches] thick), padding and covering beams, adding spring support to beams and vaulting horses, and flattening the top profile of the horse.

Gymnastics

In socialist societies such as the former Soviet Union, other Eastern European countries, China, and Cuba, young children selected on the basis of body type and other physical attributes may be given opportunities to develop into competitive gymnasts through participation in state-supported training facilities and special schools. Under economic and governmental situations existing in countries such as the United States, the development of young gymnasts has been carried out in schools and organizations such as Turners, Sokols, and YMCAs. However, the intensity and level of work required to produce elite gymnasts today is available only in private training facilities, usually paid for by parents. Recognizing the financial cost of these private facilities, USA Gymnastics initiated a program of stipends paid to a small number of the most talented young gymnasts to offset their training costs. Male gymnasts tend to maintain and even improve performances beyond the peak age for female gymnasts, and their training may continue during college years with the support of athletic scholarships. Collegiate gymnastics is also available for females, but today college-age women are generally considered too old to be involved in the highest level of the sport. One of the most important contributions to the development of gymnastics in the United States was the establishment of the USGF Junior Olympics program, which provides compulsory exercises and guidelines for several levels of age-group competition for both girls and boys.

Modern Rhythmic Gymnastics (Modern Gymnastics)

The women's sport of rhythmic gymnastics has appeared in its current form in the Olympic Games since 1984. Four of the five possible activities (ball, hoop, clubs, ribbon, rope) are contested to determine an all-around winner. Rope was omitted in 1984, ball in 1988, and ribbon in 1992. Six-member team exercises are performed in the Modern Gymnastics World Championships but not, after 1956, in Olympic competition. Competitors must move vigorously within a square floor area measuring 12 meters (40 feet) on each side, performing dance skills and exhibiting grace, balance, and flexibility, while manipulating and maintaining control of their apparatus. They must use all of the area, involve the entire body and handle the apparatus with both left and right hands, and move in harmony with the motion of the hand apparatus and corresponding to the rhythm and mood of the music. Time limits are used for both team and individual exercises and there are special requirements for skill difficulties.

In the 1984 Olympic Games 19 countries were represented (2 entries are allowed per country), and Canada, Romania, and West Germany won the gold, silver, and bronze all-around medals. In both 1988 and 1992, 23 countries were represented, and the Soviet Union (called the Unified Team in 1992) won both the gold and bronze. In 1996 Spain won the team gold, Bulgaria the silver, and Russia the bronze. Modern Gymnastics World Championships have been held since 1963.

Gymnastics Festivals

A remarkable European tradition is that of gymnastic festivals involving huge numbers of athletes of all ages, the emphasis being on participation rather than competition. In the Gymnaestradas, Turnfests (Turnverein associations), and Slets (Sokols), thousands of performers participate in mass demonstrations, team and individual competitions, and workshops involving rhythmic and artistic gymnastics, acrobatics, folk dancing, and related activities. In the 1965 Gymnaestrada in Vienna, more than 10,000 athletes from over 30 countries (perhaps 80 percent women) participated. In 1975 in Berlin, even with a boycott by Eastern Bloc countries, over 12,000 athletes (including a 2-year-old and a group from Sweden averaging 50 years old) from 36 countries presented 312 Gymnaestrada performances for the enjoyment of 250,000 spectators. Turnfests and Slets are also held in the United States. In the fourteenth American Sokol Slet, held in 1977, more than 3,000 athletes from 70 American and Canadian Sokol units took part and over 1,000 competed. Reports of this event noted that the last Sokol Slet in Czechoslovakia had 275,000 athletes and 350,000 spectators.

—Richard V. McGehee

See also Acrobatics; Turnen.

Bibliography: Bowers, Carolyn O., Jacquelyn K. Fie, and Andrea B. Schmid. (1981) *Judging and Coaching Women's Gymnastics.* 2d ed. Palo Alto, CA: Mayfield.

Cooper, Phyllis. (1980) *Feminine Gymnastics.* 3d ed. Minneapolis: Burgess.

Coulton, Jill. (1981) *Sport Acrobatics.* New York: Sterling.

Fukushima, Sho. (1980) *Men's Gymnastics.* London and Boston: Faber & Faber.

Goodbody, John. (1983) *The Illustrated History of Gymnastics.* New York: Beaufort.

International Gymnast (formerly *Modern Gymnast,* 1957–1971, and *Gymnast,* 1972–1975).

International Gymnastics Federation. (1993) *Code of Points for Artistic Gymnastics for Men.* Switzerland: FIG.

International Gymnastics Federation, Women's Technical Committee. (1993) *Code of Points for Artistic Gymnastics for Women.* FIG.

Laptad, Richard E. (1972) *A History of the Development of the United States Gymnastics Federation.* U.S. Gymnastics Federation.

Loken, Newton C., and Robert J. Willoughby. (1977) *Complete Book of Gymnastics.* 3d ed. Englewood Cliffs, NJ: Prentice-Hall.

Murray, Mimi. (1979) *Women's Gymnastics: Coach, Participant, Spectator.* Boston: Allyn and Bacon.

Ryan, Joan. (1995) *Little Girls in Pretty Boxes: The Making and Breaking of Elite Gymnasts and Figure Skaters.* New York: Doubleday.

Ryser, Otto, and James Brown. (1990) *A Manual for Tumbling and Apparatus Stunts.* 8th ed. Dubuque, IA: Wm. C. Brown.

Schmid, Andrea Bodo. (1976) *Modern Rhythmic Gymnastics.* Palo Alto, CA: Mayfield.

Schmid, Andrea Bodo, and Drury, Blanche J. (1977) *Gymnastics for Women.* 4th ed. Palo Alto, CA: Mayfield.

Turoff, Fred. (1991) *Artistic Gymnastics: A Comprehensive Guide to Performing and Teaching Skills for Beginners and Advanced Beginners.* Dubuque, IA: Wm. C. Brown.

USA Gymnastics (formerly *USGF Gymnastics*).

Wallechinsky, David. (1984) *The Complete Book of the Olympics.* New York: Viking.